Government and Public Administration

McGRAW-HILL SERIES IN POLITICAL SCIENCE

JOSEPH P. HARRIS, *Consulting Editor*

Noc.c.

Government and Public Administration *THE QUEST*

FOR RESPONSIBLE PERFORMANCE

John D. Millett

PRESIDENT, MIAMI UNIVERSITY

New York

Toronto

London

1959

McGRAW-HILL BOOK COMPANY, INC.

GOVERNMENT AND PUBLIC ADMINISTRATION

THE MAPLE PRESS COMPANY, YORK, PA.

To Allan, David, and Stephen

Preface

Purposefully and avowedly, this volume sets out to be a discussion of American political institutions. The focus of attention is how these institutions operate to keep the great apparatus of public administration subject to some degree of political responsibility. This is a theme of vital importance to the student of governmental institutions in general, as well as to the student of public administration in particular.

In recent years it has been especially popular among scholars to examine the phenomena of government primarily in terms of political behavior. The psychology of group dynamics in voting and in influencing the electorate, in exercising political pressure upon elected officials and upon administrative agencies, and in performing the work of government has been studied in terms of motivation, characteristics of personality, and external stimulus. To many, the "behavioral sciences" have seemed to be synonymous with the social sciences; others have considered the first indeed to have displaced the second in so far as scholarly enterprise is concerned.

The research in social psychology carried on in recent years has added immensely to our understanding of political behavior, whether it occurs in the context of the political party, the pressure group, the legislature, administrative agencies, or elsewhere. We have by no means reached the limit of knowledge about group behavior in government, or in other social organizations. We have surely made a promising beginning.

Yet, I cannot accept any implicit suggestion that our study of political behavior has eliminated the necessity to comprehend as fully as we can the operating characteristics of our formal political institutions. I cannot find that our most enthusiastic disciples of the study of political behavior have put forward any such claim. It is merely that in the excitement of discovery an exclusive claim to political insight has seemed to be suggested.

There is no need for any sense of rivalry to develop between the study of political institutions on the one hand and the study of political behavior on the other. Both are essential if we are to understand the process of government. Our political institutions set forth the framework in which political decisions are made and executed. This framework conditions and circumscribes the arena of political conflict. Moreover, this framework is in itself a matter of political debate from time to time.

Indeed, we must not forget that a concern with political institutions, with the rules of the political game, has been a preoccupation of political philosophers and statesmen throughout Western history. In our culture man has striven mightily to provide himself with mechanisms of government which would both serve his political needs and preserve his individual freedom. The study of political institutions is the study of great ideals. It is the study of man's moral sense manifest in government.

This volume is concerned with one broad aspect of American political institutions: the devices available whereby our society endeavors to make bureaucracy politically responsible. The importance of this subject scarcely seems open to debate.

There is a major and a supplemental thesis which this volume endeavors to state. The principal thesis is that there is an element of separate identity to be observed in practice between the legislature, executive, and judiciary on the one hand—the organs of political decision making—and the various administrative agencies of government which, in their aggregate, comprise the bureaucracy. It is this separate identity which, in turn, places the one set of political institutions in a position of political superiority over the other.

The secondary thesis of this volume is that administrative agencies are not to be thought of as simply an extension of the executive branch of government. This subject of constitutional status is considered in more detail in a subsequent chapter. It may be well, nonetheless, to anticipate that discussion here. We have had great difficulty in the United States in developing a constitutional doctrine adequate for the realities of administrative activity in our scheme of government. There are occasions when the legislature by statutory enactment—the Hatch Acts of 1939 and 1940 are an example—speaks of the executive branch of government as embracing all administrative agencies. Such usage is a matter of convenience and must not be interpreted as expressing any fundamental sense of constitutional acquiescence by the legislature.

The fact is that administrative agencies in our scheme of government are not part and parcel of the executive branch but constitute a distinct echelon of government subject to the separate direction of the executive, legislature, and judiciary. Administrative agencies are politically responsible to all three. And this responsibility is not channeled through any one branch; it is exercised directly.

Indeed, a basic difference between a parliamentary system of government and our American system of government is that administrative agencies are not responsible to the legislature through the intermediary of the executive but are responsible directly to the legislature on those matters which are of legislative authority.

We shall return to consideration of this subject in the pages which follow. I wish only at the outset to make clear the framework for the discussion of this volume. I believe there is a separate identity to be observed between the legislative, executive, and judicial organs of our government and the administrative agencies of our government. Furthermore, I believe it is the high purpose of our political institutions to vest substantial control and supervision over the bureaucracy in these organs of political decision making.

Essentially, this volume is intended to be a companion to my earlier book, *Management in the Public Service*.[1] In that book I endeavored to consider the bureaucracy from the point of view of the heads of operating agencies of government. That study dealt with questions of operating effectiveness to be encountered in all bureaucratic endeavor, whether the substance of the work performed be the national defense, the conservation of natural resources, the provision of public education, or the regulation of business enterprise affected with a public interest.

This volume, as I have tried to say, involves a different, and if you please, a grander theme in so far as the destiny of man is concerned. Our attention here is directed to the ways and means whereby management in the public service is kept subject to responsible political direction.

One reason why this subject is of such grave importance today is the extent of professionalization in the public service. Perhaps it was a canon of Jacksonian democracy that any citizen was competent to perform the work of government. This is clearly and potently not so today. No ordinary citizen can launch an earth satellite into orbit. No ordinary citizen can teach nuclear physics in a public high school or a public university. No ordinary citizen can design and construct a dam. No ordinary citizen can treat mental illness. The list might be prolonged indefinitely.

As the work of government has expanded, as the body of man's knowledge has grown and become ever more highly specialized, public administration has become more highly technical, requiring high competence indeed in all its endeavors. The very survival of our nation today depends upon the capacity and loyalty of those men and women who are recruited and retained in the public service.

At the same time, the democratic thesis requires that bureaucracy in its high degree of professionalization shall not become the ruler of man. To be sure, democracy as a system of government, as the operative ideal of a political way of life, is not too easy to define. Perhaps Abraham Lincoln gave us the best summary when he spoke of "government of the people, by the people, for the people." Certainly, democracy involves elements of popular participation and popular control. In a democracy, then, a pro-

[1] New York: McGraw-Hill Book Company, Inc., 1954.

fessional bureaucracy must be reconciled with popular control. That is the theme of this volume.

The idea that the study of public administration must begin with some attention to the structure of government for exercising political oversight of the bureaucracy was born for me while I was a professor in the graduate faculty of political science at Columbia University. The conception emerged from many discussions with my mentor, colleague, and friend, Professor Arthur W. Macmahon. In developing our joint interest in how the subject matter of public administration should be conceived and taught, we early fixed upon a basic division between problems of control and problems of management. Any virtue which the present volume may have must be credited first of all to Professor Macmahon.

I am indebted to Professor Joseph P. Harris of the University of California (Berkeley) for a careful reading of the entire manuscript and for his many suggestions to clarify and improve its content.

I was fortunate in persuading my former colleague, Professor Walter Gellhorn of the Columbia University School of Law, to read the four chapters of Part 4. His helpful comments have done much to ensure that this discussion of the role of the judiciary does not contain too many obvious legal errors.

And I am most appreciative of the diligence of my secretary, Miss Jane Durrell, who not only has typed the manuscript through various versions but also has prodded me to its completion.

I cannot help but be disturbed by the great gulf which exists between a simple conception of subject matter and its adequate communication to others. There is so much to discuss while striving simply to set forth a basic idea: that in the American scheme of government the legislature, executive, and judiciary are joined not only in the determination of public policy but also in the great purpose of keeping the administrative apparatus of government subject to popular direction and control. The quest for responsible performance is our guarantee that bureaucracy shall ever remain the servant of a free people.

John D. Millett

Contents

PART THREE

THE EXECUTIVE

PART FOUR

THE JUDICIARY

CONCLUSION

Introduction

Chapter 1

Politics and Administration

Politics is a word of noble meaning. It expresses the whole range of man's endeavor to govern himself, to provide a structure and practice for the exercise of political power. In a totalitarian political system, all power is by definition political. In a pluralistic political system, power is exercised by many instruments of society. Government then becomes one of these instruments. Political power in such a society may be extensive, but does not exercise an exclusive control over the behavior of man.

The study of political systems in Western culture is concerned primarily with the ends and means of political power. Over and over again this study has stressed two great goals for Western man: how to harness the exercise of political power to the advancement of the general welfare of society rather than to the gratification of the baser drives of a few persons in society; and secondly, how to restrain the exercise of political power in such ways as to recognize the worth of the individual in society. These themes challenged the thought of Plato and Aristotle; they illuminated the exposition of Roman law set forth by Cicero; they have continued down to the present day to excite the concern of our great political thinkers.

Politics then is a word which embraces all aspects of the study of government. It includes the theory of governmental purpose and practice. It is concerned with governmental structure and relationships. It refers to the policy and program of governmental operation. It extends to the dynamics of political power: who wields power; how power is attained and retained by political leaders; how power is exercised in practice in the conduct of governmental affairs. Politics is synonymous with government. The study of politics is the study of the art and science of government.

Because politics means power over the life and fortune of man, and because that power has so often been exercised even in Western culture for the benefit of a few at the expense of many, the word politics often has a connotation of evil. In our own country, politics often means manipulation of political power by certain persons or groups for special benefit or privilege. It often refers to the strategy and tactics of political leaders whose scheming serves egoistic ends and proceeds through deceit, misrepresentation, and force. It is often thought of as dishonesty, graft, immunity from legal accountability, corruption, and personal or group aggrandizement.

Aristotle observed that man was by nature a political animal. We know from experience that political power is essential to the life of man in society. The theorist may conceive of an anarchy in which society dispenses with the exercise of political power. The student of government knows that there is no record of the continued existence of any society or civilization in which political power was absent. Society implies social organization, and social organization requires among other characteristics the exercise of political power.

Political commentators in Western culture have long observed that political power is subject to abuse. It is this abuse which has led to the distrust of government, and to a popular idea in our own country on occasion that political power is evil or somehow degrading. Yet rational reflection quickly leads us to the realization that political power cannot be rendered free from abuse by ignoring its exercise or by wishing that it did not exist. Rather, in practical ways we have sought to surround the exercise of political power with various safeguards, and on occasion we "throw out the rascals" and install a new political leadership which promises a "clean" operation of government in the general interest.

There is no profit for Americans in belittling the exercise of political power. Rather there is the necessity to keep the exercise of political power within reasonable limits and under reasonable leadership. In other words the prevention of gross abuse in political power means some degree of control over the exercise of political power.

THE RESTRAINT OF POLITICAL POWER

The control of political power is a basic concept of the American system of government. This control begins with the idea of liberty. A society which believes that the individual is more than a cog in a machine, which believes that every person has by the fact of his life an inherent element of individual dignity and worth—such a society has begun to circumscribe the role and conduct of government.

Western political tradition has long embraced the idea of liberty, even if it has been somewhat less than successful on occasion in practicing its profession of faith. The Judaeo-Christian religious heritage of our culture laid a firm foundation for the idea of individual worth. The doctrine of a natural law providing man with certain unalienable rights, of which life and liberty were foremost, had a religious as well as a rational exposition. The assumption that all men were created equal in the sight of God and under the law of man did much to shore up the idea of liberty. The Levelers of seventeenth-century England declared: "the poorest he that is in England hath a life to live as the richest he." Equality and its political counterpart, liberty, have made government appear as servant rather than master in society.

In the second place, the concept of a general welfare as something more than the interest of any particular person or group in the state has done its part also to encourage a restraint in the use of political power. The preamble of the Constitution of the United States declares that the purpose of the federal government is to "establish Justice, insure domestic Tranquility, provide for the common defense, promote the general Welfare, and secure the Blessings of Liberty. . . . " The general welfare has never been a simple concept to define. Yet this difficulty is no justification for concluding that the phrase is meaningless. To the contrary, the belief is deep-seated in the American practice of government that political action shall be directed to the general welfare, and that this general welfare embraces the community at large. For any particular segment of society through political action to profit extensively and continuously at the expense of other segments violates our sense of justice, equity, and fair play.

The idea of the general welfare as the goal of political action admits the possibility that the work of government shall not be destructive of the best interests of man but on the contrary may advance those interests. All governmental activity is not to be condemned just because it is governmental. Rather, we ask that all governmental activity be subject to a rigorous test, the test of the general welfare. And obviously the idea of the general welfare cannot be static. It necessarily changes with the changing conditions and circumstances of man. The idea of the general welfare in a simple agrarian society may be very different indeed from the idea of the general welfare in a complex, industrialized, highly technical, and urbanized society.

In the third place, political power is restrained in our society by the concept of limited government. In essence, we hold that there are certain matters of substance and of procedure which are beyond the competence of government to perform. Our federal Constitution sets forth certain types of political action which the government is not to undertake. It is not to grant any title of nobility. It is not to pass a bill of attainder or an ex post facto law. It is not to impose any duty or tax on exports. It may not divide one state into several without the state's consent. It is not to abridge freedom of the press or of speech. It is not to establish a religion. These are all fairly specific manifestations of political power which our government is prohibited constitutionally from undertaking. Beyond these details is the proposition that community and state are not identical; hence many social and economic activities of the community can and should be carried on with only such minimum control as is necessary to protect the welfare of the community at large. Ours is not an all-competent government, and thus we endeavor to prevent the exercise of an all-competent political power.

In addition, our governmental system is limited in terms of procedure. Our bill of rights sets forth a number of procedural safeguards for the individual in his relationship to government. His property may not be taken for a public use without just compensation. He is not to be deprived of his life, liberty, or property without due process of law. He shall be secure against unreasonable search and seizure. He shall not be compelled in any criminal case to be a witness against himself. In all criminal prosecutions he shall enjoy the right to a speedy and public trial, shall be informed of the accusation against him, shall have the assistance of counsel in his defense, and shall be entitled to summon witnesses in his favor. Ours is not just a government, then, which is restrained in matters of substance. It is limited in how it proceeds to carry out its functions.

An essential operative ideal of our governmental system accordingly is that political power can and should be restrained. We have sought this great end by recognizing the worth of the individual and by proclaiming the goal of liberty for the person. We have sought this great end by insisting that political power, when exercised, shall be directed toward the general welfare. And we have sought this great end by acknowledging a difference between the community and the state, thus reserving substantial areas of human endeavor for the free play of competing groups under a minimum of political control.

POLITICS AS GOVERNMENTAL STRUCTURE

Government must be accepted as necessary to man in society. Yet the restraint of political power is essential if man in society is to enjoy some degree of individual freedom and dignity. In the Western tradition the reconciliation of political power and liberty has been sought through a machinery of government which is usually described as constitutionalism. Man has endeavored through great written documents and through political custom and usage to construct a framework of government which will both advance the general welfare and preserve the blessings of liberty.

Political philosophers have on occasion attempted to formulate an ideal system of government, a utopia. Other philosophers have identified and justified desirable political developments with a resort to historical evidence or "right reason." Men of affairs have had to establish, modify, and operate a political system which would achieve the goals of the philosopher and suit the current mood of important elements of society. Under the impact of various forces—victory or defeat in war, the availability of natural resources, technological developments, the impact of competing cultures, migration and commerce, skillful leaders, and wise counselors—governments have been instituted among men and have performed their varied tasks. Yet in Western culture these developments have evidenced a certain common goal: a system of government which would preserve and advance democratic values.

Political power in any society is structured. It cannot exist or function without a more or less formalized arrangement. Some of this structure may be prescribed in writing. Much more is apt to be unspecified in any formal documents but rather to represent tradition and operative ideals. No one can claim to know the essence of government simply from the written word. He must examine the practice as well.

There are at least three essential features to any structure of government. The first of these is a system for the transmission and exercise of political power. The second comprises organs of decision making. The third is a bureaucracy, or administrative apparatus. All three of these will be found in even the most rudimentary forms of government. Indeed, it may be said that government scarcely exists without these component elements.

The system of power is a social phenomenon. It reflects the status of various classes in a society and the degree to which they have access to the exercise of power. Aristotle long ago observed that the supreme authority in states must rest in the hands of one, a few, or many. He then defined "true forms" of government as those which governed with a view to the common interest, whereas he termed "perversions" those forms which ruled with a view to the private interest. The true forms were accordingly kingship, aristocracy, and constitutional government. The perversions were for government by one, tyranny; by a few, oligarchy; and by many, democracy. It makes no difference today that we do not accept the particular words which were used by Aristotle. The basic observation is of continuing importance.

In the social structure of a hereditary monarchy, political power may be wielded by the king, or in the name of the king by a hereditary aristocracy or a privileged bureaucracy. In the social structure of feudalism, political power may be atomized among many hereditary nobles and successful military leaders. In a republic, political power may be exercised by a few (an elite) or by many. These are the basic systems for the transmission and exercise of political power.

The decision-making organs of government are usually described today as dictatorial, parliamentary, or legislative-presidential. In an absolutism, the word of the dictator and his clique is law. His decisions constitute the basic direction for political action. In a parliamentary government, the decisions of the legislative body provide the determinations for general governmental policy. In a legislative-presidential system of government, the power of political decision making is held by both legislative and presidential instrumentalities. There may be combinations and modifications of these basic types. A few words of description cannot ever suggest the subtleties of the actual decision-making process in any type of government.

The system for the exercise of political power and the structure for decision making are necessarily highly interrelated in a society. It is possible to have a parliamentary structure of government for decision-making purposes which, in terms of the realities of the system for exercising power, represents an oligarchy or elite. Or a parliamentary structure may represent a democratic system of power. Similarly, a legislative-presidential structure may be the instrumentality of an oligarchical power system or of a democratic power system. Simply because any particular society claims to have parliamentary organs for decision making does not necessarily indicate that it has a democratic system for the exercise of political power.

Our focus of attention in this volume is, of course, American government. In this country the system for the transmission and exercise of political power is democratic. In addition, it is highly decentralized. The individual citizen has the privilege of voting for those officeholders who constitute the organs of decision making. Furthermore, the political parties which provide the vehicle for presenting candidates are organized on a local basis, the higher levels of governmental decision making being paralleled by federations or combinations of these local units of our political parties.

The organs of decision making in our country are legislative, executive, and judicial. If it has come to pass in practice that on occasion the executive seems to dominate among these three in the process of decision making, it does not follow that the other two organs of government are unimportant. Indeed, there have been times when the legislative organ has dominated, and in our particular structure it is always a governmental organ of great potential and actual importance.

BUREAUCRACY

The third essential element of government is a bureaucracy, or administrative apparatus. This word bureaucracy, like so many in the lexicon of politics, is one of varied meaning. For example, it has been employed by one writer in an economic sense: the performance of activities with no cash value in the market place.[1] In a competitive economy presumably control is exercised over all producers by the device of the market place. The test of utility and efficiency is the dollar of the consumer who, by his

[1] Ludwig von Mises, *Bureaucracy* (New Haven, Conn.: Yale University Press, 1944).

individual purchases, rewards those who best meet his needs and rejects others. Even in the large-scale industrial enterprise of today, operated in large part by professional managers, the profit incentive based upon survival in a competitive market serves as a constant stimulus and a definite restraint. In the public service, where only government operates, there is no such close and continuing scrutiny of utility and efficiency. But this is a fairly technical and little-used definition of bureaucracy.

A second meaning of bureaucracy is synonymous with large-scale organization. As characterized by the German sociologist, Max Weber, bureaucracy consists of certain common features, such as a continuous organization of official functions bound by rules, a specified sphere of competence, organization of officers according to the principle of hierarchy, a separation of administration from ownership or control, the selection of personnel on the basis of technical qualifications, the appointment of personnel, the formulation and recording in writing of administrative rules and acts, systematic discipline and status, and status expressed in terms of career position and salary. Weber recognized that such bureaucratic organization might characterize many different kinds of social groups, from government to business and the church.[2] Yet when the word bureaucracy is used, most of us think of government, and specifically of the administrative apparatus of government.

Certainly there is no denying that we live in an era of large-scale administrative organization. In this sense bureaucracy is with us, and will no doubt remain so while our present society survives. In 1900 our federal, state, and local governments in the United States employed one million persons. By 1950 the number had grown to over seven million.[3] Whereas one out of every twenty-five employed persons worked for government in 1900, by 1950 the proportion was one out of every eight employed persons. Total expenditures by government in 1900 came to around 1.5 billion dollars; by 1950 they were over 60 billion dollars. In terms of dollars of constant purchasing power, expressed in 1929 price levels, the expenditures of government in the United States increased from some 3 billion dollars around 1900 to some 40 billion dollars in 1950. Whereas in 1900 governmental expenditures amounted to about 9 per cent of national income, in 1950 they amounted to 25 per cent. Expressed in a somewhat different way, the input of labor and capital devoted to the operation of government was about 5 per cent of national input in 1900; in 1950 it was around 15 per cent.[4]

[2] Max Weber, "The Essentials of Bureaucratic Organization: An Ideal-type Construction," in Robert K. Merton, Ailsa P. Gray, Barbara Hockey, and Hanan C. Selvin, *Reader in Bureaucracy* (Glencoe, Ill.: Free Press, 1952), p. 18.

[3] These and subsequent figures in this paragraph are taken from Solomon Fabricant, *The Trend of Government Activity in the United States since 1900* (New York: National Bureau of Economic Research, Inc., 1952).

[4] *Ibid.,* p. 25.

We are not concerned here to defend or denounce this trend. It may be worthwhile, nonetheless, to mention certain conclusions reached by the author of a careful economic analysis of these developments. Fabricant found that hardly any kind of government activity declined between 1900 and 1950. There was considerable variation in the rate of growth among activities, however, some, such as national defense, highways, and public welfare, expanding more rapidly than others. The most important factor in the expansion of governmental employment and expenditure occurred not from new governmental activities but from a growth of governmental activities already in existence in 1900.[5] Although governmental activity did expand in relation to private activity in such fields as social welfare service, housing, higher education, and finance, and although there was an expansion of governmental activity into such business enterprises as electric power and other local utilities, banking, and liquor stores, nevertheless these increases in government activity, substantial as they were, were not "a major factor in swelling government operations."[6] The major factors accounting for the expansion of governmental administration were first of all the growing concern for national defense, joined with other factors such as population increase, economic growth and urbanization, depression and the concern for economic security, advancing science and technology, and the economic insecurity of agriculture.[7] Whether we like it or not, governmental bureaucracy, in the sense of large-scale activity and organization, is a characteristic of our time.

There is a third meaning often associated with the term bureaucracy. It is a derisive meaning, bearing a connotation of critical disapproval. Bureaucracy in this sense stands for certain features such as slow action (delay), a high regard for picayune detail (red tape), a reluctance to make decisions (a tendency to pass the buck), a high degree of caution (lack of initiative), a concern for precedent and a fear of change (non-progressive), a plethora of paper work, and a passion for status and security.[8] No doubt large-scale organization does have a tendency to breed many of these characteristics, although a determined leadership may mitigate, if not eliminate, many of the grossest evidences of such failures. If bureaucracy behaves in this contemptuous sense of the word bureaucratic, the fault may often be laid at the door of many legal restrictions surrounding the public service as well as the prevalence of a political leadership which rewards caution and punishes innovation and action.

Then there is a fourth meaning to the word bureaucracy—a meaning which is of special importance to us in this volume. Bureaucracy may

---

[5] *Ibid.*, pp. 82–83.   [6] *Ibid.*, p. 111.   [7] *Ibid.*, chap. 7.
[8] Cf. John H. Crider, *The Bureaucrat* (Philadelphia: J. B. Lippincott Company, 1944).

refer to the exercise of political power by the administrative apparatus of government. We shall come back to this concern in a moment.

It appears today that the most common usage of the term bureaucracy is simply as a reference to the large-scale organizational machinery which is required to do the work of government. It is a mistake to think that bureaucracy is something new. An army is a bureaucracy, a large-scale organization for performing the aggressive and defense policies of a nation. Governments have always had a system of tax collectors—this is another part of bureaucracy. When kings had clerks to keep records for them, when the Romans established means for building roads, when the decision-making organs of government determined to send representatives to foreign countries and in turn to receive the representatives of other nations, bureaucracy was born. No government outside a primitive society can exist without some degree of administrative machinery.

Indeed, it has not been too unusual for the administrative apparatus of government to continue more or less unchanged when the system of political power or the structure of government in a society is undergoing change. The bureaucracy which was built up under the Roman republic was continued and strengthened under the empire. In France, the administrative apparatus of the state in a brief period of time passed from the control of the *ancien régime* through revolution to military dictatorship, monarchical restoration, and parliamentary republicanism. In Germany in another short space of time, the bureaucracy has watched the transformation of power from Prussian militarism to republicanism to Nazism and now back to republicanism in West Germany.

BUREAUCRACY AND POWER

A crucial question of government in all ages and places of Western society has been the part bureaucracy should and does play in the system of political power. The ideal model or construct of bureaucracy has been to picture the administrative apparatus of government as politically neutral. The thesis is that the bureaucracy is properly subordinate to the organs of governmental decision making just as the organs of decision making in turn are subordinate or responsive to the system of political power.

Thus in essence the state is pictured as an interlocking series of relationships. There is first, as we have mentioned, a system of political power. There are secondly organs of decision making through which this power system operates. There is thirdly an administrative apparatus for the performance of the determinations of the decision making organs of government. The bureaucracy is thus conceived as servant, not master, within the operation of the state.

It is no simple matter, however, to divide political society into these component elements of political power, governmental decision making, and administrative performance. Government is much too pervasive in human life to be divided into neatly compartmentalized units. And government is far too complicated in operation always to be observing some finely constructed preconceived models. The distinctions we make here are for convenience of discussion and understanding. It does not follow that these distinctions necessarily represent the full detail of operational practice.

Yet in the history of Western society it is doubtful if there has ever been a nation which was governed over any important period of time or to any substantial degree by its bureaucracy. Certainly there have been instances where bureaucracies have exercised considerable influence in guiding the policy of the decision-making organs of government, whether these represented dictatorial, aristocratic, or democratic power.[9] It is difficult to conceive of bureaucracy as not influencing governmental decision making, and in turn influencing the system of political power. Bureaucracies are composed of persons who specialize in the work of government. They develop a particular competence, and from their experience and knowledge they must necessarily suggest desirable lines of governmental policy.

There is a great difference, however, between influencing the conduct of government and wielding governmental and political power. There is a difference between the power to advise and the power to decide. Bureaucracies must be expected to advise. It is when they possess also the power to decide that bureaucracies become a factor in the system of political power.

For a bureaucracy to wield political power in a state, several special conditions would have to obtain. For one thing, all the important positions in the bureaucracy would have to be held by persons having a common social status, a more or less common political point of view, and a distinctive political purpose within the state. In addition, the system of political power would have to be so structured in the state that this bureaucratic element was dominant, able to make its purpose effective. Furthermore, the organs of decision making would have to be synonymous with the administrative apparatus or incapable of any independent action.

As we have said, it seems doubtful if in the history of Western states there has ever been a nation where these conditions obtained over any considerable period of time. Yet this absence of any extensive experience with bureaucracy as the wielder of political power and as the decision-making organ of government does not necessarily mean that we need not

[9] For a discussion of the definition of bureaucratic power and a brief account of its history, see Arnold Brecht, "How Bureaucracies Develop and Function," *Annals of the American Academy of Political and Social Science,* vol. 292 (March, 1954), p. 1.

fear the possibility of such an occurrence. Bureaucracy in this political power connotation may ever be a political danger in government.

There are some who profess to see the menace of bureaucracy—that is, of a politically dominant bureaucracy—in the sheer size of governmental activities today. Perhaps there is a point at which the very size of the administrative activities of government will become a threat to the continued existence of a democratic polity. Perhaps the administrative work of government could become so extensive that administrative leadership could control the voting of all governmental employees, or otherwise take action hostile to our democratic political system. Just what connection there is between size and a politically dominant bureaucracy, no one today knows. It is sometimes said that whenever government comes to dominate one-third, or one-half, or two-thirds of the economy, our prevailing political system will collapse. Today, our government requires for its purpose from one-quarter to one-third of all economic output. In one year during World War II, in 1944, government took 48 per cent of all production of goods and services. Yet it would be an exaggeration to say that our political system had collapsed or was on the verge of disintegration.

This is not to suggest that there is no possible relationship between size of governmental administrative activity and a politically dominant bureaucracy. This author believes there probably is some such relationship. But no one at this time knows exactly what that relationship may be.

Charles S. Hyneman has identified five ways in which the bureaucratic apparatus of a modern democratic government might undermine or even destroy that government. One way would be for the administrative organization to dominate popular elections. Another way would be for the bureaucracy to misinform the public about the issues confronting government. A third way would be to initiate and administer policies and programs contrary to the public will. A fourth way would be to fail to advise and assist party leaders in the formulation and administration of public policy. And a fifth way would be to cause the people to lose all faith in government by a failure to perform the necessary work of government.[10]

No doubt any one of these tactics employed by a coherent, purposeful group of administrative leaders could have the result of undermining or destroying our democratic political system. Such a leadership group would have to be united within itself, have the devoted loyalty of subordinate workers, and be determined to seize and wield political power in the state. Such power might either be sought directly or be used to favor one particular political faction within society over any other faction.

The threat of such a possible eventuality is present in the modern state. How real the threat is in actuality is the subject of our concern in this volume.

[10] Charles S. Hyneman, *Bureaucracy in a Democracy* (New York: Harper & Brothers, 1950), pp. 26–35.

The Safeguards against a Politically Powerful Bureaucracy. There are several possible safeguards against the menace of a bureaucratic disposition to seize control or to influence the exercise of political power. One is political tradition. If society through its culture patterns and educational indoctrination achieves a high regard for the democratic way of life, then the membership of the bureaucracy is likely to reflect these attitudes, too. This is especially so in a bureaucracy whose selection practices bring into governmental organization a wide cross section of society. Any bureaucratic group which tends to be self-selective or to be drawn from one social stratum can be a potential source of danger. But if social tradition cultivates a loyalty to democratic practices and if persons from varied social groupings are brought into the bureaucracy, this danger can be limited if not eliminated.

There is another safeguard. A bureaucracy organized into a small number of clearly defined, highly integrated agencies might in time become a bureaucracy which a few key individuals could dominate. Apart from the factor of federalism which makes this more difficult in our country, the organizational structure of administrative agencies in America tends to embrace a variety of types and a considerable number of units. From time to time a good deal is said about "integration" of administrative structure. Certainly some degree of rationalization, which brings common activities of a closely related nature together, may be badly needed from time to time. Yet a variety of types and a multiplicity of administrative units reflects certain pluralistic features of our social structure, and this in turn may be a strong shield against the danger of bureaucratic power.

The primary safeguard against a politically dominant bureaucracy, however, is the effective functioning of the organs of decision making within the governmental structure of a society. If the basic determinations about what the bureaucracy shall do and how it shall proceed to accomplish its assignment are made outside the bureaucracy itself, and if the bureaucracy loyally subordinates itself to these organs of decision making, then the bureaucracy is subject to external direction and control. Such a bureaucracy is not then a politically dangerous instrument but an essential participant in the process of government.

DECISION MAKING AND POLITICAL POWER

Most studies of government in general and of American government in particular tend to concentrate attention upon the transmission and exercise of political power or upon the organs of decision making. In our country the study of the system of political power involves an examination of the social composition of the electorate and of its behavior, the structure and operation of political parties, the process of nominating and electing candidates to public office, the characteristics of political party leadership, and the relations between parties and important interest groups in society. This is the exciting stuff of democratic politics.

The study of the organs of decision making in our country is concerned with the distribution of governmental power among legislature, executive, and judiciary, and with the sharing of governmental power between a federal government for the nation as a whole and forty-nine state governments. In turn, although in a somewhat different relationship, the state governments share power with local units of government. This structure of government has been much described and often analyzed in terms of the collaboration and friction which attends the functioning of these various parts.

Furthermore, it is the political system which elects legislators and executives and which directly or indirectly selects the judges who comprise the judiciary. Political parties influence the organs of decision making. Interest groups likewise influence the behavior of the legislators and executives. The close working relationship between the system of political power and the organs of decision making has often been disclosed in the writing about American government.

The relationship of the bureaucracy to the system of political power is less well known. It has been evident for some time that political parties in our country have exerted a considerable impact upon administrative performance. Before civil service restrictions in the appointment, promotion, and retention of personnel became widespread, a goodly number of appointments to administrative positions were contrived through political party channels. Political leaders have often been concerned to influence administrative action, whether it was the purchase of land and the construction of buildings, the handling of criminal charges against individuals, or the location and distribution of governmental services.

Administrative officials who were interested in the development of their particular field of activity, whether it was public health, or education, or national defense, have often cultivated friendly relationships with political leaders. These relationships have assisted administrators in obtaining the appropriations they needed or other support in crucial matters. Indeed, it is well known that in some types of administrative activity administrative agencies and one or more interest groups have become almost identical. It is not impossible for interest groups to achieve a substantial domination of certain administrative agencies.

These relationships are apt to obscure an important characteristic of our system of government. In terms of the formalities of the governmental process the direction and control of the bureaucracy rests with the organs of decision making which have been duly constituted for this purpose. The direction and control exercised by other means is either informal or indirect. The responsibility for maintaining an external restraint on bureaucracy remains with the organs of decision making. How these organs proceed to effect that external restraint is the subject of this volume.

It should not be necessary to dwell at length upon the incompatibility of a politically dominant bureaucracy and a democratic polity. A free society requires a system of political power which is diffused rather than concentrated, a system in which politically citizens are equal. If any one element of society becomes politically dominant, then it may be in a position to crush its opponents and stifle freedom. A democracy cannot tolerate any political elite on a continuing basis. A democracy cannot tolerate a bureaucracy whose goal is the exercise of unrestrained political power rather than the proper performance of the duly determined and assigned activities of government.

A free society is committed to freedom. On the one hand, this involves the restraint of political power. On the other hand, it involves the provision of opportunity for the individual to develop and use his talents. Within the family we encourage youth to learn and to do. Within our economy, our churches, our various social groupings, we provide many different units in which the individual may find his place and his satisfaction. Freedom is served by a pattern of competing social groups. Furthermore there is considerable social mobility, so that individuals may rise to positions of trust and leadership upon the basis of personal merit. Widespread educational opportunity has helped to neutralize the advantages of family wealth and status. Freedom is thus served by a social structure in which class lines have not been irrevocably drawn. Moreover, our economy has emphasized productive growth and the widespread distribution of material rewards. Economic security has been achieved within the framework of an expanding economy. Freedom has thus been served by continued economic growth shared by many, not just a few.

A democratic polity is part of a free society. It embraces a widely qualified electorate, political parties free to organize and to present candidates and issues as they see fit, adequate methods of informing the electorate, free elections, and the existence of organs of decision making which are politically responsible to the people. A democratic polity could not survive if the bureaucracy were to escape from political responsibility to the people through the organs of decision making.

To be sure, we do not suppose that the American arrangements for a free society and a democracy are necessarily perfect. In a society of something less than perfect men and women, we must expect institutions and practices which are less than perfect. If the operative ideals of a society are just so much window dressing, then that society is no longer true to its profession of faith. What counts is not the gulf between operative ideals and practice. What counts is whether a people acknowledges its faults and imperfections and strives slowly to improve.

At the beginning of his academic career Woodrow Wilson wrote a brilliant little essay on the "study of administration."[11] In the course of his discussion Wilson declared that "there should be a science of administration which shall seek to straighten the paths of government, to make its business less unbusinesslike, to strengthen and purify its organization, and to crown its duties with dutifulness." It is the last of these objectives in the study of administration which we are here concerned to explore. How do we crown the duties of the bureaucracy with dutifulness? Is the quest for politically responsible behavior by a bureaucracy in our system of government an illusion? Or do the organs of decision making in our structure of government provide effective means for direction and control over the administrative apparatus? Upon the answer to these questions depends in considerable degree the future of a democratic polity in our country.

[11] *Political Science Quarterly,* vol. 2 (June, 1887), p. 197.

PART ONE

The Constitutional Framework
of Public Administration

Chapter 2

The Constitution and Public Administration

Our system of government in the United States rests upon constitutional prescription. One legacy of our Western political heritage is a high regard for law. Indeed, we are convinced that freedom is possible only under law. Nor is law simply a matter of defining the relationships of man to man in society. We have given law an even greater task: to define the relationship of government to man.[1] To this end constitutionalism provides the means. The central role of constitutionalism, or of constitutional democracy, in establishing the essential framework of government is one of the great themes in the political development of Western society.[2]

When the federal Constitution of 1787 was written, two goals were foremost in the political thinking of the day. One was to provide an effective means of common political effort by the thirteen states which had so recently acquired independence from Great Britain. The other objective was to establish a central government, even as they had undertaken to do in each of the thirteen states, which would be limited in scope and safe for men's liberties. The governments established in the first decade of independence reflected the political ideas current in eighteenth-century America. These governments reflected too the conditions of society with which the men of that day were familiar.

American constitutionalism has been primarily concerned with the second of the three essentials of government mentioned in the preceding chapter. State constitutions and the federal Constitution provide organs of decision making as a part of the system of government. These constitutions have little to say about the structure of political power or the operation of political parties. And they have little to say about bureaucracy. These omissions are noteworthy. Little has been done in the inter-

[1] Cf. Edwin W. Patterson, *Jurisprudence: Men and Ideas of the Law* (Brooklyn, N.Y.: The Foundation Press, 1953).

[2] Cf. Frederick Watkins, *The Political Tradition of the West* (Cambridge, Mass.: Harvard University Press, 1948), especially chap. 6.

vening years, however, to enlarge the scope of our formal constitutional documents. Tradition, common practices and understandings, and occasional legal enactments have rounded out the governmental system as a whole. Our "living Constitution," as Howard Lee McBain termed it, has seemed to meet the needs left unresolved or not foreseen by the Founding Fathers.

There are various reasons why the federal Constitution left matters of political power untouched. For one thing, qualifications for voting were considered a question to be determined by each state. The federal Constitution was content then to state only that whatever person was competent to vote for any office in a state should be eligible to vote for officials to be elected under the federal system: representatives and presidential electors. Subsequently by amendment, the Constitution has restricted the states from denying suffrage to any person on account of race, color, or previous condition of servitude, or on account of sex. And the popular election of senators was further achieved through amendment. Laws enacted by the Congress have dealt with corrupt voting practices and with contributions to the support of political parties. For the most part, however, matters of voting qualifications, the conduct of elections, and the structure and operation of political parties have been left to state determination.

In addition, at the time when the federal Constitution was written there was a good deal of uncertainty about the proper place of political parties in our system of government. As indicated in no. 10, perhaps the most celebrated essay of *The Federalist,* James Madison suggested that the Republic would be well advised to control the effects of "faction." Yet early in our national history political parties began clearly to emerge. They are now accepted as an indispensable element of our democracy.

Even the state constitutions, written or rewritten as most of them have been since the end of the eighteenth century, tend to deal with the trivia of political party operation. State laws set forth the important legal provisions governing voting and political activity, whereas custom and usage provide the important features of the transmission and exercise of political power in our society. This is not our principal interest here, however.

BUREAUCRACY IN THE FEDERAL CONSTITUTION

It is revealing of the political thinking and of the rudimentary governmental needs of the day that the federal Constitution should have so little to say on the subject of public administration. Indeed, it is fair to say that our federal Constitution assumes the existence of a bureaucracy rather than provides for it. Such mention as does occur of the subject is entirely indirect or oblique.

In defining the powers of the President in Article II, Section 2, the

Constitution says that "he may require the opinion, in writing, of the principal officer in each of the executive departments, upon any subject relating to the duties of their respective offices." Farther along in the same section the Constitution sets forth the appointive power of the President in these words: " . . . and he shall nominate, and, by and with the consent of the Senate, shall appoint ambassadors, other public ministers and consuls, judges of the Supreme Court, and all other officers of the United States whose appointments are not herein otherwise provided for, and which shall be established by law; but the Congress may by law vest the appointment of such inferior officers, as they think proper, in the President alone, in the courts of law, or in the heads of departments."

Two aspects of these provisions just quoted from Article II of the Constitution should be particularly noted. For one thing, the article does not specifically mention the creation of either "executive departments" or "departments." It simply implies that such agencies will be set up by referring to their heads whom the President may consult in writing, and in whom the Congress may by law vest the power to appoint "inferior officers." Neither of these references to administrative agencies is very explicit. Why does one reference use the expression "executive department" and the other merely the single word "department"? Is there some distinction implied by this differing terminology or is it simply an accident of phraseology? Is there a suggestion here that all administrative agencies must be labeled either executive departments or departments? Is there any particular implication for administrative organization contained in these oblique references? No one can answer such questions as these. There is no authoritative source for providing the answers except continued practice as reflected in legal enactments, presidential attitudes, court decisions, and general acceptance.

A second aspect of this constitutional language is again an indirect one. The words refer to "all other officers of the United States . . . which shall be established by law." Here is the strong implication that officers of the United States must be provided for by law, that is, by enactment of the legislature. In an article which is concerned to set forth the power of the executive the wording appears to suggest that the President shall not create "officers of the United States." Only the legislative process, in which to be sure the executive participates, is capable of establishing such positions.

Yet Article I of the federal Constitution which provides for the legislative power says nothing specifically about administrative agencies. The important section of Article I is, of course, Section 8 enumerating the scope of the legislative authority of the federal government. This section refers to subjects, not to agencies. It speaks of the collection of taxes, the coinage of money, the establishment of post offices, the issuance of patents and copyrights, the support of armies, and the maintenance of a navy. There are other items as well, terminating in a clause which authorizes the Congress to make all laws "necessary and proper for carrying into execution the foregoing powers, and all other powers vested by this Constitution in the government of the United States, or in any department or officer thereof." Here again, instead of any direct provision therefor, is an assumption that administrative agencies will have to be created for the operation of the federal government.

In their eloquent defense of the Constitution, the authors of the collection of papers known as *The Federalist* had little to say about public administration. In essay no. 72, Hamilton commented upon the administrative role of the President, but he appeared to be more concerned about "the stability of the system of administration," which he connected with the term of the President in office, than with the constitutional status of administrative agencies. In a subsequent essay, no. 84, Hamilton enumerated the "principal departments of the administration under the present government" and expressed the opinion that these same agencies would be required under the new government. Yet his major preoccupation appeared to be the practical problem of prospective cost in operating the new central government established by the federal Constitution.

It would be erroneous to assume that the men who framed the Constitution of 1787 were ignorant of administrative problems or belittled the importance of public administration. To be sure, the administrative agencies set up under the Articles of Confederation were few and rudimentary. The authority of the central government was limited. Society was largely commercial and agrarian; population was sparse and scattered the length of the Atlantic seaboard from Maine to Georgia. Overland transportation was slow, dependent upon few roads and upon horse- or oxen-drawn vehicles. Communication was likewise slow. Even in the states governmental services were not extensive. There was little need for or disposition toward governmental administration in eighteenth-century America.

Yet such evidence as is to be found in the federal Constitution itself and in other contemporary documents suggests the conclusion that in 1787 the necessity for public administration as a feature of government was taken for granted. Administrative agencies were in existence at the time. Their continuance, perhaps their expansion, was assumed. Perhaps the menace of a politically irresponsible bureaucracy seemed somewhat remote at that time, but the danger was undoubtedly known to men well-read in the political thinking of their own age and of earlier times.

The governmental challenge of 1787 was not administrative. The basic problem was to establish an effective national government for a new-born nation, to provide organs of decision making competent to meet the needs of the day and even to cope with the developments of the future. One of the tasks of this framework of government was to provide adequate and effective supervision for the administrative agencies of government. This concern was certainly present in the provisions for an executive branch in the new federal government modeled in large measure from the executive branches already existing in the state governments of that day. The constitutions as written were thought to provide the organs of decision making necessary to operate a government, including the establishment and supervision of a bureaucracy.

Some understanding of the attitude of the Founding Fathers is to be obtained from one of the celebrated cases decided by the Supreme Court of the United States with John Marshall as Chief Justice. In the case of *McCulloch v. Maryland,* the authority of the federal legislature to charter a national bank was challenged.[3] In so far as the specific issue was concerned Marshall found his guidance in the last clause of Section 8 of Article I empowering the Congress to make all laws necessary and proper for carrying into execution the other authority set forth in the Constitution. In the eyes of Marshall, the national bank was not just a private agency chartered by the federal legislature. It was an administrative agency necessary for the performance of duties constitutionally specified as coming within the competence of the Congress. Thus was acknowledged the implied assumption of the federal Constitution that administrative agencies would be created by law as deemed necessary and in such form as the legislature and executive might deem appropriate.

Beyond the immediate issue Marshall saw an even more fundamental proposition. The Chief Justice characterized the Constitution of the United States as "intended to endure for ages to come, and, consequently, to be adapted to the various *crises* of human affairs." He thus implied that the Constitution as fundamental law was expected to grow, to take on new meaning with changing circumstances, while the original words remained unchanged and the great principles of governmental framework continued to function unimpaired. All the administrative problems of a later day did not have to be specifically anticipated by the federal Constitution in order for that document to provide the essential elements of a government adequate to cope with the bureaucracy of our own day.

PUBLIC ADMINISTRATION AND THE STATE CONSTITUTIONS

Before we proceed further, it may be well to pause briefly to say something about state constitutions. In essentials the constitutions for our state governments do not differ in many respects from the federal Constitution. The state constitutions have been more often rewritten, they provide many more details, and they embrace a relationship between state authority and local units of government somewhat different from that which exists between the federal government and the states. Otherwise, state constitutions

[3] *McCulloch v. Maryland,* 4 Wheat. 316 (1819).

serve much the same purpose and express much the same fundamentals of government as does the federal Constitution.

Of the forty-nine state constitutions, only two—those of Massachusetts and New Hampshire—antedate the federal Constitution of 1787 and have not been subsequently rewritten. Of the thirty-one other states becoming a part of the United States before 1860, all but three have rewritten their constitutions at least once and some have rewritten them more times. The result of these revisions has been to include more detail, much of it dealing with administrative officials. It is rather common, for example, for state constitutions to specify that there shall be such state officials in addition to the governor as a secretary of state, a treasurer of state, an attorney general, and an auditor of state, all of whom are popularly elected. In some instances, state constitutions have gone further and provide for a board of regents for a state university and on occasion for a state board of education. In revisions which have occurred since 1900 there has been some tendency to reduce the number of separately elected state officers and to vest an increased authority for administrative supervision in the chief executive.

Actually, most state constitutions say very little about the administrative agencies of state government. It is assumed rather than explicitly set forth that the legislature may by law create such administrative agencies as it may deem necessary. The governor is often given the "supreme executive power" and may require from other officials in the executive department their opinion in writing. He is to see that the laws are faithfully executed. Just what such provisions mean in practice only custom and changing circumstances of political and personal fortune can determine. State constitutions, then, tend to deal with such matters as voting and the conduct of elections, public debt, county and township organization, finance and taxation, the creation of corporations under general law, the organization of cities and other incorporated units of local government, and various miscellaneous provisions. Sometimes, as in New York, the constitution may actually set forth the major administrative agencies of state government. Yet little if anything is said about the status of administrative agencies as such.

CONSTITUTIONAL CONCEPTIONS OF GOVERNMENT

For the most part federal and state constitutions are concerned with establishing a framework of governmental organs for decision making. This framework is usually described as a system for the separation of power. In eighteenth-century political thought government was conceived as having three somewhat different, if interrelated, elements. The federal Constitution of 1787 spoke of "all legislative powers," "the executive power," and "the judicial power." The classical statement of the prevailing idea of the time was contained in the Massachusetts Constitution of 1780 which declared: "In the government of this commonwealth the legislative department shall never exercise the executive and judicial powers or either of them; the executive shall never exercise the legislative and judicial powers or either of them; the judicial shall never exercise the legislative and executive powers or either of them: to the end it may be a government of laws and not of men." To be sure, in practice, the separation of governmental power into legislative, executive, and judicial component parts is not absolute. Our constitutions provide for a co-mingling of power, such as executive participation in the enactment of laws, and legislative participation in the appointment of administrative officials.

The structure of American government recognizes nonetheless three different sets of institutions exercising governmental power. The legislative is one institution, very different in its selection, numbers, procedure, and authority from the other two institutions. Similarly, the executive and judicial institutions are quite different in their characteristics from any of the other two. The separation of power in our constitutional democracy is a separation of organs possessing decision-making authority.

There are other characteristics of the American scheme of government which must be mentioned in passing. A bill of rights and other provisions clearly indicate that government is not all-powerful but limited both in the substance of what it may do and in the procedure for exercising its authority. The nature of these limitations has been referred to in the preceding chapter. In addition, ours is a federal scheme of government, comprising a central government for the nation as a whole and forty-nine constituent governments each of which possesses the residual power not vested in the central instrument and not specifically prohibited. We shall have something more to say about this federal system and its administrative implications in the next chapter.

Our American constitutions are concerned to set forth a basic framework of government which is conceived to be adequate to the governmental needs of man in society and at the same time protective of his individual liberties. The kind of structure thought proper for this purpose two hundred years ago and still functioning today embodies the existence of a legislature, an executive, and a judiciary. Each is a distinct entity, different from the other and independent in its status. No one branch is thought of as inherently superior to another; no one branch is expected to be dependent for its authority or its existence upon another. Each is thought of as exercising a different part of the sum total of governmental power. All three are essential to the existence and operation of government.

If the legislature, executive, and judiciary encompass the substance of governmental power, what then is the constitutional position of administration? We cannot turn to our constitutions themselves for a clear and definite answer to this question. The fact is that our constitutions do not undertake to provide any answer. The explanation must be something more than the meager administrative activity of the eighteenth century, as we have already commented. It appears that those who wrote our constitutions assumed that there was no problem to worry about, that any question about the constitutional status of administrative agencies could be answered readily and easily enough if only an adequate basic framework of government was brought into existence. It is subsequent students of government, and even political leaders and judges, who have had reason to ponder the issue with the growth of the modern administrative state.

IDEAS OF CONSTITUTIONAL STATUS

In *The Federalist,* no. 72, Alexander Hamilton began:

> The administration of government, in its largest sense, comprehends all the operations of the body politic, whether legislative, executive, or judiciary; but in its most usual and perhaps in its most precise signification, it is limited to executive details, and falls peculiarly within the province of the executive department. The actual conduct of foreign negotiations, the preparatory plans of finance, the application and disbursement of the public moneys in conformity to the general appropriations of the legislature, the arrangement of the army and navy, the direction of the operations of war—these, and other matters of a like nature, constitute what seems to be most properly understood by the administration of government. The persons, therefore, to whose immediate management these different matters are committed, ought to be considered as the assistants or deputies of the chief magistrate, and on this account, they ought to derive their offices from his appointment, at least from his nomination, and ought to be subject to his superintendence.

In writing about that initial and formative period when the federal government was just starting, Leonard D. White has pointed out that much administrative authority was vested directly in the Chief Executive by law.[4] Except for the Treasury Department, the President was authorized to prescribe the duties of the heads of departments. Department heads, moreover, were expected to act in accordance with the President's instructions. In addition, many details were left to the Chief Executive, such as signing patents and approving contracts for the construction of lighthouses. Certainly, in the early days of the Republic, the President was by law made a principal administrative officer of the federal government. In turn, the Chief Executive was inclined to look upon department heads as his assistants, helping him in the exercise of the executive power.

At the same time, as Secretary of the Treasury, Hamilton went far beyond the inclination of the President in formulating public policy for

[4] Leonard D. White, *The Federalists* (New York: The Macmillan Company, 1948), especially pp. 17–20, and chap. 3.

congressional enactment. Indeed, Hamilton appeared determined to make his position that of a legislative leader, and to a very real degree the President became an impartial chief magistrate and Hamilton a kind of prime minister. When Jefferson became President, the situation was quite different. The President himself was the party leader. More than this, Jefferson was concerned to slow up the process of building a strong administrative organization in the hands of the central government. The very fact that Jefferson had a determined view about the desirable course of political events made the Presidency itself a different kind of office from what it had been under Washington and then under Adams. In a sense, Jefferson made the Presidency more important politically and less important administratively than it had been under Washington.[5]

In any event, it early became an accepted practice to look upon administration and executive power as one and the same. To this very day, there is a disposition in many quarters to speak of the executive branch of government as encompassing all, or almost all, administrative agencies. Thus in 1947 and again in 1953, Congress in passing legislation to create a special agency to study administrative organization labeled the body "The Commission on Organization of the Executive Branch." In 1937, the President's Committee on Administrative Management had no doubt when asserting: "The President is chief executive and administrator within the Federal system and service."[6]

Yet a somewhat different position has been declared from time to time. Under President Jackson a dispute arose between the Postmaster General, Amos Kendall, and the Congress over a claim rendered by one Stokes as a contractor for carrying mail. Both the Postmaster General and the President believed the claim to be fraudulent. Congress by law directed the Solicitor of the Treasury to settle the claim and the Postmaster General then to pay the claim so established. Kendall finally credited Stokes with part of the claim but not all of it. He was sued for the balance. Kendall argued that as head of a department he was subject to the direction and control of the President, and that even in the light of statutory enactment he was not obliged to act contrary to instructions from the President. The Supreme Court of the United States refused to accept this reasoning. To accede to Kendall's argument, the Court declared,[7]

> . . . would be vesting in the President a dispensing power, which has no countenance for its support, in any part of the Constitution; and is asserting

---

[5] Cf. Lynton K. Caldwell, *The Administrative Theories of Hamilton and Jefferson: Their Contribution to Thought on Public Administration* (Chicago: University of Chicago Press, 1944). See also Leonard D. White, *The Jeffersonians* (New York: The Macmillan Company, 1951).

[6] President's Committee on Administrative Management, *Report with Special Studies* (Washington: Government Printing Office, 1937), p. 2.

[7] *Kendall v. Stokes,* 12 Pet. 610 (1838).

a principle, which, if carried out in its results, to all cases falling within it, would be clothing the President with a power entirely to control the legislation of Congress, and paralyze the administration of justice. [The Court went on to say] . . . it would be an alarming doctrine, that Congress cannot impose upon any executive officer any duty they may think proper, which is not repugnant to any rights secured and protected by the Constitution; and in such cases, the duty and responsibility grow out of and are subject to the control of the law, and not to the direction of the President. [The Court added] The law is supreme in the United States and is binding upon administrative officers. Apart from the Constitution itself, this emanates primarily from statutory enactment, which originates in the legislature.

Within a two-year span President Pierce received two somewhat different opinions on this same matter from his Attorney General, Caleb Cushing. In his first opinion the Attorney General declared that heads of departments had a responsibility to Congress. He pointed out that they were created by law and that most of their duties were prescribed by law. The legislature might at all times call upon department heads for information or explanation in matters of official duty and might "as it sees fit interpose by legislation concerning them, when required by the interests of the government."[8] A year later the Attorney General declared that no head of a department could lawfully perform an official act against the will of the President. If this were not so, the Attorney General said, "Congress might by statute so divide and transfer the executive power as utterly to subvert the government."[9]

Many years later, speaking of the Federal Trade Commission, the Supreme Court called it "an administrative body created by Congress to carry into effect legislative policies embodied in the statute in accordance with the legislative standard therein prescribed, and to perform other specified duties as a legislative or as a judicial aid. Such a body cannot in any proper sense be characterized as an arm or an eye of the executive."[10] It also spoke of the Commission as "charged with no policy except the policy of the law," and accepted the proposition that a Commission member was an "officer who occupies no place in the executive department and who exercises no part of the executive power vested by the Constitution in the President."

These opinions express conflicting legal conceptions about the status of administrative agencies in our scheme of government. At the least they indicate some confusion in fixing the respective relationship of legislature and executive to administrative agencies. The legislature has a certain role to perform. The chief executive still another. A line of demarcation in the scope of these respective branches of government has not been easy

[8] 6 Opinions of the Attorney General 326 (1854).
[9] 7 Opinions of the Attorney General 453 (1855).
[10] *Humphrey's Executor v. United States,* 295 U.S. 602 (1935).

to formulate in terms of a clear and consistent doctrine of constitutional status.

Thirty years ago a distinguished political scientist, W. F. Willoughby, thought that the solution to the problem of the constitutional status of administrative agencies lay in drawing a sharp distinction between executive power and administrative power.[11] Willoughby declared that the executive power was that of "representing the government as a whole and of seeing that all its laws are properly complied with by its several parts." On the other hand, "the administrative function, that is, the function of direction, supervision, and control of the administrative activities of the government, resides in the legislative branch."[12] Willoughby likened the authority of the legislature to that of a board of directors in a business corporation. Impressed as he was by the extent of the authority exercised by the legislature over administrative activities, organization, procedure, and expenditure, Willoughby could see no other interpretation of constitutional status which would fit the stubborn facts of actual practice.

Accordingly, Willoughby was led to declare that constitutionally the President "possesses no administrative authority."[13] Instead, he argued that in relation to the heads of administrative agencies the power of the President was limited only to making sure that the orders given them by law were "duly enforced." Willoughby then went on to advocate that as a matter of administrative efficiency the legislature should by law confer upon the Chief Executive the powers of a "General Manager." He wanted the legislature to provide by law that "the line of administrative authority" should run from agency heads to the Chief Executive to the legislature and not directly from agencies to legislature. The President as General Manager should control institutional services, such as care of plant, procurement and distribution of supplies, and the keeping of accounts. The President should prepare the budget. But in all these activities the Chief Executive would be "strictly a subordinate of the legislature, the agent through which the latter exercises the powers of general administration."[14]

A different position holds that all administrative agencies are themselves simply subordinate elements of the executive branch of the government. Did not the federal Constitution refer to heads of "executive departments"? Has not the legislature itself enacted laws which in effect equate the executive branch with the sum total of all administrative activity? And in a tripartite structure of government where would one expect to find administrative agencies except as a part of the executive branch? Arguments such as these have been put forth to maintain that executive and administration are synonymous in our scheme of government.

[11] W. F. Willoughby, *Principles of Public Administration* (Washington, D.C.: Brookings Institution, 1927), chaps. 2 and 3.
[12] *Ibid.*, p. 11.   [13] *Ibid.*, p. 36.   [14] *Ibid.*, p. 49.

This position was advocated by the President's Committee on Administrative Management in 1937.[15] It said that the work of the executive branch was badly organized and declared: "The whole Executive Branch of the Government should be overhauled and the present 100 agencies reorganized under a few large departments in which every executive activity would find its place."[16] Subsequently the Committee asserted that the Constitution "places in the President, and in the President alone, the whole executive power of the Government of the United States."[17] The Committee then acknowledged that the administrative organization to carry out "the executive power" rested upon statutory law. It proceeded to characterize the structure of the executive branch, meaning the structure of administrative agencies, as inefficient, as a "poor instrument for rendering public service," and as thwarting democratic control.[18]

Without making its position entirely explicit, the President's Committee, as the above expressions of point of view indicate, conceived of the executive branch not just as the President but rather as the sum total of administrative activities. Yet the Committee realized also that the reforms it was advocating could not be accomplished by the President alone. It urged that Congress be satisfied to determine "the broad outlines of reorganization" by creating executive departments and by adopting "the general policy that all administrative operating agencies be brought within these large executive departments."[19] But the Committee seemed also to anticipate that this proposal might not be entirely acceptable to the Congress.

Confronted with the inescapable fact that the Congress created by law all "executive departments" as well as other administrative agencies, and realizing that the success of its own recommendation depended upon legislative enactment, the President's Committee faced a crucial dilemma. On the one hand, the Committee was committed to the proposition that the executive branch of the federal government embraced all administrative activities. On the other hand, the Committee confronted the necessity of congressional action in order to carry out its proposals. The Committee then proceeded to develop a surprising constitutional doctrine, the doctrine of "accountability of the executive to the Congress."[20] Just where it found this doctrine or how it arrived at such a proposition, the Committee did not say. It opened its discussion with these words:

Under the American system the Executive power is balanced and made safe by freedom of speech, by elections, by the protection of civil rights under an independent judiciary, by the making of laws which determine poli-

[15] President's Committee on Administrative Management, *op. cit.*, p. 2.
[16] *Ibid.*, p. 4.   [17] *Ibid.*, p. 31.   [18] *Ibid.*, pp. 32–33.
[19] *Ibid.*, p. 49.   [20] *Ibid.*

cies including especially appropriations and tax measures, by an independent elective Congress, and by the establishment of Executive accountability.

The Committee went on to assert that the preservation of the principle of the "full accountability of the Executive to the Congress is an essential part of our republican system."[21] It suggested first that accountability would be achieved through proper executive coordination of administrative activities. The Committee then spoke of the importance of the legislature and of the work done by committees in considering pending bills and in conducting investigations. "It is with full realization of the necessity of continuing and preserving this important function of the Congress and its committees that we suggest the necessity for improving the machinery of holding the Executive Branch more effectively accountable to the Congress."[22] The Committee said that "detailed legislative requirements" on organization and operation of the administrative machinery absolved the head of a department and then the President from his executive responsibility. The President's Committee saw as a solution: "The Executive then should be held to account through an independent audit made by an independent auditor who will report promptly to the Congress his criticisms and exceptions of the actions of the Executive."[23]

Apart from the prescription, we may note two major aspects of the position put forth by the President's Committee on Administrative Management. First, the Committee appeared to equate the President and all administrative agencies as together constituting the executive branch of government. Secondly, the Committee announced a new constitutional doctrine of presidential accountability to the Congress for the conduct of administrative agencies. These two propositions entail governmental complexities which neither the President's Committee in 1937 nor others have been able to resolve.

Some political scientists have taken positions similar to that of the President's Committee on Administrative Management but have argued in terms of preferable practice rather than of constitutional prescription. Thus, one writer has set forth his "working bias" in these terms: "An administrative agency should be responsible to the legislature, but only through the chief executive, and primarily for broad issues of public policy and general administrative performance."[24] The author goes on to point out that administrative agencies "must be answerable in some sense to *both* the chief executive and the legislature."[25] He then poses the issue as whether this dual responsibility shall be structured in terms of an agency being directly and separately responsible to the legislature and the chief

[21] *Ibid.*   [22] *Ibid.*   [23] *Ibid.*, p. 50.
[24] Arthur Maass, *Muddy Waters* (Cambridge, Mass.: Harvard University Press, 1951), p. 8.
[25] *Ibid.*, p. 9.

executive, or shall an agency be responsible to the legislature through the chief executive? This question is then answered by this particular student of government in terms of the second arrangement being the preferable practice.

The arguments in favor of indirect responsibility are both political and technical in nature. If administrative agencies are responsible to the legislature only through the chief executive, then there is one rather than two sources of official communication and command. Conflicting instructions may be avoided, and administrative action be sure and certain rather than confused and contradictory. Coordination of agencies having common concerns is more readily achieved if there is only one source of command. The executive is better equipped than the legislature for the supervision of administrative agencies. The executive can present balanced and consistent programs to the legislature for consideration, and legislative action can be better informed and clearly focused on major issues.[26]

Opposed to this line of reasoning are two major arguments. One is that since the legislature must set forth the broad outlines of public policy to be carried out by administrative agencies, this necessarily entails some degree of supervision over them. The other is that if legislative responsibility is to be exercised through the executive, does this not make the executive subordinate to the legislature, contrary to the framework of government established by our constitutions?

The various ideas and concepts just cited illustrate an important confusion in the constitutional prescription of American government. Unquestionably those who drafted the federal Constitution and our state constitutions intended to provide an adequate arrangement for the supervision of bureaucracy. No one contemplated the possibility of a politically irresponsible administrative apparatus. Rather, it was thought that the scheme of government set up for decision making would be competent to supervise the bureaucracy and ensure its behavior in accordance with instructions from the legislature and executive. How this arrangement would work in practice seems to have given little concern to those who wrote our constitutional documents.

CONCLUSION

The doctrine of the separation of legislature, executive, and judiciary is a fundamental characteristic of the American structure of government. There is no equally clear and distinct doctrine of the constitutional status of the bureaucracy within this system of government. Important phases of supervision over administrative agencies are exercised by the legislature. Equally important but different phases of supervisory authority are exercised by the executive. The same is true of the judiciary. Indeed, we may say that each branch of government exercises vital authority over the

[26] *Ibid.*, pp. 9–11.

conduct of administrative agencies. The nature of that authority is peculiar to the nature and attributes of each separate branch of government: legislative, executive, and judicial.

The practice of political supervision of the bureaucracy has continually outstripped our ability to theorize about this actual practice. We have undertaken the quest for politically responsible bureaucracy without the benefit of any clear-cut, precise doctrine of administrative responsibility. This is one of the noteworthy features of American government.

In the absence of any definite doctrine of constitutional status on the part of our administrative agencies, some students of government and others have proclaimed that all administrative agencies are a part of the executive branch. The difficulty with this concept is that it does not adequately deal with the role of the legislature in our scheme of government. If the legislature is to be properly recognized as the vital factor which it is in providing the statutory basis of administrative action, including appropriations, then are administrative agencies responsible to the legislature only through the executive? Any such conception of executive status might well become destructive of the whole idea of executive independence which is the essence of our scheme of government. But the price of executive independence under our scheme of government is a limited scope of power for the executive. If the executive were all-powerful in relation to the bureaucracy, then in turn he would have to be subordinate in power to the legislature. This is the arrangement in a parliamentary scheme of government. This is not the American scheme.

It would be equally destructive of executive status to conceive of the executive's role as that of an agent of the legislature. Constitutions, not statutory law, vest power in the executive. As we shall note later, law may amplify or supplement that power, but it cannot fundamentally alter it. Otherwise, separation of power would no longer be the fundamental characteristic it is in our scheme of government.

We cannot look to constitutional doctrine to find an answer to the question: How do we keep the bureaucracy politically responsible in America? Rather we must look to practice. And in practice, as we shall observe, all three branches of government, legislative, executive, and judicial, have major roles to play in maintaining politically responsible behavior. Each such role is different; each operates directly upon administrative agencies. In a sense, administrative agencies are responsible in varying ways to all three branches of government.

We may reasonably think of the bureaucracy in our system of government as being a kind of separate element, apart from the three basic organs of decision making in our governmental structure but subordinate to all three. Yet such an interpretation of status is not founded in constitutional prescription. It is founded in the political practice of American government. It is that practice which points the way in the quest for responsible performance of the bureaucracy.

Chapter 3

Federalism and Public Administration

The American system of government entails more than a separation of power among legislative, executive, and judicial branches. It also involves a sharing of power between two levels of government: a federal level and forty-nine state governments. Necessarily, the work of public administration in our country must be performed within the context of this federal system.

The most important problem of a federal system is the allocation of authority between central and constituent governments. In terms of constitutional prescription, our central government is one of enumerated powers; the state governments possess residual powers including the so-called police power to enact laws concerning the health, safety, morals, and welfare of the people. The Founding Fathers were especially concerned to give the central government authority over foreign affairs, national defense, and the regulation of commerce among the states, together with the power to raise directly the funds necessary for the support of these activities. In time, and under the impact of changing social and economic circumstances, the authority of the central government has proved quite extensive indeed. Today it is fair to say that our central and state governments no longer divide governmental power but exercise a concurrent power.[1]

In a federal system the first issue to arise is a political one: when a public concern is sufficiently grave to warrant governmental action, shall that action be federal or state in nature? A corollary issue is the competence of the federal government within the range of its power to take action. This is a constitutional question which may eventually be decided by the judiciary, or by amendment of the Constitution. But a federal system in practice poses a special administrative issue as well. Because of the

---

[1] Cf. Arthur W. Macmahon (ed.), *Federalism: Mature and Emergent* (New York: Columbia University Press, 1955).

peculiar nature of the distribution of power between federal and state governments, it is not unusual for the central government to manifest an interest in some particular public problem along with the state governments. A federal administrative agency is then set up not to displace state agencies but to complement and supplement their work.

The point is just this. A federal system of shared political power necessarily results in a system of shared administrative activity. To some persons, especially those unfamiliar with a federal structure of government, it is confusing indeed to find central, state, and even local administrative agencies concerned with some particular activity but not formally subordinate one to the other. Administrative authority follows the decisions of political desirability and constitutional sanction. Many administrative agencies of the federal government find that their role is not to command but to persuade and stimulate state and local governmental administrative agencies to do their work in the most proficient way possible. An intricate set of administrative interrelationships is one of the consequences of a federal system of government.

DETERMINATION OF A FEDERAL OR NATIONAL INTEREST

As our political history has unfolded, various reasons have been advanced why the central government should evidence a concern with a particular subject. The emergence of a national economy within our country has been a major factor, for example, in encouraging national government action on economic matters. Sometimes, only the national government has possessed both the authority and the scope for successful action. Thus in 1886 the Supreme Court held that a state could not regulate the rates charged by a railroad for commodities shipped in interstate commerce.[2] If there was to be regulation of rates charged by common carriers for commodities shipped in interstate commerce, then the authority must be exercised by the central government. The direct consequence of this decision was the passage of the Interstate Commerce Commission Act of 1887. Similarly, only the central government can coin money and so endeavor to affect the price level and the functioning of the economy by altering the monetary supply.

Other factors have encouraged national government action rather than that of state government. The economic resources of individual states have varied a great deal. Central action has then been sought as a means of fixing a minimum standard of performance, together with a minimum expenditure of funds for some governmental service. In recent years, moreover, because of its preemption of the personal and corporation income tax, the tax resources of the federal government have appeared more

---

[2] *Wabash, St. Louis and Pacific Railroad Co. v. Illinois,* 118 U.S. 557 (1886).

remunerative and more equitable than those of state and local governments. Some persons, therefore, seek to "equalize" economic differences among states by using national tax income to support services otherwise exclusively state and local.[3] Furthermore, there is always the possibility that forty-nine state governments will take conflicting or competing action on a particular subject. Thus, it has been urged on occasion that the national government ought to have the authority to pass a divorce law in order to eliminate the varied standards on this subject which exist among different states. In order to have an effective inheritance tax, it was necessary to obtain national action to avoid the likelihood that some states would use the absence of such a tax as a means to promote their own economic advantage.[4] Sometimes, too, it has been suggested that federal administrative operation was more efficient or less corrupt than that of some of the states.

In any event, various reasons may be advanced from time to time for federal government policy and administration in some particular field of interest. But in each such instance federal jurisdiction has had to be established or defended by reference to one of the provisions set forth in Article I, Section 8, of the Constitution. In this process, apart from the clauses having to do with national defense, foreign affairs, and the regulation of commerce among the states, one clause in particular has had special importance. The very first clause in Section 8 declared that Congress should have power "to lay and collect taxes, imposts, and excises, to pay the debts and provide for the common defense and general welfare of the United States." This taxing power of the federal government has been construed in a broad sense. Indeed, the production of revenue may be only an incidental element of tax legislation. A protective tariff is primarily expected to provide protection for American products against foreign competition; the receipt of income for the government is of secondary importance. Moreover, the taxing power may be used for regulatory purposes, as to control traffic in narcotic drugs. In some instances, the Supreme Court has reasoned that this taxing power has been pushed "too far," as when legislation was passed by Congress taxing products made in factories employing child labor and when a special tax was levied upon liquor dealers conducting their business in contravention

---

[3] This position was put forth with some vigor by the Advisory Committee on Education in 1938 in its *Report* (Washington: Government Printing Office, 1938) urging federal financial assistance for education. Much the same sort of argument was repeated in 1947 by the President's Commission on Higher Education in its report *Education for American Democracy* (Washington: Government Printing Office, 1947).

[4] The state of Florida has a constitutional prohibition against the enactment of an inheritance tax by the state legislature if the federal government should ever abandon this tax.

of state laws.[5] Yet a tax upon all persons "engaged in the business of accepting wagers," the "gamblers' occupational tax," as well as a tax upon all wagers, has been upheld by the court.[6]

These intricacies of when is a federal tax a constitutional federal tax are not so important to public administration as a more far-reaching interpretation of the taxing power. Article I, Section 8 empowers Congress to levy taxes to pay off debts and to provide for the national defense and the "general welfare." There has been much debate about the proper interpretation of this language. Does the power to *tax* for the general welfare imply the power to *spend* for the general welfare? And in so far as the federal government is concerned, is there no limitation upon what the legislature may decide is desirable expenditure for the general welfare? Although there was some uncertainty or vacillation on the part of the Court in 1936 when processing taxes were ruled unconstitutional as a regulation of agriculture, in general it must be said today that the Supreme Court has in effect eliminated any constitutional objection to the "power to spend."[7]

The national legislature, in the exercise of its legislative wisdom, must decide both for what particular purposes and how much the federal government shall spend for the benefit of the general welfare. To date this legislative, or political, question has been decided in favor of a great array of objects, such as the construction of automobile highways, the operation of an agricultural extension service, the support of agricultural experiment stations, the provision of lunches to school children, the operation of employment offices, the construction of school buildings in areas "affected" by the location of military posts and atomic energy or other federal installations, the administration of relief assistance to the aged, the blind, and dependent children, the construction of hospitals, the support of health services, the construction of low-cost public housing, and aid in the development of airports. In each such instance, Congress has decided that it is in the interest of the public welfare to spend federally collected taxes for the complete or partial operation of these particular government services. In each such instance, the federal government has necessarily had to establish administrative machinery to effect the purpose of the legislation. In almost all such instances, the federal government has set up administrative machinery which carries on activities closely related to activities also carried on by state governments.

---

[5] *Bailey v. Drexel Furniture Company,* 259 U.S. 20 (1922); and *United States v. Constantine,* 296 U.S. 287 (1936).

[6] *United States v. Kahriger,* 345 U.S. 22 (1953).

[7] The leading cases on this subject are *Massachusetts v. Mellon,* 262 U.S. 447 (1923); *United States v. Butler,* 297 U.S. 1 (1936); *Steward Machinery Company v. Davis,* 301 U.S. 548 (1937); *Helvering v. Davis,* 301 U.S. 619 (1937); and *Alabama Power Company v. Ickes,* 302 U.S. 364 (1938).

Financial support is not the only mechanism by which the federal government asserts a federal interest in a particular subject. During many years of our political history, an even more common practice was for the federal government to establish an administrative agency to collect statistics or otherwise to provide information about some subject. Among the administrative agencies of the federal government originally created with this purpose in mind, we may mention the Bureau of Agricultural Economics, the Bureau of Foreign Commerce, the Bureau of Labor Statistics, the Children's Bureau, and the Women's Bureau.

The constitutional authority for much of the administrative work of the federal government is derived from the power to tax for the general welfare. In practice, this power has been widely used to carry out a great variety of administrative undertakings. Yet there is a continuing possibility that the exact nature of the administrative authority being exercised will not be clearly understood by legislators, special interest groups, administrators, and the interested public at large. Federal administrative authority based upon the constitutional power to promote the general welfare through the expenditure of public funds is not quite the same thing as authority to promote the general welfare through the commerce power. At the same time, this spending power, as we have mentioned before, frequently if not always involves federal administrative agencies in extensive relationships with state and local administrative agencies. A great deal of effort, therefore, is needed to avoid any unnecessary duplication or conflict of administrative endeavor.

The decision when to spend for the general welfare is a legislative decision. For example, is it desirable for the federal government to set up a general system of financial support for education? Constitutionally, there can be no argument today about this question. If Congress believes it desirable to establish federal aid to education, there can be little doubt about the constitutional authority to take such action. But whether Congress should take such action or not is a profoundly important issue of public policy, of political argument. Many different groups are vitally interested, from school administrators, parents and teachers, and taxpayers to those concerned about federalism as a governmental scheme. It should be pointed out that just because the federal government has the *constitutional authority* to spend for the public welfare, as in a field such as support of primary and secondary education, it does not necessarily follow that the legislature will decide that it is *desirable* to spend for this purpose.

CONCERN ABOUT EXPANSION OF FEDERAL AUTHORITY

In recent years in particular there has been a good deal of concern about the development of more and more federal activities impinging upon state authority. This concern led President Eisenhower to address a special message to the Congress on March 30, 1953, on the subject. In this message he said:[8]

> The present division of activities between Federal and State Governments, including their local subdivisions, is the product of more than a century and a half of piecemeal and often haphazard growth. This growth in recent decades has proceeded at a speed defying order and efficiency. One program after another has been launched to meet emergencies and expanding public needs. Time has rarely been taken for thoughtful attention to the effects of these actions on the basic structure of our Federal-State system of government.
>
> Now there is need to review and assess, with prudence and foresight, the proper roles of the Federal, State, and local governments. In many cases, especially within the past 20 years, the Federal Government has entered fields which, under our Constitution, are the primary responsibilities of State and local governments. This has tended to blur the responsibilities of local government. It has led to duplication and waste. It is time to relieve the people of the need to pay taxes on taxes.

The President went on to say that the "major mark of this development" had been the growth of federal grants-in-aid to state governments. He mentioned that there were over thirty such grant programs, spending over two billion dollars a year and comprising almost 25 per cent of state government revenues. He urged the creation of a Commission on Intergovernmental Relations to study the situation and if possible to propose clear lines of authority to define the areas of action for the federal and state governments in such fields as health, education, and social security. He asserted: "The maintenance of strong, well-ordered State and local governments is essential to our Federal system of government."

As a result of President Eisenhower's recommendation, Congress in 1953 authorized the creation of a Commission on Intergovernmental Relations composed of fifteen members appointed by the President, five appointed by the Speaker of the House, and five appointed by the President of the Senate. The Commission submitted its official report to the President in June, 1955.

If some had thought that there might be a ready solution to the problem of federal-state relationships in the twentieth century, the report of the Commission on Intergovernmental Relations must have been a disappointment. The Commission pointed to the continuing vitality of state and local governments as evidence that the federal system still functioned. As a system, the division of governmental effort between federal and state component parts was vital to American freedom and should be preserved. At the same time the Commission acknowledged that there were few governmental problems today in which some national interest might not arise. All the Commission could do was urge that the need for national participation in any field of activity be carefully appraised, and

[8] *Congressional Record*, vol. 99, part 2, p. 2459,

that when national participation was decided upon, such participation be held to the minimum required to achieve the objective. As a general pattern the Commission asserted that the nation's civic responsibilities should be divided so that we:[9]

> Leave to private initiative all the functions that citizens can perform privately; use the level of government closest to the community for all public functions which it can handle; utilize cooperative intergovernmental arrangements where appropriate to attain economical performance and popular approval; reserve National action for residual participation where State and local governments are not fully adequate, and for the continuing responsibilities that only the National government can undertake.

Beyond so general a prescription, however, the Commission was not prepared to go. It reviewed the history of constitutional limitations upon the authority of the central government and concluded that divisions of federal and state activity were now a matter primarily of public policy as determined by the legislature rather than of constitutional doctrine. The Commission called attention to the need to improve state government and state administration if demands for federal action were to be reduced. It identified the major activities of the federal government and then mentioned various circumstances which brought about national government action, among them, activities which could not be handled within the geographical jurisdiction of a state, such as the regulation of radio and television, and the failure of states to protect basic political and civic rights belonging to all citizens of the United States. The Commission was unable to find any hard, clear-cut distinction between problems of state and problems of national concern. The most it could do was to suggest continuing assessment of federal-state relationships. It did not see any possibility of a complete separation of tax resources for various levels of government.

Leonard D. White has suggested that, in the interests of strengthening state governments as constituent parts of our federal system, certain services now operated with federal assistance should become entirely state responsibilities. He has proposed particularly that vocational education, vocational rehabilitation, soil conservation (not a grant-in-aid program), and highway construction become exclusively state activities. But in making these proposals, White acknowledged that he was uncertain whether they were practically or politically feasible.[10]

Once the federal government asserts an interest in a particular activity and assumes all or part of the financial burden in providing that service, any change in the situation is difficult to make. State government officials

---

[9] Commission on Intergovernmental Relations, *A Report to the President for Transmittal to the Congress* (Washington: Government Printing Office, 1955), p. 6.

[10] Leonard D. White, *The States and the Nation* (Baton Rouge, La.: Louisiana State University Press, 1953), p. 77.

themselves are reluctant to take over the entire burden of a shared activity when it means that new state taxes must be enacted. At a time when the tax resources of the federal government are hard pushed to meet national defense needs and international requirements, any state hope for a relaxation of federal revenue collection with a corresponding advance in state taxation is a dim one.

GRANTS-IN-AID

The grant-in-aid is a major device for sharing the expenditure in support of an activity operated by another level of government. The grant-in-aid, however, is not the only mechanism for such financial assistance. Another procedure is for one government to share its revenues with another government. The national government has done this in a few instances, such as revenues obtained from utilization of mineral and timber resources on public lands. Some state governments share sales tax and other tax income to a considerable degree with local units of government, including school districts. Still a third kind of financial assistance is the repayable loan which the national government may make to state and local governments. This has been done in aiding public housing, slum clearance, and other public works projects.

The history of federal grants-in-aid falls into three fairly distinct periods.[11] In the period from 1785 to 1914—beginning even before the Constitution of 1787 was written—the chief concern of the central government was financial support for education and agriculture. In the ten-year period from 1919 to 1929, the chief concern was highway construction, an adjunct of the booming automobile industry in this country. With the advent of the Depression down to the present day, the principal objects of attention have been public welfare and social security. In the fiscal year ending June 30, 1953, some 90 per cent of the 2.7 million dollars spent on federal aid was divided among six programs: public assistance (51 per cent), highways (19 per cent), unemployment compensation (7 per cent), school lunches (5 per cent), hospital construction (4 per cent), and school construction and operation in areas affected by defense activities (4 per cent).

In the very early years of the national government, Congress gave vast tracts of public lands to the states for educational, transportation, and reclamation purposes. In 1837, a 28-million-dollar surplus in the federal treasury was divided among the states, ostensibly as a loan but without any intention of demanding repayment. In 1862, the Morrill Act provided grants of public lands to the states to aid them in developing colleges for teaching agricultural and mechanical arts, "without excluding other scientific and classical studies, and including military tactics." In 1887, Con-

[11] Commission on Intergovernmental Relations, *op. cit.,* chap. 5.

gress began direct money grants to state agricultural experiment stations and in 1890 started financial support for instruction in the land-grant colleges.

In the decade from 1911 to 1920, state forest services, agricultural extension work, vocational education, and vocational rehabilitation were added to the list of state programs receiving financial assistance from the federal government. The Federal Aid Road Act of 1916 was the most important piece of legislation, however. This law, with its amendments in 1921, established administrative machinery entailing careful direction and supervision of state highway construction in return for federal funds.

In 1920, the Sheppard-Towner Act authorized the grant of federal funds to states to assist them in promoting infant and maternity hygiene. Although the grants were discontinued in 1929, they were renewed under the Social Security Act of 1935. In 1933 in the Wagner-Peyser Act, Congress authorized annual appropriations for grants to states to establish and maintain public employment offices. In that same year the Federal Emergency Relief Act provided grants to states to meet relief needs. The Social Security Act of 1935 made federal financial assistance available to states in giving aid to the needy aged, the blind, and dependent children. In addition, the act authorized the federal government to pay the entire administrative cost for state unemployment compensation laws. In 1937, the Wagner Public Housing Law placed federal assistance to local communities for low-cost housing on a definite legal basis; this legislation was modified and extended by amendments passed in 1947. In the period since the end of World War II, federal grants-in-aid have been extended to airport construction, hospital construction, school construction, the provision of school lunches, civil defense, water pollution control, and shore erosion control.

Many different factors have influenced the inauguration of federal grants-in-aid. In some instances, the national government has sought to ensure the performance of certain activities by the states, as in agricultural education, highway construction, and old-age assistance. When the Wagner-Peyser Act was passed in 1933, twenty-three states had employment services with a total of 192 offices in 120 different cities. Within five years after the passage of the law, all but one of the forty-eight states had set up employment services, operating 1,300 offices.[12] A nationwide program has usually been desired by the advocates of such action. But grants-in-aid have also been used to inaugurate new government activities, as in agricultural research and in public housing. The Federal Emergency Relief Act was passed in 1933 in order to prevent the almost complete

[12] Raymond C. Atkinson, Louise C. Odencrantz, and Ben Deming, *Public Employment Service in the United States* (Chicago: Public Administration Service, 1938), pp. 22–23.

collapse of state relief activities, whose financing and administration were completely inadequate to the load of the time.

Arguments for and against the Device. Much has been said for and against federal grants-in-aid.[13] It is claimed that the device is a useful one for bringing the national, state, and local governments together in a common enterprise. National financial assistance is needed to help support many essential services of state and local governments. Federal aid is a means for equalizing differences among states in their ability to finance government services. Federal supervision has improved the standards and conduct of state administration. Finally, it is said that federal aid is a desirable substitute for direct administration by the national government. On the other hand, the opponents of federal aid assert that the device is used to extend national government authority in fields which properly should be the exclusive concern of state governments. Federal tax funds are thereby spent for local rather than for national purposes. Federal aid places an unfair burden upon those states whose citizens are taxed to operate government activities in other states. Furthermore, federal aid may lead to governmental extravagance, or at least to a distortion in the pattern of state government expenditures. Finally, federal aid leads to centralized control over many government services which should be left to varied and local direction.

The constitutional prescription of federalism in our governmental structure probably has made the grant-in-aid relationship essential to the effective functioning of the system. For various reasons national government participation in the financing and administration of some governmental activity may be desired. The grant-in-aid has proved a useful device for such national-state cooperation. The federal system has been no bar to the development of this joint relationship. It is a matter of government policy how extensively the device shall be used.

Financial Aspects. A good deal of argument has arisen from time to time about the financial aspects of federal grants-in-aid. Much of this same debate may also arise in regard to state grants to local governments.[14] In the first place, when the central government extends financial assistance to the local unit, how shall the amount of this aid be determined? There are several possible answers. A given amount of assistance may be divided among the states on a population basis. This was used, for example, in making the land grants for educational purposes under the Morrill Act of 1862. Population is a major factor also in apportioning funds for vocational education, airports, hospitals, school lunches, and

---

[13] The arguments are summarized in *Federal Grants-in-Aid* (Chicago: The Council of State Governments, 1949), pp. 41–42.

[14] See Report of the Committee on State-Local Relations, *State-Local Relations* (Chicago: The Council of State Governments, 1946), parts 3 and 4.

child welfare. In these instances there is an obvious relationship between the program provided, financial assistance, and the numbers of people residing within a state. In addition to the population factor, two federal programs—highway and airport construction—have added another factor, the geographical size of a state. In a few programs—support of the land-grant college, agricultural extension, maternal and child welfare, and aid to crippled children—Congress has specified that a lump sum of equal amount is to be given to each state regardless of other factors. Yet another way of determining the amount of federal aid is for Congress to offer to match any state expenditure, subject perhaps to an upper limit. This has been done, in the programs of assistance to needy persons over sixty-five years of age, to dependent children, to the blind, and to the disabled. Finally, the national government may endeavor to allocate funds among the states on the basis of some calculation of relative need. The usual method of calculating need is the difference in per capita income payments among states. Public health and hospital funds, vocational rehabilitation grants, and school-lunch grants have been made according to a formula weighted to indicate the relative financial well-being of various states.

Apart from the problem of the basis for allocating funds, a major concern is whether the states shall be expected to match federal funds, and if so, to what extent? The basic issue is whether federal financial support of a program shall be a relatively major or minor part of the total expenditures for an activity. For example, under the program for support of agricultural experiment stations, the national government has allotted a uniform $90,000 to each state, and then has required an even matching of dollar for dollar of the remaining expenditures. Actually, in practice, state governments have tended to spend anywhere from two to three or four times the amount of the federal allocation in support of agricultural experiment stations.[15] On the other hand, of the national government's some 30 to 40 million dollars a year given for the support of agricultural extension services, only about 5 million must be matched by the states. In practice, the tendency has been for the states to match or even to exceed the amount of federal aid.[16] In the field of vocational education, an equal matching is required for each dollar of federal assistance; here again the states and local governments tend to spend about twice as much as they are actually required to expend. Under regulations of the Surgeon General, state and local governments must spend one dollar for every two dollars of federal grants for public health purposes. Under the National School Lunch Act of 1946, all states whose per capita income exceeded the national average had to match the federal grant dollar for dollar up to 1951, and then spend 1½ dollars for each dollar of federal aid up to

[15] Richard G. Axt, *The Federal Government and Financing Higher Education* (New York: Columbia University Press, 1952), p. 95.
[16] *Ibid.*, p. 71.

1955. For states whose per capita income was less than the national average, the formula permitted a differential, so that some states had to spend only 50 cents for each dollar of federal aid. Variations in these matching requirements occur in other legislation.[17]

Unless an exact formula for matching is written into a grant-in-aid program, pressure is likely to be placed upon administrative officials of the federal government to assume more and more of the total cost. Even though the circumstances were unusual, this was the experience, for example, of the Federal Emergency Relief Administration between 1933 and 1935. In some states the federal government found itself assuming up to as much as 98 per cent of the total relief expenditures; in several instances federal participation was 75 per cent or more.[18] The federal government abandoned the entire program in 1935 because of the complete breakdown in matching requirements.

Since a grant-in-aid program is ordinarily thought of as a joint enterprise, some sharing of total expenditures for a service is to be expected. It is not a simple matter, however, to determine just what the basis of this sharing should be. The simplest solution is to expect an exact matching. But this answer may not always be consistent with the purpose of the program. States differ in financial well-being. In 1953, for example, whereas the average income payment per person for the United States as a whole was $1,676, in thirty states income payments per capita were below this amount. In two, Mississippi and Arkansas, the average income per capita was below $1,000. There were three states where the average was between $1,000 and $1,100 a year; four were between $1,100 and $1,200; four between $1,200 and $1,300; six between $1,300 and $1,400; four between $1,400 and $1,500; five between $1,500 and $1,600; and two over $1,600 but less than the national average of $1,676. At the other extreme there were seven states where per capita income in 1953 averaged more than $2,000, the highest being Delaware with $2,256. There were two states where the average was more than $1,676 but less than $1,700; five states between $1,700 and $1,800; two between $1,800 and $1,900; and two between $1,900 and $2,000. We do not have a uniform degree of economic development or an equalized distribution of economic resources state by state within the United States.

This situation being true, it is relatively easier for some states to expend funds on a basis of equal matching than for others. Moreover, this relative difference may be the exact opposite of the intention of a national program. For example, apart from its purpose in promoting increased consumption of agricultural products, the objective of the national school-

---

[17] For a summary of matching requirements, see Commission on Intergovernmental Relations, *op. cit.*, pp. 305–307.

[18] Edward A. Williams, *Federal Aid for Relief* (New York: Columbia University Press, 1939), pp. 217–218.

Table 1. State Comparisons of Benefits from Federal Grants

State	Total federal tax payments, million dollars	Total grants received, million dollars	Grants as per cent of tax payments	1953 per capita income	Grants as per cent of total income payments
United States	69,857	2,722	3	1,676	1.03
Alabama	679	57	8	1,021	1.80
Arizona	310	24	8	1,488	1.79
Arkansas	364	48	13	953	2.68
California	6,458	260	4	2,008	1.08
Colorado	649	46	7	1,652	1.96
Connecticut	1,427	24	2	2,132	0.53
Delaware	330	6	2	2,256	0.75
Florida	1,152	57	5	1,352	1.31
Georgia	923	84	9	1,162	2.04
Idaho	212	15	7	1,448	1.74
Illinois	5,239	124	2	2,038	0.68
Indiana	1,746	49	3	1,751	0.67
Iowa	947	45	5	1,546	1.12
Kansas	748	44	6	1,590	1.39
Kentucky	761	55	7	1,146	1.62
Louisiana	797	101	12	1,240	2.89
Maine	305	17	5	1,364	1.38
Maryland	1,315	31	2	1,806	0.68
Massachusetts	2,477	80	3	1,792	0.92
Michigan	3,447	101	3	1,916	0.78
Minnesota	1,186	56	5	1,524	1.21
Mississippi	344	42	12	830	2.33
Missouri	1,758	97	6	1,631	1.47
Montana	243	19	8	1,690	1.86
Nebraska	535	22	4	1,558	1.05
Nevada	112	11	10	2,201	2.56
New Hampshire	226	9	4	1,586	1.07
New Jersey	2,715	45	2	2,035	0.43
New Mexico	227	23	10	1,337	2.30
New York	9,646	199	2	2,110	0.62
North Carolina	998	59	6	1,078	1.31
North Dakota	179	17	10	1,270	2.19
Ohio	4,254	104	2	1,942	0.64
Oklahoma	696	78	11	1,310	2.66
Oregon	733	29	4	1,718	1.05
Pennsylvania	5,139	107	2	1,778	0.57
Rhode Island	396	14	3	1,705	1.00
South Carolina	468	43	9	1,092	1.80
South Dakota	182	19	10	1,296	2.23
Tennessee	872	63	7	1,156	1.66
Texas	3,105	156	5	1,468	1.29
Utah	250	21	9	1,484	1.92

Table 1. State Comparisons of Benefits from Federal Grants (Continued)

State	Total federal tax payments, million dollars	Total grants received, million dollars	Grants as per cent of tax payments	1953 per capita income	Grants as per cent of total income payments
Vermont	125	8	6	1,382	1.56
Virginia	1,100	47	4	1,350	0.99
Washington	1,211	64	5	1,846	1.40
West Virginia	535	37	7	1,245	1.53
Wisconsin	1,566	51	3	1,694	0.86
Wyoming	143	10	7	1,654	1.98

SOURCE: Commission on Intergovernmental Relations, *A Report to the President for Transmittal to the Congress* (Washington: Government Printing Office, 1955), Appendix, Tables 9, 4, 7, and 8.

lunch program is to provide school children with a nutritious lunch at minimum cost. The need for such a lunch at low cost is likely to be greater in a state with relatively low average income payments per individual than in a state with relatively higher averages. For this reason, the 1946 law introduced a calculation of need based upon differences in per capita income in setting forth a matching requirement for the support of the school-lunch program.

An allocation formula based upon state uniformity, area, or relative need immediately introduces another problem. The fact that states have differing degrees of economic wealth, whereas the federal tax system is geared to a considerable degree upon ability to pay, has produced an inequality among states in the benefit derived from federal assistance. On a per capita basis, the state governments by no means share equally in the receipt of federal grants. In 1953, the average grant to states per capita for the whole United States was $17.19. There were eighteen states in that year in which the average per capita grant was less than this national average. The thirteen states with an average per capita grant above $25 were all located west of the Mississippi. The twelve states where the grant was less than $15 per person were all east of the Mississippi.

It is often pointed out that some states contribute a good deal more in federal taxes than they receive back in federal grants. Whether this is a proper criticism or not, depends upon one's basic assumption. The fact that returns from grants-in-aid are not proportionate to tax contributions is beyond question. A study of such data as those in Table 1 clearly reveals a number of disparities. There were seven states in which the federal grants-in-aid in 1953 amounted to 10 per cent or more of total federal tax payments originating in those states. Four of these seven states were in the lowest twelve states in so far as per capita income payments were concerned. Geographical location as well as differences in wealth result in disparities among federal benefits. Program formulas have been devised to this end. In general, the wealthiest states north of the Ohio and east of the Mississippi tend to benefit the least from federal grants-in-aid. Thus, the states receiving in benefit only 2 per cent of their tax contributions include Connecticut, Delaware, Illinois, Maryland, New Jersey, New York, Ohio, and Pennsylvania. These states all ranked among the first thirteen states in the United States in so far as per capita income payments were concerned. Obviously, grants-in-aid have been devised to make some differentiation among states based upon differences in wealth as indicated by variations in per capita income received.

Some persons do not accept the equalization of relative abilities to support government services among various states as a desirable element of public policy. Others point out that it has been impossible to develop an exact or even adequate index of relative fiscal capacities of various governmental units. The federal device of comparing per capita income payments per state is only an approximate indication of varying fiscal capacity. The common state practice of comparing per capita real property assessments is even more dubious, since assessment practices tend to vary so widely among various local units of government.

The Committee on Federal Grants-in-Aid of the Council of State Governments in 1949 concluded that unadjusted per capita income should not be used as a measure of varying fiscal capacity on the part of states, but that at least federal tax withdrawals should be reflected by deducting individual income tax collections from the per capita income figure. In addition, the committee suggested that the range of variability in matching proportions of federal grants should be confined within rather narrow limits. Three reasons were given for this opinion: the lack of a reliable index of relative fiscal capacities, the danger of too much participation and control by the national government, and the undesirability of carrying the concept of equalization beyond a "reasonable" point. In applying this conclusion, the committee proposed that in those programs where a fifty-fifty participation by the federal and state governments was desirable, a variation up to 66⅔ per cent federal participation should be the maximum. And the committee argues that the formula for variable grants should be fixed by legislation and not be left to administrative discretion.[19]

ADMINISTRATIVE SUPERVISION UNDER GRANTS-IN-AID

Grants-in-aid involve more than financial assistance to states by the federal government or to local units by state governments. They may, and

---

[19] *Federal Grants-in-Aid*, pp. 117–118.

today usually do, carry with them some degree of administrative supervision. The extent of this supervision varies under different legislation.[20]

In making the original grants of land for agricultural colleges, Congress by law laid down numerous conditions which states were to observe. Yet no machinery was provided for ensuring compliance with these instructions. In providing money grants to the states for agricultural colleges, the Morrill Act of 1890 empowered the Secretary of the Interior to determine whether each state was entitled to its share of the annual appropriation. Later inquiry after 1912 revealed that the original act had been consistently violated in a number of states and that all states had violated the legislation at some time. Maladministration of the land grants was a major reason why Congress was willing to include more strict controls over state performance when making subsequent grants. Thus the Morrill Act of 1890 said that if the Secretary of the Interior found that a state was not adhering to the conditions of the act, further payments were to be withheld. In 1894 the Secretary of Agriculture obtained legislative authority to inspect the accounts and the operations of agricultural experiment stations. The Smith-Lever Act of 1914 providing grants-in-aid to support agriculture extension services specified that the Department of Agriculture was to approve plans for state work. Subsequent legislation extending the grant-in-aid device has provided a full array of supervisory techniques.

Some federal legislation sets forth requirements in state administrative machinery if a state is to qualify for federal financial assistance. Thus, the 1914 law on agricultural extension work specified that the program was to be carried on "in connection with" the land-grant colleges. Similarly, the 1920 law on vocational rehabilitation required states to set up a state board for vocational rehabilitation. There are other examples. Sometimes, federal administrative agencies seek to influence state administrative machinery through administrative order. The federal employment service act of 1933 required each state to select its employment service personnel under a merit system. In 1939 similar requirements were added to the federal social security law.

All federal agencies administering grant-in-aid programs find personnel problems a chief cause for concern. They utilize many different pressures to insure satisfactory personnel practices by state agencies. Under the Smith-Lever Act of 1914 the Department of Agriculture entered into an official understanding with state colleges providing that the colleges would select directors of extension service who were satisfactory to the Department of Agriculture. This in effect gave the Department a veto over state personnel. Most federal agencies through informal contact endeavor

---

[20] In the comments which follow I have relied heavily upon V. O. Key, Jr., *The Administration of Federal Grants to States* (Chicago: Public Administration Service, 1937).

to influence personnel practices and even the appointment of key personnel. When partisan politics leads to a particularly unsatisfactory situation, a federal agency may threaten to withhold funds.

In general, federal agencies have four particular techniques for supervising the state operation of grant-in-aid activities. These are

1. Prior approval of state plans for operations
2. Reports
3. Field inspection
4. Audit of state expenditures

Some federal agencies, such as the Bureau of Public Roads, require state agencies to submit preliminary and final plans and specifications for individual projects before beginning any actual work. Other agencies, such as the U.S. Employment Service, prescribe a standard plan of operation, which each state agency must prepare annually, covering such subjects as organization, personnel, equipment and lay-out of offices, procedures, and other subjects. In other instances a plan is a general scheme of operation which need not be submitted annually but remains in effect until a modification is proposed and approved.

In the second place, most federal laws require state agencies to render such reports to the federal supervising agency as it may prescribe. These reports may be of two kinds: operating reports and financial reports. Operating reports ordinarily give some statistical record of progress or accomplishment and may be accompanied by a narrative record of problems and achievements. For example, the U.S. Public Health Service has obtained elaborate statistical data on public health in each state in addition to material on actual health activities. The Department of Agriculture has prescribed the actual form of accounts to be maintained by experiment stations and state extension services. Other federal agencies simply specify the kind of financial data which they wish to receive. Since many grants are made under different acts, such as four different laws governing agricultural research, the states are required to keep separate accounts for each grant.

The approval of plans and the receipt of reports are in themselves inadequate as a guarantee that state administrative performance meets all federal requirements. In consequence federal supervisory agencies have uniformly established some system of inspection and visitation as a means of personally checking upon state operations. The term inspector is often avoided in preference for such designations as consultant, agent, and representative.

The audit is a specialized type of inspection designed to ensure that the federal funds granted the state have been spent as prescribed by federal law and regulations. Often broad questions of legal interpretation may be raised by such inspections. Thus, the Social Security Act specified that federal grants should be used for assistance payments and for the cost of administering a state plan but for no other purpose. Administrative audit and decision must then define costs of administration under the act. The audit is a means of ensuring that necessary accounting and financial procedures are being observed, that all financial transactions are carefully recorded, and that the requirements surrounding the receipt of a grant are fully observed. In some instances the administrative agency may even disallow certain state expenditures on the grounds that they were illegally made. This may lead to a reduction in future grants.

The ultimate sanction in the grant-in-aid system is, of course, federal authority to withhold financial assistance to a state. The Morrill Act of 1890, for example, provided that the Secretary of the Interior might withhold grants if he found any state failing to abide by the provisions of the law. The Social Security Act of 1935 established specific causes for withholding state grants, and required the Social Security Board to give notice and an opportunity for hearing before it found that a state was failing substantially to comply with a provision of the statute. Under the unemployment compensation provisions of the law if a state "in a substantial number of cases" denied unemployment compensation to individuals entitled to it, then federal financial assistance might be withdrawn.

Occasionally an agency may suspend payments temporarily as a means of forcing compliance with federal regulations. This has also been done by the Department of Agriculture.[21] For a time in 1935 all public roads projects coming from the state of Georgia were rejected until Governor Talmadge strengthened the highway department.

The Federal Emergency Relief Administration actually took over the entire administration of relief in six states between 1933 and 1935 when states refused to carry out their responsibilities under the relief system. For example, evidence of corrupt political interference in relief operations in Ohio led the FERA to assume complete control of relief administration in March, 1935. But the Federal Emergency Relief Act was the only law which ever authorized the federal administrative agency to take over actual administration under specified conditions.

Obviously withholding federal funds is a drastic action. In most instances a mere threat is sufficient to bring about state administrative compliance. At the same time, such action can only be taken when federal agencies are fairly certain that they will be upheld by Congress. Federal supervisory agencies withhold funds as a last resort and only after long-continued maladministration within a state. But even if the sanction is at best a double-edged sword likely to cut the federal agency as well as the

---

[21] On the role of the Department of Agriculture in the whole field of grants-in-aid, see Carleton R. Ball, *Federal, State and Local Administrative Relationships in Agriculture* (Berkeley, Calif.: University of California Press, 1938).

state, nonetheless it is an important influence for effective state administration.

Whether these various means of administrative supervision by federal agencies over state governments are desirable has also been much debated. In general, we may say that federal financial assistance must mean some degree of administrative supervision. The national government cannot be expected to appropriate funds for some purpose and then surrender the power to make certain that that purpose is actually carried out. Financial support brings with it administrative supervision.

CONCLUSIONS OF COMMISSION ON INTERGOVERNMENTAL RELATIONS

In reviewing the record of federal grants in 1955, the Commission on Intergovernmental Relations spoke of the grant as a "fully matured device of cooperative government."[22] It mentioned that the elements of a grant system were now well established: defined objectives, apportionment and matching formulas, the requirement of certain conditions and minimum standards, the prescription of sanctions, and the provision of administrative supervision. The Commission set forth certain "broad principles" which it said should be used in determining when to use the grant-in-aid. First, the grant should be made or continued only for a clear and important national objective. Secondly, when it is decided that national participation in an activity is desirable, the grant-in-aid should be employed only when it is found to be the "most suitable form" of such participation. Thirdly, the grant should be carefully designed to achieve its objective.[23]

The Commission pointed out that where the national objective could be achieved by some statistical, informational, or research service, this form of activity was preferable to direct administrative participation. In most instances the grant-in-aid was employed to launch or expand services for which a state or local government was regarded as primarily responsible. For the most part grants have had the effect not only of augmenting state government services but also of improving state government administration.[24] Yet the Commission pointed out that the grant-in-aid could be an expensive way of stimulating service when only a few states were not providing "reasonably adequate service." In a number of instances, state budget officers reported their belief that grants-in-aid did distort state budgets, either by fixing a somewhat different pattern of expenditures for the state or by producing a certain inflexibility of expendi-

[22] *Op. cit.,* p. 120.

[23] *Ibid.,* p. 123.

[24] *Ibid.,* p. 126. Cf. Commission on Intergovernmental Relations, *Summaries of Survey Reports on The Administrative and Fiscal Impact of Federal Grants-in-Aid* (Washington: Government Printing Office, 1955).

tures over a period of time.[25] The fact that many grants are highly specialized in nature has produced some administrative difficulties for states, such as the creation of separate administrative units just to handle the federally aided program.

The Commission called attention also to the difficulty in fixing the amount of funds to be granted to each state. Highway needs vary with the size of a state, health needs may vary according to population, public assistance needs may vary with changing circumstances in particular segments of the economy. The Commission expressed the point of view, however, that the federal government "should not attempt to equalize fully state fiscal capacities." It added: "Equalization for its own sake might involve the national government in all manner of governmental activities. Once embarked upon such a comprehensive governmental program, it would be difficult to establish a logical stopping point."[26] Yet where it seemed apparent that national objectives were not likely to be realized in low-income states, some kind of equalizing formula was appropriate.[27] In these instances low-income states should be granted more funds in relation to program need than high-income states and should be required to provide less in the way of matching funds.

Finally, the Commission reviewed some of the administrative difficulties encountered in utilizing the grant-in-aid device. The central administrative issue was the degree of control to be exercised by the federal supervisory agency. Some persons have felt that in certain programs at least the control has been so stringent as to make state agencies mere agents of federal administration. Others pointed out that a federal grant missed its purpose unless there was sufficient federal supervision to ensure accomplishment of the desired results. A grant-in-aid program may set forth certain standards to be realized through state administrative performance. Some programs require federal approval of state operating "plans." If a federal agency endeavors to anticipate all the problems state agencies will meet, rules and instructions become overly detailed and burdensome to execute. If great discretion in operation is left to state agencies, the federal government opens the way to criticism for laxity in supervision. Administrative reporting and inspection are customary techniques of supervision but are not entirely adequate in the absence of some clearly defined limits. The Commission had no certain solution to these difficulties. It could only point out that federal officials should make certain that the purposes of a program are realized but should refrain from imposing their own ideas beyond the essential minima of state performance. "In their dealings with State agencies, Federal officials must distinguish clearly between what is

[25] *Ibid.*, p. 110.
[26] *Ibid.*, p. 129. Cf. Commission on Intergovernmental Relations, *A Survey Report on The Impact of Federal Grants-in-Aid on the Structure and Functions of State and Local Governments* (Washington: Government Printing Office, 1955).
[27] *Ibid.*, p. 135.

required as a condition of Federal aid and what is merely recommended or suggested."[28]

COOPERATIVE RELATIONSHIPS

Even where the federal government does not participate in a state service by means of a financial subsidy, the federal system gives rise to many informal relations between the administrative agencies of the national government and those of state governments. One instance of this sort has been the work of the Tennessee Valley Authority. In the course of operating its programs of flood control, navigation promotion, and electricity generation, the TVA has developed a wide range of cooperative undertakings with state and local agencies in the area. Because it was engaged in fertilizer production at the Muscle Shoals nitrate plant built during World War I, the TVA has worked closely with official farm agencies in developing farm demonstration areas. In order to encourage industrial growth and hence a market for its power, the TVA worked with state universities on engineering and agricultural research. The TVA also did much to encourage the enlargement of public health programs in the several states of the region.[29]

On some occasions, administrative agencies of the national government utilize the administrative machinery of state governments in carrying out their work. An outstanding example occurred during World War II. The Office of Price Administration used the gasoline tax machinery of the states to help it in enforcing gasoline rationing. The state organization for collecting gasoline taxes already had worked out detailed relationships with gasoline distributors and it was relatively simple for them to collect ration stamps as well. The arrangement for this cooperative administration was handled informally through a voluntary association of state tax officials.[30]

The Work Projects Administration of the 1930s was an agency operated throughout the country by administrative officials of the national government. At the same time, the WPA had many close operating relationships with state and local government agencies. In the first place, the WPA drew its labor supply primarily from state and county welfare agencies. In the second place, many of the work projects it undertook were sponsored by state and local governments, which contributed the cost of some of the materials and even provided necessary supervisory personnel.

[28] Ibid., p. 141. For a general account of federal grants-in-aid, see Commission on Intergovernmental Relations, A Description of Twenty-five Grant-in-Aid Programs (Washington: Government Printing Office, 1955).

[29] Cf. David E. Lilienthal, TVA—Democracy on the March (New York: Harper & Brothers, 1944).

[30] George H. Watson, "State Participation in Gasoline Rationing," Public Administration Review, vol. 3 (Summer, 1943), p. 213.

There are hundreds of other examples. State game wardens have been deputized by the national government to help enforce the Migratory Bird Act. Sometimes foresters of the U.S. Forest Service act as state game wardens. Joint efforts of national and state officials have characterized the enforcement of narcotics laws, of grain standards, of plant quarantine, of liquor control, and of many other activities.[31] There are over four hundred joint boards set up by the Interstate Commerce Commission and state utility bodies to handle common interests in motor carrier regulation.

Sometimes state legislatures "incorporate by reference" federal legislation into state law. This has been done, for example, by providing that federal law setting standards for foods and drugs shall be a part of state law as well. Meat-packing standards enforced by the national government have also been enacted as law by state governments. Standards of mine safety have been treated the same way. There have even been instances where state law has empowered administrative officials of the national government to enforce state legislation in various fields such as those mentioned above. Contracts between federal and state agencies for scientific research and engineering surveys have become especially common in recent years. In these and other ways, joint action by national and state officials has been made possible and even encouraged.[32]

INTERSTATE COOPERATION

In many instances the national government has been called upon to undertake tasks because the work to be done could not be handled satisfactorily by state governments acting individually. In practice, two other possibilities have developed besides action by the national government under these circumstances. One is commonly known as "uniform state action," the other is the interstate compact.

Originally established in 1892, the National Conference of Commissioners on Uniform State Laws has included representatives from all states. The work of the conference has been to draft legislation on various subjects which might then be enacted by state legislatures. Such legal uniformity is advantageous to business corporations carrying on activities in a number of states. It has also been useful in avoiding undesirable kinds of interstate competition or rivalry for business or other advantages. An outstanding accomplishment of the conference has been the framing of a Uniform Negotiable Instruments Act enacted by the forty-eight states. Uniform laws have also been drafted and enacted by some states on such subjects as warehouse receipts, transfer of title to personal property, the

[31] See Jane Perry Clark, *The Rise of a New Federalism* (New York: Columbia University Press, 1938).

[32] See Commission on Intergovernmental Relations, *A Report to the President for Transmittal to the Congress,* chap. 3.

regulation of the use of narcotic drugs, the execution of wills, desertion and nonsupport, and illegitimacy. A recent major project was the completion of a Uniform Commercial Code.

The interstate compact is a kind of formal agreement, or "treaty," entered into by two or more states to govern some common interest. The first major agreement of this sort in the United States was the Colorado River Compact entered into by the states of Arizona, California, Colorado, Nevada, New Mexico, Utah, and Wyoming in 1922 and approved by Congress in 1928. This compact set forth the division of water rights for the respective states which became effective with the completion of the Hoover Dam in Boulder Canyon. This compact was rewritten in 1948. Another outstanding early compact was the agreement between New York and New Jersey which, in 1921, set up the Port of New York Authority. In the intervening years, more and more compacts have been prepared on stream pollution, sanitation, and other water problems. Efforts to adopt interstate compacts on subjects like minimum wages for women and children and the elimination of child labor were failures, however. One of the most interesting recent extensions of the device has been in the field of higher education, where thirteen Southern states have joined together to plan a common program for the improvement and economic operation of their colleges and universities.[33] A somewhat different kind of arrangement is being tried among a number of Western states.

Certainly, there are alternatives to the demand that the national government undertake to perform certain functions. It is up to the states to explore those possibilities of joint action within the structure of federalism which are available to them.

CONCLUSION

The American system of federalism creates a structure of government which imposes certain peculiarities for administrative action. When the national government through the legislature and the executive decides upon a desirable public policy, it must first be satisfied on the score of its constitutional authority to take action. Subsequently, that authority may be reviewed and upheld, modified, or rejected by the judiciary.

When the national government undertakes a program, it has the choice of creating its own administrative machinery or of working through state agencies. There are various advantages to the first practice: larger and more economical areas of administration than those provided by state boundary lines, uniformity of administrative action, and the treatment of the nation as one unified whole. A grant-in-aid system raises complicated questions of financial sharing and administrative control. Critics also

[33] See Frederick L. Zimmerman and Mitchell Wendell, *The Interstate Compact since 1925* (Chicago: The Council of State Governments, 1951).

often point out that grants for specific purposes tend to suggest that the states should regard these services as more important than other services not so aided. On the other hand, state government officials often find the grant-in-aid of desirable fiscal assistance as well as an amenable extension of federal activity.

It must be remembered that our federal system is first of all a matter of fundamental structure of government. Secondly, it is the framework for the political organization of the nation. National legislators are elected from the constituent states. These legislators are naturally interested at all times in the work of national administrative agencies as they affect their own states and subdivisions. They expect "equal" expenditure and "equal" development of a government service. This is understandable.

Federalism—a structure of central and constituent units of government —is a fundamental element of American government. This feature must then necessarily influence the development and operation of all government administrative services. In turn administrative officials of the central government must be constantly alert for opportunities of intergovernmental cooperation in common tasks and common interests. The structure of federalism establishes a part of the basic framework within which administrative policies and operations are supervised and controlled within the United States.

PART TWO

The Legislature

Chapter 4

The Legislative Power

Article I of the federal Constitution begins with the simple words: "All legislative powers herein granted shall be vested in a Congress of the United States, which shall consist of a Senate and House of Representatives." The next section provides details about composition and membership of the House of Representatives, a third section does the same for the Senate, a fourth section concerns meeting, a fifth deals with procedure, a sixth concerns compensation and privileges, and a seventh section provides for the passage of bills, including the arrangement for presidential approval. Section 8 of Article I of the Constitution sets forth the powers of Congress, which are in effect the subject-matter concerns of the federal government. Section 9 imposes certain restraints upon legislative action, and Section 10 provides certain restrictions upon the states. Nowhere does Article I endeavor to define what the legislative power means in scope.

The men who wrote the federal Constitution were convinced that there was no need to spell out legislative power in any detail. The citizens of the various states were familiar with their own legislatures. As colonies, each of the thirteen had had its own colonial legislature. Legislative power was a familiar concept. Why should any effort be made to define it?

Actually, the national legislature has a number of somewhat different duties conferred upon it by the Constitution. For one thing, it may propose amendments to the Constitution; indeed, of the twenty-two amendments which have been adopted, all have originated with the Congress. In the second place, the Congress has an electoral function. Under the Constitution it is charged with the duty of receiving and counting the votes of the electoral college cast for President and Vice President of the United States. It is the Congress and only the Congress which can officially declare the election of a President. If no person receives a majority of the electoral votes, then it is the House of Representatives which must elect a President, each state for this purpose having but one vote. In both

1801 and 1825 the House of Representatives did elect the President, and in 1876 the Congress had to decide which of two sets of electoral votes from several states to count. In the third place, the Congress is a high court of justice for the impeachment of the President, judges, and other important public officials. In the fourth place, the Senate has special authority to confirm major appointments of the President and to approve treaties negotiated by the President. In all of these respects the Congress is not an ordinary legislative body.

Yet, in spite of these somewhat peculiar and nonlegislative functions, the primary business of the national Congress, and of state legislatures as well, is legislation. The legislature speaks through the enactment of law. Its reason for existence is to make great decisions of government which shall become the law to be administered by administrative agencies and to be observed by citizens and all other inhabitants of the nation. The fundamental determinations about what government shall and shall not do in our society are embodied in legislation. Here is the beginning of public policy in action.

In his second treatise on government John Locke began one chapter with these words:[1]

> The great end of men's entering into society being the enjoyment of their properties in peace and safety, and the great instrument and means of that being the laws established in that society, the first and fundamental positive law of all commonwealths is the establishing of the legislative power, as the first and fundamental natural law which is to govern even the legislature.

Locke thus thought of constitutionalism as assuming first the task of creating the legislative power. This American constitutionalism has done. Locke went on to declare:[2]

> This legislative is not only the supreme power of the commonwealth, but sacred and unalterable in the hands where the community have once placed it. Nor can any edict of anybody else, in what form soever conceived, or by what power soever backed, have the force and obligation of a law which has not its sanction from that legislative which the public has chosen and appointed; for without this the law could not have that which is absolutely necessary to its being a law, the consent of the society, over whom nobody can have a power to make laws but by their own consent and by authority received from them; and therefore all the obedience, which by the most solemn ties any one can be obliged to pay, ultimately terminates in this supreme power, and is directed by those laws which it enacts.

Locke declared that a legislature could not assume for itself arbitrary power. It was bound by natural law to recognize the liberties and property of the individual citizen. Moreover, it was obliged, he declared, to proceed

[1] John Locke, *Of Civil Government*, Everyman's Library ed. (London: J. M. Dent & Sons, Ltd., 1924), p. 183.
[2] *Ibid.*, pp. 183–184.

by promulgating "standing laws," that is, general rules of conduct to be observed by all in like circumstances and conditions. "Absolute arbitrary power, or governing without settled standing laws, can neither of them consist with the ends of society and government. . . . "[3] Locke also declared that the legislative power, being itself a delegated power from the people, could not then be delegated to other hands. It was in large part from Locke that the Founding Fathers derived their ideas about government embodied in American constitutionalism. The legislative power was molded in a cast familiar to eighteenth-century political thinking.

LAW AND LEGISLATION

At the outset it may be desirable to draw certain elementary distinctions between law and legislation in our governmental practice. The two are by no means the same. Legislation is the enactment of a legislature. It takes precedence in our society over any other form of law except the provisions of the Constitution itself. But in our system of government the courts enjoy the authority to decide when a statute is in conflict with the provisions of a state or the federal Constitution. Accordingly, the supreme law of the land is the Constitution as interpreted by the courts. Statutory enactment enjoys a second rank in our lawmaking.

The law to be observed by the citizen is more than statutory, however. A great body of law is judge-made. This is especially true of the common law. Legislative enactment may repeal or modify elements of the common law, but much of the relationship of citizen to citizen and even of the citizen to government is embodied in opinions of courts which have come down through the centuries. In addition, the legislature may speak in broad terms of public policy, leaving many rules and regulations specifying details or circumstances of law enforcement to the chief executive or to administrative agencies. These supplementary rules and regulations have the force of law. Moreover, the federal Constitution also specifies that "all treaties made, or which shall be made, under the authority of the United States" shall be included within the "supreme law of the land." This last provision has caused a good deal of controversy in the United States, since it is not clear from the wording whether the federal government might make a treaty which would in effect transfer authority from state governments to the central government.[4] Nonetheless, treaties made by the President and approved by a two-thirds vote of the Senate have the force of law. Finally, within the appropriate limits of the executive power, the Chief Executive may also take action which has the force of law.

[3] *Ibid.*, p. 186.
[4] The Supreme Court appeared to say this could be done in one case, *Missouri v. Holland*, 252 U.S. 416 (1920).

Law, then, is not the exclusive province of the legislature. There are other law making agencies. But within the terms of our Constitution, it is correct to say that the legislature is the supreme law making authority under our system of government. Other law making power, with the exception of that of the Chief Executive within his executive authority, is subordinate to that of the legislature. Even judge-made law, apart from constitutional interpretation, may be changed by statutory enactment. It is the voice of the legislature which speaks with final authority in the determination of law.

In essence, law is a statement of major purpose and a standard of conduct. It is sometimes common practice among legal students to draw a distinction between "private law" and "public law." This distinction is somewhat different from that which is made in practice by Congress itself in enacting legislation. A "private" bill as considered by Congress is one concerned with some individual person or condition; usually it authorizes payment of some damage claim or admits some named individual legally to residence within the United States. But in customary legal terminology private law is concerned with the rights and duties of individuals in their relation one to another. The law of contracts is in this sense private law. Public law, on the other hand, deals with the administrative activities of government and with the relations of the citizen to government. The law we are concerned with in this volume is public law.

THE LAW AS PUBLIC POLICY

In terms of the politics of public administration, the manifestation of legislative power which is of utmost importance is the enactment of public policy. We are not concerned here with the mechanics of legislative procedure; nor can we begin here to pursue the many ramifications of how legislators are chosen and of how pressures are brought to bear to influence legislation.[5] Our interest must necessarily center upon the various ways in which the legislative power affects the work of administration in the American scheme of government.

The source of administrative authority is law, law enacted by the legislature authorizing the performance of certain specified governmental activities, establishing particular goals for administrative endeavor, prescribing methods and procedures to be employed. Public policy is an amalgam of many forces. The chief executive may urge certain action. Heads of administrative agencies may advocate desirable legislation. Party leaders in the legislature may develop a program for enactment. Pressure groups

[5] On these matters, see especially James M. Burns, *Congress on Trial* (New York: Harper & Brothers, 1949); Stephen K. Bailey and Howard R. Samuel, *Congress at Work* (New York: Henry Holt and Company, Inc., 1952); and Bertram M. Gross, *The Legislative Struggle* (New York: McGraw-Hill Book Company, Inc., 1953).

may urge adoption of one or more types of laws. Individual members of the legislature may become interested in some problem and over a period of time organize support for their ideas. Legislative committees and their staffs may frame measures for consideration. In all of these and other ways, public policy is born, modified, and on occasion, abandoned.

Not all public policy is necessarily the result of legislative enactment. Policy goals for administrative action may be set in particular circumstances by the chief executive. Statutes do not always cover all possible situations which may confront an administrative agency. There is thus room for possible executive direction. In certain fields, notably in foreign relations and national defense, by constitutional prescription, the Executive enjoys broad authority to establish policy goals. Yet it remains nonetheless true that public policy almost always begins in statutory enactment which authorizes government action, sets goals for administrative activities, and prescribes methods and procedures.

American political history is in large part the story of public policy development centering in pressures and forces resulting in particular legislative enactment: the adoption of a protective tariff, the assumption of state debts, the embargo of trade with belligerent nations, the promotion of internal improvements, the settlement of land, the containment of slavery, the encouragement of agriculture, the resumption of specie payment, the regulation of public utilities, the control of trusts, the requirement of proper labeling of food and drugs, the conservation of natural resources, the control of floods, the development of water power, the irrigation of arid lands, the protection of Indians, the organization of a national banking system, the promotion of public health, the adoption of a social security system, the protection of collective bargaining, the financial support of low-cost housing—these and hundreds of other important laws are the subject matter of stirring political controversy. But equally important they are the origin of various administrative activities of the federal government.

Public policy is not just a matter of a broad determination that some situation or circumstance requires government action. There are issues of strategy as well. Suppose legislators are agreed that the conduct of agriculture is a matter of major national concern. How shall this interest be evidenced? A first step was to authorize the collection of agricultural statistics in order to provide information about this important segment of the nation's economy. A next step was to encourage agricultural education by providing grants to states with which to help maintain agricultural schools. Afterwards grants were made for an agricultural extension service to bring consultative advice to the farm itself. Another step was to promote agricultural research in order to advance the knowledge to be taught to farmers. Then it was decided that farmers needed their own specially designed banking system to provide mortgage financing, production credit, and other needs. Farm groups sought some protection in the process of marketing cattle; stockyard regulation then began. Uniform marketing standards for grains, tobacco, and other products were sought through legislation. Then a drastic reduction in farm prices presented the problem of the general economic well-being of farming as a business enterprise; there followed elaborate arrangements for price supports, soil conservation payments, and other devices. The story of farm legislation in the United States is a record of identification of various needs and the inauguration of various methods for meeting those needs. The story of such farm legislation is equally a record of the establishment and development of various types of administrative machinery to carry out the objectives of public policy.[6]

It must be emphasized again that not all public policy is a matter of legislative enactment. A President like Theodore Roosevelt may decide to withdraw certain public lands from the legal right of individual homesteading or purchase in order to conserve forest and other vital natural resources. The judiciary may decide that when one particular business enterprise dominates half of a market it is by that fact alone evidencing a restraint of trade. An administrative agency may decide that no discrimination between races shall be practiced on a military base. These are important decisions not embodied in statutory enactment. Yet in most such cases it is statutory enactment in authorizing some government program or establishing some administrative agency which affords the opportunity for the exercise of executive, judicial, and administrative policy making.

Legislative enactment of public policy is important for many reasons. The first factor is that in a democracy there is a general expectation that most fundamental issues of public controversy will be settled by legislative action. Although there are times and occasions when the Chief Executive may command widespread popular support for some executive action— President Jackson's order to withdraw national government deposits from the Second United States Bank is a good example—nonetheless there remains the general expectation that the people's representatives in the legislature shall determine fundamental questions of public policy. And such determination means statutory enactment. In many instances general public support for a given policy will ordinarily be more widespread and easier to mobilize if the legislature has spoken with a statute. To be sure, it does not always follow that a law will be obeyed just because it is a statute enacted by the legislature. Nor does it follow that a public policy will necessarily be widely accepted simply because it is embodied in a statute. The point nonetheless remains that public policy pronounced through legislative enactment will often command greater acceptance than

[6] Cf. Murray R. Benedict, *Farm Policies of the United States, 1790–1950* (New York: The Twentieth Century Fund, Inc., 1953).

public policy promulgated by the Chief Executive or decided by the judiciary.

In the second place, there is a certain type of public policy which can be pursued only if it is embodied in statutory enactment. In our particular scheme of government it is not always easy to say just where the dividing line is to be drawn between legislative and executive policy making. The simplest illustration is supposed to be the public policy of war. The federal Constitution says (Article I, Section 8) that the Congress shall have power "to declare war." President Lincoln mobilized the armed forces of the United States in 1861 without a declaration of war; indeed the Civil War legally was never acknowledged to be more than an armed insurrection against the national government. President John Adams was involved in an undeclared war with France; President Jefferson was involved in an undeclared war with the Moslem areas on the southern shores of the Mediterranean. President Truman committed the United States to an undeclared war in Korea. President Franklin Roosevelt adopted a number of policies in 1940 and 1941 which officially were known as all aid to the Allies "short of war." Yet even when we acknowledge the numerous exceptions, the generalization remains true that many important public policies can become public policy only upon enactment by the legislature. Again recognizing that there are possible exceptions, we may say that any new activity by government, any important change in government activity, any substantial expenditure of public funds for some particular objective—decisions of this sort involving public policy become legal or official policy only after enactment by the legislature.

There is a third important factor in the statutory enactment of public policy. Administrative agencies to carry out public policy are ordinarily created only by law. Sometimes the legislature may authorize the executive to establish administrative agencies to carry out some public policy; this is especially likely to occur in a period of war or of other national emergency. Sometimes the legislature may authorize the executive to make changes in administrative agencies or even to serve as the legislative agency in drafting and submitting "reorganization plans." Generally, however, administrative agencies are authorized by laws passed by the legislature. Much of public policy is not self-executing. It takes administrative agencies to translate broad purpose into everyday action, to give concrete meaning to what are otherwise pious declarations. If public policy is to be meaningful, it will usually require an administrative agency to carry it out. And administrative agencies are created most commonly by acts of a legislature.

In the fourth place, legislatures will usually refuse to appropriate funds for the operation of an administrative agency unless the work it performs has been authorized by law. Here again, under somewhat unusual circumstances, it is possible to find exceptions. Yet as a general rule, appropriations follow statutory enactment. Indeed, in the Congress, both houses have standing rules which make it possible for any individual member to object on the floor that a pending appropriation has not been authorized by law. If this objection is sustained by the presiding officer or the house as a whole, then the item objected to is stricken from the appropriation measure. Under these circumstances, administration of a public policy may be effectively halted or curtailed if it is possible to object that some appropriation item is directly related to a program or activity not authorized by law. It is not easy to make such an objection, or to have such an objection sustained by the legislative body, but the possibility of such objection reinforces the need to embody fundamentals of public policy for administrative enforcement in statutory enactment.

The heart of public administration, then, is public policy. And public policy is most frequently set forth in our government by legislative enactment. The legislative power is both the fount of public policy and the origin of administrative activity.

DEFICIENCIES IN THE LEGISLATIVE POWER

Any detailed study of legislatures as they are organized and as they operate in the United States will necessarily point to a number of deficiencies. In terms of population, a number of parts of the United States are overrepresented in the Senate, where each state is equally entitled to two members. The districts from which members of the federal House of Representatives are elected are determined by the state legislatures. Sometimes redistricting is delayed after a decennial census, and sometimes districts are drawn in the hope of favoring one political party as against another. In many state legislatures, rural counties or rural parts of the state are substantially overrepresented as against urban areas.

Most state legislators receive only nominal compensation for their duties and must carry on their businesses or professional work while serving in the legislature. In the national legislature, the compensation provided by no means meets the cost of maintaining two residences and of serving the home electorate in many expected ways, such as speechmaking, handling complaints, and contributing to various causes. The time demands made upon individual legislators are great, and it is little wonder that they frequently have almost no opportunity to acquaint themselves with the details of many problems facing the legislature.

The greatest difficulty which confronts a legislature in the determination of public policy, however, is the matter of obtaining agreement among a numerous membership. Partly, the final agreement is a matter of leadership, the member subordinating his own personal opinions to the decision of the executive, to the decision of the small group of legislative leaders, or to the decision of both. Partly, agreement is a matter of compromise, a law embodying various points of view and even various interests. Partly, agreement is a matter of broad generality which avoids specific details on which individual differences of opinion so readily focus. These difficulties in obtaining legislative consensus in the formulation and declaration of public policy have two major consequences for public administration.

One is that administrative agencies are frequently entrusted with a public policy to enforce which has not been clearly defined and which by no means represents a general legislative consensus. Under these circumstances the administrative agency may necessarily have to proceed with caution in carrying out its assigned task, consulting widely with interest groups and with individual legislators in an effort to avoid widespread attack. A failure to proceed with such caution may mean extensive legislative and other criticism. The adoption of a cautious procedure may make administrative accomplishment slow; it may even mean failure to achieve any real purpose at all.

Another difficulty is that administrative agencies are often reluctant to seek legislation which will clarify their objectives and procedure. If the legislature is asked to express its purpose more clearly, it may fail to do as well as before. If the legislature is asked to modify existing statutes, it may review all previous law and decide that many provisions ought to be changed. Then the legislature may not be able to agree on the changes and the resulting statute may be an emasculated one indeed. Or the legislature may take the occasion to air all accumulated grievances until what has been accomplished by an administrative agency is lost sight of in the chorus of disapproval which receives so much attention.

It is no simple task for a legislature to formulate and enact public policy. It is no simple task for a legislature to clarify its purpose or to bring governmental programs and activities up to date. It is no simple task for a legislature to modify provisions of law which create administrative complexities and even inefficiencies. The legislature is the source of public policy, but the product is not always a clear and simple statement of public policy for administrative agencies to carry out.

THE EXTENT OF LEGISLATIVE POWER

Frequently in reading about government one is likely to encounter expressions such as the "sanctity of law," the "majesty of law," or the "supremacy of the law." Such phrases are intended to convey a sense of the high regard our society gives to its statements establishing standards of conduct or setting forth broad purposes of the state. Sometimes this same regard by transference attaches itself to the legislative body itself. Then we are apt to find expressions such as the "supremacy of the legislature."

To be sure, statutory law is in the first instance the product of the legislature. And it is statutory law which sets forth the public policy of administrative endeavor in our government. But the supremacy of the law should not be confused in our system of government with the supremacy of the legislature. As we have already pointed out, the law as it is known in American jurisprudence is not exclusively statutory, that is, is not exclusively the product of the legislature. Indeed, the supreme law is the Constitution, and no legislative body in our government enjoys the privilege of writing the Constitution to suit its ideas of the moment. Nor is interpretation of the meaning of a constitution, federal or state, an exclusive function of the legislature.

The legislative power is important, vastly important in American government. But the legislative power is not all-powerful. The legislative power is part of a triumvirate of power. The legislature shares power with the executive and the judiciary. The legislature cannot claim power beyond the limits of what is definitely legislative in nature. In other words, there are limits to legislative power.

Yet it is not easy to fix definite limits to legislative power. To be sure, the constitutional system of American government fixes certain limits. The legislature may not encroach upon executive power or judicial power. It may attempt to do so; the resistance of the other two branches is expected to remind the legislature that it does have limits to its power. Another limitation is that the legislature may not enact an unconstitutional law. There is of course no way to prevent a legislature from writing any law it so desires. But it was early decided by the Supreme Court of the United States that the judiciary would not enforce a law which, in the judgment of the Court, contravened the provisions of the Constitution.[7] In effect, a statute held by the Court to violate the requirements of the Constitution has no legal force or effect. Here again is an important limitation upon the legislature.

There is still a third limitation which in a sense arises from the two just mentioned. Or perhaps it is more accurate to say that this third limitation is just another way of restating the first two. The item is so vital, however, that it deserves separate mention. The legislature must exercise its legislative power in a manner appropriate to the nature of the legislature. As we have said, legislative power is not the same as governmental power. The legislature does not possess the power to govern in our country. It possesses only the power to behave as a legislature.

This means that the legislative power must speak through the enactment of law. The legislative power is not a power which rests in one individual legislator. It is not a power which rests in any one legislative committee. It is not a power which may be exercised by criticism in a report or in debate. It is not a power which may be exercised by appointment of per-

[7] *Marbury v. Madison,* 1 Cranch 137 (1803).

sonnel, or by the arbitration of disputes between individuals. It is a power which evidences itself in the passage of a law.

Now this limitation of legislative action only by law is not a simple one. The ramifications of the power of statutory enactment are many. The legislature, and this means its committees, must be able to inform itself about situations and circumstances which may require legal remedy. Moreover, although the individual legislator does not speak for the legislature as a whole, there is no sure means for deciding when the legislator is acting as an individual and when indeed he may be voicing sentiments common to many legislators, perhaps to a majority or more of all members. Furthermore, statutory enactment may seek to do many things. Laws are not confined to broad statements of public policy. They may and frequently do deal with a multitude of details, including details of how public business shall be transacted. A legislator or a committee which is dissatisfied with the conduct of public administration may convince the legislature that it should enact restricting legislation which will specify in detail how work shall be done in the future. Even when the legislature is dissatisfied with court action, it may enact laws changing court structure, court procedure, or court jurisdiction. The extent of legislative interest is great, indeed, and may lead to many different kinds of laws.

For this reason administrative officials spend a great deal of time doing their best to satisfy individual legislators about various aspects of public business. It is natural that this should be so. The interest of one legislator may readily become the interest of many legislators. More than this, any action regarded as an insult by an administrative agency to a legislator will quickly be resented by other legislators, regardless of party affiliation. Administrative officials are then well advised to give careful attention to the complaints and criticisms of the individual legislator. The price of refusal may be the enactment of law which will make administrative operations more inflexible, more time-consuming, more difficult to perform.

The fact still remains that the legislature speaks officially through the enactment of law. And this is a process which requires the action of the entire membership. The legislature may speak with many voices, but it acts in a single way, the passage by majority or greater vote of a statute or resolution. The legislative product is legal language, language expressing public policy, creating administrative agencies, and determining operating practices.

The legislative power is a vital power in the American scheme of government. It is more than the origin of administrative authority. It is more than the source of funds for administrative operation. It is a continuing check upon how administrative authority shall be exercised and how administrative operations shall be conducted.

Chapter 5

The Legislature as Source
of Administrative Authority

The legislative process in our scheme of government is somewhat different from the legislative power. For example, the chief executive under our federal and state constitutions participates in the legislative process. He is expected to recommend desirable legislative action from time to time. He may also disapprove bills enacted by the legislature, although this veto may usually be overridden by a two-thirds vote of the legislature. Similarly, administrative agencies may participate in the legislative process by recommending action, by providing information, by answering criticisms. Many groups also participate in the legislative process. Many persons may propose. It is the legislature which disposes. And in the process of disposing, the legislature gives rise to administrative authority.

Not every statute passed by a legislature necessarily involves administrative authority. Often law simply expresses rights and obligations in the relationship of one citizen to another. For example, a law which requires every person who owns an automobile to carry liability insurance sets forth an obligation which is not enforced by some particular administrative agency of state government unless and until an accident actually occurs. Sometimes a law is enforced through the ordinary law-enforcement machinery, which means the system of police force, prosecuting attorney, and court of law. A law making some action a crime, such as the transportation of a stolen automobile across state lines, falls in this category. To be sure, the multiplication of such laws may frequently require an enlarged police force, an augmented district attorney's staff, and even an increased number of judges, but this kind of legislation does not establish new forms of administrative action.

On the other hand, many pieces of legislation do require new administrative bodies if the purpose of the law is to be carried out. If a patent is to be awarded to inventors of new and useful articles, there must then be an agency to decide in the first instance when an article is both new and useful. If an individual is to operate an automobile only after he has obtained an operator's license, then there must be an agency to issue the license. If the federal government is to develop atomic energy as a military weapon, then there must be some agency responsible for this task. Taxes cannot be collected, births cannot be recorded, roads cannot be built, schools cannot be operated, armed forces cannot be maintained without administrative agencies to perform the specialized functions involved.

Sometimes, a legislature may move from one kind of law enforcement machinery to another. For example, in 1890 when Congress enacted the Sherman Antitrust Law it provided that combinations in restraint of trade should be illegal. The enforcement of this policy was left to the Department of Justice by bringing both criminal and civil suits in a federal district court. Then in 1914, apparently dissatisfied with progress in law enforcement under the Sherman Act, Congress passed the Federal Trade Commission Act which in sweeping language forbade all "unfair methods of competition" and authorized a new administrative agency specifically to enforce this prohibition.[1] A political leader and supporting groups may insist, as did President Wilson in 1914, that statutory purpose can be effectively accomplished only by creating new and specialized administrative machinery.

There has been some concern from time to time about whether chief executives or individual legislators take the leading role in formulating and advocating the enactment of new legislation. In the past twenty-five years in particular, many persons have concluded that the initiation of legislation has fallen primarily into the hands of the chief executive. In the early days of the New Deal, especially from 1933 to 1936, it seemed that the President of the United States had become the source of most major proposals for law considered by the Congress. Actually, such a view is superficial, and frequently overlooks the many other forces besides presidential interest which produce laws in this country. The emergency economic circumstances existing in 1933 tended to encourage enactment of law in a shorter space of time than might otherwise have been the case, but the period produced few if any new ideas which had not been discussed for some time before 1933.

Lawrence H. Chamberlain in 1940 set out to explore the origin of 90 major pieces of congressional legislation enacted between 1890 and 1940.[2] He examined such fields as business law, tariff law, labor legislation, national defense, agricultural law, banking and currency, immigra-

---

[1] For a review of policy and administration in this field, see George W. Stocking and Myron W. Watkins, *Monopoly and Free Enterprise* (New York: The Twentieth Century Fund, Inc., 1951).

[2] Lawrence H. Chamberlain, *The President, Congress, and Legislation* (New York: Columbia University Press, 1946).

tion, conservation, and railroad law. His list included 24 major statutes enacted between 1933 and 1940 under the New Deal. He concluded that presidential influence was preponderant in the initiation of passage for 19 measures, including 8 laws passed under the New Deal. The influence of individual legislative leaders was preponderant in the initiation of passage for 35 major pieces of legislation, including 2 laws passed under the New Deal. In the instance of 29 other laws, including 13 laws passed under the New Deal, the influence of the President and of legislative leaders was so intermingled that initiation of passage must be described as a joint responsibility. In the final 7 instances, the laws were initiated preponderantly by the pressure of some particular interest group.[3]

One comment of Chamberlain deserves to be quoted in full:[4]

> One of the points brought out most clearly by the case studies set forth in the preceding chapters was the depth of the legislative roots of most important statutes. For instance, a law is hailed as something new at the time of passage but further examination reveals that the proposal had been discussed more or less continuously in Congress for several years. Presidential attention had led to its elevation from the obscurity of just another bill to the prominence of an administration measure. Administrative experts had participated by drafting a new bill but there was not very much in the new bill that had not been present in one or more earlier drafts. At all events, driven by the power now behind it, the bill becomes law without great difficulty or delay, while in the absence of presidential action years might have gone by without its adoption. The law is allocated to the category of presidential influence because its passage in final form was certainly not assignable to any other instrumentality. But the influence of what had taken place in Congress cannot be ignored. Had the initial proposal not been introduced and discussed, the final act might not have come when it did or it might have emerged in quite a different form. There is no way in which this preliminary activity can be assessed and it would be futile to attempt its measurement but its importance is genuine.

Chamberlain then reports that of the 90 laws examined by him, no less than 77 had originally been bills introduced by an individual legislator without endorsement from the President. Many of these bills had been considered by congressional committees several times. In the 19 cases classified as coming in the category of preponderant influence by the President, 12 had been originally initiated by some legislator. Of the 29 laws classified as the product of joint presidential-congressional influence, 26 had been originally introduced without presidential support.

These facts underline the fundamental role of the legislature in the determination of public policy. Pressure groups, the chief executive, administrative agencies may propose; we repeat, it is the legislature which

[3] This tabulation will be found, *ibid.*, pp. 450–452.
[4] *Ibid.*, pp. 453–454.

disposes. To be sure, administrative agencies are apt to be especially active in suggesting modifications and extensions of existing public policy. Administrative experience almost always reveals certain imperfections in statutes. Legislators are usually amenable to proposals for minor corrections in laws. But fundamental legislation may actually originate to a lesser extent in administrative agencies than is often commonly assumed.

The basic proposition to appreciate then is that in our system of government all administrative authority rests upon statutory enactment passed by our legislatures. Moreover, under the doctrine of separation of power, legislators have both extensive discretion in determining what is desirable public policy and great freedom in deciding what provisions of law shall be written into the statutes. Under a parliamentary system of government, prime minister and cabinet may largely control public policy and the content of law. This is not true under our system of government. Legislators individually and collectively have much greater direct control over the statutes which specify what administrative agencies may do and how they shall do it.

TYPES OF LEGISLATION

Legislative assemblies in the United States enact four broad types of laws affecting the operation of administrative agencies:

1. Substantive laws: those which express general purpose or set forth the goals of administrative action and the authority to be exercised.
2. Structural laws: those which set forth the organizational framework of administrative agencies.
3. Procedural laws: those which specify how administrative agencies shall conduct their business, including the preparation of budgets and the maintenance of accounts, the appointment of personnel, the procurement of supplies, the reimbursement of travel expenses, etc.
4. Appropriation laws: those which specify periodically what administrative agencies may spend in the performance of their legal duties.

We shall examine the second and fourth types of laws in subsequent chapters. In the present chapter we shall confine our attention to the first and third types. In brief we may say that substantive legislation is usually positive in tone, specifying what an administrative agency is supposed to accomplish. Procedural legislation is usually restrictive in character, specifying limitations about how an administrative agency is to carry on its work. The classification outlined here is intended solely to assist in understanding the variety of administrative dependence upon law. Legislatures themselves do not draw hard and fast lines between the types of laws enumerated above, except between general statutes and appropriation laws. Indeed, in enacting a law setting forth some new public policy, it is

common for the legislature to state organic authority, organizational structure, and even administrative procedure all in one statute.

SUBSTANTIVE LEGISLATION

To undertake to discuss the substantive law which legislatures enact
would be the same thing as trying to describe most of the whole existing
body of statutory law in the national government or in any of the state
governments. Organic legislation in a state has to do with the powers of
municipal corporations, public education, public health, the operation of
penal institutions, the construction and maintenance of public highways,
the regulation of public utilities, alcoholic beverage control, employer-
employee relations, public welfare, unemployment compensation, sales
taxes, and hundreds of other subjects. Every one of these laws vests certain degrees of authority in some administrative agency of state government. The substantive legislation of the federal government embraces
such subjects as the conduct of foreign affairs, the collection of income
taxes, the conservation of forests, the regulation of commerce "among the
states," custodianship over Indians, the development of water resources,
soil conservation, the promotion of public housing, the national defense,
and many, many other items. It is impossible to characterize this substantive legislation except to say that today it is extensive, varied, and
essential to all administrative operation. Perhaps one or two special features of substantive legislation might be noted in passing.

Increasingly today, it is common for the substantive law of the federal
Congress to begin with a general declaration of policy. For example, the
Employment Act of 1946 begins with the statement:

> . . . it is the continuing policy and responsibility of the Federal Government
> to use all practicable means . . . for the purpose of creating and maintain-
> ing, in a manner calculated to foster and promote free competitive enterprise
> and the general welfare, conditions under which there will be afforded useful
> employment opportunities, including self-employment, for those able, willing,
> and seeking to work, and to promote maximum employment, production, and
> purchasing power.

This is a very broad statement of policy indeed, but its meaning is not
our concern here. Rather, we may observe that such a declaration provides a general expression of purpose or objective for the guidance of an
administrative agency. A declaration of purpose does not confer specific
authority upon administrative officials. It simply gives them some guidelines for action.

The actual substance of administrative authority is contained in the
more specific sections and clauses of statutory enactment. Usually this
authority is of two kinds. It may be regulatory in nature, conferring the

power to impose standards of conduct upon certain individuals or groups. This power may be exercised through the issuance or revocation of licenses, the promulgation of orders specifying particular behavior (to cease and desist from an unfair trade practice or to charge only a stated price), the determination of standards of work or service performance, and the imposition of tax or other obligations. Regulatory authority may also involve the power to inspect in order to ensure conformance with the required standards of conduct. Enforcement of such authority usually rests in the final analysis with a court of law. We shall have more to say about this later. But increasingly in our society, administrative authority tends to be service-directed in intent rather than regulatory in scope. Substantive law states the services government shall render, the beneficiaries to be served, the scope of services to be provided, and the conditions or circumstances of service.

Substantive legislation may be in perpetuity, or until amended. Or it may have only a specified life span. Thus the authority of the President to enter into trade agreements with other nations whereby our tariff rates are lowered has never been conferred for more than three or four years at a time. The authority of the Selective Service System to designate young men to serve in the Armed Forces of the United States in peacetime has been limited to three- or four-year periods of time. During World War I and again in World War II, the period of applicability of most legislation was fixed as the "duration" plus six months. Sometimes the life of an administrative agency or of a particular program may be limited by the provision that only so much money may be spent. Thus, the "college-housing" provisions of the Federal Housing Act of 1950 authorized loans up to a total of 300 million dollars to public and private institutions of higher education. When this amount had been committed, extensions of lending authority were necessary to keep the program in operation.

A legislature often prefers to place time or other limitations upon some government service for several reasons. If a program or regulation is likely to be unpopular, or to be unusual in scope, then by fixing a time limit the legislature ensures that it will review the whole operation before it can continue. Sometimes, moreover, the legislature may be undecided about the desirability of a program but be willing to experiment. A time limit then ensures that a complete review of experience will take place before a continuation is authorized.

There are also certain drawbacks to this legislative practice. When substantive laws are only temporary, then the legislature must reconsider a subject at some particular time regardless of the burden of other problems. It may happen that the review is actually perfunctory because of the press of other matters. Moreover, if too many laws must be reviewed at a session of the legislature, then there will be little time to consider new business. From the point of view of the administrator, a temporary program imposes numerous burdens. All operating plans and all personnel appointments have to be merely temporary in duration. And preparing the case for continuation of an activity may consume as much time as actually directing its performance.

In the fourth place, substantive legislation includes positive provisions enabling a program to be carried out. Apart from any organizational structure which the law may specify, it is absolutely essential for legislation to authorize the appointment of personnel and the expenditure of public funds if government regulation or service is to be performed.

Such general characteristics as these are to be found in all substantive legislation authorizing administrative activity. The legal provisions for government regulation and government service are necessarily influenced by the peculiarities of the particular concern giving rise to legislative action. One or two particular problems involved in this legislation will be examined later. Otherwise, the details of legislation upon which administration is based must be studied individually in terms of the subject matter dealt with.

PROCEDURAL LEGISLATION

From time to time legislatures also pass laws fixing the methods by which public business shall be conducted. Usually these laws are restrictive in nature, setting forth certain practices which are prohibited or establishing specific procedures which must be followed. Often these laws have arisen from abuses in administrative conduct which may have occurred in some agency. Occasionally a law endeavors to correct a time-honored practice which is no longer publicly acceptable.

In practice, this procedural legislation in the federal government and the states usually covers the following subjects:

1. Procedure employed in regulatory administration
2. The custody and expenditure of public funds, including budgeting and accounting
3. The conduct of legal business
4. Construction of public buildings
5. The purchase of supplies
6. Public printing
7. Personnel transactions from appointment and promotion to tenure and retirement

There is no need to review here in detail the content of such legislation. Much of it in the states and in the federal government is quite similar in nature. Legislation for regulatory administration usually specifies that rules affecting individuals shall be adopted only after notice and hearing. In addition, adjudication must proceed only upon notice of charges, the provision of a hearing, the right of representation, and the right of an appeal. In so far as the other matters are concerned, they usually require competitive open bidding in awarding construction contracts and in purchasing supplies, the appointment of personnel by competitive examination, the disbursement of government funds only upon the basis of properly prepared vouchers, the restriction of the conduct of government legal business in the courts to the attorney general or an attorney designated by him, and similar arrangements.

Procedural legislation has its special problems. Sometimes a legislature wishes to restrict administrative discretion to a degree which will make the conduct of public business almost impossible. For example, to use an illustration from a subject to be discussed later, when procedural legislation in regulatory administration was first proposed, it was feared that the legislature was endeavoring to provide for unlimited review of all administrative actions in the courts. Such a result could have meant that regulatory agencies would have to pursue every case through a lengthy process of judicial review, with attendant delays and reduction in the scope of regulatory activity. As a result of prolonged consideration, with an opportunity for administrative agencies to present their point of view at some length, laws were written which in general appear to be working with some degree of satisfaction, both for those affected by administrative regulation and for the agencies themselves.

It may be said, indeed, as a general proposition that procedural legislation when it is first introduced is usually much more restrictive in nature than the actual law which is eventually passed. Legislators endeavor to get at every possible faulty practice, real or imagined. The result is apt to create new and unintended complications in the public business. For example, in writing legislation allowing payment of travel expenses for the family and the household goods of a government employee assigned overseas, members of Congress wanted a provision that such an employee would agree to remain in government service for at least twelve months after the move. But this would have made it virtually impossible for an agency to fire an employee once he had been moved overseas and the government had paid his expenses. Moreover, the law might have made it impossible for the State Department to reassign its personnel except every twelve months, even when unexpected or emergency situations arose. The committee considering the law (eventually Public Law 600 of the Seventy-ninth Congress, approved August 2, 1946) agreed to modify the twelve-months provision by inserting the words "unless separated for reasons beyond his control" and to exclude the Foreign Service entirely.

Sometimes a legislature enacts a law requiring the head of a department personally to sign all appointment papers. This is all right when an agency is small. It may become an impossible situation when an agency begins to number two thousand or more employees. Administrative operation in a large agency requires that agency to establish proper procedures and to obtain competent officers to handle personnel transactions. The actual department head must depend upon these officials and procedures. If in fact he does sign appointment papers, he does so as a matter of pure routine. Yet legislators often do not understand or sympathize with such a situation in large administrative agencies.

On the other hand, legislators frequently find situations where the work of an administrative agency has been mismanaged, either by sins of venal intent or of stupid inadequacy. It is natural that a legislature should want to correct such situations by law. After all, the business of a legislature is passing laws. The very fact that a legislature tends to have primarily a legal relationship to public administration encourages it to think in terms of handling any unsatisfactory occurrence through some new law. Actually, the spotlight of publicity, a warning of possible legislation, or the revelation of a bad situation to the chief executive—any of these actions short of passage of a law itself may be sufficient to produce a needed change. Legislative power is substantial power indeed. Legislators sometimes do not appreciate how much can be accomplished without enactment of a law, in so far as the procedural aspects of public administration are concerned.

In the last resort, however, the legislature is largely responsible for the way in which public business is performed. In general, procedural legislation has been directed at improving the moral tone and efficient conduct of public administration. Many of the details, however, have hampered or impaired the effective performance of the public service, requiring greater attention to procedures than to the substance of administrative action.

LEGISLATIVE PARTICIPATION IN ADMINISTRATION

Laws providing the legal authority for administrative action and specifying how public business shall be conducted have not always been entirely satisfactory to legislators themselves. From time to time, they have sought a more active role by providing for some direct participation in the administrative process. Sometimes this injection of the legislature into administration has been directed essentially toward greater control of the expenditure of funds. Examples of such attempts will be noted in a later chapter. But the legislature may manifest its administrative interest in other than simply expenditure matters.

To a very real degree, one of the major difficulties a legislature confronts in drafting any law is how it can clearly express its intent. More and more, a legislature must of necessity express its consensus in very broad language. "Unfair methods of competition" shall be prohibited. But exactly what are unfair methods of competition? If an industry bases its prices upon a charge at a particular production point plus transportation to the point of sale, is this unfair? Is this unfair when in practice an industry is actually manufacturing much of the product it sells at points far distant from the actual "basing point" upon which selling prices are calculated? Neither the antitrust laws nor the Federal Trade Commission Act says anything about basing-point pricing. It was an administrative agency, the Federal Trade Commission, which decided that the cement industry had maintained "a combination . . . to hinder . . . and restrain competition in price . . . made effective by . . . what is known as a multiple basing-point system of pricing."[5] Eventually, the Supreme Court upheld this decision.[6]

The particular controversy about basing-point pricing is not important here. The situation is that when a legislature passes general laws it cannot anticipate the wide variety of circumstances which may then or subsequently be involved in the administration of the law. If every known detail were to be covered, laws would seldom if ever be completed or enacted. And if a law had to be amended every time it was extended to some new circumstance not known when the law was originally passed, our legislatures would be preoccupied three hundred sixty-five days a year in revising existing statutes. A legislature has to express general purpose in broad language and leave the details to administrative discretion.

There are, of course, several ways in which a legislature may express its interest and desires in administration without resorting to legislation. "Legislative history" is an important factor in the subsequent administration of any law. During the time when the committees of the legislature are considering a measure, administrators and others may be asked how they would interpret the meaning of particular phrases. These answers are often a "pledge" of administrative intention. In reporting a bill to the whole house for vote, a committee usually explains the purpose and even suggests how the law will be administered. These statements are often considered as "binding" upon the administrators who subsequently are assigned the responsibility of enforcing the law.

Moreover, in considering later amendments to substantive legislation, in appropriation hearings, and in any legislative inquiry into administrative behavior, legislators have various opportunities to express their opinions about how a law should be applied to specific situations. All of these influences can be quite substantial in public administration. None involves necessarily a far-reaching rewriting of substantive legislation to cover various details of administration.

But these various influences at times seem inadequate to legislators. Accordingly, they seek ways in which they can ensure a direct voice in the administration of some particular legislation. The objective in these

[5] In the matter of the Cement Institute, 37 FTC 87, at p. 102.
[6] Federal Trade Commission v. Cement Institute, 333 U.S. 683 (1948).

cases is almost always the same. The legislature wishes to make certain that it will be consulted, or at least informed, about how some particular administrative discretion is being exercised. The devices utilized have been calculated to achieve this result. Then, if any substantial body of legislative opinion is opposed to some administrative action, presumably the legislature may intervene by law to effect a change.

For example, the Alien Registration Act approved June 28, 1940, introduced a new procedure in the handling of deportation cases. Up to this time Congress had refused by law to permit any such administrative discretion. First in 1917 and then again in 1924, Congress had enacted laws directing the mandatory deportation of various categories of aliens who had entered the United States illegally. Persons who had entered the country at a time when immigration requirements were only laxly enforced, those who had overstayed temporary permits, aliens who had been smuggled in as children—these and others were subject to immediate expulsion any time they were apprehended, regardless of their personal circumstances or the conditions which might then exist in their land of origin. Legally, the only way to avoid such deportation was for the alien to interest an individual legislator in his plight and to obtain a private law permitting him by name to remain in the United States. A Secretary of Labor sympathetic with the plight of many aliens subject to deportation directed postponement of expulsion while such bills were pending and in other instances encouraged brief exit and legal reentry. Then in 1940 Congress provided that in the case of an alien who was deportable under existing law but who had proved "good moral character" for the preceding five years, the Attorney General might suspend deportation, provided that deportation would result in "economic detriment" to a citizen or a legally resident alien. If such deportation were suspended for more than six months, the Attorney General was to report the facts of the case to Congress. By concurrent resolution, Congress might then disapprove of the suspension. If Congress took no action during the session when the case was reported, the alien was thenceforth to be regarded as legally resident in the United States.[7] This law has remained in effect since that day and has permitted Congress to review the application of the suspensory discretion of the Attorney General in deportation matters affecting individual aliens. Congress has retained a "veto" over the administrative acts of the Attorney General.

The Atomic Energy Act approved August 1, 1946, included provisions for industrial, commercial, or other nonmilitary use of fissionable material under license from the Atomic Energy Commission. No such license can be issued, however, unless the Commission first prepares a report to the

---

[7] For a detailed account of this legislation, see Harvey C. Mansfield, "The Legislative Veto and the Deportation of Aliens," *Public Administration Review,* vol. 1 (Spring, 1941), p. 281.

President stating all the facts bearing on such use. The President must then transmit the report to Congress and the report must lie before Congress for a period of ninety days while Congress is in session. Only after these steps have been complied with is it legal for the Commission to issue a license for the industrial or commercial use of fissionable materials. This arrangement provides Congress with an opportunity to review proposed administrative policy and to pass legislation modifying or repealing that policy if it so desires.[8]

The two examples given here illustrate methods of ensuring direct legislative review of administrative action. The first involves review of administrative discretion in suspending the deportation of individual aliens; by concurrent resolution Congress has provided itself with the means of reversing any individual case when it believes this desirable. In the second instance, Congress has undertaken to review administrative policy before it is applied by the issuance of individual licenses to utilize atomic energy for industrial or commercial purposes. Both methods make use of devices essentially "legislative" in nature. Both procedures ensure administrative consultation with appropriate committees of Congress.

One difficulty with these practices is that they tend to encourage a legislature to seek ever more and more direct participation in the administrative process. For example, the territorial legislature of the Philippine Islands, while that area was still a territory of the United States, enacted various laws for the administration of government-owned and -operated corporations. In the case of a coal company the act stated that the voting power of the government-owned stock should be vested in a committee consisting of the Governor General, the President of the Senate, and the Speaker of the House of Representatives. In this instance there was, of course, an additional complicating factor not present in the United States proper. In the Philippine territorial government, the Governor General was American, whereas the two legislators were Filipino. In any event, the constitutionality of this arrangement was challenged and carried all the way to the Supreme Court of the United States. The Court decided that the law was unconstitutional since it endeavored to give executive power to two members of the legislature.[9]

This case has served as a constant reminder to the Congress, and to state legislatures, that the Court will review with care those instances in which the legislature endeavors to participate in administration. There is some dividing line between what is a legitimate exercise of legislative power and what is a legislative invasion of executive or administrative power. The legislature, or any of its members, may not serve as administrators. The legislature under our system of government is expected to speak through legislation.

[8] Sec. 7(b) of the Atomic Energy Act, 60 Stat. 755.
[9] *Springer v. United States,* 277 U.S. 189 (1928).

From time to time legislative concern with the administration of laws tends to invade the role of the chief executive in supervising administrative performance. Since it is not always easy to draw clear and distinct boundary lines between legislative, executive, and judicial power, the danger of trespass is ever present. Because it is the source of that authority which administrative agencies wield, it is natural for the legislature to want to ensure that these agencies do exercise authority as the legislature intended. But the Founding Fathers were concerned about the possibility of legislative tyranny even as they were concerned about executive dictatorship or judicial absolutism. The power to see to it that the laws are "faithfully executed" was vested in the Chief Executive rather than in the legislature. A precise definition of legislative competence limits the legislature to the responsibility of speaking only through law duly enacted. In practice, the legislature can and does move beyond this. And on occasion chief executives complain about invasion of their responsibilities.

For example, on January 24, 1933, President Herbert C. Hoover vetoed an appropriation bill passed by Congress because it contained the proviso that "no refund or credit in excess of $20,000 shall be made without the approval" of the Joint Committee on Internal Revenue Taxation. This committtee had been created by Congress in 1926 with five members from each house; it had a staff of its own employees. Under the Act of February 26, 1926, establishing the committee, the Secretary of the Treasury was directed to report to the committee all large refunds of personal or corporation income taxes before they were actually made. Presumably the committee was to be given an opportunity to review the facts and if dissatisfied with a case to veto the action by law. In 1933 Congress moved beyond this arrangement to an actual provision that no refund could be made without the specific and formal approval of the Joint Committee. In vetoing this bill, President Hoover relied heavily upon an elaborate opinion prepared by the Attorney General.[10] "The proviso," wrote the Attorney General, "attempts to entrust to members of the legislative branch, acting *ex officio,* executive functions in the execution of the law." He went on: "If it be an executive or judicial function, clearly a joint committee of Congress may not execute it, and if it is a legislative function, it is equally clear that a joint committee may not perform it."

On May 17, 1948, President Harry S. Truman returned to the Senate without his signature a bill which would have amended the Atomic Energy Act to authorize the Senate members of the Joint Committee on Atomic Energy to direct the Federal Bureau of Investigation to investigate any person nominated by the President for a position under the law where such appointment required senatorial approval. The director of the Federal Bureau of Investigation would have been required to report the results

[10] 37 Opinions of the Attorney General 36.

of such inquiry to the Senate committee in writing. President Truman termed the bill "an unwarranted encroachment of the legislative upon the executive branch." The President expressed the opinion also that the bill would impair the investigative function by making public sources of information which ought not to be revealed. He argued that the President's own investigation of a prospective appointee was thorough. He concluded by observing: "Although I have no desire to keep from Congress information which it should properly have, I must emphasize that the provisions of this bill are completely incompatible with the necessities of the operation of our government and with the national security."

Constitutional doctrine must be the final arbiter of proper legislative action as against an improper invasion of executive authority. Occasionally legislative-executive disagreement about the appropriate boundary lines of their respective power may present a justiciable issue which can be resolved in the courts. But constitutional doctrine is more than a matter of constitutional law spoken by the Supreme Court of the United States, or by the supreme courts of the states. Of primary importance are the attitudes of mind and the habits of self-restraint which long practice has produced in our legislatures and our chief executives. On the one hand, legislatures need, and usually possess, a clear understanding of what a legislature can appropriately do in defining administrative authority and in setting forth legislative expectations. Chief executives must necessarily acquire a sympathetic reaction to legislative sensibilities, while at the same time resolutely resisting any attempt to undermine executive authority.

One source of confusion arises from the inherent difference in composition between a legislative assembly and the chief executive of nation or state. The legislature is a numerous body, composed of many persons. The chief executive is a single individual. Moreover, the point of view of any one legislator is apt to be particularistic, expressing the sentiments and aspiration of a local area or of some one group in society. The chief executive is not necessarily immune from these same influences, but in his one person there is apt to be of necessity a broader point of view. In a legislature consensus finds expression in a law. In the chief executive consensus finds expression in one person's determination of an order, directive, or opinion. It is somewhat simpler and speedier for a chief executive to express consensus than for a legislative body to do so. One individual legislator, or even one committee of legislators, no matter how influential, still cannot express legislative consensus.

CONCLUSION

The source of administrative authority in our system of government is first of all legal, resting upon legislative enactment. Legislatures may be responsive in their actions to the suggestions of a chief executive, administrative officials, and of interest groups. In the end, it is the legislature itself which must speak.

The substantive purposes or objectives which administrative agencies are expected to accomplish are expressed primarily through law. The administrative methods or practices to be followed in the transaction of government business are to a large extent embodied in law. And legislatures determine other characteristics of administration, such as organization and magnitude of operation.

Legislative interest does not end with the enacted law. It embraces the way in which administrators exercise their discretionary authority, the way in which they carry on their business, and how they spend the funds available to them. There are appropriate, or constitutional, methods by which this interest may be asserted, and there are inappropriate, or unconstitutional, methods. Legislatures have learned from experience what they can and cannot properly do. The law is supreme, under the Constitution. But legislatures and legislators are not necessarily supreme. This is part of the genius of American government.

Chapter 6

The Legislature as
Architect of Organizational Structure

Legislative interest in administration is not just a matter of authorizing policies and programs for administrative action. The legislature is concerned also with the administrative organization for carrying out the policies and programs of government. Indeed, we may say as a general proposition that politically and legally our legislative assemblies are as much interested in how the work of government shall be doen as they are in what the work of government shall be.

It is customary for any legislation authorizing some new activity by government to give considerable attention to necessary administrative arrangements. For example, the Atomic Energy Act of 1946 was a major piece of national legislation authorizing programs to encourage private research and development, to control the dissemination of scientific and technical information about atomic fission, to conduct public research and development in atomic energy, and to control the production and use of fissionable material. Finally, the act authorized a "program of administration" which would carry out the policy and programs previously mentioned and "which will enable the Congress to be currently informed so as to take further legislative action as may hereafter be appropriate." But the 1946 law went beyond this. The first section of the law after the declaration of policy had to do with the organization of an Atomic Energy Commission. Subsequent sections then dealt with such substantive matters as research, the production of fissionable materials, the control of materials, military applications of atomic energy, the utilization of atomic energy, international arrangements, control of information, and patents and inventions. Thus, it is customary for organizational provisions and substantive authority to be set forth in the same piece of legislation. More than this, it is not unusual for organizational arrangements to receive as much legislative attention as problems of administrative authority.

Legislative interest in organizational structure extends to a number of questions which must be answered each time government increases the scope or range of its activities. In a sense we may say that there is no aspect of administrative organization to which a legislature may not at some time give attention. Even so, it is possible to enumerate certain basic questions which tend to receive the major proportion of legislative interest. These particular questions as enumerated here may not exhaust the matters which receive legislative attention, but they will at least indicate the comprehensive nature of that attention.

First, shall a program being initially authorized or extended be assigned for administrative performance to a newly created agency or to an existing administrative agency?

Second, what shall be the relationship of an administrative agency to the chief executive?

Third, shall an administrative agency be headed by a single individual or by a board or commission?

Fourth, under what circumstances and conditions shall the legislature establish a corporate form of organization?

Fifth, to what extent shall the legislature specify the internal organization of an administrative agency?

Each of these questions requires some extended comment. Before turning to these, however, we should note one important qualification. To the extent that administrative organization is specified in a state constitution, the discretion of a state legislature in answering the questions listed above is circumscribed. Moreover, state laws on local affairs and city charters usually set forth many details of administrative structure for municipal government. Hence, the discretion of a local council may be decidedly limited. But within the appropriate restrictions applying to it, the legislature at all levels of government must answer basic questions about administrative organization for the activities it authorizes.

NEW VERSUS EXISTING ORGANIZATIONS

Except when a government is newly established, a legislature is confronted with an existing array of administrative agencies. As the work of government grows, the legislature must then face the problem whether to assign some new or expanded program to an agency already in operation or to create a wholly new agency.

A number of political reasons have encouraged legislatures to favor a constant expansion in the number of administrative agencies of government. For one thing, a new agency usually means more administrative positions to be filled by appointment. There is more prestige and status for the administrative head of an activity if the agency is separate from an existing agency. These dual concerns for jobs and status frequently play a major part in motivating the organizational thinking of a legislature. If the dominant political party desires to create new positions, and if there is some interest in giving top status to an individual known to be likely to be appointed to head an activity, then the legislature may be willing to create a new administrative agency.

There are other political factors which may also be influential. Certain leading legislators may be hostile to some particular person who is head of an agency. They may then oppose adding new programs to that agency. On the other hand, legislative leaders may have special confidence in a particular administrator and be quite willing to enlarge the scope of his duties. Sometimes these attitudes of hostility and friendliness apply to a whole agency rather than just to the individual head of an agency. Furthermore, interest groups often affect legislative attitudes about organizational structure. The larger the number of interests coming within the jurisdiction of a single government agency, the less influence any one interest group is likely to exercise. Here is a good reason for an interest group to favor a separate agency.[1]

There are times when a legislature must embark upon some new type of administrative endeavor. This is especially true in time of war; it occurred also under the crisis of prolonged depression during the decade of the 1930s. In passing the original legislation for such new government programs as control of agricultural production, social security, and relief of the unemployed, Congress provided for so-called emergency agencies. In due course it was expected that the need for some of these measures would pass and the administrative agency could be abolished. There is a prevailing belief among many legislators that it is relatively easy to end the life of a separate administrative entity. Therefore, it is sometimes argued, a short-range program of government should never be entrusted to a permanent administrative organization but should be kept separate.

A few examples will suffice to suggest the varied, and even contradictory, reactions of legislators to organizational situations.

In 1942, President Roosevelt appointed Jesse Jones as Secretary of Commerce. For the ten years preceding Jones had been head of the Reconstruction Finance Corporation; since 1939 he had headed the Federal Loan Agency which was in reality the RFC. Because of widespread legislative confidence in Jesse Jones, the President at the same time by executive order issued under the First War Powers Act of December 18, 1941, provided that the RFC should become a part of the Commerce Department. Immediately after his inauguration for the fourth time in January, 1945, President Roosevelt dismissed Jesse Jones as Secretary of Commerce and appointed the former Vice President, Henry A. Wallace, to the position. Before the Senate was willing to confirm this appointment,

[1] Murray Edelman, "Governmental Organization and Public Policy," *Public Administration Review,* vol. 12 (Autumn, 1952), p. 276.

Congress passed a law approved February 24, 1945, separating the RFC from the Department of Commerce. The RFC had been merged with the Department of Commerce because of a personality situation rather than because of any belief that the activities involved were necessarily closely related to those performed by that department. Three years later the corporation was removed from the jurisdiction of the Department of Commerce by law because of legislative distrust in the personality of a new appointee as head of the department.

In the Atomic Energy Act of 1946, Congress provided for a separate administrative agency to carry on research, development, and production of fissionable materials, and especially of the atomic bomb. During World War II the atomic bomb program had been administered by the Department of War. Indeed, a major reason for assigning this activity to the department had been a belief that so large an undertaking could best be carried on effectively and in secret only by the War Department. At the end of the war there was a widespread feeling among legislators that a continuing program in atomic energy should not be conducted under military jurisdiction. This attitude prevailed even though it was recognized that the major application of atomic energy for some time to come would continue to be military. A good many scientists who had played a leading part in producing the atomic bomb were restive under military administration. There was a belief that many Army officers did not fully appreciate civilian scientists as individuals and were not entirely sympathetic to scientific research. There was some fear also that atomic research and production under military auspices would not give adequate attention to the peacetime, or nonmilitary, utilization of atomic energy. For these and other reasons Congress was readily persuaded to separate atomic energy administration from the Department of War. At the same time the law contained elaborate provisions for military liaison.

In June, 1947, Secretary of State George C. Marshall proposed that the United States should adopt a new program of providing economic assistance primarily to the nations of Western Europe. The result was the passage of the Economic Cooperation Act of 1948. The law established a separate agency to be known as the Economic Cooperation Administration, to be headed by an administrator who was to "have a status in the executive branch of the government comparable to that of the head of an executive department." It was recognized that this legislation was a major element in the foreign policy of the United States; indeed it had been the State Department which had developed the basic plans for the entire endeavor. The law simply asserted that "the Administrator and the Secretary of State shall keep each other fully and currently informed on matters, including prospective action, arising within the scope of their respective duties which are pertinent to the duties of the other." Yet Congress would not provide that the new program should actually be administered by the Department of State. Partly, this position reflected a continuing distrust of the State Department among certain members of Congress. It was felt that the Foreign Service was not too readily adaptable to the administration of broad economic efforts. Partly, the action reflected especially the known desire of Senator Arthur Vandenberg, then head of the powerful Senate Committee on Foreign Relations, to have a separate agency to which a prominent Republican might be appointed as head. Since the Congress at the time of the passage of the legislation was controlled by the Republican members, this desire prevailed.

Subsequently, we may note that in 1954 Congress, in providing an appropriation for the successor agency to the ECA, the Foreign Operations Administration, specified that it must be liquidated by June 30, 1955. No doubt this action expressed primarily a widespread legislative feeling that the United States could and should not continue indefinitely to provide economic assistance to foreign nations. Yet in his budget message to Congress on January 17, 1955, President Eisenhower recommended that 1.1 billion dollars be spent in the next fiscal year for economic assistance to other countries. It was generally recognized, indeed, that economic aid was not going to come to any abrupt end on June 30, 1955. Rather, the administration of military assistance was transferred to the Department of Defense, which had played the major role in the administration of this form of economic aid from the beginning, and the technical assistance or technical cooperation program was transferred to the State Department. In this instance Congress was apparently satisfied to have abolished the separate agency as a means of satisfying a widespread sentiment that a program ought to come to an end, while actually continuing a substantial part of the program under the jurisdiction of two major executive departments.

In general, agricultural interest groups in the United States have favored a single integrated agency to administer all kinds of agricultural programs, from research and statistics and education to soil conservation, marketing controls, and farm housing. At various times certain specialized programs have been placed under separate agencies, such as the Resettlement Administration and the Rural Electrification Administration. As of 1957 the Farm Credit Administration was the only important federal agency serving farmers which had not been incorporated within the framework of the Department of Agriculture.

As early as 1887 the federal government entered the field of transportation regulation with the creation of a separate regulatory body, the Interstate Commerce Commission. During World War I the federal government created a shipping board, but permanent legislation on maritime policy did not follow until an act of June 29, 1936, established a new separate agency, the U.S. Maritime Commission. This agency was abolished by a reorganization plan of 1950 which set up a Maritime Administration and a Maritime Board in the Department of Commerce. Similarly, an act of June 23, 1938, created a Civil Aeronautics Authority to promote the development of commercial air transport and to regulate aeronautical safety. A reorganization plan as early as 1940 divided the authority into a Civil Aeronautics Administration and a Civil Aeronautics Board located within the Department of Commerce.

From time to time various bodies studying transportation organization have pointed out that railroads were subject to the jurisdiction of one agency, merchant shipping to another, and commercial aviation to still a third. Thus, for example, a study by the Brookings Institution prepared for the (Hoover) Commission on Organization of the Executive Branch of the Government in 1948 was reported to have declared that it was "necessary in order to achieve the declared regulatory objectives of impartial treatment of all forms of transportation, non-discriminatory rates, workable competition, and the integration of the several forms of transportation into an efficient, economical, and progressive national system" to establish a consolidated transportation regulatory agency.[2]

There has been little opposition by the commercial maritime and aviation interests to the location of the administrative agency concerned with their affairs within the structure of the Department of Commerce. There has been vociferous opposition to the suggestion that the Interstate Commerce Commission or a new consolidated regulatory commission should assume major jurisdiction over their affairs. Indeed, the activities in the three fields are essentially different. Federal government interest in railroad service is primarily regulatory in nature, concerned to prevent discrimination in railroad charges and to ensure minimum desirable standards of service. The federal government interest in merchant shipping and commercial aviation is essentially promotional in character, providing financial assistance and service aids to both forms of transportation. The Department of Commerce has tended to be promotion-minded. The Interstate Commerce Commission is regulatory-conscious. The business groups affected have developed different attitudes and different types of adjustment to government concern with their operations. Thus there has been little basis for administrative consolidation for these three different industry groups.

There is no ready answer to this question whether the legislature should create new agencies or expand others. Legislators are not necessarily interested in technical reasons why one particular activity should be merged with another. They are not readily persuaded to action by a statement that agencies with related tasks ought to be placed under common supervision in order to achieve harmonious programs or to ensure economy of administrative overhead. This caution does not result from any indiffer-

---

[2] The quotation is from a statement by Commissioners Brown and Pollock in Commission on Organization of the Executive Branch of the Government, *Regulatory Commissions* (Washington: Government Printing Office, 1949), p. 19.

ence or hostility on the part of legislators to such objectives as administrative efficiency. The fact is that activities of government are not established for technical reasons. They are authorized because of the demands of an articulate and influential segment of the public or because of the need to respond to some extensive public concern or distress. The factors which induce legislative action on some subject will usually predispose the legislature also to some particular point of view in so far as administrative status is concerned.

RELATIONSHIP OF AN ADMINISTRATIVE AGENCY
TO THE CHIEF EXECUTIVE

A second set of problems for a legislature involves the determination of the relationship which an administrative activity shall have to the chief executive. The full ramifications of this issue cannot be considered here, since the powers of administrative supervision vested in the chief executive will be discussed in a subsequent chapter. Certainly it is a basic doctrine of our constitutional system of government that the legislature cannot dilute or circumvent the constitutional powers of the chief executive. To the extent that a constitution vests authority over administrative agencies in the chief executive, any law which endeavors to alter that authority is unconstitutional.

Yet in actual practice, in two or three types of situations, the problem has arisen of "insulating" certain administrative agencies from the ordinary administrative authority of the chief executive. We may ignore this question in so far as it affects so-called legislative agencies. In the federal government, for example, the Library of Congress, the Architect of the Capitol, and the General Accounting Office are often referred to as legislative agencies. In so far as the ordinary tasks of governmental administration are concerned, the general question of organizational relationship to the chief executive has arisen primarily in two fields: regulatory administration and educational administration.

Obviously, where an administrative agency is separately provided for by a state constitution or a municipal charter, a legislature cannot by itself undertake to alter the relationship of these officers to the chief executive. On occasion, a legislature may have a choice in deciding whether to vest a particular activity in an agency subject to the supervisory authority of the chief executive or to vest the activity in one of the separately elected officials. If the legislature is dominated by the same party as that to which the governor belongs, the answer may favor the governor. But even where the legislature and governor are of different party persuasion, the legislature may nonetheless be reluctant to increase the authority of one of the separately elected officials. The reason is simple. The incumbents of the separately elected posts are all likely to be politically ambitious. One or more may be eager to run for other elected office, such as for governor or

United States senator. A legislature which adds to the authority of any one such officer tends in effect to give a boost to his political ambition. Often a legislature will carefully avoid any such apparent favoritism.

In the federal government the question about desirable relationship between administrative agencies and the Chief Executive centers in regulatory administration and involves the matter of executive authority to remove the members of a regulatory board. The whole subject of executive authority to appoint and remove administrative officials will be considered in more detail later. Only the essence of the issue need be mentioned here.

The problem here is whether it may be desirable in some particular instance to give an administrative agency some degree of independence from presidential control. It appears to be commonly accepted that if the legislature specifies in substantial detail what an administrative officer is to do, then the President cannot command him to do otherwise. Robert E. Cushman has set forth this conclusion in these words: "The weight of opinion (there being no judicial decision in point) is that the President cannot validly review a quasi-judicial decision reached by one of his subordinates in pursuance of statutory authority."[3] It follows that to the extent Congress limits the discretion of an administrative officer by statutory provision, it does in effect limit the supervisory authority of the President himself.

For this reason Congress frequently has a definite motivation to prescribe a considerable range of policy, program, and administrative detail into law. Much depends upon the prevailing attitude of the legislature toward the Chief Executive. If the attitude generally is one of considerable public confidence in a President, and if in turn Presidential prestige and leadership are influential with the Congress, then legislation may be passed which sets forth broad ends of public policy only. In these circumstances, the administrative officer entrusted with the operation of a program must necessarily obtain a large measure of direction from the Chief Executive. In a reverse set of circumstances, the administrative officer may in effect obtain a substantial measure of "independence" from the President's supervisory authority. But this does not mean that the administrative officer obtains a special kind of discretionary power. It means only that the legislature has by statutory prescription left little administrative discretion at all.

As we have said, the problem of discretion has arisen primarily in the realm of regulatory administration.[4] Usually, regulatory authority has been

[3] Robert E. Cushman, *The Independent Regulatory Commissions* (New York: Oxford University Press, 1941), p. 454. The basic decision of the Supreme Court on this subject is the Kendall case of 1838, referred to in chap. 2.

[4] On regulatory administration in general, see George A. Graham and Henry Reining, Jr., *Regulatory Administration* (New York: John Wiley & Sons, Inc., 1943).

vested in a board or commission. Cushman has defined the issue in this way: "From a practical point of view the only way in which Congress can make the regulatory commissions independent is by limiting the discretionary power of the President to remove their members from office."[5] Here we need add only that it appears now to be established that Congress can limit the President's power to remove a regulatory official. If the law specifies that an officer shall be removed only because of neglect of duty or because of malfeasance in office, with due notice and hearing on the charges—and if the officer is a regulatory official—then the President can exercise his power of removal only in accordance with the specified standards and procedure.

The purpose in conferring this special status upon regulatory bodies is to be found in the peculiar nature of the regulatory process. The regulatory agency is ordinarily headed by a board rather than a single individual. The board or commission members are appointed for fairly long periods—five, seven, or nine years being most common. Terms of office overlap so that only one person retires in any one year. Continuity of policy is thus supposed to be advanced. The provision about removal is a further safeguard to encourage "independent" action by members. Since the authority of the regulatory commission is often described as "quasi-judicial," involving the application of broad standards of public policy to particular individuals or groups, the commission is expected to judge each case on its merits and in accordance with the evidence presented. A chief executive, it is held, should not desire to substitute his judgment in these individual cases for the considered decision of a regulatory commission.[6]

In any event, we may say that in practice a legislature may and does confer a peculiar status upon a regulatory body which gives it a position of some "independence" from executive supervision. The real degree of this independence may easily be exaggerated. Moreover, few if any chief executives are likely to desire to interfere in individual case decisions in any event. But a legislature can include certain organizational provisions in a law setting up a regulatory body which makes the agency different in status from those carrying out other programs.

At the state and local levels of government the question of administrative structure appropriate for the function of public education has given rise to some discussion. In most local school districts throughout the

---

[5] Cushman, *op. cit.*, p. 454.

[6] There has been a great deal of discussion about the peculiar status of regulatory commissions, beginning with the report of the President's Committee on Administrative Management in 1937. In addition to the Cushman book, the interested student should consult James M. Landis, *The Administrative Process* (New Haven, Conn.: Yale University Press, 1938); I. L. Sharfman, *The Interstate Commerce Commission,* vol. IV (New York: The Commonwealth Fund, 1937); James W. Fesler, *The Independence of State Regulatory Agencies* (Chicago: Public Administration Service, 1942); and Marver H. Bernstein, *Regulating Business by Independent Commission* (Princeton, N.J.: Princeton University Press, 1955).

United States, state education laws provide for separately elected boards of education. This means that school boards are responsible only and directly to the voters. Mayors and city councils usually have no supervisory control over local school administration, even though support of the school system tends to be the largest single item of local expenditure. To the extent that some degree of joint action or common endeavor is desirable between school administrators and other public officials, such as recreation or health or welfare or public works administrators, voluntary cooperation is the only basis of relationship.

In a few large cities, such as New York, the school board is not separately elected but appointed by the mayor. This arrangement has been established in the belief that in a large municipality voters are not likely to know very much about individual candidates for election to a school board, and that a more representative group will be obtained by appointment rather than by election. As of 1950, thirty-nine of the forty-eight states either had no state school board or the governor appointed all or a majority of the board members. But in recent years there has been an increasing tendency for voters to adopt constitutional amendments providing for elected state boards. Here again the argument centers on whether direct popular election or gubernatorial appointment is more likely to provide able and representative members.

The argument of most professional school administrators has usually been that popular election is the preferable method of selecting both local and state school board members. The idea of an appointed board has been feared, lest this in turn result in the exercise of supervisory control over education by a mayor or governor. It is generally argued that public education is a unique task of government. Its work touches the lives of almost all families with children and affects the welfare of society as a whole in a vital spot, the nurture of youth. This far-reaching endeavor, it is said, should not be left to the control of a chief executive whose primary concern is political power and whose personal interest may not extend to education. Rather, school administration should come under the joint leadership of a lay board of outstanding citizens and of a professionally trained and experienced school administrator. In the effort to ensure the election of proper personnel to a school board, it is quite common to provide for election on nonpartisan ballots, often at special times, and to provide no compensation for board members.

Prominent minority groups—racial, religious, or national—have sometimes declared, however, that appointment by a chief executive is preferable to popular election in selecting members of a school board. If party labels were used in school elections, political leaders would be careful to put forth a slate of candidates with a balanced appeal to voters of various backgrounds. When the election of a school board is by nonpartisan ballot, the group which best succeeds in arousing popular interest in school candidates and which persuades citizens to vote for certain particular persons is very apt to elect all or almost all members of the school board. If special elections are not held for school board members, and if members are chosen by partisan ballot, then it is argued that voters tend to concentrate their attention upon the most exciting part of the contest, which will usually center in the race for mayor, governor, president, or senator. Under these circumstances school board members are apt to be elected on the "coattails" of some other candidate, or to be elected as the result of "landslide" enthusiasm for a particular political party.

Without endeavoring further to discuss the merits of elected versus appointed members of school boards, we may nonetheless observe as a general proposition that there is a widespread popular hostility to supervision of school administration by a chief executive. Most school laws confer a substantial degree of administrative and fiscal independence upon school boards. This practice is the result of years of conviction on the part of many groups that school administration should be conducted under different arrangements from those characterizing other activities of local government. It does not matter that many other functions of local government such as public health, public welfare, public works, and even police administration have become highly professional and specialized in nature. School enthusiasts—professional and lay—nonetheless insist that school administration is different. No matter how it may be argued that all aspects of local government should be brought under common executive supervision in order to ensure efficient operation,[7] school enthusiasts are determined that at least the public schools must be kept away from the influence of a chief executive. To a substantial degree this attitude is a prevailing canon of political faith in the United States.[8]

Much the same attitude prevails in so far as higher education is concerned at the state level of government. State universities are generally administered by lay boards of trustees plus a full-time professional head. A great deal of educational and administrative discretion has been vested in these boards by law or even by constitutional provision. Chief executives have usually been reluctant to assert any extensive supervisory authority over state universities because of prevailing popular hostility to such an effort as expressed in statutory enactment.

THE SINGLE- VERSUS THE MULTIPLE-HEADED AGENCY

Still another major political question in the determination of administrative structure is whether an agency shall be headed by a single administrator or by a board. In the early years of our federal republic, Con-

---

[7] See the arguments set forth in N. B. Henry and J. B. Kerwin, *Schools and City Government* (Chicago: University of Chicago Press, 1938).

[8] Cf. Frederick C. McLaughlin, "Local Government and School Control," *School and Society,* vol. 75 (Apr. 5, 1952), p. 211.

gress established almost exclusively agencies with a single individual as head. Between 1776 and 1789 the Continental Congress had set up committees and boards of its own members to carry on administrative duties.[9] It was generally accepted that experience with these had been unhappy; the defects of administrative structure under the Articles of Confederation were powerful factors leading to the adoption of the federal Constitution. With this experience much in mind, it was natural for Congress after 1789 to favor single-headed administrative agencies. Alexander Hamilton in particular was one of the most determined advocates on this score.[10] Although there was some experimentation with boards down to the Civil War, notably at the bureau level in both the Treasury Department and the Navy Department, by 1860 it was generally accepted that single-headed control of administrative activities was preferable.[11]

After the Civil War, legislative thinking began to alter. The Pendleton Act of 1883 created a Civil Service Commission of three members. In 1887, legislation was passed establishing an Interstate Commerce Commission of five members. In 1913, in passing new legislation for supervision of the national banking system, Congress provided for a Federal Reserve Board of seven members, two serving ex officio. A second regulatory commission, the Federal Trade Commission, was established in 1914. During World War I, several government corporations were set up headed by boards of directors. In the intervening years, the number of boards and commissions in the federal government has tended steadily to increase. Perhaps the most important such body set up after World War II was the Atomic Energy Commission.

Interestingly enough, the trend has been somewhat different in our state and local governments. Here, during most of the nineteenth century, it was customary to have boards for education, health, welfare, road, and even police administration. Except in the field of education, this trend has been reversed, and the prevailing practice is to have single-headed agencies in these fields, sometimes with an advisory board attached. To be sure, there are still many boards and commissions in state and local government, but in relative terms the proportion of government services operated by boards has tended to decline.

Apart from the government corporation, which we shall discuss in a moment, the argument in favor of board administration is usually three-fold. First, it is claimed that the vital importance of a particular activity, especially as it may affect the lives and fortunes of individuals, is best entrusted to the judgment of a group rather than to the decision of a single person. Our appellate judicial bodies are always courts of from

[9] Lloyd M. Short, *The Development of National Administrative Organization in the United States* (Baltimore: Johns Hopkins Press, 1923), pp. 37–51.

[10] *Ibid.*, p. 53. Cf. also Leonard D. White, *The Federalists* (New York: The Macmillan Company, 1948), pp. 90–92.

[11] *Ibid.*, pp. 219–220.

three to nine judges. In the regulatory process, where issues of entrance or continuation in business or a profession are involved, or where matters of business prices and profits must be determined, we feel safer with a board than with one person in the seat of authority. We believe there is more likelihood of fairness from a group. This fundamental premise is deep-seated in our political tradition and is evidenced, for example, in our attachment to trial by jury. A second argument is that there is more wisdom in a group than in a single individual. When the Atomic Energy Commission was established in 1946, almost no one in the President's office or in Congress was inclined to question the desirability of placing this function under a board. It was thought that in such a new undertaking with immeasurable ramifications and with unknown potentialities, only the judgment of a board could be trusted. Moreover, some persons, especially some scientists, felt that the experience under military command had been unhappy. They were therefore inclined to favor a different arrangement which they thought a board would ensure. Furthermore, as a part of this proposition about wisdom, a board may be advocated by various groups in the expectation that a representative of their number may be appointed and so ensure the presentation of their particular point of view. A third argument in favor of a board is the feeling that somehow this will eliminate "politics" from an agency. Just what politics means in this context few persons ever make explicit. Often a law provides that not more than a bare majority of the membership of any board shall come from a single political party. Presumably where several persons of equal authority are present, and these belong to different parties, there will be less inclination to indulge in political chicanery involving appointment to office on a spoils basis or the granting of special privileges to a favored clientele.

There have been three primary arguments against the multiheaded agency. The first is that it tends to dilute or obscure political responsibility for direction of an agency's work. When an administrative activity is headed by a single person, he and he alone must accept responsibility for all basic policies of operation. Popular dissatisfaction with work objectives or performance can then be expressed through pressures which result in replacement of the agency's head. This kind of simple solution to dissatisfaction with an administrative agency is not available in the case of an agency headed by several persons. In the second place, a multi-headed agency may encourage vacillating or ineffective direction of work. The reasons for this are primarily technical in nature. A good deal of organizational experience has indicated that agencies run by several persons are apt to have uncertain or confused lines of communication, channels of command, and divisions of work assignment. A famous Army general, George D. Goethals, builder of the Panama Canal and Army supply chief during World War I, is supposed to have remarked on one occasion that all boards are "long, narrow, and wooden." In any event, if it be true that boards tend to weaken an agency's work accomplishment—this is an assumption by no means conclusively demonstrated by our present-day knowledge—then this failure may have political repercussions. In 1954 and 1955, for example, and again in 1957 there was some fear evidenced that basic differences over policy and program among the commissioners of the Atomic Energy Commission were impairing the work efforts of that agency. Certainly any failure on the part of the AEC to push forward on the research, production, and utilization of atomic energy, especially for national defense, could have dire political consequences for the nation as a whole, for individual political leaders, and for the political party directing the nation's affairs. A third argument has been that boards do not in and of themselves necessarily ensure integrity in administrative operations. There have been instances where members of a board, even though ostensibly of opposing political affiliation, have in fact collaborated in administrative venality. The essence of the argument about taking some administrative work "out of politics" is that when one politician is set to watch two other politicians, nonpolitical administration results. Actually, the consequence may just as well be that one politician watching over two other politicians may bring about intensified political administration. There are more people to be satisfied. Integrity is primarily a personal attribute and cannot be produced by mechanical arrangements of organizational structure.

Sometimes a legislature may be induced to create a board to take "politics" out of a troublesome sphere of legislation. For example, in local government, planning boards were created at the turn of the century in the belief that such boards could manage to lay out long-term capital development programs without resorting to legislative logrolling or executive compromises. But several decades of experience have suggested that although these planning boards succeeded in preparing elaborate planning reports, they seldom if ever succeeded in preparing a plan which was put into effect.[12] To a few, this has meant that planners should be given more political power. To others, it has demonstrated the futility of endeavoring to short-cut or bypass the legislative process. More and more, we have come to realize that basic policy decisions must be made within our scheme of government by legislatures and chief executives and that administrative agencies may advise and administer but cannot usurp the role of either.[13]

Such are the arguments for and against single-headed agencies versus multiheaded agencies. The resolution of the argument in the case of any particular administrative situation is a political question which must first

[12] Cf. Robert A. Walker, *The Planning Function in Urban Government,* rev. ed. (Chicago: University of Chicago Press, 1941, 1950).

[13] Charles S. Ascher, "City Planning, Administration—and Politics," *Land Economics,* vol. 30 (November, 1954), p. 320.

of all be provided by the legislature. The members of our elected assemblies must make the best judgment they can in each case where this question of administrative organization arises.

CORPORATE FORM OF ORGANIZATION

A special organizational problem is posed by the government corporation. By this term we ordinarily mean an agency with a special kind of administrative status created to operate an enterprise which has business functions. There are at least two other kinds of government corporations, however, which we shall omit from our discussion here. One is the municipal corporation, which in reality is a local unit of government. The other is the educational corporation, which has been used in most states to perform the function of higher education. In its dormitory, and certain other, activities this educational corporation does partake of the characteristics of the government corporation which is our interest here.

There is a difference between the corporation chartered by government for the benefit of a group of individuals who join together to carry on some activity, and the government corporation which is created as an administrative agency of the state. Actually, in American history, the first experience with government corporations was a mixture of the two types. The First Bank of the United States was chartered by Congress in 1791 and received 20 per cent of its capital from the United States Treasury. The Second Bank, chartered in 1816, was similarly supported. In 1902 by an act of Congress the President was authorized to acquire all the rights, privileges, and properties of the New Panama Canal Company of France for a sum not to exceed 40 million dollars. Thus the national government acquired a private corporation by direct purchase and thereafter directed its operations by virtue of this ownership.[14] In 1916, the Federal Farm Loan Act provided for the creation of twelve Federal Land Banks in which government ownership of capital stock was intended to be only temporary. By 1919, the government investment was only one-third of the total. The Depression reversed this trend, however, and by 1945 the government's proportion was 60 per cent. By 1955, this capital stock was held entirely by national farm loan associations.

These early federal experiments with government corporations were mostly in the nature of mixed enterprises. The New Panama Canal Company was a private enterprise purchased by government because of its role in an important phase of our national defense and foreign relations. In the states during the first half of the nineteenth century particularly there was also a substantial degree of state government capital participation in road, canal, and railroad corporations.

[14] See Marshall E. Dimock, *Government-operated Enterprises in the Panama Canal Zone* (Chicago: University of Chicago Press, 1934).

During World War I five government corporations were set up: the Emergency Fleet Corporation, the U.S. Grain Corporation, the War Finance Corporation, the U.S. Housing Corporation, and the U.S. Sugar Equalization Board.[15] These were placed in liquidation soon after 1919. But in 1923 Congress created by law twelve Federal Intermediate Credit Banks for the benefit of farmers, the capital stock in which was wholly provided by the government. In 1924 Congress passed legislation creating an Inland Waterways Corporation, which was operated by the federal government until it was sold to private interests on September 19, 1953.

The Depression brought substantial new uses of the corporation device. The first was the Reconstruction Finance Corporation, set up in 1932 and finally placed in liquidation under an act approved July 30, 1953. The next and perhaps most noteworthy addition was the Tennessee Valley Authority (TVA) created by an act of Congress approved May 18, 1933. The Federal Deposit Insurance Corporation was established by the Banking Act of June 16, 1933. Thereafter a number of government corporations were created by executive or administrative action. A Commodity Credit Corporation was created by Executive order on October 16, 1933; an Export-Import Bank by Executive order on February 2, 1934; an Electric Home and Farm Authority, Inc., to work in the Tennessee Valley was authorized by Executive order on December 19, 1933. Administrative officials took steps to incorporate other enterprises under the laws of the state of Delaware. In the period from March, 1933, to June, 1934, as many as fourteen new government corporations were established within the federal government.[16]

The device of the government corporation was much discussed during the 1930s. The best-known short statement of purpose for a government corporation was expressed by President Roosevelt in his message to Congress on April 10, 1933, urging creation of the TVA. He urged that the new agency be a "corporation clothed with the power of government but possessed of the flexibility and initiative of a private enterprise." The "flexibility" of the government corporation is manyfold. Having received an initial appropriation of capital, the government corporation may commit its funds in such a way as to obtain income from its investment. This income may be retained by the corporation rather than paid into the Treasury as miscellaneous receipts. Thus the corporation is freed from the need to obtain annual operating appropriations from the legislature. Plans for development can be made over a period of time and carried out within the limits of available income. In the federal government, corporations have been subjected to a different kind of audit control from that of

[15] Cf. Harold A. Van Dorn, *Government-owned Corporations* (New York: Alfred A. Knopf, Inc., 1926).

[16] For the names and essential facts about these corporations, see Lawrence F. Schmeckebier, *New Federal Organizations* (Washington, D.C.: Brookings Institution, 1934).

ordinary agencies. Moreover, the TVA was permitted to establish its own separate personnel system, and originally this was a good deal superior to many of the usual personnel practices in the federal government. The government corporation usually could sue and be sued in its own name.[17]

The extensive, and almost indiscriminate, use of the government corporation during the 1930s also produced a good deal of public criticism. It was charged that the President and department heads were creating corporations to carry on activities not authorized by Congress. Since many corporations were able to operate from earned income, it was said that they escaped annual scrutiny by Congress through the appropriation process. In addition, the financial transactions of the government corporation were not being examined by the General Accounting Office. Moreover, the corporation was being set up to engage in activities which were not essentially different from those of other agencies. The financial justification for a government corporation was that its operations were income-producing. This criterion, however, was not always being observed. The use of state laws to incorporate federal government activities was questioned, as by the President's Committee on Administrative Management in 1937. The President's Committee also wanted all government corporations placed under regular civil service restrictions. The exemption of government corporations from state and local taxation was criticized, especially in the case of the TVA.[18] Moreover, there was a great deal of concern whether the federal government was about to embark upon extensive competition with private enterprise through the device of the government corporation.

Various criticisms of the government corporation, coming especially from the Joint Committee on Reduction of Non-essential Expenditures set up by Congress in 1941, resulted in the passage of the Government Corporation Control Act of December 6, 1945.[19] First of all, the law specified that all government corporations must prepare a "business-type budget, or plan of operations" to be submitted to the President and by him to be transmitted to Congress as a part of his budget message.

[17] In its report in 1937, the President's Committee on Administrative Management declared that the government corporation was an "effective device for not only emergency purposes but for the continuing operation of a variety of economic services." It identified the "peculiar values" of the government corporation as "freedom of operation, flexibility, business efficiency, and opportunity for experimentation." President's Committee on Administrative Management, *Report with Special Studies* (Washington: Government Printing Office, 1937), pp. 43–44.

[18] This particular criticism was met by Congress in 1940, when Congress authorized the TVA to make payments in lieu of taxes to state and local governments in the Tennessee Valley area. See Alexander Edelman, "Public Ownership and Tax Replacement by the Tennessee Valley Authority," *American Political Science Review,* vol. 35 (August, 1941), p. 727.

[19] For a general discussion of the history and provisions of this law, see C. Herman Pritchett, "The Government Corporation Control Act of 1945," *American Political Science Review,* vol. 40 (June, 1946), p. 495.

Secondly, these "budget programs" of government corporations were to be "considered" each year by Congress, but this was not to be construed as meaning that a corporation might not finance its own activities as authorized by law without regard to the time limits of a fiscal year. In the third place, all financial transactions of corporations were to be audited by the General Accounting Office "in accordance with the principles and procedures applicable to commercial corporate transactions." In the fourth place, no new government corporations were to be created except upon authorization by Congress, and any corporation set up under the laws of the District of Columbia or of a state had to receive a charter of incorporation from Congress or cease to operate by June 30, 1948. Certain other miscellaneous provisions of the law need not concern us here.

Government corporations by no means came to an end with the passage of the Government Corporation Control Act of 1945. A Congressional report in 1954 listed seventy-eight active government corporations as of that date, as well as sixty-three inactive or terminated corporations.[20] Under the act, Congress gave new charters to five corporations previously created or operating under executive or administrative authority. In 1953, Congress provided for the liquidation of the Home Owners Loan Corporation and the Reconstruction Finance Corporation formerly authorized by legislation.

The most important single provision of the Government Corporation Control Act was the requirement that only the legislature might authorize a government corporation. Although many department and agency heads enjoy a good deal of discretion in setting up the required administrative structure for their activities, they may not hereafter organize a government corporation. Only Congress can create such an administrative agency. Thus it has become a legislative determination to decide when and under what circumstances a government corporation shall be established.

What are the prerequisites for a government corporation? Certainly, the most important single criterion is the nature of the financial operation involved. If the activity is one requiring a sizable capital outlay and the imposition of charges for the service rendered, then there is good reason to consider the possibility of a government corporation. The advantage of the government corporation is that its financial operations can be placed on a self-contained basis. The volume of receipts usually fixes the magnitude of expenditure. A balancing of income and outgo is thus encouraged. Moreover, the government corporation can accumulate a surplus of income over outgo and carry this balance over from one year to another. This is a privilege which the ordinary government agency does

[20] Senate Committee on Government Operations, *Audit Reports of Government Corporations and Agencies* report no. 861, 83d Cong., 2d Sess. (Jan. 20, 1954).

not enjoy. When an agency operates with appropriated funds, any un-committed balance at the end of a single fiscal year normally lapses and is no longer available for use.

It is not necessarily required that a government corporation must be able to balance service charges and expenditures in order to justify the corporate form of organization. It may be desirable public policy in the operation of a public utility, for example, to render the service at a charge less than cost. Such a practice certainly demands careful justification. But even in the case of a subsidized operation, the corporate form may be desirable if a substantial proportion of the income is obtained from service charges.

Should all income-producing activities of government be organized as corporations? The largest public utility in the country, the U.S. Post Office, is not set up as a government corporation. Occasionally there has been some proposal of this sort. The Hoover Commission was not willing to go quite this far in 1949 or again in 1955. Instead it recommended that the provisions of the Government Corporation Control Act of 1945 be applied to the Post Office Department which would remain an execu-tive department.[21] In 1955 the second Hoover Commission recommended that all lending agencies of the federal government also be brought under the provisions of the Government Corporation Control Act.[22] For all practical purposes except the formality of the designation these recom-mendations would make government corporations of both the Post Office and the lending agencies.

On the other hand, Congress has become somewhat sensitive to any proposal to create a new government corporation. Partly this reflects a concern for government encroachment upon private enterprise. Partly it reflects some distrust of the degree of fiscal independence enjoyed by the government corporation. In its 1954 report, the Government Operations committee spoke approvingly of the fact that Congress had rejected pro-posals to set up government corporations under the Defense Production Act of 1950, the Small Defense Plants Act of 1951, and the Economic Cooperation Act of 1948.[23] Certainly it is evident that under circumstances existing in the 1950s the legislature would scrutinize with care any pro-posal to establish a new government corporation.

At the state and local levels of government there is mixed practice in creating separate government corporations. Many municipal public utili-ties such as water supply operate financially as self-contained activities but without formal creation as a separate government corporation. Usu-

[21] Commission on Organization of the Executive Branch of the Government, *The Post Office* (Washington: Government Printing Office, 1949), p. 14.

[22] Commission on Organization of the Executive Branch of the Government, *Lending Agencies* (Washington: Government Printing Office, 1955).

[23] *Audit Reports of Government Corporations and Agencies*, p. 9.

ally, a municipal utility operates as a board or department of municipal government. On the other hand, turnpike commissions in various states have almost all been established as separate, formal government corporations.[24] Perhaps the best known of all government corporations at the state and local level of government is the Port of New York Authority set up by interstate compact between New York and New Jersey.[25]

A special problem involving the government corporation is the use of a board of directors as head of the operation. Where such a board serves full time, various difficulties are apt to arise in determining just what shall be the respective administrative duties of each board member. There is much to be said for board members who serve ex officio. In this way the board members do not have direct internal administrative duties in the operation of the corporation itself. At the same time they can represent broad policy points of view which should be expressed in the work of the corporation. This may be especially desirable when a corporation functions within the framework of a department or has duties closely related to the work of two or more departments and other agencies. An alternative to this arrangement is to have a citizen or lay board of directors who do not serve on a full-time basis.

The government corporation is an important organizational device for public administration. Its use depends, however, upon legislative willingness to create such an instrument for the performance of some particular public service.[26]

[24] In 1954, a report in New York State revealed that between 1921 and 1953 the state legislature had created thirty-three public corporations mostly having to do with parkways and water supply but ranging from a Dormitory Authority to the New York City Transit Authority. In addition, fifty-five local governments had established local housing authorities under the state public housing law. Temporary State Commission on Coordination of State Activities, *Report for the Year 1953–1954*, Leg. Doc. 55 (Albany: Williams Press, Inc., 1954), pp. 93–94. This document contains an excellent discussion on the government corporation.

[25] See Erwin Bard, *The Port of New York Authority* (New York: Columbia University Press, 1939).

[26] In addition to the monographic and other literature previously cited on the government corporation, the following also should be mentioned: *Reference Manual on Government Corporations*, prepared by the General Accounting Office and published as Sen. Doc. 86, 79th Cong., 1st Sess. (1945); Sidney D. Goldberg and Harold Seidman, *The Government Corporation: Elements of a Model Charter* (Chicago: Public Administration Service, 1953); Marshall E. Dimock, *Developing America's Waterways* (Chicago: University of Chicago Press, 1935); John McDiarmid, *Government Corporations and Federal Funds* (Chicago: University of Chicago Press, 1938); Ruth G. Weintraub, *Government Corporations and State Law* (New York: Columbia University Press, 1939); C. Herman Pritchett, *The Tennessee Valley Authority* (Chapel Hill, N.C.: The University of North Carolina Press, 1943); Harold Seidman, "The Government Corporation: Organization and Controls," *Public Administration Review,* vol. 14 (Summer, 1954), p. 183; and Marshall Dimock, "Government Corporations: A Focus of Policy and Administration," *American Political Science Review,* vol. 43 (October and December, 1949), pp. 899 and 1145.

SPECIFICATION OF ORGANIZATIONAL DETAIL

A fifth problem for the legislature is to decide the degree to which it shall specify organizational detail in the legislation which it enacts. Here practice has varied a good deal in recent years. One extreme was represented by the Emergency Relief Appropriation Act of April 8, 1935. This legislation appropriated $4,880,000,000 for a nationwide work-relief program but said nothing about organizational arrangements. The law simply said: "In carrying out the provisions of this joint resolution the President is authorized to establish and prescribe the duties and functions of necessary agencies within the government." This was perhaps as broad a delegation of organizational power to the President as has ever occurred in our political history. It is a delegation which under ordinary circumstances a legislature would not be willing to make. It was a delegation which is not likely to be repeated on many occasions. For example, when the Economic Cooperation Act of 1948, and again when the Mutual Security Act of 1951, were enacted, the legislation provided for a general outline of organizational structure, even though the President's special role in the conduct of foreign relations was duly acknowledged.

A different kind of situation is illustrated by the Atomic Energy Act of 1946. Here the law not only specified that there should be a commission of five members in charge of the program, but also established the position of general manager and set up divisions of research, production, engineering, and military application. The law fixed the salaries for these division directors and required that the director of the Division of Military Application had to be a member of the Armed Forces. This same kind of situation is illustrated by the Army Organization Act of 1950. The law provided that there should be a Chief of Staff, a Vice Chief of Staff, not to exceed three Deputy Chiefs of Staff, and not to exceed five Assistant Chiefs of Staff, a Chief of Engineers, a Chief Signal Officer, an Adjutant General, a Quartermaster General, a Chief of Finance, a Chief of Ordnance, a Chief Chemical Officer, a Chief of Transportation, a Surgeon General, a Judge Advocate General, a Chief of Chaplains, an Inspector General, and a Provost Marshal General. In addition, the law specified that there should be at least twelve "branches of the Army" and designated them by name. Even so, this law conferred upon the Secretary of the Army far more authority to organize the Army than had been enjoyed under previous legislation.

As one studies the laws of the United States, one finds a variety of practice extending throughout the whole range of administrative activity. When the Department of State was created in 1789, the original legislation simply made provision for a chief clerk and other clerks in addition to the secretary who was to be head of the department. In large part the internal organization of the department has not been specified by law, except for a Director General of the Foreign Service. When the Treasury Department was created in 1789, however, the law provided for a comptroller, auditor, treasurer, a register, and an assistant to the secretary, in addition to the secretary himself, who was "to be deemed the head of the department." From time to time, thereafter, other offices were added, such as the Comptroller of the Currency in 1863, the Commissioner of Customs in 1849, a Supervising Surgeon General of the Marine-hospital in 1870, a Director of the Mint in 1873, and a Director of the Budget in 1921. As one goes through the list of executive departments, he will find that most bureaus have been created by law. For the most part, the internal organization structure of separate government agencies apart from the executive departments has seldom been prescribed. This is true of such agencies as the Veterans' Administration, the various regulatory commissions, the Selective Service System, and the TVA.

Interestingly enough, one aspect of administrative organization in which legislators as individuals are much interested seldom is mentioned in the laws enacted by Congress. This is the matter of field offices. Nearly all federal administrative agencies find it necessary to create field offices in various parts of the United States. The number and location of these offices is almost always left to the discretion of administrative officers. The reason is obvious. If Congress undertook to specify the number and location of field offices, each senator and representative would expect an office—or a fair proportion of all offices—to be located in his state or district. Since any effort by Congress to specify field offices would have to be undertaken on the basis of log-rolling, or of mutual reciprocity, the legislature has wisely decided to leave this phase of organizational practice to administrative discretion. This does not mean, however, that the head of an agency has freedom to locate field offices as he sees fit. Rather, it means that legislative interest is manifest in other ways than by statutory prescription.

Much the same sort of situation exists in state law as has been described here for federal law. Sometimes state law sets forth details of administrative organization, and at other times a great deal of latitude is left to heads of administrative agencies. If some particular aspect of organization comes to the attention of individual legislators, statutory enactment on the matter may follow. Otherwise, department heads are left fairly free to determine internal organizational structure as seems desirable.

Sometimes the question is raised whether some standard might be formulated for the guidance of legislators in enacting legislation on organizational matters. For example, it might be suggested that legislators should concentrate their attention on clarifying the objectives of a government program to the fullest extent possible. Apart then from providing that the program should be administered by an existing agency or by a new one named in the law, a legislature might well leave all further organizational detail to the discretion of the head of the agency, subject to the approval of the chief executive, if the legislature is disposed to place this check upon administrative discretion. This kind of advice to legislators is easily defensible from a technical point of view. Administrative discretion in matters of organizational structure makes for a desirable degree of flexibility in meeting changing circumstances or changing concepts of effective organization. The defect in such counsel to a legislature simply is that it approaches the problem from a nonlegislative point of view. In so far as the purely technical matter of organization is concerned, a maximum degree of organizational discretion vested in the head of an administrative agency is quite useful. But legislators are seldom interested in the technical point of view. Theirs is a political interest.

We may conclude as a purely pragmatic matter that a legislature will evidence such interest in organizational detail as is of political interest at the time. Much depends upon the particular circumstances of the moment. One committee chairman may be more concerned about organizational practices than another. An interest group concerned with a particular piece of legislation may wish to have certain particulars of organization expressly set forth in law. Another interest group may wish to leave all matters of organization for later negotiation with the head of the administrative agency. Persons who have the "ear" of influential legislators may want certain organizational details embodied in law. Other persons, equally enjoying the confidence of legislative leaders, may advise that organization be left to administrative discretion. Administrative officers frequently have considerable influence with legislators, too. If a department head has close working relations with the head of a legislative committee or other leaders, he may be successful in persuading the legislature to leave organizational matters to his own decision. If the head of a bureau or of some other group in an agency can interest influential legislators in his point of view, he may obtain legal specification of certain details of organization which thus are removed from the discretion of the department head. Since the department head is a politically appointed official, selected by the chief executive, legislators are often motivated to circumscribe his organizational discretion.

To be sure, one can observe as a matter of historical trend that legislatures have tended in recent years to leave somewhat more discretion in matters of organization to department heads than was formerly the practice. Partly, this reflects the growing complexity of legislative interests and the exigencies of the legislative timetable. Organizational matters require more attention than a legislature may be prepared to give them. Partly, this trend reflects some legislative willingness on occasion to leave organizational details to administrative decision on the basis of judgment about the most effective practice. In an era of large-scale governmental expenditure, efficient administration may also be politically desirable. There is much to be said for continuation of the trend.

SUMMARY

Administration is so vital a part of the exercise of governmental power that a legislature is necessarily and properly concerned with its organizational structure. The legislative point of view is a political point of view, concerned with the varied and often conflicting power ambitions of individuals, interest groups, and heads of administrative agencies. These ambitions and conflicts are resolved by law to the best of the ability of the legislature. The resolution is expressed by some specification of administrative detail, or by the omission of such detail.

The most common conflicts on matters of organization tend to cluster around five problems. In the first place, in so far as organizational status is concerned, the legislature may choose to locate a new activity within an existing agency, or to create a new agency for a new activity. Or, it may leave the entire matter of organizational arrangement to the discretion of the chief executive. Ordinarily this third choice is seldom exercised. Secondly, the legislature may endeavor, within the limits of constitutional doctrine, to limit the supervisory authority of the chief executive. This has been especially the case in regulatory administration and in educational administration. Thirdly, the legislature must decide whether an agency shall be headed by a single individual or by a board. Both have been adopted. In the fourth place, the legislature must decide whether an administrative agency shall be given the special attributes of a government corporation. And in the fifth place, to varying degrees a legislature may decide to specify the internal organization of an administrative agency. In resolving these choices, a legislature reveals the extent of the political interest which centers at a particular time in the organizational structure of a particular administrative activity.

Chapter 7

The Legislature and Administrative
Reorganization in the Federal Government

Legislative action in creating administrative agencies results in the existence of a considerable number and variety of organizations. This is especially true in the federal government, but number and variety characterize the administrative structure of state and local government as well.

In 1955 the second Hoover Commission reported that the total number of "executive agencies" in the federal government came to sixty-four.[1] The United States government organization manual for 1956–1957 listed seventy-one administrative agencies other than those under the legislative branch, the judicial branch, and the Executive Office of the President.[2] In so far as variety is concerned, outside the legislative and judicial branches, the official organization manual of the federal government classifies administrative agencies into three kinds: the Executive Office of the President, executive departments, and independent agencies (that is, independent of an executive department). This is a classification whose principal virtue is its noncontroversial character.

A somewhat more elaborate classification of administrative agencies is presented in Table 2. Here administrative agencies have been divided into two broad types: (1) central coordinating and service agencies, which exist primarily to assist the President in his various administrative responsibilities or to facilitate the work of other agencies, and (2) the operating agencies which carry on the various programs authorized by the Congress from time to time. These operating agencies in turn have been divided into four groups: (1) executive departments, (2) separate administrative agencies, (3) regulatory commissions, and (4) miscel-

---

[1] Commission on Organization of the Executive Branch of the Government, *Final Report to the Congress* (Washington: Government Printing Office, June, 1955), p. 11.

[2] *United States Government Organization Manual 1956–57* (Washington: National Archives and Records Service, 1956).

Table 2. Types of Administrative Agencies in the Federal Government, January, 1958

	Civilian employment, 1958
Central Coordinating and Service Agencies	
1. The White House Office	407
2. Bureau of the Budget	437
3. Council of Economic Advisers	32
4. National Security Council	64
5. Central Intelligence Agency	...
6. Office of Defense Mobilization	243
7. U.S. Civil Service Commission	4,107
8. General Services Administration	27,524
Operating Agencies	
I. Executive Departments	
1. Department of State	34,397
2. Department of the Treasury	78,498
3. Department of Defense	1,600
a. Department of the Army	405,628
b. Department of the Navy	364,137
c. Department of the Air Force	311,526
4. Department of Justice	30,523
5. Post Office Department	535,421
6. Department of the Interior	48,862
7. Department of Agriculture	85,249
8. Department of Commerce	52,187
9. Department of Labor	5,807
10. Department of Health, Education, and Welfare	53,364
II. Separate Administrative Agencies	
1. Atomic Energy Commission	6,787
2. Board of Governors of the Federal Reserve System	579
3. Export-Import Bank of Washington	206
4. Farm Credit Administration	875
5. Federal Civil Defense Administration	1,295
6. Federal Deposit Insurance Corporation	1,191
7. Federal Home Loan Bank Board	796
8. Federal Mediation and Conciliation Service	319
9. Housing and Home Finance Agency	9,688
10. National Advisory Committee for Aeronautics	7,696
11. National Science Foundation	298
12. Panama Canal Company and Canal Zone Government	14,820
13. Railroad Retirement Board	2,522
14. Saint Lawrence Seaway Development Corporation	37
15. Selective Service System	6,296
16. Small Business Administration	1,310
17. Tennessee Valley Authority	14,674
18. United States Information Agency	10,989
19. Veteran's Administration	174,657

Table 2. Types of Administrative Agencies in the
Federal Government, January, 1958 (Continued)

	Civilian employment, 1958
Operating Agencies	
III. Regulatory Commissions	
1. Civil Aeronautics Board.................................	672
2. Federal Communications Commission......................	1,204
3. Federal Power Commission..............................	708
4. Federal Trade Commission..............................	727
5. Interstate Commerce Commission........................	2,253
6. National Labor Relations Board.........................	1,124
7. Securities and Exchange Commission.....................	838
8. Subversive Activities Control Board......................	33
9. United States Tariff Commission.........................	216
10. Federal Coal Mine Safety Board of Review.................	8
IV. Miscellaneous Boards and Agencies	
1. American Battle Monuments Commission..................	540
2. Indian Claims Commission..............................	17
3. National Mediation Board..............................	102
4. National Gallery of Art.................................	327
5. Smithsonian Institution.................................	853
6. Tax Court of the United States..........................	150
7. Foreign Claims Settlement Commission of the United States....	93
8. Renegotiation Board...................................	332
9. Board of Commissioners, United States Soldiers' Home........	1,007
10. Virgin Islands Corporation..............................	567

laneous boards and agencies. Altogether forty-nine operating agencies are listed here. This enumeration omits certain temporary agencies in existence in 1958, the government of the District of Columbia and certain corollary bodies, such as the National Capital Housing Authority and the National Capital Planning Commission, and two or three interagency committees. Indeed, in addition to the absence of any accepted scheme for classifying the administrative agencies of the federal government, there is no standard definition of what constitutes an administrative agency of the federal government.

Federal administrative organization has other characteristics besides number and variety. Administrative agencies differ a great deal in size, as the figures on numbers of employees at the beginning of the calendar year 1958 will indicate. Some agencies are headed by individual administrators, others by boards or commissions. Some agencies trace their history to the early days of the Republic; others are of recent origin. Each year one or two agencies may disappear while new ones are created. There is nothing static about government administrative organization.

CRITICISMS OF ADMINISTRATIVE STRUCTURE

The structure of federal administrative agencies has been criticized from time to time on several grounds. First, it has been said that these various agencies often perform closely related activities, which ought to be grouped together under common supervision in order to prevent overlapping or duplication of function, and in order to promote improved coordination. For example, the second Hoover Commission in 1955 reported:[3]

> Our task force studies show that Federal medical services are carried on by 26 different executive agencies; legal services by 54 agencies; research and development by 29 agencies; lending, guaranteeing, and insurance activities by 104 agencies and instrumentalities; transportation by 22 agencies.

Secondly, it is said that too many administrative agencies are separately subject to the supervision of the Chief Executive. For example, back in 1937 the President's Committee on Administrative Management declared:[4]

> The structure of the Government throws an impossible task upon the Chief Executive. No President can possibly give adequate supervision to the multitude of agencies which have been set up to carry on the work of the Government, nor can he coordinate their activities and policies.

In 1955 the second Hoover Commission expressed the opinion that of 64 government agencies counted by it,[5] the President had

> . . . unavoidable direct responsibility for about 31, but the remaining 33 are of such diverse character and duties that few of them lend themselves to relocation in other existing agencies. [It then proposed that in order to] solve the problems arising out of the sheer inability of the President to give them adequate personal supervision, and to lighten the load upon him, the President should direct these remaining 33 agencies to report to some official in the executive office whom he may designate.

A third major criticism of administrative structure was voiced by the President's Committee on Administrative Management in 1937. The Committee called attention to the fact that since 1887 the Congress had set up a dozen "independent regulatory commissions to exercise the control over commerce and business necessary to the orderly conduct of the Nation's economic life." These commissions, the Committee pointed out, had been given broad powers to determine desirable regulatory policy;

---

[3] Commission on Organization of the Executive Branch of the Government, *Final Report to the Congress,* p. 11.

[4] President's Committee on Administrative Management, *Report of the President's Committee* (Washington: Government Printing Office, 1937), p. 32.

[5] Commission on Organization of the Executive Branch of the Government, *op. cit.,* p. 17.

they had authority to inquire into the conduct of particular individuals or corporations and to file charges of violation of government law; and they had powers "similar to those exercised by courts of law, to pass in concrete cases upon the rights and liabilities of individuals under the statutes." The Committee declared that "in reality" these commissions were "miniature independent governments."[6] The Committee then characterized the regulatory commissions in these words:[7]

> They constitute a headless "fourth branch" of the Government, a haphazard deposit of irresponsible agencies and uncoordinated powers. They do violence to the basic theory of the American Constitution that there should be three major branches of the Government and only three. The Congress has found no effective way of supervising them, they cannot be controlled by the President, and they are answerable to the courts only in respect to the legality of their activities.

The President's Committee went on to assert that the independent regulatory commissions suffered from an "internal inconsistency, an unsoundness of basic theory." In so far as their responsibilities involved policy determination and "administration," the Committee said, the commissions should be under the direct supervision of the President. In so far as their responsibilities involved "important judicial work," the commissions ought to be "wholly independent of Executive control." The President's Committee then put forth the suggestion that regulatory agencies be "set up" within executive departments but that their work be divided into an "administrative section" and a "judicial section." The administrative section would be a regular bureau or division of a department headed by a single individual. The administrative work would then be subject to control by a Cabinet Secretary, and through him by the President. The judicial section, on the other hand, would be headed by a board whose purely "housekeeping" duties would be handled by the department in which it was located. The board members would be appointed by the President and confirmed by the Senate "for long, staggered terms" and would be removable only for cause as specified in the statute. The decisions of these boards would not be subject to review by the department head or the President but could be appealed only to a court of law.[8]

This proposal by the President's Committee precipitated a long, and at times bitter, debate about desirable administrative structure for the regulatory activities of government.[9] There were those who vigorously asserted

---

[6] *Report of the President's Committee*, pp. 39–40.

[7] *Ibid.*, p. 40.

[8] *Ibid.*, p. 41.

[9] For a general history of the commissions and some discussion of their administrative status, see Robert E. Cushman, *The Independent Regulatory Commissions* (New York: Oxford University Press, 1941). On state experience, see James W. Fesler, *The Independence of State Regulatory Agencies* (Chicago: Public Administration Service, 1942).

that government regulatory activity could only be carried out effectively by an agency which did combine policy formulation, investigation, and decision-making functions.[10] A separate inquiry into the regulatory powers exercised by commissions and by other government agencies was completed in 1941. This study proposed that the regulatory agencies adopt an internal organizational structure which would clearly differentiate between investigative and adjudicative powers.[11] Subsequently, much attention was given both to this matter and to the possibility of a somewhat enlarged scope of judicial review over regulatory agencies.

In 1955 the second Hoover Commission returned to the subject. The Commission declared:[12]

> A principal characteristic of the administrative process is the concentration in a single instrumentality of investigative, prosecuting, and adjudicatory functions. . . . This concentration of functions tends to depart from the traditional principle that no one shall be a judge in his own cause. . . . The Administrative Procedure Act sought to achieve an internal separation of functions at the hearing level. . . . We propose that such internal separation of functions be applied to agencies themselves as well as to hearing officers.

The second Hoover Commission proposed the establishment of an Administrative Court of the United States. This court was to be divided into three sections: a tax section which would take over the jurisdiction of the Tax Court of the United States; a trade section which would handle the adjudicatory work of the Federal Trade Commission, the Federal Communications Commission, the Civil Aeronautics Board, the Federal Power Commission, and certain other agencies; and a labor section which would handle the adjudicatory work of the National Labor Relations Board.[13] The Hoover Commission said nothing about the future status of these agencies whose adjudicatory authority would thus be transferred to the new Administrative Court; whether these agencies should still be headed by boards or by single administrators and whether the agencies should be absorbed into executive departments or remain separate were matters left for someone else to decide. In any event, in the past twenty years a

---

[10] See particularly James M. Landis, *The Administrative Process* (New Haven, Conn.: Yale University Press, 1938); I. L. Sharfman, *The Interstate Commerce Commission,* vol. IV (New York: The Commonwealth Fund, 1937); and the Brookings Institution report of 1937 contained in Senate Select Committee to Investigate the Executive Agencies of the Government, Sen. Report no. 1,275, 75th Cong., 1st Sess., pp. 769ff.

[11] See Attorney General's Committee on Administrative Procedure, *Administrative Procedure in Government Agencies,* Sen. Doc. 8, 77th Cong., 1st Sess. (1941).

[12] Commission on Organization of the Executive Branch of the Government, *Legal Services and Procedures: A Report to the Congress* (Washington: Government Printing Office, March, 1955), pp. 61–62. A more detailed discussion of the subject will be found in the *Task Force Report on Legal Services and Procedures* (Washington: Government Printing Office, 1955).

[13] *Ibid.,* pp. 87–88.

good deal of attention has been given to the organizational status and powers of regulatory commissions.

In the fourth place, criticism has often been leveled at the internal organization and operation of individual agencies, or at major administrative processes such as budgeting, personnel, and supply. For example, it has been said that a particular agency was poorly organized to get work done promptly and economically, or that the management staff was inadequate to provide central direction, or that work procedures were cumbersome and expensive. Or it has been said that the budget process did not provide adequate information about government programs, that personnel practices did not attract and retain top talent in administrative positions, and that purchasing procedures were weighted down in too much paper work and petty routines.

In brief summary, these are the major criticisms which have been made from time to time about the organizational structure of government administrative agencies. Such criticisms have been made about federal, state, and local agencies. To be sure, these various types of critical comment involve many details. Moreover, certain basic assumptions and even certain unexpressed premises underlie these criticisms.

THE MEANING OF REORGANIZATION

The criticisms which have been made of government administrative structure and practice necessarily imply that there are known to be better methods for performing government work. These implied or proposed reforms have generally been expressed by a single term, reorganization. Actually, the word in its literal sense means only a change in organizational arrangements or procedures. Presumably, however, a change must be an improvement.

The two terms most commonly associated with the word "reorganization" are economy and efficiency. Unfortunately, here we are confronted with terms which have no clear-cut meaning. In its usually acceptable sense, economy means to reduce costs or expenses. For this reason many advocates of reorganization needs must claim positive "savings" which would result from the execution of their proposed changes. For example, the second Hoover Commission in 1955 tabulated some 5.5 billion dollars of annual "savings" which could be realized in the expenses of federal administrative agencies if the Commission's recommendations were adopted in full.[14]

Yet experience has indicated that such estimates of savings are seldom if ever actually realized in practice. This has led legislators and others from time to time to declare that claims of savings or of economy arising from administrative reorganization are a snare and a delusion. In reality,

[14] *Final Report to the Congress,* pp. 19–20.

those who undertake administrative reform rarely have an opportunity to demonstrate conclusively that their improvements have "saved" government funds, that is, have resulted in an actual decrease in the expenditures of their agency. There are two vital reasons why this happens. For one thing, the work of a government agency seldom if ever remains static. At the very time an administrator is carrying out some major organizational change, the legislature may be in the process of enacting some new legislation directing the agency to do additional work. Or, the administrative staff of an agency may be in the process of deciding that changing conditions require an expansion in the agency's work objectives. Population change, changes in the functioning of the economy, technological change, change in foreign relations—any or all of these in combination may have a profound impact upon the program and work load of governmental agencies. Under such circumstances a program of administrative reorganization cannot be expected to demonstrate an actual over-all reduction in expenditures.

In the second place, almost every government agency lacks sufficient financial resources to do all the work expected of it. Any economies introduced are almost immediately absorbed into new levels of service. A road department repairs more roads faster or more frequently. A school system adds to its instructional program. A police department gives more attention to preventing juvenile delinquency. A health department steps up its fight against communicable disease or its preventive medicine program. In every government agency there is almost always a backlog of important and useful work to be done just as soon as funds are available. For both of these reasons it is difficult for administrators to demonstrate in the one conclusive way—an actual curtailment of expenditures—that a particular administrative reorganization has resulted in measurable economy.

In truth, it now seems clear that economy in governmental administrative costs can be obtained in only one way. That is, for circumstances to be such that an actual curtailment of service becomes possible. If an effective program for international disarmament were to be agreed upon and duly carried out, then there might be an actual reduction in the necessary governmental outlays for national defense. In an economy of nearly full employment, there can be a reduction in the expenditures for poor relief and various other kinds of social service. As government debt is paid off from a surplus of income over current expenditures, or from a cessation of borrowing, then debt service costs can be reduced. In all these instances, economy can and does become possible.

It seems likely that some advocates of so-called government reorganization have been less interested in changes in administrative structure and procedure than in an actual curtailment of government services. The problem, then, is not administrative reorganization but basic governmental policy. For example, the costs of medical service under the Veterans' Administration can be reduced if it is decided to provide hospital and medical care to veterans only for a service-connected disability, i.e., not any illness or disease. The first Hoover Commission in 1949 recommended that the legislature settle the "basic question" of who is to benefit from government medical service.[15] This is not a recommendation about organization; this is a recommendation about policy underlying government service. But undoubtedly a change in such policy could result in an economy in governmental expenditures.

These comments on the concept of economy are not to be considered as criticism of the idea of administrative reorganization. The point is that the claim that any particular administrative change as such will reduce government expenditures is often quite difficult to demonstrate.

The second argument in favor of reorganization is that of efficiency. In the usual sense in which the term is used, it has a connotation drawn from engineering, the ratio of input elements to output in any enterprise. Greater efficiency is realized under any set of circumstances in which output increases while input remains constant, or in which output increases more rapidly than input, or in which output decreases more slowly while input declines more rapidly. In any one of these situations, the ratio of output to input becomes larger, and so we say efficiency has been improved. This engineering concept of efficiency can be applied with some degree of exactness in most business enterprises where there is a physical unit of output, such as automobiles built or kilowatthours of electric energy produced, and where input elements (or their costs) can be calculated with a considerable degree of exactness. The difficulty is that these conditions are not always present in governmental administrative enterprises. What is an "educated" child? What is "adequate" national security? What is a "proper degree" of public health? And although the number of governmental employees engaged in any enterprise is readily ascertainable, along with the total costs of their compensation, how do you calculate government overhead?

These difficulties can be overcome in various ways. And in many types of government service some unit of output is calculable. Wherever it is possible public administrators tend to keep fairly elaborate records of their work accomplishments and to make cost analyses. Where such circumstances permit, administrators may be able actually to calculate improvements in efficiency. Units of output divided by man-hours of labor input can indicate increasing or decreasing efficiency in the operation of a particular government service. And administrative changes which do result in an increased workload output with declining labor input per unit may fairly claim to have realized greater efficiency.

[15] Commission on Organization of the Executive Branch of the Government, *Medical Activities* (Washington: Government Printing Office, March, 1949), p. 23.

Indeed, the customary argument today in favor of administrative reorganization is that of improved efficiency. This is a far safer, more realizable claim than that of economy. The difficulty in this claim of efficiency is that so often it is not measurable in any concrete way. Often efficiency is and can be only a subjective claim put forth by the advocates of administrative change, and just as vehemently denied by those who oppose any particular change.

In 1937 the President's Committee on Administrative Management set forth a different concept of efficiency from the one just outlined. The Committee declared: "The efficiency of government rests upon two factors: the consent of the governed and good management." By implication the "consent of the governed" was to be realized through a "streamlined" executive branch, competently managed by the President. The Committee declared:[16]

> Fortunately, the foundations of effective management in public affairs, no less than in private, are well known. . . . Stated in simple terms these canons of efficiency require the establishment of a responsible and effective chief executive as the center of energy, direction, and administrative management; the systematic organization of all activities in the hands of a qualified personnel under the direction of the chief executive; and to aid him in this, the establishment of appropriate managerial and staff agencies. There must also be provision for planning, a complete fiscal system, and means for holding the Executive accountable for his program.

In effect, the President's Committee on Administrative Management declared that efficiency was to be achieved through "systematic organization," "qualified personnel," and the establishment of "appropriate" managerial or staff agencies. These may well be the principal means to efficiency, but we would insist that these are means to efficiency rather than evidence of efficiency itself. It may well be that efficiency cannot be realized except through systematic organization, qualified personnel, and managerial agencies. But these particular characteristics of an administrative agency may not in and of themselves demonstrate the actual existence of greater efficiency in operation.

In 1947 the first Hoover Commission endeavored to define "the essentials of effective organization of the executive branch." The Commission then went on to declare:[17]

> The President, and under him his chief lieutenants, the department heads, must be held responsible and accountable to the people and the Congress for the conduct of the executive branch.

[16] President's Committee on Administrative Management, *Report of the President's Committee,* p. 3.

[17] Commission on Organization of the Executive Branch of the Government, *General Management of the Executive Branch: A Report to the Congress* (Washington: Government Printing Office, February, 1949), p. 1.

Responsibility and accountability are impossible without authority—the power to direct. The exercise of authority is impossible without a clear line of command from the top to the bottom, and a return line of responsibility and accountability from the bottom to the top.

The wise exercise of authority is impossible without the aids which staff institutions can provide to assemble facts and recommendations upon which judgment may be made and to supervise and report upon the execution of decisions.

These words appear to restate much the same point of view as that embodied in the report of the President's Committee in 1937. The second Hoover Commission in 1955 expressed a somewhat different set of objectives. In addition to savings, the Commission reported that its recommendations were designed to preserve the national security, to maintain the functioning of all necessary agencies making for the common welfare, to stimulate fundamental research, to improve efficiency and eliminate waste, to eliminate government competition with private enterprise, and to strengthen the economic, social, and governmental structure.[18]

These were obviously very broad goals indeed. Yet they expressed in succinct style basic premises of much of the thinking which has motivated administrative reorganization in the United States.

THE REORGANIZATION MOVEMENT

The modern interest in governmental administrative reorganization began with the Taft Commission on Economy and Efficiency set up in 1910. This commission was not the first attempt at administrative improvement in the federal government. In 1888 a Senate Select Committee known as the Cockrell committee submitted a number of recommendations for administrative reform. In 1893 Congress established a commission of three representatives and three senators known as the Dockery Commission. This body retained a staff of experts which helped in proposing a number of improvements in administrative operations. In 1905 President Roosevelt appointed Assistant Secretary of the Treasury C. H. Keep to study administrative procedures and to suggest improved "business methods" in the executive departments.[19]

The Taft Commission, aided by a sizable staff of experts, recommended the introduction of a systematic budget system in the federal government and advocated continuing study of personnel practices. It also examined office procedures, purchasing methods, and desirable consolidations of

[18] Commission on Organization of the Executive Branch of the Government, *Final Report to the Congress* (Washington: Government Printing Office, 1955), p. 22.

[19] This historical outline has been taken from Select Committee on Government Organization, *Remarks by Members of . . . on Government Organization*, 75th Cong., 1st Sess. (Sept. 6, 1937), pp. 19–21.

administrative bureaus. The Taft Commission was largely responsible for the eventual passage of the Budget and Accounting Act of 1921.

In December, 1920, Congress created a Joint Committee on Reorganization composed of three representatives and three senators. In May, 1921, Congress passed a resolution authorizing the President to name a "representative of the executive to cooperate with the joint committee." The President's representative, Walter F. Brown, appears to have directed most of the work. In 1922 a number of proposals for departmental reorganization were approved by the President, including the creation of a Department of National Defense. A year later these proposals were endorsed by President Coolidge, and in 1924 a leading member of the Senate, Reed Smoot of Utah, strongly urged passage by Congress of an administrative reorganization bill embodying most of the Brown suggestions. The Congress took no action.

In 1929 President Hoover proposed to the Congress that it pass legislation delegating authority to the President to accomplish administrative reorganization. Mr. Hoover had reached the conclusion that the Congress could not and would not enact a law reassigning bureaus of related activities under common supervision or consolidating various agencies. In 1931 President Hoover repeated his suggestion, and on February 17, 1932, he sent a special message to the legislature urging adoption of his point of view. As a result of Depression pressures, the Congress added a title to the legislative appropriation act of June 30, 1932, commonly known as the Economy Act of 1932, authorizing the President to reduce government expenditures and to increase efficiency by regrouping and consolidating administrative agencies. But the President was required to submit his executive orders on reorganization to the Congress; if either house within sixty days passed a resolution of disapproval, then the executive order was null and void. When President Hoover submitted eleven executive orders in December, 1932, a month after his defeat for reelection, a Democratic House of Representatives passed a resolution of disapproval of all the orders.

In March, 1933, by two appropriation acts the incoming President, Franklin D. Roosevelt, was given a broader power of reorganization, with the provision that executive orders were not to become effective until sixty days after their submission to Congress. This time nothing was said about how the Congress might disapprove the orders, and nothing was said about the orders having to lie sixty days before Congress while it was in session. In fact, the principal order submitted by President Roosevelt under this law was dated June 10, 1933, just six days before Congress adjourned. Actually President Roosevelt did little with his authority under the 1933 economy laws, and their provisions expired in 1935.

In 1936, in part prompted by congressional action to study administrative reorganization, President Roosevelt appointed a President's Committee on Administrative Management to study administrative problems. A Senate Select Committee under the chairmanship of Senator Harry A. Byrd proceeded to make its own separate inquiry into the same subject.

On January 12, 1937, President Roosevelt transmitted the report of his Committee on Administrative Management to the Congress with an accompanying message endorsing the Committee's proposal.[20] This report took the point of view that the Chief Executive was the principal agency for exercising popular control over the administrative work of government. It identified two great needs: (1) to bring the number of administrative agencies within "manageable compass" through reorganization and (2) to equip the President with administrative machinery to help him in exercising effective supervision over all administrative agencies of the federal government. In so far as administrative reorganization was concerned, the Committee proposed that the Congress create two new executive departments and then authorize the President to regroup bureaus within this basic structure. The President's Committee also recommended notable changes in budgeting, accounting, and personnel practices. This 1937 report was a landmark document in the whole reorganization movement.

The Senate committee staff, the Brookings Institution, also submitted a series of fourteen studies dealing with a variety of government activities, such as financial administration, transportation activities, the promotion of commerce and industry, and public welfare.[21] These studies differed in some details from those undertaken by the President's Committee. The principal difference, however, was in point of view. The Senate report emphasized that administrative reorganization was a legislative task to be carried out by law enacted by the Congress.

In the subsequent legislative debate about administrative reorganization three major issues appeared. One was the desirability of a change in the status and authority of the General Accounting Office. This will be considered in a later chapter. A second issue was the status of the "independent" regulatory commissions. The third was that of the extent of reorganization authority to be conferred by the Congress upon the President.[22]

Eventually, the Reorganization Act of April 3, 1939, authorized the President to regroup and consolidate administrative agencies according to major purpose in order to reduce expenditures, increase efficiency, to eliminate overlapping and duplication of effort, and to reduce the number

[20] President's Committee on Administrative Management, *Report of the Committee with Studies of Administrative Management in the Federal Government* (Washington: Government Printing Office, 1937).
[21] Senate Select Committee to Investigate the Executive Agencies of the Government, *Preliminary Report,* 75th Cong., 1st Sess. (1937).
[22] Cf. Lewis E. Merriam and Laurence F. Schmeckebier, *Reorganization of the National Government* (Washington, D.C.: Brookings Institution, 1939).

of separate administrative agencies. Certain restrictions were placed upon
this authority, however. The President was not to abolish, transfer, or
change the designation of an executive department, nor was he to create
any new executive department. In addition, the President's authority was
not to extend to a specified list of agencies including the Civil Service
Commission, the Army Corps of Engineers, the Veterans' Administration,
the General Accounting Office, and some six regulatory commissions. And
the President was to propose his changes in reorganization plans which
were to lie before Congress for sixty days while the legislature was in session. During this period the Congress by concurrent resolution of both
houses might veto a reorganization plan.[23]

During 1939 under this authority President Roosevelt submitted three
reorganization plans which established in effect the Executive Office of
the President, three new administrative agencies (the Federal Security
Agency, the Federal Works Agency, and the Federal Loan Agency), and
made certain other shifts. None of these plans aroused any particular
opposition in Congress and each was permitted to become law. In 1940
the President submitted three additional plans, one of which was controversial in nature. The Civil Aeronautics Authority, a separate agency
set up by law in 1938 with both service and regulatory duties, was divided into a Civil Aeronautics Administration under the Department of
Commerce and a Civil Aeronautics Board "attached to" the department.
The House of Representatives voted disapproval of this change, but the
Senate, voting shortly after the Nazi invasion of the Lowlands and
France, sustained Presidential leadership by refusing to adopt the concurrent resolution. The Reorganization Act of 1939 expired in 1941. The
attention of the nation was now concentrated on the problems of World
War II.[24]

POSTWAR DEVELOPMENTS

Even before the Japanese surrender, President Truman on May 24,
1945, in a special message to Congress, recommended permanent legislation giving the President authority to accomplish administrative reorganization, subject to veto by concurrent resolution of the Congress. The
Reorganization Act of December 20, 1945, again authorized the President
to prepare reorganization plans consolidating and regrouping administrative agencies. Again he might not abolish an existing executive department
or create a new one. This time the General Accounting Office was declared to be a part of the legislative branch of government, and the

[23] Cf. John D. Millett and Lindsay Rogers, "The Legislative Veto and the Re-
organization Act of 1939," *Public Administration Review,* vol. 1 (1941), p. 176.
[24] For convenient summaries of wartime experience, see Bureau of the Budget,
The United States at War (Washington: Government Printing Office, 1946); and
Luther H. Gulick, *Administrative Reflections from World War II* (University, Ala.:
University of Alabama Press, 1948).

agencies exempted from presidential reorganization authority were limited in number to seven. Once more reorganization plans were subject to disapproval by concurrent resolution of the Congress. The duration of the legislation was limited to April 1, 1948.

During 1946 President Truman submitted three reorganization plans to the legislature. These abolished the Social Security Board in favor of a single administrator, consolidated certain land-management agencies in the Department of the Interior, continued a consolidated wartime National Housing Agency as a permanent administrative device, and made other changes. The House of Representatives voted disapproval of all three plans, but the Senate concurred only in disapproval of the first plan involving the housing agency. The reason was that permanent housing legislation was then pending and it was felt that administrative arrangements should be provided in this law rather than by reorganization plan.

In 1947 President Truman submitted three more reorganization plans to the Congress. One of these created a Housing and Home Finance Agency much along the lines of the 1946 plan; this time the Senate rejected a resolution of disapproval passed by the House of Representatives. Permanent new housing legislation was at this time bottled up in the House of Representatives. The Congress did reject, however, the plan transferring the employment service from the Federal Security Agency to the Department of Labor. There was considerable opposition to the location of an agency serving both employers and employees in a department presumably dedicated to the interests of employees alone. In 1948 another reorganization plan along similar lines was likewise disapproved by Congress. Of seven reorganization plans under the 1945 law, the House of Representatives voted to disapprove six; the Senate went along in disapproval of three.

The most important administrative reorganization after World War II was accomplished by direct legislative action. This was the National Security Act of July 26, 1947, creating a new device known as the National Military Establishment. It brought three executive departments—two existing (Army and Navy) and one new (the Air Force)—under common direction. Subsequently, by amendments approved August 10, 1949, the National Military Establishment gave way to a single executive department, the Department of Defense, composed of the three "military departments": Army, Navy, and Air Force.[25] The point is that so far-reaching an innovation in the administrative structure of the federal government could be accomplished only through the legislative process of Congressional action and presidential approval.

As a result of the general election of November, 1946, the Republican party gained control of the Congress for the first time in sixteen years. One result was the passage of a statute establishing a Commission on

[25] Cf. Elias Huzar, *Reorganization for National Security* (Ithaca, N.Y.: Cornell University School of Business and Public Administration, 1950).

Organization of the Executive Branch of the Government composed of
four persons appointed by the Speaker of the House, four appointed by
the President of the Senate, and four appointed by the President of the
United States. The law declared that it was the policy of the Congress "to
promote economy, efficiency, and improved service" in the work of
government agencies by "(1) limiting expenditures to the lowest amount
consistent with the efficient performance of essential services . . . ; (2)
eliminating duplication and overlapping of services . . . ; (3) consolidating services, activities, and functions of a similar nature; (4) abolishing
services, activities, and functions not necessary to the efficient conduct
of government; and (5) defining and limiting executive functions, services,
and activities." With the appointment of former President Herbert C.
Hoover as a member of the Commission and his subsequent election as
chairman, the enterprise was henceforth to be known as the Hoover
Commission.[26]

During 1947 and 1948 the Hoover Commission, under twenty-two
"task forces," carried on an extensive series of studies which dealt with
such subjects as budgeting, personnel, national defense, foreign affairs,
public welfare, public works, medical services, the Post Office Department, the Department of Agriculture, and the Executive Office of the
President. Beginning February 5, 1949, the Hoover Commission transmitted to the Congress a total of nineteen reports, including a final report,
containing a total of 273 different recommendations. It remained for the
legislature to act upon this broad array of suggestions for improvement
in the administrative operation of the federal government. Altogether the
proposals of the Hoover Commission would have resulted in reducing
some sixty-five agencies under the supervision of the President to about
one-third that number. The Commission did not try to make any official
estimate of the economy which would have resulted from the adoption of
all its recommendations.[27]

One study of accomplishments resulting from the Hoover Commission
has reported that of the 273 proposals, 116 had been fully carried into
effect by 1954, 35 more had been mostly accomplished, and 45 partially
put into effect.[28] It was further stated that altogether 25 per cent of the
total recommendations could have been realized by reorganization plans,
40 per cent by legislation, and 35 per cent by the action of department
and agency heads.[29] A major result certainly was the enactment of amend-

[26] Cf. Ferrel Heady, "A New Approach to Federal Executive Reorganization,"
American Political Science Review, vol. 41 (December, 1947), p. 1118.

[27] For a good summary discussion of the Hoover Commission reports, see Ferrel
Heady, "The Reports of the Hoover Commission," *The Review of Politics,* vol. 11
(July, 1949), p. 355. Cf. also Emmette S. Redford, "The Value of the Hoover Commission Reports to the Educator," *American Political Science Review,* vol. 44 (June,
1950), p. 283.

[28] Ray Harvey, Louis W. Koenig, and Albert Somit, *Achievements in Federal Reorganization* (New York: Citizens Committee for the Hoover Report, 1955), p. 16.

[29] *Ibid.,* pp. 15–16.

ments to the National Security Act abolishing the National Military Establishment and creating in its place the Department of Defense. Another major accomplishment was the Federal Property and Administrative Services Act of June 30, 1949, establishing a new agency, the General Services Administration. Important budget and personnel improvements followed upon the heels of the Hoover reports. The Commission, moreover, was instrumental in persuading the Congress to pass the Reorganization Act of 1949.

THE REORGANIZATION ACT OF 1949

As early as April 1, 1948, President Truman had called attention to the fact that the reorganization law of 1945 expired as of that date. The Congress was not then disposed to extend the life of the legislation, let alone make it "permanent" as requested by the President. On January 13, 1949, former President Hoover, on behalf of the Commission he headed, sent identical letters to both houses of Congress urging enactment of a new reorganization statute. President Truman repeated his earlier request in a special message on January 17. From this effort came the Reorganization Act of June 20, 1949.

Once again the statute authorized the President to prepare reorganization plans consolidating and regrouping administrative agencies. Once again no reorganization plan might abolish an executive department. Once again the statute was limited to a definite period of time, expiring April 1, 1953, or somewhat beyond the Presidential term of office. But in two important respects the Reorganization Act of 1949 differed from its predecessors. First of all, apart from the General Accounting Office which again was declared to be a part of the legislative branch, no agencies were specifically exempt from presidential authority to include in a reorganization plan. But, and this was the second difference, the law now made it easier for the Congress to veto a presidential reorganization plan. Under the 1939 and 1945 laws, the Congress could disapprove a reorganization plan only by a concurrent resolution requiring a majority vote by both the House of Representatives and the Senate. Under the 1949 law, the Congress might disapprove a reorganization plan by resolution passed by the "affirmative vote of a majority of the authorized membership" of either House. Thus, one house acting by itself could veto presidential reorganization. But the vote had to be by majority of the total membership of the house, not simply by a majority of those present and voting on the issue. In addition, the President was now directed to specify the reduction of expenditures which might result from a proposed reorganization.[30]

During 1949 President Truman submitted eight reorganization plans

[30] Cf. Ferrel Heady, "The Reorganization Act of 1949," *Public Administration Review*, vol. 9 (Summer, 1949), p. 165.

to the Congress. Only one of these was disapproved. This was a plan changing the name of the Federal Security Agency to Department of Welfare and giving it the status of an executive department. The objection was made in the Senate that the designation did not adequately evidence the scope of the proposed department's work. In addition Plan No. 8, which would have established a Department of Defense, was disapproved by a section of the statute of August 10, 1949, which itself created this department. Interestingly enough, this time the Congress did not object to locating the Bureau of Employment Security in the Department of Labor.

On March 13, 1950, President Truman submitted twenty-one reorganization plans to Congress. All were described as effecting recommendations of the Hoover Commission. Reorganization had now become a large-scale proposition. These proposals received a mixed reception in the legislature. One plan was disapproved because of a drafting defect. A plan to create an additional assistant secretaryship in the Department of Agriculture was disapproved, although the proposal for other departments was accepted. This action presumably reflected legislative reaction to Secretary Brennan and his controversial plan for agricultural subsidies. Also disapproved were three other plans which would have increased the administrative authority of chairmen of certain regulatory agencies. In one instance the Senate voted disapproval of a reorganization plan but the majority was less than forty-nine, a majority of the total membership. Altogether then, sixteen of the President's twenty-one proposals became effective.

During 1950 President Truman submitted six more reorganization plans to the legislature. One of these was a corrected version of an earlier plan which had been disapproved. One of these plans now proposed a new executive department to be known as the Department of Health, Education, and Security. Again, it was disapproved. Another plan transferring an activity from the Reconstruction Finance Corporation to the Housing and Home Finance Agency was also disapproved. Thus of the remaining group of six proposals submitted by the President in 1950, two were disapproved.

During 1951 President Truman proposed a single reorganization plan changing the internal operation of the Reconstruction Finance Corporation. During the preceding year a Senate investigation had revealed several indications of mishandling of loan applications. There was much discussion about whether the RFC was to be considered a permanent agency of government. In the end resolutions of disapproval received less than the majority of all members and so failed to pass.

In 1952 President Truman submitted five reorganization plans to the Congress. The first of these abolished the sixty-four positions of Collector of Internal Revenue through the United States, a post filled by appointment of the President with approval of the Senate. A number of scandals had just been revealed in the operation of the Bureau of Internal Revenue. Far-reaching changes seemed called for. The legislature agreed, since resolutions of disapproval were defeated in both chambers. Three other plans then dealt with the appointment of first-, second-, and third-class postmasters, collectors of customs, and United States marshals. The President proposed to take all of these positions "out of politics." All three plans were disapproved by the Senate. Among other things it was said that the President was trying to change existing laws on appointment of personnel through reorganization plans. A fifth reorganization plan in 1952 increased the authority of the commissioners of the District of Columbia to effect administrative changes. There was no opposition to this plan.

THE EISENHOWER ADMINISTRATION 1953–1957

When Dwight D. Eisenhower was inaugurated as President on January 20, 1953, there still remained about six weeks before the April 1 termination date of the Reorganization Act of 1949. On March 12 President Eisenhower submitted a reorganization plan to the Congress abolishing the Federal Security Agency and replacing it with a new executive department, the Department of Health, Education, and Welfare. The plan became effective. In addition, President Eisenhower submitted a second plan accomplishing a reorganization within the Department of Agriculture.

In the meantime in his first address to the Congress on February 2, 1953, the President asked the legislature to extend the duration of the 1949 law by eighteen to twenty-four months. The legislation was then extended to April 1, 1955, without any other substantive change.

With this extension of authority President Eisenhower submitted eight more reorganization plans to the Congress during 1953. Of these eight proposals only three came up for a vote of disapproval in the House of Representatives, where all three were sustained. Apart from provisions affecting the Executive Office of the President itself, none of these proposals was particularly controversial. Two more plans submitted to the legislature in 1954 aroused no opposition either.

THE SECOND HOOVER COMMISSION

With the inauguration of a Republican President for the first time since 1929, congressional leaders believed that the time was propitious for another large-scale study of federal administrative reorganization. The result was the passage of a new law approved July 10, 1953, creating another Commission on Organization of the Executive Branch of the Government similar to the one set up in 1947. Once again Herbert C. Hoover was appointed to the Commission and became its chairman. The 1953 law differed in one important respect from the 1947 act; it expanded the statement of policy to include the elimination of nonessential services and activities competitive with private enterprise. Once again the Commission carried on its investigative activity through "task forces" composed of distinguished business and professional leaders. This time studies were undertaken on such subjects as budgeting, personnel, intelligence activities, legal services and procedures, medical services, overseas economic activities, subsistence services, water resources, and business organization of the Department of Defense.

Between January and June, 1955, the second Hoover Commission issued seventeen reports and a final report. For the most part they dealt with the same subjects as in 1949, the principal additions being reports on business activities of the Department of Defense, property management, food and clothing, overseas economic operations, and intelligence activities. Altogether 314 specific recommendations were submitted. In many instances these simply went on from where the earlier reports left off. But in some instances the Commission gave greater attention to matters of public policy than to the questions of administrative conduct.[31]

One example may serve to indicate the broader scope of the mandate given to the second Hoover Commission. In studying the whole broad subject of federal government participation in water development projects, the Commission urged Congress to adopt a comprehensive national water policy comprising nine points: (1) that water resources should be developed to assure their maximum use and contribution to the public welfare; (2) that water resources development should generally be undertaken by locally or regionally created drainage districts; (3) that federal participation be undertaken only when the national interest was clearly involved and where projects were of a magnitude or complexity beyond local or private enterprise; (4) that when participating in water resources development, the federal government recognize state laws and rights; (5) that the federal government provide advisory assistance to state and local water development projects; (6) that federal participation in a project be approved only when there was substantial evidence that a project was economically justified and essential to the national interest; (7) that one agency only in the federal government be charged with collecting and reviewing hydrological data; (8) that all federal agencies administering revenue-producing projects pay all cash revenues into the Treasury and operate solely on the basis of annual appropriations; and (9) that rates for the sale of federally generated power be fixed by the Federal Power Commission.[32] These were far-reaching proposals, involving among other

[31] Cf. William R. Devine, "The Second Hoover Commission Reports: An Analysis," *Public Administration Review,* vol. 15 (Autumn, 1955), p. 263.
[32] Commission on Organization of the Executive Branch of the Government, *Water Resources and Power* (Washington: Government Printing Office, 1955).

things a substantial change in the authority vested in the TVA. The Congress showed no disposition to attempt writing so comprehensive a water development policy along these lines. The legislature preferred to continue handling water projects as under existing statutes.

The largest single task of the second Hoover Commission was its study of the "business organization" of the Department of Defense. On this subject, the Commission issued five separate reports, including business enterprises, depot utilization, research and development, food and clothing, and general organization. In these studies several improvements in both administrative organization and operating procedures were proposed, together with several policy proposals such as the possible repair of Naval vessels in private shipyards and the curtailment of military commissary and post exchange services. The organizational proposals were the most far-reaching of any resulting from a number of studies of military procurement and supply operations made after World War II.

In its final report in June, 1955, the second Hoover Commission said that some fifty of its recommendations could be carried out through presidential reorganization plans; another 145 could be carried out by department and agency heads within their discretion; some 167 proposals, however, would require legislative action. The categories as reported overlapped in several instances. The Commission declared that if all of its recommendations were adopted, some 5.5 billion dollars might be saved. The largest single item, however, one of 4 billion dollars, was a savings to be realized by a change in the method of preparing budget estimates from an obligational basis to an accrued expenditure basis.[33] The effectiveness of the work of the Hoover Commission depended upon the extent to which there was executive and legislative agreement with its proposals and a consequent willingness to implement its recommendations.[34]

In March, 1955, the Congress extended the duration of the Reorganization Act of 1949 to April 1, 1957. This was an action recommended by the second Hoover Commission. During 1955, however, President Eisenhower submitted no plans to the legislature. In 1956 he proposed only one plan involving a strengthening of research and development organization in the Department of Defense. In 1957 one plan was also submitted dealing with the further liquidation of the RFC. There was no opposition to either proposal.

On April 1, 1957, the President proposed that the Reorganization Act

---

[33] Commission on Organization of the Executive Branch of the Government, *Final Report to the Congress* (Washington: Government Printing Office, 1955).

[34] By the end of 1956 it was reported that the Congress had enacted about one-third of the legislative proposals submitted by the second Hoover Commission; the President had taken action on about half the recommendations requiring executive or administrative action. Senate Committee on Government Operations, *Action by the 84th Congress on the Second Hoover Commission Reports,* Sen. Report no. 95, 85th Cong., 1st Sess. (Feb. 25, 1957).

of 1949 be extended to April 1, 1961. Such legislation was then passed by the legislature in June, 1957.

THE MOVEMENT FOR STATE ADMINISTRATIVE REORGANIZATION

The movement for administrative reorganization within the federal government has been paralleled to some degree in almost every state of the United States, as well as at the local level of government. For instance, as a result of the example of the first Hoover Commission, seventeen states created special commissions or committees to study administrative reorganization. These were often popularly referred to as "little Hoover Commissions." Some ten other states at the same time charged legislative councils or other agencies with the task of surveying administrative structure.[35]

In fact, the movement for state administrative reorganization began as early as 1909 or 1910.[36] Governor Charles E. Hughes of New York, later Republican nominee for President and Chief Justice of the United States, in his 1910 message to the state legislature, proposed a reorganization of administrative structure. Under the leadership of Governor Frank O. Lowden, Illinois was the first state to carry out a comprehensive scheme of administrative reorganization in 1917. As of 1938, A. E. Buck of the National Institute of Public Administration found that twenty-six states had remodeled their administrative structure in some degree, three by constitutional amendment and twenty-three by statutory enactment.[37] New York State, under the leadership of Governor Alfred E. Smith, adopted a general plan of reorganization through a constitutional amendment in 1925. Many state reorganizations by statute were effected during the Depression decade of the 1930s.

Efforts at administrative reform continued in the states during the 1940s.[38] In Missouri during 1945 and 1946, between seventy and eighty boards and agencies were consolidated into thirteen executive departments. A considerable consolidation of administrative agencies was realized also in Louisiana and Utah. In both Montana and North Dakota, however, reorganization plans were rejected. Tax reforms and fiscal improvements were carried out in Colorado, Illinois, and Utah. Civil service reforms were another feature of state reorganization efforts. After a revision of its constitution adopted in 1947, an extensive reorganization of administrative agencies was carried out in New Jersey, which consolidated

[35] Herbert R. Gallagher, "State Reorganization Surveys," *Public Administration Review,* vol. 9 (Autumn, 1949), p. 252.

[36] A. E. Buck, *The Reorganization of State Governments in the United States* (New York: Columbia University Press, 1938), p. 6.

[37] *Ibid.,* pp. 8–9.

[38] Cf. Lynton K. Caldwell, "Perfecting State Administration, 1940–1946," *Public Administration Review,* vol. 7 (Winter, 1947), p. 25.

administrative agencies into fourteen executive departments.[39] In Michigan in 1948 a major change in state administrative practice was introduced by the establishment of a department of administration with strong fiscal control over the work of other administrative agencies.[40]

State governments have had their problems in administrative reorganization. As we have observed before, many state constitutions create a number of administrative agencies. Any change in the status of these bodies can be brought about only through amendment of the state constitution. Interestingly enough, no state has enacted a procedure similar to that provided in the federal Reorganization Act either of 1939 or of 1949 for accomplishing administrative reorganization. Bitter political pressures have been present in state reorganization battles even as they have in the federal government. Pressure groups in state government have resisted the consolidation of agencies in which they are particularly interested. The idea of strong executive domination of government has often been attacked in the state as well as in the federal government.[41] Many of the "little Hoover Commissions" produced no tangible results. Thus in Michigan a Joint Legislative Committee on Reorganization of State Government set up in 1949 made a number of studies of the state's some 115 agencies. Little if anything was accomplished, seemingly for a variety of reasons such as legislative indifference, a pattern of legislative-executive conflict, fear of a reduction in patronage, the ambition of some legislative members to run for state administrative positions, and the inability of reorganization advocates to demonstrate any definite or dramatic reduction in governmental costs.[42] These are difficulties which have blocked administrative change in many other states as well.

THE ISSUES OF ADMINISTRATIVE REORGANIZATION

The story of administrative reorganization, which has been told here in some detail, raises a number of issues which are essentially political in nature, that is, issues which involve political conflict between various groups in society. Such issues must necessarily be resolved through the political institutions of society, focusing especially upon legislative bodies.

1. *The Issue of Economy.* The first political problem of administrative reorganization has been the whole matter of the cost of government services and the prospect for reduction. The verdict today of most students

[39] Bennett M. Rich, "Administrative Reorganization in New Jersey," *Public Administration Review,* vol. 12 (Autumn, 1952), p. 251.

[40] John A. Perkins and Frank M. Landers, "Michigan Seeks Better Management," *State Government,* vol. 21 (September, 1948), p. 184.

[41] Cf. John A. Perkins, "Reflections on State Reorganizations," *American Political Science Review,* vol. 45 (June, 1951), p. 507.

[42] Frank M. Landers and Howard D. Hamilton, "State Administrative Reorganization in Michigan: The Legislative Approach," *Public Administration Review,* vol. 14 (Spring, 1954), p. 99.

of government would probably be that voiced by Joseph P. Harris: " . . . no substantial reductions in the cost of government have been accomplished through administrative reorganizations."[43] After all, administrative costs are usually only a small fraction of the total expense involved in the performance of any service. Structural or procedural improvements in administrative operation which reduced administrative costs by 10 per cent would reduce over-all costs by only 1 or 2 per cent. Such savings, as we have mentioned at the beginning of this discussion, can be quickly absorbed by improved service. Such savings are not necessarily unimportant, even if they are not spectacular. Yet as a rule, such savings are not sufficiently dramatic to overcome the forces opposed to administrative change.

Joseph P. Harris has argued that the real economy from improved administrative organization may be realized through the more careful development of balanced and consistent policies and programs. When agencies performing closely related activities are brought together under common direction, some duplication or conflict in programs can be avoided. Here again, the change may not be evidenced by any actual reduction in government expenditure but by enlarged service. In other words, efficiency rather than economy may result. Yet this over-all improvement may be of little satisfaction to the clientele which benefits from the policies and programs which were altered.

The fundamental issue which is most likely to lurk in any discussion of administrative reorganization is that of the volume and scope of governmental services. Ours is an economy of private enterprise; ours is a society in which voluntary association performs many services. In a highly complex economy and society governmental activities have tended to grow in magnitude. In this situation a good deal of concern about the impact of current developments upon traditional beliefs and practices is natural. Thus, the second Hoover Commission frankly declared that one of its goals had been to eliminate or reduce government competition with private enterprise. The difficulty is that when any small appointed group undertakes to examine the desirability of particular governmental policies and programs, it tends to substitute its judgment for that of elected representatives. Certainly any group is entitled to its opinion about the scope or magnitude of governmental activity. But that opinion must be tested by the degree of opposition which it arouses, or by the degree of positive acceptance which it commands. We have no final way of determining this degree except through our legislative assemblies.

The fact nonetheless seems clear that any real economy in government can only be achieved through a reduction in the magnitude and scope of

[43] Joseph P. Harris, "Wartime Currents and Peacetime Trends," part of a symposium on Federal Executive Reorganization Re-examined, *American Political Science Review*, vol. 40 (December, 1946), p. 1151.

government services. Administrative reorganization may be a technique for getting at this basic problem, but in practice it has now been demonstrated as an inadequate device for achieving economy. The advocates of administrative efficiency are poorly advised to present their argument in terms of economy. The advocates of curtailed government activity do the cause of administrative efficiency little benefit when they seek their ends through the guise of administrative reorganization.

2. *Strengthening the Administrative Role of the Chief Executive.* If economy is a questionable objective for administrative reorganization, then what shall be the purpose of all this effort? There can be no question but that a major result, if not always an explicitly avowed goal, of administrative reorganization has been to strengthen the administrative authority of the chief executive. The President's Committee on Administrative Management in 1937 was frank to admit that this was its first consideration. And it argued its case in terms of democratic theory and constitutional prescription.

In essence the argument is this: Under the American system of government the chief executive has been vested with the power to keep the administrative work of government under continuing surveillance. The chief executive is today a popularly elected official who must face public approval or disapproval for his acts after four years in office and must surrender his position (in the federal government) after eight years. The chief executive enjoys substantial constitutional power to supervise administration. He enjoys popular support as the basis for determining what policies shall be carried out. He is an effective avenue for popular control over large-scale administrative effort. Indeed, the argument implies, even if it does not explicitly assert, that the chief executive is really the better means for keeping government administration under popular direction, better than the legislature.

Under modern circumstances, the argument then goes, two conditions are necessary if the chief executive is properly to fulfill his constitutional and democratic responsibility. The chief executive must have help; that is, his position must be institutionalized. The second condition is that governmental administrative activities must be brought together under a limited number of executive departments, each headed by an official appointed and removable by the chief executive. Only in these ways can the chief executive make his influence effective.

There are two complications to this line of reasoning, no matter how cogent it may be. The first is that the legislature is often unwilling to accept the major assumption that the chief executive is the only effective avenue for popular control over the bureaucracy. Legislative members are popularly elected. They exercise considerable oversight of administrative activity. They can change policies or programs which are unsatisfactory by law. And such action by law is preferable democratic procedure, so they assert, than executive order. In the second place, the chief executive can enjoy only such institutional assistance as the legislature sees fit to provide him. And if the legislature does not desire to place all administrative activity in the hands of department heads appointed and removable at will by the chief executive, then there is little the chief executive can do about it. Suppose the regulatory commissions do exercise substantial policy-making authority; suppose they do tend to develop policy on a case-by-case approach arising out of adversary proceedings; suppose they do not take an over-all, long-range view of policy goals; are these conditions necessarily to be deplored?[44] Why assume the chief executive or one of his political lieutenants would necessarily do a better job; that is, a job politically better accepted.

It may also be argued that today only the chief executive is in a position to see governmental operations as a whole. Legislatures work by committees, and legislative leadership is almost always diffused and frequently in disagreement. Only the chief executive can speak decisively and act expeditiously. But under all except the most critical circumstances our democracy does not especially value decision or expedition.

As we shall note more fully later, chief executives have gained in administrative effectiveness through the reorganization movement, but it is easy to understand why legislatures have not been overly enthusiastic about this development. It is interesting to note that in the long history of federal reorganization there was a notable reluctance to create a new executive department. Finally, in 1953 the Congress permitted creation of one new department, the Department of Health, Education, and Welfare, after twice disapproving similar proposals of President Truman, not to mention the suggestions of Presidents Coolidge, Hoover, and Roosevelt. The legislature appeared to prefer other administrative devices than that of an executive department. In this way, among others, fear of executive aggrandizement has been voiced by legislatures.

3. *Administrative Consolidation.* Another objective of administrative reorganization has been to bring about a consolidation or integration of government activities having some common or related interest in so far as either clientele, geographical area, function, or technique of operation is concerned. This objective has been given general approval several times by the Congress, as when the two laws establishing the Hoover Commissions spoke of eliminating duplication and overlapping of services and of consolidating activities of a similar nature. The Reorganization Acts of 1939, 1945, and of 1949 spoke of grouping and consolidating agencies

---

[44] For a discussion of policy making by a regulatory commission in a particular field of work, see Charles R. Cherington, *The Regulation of Railroad Abandonment* (Cambridge, Mass.: Harvard University Press, 1948); cf. also the review of this book by Ernest W. Williams, Jr., "Program Planning and Regulatory Action," *Public Administration Review*, vol. 9 (Spring, 1949), p. 125.

and functions of government as nearly as possible according to major purpose.

The advocates of reorganization contend that such consolidation will bring about a number of desirable ends. The burden of direct supervision by the President is lessened by interposing a new level of supervision, which may indeed be more effective because it will be more concentrated. The same argument may be used in favor of bureau consolidations within a single department. Such consolidation and more effective supervision can result in the elimination of inconsistent policies, the better control of programs in terms of magnitude and scope, the better realization of a common purpose, and the more effective utilization of physical facilities. These are powerful arguments for increased administrative efficiency.

The problem can be illustrated by two outstanding examples in the federal government. In the field of water resources, it has long been notorious that two different agencies have been concerned with river development for navigation, power generation, and irrigation. These agencies are the Army Corps of Engineers and the Bureau of Reclamation, which operates in seventeen Western states. (Other agencies with direct or indirect similar interests are the Federal Power Commission, the Fish and Wildlife Service, the Department of Agriculture, and the TVA.) Both Hoover Commissions declared that there were conflict and duplication of interests between these agencies. The Corps of Engineers may undertake projects with a primary interest in navigation, but it may provide irrigation benefits without having to assess a major part of the cost to the beneficiaries and without any acreage limitation. The Bureau of Reclamation is supposed to recover as much cost as possible and to assist only "family-sized" farms, 320 acres in community property states. As a result in the same river valley, as in the Columbia and in the Missouri, both agencies will construct and operate dams. Yet the various interest groups concerned with the policies of these two agencies have successfully resisted any effort to consolidate them. No President from 1939 to 1957 has had the temerity to propose such a consolidation. Indeed, it was illegal to propose it until the 1949 reorganization law was written.

A similar story could be told in the field of the management of Western lands as between the National Park Service and the U.S. Forest Service. The suspicion and even hostility between these two agencies goes back to the famous Ballinger-Pinchot controversy of 1911 during the Taft administration. Yet the two agencies perform much the same kind of work and deal with the same clientele. But tradition has it that the Forest Service has been more conservation-minded than the Department of the Interior, and administrative consolidation, it is feared, might well aid the "predatory-minded" grazing, timber, and other private groups.

In reorganization matters it is not unusual to find chief executive, department heads, and some legislative supporters lined up in opposition to some particular legislative committee or subcommittee, one or more bureaus or agencies affected by a change, and the economic, professional, or regional interest groups concerned with the activity in question. Clientele groups are sensitive to any proposal which might somehow alter their customary avenues of influence in determining administrative policy. Administrative agencies fear changes in status which might affect their operation or future importance. Legislators are quickly enlisted in the conflict. Of such is the stuff of political controversy in administrative reorganization.[45]

4. *Procedure in Administrative Reorganization.* Finally, because administrative reorganization is controversial, there has been disagreement, too, about how it shall be accomplished. In the federal government this disagreement has centered about the degree of initiative to be entrusted to the Chief Executive. In the state government the disagreement has centered about how a chief executive can induce a legislature to act, especially whether to proceed on only a piecemeal basis.

The Economy Act of 1932 finally accepted the principle that the Chief Executive should propose administrative change and the legislature should approve or disapprove. But the Congress has been unwilling to make such legislation permanent. Rather it has preferred to extend the Reorganization Act of 1949 on three different occasions, 1953, 1955, and 1957. In this way the legislation might in effect become permanent. Yet either house of Congress may individually block a reorganization plan.

In the states, administrative reorganization has, for all practical effect, become a matter of executive prestige and influence. A powerful chief executive with a great deal of political and popular support may carry administrative reorganization through the legislature or a referendum. Legislative initiative in state reorganization has been largely nonexistent.

In no aspect is the politics of public administration more sharply or more clearly revealed than in the politics of administrative reorganization.

[45] Cf. Avery Leiserson, "Political Limitations in Executive Reorganization," *American Political Science Review,* vol. 41 (February, 1947), p. 68.

Chapter 8

The Legislature as Provider of Funds

The "power of the purse" was recognized in colonial America as a potent instrument of government. The early representative assemblies of the colonies were quick to assert the privileges and prerogatives won by the English Parliament in its struggle with the Stuart kings. Demands by the royal governors that the colonial legislatures pass permanent revenue acts were actively and successfully resisted. The colonists quickly realized that in their control of revenue and appropriation measures they held their only sure guarantee of continual participation in the process of government. In 1748 the New York legislature compelled the royal governor to surrender his attempt to exercise executive prerogative in tax and appropriation matters. Similar instances occurred in Massachusetts, Pennsylvania, and the Carolinas.[1]

When the Declaration of Independence turned to an enumeration of the "repeated injuries and usurpations" of the King of England, it included the dissolution of representative houses "for opposing with manly firmness his invasions on the rights of the people" and his attempts to impose "taxes on us without our consent." It occasioned no surprise that Article I of the Federal Constitution of 1787 should include the provision: "No money shall be drawn from the Treasury but in consequence of appropriations made by law." The extensive defense of the Constitution prepared by the authors of *The Federalist* papers contained no reference to this provision. In paper no. 30 Hamilton observed: "Money is, with propriety, considered as the vital principle of the body politic; as that which sustains its life and motion, and enables it to perform its most essential functions." But the issue of the day was not whether the legislature should control the purse strings of government. This proposition was too obvious to require comment. The argument centered solely about

[1] Alfred H. Kelly and Winfred A. Harbison, *The American Constitution: Its Origins and Development*, vol. I (New York: W. W. Norton & Company, Inc., 1948), chap. 2.

whether the new federal government should have a power to tax independent and separate from the taxing power of the states. The adoption of the Constitution settled the question.

It is then a well-accepted essential of American constitutional government that the legislative body shall determine how much government shall spend and for what purposes government shall spend these amounts. Since government in action means primarily the operation of administrative agencies, the scope and magnitude of administrative effort is determined by legislative enactment.

ESSENTIALS OF THE APPROPRIATION PROCESS

The process by which the legislature in our system of government provides funds for the operation of administrative agencies has certain common and basic features. The first is that appropriations shall be made to administrative bodies only to carry out purposes previously authorized by law. Fundamentally, an appropriation measure is different from, and subordinate to, the substantive legislation which establishes the policies, programs, and machinery of government. Some legislative assemblies in America have a rule which prohibits substantive or positive legislation in an appropriation bill. Furthermore, a particular appropriation may be subject to a point of order and to automatic elimination from the bill if it can be demonstrated that the purpose involved is not one previously authorized by law. Actually, these "rules of the game" are occasionally honored in the breach rather than in the observance. Nonetheless the basic concept remains that an appropriation law is designed simply to provide funds to administrative agencies for purposes which have already been given legislative sanction.

Secondly, the federal Constitution and most state constitutions contain a provision requiring all "bills for raising revenue" to originate in the House of Representatives. The Senate is then free to amend or reject as it may see fit. The Founding Fathers, reflecting upon their colonial experience in which lower chambers were popularly elected and upper chambers usually appointed, believed that tax measures above all others vitally affected the lives and well-being of the citizenry and that these bills should accordingly be introduced in and passed by that body which most widely represented the citizenry. By constitutional custom it has become traditional that appropriation laws likewise shall originate in the lower house of the legislative assembly.

In the third place, appropriations are usually made for a limited period of time. Colonial governors had often urged upon the assemblies that they should vote appropriations upon a permanent or continuing basis. The legislature of England and then the assemblies of colonial America early learned that no arrangement was better calculated to ensure their regular meeting than that of voting periodic appropriations. This conclusion found expression in the federal Constitution by the provision that the Congress, among other powers, should have the power "to raise and support armies, but no appropriation of money to that use shall be for a longer term than two years." Actually, the Constitution itself prescribed that the Congress should "assemble at least once in every year." The result was that, in practice, appropriations came to be made on an annual basis, even for the military forces. Since most state legislatures meet only every other year, state appropriations are made on a biennial basis. But it is generally accepted practice that appropriations shall be made to administrative agencies only on a periodic basis.

In the fourth place, administrative agencies are expected to perform their work in strict accordance with the provisions of appropriation law. This means a careful observance of the limitations upon total amount which an agency may spend and equal observance of any sublimitations which may be imposed. It also means that funds shall be spent only for the purposes appropriated. The legislature has theoretically two sanctions for ensuring this desired administrative behavior. One is the use of an auditor or comptroller independently to review the administrative handling of appropriated funds. We shall examine this practice in the next chapter. The other is to curtail or otherwise to restrict appropriations subsequently made to an offending agency. This is a powerful sanction indeed, more powerful perhaps than is commonly realized. Since administrative activities represent services for which there is a popular demand and expectation, legislators often believe that they have no alternative except to provide funds for administrative operation. Yet an agency which abuses its fiscal trust may be abolished by law and replaced by another agency, or it may have its appropriation reduced until the offending practice is eliminated, or it may have restrictions on expenditure written into the appropriation act. These are possible expressions of legislative complaint or even hostility which administrative officers are usually eager to avoid.

Finally, it must be emphasized that the appropriation process provides a legislature with a continuing opportunity to review administrative policy. Presumably, in so far as the legislature is concerned, public policy affecting the operation of administrative agencies is determined through substantive law. In practice, the reality is more complicated than this. Appropriation committees review policies set by law and policies determined by administrative discretion when they consider appropriation measures. Sometimes this practice has been criticized as enabling appropriation committees to move out beyond their "proper" sphere into the determination of matters which should be written into substantive law or into the determination of matters of detail which should be left to administrative discretion. It is complained on occasion that the appropriation committees have become the most powerful committees in the legislature.

There is probably little which can be done to restrict the scope of concern of appropriation committees if it were desirable to do so. Actually, the appropriation committees often are the only legislative committees which to keep administrative activities under close and continuing surveillance. The "subject-matter" committees sometimes do this, but not always. Moreover, there is no reason why legislative interest in public policy should end with the enactment of a law. The legislature certainly will wish to keep in touch with future developments and suggest modifications in policy as a governmental program proceeds. In the process the legislature has an opportunity to express its ideas about developing policy and even to override executive and administrative decisions, as was done during World War II when the Congress, through appropriation measures, prevented the Agriculture Department from using the soil conservation program as a means of paying production subsidies to farmers.[2]

During emergency conditions such as World War II, the Congress may relax its careful scrutiny of appropriation requests, especially for the military agencies. Thus, with only a general explanation of what was under way the appropriation committees approved the large sums of money needed for the atomic bomb project. The prevailing attitude of the legislature was to give the military agencies all the funds they requested. The wartime central control agencies dealing with industrial production and raw materials, manpower, and price control usually received what they needed. On the other hand, the appropriations committees of the Congress used the war period as the reason to terminate such agencies of the 1930s as the Work Projects Administration, the National Youth Administration, the Civilian Conservation Corps, and the National Resources Planning Board.[3]

The appropriation process is the heart of governmental administrative operation; it is therefore a vital, recurring opportunity for legislative review, comment, and modification of administrative performance.

ESSENTIALS OF APPROPRIATION PROCEDURE

Most governmental jurisdictions throughout the United States have now accepted the principle of executive preparation of the budget. The chief executive has been authorized by law (in the federal government and some states), by constitutional prescription (in other states), or by charter provision (in most cities) to present the legislature with a budget program for the next ensuing fiscal year. Since many governmental units operate on a fiscal year beginning July 1, the chief executive ordinarily presents his budget proposals shortly after January 1 of a year or biennium. This

[2] David C. Knapp, "Congressional Control of Agricultural Conservation Policy: A Case Study of the Appropriations Process," *Political Science Quarterly,* vol. 71 (June, 1956), p. 257.

[3] Cf. Roland Young, *Congressional Politics in the Second World War* (New York: Columbia University Press, 1956), pp. 43–53.

leaves the legislative chambers approximately 5 or 5½ months at the most in which to determine their own action.

Usually the chief executive's budget is an official request for appropriations with which to operate administrative agencies. The budget document then follows closely the customary form of appropriation legislation. Sometimes as in the case of the federal budget, the chief executive may even set forth his suggestions for revision or modification of the language contained in the previous appropriation law or laws. But the initiative in the appropriation process now lies definitely with the chief executive. The legislature is a kind of "court of review" which decides whether to increase or decrease the appropriation recommendations submitted by the chief executive.

Only at the local level of government has there been any extensive practice of separating budget appropriations into current operating and capital expenditure items. The two are generally, almost hopelessly, intermixed in the appropriation laws of the federal government. Many state legislatures to an increasing degree are beginning to consider items of capital expense apart from current operating needs. State practice does not appear yet to be as well defined, however, as the usual procedure in local governments. The explanation may lie in the difference in fiscal arrangements at different levels of government. In local governments current operating expenses, less miscellaneous receipts and subventions from the state government, are ordinarily met by a corresponding general property tax. Capital expenditures on the other hand are defrayed from borrowing. The local council then tends carefully to differentiate the current expense from the capital improvement appropriation. Most state constitutions prohibit legislative borrowing, at least without a popular referendum. As a result since all items of expenditure must be met from current tax receipts, there is little encouragement to distinguish current operating from capital expenditure items. In the federal government appropriations are considered apart from revenue legislation, with the result again that there has been little incentive to handle capital expenditures differently from current requirements.

In state and local governments the legislature ordinarily considers and passes each year or each biennium a single appropriation law. At the local level of government the appropriation act furthermore fixes the rate of the general property tax in the community. In the federal government the Congress usually considers some twelve or thirteen so-called regular appropriation bills, along with some half-dozen supplemental or deficiency appropriation measures. The result is that only by periodic publication of a table of appropriation bills in the *Congressional Record* does the Congress have any general indication of the total amount of funds which it has appropriated.

In the federal legislature the appropriation bill is printed only after the House Committee on Appropriations has decided what amounts it wishes to recommend for appropriation for each item. In many state and local government legislatures the appropriation bill is printed in the amounts as recommended by the chief executive, and the house committee on finance submits amendments to the executive proposals for the vote of the legislative chamber as a whole. Perhaps this difference in practice gives greater prestige to the budget of the chief executive at the state and local level of government than in the federal government; in practice the difference tends to be relatively unimportant.

As with other pending measures, legislative committees obtain most of their information about appropriation items through public or "executive session" hearings. Administrative officials of the agency involved appear in person to provide a brief explanation of their appropriation requests and then to answer such questions as committee members may desire to ask. Sometimes administrative officials are encouraged to criticize the recommendations of the chief executive and to ask for more funds. This is often the case with some program which enjoys a good deal of popular approval or which has strong backing of some influential interest group. Thus, there has been a disposition from time to time for the Congress to provide greater appropriations for the Air Forces than had been recommended by the President. This was evident, for example, in 1948 when the Congress almost doubled the contract authorization of the Air Force beyond the original recommendations submitted by President Truman.[4] Other times an appropriation or finance committee may evidence a highly critical attitude toward a particular administrative official or a particular administrative agency. The result is then likely to be some reduction in the appropriation.

Much of the legislative attitude as revealed in appropriation hearings may be a matter of chance. If public attention has been dramatically focused upon some particular agency or activity, such as the state of veterans' hospitals or of mental health institutions, then an administrative officer may expect a good deal of questioning. He may even be urged to ask for more funds. If there has been a good deal of public criticism directed toward the overseas informational program or international economic assistance, then administrative officials can expect a good deal of critical questioning and an almost certain reduction in the appropriation request. Some agencies may receive a more or less perfunctory hearing. The practice varies with the varying political issues of the day.

For the most part committee members have only such information upon which to act as they may obtain from questioning administrative officials. Rarely do representatives from interest groups and others ask to be heard at appropriation hearings. It may thus appear that the data for committee action is decidedly one-sided. How far this may actually be true is ques-

[4] Elias Huzar, *The Purse and the Sword* (Ithaca, N.Y.: Cornell University Press, 1950), pp. 177–178.

tionable, however. Committee members over a period of years come to know administrative officials fairly well and have decided whom to trust and whom to treat with some skepticism. Moreover, committee members reflect prevailing legislative and popular attitudes toward individual administrative officers and agencies. Often these attitudes have considerable justification in fact. In addition to such staff information as they may have, appropriation committees often have the advantage of informal consultation with the budget officials of the chief executive. Legislative action is not so uninformed or haphazard as the procedure on the surface might suggest.

In general, appropriation bills, when reported to the lower chamber of the legislative assembly, receive a "right of way" for immediate consideration and action. Thus in the House of Representatives of the Congress an appropriation measure enjoys privileged status and may be brought before the House for debate and passage at any time by the chairman of the Appropriations Committee. In this way the essential nature of appropriation measures is acknowledged. The actual floor debate on an appropriation bill is seldom lengthy. With very few exceptions, which occur only under unusual circumstances, the chamber as a whole accepts the recommendations of the committee.

Ordinarily, the Senate Committee on Appropriations gives much less extensive consideration to an appropriation bill than does the House Committee. The Senate Committee tends to review only those appropriation actions to which administrative officials wish to take some strong exception. Subsequently, the upper chamber as a whole is disposed to accept the action of its committee. Senate consideration of appropriations is more perfunctory and much shorter in duration than House action.

Such adjustments as may be necessary between House and Senate action on appropriation measures are handled in a conference committee, as with other bills. The committee report then becomes the version finally enacted by the legislature and presented to the Chief Executive for his approval.

Except where the chief executive may enjoy the authority to veto items of the appropriation bill, legislatures seldom find it necessary to pass an appropriation over executive disapproval. The appropriation measure then becomes the law which sets forth the official amounts which an administrative agency may spend in the performance of its assigned task.[5]

APPROPRIATIONS AND FISCAL POLICY

As mentioned earlier, in the federal government prevailing legislative practice is for the Congress each year to pass not one but several appro-

[5] For a penetrating discussion of the appropriation process see Arthur W. Macmahon, "Congressional Oversight of Administration: The Power of the Purse," *Political Science Quarterly,* vol. 58 (June and September, 1943), pp. 161 and 380.

priation measures. In 1957, during the first session of the Eighty-fifth Congress, for example, the legislature passed fourteen regular appropriation bills. One bill, that for defense, appropriated over 33.7 billion dollars out of total regular appropriations of 59 billion dollars. The next largest amount was the some 5 billion dollars appropriated for various independent agencies. Five other appropriation bills each contained funds over a billion dollars for the fiscal year 1958. These were the Treasury–Post Office appropriation (3.9 billion), the Labor–Health, Education, and Welfare appropriation (2.9 billion), the Agriculture appropriation (3.7 billion), the mutual security program (3 billion), and the appropriation for the Atomic Energy Commission (2.3 billion).

The appropriation for the Interior Department amounted to 456 million dollars, that for the Commerce Department to 598 million dollars, the one for the State and Justice Departments and the federal judiciary to 563 million dollars, and that for public works (most river and harbor projects) to 858 million dollars. The appropriation for general government, including the White House and executive staff agencies amounted to some 16 million dollars; the appropriation to support the Congress and various so-called legislative agencies (such as the Government Printing Office and the General Accounting Office) came to nearly 105 million dollars. Although the total appropriation for operation of the government of the District of Columbia was nearly 196 million dollars, only 22.5 million dollars of this was contributed from the United States Treasury.

Accordingly, in 1957 the Congress passed fourteen regular appropriation laws providing for the work of the federal government during the next fiscal year. In addition, the legislature that year enacted three deficiency appropriations to augment the funds available to administrative agencies during the then current fiscal year ending June 30, 1957. Finally, the legislature passed four laws supplementing the appropriations already made for the fiscal year beginning July 1, 1957.

The major characteristic of this particular federal appropriation process is its disjointed nature. Appropriation totals carried in one bill have no relationship to those provided in other bills, and the entire total is not necessarily related to the amount of anticipated tax receipts. This arrangement has occasioned a good deal of legislative and other criticism from time to time.

The Legislative Reorganization Act of August 2, 1946, contained provisions in section 139 for a "legislative budget." The act set forth that the Committees on Ways and Means and on Appropriations of the House of Representatives and the Committees on Finance and on Appropriations of the Senate were authorized "and directed" to meet jointly at the beginning of each regular session of Congress and "after study and consultation" to report to each house a "legislative budget" for the ensuing fiscal year, including total receipts and expenditures. The law also provided that a concurrent resolution should be passed declaring the legislative intention to appropriate a certain maximum amount, and to increase or decrease the public debt by the corresponding difference between expenditures and receipts. The law also suggested that the two appropriation committees should seek to simplify the existing appropriation measures.

Actually, the contemplated procedure for a legislative budget has never been put into effect since 1946. In 1948, a concurrent resolution on appropriation totals was adopted by the Congress but was then promptly ignored by both appropriation committees as they began the process of considering the individual items of proposed expenditure. In 1949, the reorganization law was amended to give the joint committee until May 1 rather than February 15 for reporting out a "legislative budget." The change made no difference. The law was simply ignored by the Congress itself.[6]

The fact is that the scheme for a legislative budget, as written into the Legislative Reorganization Act of 1946, appears to be unworkable in practice. Congress is accustomed to a particular appropriation procedure. Under this procedure the House Appropriations Committee regularly divides up various parts of the President's budget among ten or twelve standing subcommittees. Each subcommittee then reviews the requested appropriations with some care and calls the proper administrative officials before it for questioning. In this process the subcommittee arrives at a judgment about desirable expenditure levels for various administrative activities. This judgment expresses the consensus of subcommittee members as they in turn reflect prevailing political sentiment in and outside the Congress.

Any procedure which endeavors to obtain an expression of legislative opinion before this process of subcommittee consideration and consensus has been completed seems unworkable. Neither the subcommittee nor the entire committee can bind itself to a premature judgment which at best is only an opinion rendered before detailed review of appropriation requests has been undertaken.[7]

Still a further attempt at appropriation reform was made in 1950 in keeping with the spirit of the 1946 legislative reorganization act. In that year the House of Representatives passed an omnibus appropriation bill, that is, a measure which put together all the customary ten or twelve regular appropriation bills in a single measure. The arrangement proved unwieldy. In January, 1951, the House Appropriations Committee voted to abandon the omnibus bill and to return to the separate consideration

[6] For an account of 1947 and 1948 experience, see Floyd M. Riddick, "The First Session of the Eightieth Congress," *American Political Science Review*, vol. 42 (August, 1948), pp. 686–687; and "The Second Session of the Eightieth Congress," *Ibid.*, vol. 43 (June, 1949), pp. 489–490.

[7] Cf. Bertram M. Gross, *The Legislative Struggle* (New York: McGraw-Hill Book Company, Inc., 1953), pp. 436–438.

of individual measures. The omnibus bill was, as its name suggested, a consolidation of all the parts into an unrealistic whole. The subcommittee members did their work as before. They reported their recommended action. The Committee on Appropriations as a whole did not undertake to review these recommendations as a unit. When the House of Representatives as a body took up the measure, the debate was unsatisfactory. There was even less time for considering the whole than there was for considering the parts. Nor did members have any major ideas to discuss in so far as the grand total of all appropriations was concerned. Individual legislators were interested in individual parts of the appropriation measure. Although there are some complaints from time to time by certain legislators about piecemeal consideration of appropriations and some urging to repeat the omnibus experiment, these sentiments have apparently not commanded any widespread support in the Congress.[8]

The criticism continues to be made that the Congress in appropriating funds for the various activities of government lacks any systematic method for considering expenditures in relation to government fiscal policy as a whole. One student of budgetary practice has written: "In short, the main objectives of the budgetary process are inadequately emphasized in congressional procedures."[9] He goes on to enumerate these main objectives as effective consideration of administrative efficiency, the achievement of a unified program of expenditures in terms of a "best total result," and the explicit correlation of expenditures and revenues. In terms of these particular objectives it may well be that the appropriation process in the federal government, as well as at other levels of government, leaves something to be desired. But it may also be that the formulation of such objectives for the legislative appropriation process is itself quite unrealistic.

We may accept the proposition here that governmental fiscal policy is today one of the most important decisions of government. The size and objects of governmental expenditure, the magnitude and kinds of taxes levied, the expansion or curtailment of governmental debt, the control of currency and credit, the supervision of banking operations—these and other decisions in the realm of fiscal policy have a profound impact upon the functioning of our economy and upon the material well-being of our nation. But it must not be supposed that fiscal policy is some highly developed body of economic knowledge to be applied in any given condition or circumstance with the precision which we now use in controlling the temperature of our homes or offices. Fiscal policy is not a clearly defined body of economic precepts. Many proposals for a particular fiscal procedure at a particular time are subjects of disagreement among professional economists. Moreover, influencing as they do the welfare of all

---

[8] *Ibid.,* pp. 438–440.
[9] Arthur Smithies, *The Budgetary Process in the United States* (New York: McGraw-Hill Book Company, Inc., 1955), pp. 146–147.

of us, matters of fiscal policy are necessarily important matters of political debate.

It seems evident that in the federal government, and in the state governments as well, the legislature is little interested in achieving a general control of fiscal policy or even of governmental expenditures. The initiative in fiscal policy and in the magnitude of governmental outlays has fallen to the chief executive. A legislature could gain a substantial degree of general influence over governmental fiscal policy only if it were substantially to alter the appropriation procedure. Rather, legislatures appear primarily to prefer to exercise a control in detail over expenditures by administrative agencies, and legislative procedure is adapted to this limited objective.[10]

ADMINISTRATIVE RESTRICTIONS

Appropriation legislation is not simply a matter, however, of specifying certain amounts of money which administrative agencies may spend. Beyond this, appropriation laws often contain particular limitations or restrictions upon the exercise of administrative discretion in expenditures.

In passing we should, of course, understand that any appropriation law is restrictive in the sense that it fixes a limit beyond which an administrative agency may not legally go in spending funds to accomplish its basic purposes. In practice there are two broad types of appropriation law, the lump-sum appropriation and the line-item appropriation. In the first type of law the legislature appropriates a certain amount as a whole to meet the expenditures of an agency. The division of this amount among personal services, supplies, equipment, travel, and other objects remains for administrative determination. In the line-item appropriation the law lists all the personnel of the agency and the salary to be paid each position during the next year, as well as setting forth exactly what amounts may be expended for supplies, travel, utility services, repair of buildings, etc. It is even possible to have a combination of the lump-sum and the line-item appropriation in the same law.

The line-item is obviously more restrictive of administrative discretion than the lump-sum appropriation. The administrative officer must strictly follow the number and salaries of personnel as sepecified in law, subject to such adjustment as the chief executive or department head may be empowered to authorize. Under the lump-sum arrangement, the responsible administrative officer of the agency receiving an appropriation may make shifts in the use of funds within such limits as are not likely to incur

[10] For a good brief account of the usual criticisms made of the legislative appropriation process see *Control of Federal Government Expenditures: A Statement on National Policy* (New York: Committee for Economic Development, January, 1955).

subsequent legislative criticism. These restrictions just mentioned are inherent in the very nature of appropriation legislation.

But a legislature may go farther if it is so disposed and specify that certain restrictions are to be observed in the expenditure of funds. This is especially apt to be the case in making lump-sum appropriations. Federal government practice is of the lump-sum type. In order, therefore, to make clear certain restrictions which it expects administrative officers to observe in expending these lump sums, the Congress frequently attaches language to guide and curb administrative discretion.

It has not been unusual for Congress to set forth that only a certain amount of a total appropriation may be spent for personal services in the District of Columbia. This is a way of limiting the personnel to man the central government office. General legislation provides that a government agency may buy passenger automobiles and passenger airplanes only as these are specifically authorized by law. Therefore, if an agency wants to spend a part of its appropriation for automobiles or airplanes, it must seek a specific statement of the number of such vehicles to be purchased under a particular appropriation.

In one appropriation act for the fiscal year 1948 the Congress inserted a restriction that not more than 20 per cent of all employees of a particular agency could be paid more than $4,500 a year. In this instance the agency involved was compelled to discharge over 500 employees in order to bring its salary structure down within the limit thus directed. Another somewhat involved amendment was inserted in most appropriation laws for the fiscal year 1952. This amendment provided that not more than 75 per cent of the budget estimates as submitted to the Congress for the compensation of information specialists should actually be expended in compensation of such personnel. The purpose of this provision was to cut down the number of information specialists employed by the federal government. In effect the Congress was saying that federal administrative agencies spent too much money on public relations and public information activities and this amount should be reduced. On another occasion the Congress inserted the limitation that no part of an appropriation contained in a law should be used to pay compensation of any employee engaged in personnel work in excess of a ratio of one personnel worker for every 115 employees. In this instance the Congress was saying that personnel offices in various administrative agencies were overstaffed. It therefore established a limit to be observed in performance of personnel duties.

Beginning in 1946 the Congress inserted in appropriation laws a general restriction that no part of any appropriation contained in the act could be used to pay a salary or wage to any employee who engaged in a strike against the United States government or who belonged to any organization of government employees that asserted the right to strike against the government. Thus, rather than by general legislation, the Congress in effect made any strike of government employees illegal.

The practice of including limitations in appropriation acts specifying purposes for which the money may not be used led to one attempt during World War II to name specific persons who should not receive any compensation. This was an effort by the Congress to discharge certain government employees through the appropriation process. In 1943 the House Committee on Appropriations was authorized to investigate persons in the employ of executive departments "unfit" for government service because of "past association or membership in or with organizations whose aims or purposes are or have been subversive to the government of the United States." In that year one representative proposed an amendment to the Treasury and Post Office appropriation bill listing thirty-eight persons by name who should not be compensated from that particular appropriation. Only one of these was at the time employed by a department covered in the bill. This particular amendment was rejected, but an amendment designating the one person employed by the Treasury was approved, although it was dropped a few days later. Previous efforts at naming specific individuals had also been killed in the Senate. A subcommittee of the appropriations committee reported on April 21, 1943, that it had found two persons guilty of "subversive activity" and so unfit for continued government employment. About a third person, an employee of the Federal Communications Commission, the committee said it had not found sufficient evidence to support a recommendation of unfitness. On May 14, the committee reported that the Secretary of the Virgin Islands was unfit for government service but exonerated two employees in the Department of the Interior. Since both the Federal Communications Commission and the Department of the Interior refused to dismiss the men declared guilty of subversive activity by the House Appropriations Committee, the committee offered an amendment to a Deficiency Appropriation Act providing that no money in the Act could be used to pay the salaries of the three men. The Senate rejected this limitation but in the end was compelled to accept a compromise whereby no salary was to be paid to the three men after November 15, 1943, unless they were appointed by the President subject to confirmation by the Senate. The President had no choice but to accept the measure, although he protested verbally against the rider.[11] All three men then brought suit in the Court of Claims for salary, questioning the constitutionality of this particular action. The Supreme Court later ruled that the attempt to purge employees by denying them compensation by name was unconstitutional.[12]

[11] See Robert E. Cushman, "The Purge of Federal Employees Accused of Disloyalty," *Public Administration Review*, vol. 3 (Autumn, 1943), p. 297; and Frederick L. Schuman, "Bill of Attainder in the 78th Congress," *American Political Science Review*, vol. 37 (October, 1943), p. 819.

[12] *United States v. Lovett*, 328 U.S. 303 (1946).

The Court declared that the action of Congress constituted a bill of attainder, inflicting punishment on named individuals without a judicial trial. The three persons involved were thus, in a sense, vindicated, but none of the three returned to federal employment.

As a rule, restrictive provisions are inserted in appropriation laws because a legislative committee is convinced that some abuse has grown up in administrative practice. An agency has too many passenger automobiles driven by chauffeurs; an agency has too many highly paid employees; an agency spends too much on travel; an agency wants to close an office in a particular city—any or all of these actions may excite legislative criticism and result in restrictions inserted in a future appropriation law. These restrictions then may be repeated for a number of years until the legislature is satisfied that the need for them no longer exists.

Appropriation laws are hence more than laws providing funds for administrative activities. They also contain many legal directions and restrictions for administrative action.

APPROPRIATION LAWS

In the federal government the result of legislative consideration of appropriation requests is a set of laws containing minor details and extensive authorizations of administrative operation. No matter how much attention is given in any one year to rationalizing appropriation bills, the laws passed by the Congress still contain large and small sums of money, minor irritations of procedure, and great policy decisions.

To give an example, for the fiscal year 1957 the appropriation bill for the Department of Agriculture included thirty-six different titles or items of appropriation. Three of these titles amounted to 50 per cent of the total: one for the agricultural conservation program came to 227 million dollars; another for the disposal of special commodities held by the Commodity Credit Corporation came to over 257 million dollars; and the third for the school-lunch program amounted to 100 million dollars. There were five appropriation titles each providing more than 50 million dollars. There were eleven other appropriation titles each of which was in an amount under a million dollars. But as if this great disparity in the size of appropriation titles in a single appropriation measure were not sufficient, the Supplemental Appropriation Act of 1957 provided over $1\frac{1}{4}$ *billion* dollars with which to carry out the soil bank program approved May 28, 1956. This one item was larger than the other thirty-six appropriation titles put together.

The same kind of analysis could be made of the appropriations provided other departments. When one comes to the Department of Defense the appropriation act is even more noteworthy. To be sure, national defense is the most important, the largest, and the most complicated undertaking of the federal government. In the act making appropriations for the fiscal year 1957 there were just forty-six titles providing some 36 billion dollars of new funds to obligate. One title alone amounted to nearly 7 billion dollars for procurement of aircraft to be used by the Air Force. There were another nine appropriation titles each of which exceeded a billion dollars in amount. Thus ten out of forty-six major headings accounted for over two-thirds of the total appropriation. Yet there was one title in the act for $450,000 (the public relations activities of the Department of Defense), another for $375,000 (for the Court of Military Appeals), a third for $357,000 (for the National Board for the Promotion of Rifle Practice), and a fourth for $683,000 for management of naval petroleum reserves. Thus here again one may find breath-taking sums coupled with items involving expenditures of less than a million dollars.

To the appropriation titles as such must be added the special and general restrictions. Thus, the Department of Agriculture and the Farm Credit Administration Appropriation Act for 1957 contained numerous provisos serving as limits upon administrative discretion in the obligation of appropriations. The Agricultural Research Service was not to spend more than $7,500 of its general appropriation for salaries and expenses (in the amount of some 94 million dollars) for the construction of a building and an even smaller amount for repair or renovation. The title for the Forest Service permitted expenditure of funds for the operation and maintenance of aircraft. The appropriation for operations of the Soil Conservation Service specified that in the state of Missouri no agreement was to be made with a local soil conservation district unless it had the prior approval of a central state agency. Under marketing research, the act provided that no part of the funds made available might be expended to collect data or publish a report on the intention of farmers "as to the acreage to be planted in cotton." Among the general provisions, the law specified that the Department might purchase 645 passenger automobiles of which 622 were to be for replacement only. Except for experimental purpose no part of the appropriation might be expended "in the purchase of twine manufactured from materials produced outside the United States." Moreover, no part of the funds available to the Department might be used for the payment of salary or travel expenses of any person convicted of violating the Hatch Act of August 2, 1939, or the statute that prohibits an employee of the government from endeavoring to influence the vote of a member of Congress on any pending measure. These were by no means all of the prohibitions. The nature of these specific and general limitations may vary from time to time, but some have continued in the appropriation laws for many years.

When one turns to a state appropriation act, he finds a bulky statute of many pages containing primarily long columns of figures opposite particularly indicated purposes such as personal services (usually itemized), supplies, equipment, communication, travel, and printing. Each department and other agency of state administration is specifically mentioned, and in the case of large departments, the bureaus and divisions are likewise enumerated. Only a few general provisions usually appear, such as a limitation upon the period of availability of appropriated funds (necessary since most state legislatures appropriate for a biennium) and a requirement that funds be spent equally by quarters. Sometimes an appropriation act makes arrangement for a petty-cash fund, and many states now include a blanket proviso that any federal funds received by the state or by a local political subdivision are thereby appropriated for the purpose for which received. Some states also set up a general arrangement whereby funds may be transferred from one subitem to another, subject to some kind of control.

As passed, the federal, the state, or the local budget law becomes the operating guide for administrative agencies in the next ensuing fiscal period. The amounts as fixed in the act are absolute limits to the volume of expenditures which administrative agencies may incur. The limitations or provisions which accompany the amounts are procedural requirements or subappropriation restrictions which administrative agencies must observe. The appropriation law is a law, with all the majesty and importance of legal stipulation in our society.

LEGISLATIVE STAFF FOR BUDGET REVIEW

In the experience which our legislative bodies have thus far accumulated, a number of special problems have arisen about the appropriation process. One of these has been the matter of adequate staffing for the committees which consider the budget requests coming from administrative agencies.

Most governmental jurisdictions with an executive budget system have provided the chief executive with a budget staff to examine all budget requests and to help in preparing recommendations for the legislature. In some governments, and particularly in the federal government, this budget office is fairly elaborate, comprising a number of specialized personnel who devote their time on a continuing basis to a study of the budget programs of various administrative agencies. These budget examiners come to have a considerable familiarity with the operations of the agencies whose budget requests they scrutinize, and hence they bring a well-informed judgment to bear in rendering advice to the chief executive.

On the other hand, most appropriation or finance committees have a single chief clerk with a handful of assistants to aid them in reviewing these same administrative requests. In most states, moreover, these clerks are employed only during the legislative session itself and do not work continuously. In the federal government, in 1956, the House Appropriations Committee had a total staff of about forty persons and the Senate committee a staff of about thirty. These numbers compare with a staff of 450 persons in the Bureau of the Budget of the Executive Office of the President.

The legislative members themselves have only a limited time which they can devote to appropriation hearings. The legislature usually meets only a part of the year or of a biennium. And even if the legislator serves on only one committee, he cannot give his full time to the committee's work. The committee can meet only during that part of the day when the legislature itself is not in session. The legislator must also give a part of his time to correspondence with his constituents, to meetings with public and other groups, and to many other demands. All this means that even the best-intentioned and most determined legislator cannot master the details of administrative operation which underlie the appropriation requests from administrative agencies.

Moreover, it is often pointed out that under present circumstances the legislative committees handling appropriation bills seldom make any substantial departure from the recommendations of the chief executive. For example, the appropriations recommended by President Eisenhower in 1957 for the fiscal year 1958 came to a total of 63.9 billion dollars. The various laws passed by the Congress eventually provided a total of 59.1 billion dollars for the operation of the federal government. This was a reduction of about 8 per cent in the amount as originally presented by the President. Yet over half of this was realized by reducing contract authorizations for the Armed Forces. Legislatures usually follow executive leadership.

These arguments are put forth as substantiating the need for some change in the appropriation procedure of the legislature. And the change which is most commonly advocated is the creation of a legislative budget staff, that is, of a budget agency to function under the exclusive jurisdiction of the legislature or of a legislative committee.

A proposal recommended in 1951 by the Senate Committee on Expenditures in the Executive Departments (subsequently renamed the Committee on Government Operations) may be cited as illustrative of various proposals. In that year the Senate committee favorably reported a bill which would have amended the Legislative Reorganization Act of 1946 by establishing a Joint Committee on the Budget which in turn would have been authorized to employ such staff as it might find necessary. This joint committee would have been composed of five members each from the House and Senate Committees on Appropriations and four members each from the House and Senate Committees on Expenditures in the Executive Departments.

The 1951 proposal was passed by the Senate on April 8, 1952, but was not considered by the House. In 1953 a similar measure was again voted by the Senate on May 19, but the House Rules Committee refused to provide a special rule whereby the measure might come to the floor of the House for a vote. Again in 1955 the House of Representatives would not take action. It may well have been that the Appropriations Committee of the House had little desire to share its authority with other committees and that for this reason alone the proposal was not destined to receive favorable consideration.

On the face of it the argument in behalf of adequate legislative staffing for appropriation purposes appears to possess merit. The difficulty is that there are at least two basic weaknesses in any such proposal. For one thing, the argument presupposes that legislative supervision of administrative agencies is quite similar in nature and process to executive supervision. If one grants this premise, then the case for additional staffing may be a convincing one. But if the nature and process of legislative supervision are quite different from those of executive supervision, then any argument that both should have similar machinery loses most of its weight. In the second place, from a purely practical point of view the legislature is not without sources of information if appropriation committees desire to make use of them.

Without exploring all the reasons for the proposition here, we may assert with emphasis that legislative supervision is quite different from executive supervision of administrative agencies. The genius of the American system of separation of power is the creation of organs of government not only dissimilar in process, but also fundamentally different in nature. The legislature exercises one kind of supervisory authority over administrative agencies. That authority is legislative in character; in other words it is a kind of authority appropriate to a concept of legislative power wielded by a body of numerous representatives of the people. The executive exercises executive supervision, or authority peculiarly appropriate to a concept of executive power. Machinery necessary and desirable for the exercise of the one kind of power is by no means, therefore, necessary and desirable for the exercise of the other kind of power.

In addition, in the federal government the appropriations committees of Congress may seek the advice and assistance of officials of the executive's budget bureau. This has on occasion been done. The relationship has not been too close, however, because budget officials have sensed that executive and legislative interests in the budgetary process were not identical. Furthermore, appropriations committees to the extent that they desire to do so may make use of reports prepared by the Comptroller General.

If a legislative budget committee were to have a large budget staff, this staff would soon come to speak in the name of the committee. Moreover, the committee would have to supervise the staff closely, or the staff would come to speak for the committee. The essence of the problem is whether legislative concern with budget matters may properly be delegated to a staff. The function of budget review by a legislature is to speak political interest in the magnitude, scope, and procedure of administrative agencies. Can this political interest be equally well voiced by a staff as by elected representatives of the people? This author believes not.

Moreover, when both the legislature and the executive have staff assistance in exercising supervision of administrative agencies, the two staffs become competing bureaucracies. Unless the two agree to work together, in which case they are for all practical purposes one staff, the two rival each other in inquiring into administrative operations, report conflicting findings about the effectiveness of administrative activities, and assume divergent attitudes about the goals of administrative endeavor.

From time to time some state legislatures have experimented with building up their own staffs under a finance committee to scrutinize the executive budget. When this practice extends beyond a chief clerk to assist the committee chairman in scheduling meetings and in keeping track of committee amendments, conflict with the governor's office is apt to result. In practice, a governor's budget officer will usually work closely with the legislative finance committees to the extent the committees desire.

The idea of increasing legislative staffing for appropriation purposes is usually misconceived. Frequently it is born of extensive conflict between legislature and executive. In these circumstances legislative leaders often seek to obtain authority which is more likely to be executive rather than legislative in character. Or in other circumstances, by intensive examination of expenditure requests legislative leaders are in reality seeking political ammunition to be used against the executive. These purposes may be a part of the politics of public administration but they are not in themselves a sufficient justification to seek to alter the fundamental structure of American government.

THE BASIS OF APPROPRIATIONS

A particularly difficult problem has recently come to the forefront of attention in the federal government. A similar practice in varying degree exists at other levels of government. Because so much of the federal budget is today devoted to expenditures for national defense, this difficulty has become especially acute.

In customary government practice an appropriation by the legislature to an administrative agency constitutes authority for that agency to incur "obligations" up to the limit of the appropriation. Government spending procedure draws a sharp distinction between the obligation and the disbursement of available funds. An obligation arises when an agency hires personnel, authorizes an employee to travel, or orders supplies and equipment. An obligation, in other words, is a commitment of funds. Obligations "consume" the available appropriations; unobligated funds are the only balance which the administrator may legally commit for still further activity. An actual disbursement does not occur, however, until the end of the month when salary checks are distributed, or until an employee returns from his travel and submits his expense account, or until the ordered supplies are delivered. Thus there is always some time lag between the obligation and the disbursement of government appropriations.

In most circumstances this time lag, or lead time as it is sometimes called, is not very great and does not raise any serious problem for governmental appropriation practice. Requests for funds are submitted by administrative agencies on an obligation basis—that is, the agencies report what was available to them in the preceding year and the current year for obligation and request funds for the next year to obligate for that year's operations. At the end of the fiscal year, unobligated balances usually lapse, but undisbursed or "unliquidated" obligations remain available as the basis for continued disbursement after the year itself has ended. As of June 30—the customary end of most governmental fiscal years— an agency will still have some outstanding bills unpaid. There will be some travel obligations still not paid. Some supplies will not yet have been delivered. In the federal government under ordinary practice a legally incurred obligation is payable for two years after the end of a fiscal year. At the end of that time unliquidated obligations are canceled. Many state and local governments follow a variable practice in so far as time limits are concerned, but most auditors insist upon an early disbursement of obligations.

In the federal government the problem of unliquidated obligations became crucial in two types of situations: the procurement of military supplies and the construction of large-scale projects such as multipurpose dams for navigation, flood control, irrigation, and power generation. In state and local governments the same kind of trouble has arisen in connection with construction undertakings. For example, the Department of the Air Force may not legally contract for new heavy bombers, such as the B-52, until funds for this purpose are appropriated by the Congress. But an order for 1,000 new heavy bombers may not be completely filled until two or three years after the award of a contract. In such cases the legislature will have to provide that an appropriation shall remain available for disbursement until all of it is expended. As a result, funds pyramid in size from one year to the next, and make a balancing of income and outgo difficult to achieve, at least on paper.

This situation was reported at some length by the second Hoover Commission in 1955. It was pointed out that in the 1956 budget there was an estimate of 24.5 billion dollars to be paid out during the year from appropriations made in prior years. With the advent of the Korean War in 1950 the unexpended balances, or unliquidated obligations, had steadily mounted from 11.5 billion dollars on June 30, 1950, to a peak of 78.4

billion dollars on June 30, 1954. This was expected to decline to about 54 billion dollars by June 30, 1956.[13]

The second Hoover Commission proposed that Congress adopt a new basis of appropriating funds, called the "annual accrued expenditure" budget. Under this arrangement, for those programs with a long lead time, or lag, between obligation and disbursement, an agency would submit to Congress its proposed program for a considerable period. The Congress would appropriate only that amount actually needed for disbursement in the next fiscal year, and for succeeding years would give an administrative agency "contracting authority" for the whole program, or as much of the program as the Congress approved. To some extent this practice has actually been followed, both in military procurement and internal improvements. The Hoover Commission proposed that the practice be made general and systematic.[14]

In 1956 the Congress passed two laws intended to meet in part the difficulties which had been experienced with long-continuing appropriations. An act approved July 25, 1956, continued the practice of permitting obligations to be carried forward two years for disbursement but permitted some part of the unobligated balance as of June 30 of each year to be set aside for payment of claims and other obligations. A report of such action had to be given to the Director of the Bureau of the Budget, the Comptroller General, the Speaker of the House of Representatives, and the President of the Senate. The more important act, approved August 1, 1956, provided for "cost-based" budgets and for accounts to be kept on an "accrual" basis. This meant that in any given year the amounts to be obligated from new appropriation authority would be integrated with disbursements made from appropriations in previous years. It was especially hoped henceforth to have at least accrued expenditure data for each agency of the government showing resources acquired during the year. A beginning toward improved cost-budgeting was begun with the estimates for the fiscal year 1958.[14]

In 1958, Congress enacted a statute, approved on August 25, which added new provisions to the Budget and Accounting Act of 1921. These new sections authorized the President to determine for any particular appropriation item when a satisfactory system of accrual accounting had been developed. He might then recommend a proposed limitation upon the annual accrued expenditures an agency might make in the coming fiscal year. In this way, for certain critical appropriations involving long-term disbursement, the executive and legislature could provide contractual authority and annual accrued expenditures, rather than the customary ob-

[13] Commission on Organization of the Executive Branch of the Government, *Budget and Accounting* (Washington: Government Printing Office, 1955), p. 20.

[14] For criticism of the proposal, see George Y. Harvey, "Contract Authorization in Federal Budget Procedure," *Public Administration Review,* vol. 17 (Spring, 1957), p. 117.

ligational authority. As a result, appropriations would more nearly represent actual cash disbursement, and in any given year the budget would indicate accrued obligations from previous years as well as current operating expenditures. Just how well the new dual system of making appropriations would work out in practice, only time would tell. Even so, in passing Public Law 759 of the Eighty-fifth Congress, the legislature decided that the statute should terminate on April 1, 1962.

Sometimes criticism has been leveled also at the legislative practice of making continuing appropriations. In these instances, a legislature passes a law providing appropriations for a certain purpose on a continuing basis until the law is repealed. Thus, for example, there are federal laws which provide that a stated proportion of timber sales income or other land income in certain Western states shall automatically be turned over to local governments in the area. These constitute authorization to an agency to spend the amount involved without any further appropriation from the Congress. Some state laws similarly direct that a fixed proportion of sales tax receipts or some other income shall be distributed to local units of government or be "earmarked" only for road construction or some other such purpose.

Where these continuing appropriations exist, the legislature does not necessarily have an opportunity to consider the desirable size or immediate urgency of a particular expenditure. The privileged expenditure, in other words, escapes an annual scrutiny by the legislature. The preferable practice appears to be general legislation which authorizes a type of administrative expenditure but leaves to annual determination the question of actual amount. Although this may well be the preferable practice, as the author would indeed agree, it is often unacceptable to certain groups of citizens, who prefer a more stable basis of financing. If they can once obtain a continuing appropriation, they will not readily acquiesce in its elimination for reasons of consistency or regularity in appropriation practice.

APPROPRIATIONS TO DEPARTMENTS OR CONSTITUENT UNITS

In making appropriations for administrative operations, the legislature has three choices. It may appropriate funds for some particular purpose to the chief executive, leaving to him the task of deciding which administrative bodies shall carry out the work involved. A second possibility is to appropriate funds to the head of a department or agency and leave it to his discretion to decide how to divide the amount among operating units of the agency. The third possibility is to appropriate funds directly to the constituent operating units of a department or agency.

All three of these practices exist in the federal government. For example, appropriations for mutual security and economic assistance have customarily been made directly to the President of the United States, who in turn has assigned administration of the program to the Department of Defense, the Department of State, and other agencies. The sums here involved have generally been between two and three billion dollars per year since 1951. On a smaller scale, the Congress has usually appropriated several million dollars to the President each year with which to render assistance to state and local governments stricken by a major disaster such as floods, hurricanes, tornadoes, etc. Within the Agriculture Department the appropriation to carry out the Soil Conservation and Domestic Allotment Act of 1936, as amended, has regularly been to the Secretary. This is one of the largest component items in the department's budget, as we have commented earlier. On the other hand, within the same department appropriations are made directly to the Agricultural Marketing Service, the Foreign Agricultural Service, and the Forest Service. In state and local governments the prevailing practice appears to be for the legislative body to appropriate funds to the department or agency. Occasionally one will find appropriations to be spent at the discretion of the chief executive, or appropriations specifically mentioning a bureau or other unit of a department or agency.

The appropriation practice to be followed is entirely a matter for legislative determination. In the federal government it will be found that most of the appropriations going directly to bureaus have a history of fifty or more years of practice behind them. In the days when government was relatively much simpler than at present, Congress became accustomed to think in terms of particular bureaus in making appropriations. Under emergency circumstances such as economic depression or war, the Congress made appropriations directly to the Chief Executive or to a department head, since administrative arrangements were sometimes not yet completed or continually in a state of adjustment.

Arguments may be presented for any one of the three practices. From the point of view of the legislature, it is sometimes desirable to tie down administrative organization through appropriation detail. Sometimes an interest group distrusts the department head and wishes to circumscribe his discretion. Sometimes a legislative committee develops antipathy for a certain department head and desires to curtail his discretion. Or this feeling of antipathy may be reversed, so that a legislative committee may rebuke a bureau chief by dropping any specific mention of his unit. Sometimes administrative officers ask the legislature to earmark a part of a lump-sum appropriation for a particular purpose. This may be done as self-protection to the administrator so that he can resist pressures to commit even more funds to some one program. For example, where state legislatures usually appropriate lump-sum amounts for support of a state university, it is not unusual to find the president of the university asking the legislature to set aside a specific amount for support of the medical school program. In this way he is able to point out how much medical education costs and at the same time put limits to the total amount spent for this purpose as against teacher education, graduate instruction, business education, etc.

From a technical point of view it is argued that appropriations to a department or agency head provide some degree of internal budgetary flexibility, giving the chief administrative officer discretion in allotting funds among operating units. This budgetary flexibility to a considerable degree is lost when appropriations are made to constituent bureaus or other operating units. The department head can suggest alterations only at the time when the budget request is submitted. On the other hand, the legislature prefers less departmental discretion, since if there is conflict in expenditure plans between a department head and a subordinate, it is the legislature which may make the final decision. Such legislative decision making is time-consuming, however.

The prevailing appropriation practice appears to be a matter of historical arrangement, with periodic adjustment depending upon the influence at some time of a particular chief executive, department head, bureau chief, or legislative leader. This historical accretion, together with occasional adjustment arising from the impact of special circumstance and personality, helps to explain why appropriation legislation so often is a hodgepodge of varied arrangements.

CONTINUING CONTROL

Appropriation acts provide supervision and control of administrative operations by law. Yet this has not always been satisfactory in and of itself for legislative bodies. Frequently, the legislature has no choice except to provide funds in a lump sum for some administrative purpose. The only other choice would be to provide no funds at all. The legislature cannot anticipate every possible development which may occur, and some discretion must be left to administrative officials. But legislators are often dissatisfied to leave further action to administrative officials, supervised in turn by the chief executive. They believe that their ideas and expectations should play a part in administration, even after laws have been written and funds appropriated. The result of this attitude is that from time to time legislatures are moved to write into appropriation law some provision for continuing supervision of administrative operations.

For example, in New York State the legislature in 1921, with amendments enacted in 1927, wrote into the state finance law a requirement that administrative agencies could not spend certain types of lump-sum appropriations until a schedule of positions and salaries for expenditure under the appropriation had been approved by the governor, by the chairman of the Finance Committee of the Senate, and by the chairman of the Ways and Means Committee of the Assembly. In 1929 the legislature insisted that this provision of the law should be followed for a number of appropriations. Governor Franklin D. Roosevelt attacked the action of the legislature on the ground that it was an unconstitutional extension of legislative power and an invasion of the executive authority. At the request of the legislature the attorney general of the state brought action in the courts to prevent the comptroller from making payment without the approval of the two legislative chairmen. An intermediate court upheld the point of view of the legislature. The highest court of the state, the Court of Appeals, reversed this stand and endorsed the Governor's position. In its opinion the court declared: "This is a clear and conspicuous instance of an attempt by the Legislature to confer administrative power upon two of its members. It may not engraft executive duties upon a legislative office and thus usurp executive power by indirection."[15]

In 1948 in the Independent Offices Appropriation Act, the Congress provided that the Veterans' Administration could not use any of its funds for the purchase of a tract of land in Arlington, Virginia, or in Tallahassee, Florida, for construction of a hospital "until the Committee on Appropriations of the House of Representatives has investigated and given its approval." Presumably, this restriction was inserted because the Appropriations Committee was not satisfied with these two proposed projects but was not willing to legislate them out of the program. Instead, the committee simply arranged for further consideration without holding up the appropriation act. No one can question the power of Congress to direct by law that funds shall not be spent for a particular purpose or project. Whether Congress can delegate to a committee the authority to approve a project after the appropriation law has been enacted is more questionable. Yet it was done in this instance.

In 1955 the second Hoover Commission recommended that the Department of Defense curtail the operation of commissary stores and post exchanges serving military personnel and their dependents on military posts, bases, and stations.[16] The Secretary of Defense then indicated that he sympathized with this recommendation and that he proposed to carry it out. Members of the legislature, perhaps reflecting the opinion of some military officials and others, were not so sure that the proposed action was desirable. As a result, the Congress wrote a section 638 into the Department of Defense Appropriation Act declaring that the Secretary of Defense was not to terminate activities at a military installation if the

[15] People v. Tremaine, 252 N.Y. 27 (1929).

[16] See Commission on Organization of the Executive Branch of the Government, Business Enterprises: A Report to the Congress, May, 1955 (Washington: Government Printing Office, 1955).

Appropriations Committee of either the Senate or the House of Representatives disapproved such proposed termination.

In signing the appropriation measure on July 13, 1955, President Eisenhower sent a message to the Congress specifically protesting the terms of section 638 of the law. Except for the "imperative need" of the Defense Department for funds, he declared, he would have withheld his approval of the measure because this section constituted "an unconstitutional invasion of the province of the Executive." The President went on to say:[17]

> The Congress has the power and the right to grant or to deny an appropriation. But once an appropriation is made, the appropriation must, under the Constitution, be administered by the Executive Branch of the Government alone, and the Congress has no right to confer upon its committees the power to veto Executive action or to prevent Executive action from becoming effective.
>
> Since the organization of our Government, the President has felt bound to insist that Executive functions be maintained unimpaired by legislative encroachment, just as the Legislative Branch has felt bound to resist interference with its power by the Executive. To acquiesce in a provision that seeks to encroach upon the proper authority of the Executive establishes a dangerous precedent. I do not, by my approval of HR 6042, acquiesce in the provisions of Section 638 and to the extent that this section seeks to give to the Appropriations Committee of the Senate and House of Representatives authority to veto or prevent Executive action, such Section will be regarded as invalid by the Executive Branch of the Government in the administration of HR 6042 unless otherwise determined by a court of competent jurisdiction.

The President thus served notice that he had no intention of permitting the Secretary of Defense to carry out the letter of the law as enacted by the Congress. On the other hand, it is reasonable to expect that the Department of Defense was cautious in carrying out the original recommendation of the Hoover Commission because it had received advance notice that the legislature would scrutinize its actions carefully and might have something more to say on the subject when the time came next year to enact another appropriation law.

To be sure, under various circumstances administrative officers may find it desirable to consult with the chairman and the staff director of the appropriations committees when they are changing their plans from those originally discussed when their appropriation was pending. For example, one congressman complained that General Somervell of the Army had violated the spirit of an appropriation law during World War II when he shifted funds from a general construction appropriation to augment the specific appropriation made with which to build the Pentagon Building. General Somervell had a complete answer when he replied that he had consulted both the chairman of the House Appropriations Committee and

[17] *Congressional Record,* vol. 101, part 8, p. 10460.

its chief clerk beforehand and that the committee thus had foreknowledge of his intention. The failure of these legislative officers or of the committee as a whole to warn him against the action was construed as tacit approval.

There is, of course, one device which the legislature can certainly use if it so desires. For example, in 1949, the Congress in appropriating funds for the Atomic Energy Commission provided that no part of the appropriation should be used to start a construction project for which an estimate had not been included in the budget request for the year, or to start a construction project the cost estimate of which subsequently exceeded the cost estimate originally provided in the budget, or to continue any community facility construction project where the cost was subsequently estimated to exceed the original expectation included in the budget unless the Director of the Budget approved and submitted a detailed explanation to the Senate and House Appropriation Committees and to the Joint Committee on Atomic Energy.

This provision said nothing about prior approval by the congressional committees. It insisted only that full information be supplied the legislature when a change in budget plans on construction projects might occur. Yet this also implies that the administrators of the Atomic Energy Commission would be well advised to consult fully with legislative committee members before adjusting their budget plans.

This kind of provision can be fully justified under our Constitution, in the opinion of this author. Whether a legislature may go beyond this by attempting to control administrative action after an appropriation has been made is questionable. In some instances, as in Ohio, the legislature has set up a "controlling board" with both executive and legislative membership to approve transfers of items within the total appropriations to an agency and otherwise to provide some flexibility in the execution of appropriation legislation. The fact that this arrangement generally operates to the benefit of administrative officers has led to its widespread acceptance.

It is easy to understand why the legislature should wish to retain a continuing voice in appropriation matters. But how to distinguish between proper and improper legislative control on appropriations is less easy to determine. It is generally agreed that the legislature may impose through law such conditions and such restrictions in the expenditure of funds as it deems wise. It is equally clear that the legislature cannot undertake to exercise the functions of the executive. Somewhere between the two is a ground of uncertain constitutional practice.

CONCLUSION

The importance of the legislative role in appropriating funds for administrative activities cannot be exaggerated. Yet the limits of legislative discretion may be overstated. When the legislature authorizes particular programs of administrative operation it obligates itself to their subsequent financial support. Indeed, many laws set standards of expenditure which in effect bind the hands of appropriation committees. Legislation which sets certain standards of state support to local school districts obligates the legislature to appropriate the necessary funds. Legislation providing benefits to veterans obligates the legislature to provide the funds to pay all who qualify. In some fields such as labor and welfare legislation it is not unusual to find that from two-thirds to three-quarters of all expenditures are in effect mandatory under existing laws.

Moreover, interest group or general public concern with particular programs of government results in a legislative disposition to be fairly generous in appropriating funds. In a troubled world where national security is at best precarious, the Congress of the United States is not likely to be penurious in handling estimated appropriation requirements for national defense. Indeed, a major political issue of our day is not whether the Congress spends too much on national defense but rather whether it appropriates enough.

But appropriation practice may not always be satisfactory in enabling the legislature to see broad public policy issues in their comprehensive whole. Thus, for example, the Congress of the United States has not yet found a satisfactory means for relating income and expenditure to each other. This essential element of fiscal policy remains largely for executive formulation. Moreover there is often a disposition for appropriation committees to concentrate attention upon items to be purchased from appropriations such as personal services, supplies and equipment, etc. In these instances the legislature worries primarily about operating efficiency, and the possibility of certain abuses such as high salary compensation, excessive travel, or noncompetitive bidding. This concentration may be justified in some circumstances, but appropriations to some departments may actually be relatively unimportant in terms of items purchased. For example, it has been estimated that over 60 per cent of all disbursements by the U.S. Department of Agriculture are payments to individual farmers or to others who are not government employees at all. In these, and perhaps in all instances, the appropriation process might do well to focus more attention upon broad policy issues.[18]

To a considerable degree what appropriation committees tend to do is to size up administrators who direct various activities and to direct attention to details of operation. The administrator who makes a favorable impression upon the appropriation subcommittee usually fares pretty well. The administrator who seems to lack a command of detail, who is hesitant in answering questions, who tries to bluff or conceal facts, who belittles legislative ideas and attitudes, or who otherwise seems to be un-

[18] See Edward C. Banfield, "Congress and the Budget: A Planner's Criticism," *American Political Science Review*, vol. 43 (December, 1949), p. 1217.

cooperative can expect little cooperation in turn from the legislature. Perhaps in this respect alone the appropriation process more than justifies itself.

In any event, only the legislature under our system of government can appropriate public funds for administrative operation. The magnitude, scope, and direction of administrative effort are thereby periodically determined. The power of the purse resides in legislative hands, and is a powerful control making for administrative responsibility in America.

Chapter 9

The Legislature and Supervision
of the Expenditure of Funds

Under Article I of the federal Constitution "no money shall be drawn from the Treasury, but in consequence of appropriations made by law; and a regular statement and account of the receipts and expenditures of all public money shall be published from time to time." Yet at the same time it is the President under Article II who "shall take care that the laws be faithfully executed." The respective roles of the legislature and of the Chief Executive in carrying out the appropriation laws were not entirely clear from the wording of the Constitution, and practice has also been confused. Yet from this uncertainty has arisen in the federal government at least a theory of legislative responsibility for supervising the faithful and legal expenditure of public appropriations.

In the beginning the Congress appropriated funds for the operation of the government under a few broad purposes, such as "the civil list," the expenses of the War Department, the retirement of the national debt, and the payment of pensions to injured veterans.[1] But some members of Congress were unsatisfied with this practice and insisted upon a more exact specification. The question then arose how Congress was to ensure that its limitations were observed. Little progress was made at first in getting the Secretary of Treasury to acknowledge that he lacked authority to make transfers or otherwise to adjust sums as voted by the legislature.

In 1801 when serving as Secretary of the Treasury, Albert Gallatin proposed to President Jefferson that he counsel Congress to appropriate funds for specific purposes, to "disallow" expenditures varying from such appropriation, and to reduce discretionary authority exercised by administrative officials. These were the very practices Gallatin had fought

---

[1] The historical information which follows has been taken from Lucius Wilmerding, Jr., *The Spending Power* (New Haven, Conn.: Yale University Press, 1943).

during his years as a representative. Hamilton challenged the proposal as certain to result in administrative inflexibility and waste. Actually, the controversy was not so great as it appeared on the surface. The doctrine of specific appropriation quickly received general agreement and has remained in effect until the present day. In 1809 Congress passed a law declaring that "the sums appropriated by law for each branch of expenditure in the several departments shall be solely applied to the objects for which they are respectively appropriated, and to no other." But the law authorized the President under certain conditions to make transfers within the total amount for any department.

In the period after Jefferson's administration there was still more concern with the exact specification of purpose or object of expenditure in the annual appropriation laws. In 1817 Congress by law directed that appropriations made for military purposes were not to be transferred to any other object of public expenditure. In 1820 Congress passed further legislation designed to stop the abuse of departmental expenditure of balances carried forward as unexpended from previous years. Moreover, department heads were enjoined not to enter into contracts unless so authorized by law and unless an adequate appropriation for payment of the contract was available.

In the years between 1820 and the conclusion of the Civil War, a variety of appropriation difficulties arose. Some appropriations were used to meet the deficiency of a prior year and hence were inadequate for current operations. Appropriation measures were not passed on a regular schedule, especially since in one year the session beginning in December had to adjourn in March and the next year might run until May or June. In other instances Congress tried to be even too detailed in its appropriations, making orderly administration almost impossible. In the face of numerous complaints Congress began to relax its restrictions. Then in 1860, on the eve of the Civil War, Congress repealed an 1842 statute permitting almost unlimited discretion in the transfer of appropriations by department heads. The exigencies of war interrupted a disposition to push congressional controls over expenditures even further.

After the Civil War Congress in 1868 again attacked what it regarded as the evils of transfer; no money henceforth was to be used for any other purpose than that for which it was appropriated. In 1870 Congress passed legislation designed to end the practice of carrying unexpended balances forward from one year to another. Yet an interpretation of this new law by the Attorney General tended to defeat much of the congressional intent. Congress adopted additional legislation on the subject in 1874, and with the help of a vigorous enforcement by the Treasury Department, the new law proved fairly effective. As a result of the laws of 1868, 1870, and 1874, the abuses of mingling appropriations and of bringing forward unexpended balances were largely eliminated. Congress had thus gone far in asserting a substantial control over expenditures through the legislative process.

The next practice to command considerable congressional attention was that of spending funds so that supplemental or deficiency appropriations became necessary. In certain cases the need for additional funds was actually created by a congressional disposition toward partial or under appropriation. In 1905 Congress finally enacted a so-called Anti-Deficiency Act which directed department and agency heads to apportion appropriations on a monthly basis so that the total would be spread over the entire fiscal year. In 1906 another law directed heads of departments and other agencies to include in their estimates the full needs of a fiscal year and forbade them to submit special or additional estimates except in special circumstances. But in 1911 President Taft's Commission on Economy and Efficiency criticized excessive itemization in appropriation laws and urged instead a greater degree of administrative discretion accompanied by "such an accounting as will disclose promptly and accurately the results of the exercise of the executive discretion. . . . " Again the advent of war in 1917 required a relaxing of legislative restrictions and the appropriation of large sums of money to be expended primarily under executive or administrative discretion. In the aftermath of that war experience, Congress enacted the Budget and Accounting Act approved June 10, 1921.

Thus far we have noted efforts by Congress to restrict administrative activity through provisions of general law or of appropriation law. During all these years Congress had also sought to check administrative performance by some kind of continuing postappropriation control. As early as 1791 Congress passed a law which directed the Secretary of the Treasury to lay before Congress each year a complete report on appropriations and expenditures. A companion measure to set up committees to examine this report was defeated in the House of Representatives. In 1802 the powers of the Committee on Ways and Means were enlarged to include the duty of examining the expenditure practices and records of the "several public departments." The exercise of this authority proved beyond the capacity of the committee. Its members had neither the time nor the interest necessary for a careful audit of administrative expenditures. In 1814 Congress set up a new standing committee on public expenditures. In 1816 six standing committees were created, dividing the scope of governmental administrative activity among them. Still the committees proved an unsatisfactory device for supervising administrative activity in expending appropriated funds. In fact, the committees performed almost no work at all.

Finally, in 1876, at the end of the Grant administration, with the House of Representatives under control of Democrats, the various committees on expenditure were directed to conduct inquiries into the conduct of administrative agencies. Already a series of scandals had come to light. For a good part of the year the House committees were engaged in a grand inquest. But the actual financial operation of government played only a small part in the work of the various committees. These committees were so much associated in the popular mind with investigation of wrongdoing, to a considerable extent motivated by a desire for political advantage, that their role as supervisors of financial transactions was almost forgotten. It was through the work of the Committee on Expenditures in the Department of Justice that the "star-route" frauds were revealed in 1883. But over the subsequent years little was done.

THE BUDGET AND ACCOUNTING ACT OF 1921

President Taft's Commission on Economy and Efficiency had made the development of a national budget system its major interest. The growing movement for administrative improvement in the United States, fostered by new agencies called "bureaus of municipal research," made the achievement of an executive budget system one of its primary goals. The objective was a simple one. The chief executive should be made responsible for collecting budget estimates from all administrative departments, he should review these with care and then recommend to the legislature such sums as he thought necessary in terms of the work to be accomplished and the general fiscal situation of the government.[2] The difficulty in this proposal was the substantial additional authority for administrative supervision which it conferred upon the chief executive. For this reason the executive budget system was attacked as undermining the power of the legislature and hence the whole fabric of democratic government.[3] The answer to this argument was twofold. First, it was necessary to emphasize the role of the chief executive as an instrument of responsible government.[4] Secondly, it was necessary to develop the idea that legislative authority in budgetary matters should also be enhanced. As a result there came into being the doctrine of the legislative audit.

The case for this second idea was briefly put forth in a pamphlet published in 1915, which declared:[5]

[2] The arguments for the executive budget system and an account of the state budgetary improvement accomplishments are to be found in W. F. Willoughby, *The Problem of the National Budget* (New York: D. Appleton & Company, Inc., 1918); and *The Movement for Budgetary Reform in the States* (New York: D. Appleton & Company, Inc., 1918).

[3] Cf. Edward A. Fitzpatrick, *Budget Making in a Democracy* (New York: The Macmillan Company, 1918).

[4] Cf. Frederick A. Cleveland and A. E. Buck, *The Budget and Responsible Government* (New York: The Macmillan Company, 1920).

[5] *The Constitution and Government of the State of New York,* Bureau of Municipal Research of New York City, Bulletin no. 61 (New York, 1915), p. 84. The bureau, like other such agencies later created in other cities, was a private agency supported by citizens interested in municipal reform and improvement.

One of the prime reasons for the establishment of representative government was to call the executive to account for expenditures. . . . In some
countries the King or his immediate representatives are required to appear
personally and make the statement with respect to the expenditures under
past authorizations by the legislative body. . . . It was from this practice of
listening to a verbal statement or account of expenditures that the term
"auditing" arose. The next step in the development of a procedure for enforcing accountability through an independent audit was the appointment of
an auditing committee. . . . A third step in advance was the creation of an
auditing department or office which was made independent of the executive.

The idea seemed a simple one. The legislature should be given an
agency to exercise full-time, continuing scrutiny of the financial transactions of administrative agencies. When this agency found evidence of mal-
performance or misfeasance in office, the facts could be called to the
attention of an appropriate committee in the legislature. This committee
would then perhaps call in administrative officers to explain their behavior. The committee would decide whether administrative practice was
proper or not and presumably seek corrective action through the legislative process. Thanks to the concept of separation of powers, the legislature in the American system of government possessed no authority in
theory or practice to dismiss offending department heads and the Prime
Minister as might be done by the House of Commons in England.[6]

The Budgeting and Accounting Act of 1921 as finally drafted and
enacted in the federal government seems to have drawn upon this developing doctrine of a legislative audit. The difficulty seems to have been
that although some legislators and their advisers may have had a fairly
clear conception of what it was they wished to create, they were not very
adept at expressing this intention in the language of the law. It is the
judgment of one student that "the act was passed with almost masterly in-
attention to draftsmanship. Nearly every ambiguity of jurisdiction under
existing law was retained, and some additional ones were created."[7]

Here we are not concerned with the budget provisions of the 1921 law.
We are interested only in the creation of a new office, the General Accounting Office. In the first place, the 1921 act abolished the position of
comptroller and the positions of six auditors which had existed within the
structure of the Treasury Department. The positions of comptroller and
auditor went back to the original legislation creating the Treasury in
1789. The auditor was to receive all public accounts sent to the Treasury
by administrative agencies, examine them, certify an available balance,
and then transmit the voucher and certificate to the comptroller. The

[6] For a brief description of the work of the Comptroller and Auditor General and
the Public Accounts Committee of the House of Commons—"the original and best
developed form of the legislative type of audit"—see A. E. Buck, *The Budget in
Governments of Today* (New York: The Macmillan Company, 1934), pp. 269–276.
[7] Harvey C. Mansfield, *The Comptroller General* (New Haven, Conn.: Yale University Press, 1939), p. 67.

comptroller was to maintain the official accounts, review the actions "settled" by the auditor, and was to recover debts owing the United States. In addition, the comptroller was to countersign all warrants drawn by the Secretary of the Treasury authorizing the expenditure of public funds. During the nineteenth century two more comptrollers and other auditors were added to the Treasury Department; then in 1894 the structure returned to a single comptroller. Although their authority was substantial, both the comptroller and the auditors were subordinates of the Secretary of the Treasury and subject presumably to dismissal by the President.

The Budget and Accounting Act of 1921, as we have said, abolished these positions and created a new office called the General Accounting Office under a new head designated the Comptroller General. Little attention was given apparently to the powers vested in the Comptroller General. The language employed simply made use of the terms and practices which previously had prevailed in the Treasury Department without any particular inquiry about their propriety or feasibility when transferred to a new organization. Such debate as did occur centered on the method of appointment and the term of office for the Comptroller General. The House of Representatives favored congressional appointment; this was abandoned in the face of both constitutional and practical difficulties. Under the Constitution the appointing power is vested in the Chief Executive. Moreover, since the life of an individual Congress is only two years, no continuity in office could be realized in this way. In the end Congress provided that the Comptroller General should serve for a fifteen-year term of office and be ineligible for reappointment. In addition, the law provided that the Comptroller General could be removed from office only by impeachment or by a concurrent resolution of Congress. President Wilson vetoed the entire act on June 4, 1920, because he believed that this limitation upon the removal power of the President was unconstitutional. President Harding signed the act on June 10, 1921.

The history of the legislation would seem clearly to indicate that Congress had in mind creating an office which would provide a means for legislative supervision of administrative operations. Several clauses were written into the act suggesting this intention. The Comptroller General was directed to investigate all matters relating to the "receipt, disbursement, and application of public funds," and was annually to make a report to Congress on the work of the General Accounting Office, including any recommendations for legislation to improve the administration of public funds. The Comptroller General was also directed to make such investigations and reports as might be ordered by either house or by any committee of either house. In addition, he was to report to Congress every expenditure or contract made by any department or establishment in violation of law.[8]

[8] For the legislative history of title 3 of the Budgeting and Accounting Act of 1921 see Wilmerding, op. cit., chap. 12; and Mansfield, op. cit., pp. 65–70.

THE AUTHORITY OF THE COMPTROLLER GENERAL

The authority of the Comptroller General to advise Congress and to serve congressional committees was incidental to the broader powers inherited from earlier legislation. The Budget and Accounting Act of 1921 declared that "all powers and duties now conferred or imposed by law upon the Comptroller . . . or the six auditors of the Treasury . . . shall . . . be vested in and imposed upon the General Accounting Office." These powers were essentially four in number.

In the first place, the Comptroller General was given authority to prescribe the accounting forms and accounting systems employed by administrative agencies in handling their financial transactions. In legal theory at least the Comptroller General was thus in a position to exercise initiative in developing the entire system of governmental accounting. In any event, if he failed to exercise this leadership, he was in a position where he might disapprove administrative developments in the field of accounting if he desired for any reason to do so. More than this, his authority over governmental accounting practices was certain to be exercised from the point of view of the Comptroller General's other responsibilities. It was not likely that the Comptroller General would be particularly interested in or concerned with the accounting needs of administrative officers arising from their responsibility for operations themselves.

In the second place, the Comptroller General inherited the authority to "settle and adjust" the accounts of government disbursing officers. These words "to settle accounts" over many years of administrative practice had come to have a particular technical meaning in federal government accounting practice. By 1921 most of the executive departments and other administrative agencies had their own disbursing officials. Only in 1933 was much of this disbursing machinery centralized under the jurisdiction of the Treasury Department. These disbursing officers, who were administrative subordinates of department and agency heads, had in effect a checking account made available to them by the Treasury for the appropriation purposes applicable to each agency. These disbursing officers wrote checks—or earlier drew and distributed cash—for the payment of administrative payrolls and for the payment of contracts for supplies and other services. This disbursement occurred in accordance with the personnel and other procedures of each agency. Subsequently, the auditors in the Treasury Department and, after 1921, the General Accounting Office undertook to settle the accounts of these disbursing officers.

To settle these accounts meant to examine the vouchers for payment of government obligations and to make sure that all these transactions were in accordance with the appropriation law. If the auditor found that all transactions were within the limit fixed by appropriation law and were for purposes specified by law, then the disbursing officer received a certificate of settlement indicating that his obligation to the Treasury for the cash (or checking) account advanced to him was now "settled." If the auditor found that some disbursement exceeded the authorized amount or was for a nonauthorized purpose, then he entered a "suspension" for the particular amount in the disbursing officer's account. This was also done in case the disbursing officer failed to file all the requisite information about a payment, such as a copy of the amounts due to each individual on the payroll or a copy of the contract under which a payment was made. If the disbursing officer later supplied adequate justification for the payment, the suspension might be lifted and the account officially settled. If the auditor was still unsatisfied, then a permanent "disallowance" might be entered in the account. When a payment was thus disallowed, the Attorney General was then expected to institute suit to recover the illegal payment. The disbursing officer was personally liable for the illegal disbursement. If he could recover the payment from the payee, the money was returned to the Treasury. Otherwise, the government was expected to collect the amount from the disbursing officer personally or from his bonding company.

This whole system was obviously somewhat cumbersome and even in some ways unfair. It did set up some formidable arrangements for ensuring the integrity of government disbursements. Yet it also placed heavy responsibilities upon the disbursing officer. This official was expected to be in a position to know what was a legal and what was an illegal expenditure. This could give the disbursing officer reason for considerable delay in paying government obligations, or it could make him an influential officer in deciding the interpretation to be given the laws of Congress. Or the disbursing officer might find himself in the embarrassing position of being pecuniarily liable for acts performed in good faith in the discharge of orders received from his administrative superiors.

Actually neither situation appears to have occurred in any important degree before 1921. The auditors at that time were administrative subordinates of the Secretary of the Treasury. They were subject to removal by the President. If any real difference of opinion arose about interpretation of the law which could not be settled by a department head in consultation with the Secretary of the Treasury, then the dispute might go to the President, with such assistance from the Attorney General as he might seek. The whole dispute was thus capable of resolution among officials subject to executive supervision. After 1921 this was no longer the case. The Comptroller General now had the authority to settle accounts. He was in a position accordingly to interject his ideas about legality into the administrative process to the extent that he so desired. If there was disagreement in interpretation of law between a department or agency head and the Comptroller General, then any resolution of that conflict by the President was no longer binding. Because the Comptroller General stood beyond the sanction of the President's removal power, any disagreement would now have to go to the legislature for determination.

After 1921 many such disagreements did go to the legislature for action. A number of so-called relief bills had to be introduced at each session of Congress directing the General Accounting Office to settle particular items which had been disallowed in the accounts of some disbursing officer. It might well be argued that this situation was desirable. After all, should not the Congress rather than the Chief Executive be expected to clarify the intent of law? Apart from the constitutional issue involved in deciding just what is the meaning of the Chief Executive's responsibility to see to it that the laws are faithfully executed, there was one important objection to this process. It was time-consuming, and it put a considerable burden upon the legislature. A dispute between administrative officers and the Comptroller General might take months or even years to adjust through the legislative process of enacting clarifying legislation. And so much time might conceivably be devoted to this task as to leave little time for the consideration of new legislation.

Incidental to the authority to settle accounts was the power of the Comptroller General to settle claims against the United States. We shall have occasion later to comment about the law of torts in so far as it affects the work of administrative officers in the United States. Claims for money due an individual, partnership, or corporation from the federal government may also arise from an allegation that some amount properly owed under a contract with the government has not been paid. If a disbursing officer in his judgment saw fit not to allow such a claim, either because of an alleged failure to perform properly the services required by a contract or because of some disagreement in the interpretation of the terms of the contract, the aggrieved individual might seek satisfaction from the auditors or, after 1921, from the Comptroller General. Here there were other alternatives available to the aggrieved party, such as a suit in the Court of Claims or an appeal to a friendly legislator to support private legislation. As a result, the jurisdiction over settlement of claims was not too important a power vested in the General Accounting Office.

In the third place, the Comptroller General inherited authority to audit the financial transactions of the federal government. In actual practice, however, this authority was not very meaningful. The power to audit on the heels of the power to settle accounts was superfluous when both responsibilities were vested in the same office. Having settled an account, the General Accounting Office was not likely to review the transaction further and then find upon "audit" that the settled account was somehow improper. Or perhaps it might be said that settlement of an account meant that it was officially audited. Once the determination of legality had been made by the General Accounting Office and the disbursing officer's accounts officially settled, there was no point in that office endeavoring to examine the accounts any further. Audit was a superfluous term in so far as the work of the General Accounting Office was concerned.

A fourth power of the Comptroller General was that to countersign all warrants first signed by the Secretary of the Treasury. Here again a technical procedure in the expenditure of appropriations was involved. When the legislature passed and the Chief Executive approved an appropriation law, a system of warrants had the effect of giving official notice to administrative officers that they were now duly authorized to obligate the specified sums for specified purposes. These warrants officially placed funds to the credit of disbursing officers for expenditure. By countersigning such warrants, the Comptroller General saw to it that the notices to spend government funds were entirely proper. Although this function was in large part routine, it afforded the Comptroller General some opportunity to intervene in the process of making administrative decisions about the actual operations to be undertaken.

But authority vested in an agency means very little in the abstract. More important is the way in which such authority is interpreted and used by the individuals who exercise it. In so far as the General Accounting Office was concerned, the real impact of its operation was in large measure determined by the first person who held the post of Comptroller General from 1921 to 1936, John R. McCarl. He was disposed to assert to the utmost all the authority vested in the Comptroller General. As one student has concluded, this determination meant "controversies over the finality of administrative determinations and the continual substitution of the Comptroller General's conclusions on matters of fact and of law for those of the department heads."[9] Moreover, McCarl was more interested in his own direct exercise of control over administrative activities than he was in becoming a "tool" or "agent" of the Congress. He was disposed to correct administrative error, as he saw it, through his own authority rather than to inform Congress about the matter and obtain its judgment. Nor did he seek to develop close working relationships with congressional committees, such as the appropriation committees and the committees on expenditures in the executive departments. And he concentrated the work of the General Accounting Office in Washington where all financial transactions had to be examined and where the maximum impact of his own views could be ensured.

The very essence of the authority of the Comptroller General, as we have already noted, lies in his power to settle accounts. In practice, this authority has given officials of the General Accounting Office considerable opportunity to insist that their, and not anyone else's, interpretation of the meaning of the law shall be final and binding in the financial transactions of the federal government. For example, the U.S. Employees' Compensation Commission decided that an appropriation for "medical services

[9] Mansfield, *op. cit.,* pp. 71–72.

and supplies" should be used to purchase an artificial limb for an injured government employee. The Comptroller General disallowed the payment on the grounds that an artificial limb was not a medical supply. Even though the Attorney General ruled that the Commission's interpretation of the law was proper, the Comptroller General refused to be bound by this advice, and the Commission had to take the matter to Congress. The law was amended to uphold the position of the Employees' Compensation Commission.[10] In 1935 the Comptroller General held that a travel order authorizing reimbursement of expenses on change of station for a government employee was not valid when signed by the Assistant to the Secretary of the Interior. A legal travel order, said the Comptroller General, had to be signed by the Secretary and the Secretary could not delegate this task to his assistant even though a joint resolution of Congress approved March 28, 1918, provided that the Assistant to the Secretary of the Interior was authorized to sign such papers and documents as the Secretary might direct. While the Civilian Conservation Corps was in operation during the 1930s another conflict arose. An act of March 4, 1915, authorized the Secretary of War to determine when and where adequate quarters were not available for commissioned officers and warrant officers; when adequate quarters were not available, an officer was entitled to a rental allowance. When officers were assigned to operate CCC camps, the Secretary ruled that the barracks accommodations provided did not constitute adequate quarters and that they might, therefore, draw rental allowances. The Comptroller General subsequently disallowed these payments on the grounds that the barracks provided the officers did constitute adequate quarters within the meaning of the law.[11]

In these cases administrative officials made one interpretation of the law, the Comptroller General a different one. Administrative officials felt that, since they were responsible for carrying out provisions of the law promptly and decisively, their interpretation should be binding. The Comptroller General felt that, since he was responsible for seeing to it that no money appropriated by Congress was spent except in accordance with law, his interpretation should be binding. It must be noticed that in these and many similar cases no question of malfeasance in administrative practice was involved. The sole question was the application of general provisions of law to certain specific sets of circumstances. The judgment of the Comptroller General was binding until the Congress enacted clarifying legislation.

While McCarl was Comptroller General, he had one particular answer to administrative complaints about uncertainties and delays in handling

[10] *Ibid.*, p. 105.
[11] These last two examples have been taken from *Reorganization of the Executive Departments, Hearings before the Joint Committee on Government Organization,* 75th Cong., 1st Sess. (February–April, 1937), pp. 389–405.

their responsibilities. This answer was to encourage administrative officials to seek a "pre-audit" of uncertain financial matters. If an administrative agency would present the facts and reasons for a proposed financial transaction, the Comptroller General would rule in advance whether he thought the action was legal or not. Such a practice in effect made the Comptroller General an important element in the determination of government policy. His "pre-audit" did eliminate the subsequent danger of a possible suspension or disallowance in the accounts of a disbursing officer. But if the Comptroller General ruled in the negative in advance, an administrative agency was stopped from proceeding with a proposed line of action.

There was one particular way in which the extensive participation of the Comptroller General in administrative decisions could be eliminated. This was for Congress in passing some statute to provide that the findings of fact about financial transactions by an administrative officer should be final and should not be questioned by any other official. This was done in quite a few instances. Thus the determination of adjusted compensation payments due to veterans by the Veterans' Administration was legally placed beyond the Comptroller General's power to review. The same was true of commodity benefit and soil conservation payments as fixed by the Secretary of Agriculture. Certain other expenditures were given a similar immunity, such as those of the Supreme Court, congressional committees, and the President.[12]

In any event, it is apparent that the powers of the Comptroller General, especially as interpreted and put into practice by McCarl between 1921 and 1936, were such as to make him a vital factor in the administrative process. He could at will substitute his interpretation of what constituted a legal expenditure for that of any administrative official, including the Attorney General of the United States. Where disagreement arose, then Congress alone was able to step in and settle the issue.

In this limited sense the Comptroller General could rightfully claim to be an agent of Congress. He was certainly an independent official—removed from presidential supervision—who could interrupt any particular administrative action as he saw fit. Congress had then to be called upon to override or sustain the interpretation of the Comptroller General and so to clarify legislative intention.

CRITICISM OF THE GENERAL ACCOUNTING OFFICE

The first general criticism of the work of the Comptroller General appeared in 1934 when a leading American authority on governmental financial administration asserted that his powers were "inconsistent" and "illogical." A. E. Buck argued that the financial authority of the Treasury Department and the Bureau of the Budget had been substantially reduced

[12] Mansfield, *op. cit.*, p. 97.

by the policies and practices of the General Accounting Office. Further-more, the Comptroller General was exercising power which was essentially administrative in nature. The accounting work of the Treasury Department and of operating agencies was being duplicated by the General Accounting Office. Since the Comptroller General kept his own accounting records, there was no such thing as an independent audit in the federal government. Buck advocated that the controlling functions of the Comptroller General be transferred to the Treasury Department. He wanted a new auditing agency to take the place of the General Accounting Office.[13] Indeed, a proposal comparable to this had been embodied in the executive orders on reorganization submitted by President Hoover to Congress in December, 1932.

Then in 1937 President Roosevelt's Committee on Administrative Management leveled a major blast at the Comptroller General. In discussing fiscal management the Committee declared that there were four major defects, including "the vesting in the office of the Comptroller General, which is not responsible to the President, of the settlement of claims, the final determination concerning the uses of appropriation, and the prescribing of administrative accounting systems"; and the "absence of a truly independent and prompt audit of the financial transactions of the government, whereby the Congress may hold the Executive Branch strictly accountable."[14] The Committee also asserted that no comprehensive and adequate system of general accounts had been developed by the Comptroller General's office. Because the Comptroller General exercised essentially executive duties, his authority to control expenditures should be transferred to the Secretary of the Treasury, while the title of the Comptroller General should be changed to Auditor General, the name of his agency should be changed to General Auditing Office, and his authority should be confined to auditing expenditures.[15]

This point of view was controverted, however, by a study prepared for the Senate Select Committee to Investigate the Executive Agencies of the Government. The Brookings Institution argued that government auditing was the basis of settling and adjusting claims and accounts, and that this function had to be performed by an agency of Congress "as a necessary consequence of Congressional responsibility for public funds." Moreover, such a settlement of claims and accounts rightly meant the examination of every financial transaction of administrative officials to make sure that it was conducted under proper legal authority and that the amounts were properly chargeable. Accordingly, the Brookings Institution argued, governmental auditing could not be compared with commercial auditing. The

[13] A. E. Buck, *op. cit.*, pp. 238–244, 285–290.
[14] President's Committee on Administrative Management, *Report* (Washington: Government Printing Office, 1937), p. 15.
[15] *Ibid.*, pp. 24–25.

report concluded that the "protection of the Treasury is a responsibility imposed upon the Congress by the Constitution, and it is only through the continued watchfulness of responsible accounting officers that this responsibility can be properly discharged." The Brookings report did suggest that the designation General Accounting Office be changed to "Office of Audit and Settlement," and that the Comptroller General's title be changed to Auditor General.[16]

The controversy over the proposed reorganization legislation in 1937 and 1938 finally resulted in the elimination of any provision affecting the General Accounting Office when the Reorganization Act of 1939 was passed. The Reorganization Act of 1945 declared the Comptroller General and the General Accounting Office to be "a part of the legislative branch of the government." In the meantime, students of public administration elaborated conflicting points of view in monographic literature.[17]

For some time after the end of McCarl's term of office in 1936, the position of Comptroller General was left vacant. After one abortive effort to fill the post, President Roosevelt in 1940 nominated Lindsay C. Warren, a member of Congress from North Carolina since 1925, chairman of the Committee on Expenditures of Executive Departments, and author of the Reorganization Act of 1939. Although by no means inclined to sacrifice the role developed by McCarl, Warren was not disposed to engage in indiscriminate sniping at administrative agencies. More than this, he endeavored to work more closely with Congress by encouraging inquiries about administrative operations and by providing information to congressional committees. The urgency of war was such, moreover, that the General Accounting Office had no desire to appear in any way as interfering with administrative operations during the first half of the 1940s.[18]

Nonetheless, an interesting episode occurred in 1944. On February 15 of that year, the Office of War Mobilization released a report prepared by Bernard Baruch and John M. Hancock entitled *War and Post-War Adjustment Policy.* In the course of their discussion the two authors recommended that at the conclusion of hostilities there should be a "quick, fair, and final settlement of terminated war contracts through negotiations by the contractors and the procurement agencies." They then specifically

[16] Senate Select Committee to Investigate the Executive Agencies of the Government, *Financial Administration of the Federal Government,* Report no. 5 prepared by the Brookings Institution, 75th Cong., 1st Sess. (1937), pp. 93–102.

[17] See Mansfield, *op. cit.;* and also Daniel T. Selko, *The Federal Financial System* (Washington, D.C.: Brookings Institution, 1940).

[18] Indeed, Public Law 389 of the 77th Congress, approved Dec. 29, 1941, just three weeks after Pearl Harbor, transferred much of the legal liability for proper expenditure of funds from disbursing officers to certifying officers, and then directed the Comptroller General to relieve certifying officers from liability for "illegal" expenditures if the obligation was incurred in good faith and if the United States received value for its payment.

challenged the idea that all agreements on terminated contracts should be subject to disallowance by the Comptroller General. The authors insisted that industry would need working capital immediately in order to shift from wartime to peacetime production. Such working capital should be provided by the government through a speedy payment of amounts owed upon termination of war contracts. If these agreements were subsequently to be disputed by the Comptroller General, he might, the authors contended, "quibble the nation into a panic." They used even a more powerful phrase, warning against the danger of "unemployment by panic." The authors suggested that the Comptroller General have full power to review all settlements after they had been made, and if his office found any evidence of fraud this should be called to the attention of the Justice Department.

These recommendations, coming from two respected figures in the nation's financial world, had great weight. Moreover, their position was endorsed by both the War and Navy Departments. Over the protest of the Comptroller General, Congress provided in the Contract Settlement Act of July 1, 1944, that other provisions of law notwithstanding the functions of the General Accounting Office "shall be defined to determining after final settlement, (1) whether the settlement payments to the war contractors were made in accordance with the settlement, and (2) whether the records transmitted to it or other information warrant a reasonable belief that the settlement was induced by fraud." The Comptroller General was also authorized to examine any records of contracting agencies and to investigate completed settlements of contracting agencies in order to report to Congress whether the procedures were being followed with care, and whether they adequately protected the interest of the government.

The result of this arrangement was to remove the Comptroller General from direct participation in the settlement of terminated contracts. Administrative officers of the War and Navy Departments did not have to consult the General Accounting Office through "pre-audit" about any of their proposed settlement agreements. Nor did they have to worry lest the Comptroller General upon review of each agreement disallow a settlement payment as being illegal. If the Comptroller General disliked any particular agreement, he was free to bring his criticisms to Congress, which might then express disapproval of administrative behavior. Or, the Comptroller General might recommend a prosecution for fraud to the Attorney General, if the facts in any particular case seemed to warrant such action. The Comptroller General was not removed entirely from the process of settling terminated war contracts, but his authority was considerably curtailed. A major administrative effort was thus given special status in so far as the General Accounting Office was concerned.

Still another kind of restriction was placed upon the General Accounting Office when Congress passed the Government Corporation Control Act of December 6, 1945. One of the advantages which government corporations had generally enjoyed was freedom from the authority of the Comptroller General to "settle" their accounts. Indeed, between 1933 and 1940 the Comptroller General and the Tennessee Valley Authority had carried on a running feud about their respective jurisdictions and procedure. The original legislation of 1933 had provided only that the General Accounting Office should audit TVA expenditures. The Comptroller General then desired to carry on this audit in Washington in his accustomed manner by having copies of all financial transactions forwarded to him. The TVA argued that the law contemplated a field audit and refused to transmit records to Washington. Other disagreements involved the disbursement of funds, appropriate accounting procedures, and the application of general restrictive legislation to TVA operations.[19] The Government Corporation Control Act provided that the fiscal transactions of all wholly owned government corporations should be audited by the General Accounting Office. But the act specified that this audit was to be made "in accordance with the principles and procedures applicable to commercial corporate transactions" and was to be conducted at the places where the accounts of the government corporation were normally kept. The General Accounting Office was to report its audit to Congress each year. This time again the authority of the Comptroller General was restricted to reviewing financial transactions and reporting his findings to the legislature for action; he could not take action on his own.

Then in 1946 Congress enacted Public Law 600 of the Seventy-ninth Congress, approved August 2, 1946, which settled many of the conflicts about the interpretation of legal restrictions upon administrative agencies. This law was drafted by the Bureau of the Budget and the Treasury Department in consultation with the General Accounting Office. It covered such matters as the payment of travel expenses, the employment of consultants, the purchase of supplies, the delegation of authority by a department head to subordinates to sign papers on his behalf, and the payment of awards for useful suggestions about how to improve administrative operations.

In December, 1947, the Comptroller General joined with the Secretary of the Treasury and the Director of the Budget to establish a joint accounting program. The purpose of this program was to encourage individual agencies to develop and improve accounting practices to meet their own needs within a common framework of accounting standards and fiscal reporting. What was particularly important about this step was the Comptroller General's recognition that there were other interests besides his own to be accommodated in a government accounting system and his indication of a willingness to cooperate in the promotion of accounting improvements.

[19] Cf. Mansfield, *op. cit.*, pp. 232–244.

It appeared that to some degree the General Accounting Office under the leadership of Comptroller General Warren was seeking to cooperate with administrative agencies and to avoid some of the bitterness which had arisen during the 1930s. The Comptroller General was unwilling to alter his authority in any respect but was willing to exercise that authority with some concern for the needs of administrative agencies. In specific instances Congress also seemed willing to limit the authority of the Comptroller General or to clarify legislative intent when this seemed uncertain.

THE FIRST HOOVER COMMISSION

In 1949 the Hoover Commission on Organization of the Executive Branch of the Government called the government's accounting system "outmoded and cumbersome."[20] It was time, the Commission said, when the system "must be modernized." The Commission recommended that a new position of Accountant General be established under the Secretary of the Treasury with authority to prescribe general accounting procedures subject to the approval of the Comptroller General within the powers already conferred upon him. The Commission then criticized the practice of the GAO in requiring that all expenditure vouchers and supporting data for every financial transaction be submitted to its Washington office for examination and settlement. The Commission recommended that vouchers and supporting papers no longer be sent to Washington and that a spot sampling process be given consideration in place of a full and detailed examination.

This was as far as a majority of the members of the Commission were willing to go. They did not suggest any shift in the name or in the functions of the GAO. They asked only for a change in its operating practice. Even so, this acknowledged some dissatisfaction with the manner in which the office had been operating.

Neither the Congress nor the President took any immediate step to translate these particular recommendations of the Hoover Commission into action. Rather the joint accounting program continued as a means of bringing some improvements in government financial operations without any major alteration in organizational structure.

A major accomplishment of the joint accounting program was the Budget and Accounting Procedures Act of 1950. The first part of this act brought up to date and made more flexible various provisions on budgeting as originally written into the Budget and Accounting Act of 1921. The second part began with a general recital of accounting objectives in the federal government. It also gave legal sanction to the joint

[20] Commission on Organization of the Executive Branch of the Government, *Budgeting and Accounting* (Washington: Government Printing Office, 1949).

accounting program as a continuous endeavor to improve governmental accounting and financial reporting. The power of the Comptroller General to prescribe accounting systems for government agencies was now to be exercised after consultation with the Secretary of the Treasury and the Director of the Budget. The Secretary of the Treasury was to prepare general reports on the financial operations of the government. The existing system of setting up government accounts, of establishing disbursing accounts, and of disbursing funds might be modified by joint agreement of the Secretary of the Treasury and the Comptroller General. The Comptroller General was then authorized to discontinue his elaborate system of financial records maintained in the General Accounting Office. Finally, the act spoke of the financial transactions of government agencies being subject to audit by the Comptroller General in accordance with "generally accepted principles of auditing." Such audit might be conducted in the place or places where the regular accounting records were normally kept.

In the same year the Post Office Department Financial Control Act ended the long practice by which the official accounts of the Post Office Department had been kept by the Auditor of the Post Office in the Treasury Department and after 1921 in the General Accounting Office. In November, 1950, the Postal Accounts Division of the General Accounting Office was abolished and the Post Office Department assumed full responsibility for maintaining its own appropriate financial accounts.

THE SECOND HOOVER COMMISSION

In 1955 the second Hoover Commission reported that "great improvement" had been made during the preceding ten years in governmental budgeting and accounting.[21] The task force of the Commission enumerated some of these accounting improvements and observed that since 1948 the "organization and methods of the GAO have been substantially improved."[22] It declared that antiquated methods had been abandoned or modified. The number of personnel in the General Accounting Office had been reduced. The professional quality of the staff had been improved. The practice of keeping duplicate records of all government expenditure transactions had been discontinued. The General Accounting Office, according to the task force, "now performs modern commercial-type audits at the site of agency operations."

The Hoover Commission recommended this time that the Budget Bureau rather than the Secretary of the Treasury take the leadership in developing further improvements in accounting and reporting by admin-

[21] Commission on Organization of the Executive Branch of the Government, *Budget and Accounting* (Washington: Government Printing Office, 1955).

[22] Commission on Organization of the Executive Branch of the Government, *Task Force Report on Budget and Accounting* (Washington: Government Printing Office, 1955), p. 53.

istrative agencies. It urged, furthermore, that the administrative agencies create the position of comptroller to manage their accounting function. Other recommendations on accounting dealt with more technical matters involving the allotment system for preventing appropriation deficiencies, accrual and cost accounting, property accounting, and disbursement accounting.

In 1954, a year before the end of his term, Comptroller General Warren resigned from office because of physical disability. President Eisenhower nominated Joseph Campbell to succeed Warren. At the time Campbell was a member of the Atomic Energy Commission; previously he had been vice-president and treasurer of Columbia University.

It seems evident that by 1955 many of the objections to the work of the General Accounting Office voiced by the President's Committee on Administrative Management in 1937 had been met. The Comptroller General continued to "settle" accounts, but in practice this now meant more of an audit procedure than had earlier been the case. The Comptroller General had not surrendered his power to suspend or disallow items in the accounts of disbursing and certifying officers. But more and more his point of view was one of endeavoring to prevent fraud or malpractice rather than of imposing his point of view as against an administrative point of view of what was permissible behavior under existing statutes. The size of the office was reduced from 15,000 employees to 6,500. The General Accounting Office, moreover, began to examine general administrative practices rather than detailed financial papers. For example, it criticized questionable practices in charges paid by the Veterans' Administration for educational benefits, policies on the lease and sale of government-owned industrial plants, the operation of concessions at military posts on a rent-free basis, the expense of recreation centers for military personnel, and many other items.

In these instances it was up to the appropriate administrative officers to make changes in the face of these criticisms. Or congressional committees could take up the charges, ask for explanations, and suggest legislative change, if it so desired. Furthermore, the Comptroller General, as a result of his investigations, was asked for more and more assistance by congressional members and committees.

The continued importance of the Comptroller General, however, was illustrated again in the 1955 controversy over section 638 of the Department of Defense Appropriation Act. As we noted in the preceding chapter, President Eisenhower in a special message to the Congress on July 13, 1955, had stated that he intended to regard the section as invalid. Subsequently, in response to an inquiry from an individual member of the Congress, the Comptroller General on August 17, 1955, wrote that as an agent of the legislature it was his duty "to accord full effect to the clear meaning of an enactment by the Congress so long as it remains unchanged by legislative action and unimpaired by judicial determination." The Comptroller General then said that whenever he ascertained that expenditures had been made in contravention of section 638, he would take action to "disallow credit for such expenditures in the accounts of accountable officers, and hold such officials, and their sureties, financially liable for such payments." He added: "Also, we will furnish a full report thereon to the Congress for its consideration." Thus, the Comptroller General—and so the legislature indirectly—had the last word in the controversy over discontinuing certain business enterprises operated by the military departments.

By 1955 the Congress of the United States had acquired a powerful instrument for keeping the financial operations of government under continuing surveillance.

STATE AND LOCAL EXPERIENCE

Most other governmental units have an officer designated as comptroller or auditor. Usually he is directly elected by the voters, sometimes at the same election with a governor or mayor and sometimes with a longer term of office. This comptroller or auditor is then responsible, not to the legislative branch, but directly to the voter. Indeed, certain state constitutions provide for a comptroller or auditor in the same section as that creating the governor or mayor. In other words, it appears in many state and local units of government that the comptroller or auditor shares in the exercise of the executive power.

The authority exercised by this comptroller is that of actual positive financial administration. Even where designated an auditor, the official exercises no audit authority in the sense in which that term is used in common business practice. The governmental comptroller or auditor maintains the official expenditure accounts of the government, enters encumbrances or obligations in these records upon the basis of forms submitted directly by the various administrative agencies, and then writes the checks or otherwise directs the expenditure of public funds upon the basis of vouchers coming from administrative agencies.

In other words, many state and local governments operate upon the principle that there shall be a separate and complete determination of every expenditure from public funds both when payment is directed and when the actual disbursement occurs. This second step operates under the independent determination of a separately elected public official. The purpose of this second determination is to ensure that all expenditures remain within the limits fixed by appropriation laws and that all other legal restrictions upon public expenditure are faithfully and fully observed.

The supervisory power of this separate public official is substantial indeed. In the name of ensuring the legal propriety of every public expenditure, the comptroller or auditor may make himself an extremely important person in the entire administrative process. Much administrative discretion might thus fall under the purview of the comptroller. And in some instances, as in New York City where the framework of local government is unique, the comptroller becomes the principal policy-making official in general matters of financial administration.

In fact, however, few governmental jurisdictions have experienced the conflict which arose in the national government over the powers of the Comptroller General. The reason seems simple. The state auditor or local comptroller is a publicly elected official. He may well have ambitions to hold other elective offices; in recent years in Ohio, for example, one state auditor ran for the position of United States senator and another for the position of governor. The auditor or comptroller serves for a limited period of time and may wish to be reelected. Often—perhaps usually—the governor or mayor and the comptroller or auditor have been elected by the same party at the same time and owe common obligations to the political organization which nominated them. Under all such circumstances it is unlikely that a comptroller or auditor will endeavor to follow any line of action which will incur considerable public displeasure. This does not mean that he will blind himself to illegal expenditure of funds. This is rare. It does mean that he will usually settle any question about the legal justification for particular expenditures in such a way as will appear reasonable to administrative officers. A comptroller or auditor is not in the business of winning enemies and alienating people. When state or local administrative officials tend to make a very broad interpretation of their legal authority, a comptroller or auditor may call them to task. At the same time, he will generally endeavor to accommodate any reasonable administrative point of view.

In some states the auditor has also been given certain direct administrative responsibilities in addition to his authority to review all instructions to pay obligations incurred by administrative agencies and to determine whether actual payment shall be made. He may be given authority to supervise savings banks and trust companies, although this activity would appear to be more closely related to the authority of the superintendent of banks in a state in supervising state banking operations. He is also in some instances authorized to examine the financial transactions of county and local units of government as well as those transactions of state agencies which do not involve the expenditure of appropriated funds. In almost every state the auditor of state or the comptroller of a municipality is an important administrative official exercising substantial authority.

Even more so than in the federal government most state and local governments lack any auditing system in the sense in which that term is used in commonly accepted commercial practice. Rather, states and local governments have a dual system of disbursement in which one administrative office—the one responsible for operations—incurs obligations and then requests disbursement, and a second agency—the auditor or comptroller—actually writes the checks paying the account. The state or local government treasurer is almost completely a banking office, receiving deposits from agencies which collect taxes and fees and paying checks drawn by the auditor or comptroller.

In general, this system works with some degree of satisfaction. Even where it is revealed that an auditor has been guilty of embezzlement or actual thievery, as in Illinois in 1956, there is little disposition to change the system. Indeed in Illinois, the dishonesty uncovered appears to have resulted from the auditor's handling of the direct appropriations for operation of his own office and from his handling of his supervisory authority over state savings banks.

In most state and local governments, it is commonly regarded as desirable to have this dual system of disbursement. If there is no one then to audit the check-writing function of the auditor or comptroller, this is seldom regarded as a fatal defect. There is a disposition among legislators and others to believe that a dual system of disbursement is a necessary safeguard for administrative integrity. There then seems little need for still a third step, an independent examination of this disbursement activity after it has occurred. For the most part the dual system of disbursement works out so that payments to employees and to contractors are seldom delayed unduly.

SUMMARY

Just as it is an essential element of American government that the legislature shall appropriate the public funds to be expended by administrative agencies, so it is a common feature that this administrative expenditure shall be reviewed by some agency created by law or constitution. Administrative agencies are expected to observe faithfully the standards of compensation to personnel, the contracting procedures, travel limitations, and other legal restrictions upon the expenditure of funds. But this is not enough in itself. There must be some practical machinery by which this administrative faithfulness can be ensured.

The result of this expectation in the federal government is the position of the Comptroller General and the General Accounting Office. Administrative agencies incur obligations and the Treasury Department disburses public funds; a few administrative agencies, such as the military departments, also have this authority to disburse. The Comptroller General then settles the accounts of the certifying and disbursing officers. On occasion he has used this authority to substitute his technical judgment about what is a legal expenditure for the judgment of administrative officers. There is no systematic review of this process by the legislature itself unless and until it is called upon to arbitrate a dispute between the Comptroller General and an administrative agency.

In state and local governments there is a dual system of disbursement involving administrative agencies and a separately elected official called an auditor or comptroller. The auditor or comptroller has his duties defined by law. He is generally responsible for maintaining a separate set of administrative accounts and for deciding just what requests for payment to persons and companies by administrative agencies shall be honored. There is not often a separate review of this auditor's judgment or record-keeping except to the extent that the legislature does set up additional machinery such as a legislative committee or a joint legislative-executive board.

All this procedure is quite different from the customary audit of the commercial or business type which involves the examination or review of business financial transactions by a separate firm of certified public accountants. The auditors under this procedure keep no separate or independent administrative accounting records and do not pass upon any administrative judgment before payment is made. Rather, the auditors, retained by the board of directors, examine the accounts kept by administrative officials and determine whether the procedures and practices indicate faithful reporting of results and honesty in the handling of business funds. Any criticisms or suggestions for improvement are then reported to the board of directors or its auditing committee for action as it may see fit.

The principal criticism of government procedure in contrast with commercial procedure is that administrative officials responsible for the conduct of operations are constantly subject to the possibility that their administrative judgment—not their honesty or their accuracy—will be questioned. There is justification for this criticism, although in practice governmental auditors and comptrollers interfere a good deal less than might be supposed.

There is also criticism that in this process of settling accounts or of dual disbursement, the legislature itself obtains very little help in keeping informed about how administrative agencies are operating. Here again there is some justification for the complaint. Legislators, however, have little time or background for engaging in the technical aspects of studying an audit report, if one were available to them. Moreover, appropriation committees rather than auditing committees expect to exercise such supervision over administrative financial transactions as may be necessary.

In any event our governmental practice has devised some system for helping legislatures and for watching over the fiscal regularity of administrative agencies.

Chapter 10

The Legislature as Administrative Overseer

In the process of considering desirable legislation our legislative assemblies serve as a public forum where conflicting points of view are presented. Thus the public interested in legislative matters has an opportunity to be informed about important issues of the day. Incident to this function of debating and legislating is the function of the legislature to investigate. Probably no other phase of the work of the legislative assembly at the national level in our country has received more attention, or created more controversy in recent years, than this.

The argument, as used by the Supreme Court, is that the authority of the legislature to obtain needed information arises from the authority to legislate. The Constitution of the United States says nothing specifically about legislative investigations. The Constitution merely says that all legislative power granted therein shall be vested in a Congress consisting of a Senate and a House of Representatives. The document contains no reference to conducting inquiries, summoning witnesses, requiring the production of papers or other testimony, or punishing for contempt. The Supreme Court has held that these elements of the authority to investigate are implied by the authority to legislate.[1]

Yet in some respects the authority to investigate has become a major part of the work of the legislature. There have been those who have seen in this activity the very essence of legislative endeavor. John Stuart Mill wrote in 1861:[2]

> Instead of the function of governing, for which it is radically unfit, the proper office of a representative assembly is to watch and control the government; to throw the light of publicity on its acts; to compel a full exposition and justification of all of them which any one considers questionable; to censure them if found condemnable; and, if the men who compose the govern-

[1] *McGrain v. Daugherty,* 273 U.S. 135 (1927).
[2] *Essay on Representative Government,* Everyman's Library ed. (London: J. M. Dent & Sons, Ltd., 1924), p. 239.

ment abuse their trust, or fulfill it in a manner which conflicts with the deliberate sense of the nation, to expel them from office, and either expressly or virtually appoint their successors. This is surely ample power and security enough for the liberty of a nation.

Although Mill was thinking in terms of a parliamentary system of government, his words may be applied with few alterations to the functioning of the legislature in our own system. Woodrow Wilson saw the investigative function in this same light when he wrote: "Quite as important as legislation is vigilant oversight of administration."[3] And the legislature itself has come to a full appreciation of this situation. In section 136 of the Legislative Reorganization Act of August 2, 1946, the Congress provided:

> To assist the Congress in appraising the administration of the laws and in developing such amendments or related legislation as it may deem necessary, each standing committee of the Senate and the House of Representatives shall exercise continuous watchfulness of the execution by the Administrative Agencies concerned of any laws, the subject matter of which is within the jurisdiction of such committee; and, for that purpose, shall study all pertinent reports and data submitted to the Congress by the agencies in the executive branch of the government.

Another section of the 1946 statute (section 134) conferred upon each standing committee of the Senate authority to hold hearings, to require by subpoena the attendance of witnesses and the production of papers, to take testimony in the process of conducting investigations into any matter within the jurisdiction of the committee. Under the rules of the House three standing committees enjoy the authority to subpoena witnesses and papers at any time; other committees must obtain specific authorization from the House before they can exercise this power. The 1946 law set forth no limitations in the procedure of conducting legislative investigations.

LEGISLATIVE OVERSIGHT

The Legislative Reorganization Act of 1946 introduced the provisions of section 136 with a heading which read: "Legislative Oversight by Standing Committees." The question naturally arises of what do we mean exactly by the words "legislative oversight" of administrative agencies. What is the nature and scope of this authority in our system of government?

There is no definitive or authoritative answer to this question. Rather, it must be answered in terms of constitutional doctrine and prevailing

[3] *Congressional Government* (New York: The Macmillan Company, 1885), p. 297.

practice. In part a definition of legislative oversight must be provided by exclusion of certain elements which we know are not included within the term. Thus, obviously, the power of legislative oversight of administrative agencies is legislative in character; it does not include the exercise of powers vested in the chief executive by our constitutions. Legislative oversight does not, therefore, include the power to appoint or to dismiss principal administrative officers. It does not include the power to issue orders or instructions to administrative agencies on the conduct of their operations except as such orders or instructions are embodied in statutory enactment. It does not include the power to conduct foreign relations.

In essence, the power of legislative oversight involves simply the authority to require administrative officers to explain their actions. Any administrative officer may be asked to appear before a committee in order to answer questions about acts of commission or omission. The questioning may be as extensive or as restrictive as the committee members are disposed to make it. The inquiry may imply approbation or disapproval; individual committee members, indeed, are likely to disagree among themselves on this point. The role of the legislature is to obtain information, presumably to guide it in the exercise of its legislative power.

To be sure, legislative intent in administrative oversight goes beyond a mere desire to be informed. The power to conduct an inquiry into administrative action usually arises from a number of different motives. For one thing, in a time of crisis or when a new activity of government is begun, legislators reflect a public concern to know what is happening. Anything that happens is news, and legislators are eager to know what is actually going on. Thus, in the opening days of World War II top administrative officials found the requests for appearances before legislative committees so numerous there was scarcely time to perform their regular duties. This legislative interest implied no sense of criticism; it was curiosity mixed with concern for action, any action, at a time of crisis.

Sometimes, legislative investigation arises from charges of administrative malpractice. Such charges may come from citizens who have been aggrieved by administrative action or failure. Such charges may come surreptitiously from an employee inside an agency who believes that he has information or evidence of ethical or legal wrongdoing. Such charges may come from an employee of government who has been dismissed from office. Sometimes a newspaper man or an opposition political figure may hear gossip or rumor about administrative malfeasance. In varied ways legislators may have criticism of administrative agencies brought to their attention. It is then up to the members of the legislature to decide whether they believe the charges are important enough, or emanate from an important enough source, to deserve investigation.

The circumstances which give rise to investigation need not always involve wrongdoing in a criminal or legal sense. Sometimes, the criticism is really a matter of point of view, or of administrative policy. Some administrative officers may have an overly cautious disposition which results in charges of administrative delay and inconvenience. Sometimes administrative officials may have a particular zeal or enthusiasm for their work and ride roughshod over opposition. Their action may be entirely within the letter of the law they administer and yet arouse hostility. Thus, there were legislators during World War II who believed that many persons within the Office of Price Administration were overly zealous in the cause of price control, even though Congress itself had enacted a law in 1942 fixing the general objectives of administrative action.

Legislative oversight necessarily manifests both personal and political considerations. Many individual reputations have been made from the conduct of legislative investigations. To mention only two or three recent illustrations, we may note that Senator Thomas J. Walsh of Montana during the Teapot Dome investigation of the Harding-Coolidge era, Senator Harry S. Truman of Missouri during World War II, and Senator Joseph R. McCarthy of Wisconsin during the Truman and Eisenhower administrations made themselves personages of nationwide reputation. Since such personal attention may be a major factor in election to public office and in the pursuit of a public career, a prominent role in the conduct of a legislative investigation can be of great personal importance to a legislator.

Furthermore, legislative investigations may be motivated by general political considerations. Sometimes, an inquiry serves to express legislative distrust of the chief executive. Under our system of separation of governmental power, legislative-executive rivalry and jealousy are by no means unknown, even when nominally the legislature is led and the executive post is held by men of the same political party. When legislative and executive leadership are held by persons of opposite party affiliation, then there is a special political inducement to legislative investigation. The hope rises that "fishing" expeditions by the legislature may uncover evidence, or the appearance of evidence, which will serve to embarrass the chief executive and enhance the other party's opportunities for success at the next election. Such behavior is regarded in political circles as normal "playing of the game."

Finally, it should be noted that administrative oversight through investigation is exercised by legislative committees, not by a legislative chamber as a whole. Administrative officials are not permitted on the floor of American legislative assemblies; they have no privilege to speak there or to answer questions from the floor. Rather, administrative officials appear only at committee hearings. The result is that a segment of the legislative chamber has the benefit of seeing and hearing an administrative officer and of evaluating his testimony. This may be satisfactory when the committee involved includes legislative leaders, and when its members are representative of prevailing legislative sentiment. When the membership of a committee tends to consist primarily of a chairman and a few members (of regular attendance) with a special point of view, then an administrative officer can expect that point of view to predominate in his questioning. There is both an administrative and a public danger that this special point of view may be confused with the point of view of the legislature as a whole.

What sanction does the legislature possess with which to redress administrative wrongdoing? There are two or three possibilities of action. The legislature may enact a law to meet a situation which demands corrective action. Or the legislature may increase or decrease the appropriation to an administrative agency as a way of expressing its attitude. Or, where top personnel are appointed subject to senatorial approval, then the upper chamber may refuse to approve the appointment of an individual who has angered members (if he comes up for reappointment or appointment to a new position). Or the upper chamber may refuse to approve the appointment of a person who does not promise to take some desired corrective action. These are the formal sanctions of legislative oversight.

There are of course informal sanctions as well. An administrative officer may feel so embarrassed or so harassed by legislative investigation that he will resign from public office. Or the continuance in office of a top administrative officer may prove embarrassing politically to a chief executive and he will request or otherwise encourage that officer to resign. And public disrepute in greater or lesser degree may follow upon the heels of legislative investigation.

In our present context we are concerned only with legislative oversight of administrative agencies. Our interest here is not so broad as the scope of all legislative investigations. Many such inquiries may not be directed at administrative agencies at all, but at the behavior of labor organizations, business corporations, pressure groups, the Communists, and others. We shall center our attention, however, upon legislative activity which has as its purpose to exercise some oversight of administrative agencies.

History. The practice of legislative investigation began in sixteenth-century England. The colonial legislatures in the eighteenth century were accustomed to create committees to inquire into various matters of concern to the citizens of the New World. And in its second term the Congress of the United States asserted its authority to investigate questions of interest to it. The story of congressional investigating committees thus begins early in our political history and has been a continuing phenomenon of government.[4]

During the Civil War Congress established a Joint Committee on the

[4] On the history of investigating committees see Ernest J. Eberling, *Congressional Investigations* (New York: Columbia University Press, 1928); Marshall E. Dimock, *Congressional Investigating Committees* (Baltimore: Johns Hopkins Press, 1929); and Nelson McGeary, *The Developments of Congressional Investigative Power* (New York: Columbia University Press, 1940).

Conduct of the War which consisted of three senators and four representatives. In a very short time this committee seemed bent upon taking over the active direction of the North's war effort. For many years this committee was to represent congressional investigating authority at its most audacious extreme. A distinguished historian of the Lincoln administration has written:[5]

> By the bold ruthlessness of its leaders, by the partisan vote which created it, and by the star-chamber quality of its proceedings, the character of the committee can be gauged. In the name of promoting military efficiency, injecting energy into the service, exposing mistakes, and obtaining information for the President, this impressively busy organization conducted elaborate inquisitions, took generals and war officials away from their proper duties, stirred the country with misplaced publicity, ruined the reputations of able generals while building up their own military pets, worried Lincoln, bandied unproved charges of treason, and created dissension and distrust within the lines. Not a member had had military experience, yet the committee assumed a finality of military judgment commensurate with their marked intolerance toward men of West Point.

In the same vein but in the more colorful words of the poet, Carl Sandburg has written about the committee:[6]

> When in December Congress appointed a Committee on the Conduct of the War, Lincoln saw it as one extreme intended to check another. Its members, chiefly radical antislavery Republicans, were headstrong men of brains, courage, ability, of long training in politics and the antislavery struggle. Nothing less than genius shone and coruscated from some facets of this committee. They were to help Lincoln, and more often interfere with him, for a long time. They sniffed out waste and corruption; they cleared away stenches; they muddled, accused men wrongly, roused fear and suspicion, and left ranklings; they wrangled and bombinated; they played with the glory and despair of democracy.

There have been many other famous congressional investigations, such as the long inquiry into the Ballinger-Pinchot controversy during the administration of William Howard Taft, the inquiry into the Teapot Dome scandal of the 1920s, the inquiry into the munitions industry from 1931 to 1934, and the investigation of relief administration under Franklin D. Roosevelt in 1938–1939. In March, 1941, the Senate created a special committee to investigate the national defense program; throughout World War II this committee, under the leadership of Senator Truman, inquired into such subjects as the renegotiation of war contracts, merchant ship construction, the aircraft industry, rubber and steel capacity, the use of

[5] J. G. Randall, *Lincoln the President*, vol. II (New York: Dodd, Mead & Company, Inc., 1946), pp. 63–64.

[6] *Abraham Lincoln: The War Years*, vol. I (New York: Harcourt, Brace and Company, Inc., 1939), p. 388.

dollar-a-year men in top administrative posts, the handling of surplus property, the development of oil resources in the Yukon, and many other subjects. The Senate committee made no inquiry into the strategy or tactics of the war, but only into its administrative operations.

In the past twenty years perhaps public attention has been focused most often and most conspicuously upon the Communist threat to American political, economic, and social institutions. At various times as many as three different committees have been engaged in seeking out evidence of Communist infiltration into governmental agencies, unions, Hollywood, colleges and universities, and other groups. To a considerable degree so much excitement has been aroused by these investigations that there has been a danger many people might come to believe this to be the only preoccupation of such inquiries.[7]

In any evaluation of congressional investigating committees, the long history of their activities, the variety of inquiries undertaken, the accomplishments realized in revealing administrative ineptitude and even malpractice, the stimulus provided to improved administrative behavior, the opportunities provided for voicing criticism, and the salutary influence of the possibility of such inquiry must be balanced against the exaggerated charges, the undue excitement, and the unfair procedure arising in connection with some particular inquiries. In any event, it must be acknowledged that congressional investigations have long played a major role in American government.

THE CONDUCT OF INVESTIGATIONS

Legislative inquiries into the conduct of administrative agencies may be undertaken by special or standing committees. For many years, especially during the 1920s and 1930s, the prevailing practice was for either the House of Representatives or the Senate to set up a special or select committee whenever the chamber was disposed to make some investigation. There were several disadvantages to this arrangement. A special committee could be created only by majority vote of the chamber which authorized the inquiry. This meant that the need for an investigation had to be approved by a substantial proportion of the membership of the legislative body; it also meant that a good deal of debate often was given to the question whether the inquiry was desirable. The careful control over the legislative calendar exercised by the leaders of the House of Representatives in effect made their agreement indispensable to the authorization of an investigation. As a result, it was the Senate which played the

[7] On this whole subject, see Robert K. Carr, *The House Committee on Un-American Activities* (Ithaca, N.Y.: Cornell University Press, 1952); Alan Barth, *Government by Investigation* (New York: The Viking Press, Inc., 1955); and Walter Gellhorn (ed.), *The States and Subversion* (Ithaca, N.Y.: Cornell University Press, 1952).

major part in authorizing and carrying out special investigations, because the rules of procedure in that chamber were so much more flexible and gave so much more freedom to the individual member. Indeed, there was much criticism of the Senate during the 1920s on the ground that the freedom of its rules led to a good deal of sniping at the administration then in office.[8] Thus in the House of Representatives, a small group of leaders might succeed in preventing a special investigation whenever they were disposed to do so; in the Senate the determination of any small group of members could practically force an investigation by blocking all other legislative activity.

Custom also dictated that when a special committee was authorized the presiding officer of the chamber should appoint as chairman the member who originally introduced the resolution asking for the inquiry. Since chairmen of standing committees were selected on the basis of seniority, the only way for a junior member to become a committee chairman was to introduce a resolution calling for a congressional investigation. This was, moreover, the only way for a minority member of the Senate, for example, to become a committee chairman. And since investigating committees usually gained a good deal of attention for their chairmen, there was some competition and even horse-trading involved in getting an investigation authorized. Not so much the need to check the work of a particular administrative program as the popularity and influence of a particular legislator was at stake in getting a vote on a resolution to authorize a special inquiry.

In any event, the Joint Committee on the Organization of Congress in 1946 threw its weight against the creation of special investigative committees and proposed that henceforth investigations be carried out by the regular standing committees of both houses of Congress. This has been the prevailing practice since that time, although now another concern has been introduced. Since the regular committees are usually fairly large, an investigation is often turned over to a subcommittee. Here again a good deal of influence may be exerted in determining what member of a standing committee shall carry on an investigation. It is, of course, still possible for either house of Congress to authorize a special committee of inquiry whenever it desires to do so, as was done in both the Eighty-second and Eighty-third Congress to inquire into the work of philanthropic foundations.

Another difficulty which has arisen has been that of determining the jurisdiction of standing committees in supervising administrative agencies. In the first place, both the Senate and the House have a full complement of committees with similar assignments. When a need arises for an inquiry into a particular alleged malpractice, it is necessary to negotiate in the

---

[8] For a spirited defense of the Senate rules, see Lindsay Rogers, *The American Senate* (New York: Alfred A. Knopf, Inc., 1926).

first instance some understanding whether the appropriate House committee or Senate committee will undertake the investigation. In the second place, there is some confusion in committee assignments within each legislative chamber. Most committees have certain subject-matter jurisdiction, such as foreign affairs, banking and currency, the armed services, agriculture and forestry, interstate and foreign commerce, post office and civil service, and the judiciary. These assignments do not necessarily or exactly parallel the structure of administrative agencies in the government, and this fact may occasion some difficulty. But more importantly, it is not too easy to draw a sharp line between these subject-matter committees and the committees on appropriations and the committees on government operations.

In each house, the Committee on Appropriations is divided in turn into a number of subcommittees. Nominally, each subcommittee is concerned solely with the request for capital and operating funds presented by administrative agencies. But in the course of inquiring into the need for funds, the whole range of administrative policy and operations may come under scrutiny. Initially termed committees on expenditures in the executive departments, the two committees on government operations were supposed to be the legislative units to receive audit reports from the Comptroller General. In practice, both committees have ranged far beyond this. Indeed, Senator Joseph R. McCarthy of Wisconsin as chairman of the Senate Committee on Government Operations during the Eighty-third Congress (1953–1954) persuaded the committee to create a "permanent subcommittee" on investigation which he then used as a vehicle to further his search for subversive individuals and groups in government.[9] The result of these varied committee assignments is the possibility of a good deal of rivalry in the conduct of investigations, with a consequent harassment of administrative agencies.

In a few instances the Congress has eliminated at least one drawback in committee operations by creating a joint committee to watch over administrative activities. In recent years the best-known and perhaps most active of all such committees has been the Joint Committee on Atomic Energy which was specifically provided for in the Atomic Energy Act of August 1, 1946. Section 15 of that act set up the joint committee composed of nine members of each house and charged it with making "continuous studies of the activities of the Atomic Energy Commission and of problems relating to the development, use, and control of atomic energy."

[9] The extent of the work carried on by the Senate Committee on Government Operations was indicated in its report for 1953–1954. Committee hearings and other consideration were given to eleven executive reorganization plans, five bills on administrative reorganization, five bills on legislative reorganization, the work of the General Services Administration, the disposal of surplus property, competition of government enterprise with private enterprise, and various reports of the Comptroller General. See *Activities of the Senate Committee on Government Operations, 83rd Congress,* Sen. Report no, 4, 84th Cong., 1st Sess, (Jan, 10, 1955).

The act went on to specify that the Commission was to keep the joint committee "fully and currently informed with respect to the Commission's activities." The joint committee was authorized to appoint and compensate expert technicians and consultants as it might deem necessary. This was both a broad statement of authority to exercise legislative oversight of an administrative agency and an arrangement for joint exercise of that oversight.[10]

In a few other instances the Congress has provided for legislative oversight through a joint "board of visitors." Thus, legislation provides for a board of visitors to the United States Military Academy of nineteen members from the appropriations and armed services committees of both houses; the board of visitors to the Naval Academy consists of four senators and five representatives appointed by the presiding officer of each chamber plus the chairman of the armed services committee of each house. This practice has not been extensive, however.

In other but also rare instances the Congress may set up special inquiries to be conducted by a body on which both houses and the chief executive are represented. This was done notably in the instance of the Temporary National Economic Committee which was set up in 1938 to inquire into the laws and administration affecting industrial organization and the restraint of trade; this committee consisted of three senators, three representatives, and six administrative officials. In 1947 and again in 1953 the Congress set up a Commission on Organization of the Executive Branch of the Government with four members appointed by the Speaker of the House, the President of the Senate, and the President of the United States. The Commission on Intergovernmental Relations set up in 1953 had fifteen members appointed by the President, five by the President of the Senate, and five by the Speaker of the House. These joint arrangements for study and investigation involving cooperation of legislature and executive are rare rather than customary, however.

The question of standing committees as against special committees for the conduct of legislative inquiries is in part a matter of legislative leadership and seniority. If a place is made through the regular organization for younger legislative members of talent and vigor to exercise their abilities, the pressure for special committees lessens. If the opposite is the case, then the pressure for special committees may mount. There is no complete answer to the question of which practice is preferable. The standing committee may develop a great deal of knowledge about the work of particular administrative agencies and so have a good sense of the capacity of the existing administrative leadership. These committees may be able quickly and fairly to evaluate any charges brought against an administrative agency. On the other hand, standing committees may become com-

[10] Cf. Herbert S. Marks, "Congress and the Atom," *Stanford Law Review,* vol. 1 (November, 1948), p. 23.

placent or indifferent, or they may have such close personal relationships with the leadership of an administrative agency as to condone certain questionable administrative practices. Special committees have the virtues and the vices of members vitally interested in a particular inquiry but often having a one-sided point of view.

Sometimes, Congress or a state legislature may require that periodic reports be submitted by an administrative agency. This is a means whereby legislative members may keep themselves informed about administrative events, if they will take the trouble to read the report. Since administrators are seldom disposed to report mistakes or failures, this reporting technique is not too satisfactory. Yet congressional committees can make this practice important by holding hearings on a report. This has been the practice, for example, of the Joint Committee on the Economic Report established by the Employment Act of February 20, 1946. The Atomic Energy Act of 1946 required a semiannual report to the Congress from the Atomic Energy Commission. The Joint Committee on Atomic Energy has followed the work of the Commission so closely, however, that it is doubtful if this particular report is of much importance in furthering congressional oversight.

It should be emphasized again that legislative oversight is not necessarily synonymous with legislative investigation. Many standing committees, as just suggested, develop informal and close working relationships with administrative officials. Administrators may voluntarily consult with chairmen of standing committees in order to ascertain their attitude toward particular administrative policies. Furthermore, committee chairmen and members may from time to time visit administrative installations, inspect various administrative practices, interview administrative officers on an informal basis, and otherwise inform themselves about administrative operations. None of this activity is technically labeled "investigation"; all of it is properly regarded as legislative oversight of administration.[11]

PROCEDURE IN INVESTIGATION

The purpose of a legislative inquiry is to obtain information. Its procedure therefore is adapted to this purpose. Information may, of course, be obtained informally, through the request of an individual member of the legislature. A formal investigation entails a more or less well-understood procedure.

In the first place, a formal investigation is conducted by a committee, not by one legislator. The inquiry is conducted in the name of the com-

[11] For an interesting, if dated, account of the work of a single congressional committee, see Albert C. F. Westphal, *The House Committee on Foreign Affairs* (New York: Columbia University Press, 1942). For a more recent analysis, see Ralph K. Huitt, "The Congressional Committee: A Case Study," *American Political Science Review,* vol. 48 (June, 1954), p. 340.

mittee and reflects committee direction and interest. Moreover, both majority and minority party members are represented in the composition of the committee. This presumably provides a variety of points of view, and so ensures an adequate consideration of an issue and the revelation of all relevant facts.

In the second place, a legislative investigation ordinarily obtains information through the same process used by all legislative committees, the open hearing. Individuals are requested to answer questions, and are subject to such detailed questioning as the members of the committee may desire. Much of what may be accomplished, therefore, depends upon whether witnesses before a legislative committee are cooperative and articulate in answering questions and in explaining their point of view. Much also depends upon the skillfulness and fairness of the legislative members in asking questions.

In the third place, it must be understood that the legislative investigation is an investigation, not a trial. There is no defendant in a legislative inquiry, although this fact may sometimes be obscured. Every person appearing before a legislative committee is a witness. There is no plaintiff or prosecuting attorney. An investigation is not an adversary proceeding. It is an inquiry. The result of an investigation is a report to the legislative chamber which the committee serves. An eventual product may be new legislation. But no individual person can be convicted of a crime or sentenced to prison by a legislative committee. There is a possible exception here in the power to punish for contempt, which we shall consider below.

These essential elements of the legislative process of investigation are simple enough. In practice the conduct of legislative investigations raises many actual difficulties of procedure. The result has been a good deal of discussion and criticism about legislative investigations in recent years.[12]

To begin with it must be recognized that most legislative investigations are political in origin and motivation. Committees do not launch a full-scale inquiry unless certain legislative members believe that some administrative wrong has occurred in which there is a major public interest. The goal of an inquiry in reality may not be legislation but ammunition with which to advance the political fortunes of an individual legislator, a group, or a political party. There are accordingly problems in timing legislative inquiries so as to acquire the maximum public attention, in summoning witnesses who will create widespread interest, in giving advance information about prospective testimony, and in commenting about witnesses and testimony after the event. These political aspects are seldom too far removed from the conduct of practically all legislative investigations.

[12] Among these criticisms, see Robert K. Carr, *op. cit.;* Telford Taylor, *Grand Inquest: The Story of Congressional Investigations* (New York: Simon and Schuster, Inc., 1955); and Alan Barth, *op. cit.*

Another set of problems arises in connection with the preparation and staffing for investigations. Legislators have many responsibilities; they are busy persons. Seldom would an individual legislator have the time to prepare the details of an investigation. Accordingly, an investigating committee must depend in large part upon its staff to interview prospective witnesses, to obtain and peruse documentary evidence, and to define issues. Sometimes a committee may obtain the services of a special counsel or investigator to prepare materials for the committee. Sometimes a regular committee may use its usual staff. There is ever the danger under these circumstances that an investigation will take on the personality of the staff rather than of the committee members. Indeed, this has frequently happened in fact and some staff heads of investigating committees have attracted widespread attention and have built political careers upon such experience.

Still other problems arise in the committee handling of witnesses. It must be understood that a person summoned before a legislative investigative committee may incur a great deal of unfavorable public attention and even loss of good reputation. It may well be said that such a fate is deserved in some instances. But the fact that such consequences may result is reason for care in the exercise of legislative authority to investigate. In some instances witnesses may in actuality be treated as if they were accused of some crime and be subjected to considerable abuse by committee members. Since in a committee investigation there is no judge to insist upon decorum, only the sense of fair play of committee members themselves provides any protection to witnesses. Moreover, witnesses have complained on occasion that they were not informed about the nature or details of the evidence which had been collected against them nor given an opportunity to prepare and present a full reply.

Another set of problems has arisen about the whole subject of compulsory production of papers and compulsory testimony. This is an especially troublesome question because of the intricacies of legislative-executive relationships under our Constitution. The power of legislative committees to compel witnesses to produce papers under compulsion of a subpoena has been upheld by the Supreme Court.[13] In turn, the legislature may punish for contempt a person who refuses to answer questions put to him.[14] One basis for refusal is to plead that under the Fifth Amendment the witness need not answer if his response might subject him to criminal trial. If a witness begins to answer questions and then claims immunity, he may still leave himself open to the charge of contempt.[15]

Because of alleged abuses in investigative procedure occurring in recent years, a good deal of attention has given to the possibility of a code

[13] Cf. *McGrain v. Daugherty,* 273 U.S. 135 (1927), and *Jurney v. MacCracken,* 294 U.S. 125 (1935).
[14] Cf. *Sinclair v. United States,* 279 U.S. 263 (1929).
[15] *Rogers v. United States,* 340 U.S. 367 (1952).

of fair procedure for legislative committees. Most of the criticisms have grown from legislative practices in inquiring into the activities and membership of the Communist Party in the United States and into the activities and membership of groups alleged to be sympathetic with the Communist Party. At times these issues have also involved administrative agencies, since part of the effort in congressional inquiries has been to discover evidence of Communist membership and subversion among governmental employees. Not all the criticisms have grown out of inquiries into Communism, however. There have been incidents involving other types of inquiries as well.

The so-called abuses evident in legislative investigations have included individual actions on the part of committee chairmen in the name of the committee and in the absence of a quorum during a hearing, the taking of testimony in executive session by one member of a committee, the collection of defamatory information and its release to the press without affording the individual involved an opportunity to be heard, defamatory comments about witnesses or persons under investigation by a committee member or a member of the staff before the hearing is concluded, permission to witnesses to give defamatory testimony about others under conditions where the witness is immune from prosecution for libel or slander and is not required to provide full evidence for his testimony, the issuance of committee reports containing defamatory accusations against individuals not based upon testimony in a public hearing, the refusal to permit a witness to have advice of legal counsel, the refusal to permit a witness to refuse to answer on the grounds of self-incrimination or of confidential relationship with another person (as in the lawyer-client, priest-penitent, doctor-patient, or husband-wife relationship), the refusal to permit witnesses to read or file a prepared statement, the refusal to permit complete answers to questions, the insistence that a witness testify before radio and television, the refusal to permit a witness to testify in public, the issuance of subpoenas without adequate notice, and the nonavailability of a transcript to the witness. In some instances individual legislative committees have voluntarily adopted codes of procedure intended to meet most of these complaints. There continues to be some interest in the passage of a general code of fair procedure for congressional investigative committees and bills to accomplish this have periodically been introduced over the past ten years.[16]

An incident with which the author is familiar and which occurred after the end of World War II illustrates the need for care in the preparation and publication of reports by congressional investigative committees. The Special Committee Investigating the National Defense Program, set up

[16] For a fair and concise account of this whole subject see Will Maslow, "Fair Procedure in Congressional Investigations: A Proposed Code," *Columbia Law Review*, vol. 54 (June, 1954), p. 839.

in 1941 under the chairmanship of Senator Harry S. Truman and after 1944 chaired by Senator James M. Mead of New York, gave a good deal of critical attention to the Canol project, a War Department project for extracting and refining oil in the Yukon Territory of Canada. These investigations were completed in 1944 with the issuance of a summary report which was quite critical of the project and of the War Department official, General Brehon B. Somervell, who was chiefly responsible for its initiation and prosecution.[17] Subsequently, the Senate special committee on September 3, 1946, issued a report summarizing the work of the committee during the war. Again it referred to the Canol project as a "glaring example of waste." But for the first time, and without any public testimony on the matter, the report now coupled the name of Admiral Ernest J. King, Chief of Naval Operations during World War II, with that of General Somervell, since Admiral King had signed a letter on behalf of the Joint Chiefs of Staff stating the opinion that the project should be continued. The report declared: "This action constitutes a blot upon the record of two otherwise capable officers, which it is the duty of the committee to report and comment on to the end that there shall be in the future no recurrence of a similar type of action."[18]

We may disregard here whether the committee was fair in its assessment of the project's justification in so far as General Somervell was concerned.[19] But to have linked Admiral King to the project and to have criticized him severely on the basis of the copy of a letter in the committee's files was grossly unfair to a distinguished Naval officer and public servant. Adverse publicity was published throughout the country on the basis of this report. Admiral King protested vigorously and was subsequently given an opportunity to testify in public hearing about the matter, explaining that he had signed the letter on behalf of all his colleagues in the Joint Chiefs of Staff and not as an individual.[20] As so often happens in such instances, the explanation did not receive the same public attention as the accusation.

The responsibility for the procedure observed in the conduct of legislative investigations belongs to legislative bodies as a whole, in the first instance, and to their committee members, in the second instance. There are undoubtedly standards of fair play which it is important for the legislature to observe.

[17] *Additional Report of the Special Committee Investigating the National Defense Program,* Sen. Report no. 10, part 14, 78th Cong., 1st Sess. (Jan. 8, 1944).
[18] *Fifth Annual Report of the Special Committee Investigating the National Defense Program,* Sen. Report no. 110, part 7, 79th Cong., 2d Sess., p. 25.
[19] The author would not agree with the committee. Cf. John D. Millett, *The Organization and Role of the Army Service Forces* (Washington: Office of the Chief of Military History, Department of the Army, 1954), pp. 391–394.
[20] *Hearings before the Special Committee Investigating the National Defense Program,* part 39, 79th Cong., 2d Sess., p. 22983.

LIMITATIONS UPON THE POWER TO INVESTIGATE

The authority of a legislature to conduct investigations is not without some limitation. As would be expected under our system of government, the restraints upon this authority are imposed in the first instance by the executive and the judiciary. In the final analysis, the legislature will, of course, observe such restrictions as public opinion may impose.

The judiciary has been cautious in imposing limitations upon legislative inquiry. Yet it is recognized that the authority to conduct investigations, as an implied element of the power to legislate, must be related to the legislative process. In one recent case the Supreme Court reminded the Congress of the United States that an inquiry must be related to the task of legislating; it refused to uphold a contempt citation against a witness who had refused to reveal sources of support for his "propaganda" activities.[21] Members of the legislature have claimed from time to time that it is a proper function of investigation to reveal activities by individuals which would arouse public indignation or scorn, and also to help collect evidence which might be used in criminal prosecution.

In 1955 the Supreme Court again considered the procedure in congressional investigation in a leading case.[22] Speaking for the Court on this occasion, Chief Justice Warren reviewed the nature and scope of the investigative power once more. Although he acknowledged that the power was a broad one, he insisted once again that it was subject to limitation. The power was not to be used to inquire into private affairs "unrelated to a valid legislative purpose." It did not extend to an "area in which Congress is forbidden to legislate." The power was not to be confused with law enforcement. "Still further limitations on the power to investigate are found in the specific individual guarantees of the Bill of Rights, such as the Fifth Amendment's privilege against self-incrimination which is in issue here."

Again in 1957 the Supreme Court refused to uphold the conviction for contempt of a witness who refused to give information about certain persons active in labor union affairs and alleged to be Communists. The court held that a witness did not need to answer questions which were not pertinent to the inquiry of a congressional committee. Again the court declared that compulsory process was to be used only in furtherance of a legislative purpose. Congressional instructions about the purpose of an inquiry must be spelled out "with sufficient particularity."[23]

The courts thus recognize that there are limitations to the legislative power to investigate. Moreover, the courts will undertake on appropriate occasion to enforce these limitations. But judicial limitations in themselves are not the only ones the legislature can or must observe.

[21] *United States v. Rumely,* 345 U.S. 41 (1953).
[22] *Quinn v. United States,* 349 U.S. 155 (1955).
[23] *Watkins v. United States,* 354 U.S. 929 (1957).

The executive usually has been insistent that legislative authority to investigate shall not encroach upon the executive power. The possibility of conflict arises primarily in connection with two kinds of questions. It is generally recognized today that department heads and other major administrative officials may refuse to answer questions which would require the revelation of matters discussed with the chief executive. Moreover, the White House staff itself has usually been recognized as immune from investigation about the handling of public business on behalf of the President. Of course, a chief executive may voluntarily instruct a department head to report a discussion with him, or a chief executive may ask one of his staff assistants to present his point of view on some matter to a legislative committee. Nonetheless, it is commonly recognized that the legislature may not use its investigative power to inquire into the personal acts of the executive. A contrary position could well be destructive of fundamental constitutional principle.

A second issue has arisen in connection with legislative requests for administrative officers, primarily department heads, to produce papers involving proposals submitted for executive consideration or papers containing instructions received from the chief executive. Beyond this, the chief executive may declare that certain papers are confidential in nature and that their public disclosure would be contrary to the public interest. Here again the executive's determination has stood, even though individual legislators have from time to time objected.

Many Presidents have refused to turn over certain papers to the Congress. In 1796, the House of Representatives requested President Washington to lay before it various papers relating to the negotiation of the Jay Treaty with Great Britain. Washington refused. In 1807, President Jefferson was asked to turn over to a congressional committee such papers as he might have relating to the Burr conspiracy. Jefferson refused. In 1837, the House of Representatives set up a committee "to examine into the condition of the executive departments." President Jackson, just two months away from turning his office over to his successor, Martin Van Buren, refused to provide any of the papers requested by the committee. Earlier, in 1833, Jackson had refused to turn over to the Senate a copy of a paper he was supposed to have read to the Cabinet relating to the removal of public deposits from the Bank of the United States. In 1843, President Tyler refused to turn over a report made to him by an Army officer on the personalities of government Indian agents. In 1860, President Buchanan sent a message to the House of Representatives in which he protested a resolution passed to investigate attempts by the executive to influence the passage of legislation. In 1861, President Lincoln refused to turn over to the Congress any of the dispatches from Major Anderson to the War Department concerning the defense of Fort Sumter. In 1876, President Grant refused to provide any information about his conduct of executive duties when away from Washington. In 1877, President Hayes directed the Secretary of the Treasury to refuse to answer any questions or to produce any papers concerning the President's reasons for nominating Theodore Roosevelt to be Collector of Customs at the Port of New York. In 1909, President Theodore Roosevelt directed the Attorney General to refuse to answer any questions about the decision not to prosecute the United States Steel Corporation for violation of the antitrust laws. In 1930, President Hoover refused to turn over to the Senate Committee on Foreign Affairs any of the papers concerning negotiation of the London Naval Treaty. President Franklin D. Roosevelt in 1941 instructed the director of the Federal Bureau of Investigation not to give any files on investigations of alleged Communists and subversives to the House Committee on Un-American Activities, and on at least four other occasions issued similar instructions on matters inquired into by a congressional committee. Presidents Truman and Eisenhower took similar action on various occasions.

This brief review by no means exhausts the list of conflicts which have occurred between legislature and executive on the matter of providing information during various inquiries. The record indicates the following general propositions. First, the President's own conduct cannot be called to account through legislative investigation. Secondly, the President may refuse to transmit any papers in his own possession about matters coming to his attention. Thirdly, the President may direct department heads to withhold testimony or to refuse access to papers when in his discretion it is in the public interest to refuse such information. In general, legislative committees have avoided the issuance of subpoenas to department heads.

In 1924, when President Coolidge was confronted with a Senate inquiry into the conduct of Harry M. Daugherty as Attorney General, Daugherty requested the President's advice about his testimony. In response the President mentioned the long-established precedent that departmental files should not be opened to investigating committees when some particular disclosure would not be in the general interest. He mentioned, however, that this inquiry was being made into Daugherty's personal conduct as Attorney General. President Coolidge wrote: "I do not see how you can be acting for yourself in your own defense in this matter and at the same time and on the same question acting as my adviser as Attorney General." The President solved the dilemma by dismissing Daugherty as Attorney General, and the Senate investigation proceeded.[24]

It is clear that there are limits to the legislative power to investigate, limits imposed by concepts of fair play and by constitutional doctrine. In

---

[24] The foregoing historical information has been taken from a paper entitled "The Power of Congress to Require Testimony, Papers, and Documents from the President and the Executive Branch," inserted in the *Congressional Record* on July 26, 1955, by Senator William F. Knowland of California.

turn, these limits must be enforced by public understanding of the issues involved.

SUMMARY

No doubt legislative methods of administrative oversight are often of the blunderbuss variety. From personal inclination or political choice legislators may not behave in the careful manner with which so powerful a weapon as the investigative inquiry should be handled. It may well be, as sometimes asserted, that useful public careers have been ended and individual lives damaged needlessly and even heartlessly. Power is ever subject to abuse.

At the same time it must be acknowledged that legislative investigation is an important instrument for keeping administrative agencies in our country under surveillance and for ensuring responsible performance. The real accomplishments of legislative oversight are not to be measured in terms of scoundrels unmasked in the public service, but rather in terms of the great accomplishments of public endeavor made possible because there were ways and means of protecting the honest and devoted and of revealing the faithless public servant.

If we look back over the history of American government there are numerous instances in which legislative investigations have revealed malfeasance or other reprehensible practice in the public service. There were the Whisky Ring of the Grant administration, the "star-route" frauds brought to light during the Garfield administration, the Ballinger-Pinchot controversy of the Taft administration, the Teapot Dome scandal of the Harding administration, the WPA investigation of 1939, the Pearl Harbor inquiry of 1945–1946, the revelation of a Communist conspiracy within the public service—these and many other investigations stand to the enduring credit of legislative oversight of administrative activities.

The practice of legislative inquiry is now accepted. It may be argued that the Royal Commission device in Great Britain has accomplished the same end and on the whole done the task better.[25] But an arrangement effective in a parliamentary system of government is not necessarily the most appropriate under our own governmental structure. Although the legislative inquiry has been abused, it has nonetheless demonstrated its importance and vitality.

Administrative officials have come to realize that their actions may pass in review before legislative scrutiny at any time. Administrators have learned that in practice they stand to gain little by a reluctance to disclose information to legislative committees. Such reluctance gives rise to a

[25] Lindsay Rogers, "Congressional Investigations: The Problem and Its Solution," *University of Chicago Law Review,* vol. 18 (Spring, 1951), p. 464; and Herman Finer, "Congressional Investigations: The British System," *Ibid.,* p. 521.

natural suspicion that something must be wrong. Instead, administrators have consulted legislative members frequently about pending policies or program details, and by careful handling of all phases of administrative operation, have endeavored to avoid charges of favoritism or of actual malpractice.

In fact, in some instances administrators have desired to go further in consulting with legislative committees than the committees themselves were prepared to go. The very nature of the legislative process is such that legislators tend to want information only about the controversial or about the irregular. Legislators are often disposed to leave administrators alone when operations are proceeding along accustomed lines and when general accomplishments are more or less self-evident. Legislators are seldom much interested in the administrator or the administrative agency that is performing satisfactorily. It is the breakdown of administrative endeavor, the unusual problem, the disgruntled client, the exceptional "rotten apple" which attract legislative attention. This tendency inevitably places the legislative investigation in a somewhat peculiar position. It appears to be hypercritical of the public service.

Yet over a long period of American history legislative oversight has proved its worth as a device for helping ensure responsible and honest operation of the public service.

Chapter 11

The Legislature and Administrative Personnel

The desire on the part of the founders of the American constitutional system to limit the exercise of executive power resulted in the provision for a legislative check upon the appointment of personnel. Under the federal Constitution, the President "shall nominate, and by and with the advice and consent of the Senate, shall appoint ambassadors, other public ministers and consuls, judges of the Supreme Court, and all other officers of the United States, whose appointments are not herein otherwise provided for, and which shall be established by law." The federal Constitution continues by specifying that the Congress "may by law vest the appointment of such inferior officers, as they think proper, in the President alone, in the courts of law, or in the heads of departments."

State constitutions have often contained a similar provision. To some extent the importance of senatorial confirmation of executive appointments has been reduced through direct election of major administrative officers. In but a handful of states is the chief executive the only elected officer with executive or administrative responsibilities. But as the number of separately elected officers has diminished, legislative approval of executive appointments has tended to increase. Only a few state constitutions have been willing to vest the appointment power in the hands of the chief executive free from any legislative restriction.

Two special features should be noted in the system of legislative participation in the appointment process. First, usually this power of participation as prescribed by our constitutions extends only to one house of the legislature, the senate. Thus it is not the entire legislative body which must approve executive appointments. Secondly, the extent of senate participation in executive appointments depends upon law. The federal Constitution, for example, specifies only that the Senate shall advise and consent to the appointment of ambassadors, ministers, consuls, and judges of the Supreme Court. Otherwise, the Senate shall consent to the appointment of such other officers of the United States as may be set up by law and are not regarded as "inferior officers." Thus, the extent of Senate participation in appointments depends upon law passed by both chambers of the legislature.

The theory behind this participation of a legislative chamber in executive appointments was a simple one. The framers of our constitutional system were fearful of too much authority vested in the chief executive. Accustomed to executive power as exercised by royal governors in the colonies, they could not too well envisage the proper performance of a popularly elected chief executive. Moreover, under colonial practice a governor's council, which was sometimes an upper chamber of the legislature, had been consulted if not officially polled in matters of administrative appointments. It seemed natural, therefore, to formalize and continue the practice of a legislative check upon appointments by the chief executive.

As the practice of legislative, or rather of senatorial, approval of executive appointments has developed over the years, two major problems have been encountered. One of these has been the extent to which administrative officials of the state should be subject to senatorial approval. The other has been the exact nature of this senatorial participation. These problems have been troublesome and have led to a divergence of point of view among citizens and among governmental officials.

THE EXTENT OF SENATORIAL CONFIRMATION

The problem of the extent of the requirement of senatorial approval of appointments can best be illustrated in the case of the federal government. In the first place, the heads of all departments, commissions, and other agencies are appointed by the Chief Executive, along with deputy heads and assistant heads. The total number of such officials is somewhat over 350. In the second place, all ambassadors and ministers to foreign countries are appointed subject to senatorial confirmation. Together with certain other high diplomatic positions, such as the United States chief representative to the United Nations, the number involved here would be less than 100. In the third place, all members of the judiciary are appointed with senatorial approval; the number of federal judges in district and circuit courts and the Supreme Court is a little over 300. These would appear to be the principal officials of the United States government to which the language of the Constitution referred.

In addition, there are several important groups of officials all of whom are appointed by the President by and with the advice and consent of the Senate. All commissioned officers of the Army, Navy, Air Force, Coast Guard, Coast and Geodetic Survey, and the Public Health Service are appointed and promoted with senatorial confirmation. The number here involved as of 1955 would be over 300,000. All members of the Foreign Service in each rank must be appointed by the President with senatorial confirmation. There are about 1,300 such positions. The same is true of collectors of customs, United States district attorneys, United States marshals, and certain other posts, numbering about 200 in all. Finally, there are all first-, second-, and third-class postmasters throughout the United States appointed by the President with senatorial confirmation. The number of such positions is over 23,000.

In a single session of Congress, the first session of the Eighty-fifth Congress which met from January 3 through August 30, 1957, the President submitted 45,114 nominations to the Senate for confirmation. These were divided as follows:

Army	7,373
Navy	16,822
Air Force	12,827
Marine Corps	3,455
Postmasters	1,679
All other	2,958
	45,114

These figures would be greater in a year when a new President was inaugurated, but they may be taken as indicative of the volume of appointments requiring at least routine attention in any one given year. It will be noted that all but some 4,500 such appointments in 1957 involved officers of the Armed Forces. The fact that these forces are fairly sizable is one explanation why the number of such appointments is so large. Of the 45,114 nominations, 33 were later withdrawn, and 44,620 were confirmed.

As of 1954 about 85 per cent of all the some 2.3 million civilian employees of the federal government were under the classified civil service.[1] When it is recalled that a number of other employees, although not under the regular civil service, are nonetheless subject to their own merit system —such as the Foreign Service, the Tennessee Valley Authority, the Federal Bureau of Investigation, and the Department of Medicine and Surgery of the Veterans' Administration—the actual proportion of all civilian employees not subject to appointment on the basis of merit would be closer to 10 than to 15 per cent. And of those positions not under civil service subject to presidential appointment with senatorial approval, the proportion to the total civilian service would be less than 2 per cent today.

To be sure, the full extent of legislative participation in administrative appointments is not to be measured by the formalities of the appointment process. Depending upon various political factors—such as whether the

[1] See Commission on Organization of the Executive Branch of the Government, *Task Force Report on Personnel and Civil Service* (Washington: Government Printing Office, 1955), p. 151.

Chief Executive and members of Congress belong to the same party, whether the Chief Executive and his fellow party members in Congress have harmonious personal relations, and whether the members of Congress and the state party organization of their home state are on friendly terms—both representatives and senators may be consulted about many appointments which are formally subject to the full authority of the Chief Executive or the department head. The reason for this situation is obvious and will be mentioned again later. Because administrative action depends in so many ways upon legislative cooperation, chief executives and department heads are disposed to cement friendly relationships with the legislature through mutually agreeable appointments whenever they can make them.

Actually, then, the matter of legislative participation in administrative appointments must be understood from two points of view. One involves the formal arrangements whereby the upper chamber of the legislature is given an official voice in the approval of appointments to administrative positions. The other is the extent to which legislative members do in fact, through informal relationships, influence the appointment of personnel in administrative positions. Although there is no way numerically to measure the volume of this second type of legislative participation, it is safe to assume that it is by all odds the more important. Even in those instances where promotions to important administrative positions are made under civil service regulations, the attitude of influential legislators toward a particular individual can be the determining factor in the final selection. There is nothing necessarily undesirable about this situation. It is merely one of the ingredients of administrative life in the public service.

For the moment, however, our concern is with the extent of the formal arrangement for legislative participation in the appointment of administrative personnel. This has occasioned a good deal of comment from time to time during the history of our republic. The formal requirement for senatorial confirmation of appointments is at least a major foundation for ensuring that the appointing power shall be shared by Chief Executive and legislature.

For example, when the Emergency Relief Appropriation Act was first passed in 1935 it contained a provision that any person in any administrative organization set up under the law receiving salary compensation of $5,000 or more and located in Washington should be appointed by the President by and with the advice and consent of the Senate; any state or regional administrator receiving $5,000 a year or more was to be similarly appointed.[2] In actual practice the President interpreted the language of the law to apply only to the administrator of the Works Progress Ad-

_____

[2] Cf. Arthur W. Macmahon, John D. Millett, and Gladys Ogden, *The Administration of Federal Work Relief* (Chicago: Public Administration Service, 1941), pp. 269ff.

ministration and not to other key personnel located in the Washington headquarters. In this way the full impact of the law was avoided. But at least the idea then became current that the Congress should fix the extent of the requirement of presidential appointment and senatorial confirmation in terms of a particular level of salary compensation.

This idea was further considered at the time when administrative re-organization legislation was pending in 1937 to 1939. The proposition seemed to gain some adherents that all "policy-determining positions" should be subject to presidential appointment and senatorial confirmation. In the early months of defense and war administration between 1940 and 1943, various pieces of legislation contained a proviso that administrators receiving $4,500 or $5,000 a year should be appointed by the President by and with the advice and consent of the Senate. Then in 1943 Senator Kenneth McKellar of Tennessee persuaded the Senate to pass a bill declaring that any person in an administrative position receiving compensation in excess of $4,500 should be "deemed to be an officer of the United States, to be appointed by the President, by and with the advice and consent of the Senate, and shall not be deemed to be an inferior officer who may be appointed by the President alone or by the head of a department." The House of Representatives refused to consent to this measure and the bill never became law.[3]

Several different reasons were advanced why some such program of increased senatorial participation was desirable. In the Depression years some Senators asserted that this was the only way they could prevent administrative agencies from paying too many persons high salaries. Both during the Depression years of the 1930s and the war years of the 1940s, many new "emergency" agencies had to be created, all of which were free from civil service restrictions in appointing personnel. Senators therefore sought a check upon the bureaucracy which might otherwise be brought too completely, they feared, under executive domination. No doubt the growth of administrative offices "in the field"—that is, outside Washington —also persuaded some senators that they should take steps to ensure that the heads of field offices in their own home states would be politically friendly.

In the decade after the end of World War II, with the federal bureaucracy still large but nonetheless smaller than in the war years, with federal compensation tending to lag behind rising price levels, and with conditions of maximum employment prevailing in the nation's economy, the demands for an extension of senatorial participation in administrative appointments declined. Until circumstances should change, any widespread increase in the number of administrative positions subject to senatorial confirmation appeared unlikely.

[3] Arthur W. Macmahon, "Senatorial Confirmation," *Public Administration Review*, vol. 3 (Autumn, 1943), p. 281.

In the meantime various criticisms have been voiced about the extent of the already existing practice of formal legislative participation in appointments. In 1937 the President's Committee on Administrative Management declared that "direct appointments by the President should be reduced to a very small number of only the highest positions." The Committee went on to add that "the continued appointment by the President of field officials, such as postmasters, United States Marshals, collectors of internal revenue, and collectors of customs is not only antiquated, but prejudicial to good administration."[4] In 1955 the second Hoover Commission also made several recommendations which would have reduced the number of positions subject to senatorial confirmation. First, the Commission declared: "Political appointees should not be placed in the line of command below career administrators." It added: "Obviously, such appointments undermine the line of command and make the position of career administrator untenable."[5] Subsequently, the Commission specifically recommended that United States marshals and field positions of the Bureau of Customs and the mints be brought under civil service.[6] As we have mentioned earlier, President Truman by reorganization plan in 1952 succeeded in bringing collectors of internal revenue under civil service appointment. Similar proposals affecting postmasters, customs officials, and United States marshals were defeated in the Senate.

In dissenting from the recommendation about United States marshals and other officials put forth by the second Hoover Commission, Clarence J. Brown, a representative from Ohio and member of the Commission asserted: "I believe that both of our major political parties can continue to supply capable people to carry on the responsibilities of these positions in a satisfactory manner."[7] This expression of opinion was more than that of a single member of Congress. No doubt it reflected the prevailing attitude among members of the legislature.

From the point of view of the head of an administrative agency the practice of presidential appointment and senatorial confirmation for subordinate officials, especially those in the field, has a number of disadvantages. It means that appointments can only be made after careful consultation with the Senator or Senators from the state of residence of the individual involved. Sometimes this consultation is embarrassing in terms of relations with representatives and state political leaders. Such consultation may often entail considerable delay in finding a person agreeable to all concerned. Furthermore, the individual selected may feel a greater sense of obligation to his legislative sponsor than to his administrative

---

[4] President's Committee on Administrative Management, *Report of the President's Committee* (Washington: Government Printing Office, 1937), p. 9.

[5] Commission on Organization of the Executive Branch of the Government, *Personnel and Civil Service* (Washington: Government Printing Office, 1955), pp. 29–30.

[6] *Ibid.,* p. 82.   [7] *Ibid.,* pp. 90–91.

superior. This fact may be disruptive of internal administrative control, and even damage morale and performance because of administrative reluctance to discipline such an employee. Moreover, when the appointee proves incompetent or unsuitable for his job, then removal or transfer may have to be negotiated in the same way as the original appointment.

From the point of view of the Senator, confirmation has much to be said for it. Politically, a Senator naturally desires to reward those who have been helpful in his own election contests. Without such opportunities it might be difficult to build political organization, or at least political organization might have to find a different basis. In addition, legislators have a particular interest in their constituents and are concerned to ensure that administrative work is carried on in such a way as to give prompt and courteous service. Many legislators have not been convinced that appointment and other procedures devised within administrative agencies do produce satisfactory officials, especially in local offices. Legislative participation may help guarantee careful selection of major administrative officials. Furthermore, political reputations and reelection are often achieved through doing favors for constituents. Even if an individual appointed to administrative office has not been an active political worker, it is often useful to have such a person feel some sense of obligation for his position.

It may be important to note again that one obstacle in the extension of the practice of senatorial confirmation has been the jealousy of the lower house of the legislature. Representatives often feel that the requirement of presidential appointment by and with the advice and consent of the Senate gives the upper chamber too great an advantage. Indeed, the apprehension of representatives has resulted in a general practice whereby senators recognize that representatives shall have the primary role in clearing persons for appointment as postmaster. If it were not for this arrangement, the system of appointing postmasters might have been altered some time ago. Nonetheless, representatives have often refused to consent to legislation which would extend the practice of senatorial confirmation.

SENATORIAL COURTESY

The federal Constitution specifies that the President shall nominate, and by and with the advice and consent of the Senate, shall appoint judges, ambassadors and ministers, and the principal administrative officers of the government. This language suggests that the initiative in the selection of personnel was to be left to the Chief Executive. The consent of the Senate, by implication certainly, was to be expressed by majority vote of the membership present and voting in the upper chamber. Constitutional prescription would appear to have set forth one practice. Constitutional

custom and usage, however, have decreed a different practice. The key
to the actual system of presidential appointment is to be found in the
doctrine of senatorial courtesy.[8]

The constitutional custom of senatorial courtesy has several elements.
It means first that the Chief Executive shall consult the Senator or Senators from the state of a prospective appointee before his name is submitted
to the Senate for confirmation. Usually the purpose of this consultation
is to determine whether the nominee is agreeable to the Senator or Senators of the state concerned. This obligation to consult, of course, extends
only to Senators of the same political party as that of the Chief Executive.
The obligation to consult further suggests that a President will refrain
from submitting a name if the individual is not satisfactory to the Senator
or Senators concerned. If a Chief Executive nonetheless does nominate for
office a person who is not agreeable to a Senator, then the Senator may
inform his colleagues that he finds the nominee "personally obnoxious."
When this is stated, the courtesy of the Senate requires that the other Senators of that party—and indeed most of the entire membership—shall vote
to refrain from giving their advice and consent to the proposed appointment. The doctrine of senatorial courtesy, in other words, means that the
objection of one or two Senators can and does in effect prevent the appointment of an individual to public office. Moreover, the doctrine not
only ensures consultation by a Chief Executive; it may in practice shift
much of the initiative in determining who is a desirable appointee from
the Chief Executive to the legislature.

In practice, the standards which have been applied to senatorial confirmation have varied greatly. There is a general tradition that the Chief
Executive shall have great latitude in the selection of individuals to serve
as heads of executive departments and even as under secretaries and assistant secretaries. Unless the membership of the Senate as a whole feels
that a proposed Cabinet officer is definitely not qualified for public office,
presidential selections for these positions will receive the advice and consent of the Senate. In the past one hundred years only two persons nominated for a Cabinet post have been rejected by the Senate, one named
by President Andrew Johnson in 1867 and another named by President
Calvin Coolidge in 1925. There have been only seven such rejections in
the entire history of the United States.

In so far as ambassadors and ministers are concerned, here again the
initiative is left in practice to the President. The Senate ordinarily confirms
such appointments unless some special objection about fitness is raised.
In recent years there have been a few controversies in the Senate over
diplomatic appointments. The selection by President Franklin Roosevelt
of Edward J. Flynn, a prominent New York political leader, to be Min-

[8] Cf. Joseph P. Harris, *The Advice and Consent of the Senate* (Berkeley, Calif.:
University of California Press, 1953).

ister to Australia was withdrawn in the face of Senate hostility. One diplomatic nomination by President Truman, that of Philip Jessup to serve on a United Nations delegation, was rejected by the Senate because Dr. Jessup had been associated with the Institute of Pacific Relations, which had been declared by a Senate committee to be Communist dominated. The nomination by President Truman of Chester Bowles to serve as Ambassador to India was greeted with some opposition, but the selection was confirmed. President Eisenhower had similar difficulties with three of his selections, those of James Conant as Ambassador to Germany, Charles Bohlen as Ambassador to Russia, and of Scott MacLeod as Ambassador to Ireland; all were confirmed when brought to a vote in the Senate.

The selection of individuals to serve as heads of separate agencies and as members of regulatory commissions is also reviewed with a good deal of care by the Senate. "One of the significant features of appointments to regulatory commissions is the influence exerted by organized interest groups."[9] If a person has a reputation for taking any strong stand on regulatory matters, he is certain to be opposed for confirmation and even may be rejected. This same situation applies to persons who are nominated for reappointment to such agencies.

When it comes to the appointment of federal district and circuit court judges, the initiative has fallen almost entirely to members of the Senate. The President ordinarily plays only a slight role in the selection of judges, and the Justice Department for the most part endeavors only to make sure that individuals suggested by members of the Senate are generally qualified. On the other hand, the President is personally involved in the selection of justices of the Supreme Court. Even so, of 116 such nominations, 21 have failed to obtain the approval of the Senate.

The role of the Senate in confirming appointments in the Armed Forces, in other commissioned services, and in the Foreign Service is almost entirely routine. Such nominations are usually reported to the floor of the Senate by the chairman of the appropriate committee automatically unless some Senator has had reason to voice objection to an individual on the list. Furthermore, since representatives rather than Senators are usually consulted in the appointment of postmasters, Senate consideration of these nominations tends to be perfunctory.

When it comes to positions such as those of district attorney, United States marshal, and collectors of customs, the selection is ordinarily made by the Senator or Senators of the same political party as the President. And the courtesy of the Senate demands that these selections shall be approved by their fellow Senators.

The variety of situations which have arisen from the requirement of senatorial confirmation for certain appointments is evident from this brief review. Practically everyone is agreed that presidential appointment of

[9] *Ibid.*, p. 381.

department and agency heads and their principal associates and of members of commissions should be subject to legislative approval. The same would be true of ambassadors and judges. As we have indicated, there is a good deal of doubt whether the patronage considerations which have influenced the selection of many administrative posts such as those of district attorneys and local postmasters have in reality been helpful. Party friction and administrative disunity have often been the principal consequences. Joseph P. Harris has concluded: "On the whole, the requirement of senatorial confirmation has not elevated the standards of appointment to federal offices."[10]

As we have remarked earlier, no one would question the desirability of senatorial confirmation for presidential selection of department and agency heads, their principal associates, judges, members of commissions, and heads of diplomatic missions. In these instances the Senate has tended to apply fairly high standards of review, including the character and reputation of the nominee, his qualifications and experience, his general philosophy toward government, and his stand on particular public issues. To be sure, there have been abuses in the practice, when senatorial hearings on the qualifications and reputation of a nominee have not been carefully handled and opportunity has been afforded for airing unsubstantiated or even purely personal grievances. This occurred, for example, when Earl Warren was nominated to be Chief Justice of the United States in 1954. Moreover, the Senate standards of review appear often to subject a person with extensive experience in a field to a disadvantage because his position is well known and because he will have aroused opposition. An individual with little experience in a particular field of government activity and with no pronounced point of view on government policy is more readily confirmed. But these incidental deficiencies are relatively unimportant in terms of the larger good which senatorial confirmation tends to serve: a check upon the discretion of the Chief Executive and a public guarantee of fitness for office.

It is probably desirable to have high-ranking officers of the Armed Forces subject to senatorial confirmation—those of general and flag rank perhaps. These officers are almost always career persons who have risen through the various ranks of commissioned service and who are selected for promotion to top rank by boards of their fellow officers. In such a personnel system, senatorial confirmation may serve the useful purpose of providing some check upon the operations of what is otherwise a "closed" group.

Yet it is generally agreed by outside observers that the requirement of presidential appointment and senatorial confirmation ought not to be extended beyond the broad limits just outlined. The consequence of such extension is to transfer the initiative in selection of personnel from ad-

[10] *Ibid.,* p. 392.

ministrative to legislative hands, which obviously was not the intention of the Constitution. The resulting administrative disunity can be costly in the performance of necessary government services.

THE POLITICAL ASPECTS OF LEGISLATIVE PARTICIPATION

We have already suggested that there are political overtones in the formal arrangement whereby the legislature participates in the appointment of administrative personnel. No doubt the Founding Fathers conceived of the formal arrangement whereby the Senate would confirm certain nominations to administrative posts by the Chief Executive as a kind of check upon executive discretion. Political practice, however, produced legislative participation in administrative appointments as a necessary kind of legislative-executive collaboration in the common cause of government.

It would be an oversimplification of political history to ascribe the development of the spoils system to the peculiarities of the American structure of government. There were other factors at work. Yet it seems probable that the separation of governmental power into legislative and executive components had much to do with the development of legislative interest in administrative appointments. The executive needed leverage with which to encourage legislators to follow his leadership in the formulation of national policy. And political history suggests that Chief Executives, such as Jefferson, Jackson, Lincoln, Theodore Roosevelt, Wilson, and Franklin Roosevelt, with positive ideas about desirable governmental programs made considerable use of patronage as a means of winning legislative support. Other executives have found the appointing power equally helpful on occasion.

In turn, legislators who have taken an active part in the formulation or enactment of important programs of governmental action have a natural interest in the selection of individuals to administer those programs. Since it is the legislature which must fix program goals and from time to time determine program magnitude, members may well desire administrators sympathetic with their action. Moreover, as we have suggested, administrative appointments may be an important element in building political support or in rewarding political service on the part of legislators.

Our major interest, here, is not in the intricacies of legislative-executive relations under our system of government. We are concerned rather with the ways and means by which the legislative branch of government helps to ensure responsible behavior by administrative agencies. The question of importance to us, therefore, is whether legislative participation in administrative appointments does in fact encourage political responsibility on the part of administrators.

No reliable information is available on this subject. Many administrators have been restive when political influences have been brought to bear upon the internal, subordinate appointment of personnel. They have felt that such influence tended to undermine top administrative authority and to complicate personnel relations within an agency. There is a good deal of experience and testimony which would substantiate the prevalence of this attitude among top administrative officials of government. But few if any administrators or students have asked the other question: What kind of arrangement in the selection and retention of administrative personnel does more to advance an awareness of the political responsibility which top administrators must assume?

If political responsibility be thought of only in terms of executive responsibility, then legislative participation in administrative appointments can be a disruptive factor. It is the thesis of this volume that under the American system of government, administrative responsibility cannot be conceived of exclusively in terms of responsibility to the executive. Rather, administrative responsibility must be thought of as embracing elements of responsibility to all three branches of government, legislative, executive, and judicial. If this thesis be accepted, then the question at issue is whether legislative participation in appointments does tend to encourage an awareness on the part of administrators of their responsibility to the legislature.

This is a question which deserves extensive study which it has not yet received. Yet it is possible to suggest certain aspects of the problem which may be helpful in arriving at an answer. Even if the legislature did not participate in the selection of administrative personnel, it is doubtful indeed whether top administrative leaders would be ignorant of the importance of the legislature in the governmental process. Certainly, the power of supervision which lies in the authority to enact substantive legislation and to appropriate funds is a very real power. No administrative leader is likely to belittle the importance of this power or ignore its exercise.

Beyond this, however, there is a further factor. In matters of personnel selection the legislature does not speak by majority vote; rather, it speaks through individual influence and interest. That is, the legislator in his individual rather than in his collective capacity tends to have a voice in personnel matters. The doctrine of senatorial courtesy has even made this true in the formal process of legislative participation in personnel administration; in so far as informal participation is involved this individual and particularistic concern is equally evident. There does not tend to be a collective legislative interest in personnel matters except as this is manifest in slowing down the widespread application of civil service provisions to administrative agencies or in the provision that more rather than fewer administrative personnel shall be subject to formal legislative approval.

The point is this: In exercising the power of statutory enactment and of appropriation, the legislature must speak by majority voice. In exercising its part in personnel matters, the legislature does not speak collectively; rather individual legislators speak separately and particularly either with representatives of the executive or with representatives of top administrators. The difficulty in this situation is that legislators are not of equal status in such bargaining. Committee chairmen and other influential legislative leaders are in a position to obtain greater consideration than others. Moreover, some legislators are more interested in patronage than others. And some legislators want more attention than others if they are to be favorably inclined toward the needs and desires of a certain administrative agency.

From the point of view of the administrative agency, interest obtained on the basis of personal favors in the selection or promotion of personnel may be costly. Such interest may be short-lived and uninformed; it can easily be transferred from friendly concern to active dislike; it may be acquired at the price of the friendly disposition of some other legislator or even influential citizen. And such interest may seek still further personal and individual favor of one kind or another.

It seems reasonable then to suggest that legislative participation in administrative personnel selection is to be understood primarily in terms of legislative-executive relationships. To a lesser extent the practice reflects a need on the part of administrative agencies to win favorable response on the part of the legislature toward the interests of a particular agency, whether those interests be statutory or appropriation enactment. It seems questionable whether legislative participation in personnel matters adds substantially to the techniques by which administrative agencies are kept in the path of responsible political behavior.

IMPEACHMENT AND REMOVAL

Thus far we have been discussing legislative participation in administrative personnel matters which evidences itself in the appointment, promotion, and retention of administrative personnel. There is another interest which the legislature may have, however: the removal of administrative personnel. Individual legislators and even the legislature as a body may develop a considerable hostility toward certain administrative officials. This hostility is usually directed against top administrative personnel, but it may in practice extend to staff advisers of a department head and even to bureau officials.

In various ways a legislative body may influence the removal of administrative personnel. The federal Constitution provides that "all civil officers of the United States shall be removed from office on impeachment for, and conviction of, treason, bribery, or other high crimes and misdemeanors" (Article II, Section 4). The Constitution further provides

that the House of Representatives shall have the sole power of impeachment (Article I, Section 2), and that the Senate shall have the sole power
to try all impeachments, a conviction requiring the concurrence of two-
thirds of the members present (Article I, Section 3).

Only through the power of impeachment was the legislative assembly
of the federal government given any formal authority to remove administrative officers. In actual practice on only one occasion in the history of
the United States has Congress endeavored to impeach an administrative
officer of the government. In 1876 during the Grant administration and
as a result of the revelation that he had accepted bribes from a subordinate
employee, Secretary of War W. W. Belknap was impeached by vote of
the House of Representatives. The Secretary thereupon resigned before a
trial and conviction could be obtained in the Senate. In no other instance
has the removal of an important or minor administrative official been
sought through use of impeachment proceedings.

The legislature, however, may exercise indirect influence in seeking the
removal of administrative officials. The most obvious device is to reduce
the appropriation of an agency and let it be known that the reason is the
presence of a disliked administrative officer. This has happened on a
number of occasions, and has usually resulted in the resignation of the
official who has incurred the wrath of the legislature. Another device is to
pass a law abolishing a particular bureau or office. This, too, has been
done on occasion. The investigative power may be used to harass an administrative official and thus induce his resignation. The threat of an inquiry which will reveal unpleasant facts about an officer's personal, business, or governmental conduct may also persuade an administrator to resign. Nor are these tactics directed only toward top political officials. They
have been used against civil service personnel as well.

In one instance, as recounted earlier, the Congress has sought by appropriation law specifically to name certain officers of the government who
shall no longer receive any compensation for their services.[11] In this case
the Supreme Court subsequently held that such an action was an unconstitutional exercise of legislative power.

Finally, the legislature by fixing a term of office for certain positions
may require reappointment from time to time. If such reappointment is
subject to senatorial confirmation, the occasion may be used in effect as
a device for terminating the tenure of a particular administrative official.
This has happened on several occasions in the instance of members of
regulatory commissions and the heads of other agencies.

There are a variety of ways accordingly by which a legislature may
directly or indirectly affect the removal of administrative officers. This
device is a powerful influence in making administrative officers alert to
the status of their relations with members of the legislature.

[11] See chap. 8.

PERSONNEL LEGISLATION

The legislature is concerned with more than the extent of executive appointment with senatorial confirmation in administrative agencies. The entire system of personnel management by administrative agencies depends upon legislative enactments. Statutory law establishes the requirements of merit or career selection of employees. Legislative enactment must decide levels of compensation for the public service. Retirement and pension provisions also depend upon law. This is only the beginning of an enumeration of the many aspects of government personnel which are embodied in law. To a very real degree the quality of government service depends upon the personnel provisions made by a legislature.

The counterpart of legislative concern with participation in the selection of administrative personnel is the decision on the extent of civil service requirements in the public service. There are actually three choices open to a legislature. One is to vest appointment of a considerable number of officials in the hands of the executive subject to senatorial confirmation. A second possibility is to vest appointment of personnel in the hands of top administrative officials subject to no restriction of any kind. The third arrangement is to vest appointment of personnel in the hands of top administrative officials subject to general civil service restrictions. To some degree in the federal government the legislature decides the extent of the first of these three arrangements and has delegated to the executive the decision as to the extent of the second or third arrangement for appointment of administrative personnel.

In state and local governments no civil service system at all is possible without state legislative action. The number and type of positions to be covered by the civil service and the general type of civil service system to be established are therefore basic legislative decisions. All states today have some kind of formal merit system for the selection of at least a part of their administrative personnel, although in almost half of the states the formal system extends only to those services which receive grants-in-aid from the federal government. A formal civil service system involves such features as a job classification scheme, a standard schedule of salary compensation, the selection of employees on the basis of merit and experience or training as determined by some kind of competitive examination, an orderly procedure for the promotion or dismissal of employees, and uniform provisions on such subjects as hours of work, vacations, and sick leave. A civil service system also may include such additional elements as provision for employee training, periodic evaluation of employee performance, health services, and retirement benefits.

A major personnel problem for all levels of government has been that of salary compensation to employees. This is a basic question of legislation, because only the legislature can set standards and levels of compensation for administrative personnel. In the years since the end of World War II, legislative bodies have had to give almost constant attention to the subject of employee salary levels. In fact, legislative action has tended to lag behind advances in industrial wage rates and professional earnings, not to mention the declining purchasing power of the dollar. Personnel needs on the one hand have been countered by tax pressures on the other hand.

The first salary issue which legislatures face is whether personnel in the public service is to be paid at wage rates or salary levels generally prevailing for comparable work through a state or area. Oftentimes it has been argued that government should be a "model employer," but it seems likely that in recent years in particular government wage rates and salary levels have tended to fall behind those being paid by leading industries and commercial businesses. A second issue has been the level of compensation to be provided for top professional and administrative positions in the public service. For high administrative positions government salary compensation is usually substantially less than that received by top executive personnel in private business. For many important professional positions this is also true, especially in the health and medical field. Legislators are worried lest they provide top administrative and professional salaries to individuals whose basis of selection may be political and whose individual compensation outside the public service may possibly have been less than that provided by government.

Another matter of concern to legislatures has been the participation of public employees in political activity. This concern has been most evident in the national legislature. By the Hatch Acts of August 2, 1939, and of July 19, 1940, the Congress by statute provided that it should be unlawful for any person employed in the executive branch of the federal government to use his authority to influence an election, or to take part in political management or campaigns. This prohibition also extends to employees of state and local government paid in whole or in part from federal funds. The statute does declare that administrative employees shall retain the right to vote and to express their opinions about political subjects and candidates.

The language of the Hatch Acts is far-reaching. Nor is it any simple matter to distinguish between political management or participation in a political campaign and the free expression of opinion about political candidates and issues. The first is illegal, whereas the second is permissible behavior. The intent seems fairly obvious. It is to protect the administrative employee from political pressures to contribute to or participate in campaigns for a particular candidate for public office. It also restricts top administrative officials from using their positions as bases for conducting political campaigns. But at the same time, the legislation raises the question whether it has not, at least in its interpretation, placed substantial restrictions upon administrative employees and their voluntary participation in political affairs. When a large number of the adult population might be construed as government personnel, it is possible that this entire segment of society has been denied the privilege of participation in essential political activity. It is not easy through legislation or otherwise to draw a clear line between political exploitation of administrative employees and individual political activity.[12]

It is not necessary here to review the whole range of personnel problems which comes before a legislature from time to time for solution. It is interesting to note that of thirty-two proposals for improvement in the federal government personnel service recommended by the "task force" of the second Hoover Commission in 1955, twenty required legislative action to implement whereas another ten were listed as requiring both legislative and executive action.[13] Little in the way of improvement in civil service or general personnel management can be accomplished in the federal government except by legislative action.

CONCLUSION

In so far as the upper house of a legislative assembly must consent to appointment of top administrative personnel by the chief executive, the legislature exercises a brake upon executive discretion. Such a check is an accepted phase of our governmental process when applied to individuals selected to provide the top political leadership of administrative agencies. The extent to which this requirement of legislative approval shall operate has been debatable. Students of government and political commentators generally are agreed that the number of such positions in the public service should be small. For practical political reasons legislators have desired to extend or maintain rather than to contract the number of such positions.

In terms of the philosophy as opposed to the practical political operation of our government, the most important single personnel consideration is whether an extensive element of personnel politically selected and politically oriented is essential in administrative agencies in order to ensure responsible political behavior on the part of the bureaucracy. In 1955 the second Hoover Commission set forth certain criteria which it suggested should identify the "noncareer" or political group in administrative agencies:[14]

[12] Cf. Dalmas H. Nelson, "Political Expression under the Hatch Act and the Problem of Statutory Ambiguity," *Midwest Journal of Political Science,* vol. 2 (February, 1958), p. 76.

[13] Commission on Organization of the Executive Branch of the Government, *Task Force Report on Personnel and Civil Service* (Washington: Government Printing Office, 1955), pp. 251–252.

[14] Commission on Organization of the Executive Branch of the Government, *Personnel and Civil Service: A Report to the Congress* (Washington: Government Printing Office, 1955), pp. 31–32.

(1) Positions possessing statutory authority or executive delegation of authority to make final decisions in establishing administrative policies, programs, and objectives

(2) Positions which require the incumbent publicly to advocate new policies or to defend existing basic principles and philosophy controlling agency activities

(3) Positions of a personal or confidential nature serving non-career administrators, including personal aides, confidential secretaries, and personal chauffeurs

With these criteria the Commission also proposed that all political responsibility for the operation of a department or agency should be concentrated at the top rather than diffused throughout the organization. Whether the criteria suggested by the Commission are adequate is certainly debatable; they may well require modification in certain types of governmental services where the top leadership must include men of substantial professional competence as in educational, health, welfare, scientific, military, and similar activities.

Even so, it seems clear that extensive legislative participation in the process of selecting administrative personnel is not essential in order to ensure politically responsible behavior on the part of the bureaucracy. In this sense responsible political behavior means action guided by a sensitivity to prevailing political sentiment as voiced by legislature and executive and a willingness to be guided by proper legislative and executive direction in formulating objectives and in administering programs. This kind of responsible political behavior is as much if not more inculcated by the culture, the educational preparation, and the traditions which surround the administrative servant as by legislative participation in the selection of personnel. Legislative interest in personnel selection in our country tends to be more a consequence of the legislative-executive separation of power than the expression of concern for a responsible bureaucracy.

It would appear that the various prevailing practices enumerated in this volume whereby legislature, executive, and judiciary supervise administrative conduct do not require reinforcement by an extensive arrangement for legislative participation in the selection of administrative personnel.

This conclusion, however, should not result in neglecting the broader aspect of legislative interest in administrative personnel by which the terms and conditions of personnel management within government are determined. The legislature bears a basic responsibility for the satisfactory operation of a personnel system in conjunction with the performance of governmental administrative services.

Chapter 12

The Role of the Legislature

The power of the legislative branch in our system of government is the authority to enact into law the fundamentals of public policy which constitute the objectives of governmental activity. Beyond this, by law our legislature creates the administrative agencies which shall carry out desired activities, provides the funds for their continuing operation, and establishes the procedures by which such activities shall be administered. In the exercise of its lawmaking responsibility, the legislative branch may inquire into existing administrative policies and practices, as well as into possible new fields of legislative concern. And to the extent required by constitutional prescription or by law, the upper chamber may share in approving the appointment of personnel by the chief executive.

In this brief summary of legislative power it is the word "law" which must be emphasized. The legislative authority of government is exercised through the formal process of law. With certain exceptions—the approval of appointments, the control of expenditures, the conduct of investigations, and the exercise of various informal pressures—the legislature can only act on matters of interest and concern to it by enactment of law. It is law by which the legislature speaks. It is by law that it determines and controls the work of the administrative agencies of government. It is the law as enacted by the legislature which is supreme in the relations of public administration to society.

The authority of the legislature as the lawmaking branch of government gives the legislature great power over administrative agencies. It is the law as enacted by the legislature which administrative agencies carry out. Administrative agencies must therefore look to the law as their inspiration, their justification, and their guide. The law is superior for the administrative agency. The legislature enacts the law. In what respects then is the legislature superior to the administrative agency?

It is easy to say that the legislature enacts law and that administrative agencies enforce or carry out the provisions of law. The actual relationships which should and do then exist in practice between legislature and administrative agency are not so easy to state. In a complex society, in a highly industrialized society, political institutions must also be complex and even of considerable magnitude. And size and complexity of social problems make for difficulties in relationships.

We have observed that the legislature provides the substantive law; that is, the broad outlines of public policy which an administrative agency puts into practice. There are immense subtleties in this relationship. For one thing, the legislature does not react to public issues in a vacuum. Public issues are first of all created by some general social or economic difficulty, from juvenile delinquency to curtailment of farm income, from extensive poverty or the prevalence of disease to the exhaustion of natural resources or the burden of taxation. Social or economic difficulties become general when they begin to attract considerable discussion among various groups of people and demands for action begin to be heard on many sides. Sometimes awareness of a public problem is promoted by the chief executive; sometimes awareness of a public issue gains its strength among legislators themselves.

To what extent do administrative agencies themselves participate in this analysis of public problems and in the consideration of how to resolve public issues? The answer is that administrative participation is extensive. The chief executive may request administrative agencies to study a problem and propose a line of action. If the chief executive accepts these suggestions his "program" may indeed be the actual product of an administrative agency. But the chief executive's "program" is only a proposal until its essentials are enacted into law, until it becomes legal public policy. Administrative agencies may be requested by legislative committees to help review the chief executive's recommendations, to justify the proposals, or to comment upon alternative schemes of action. And all administrative ideas are not necessarily transmitted to the legislature only through the chief executive. The legislature may be determined to take the initiative in developing the outlines of a desirable public policy. This was done, for example, in writing the Atomic Energy Act of 1946. In these circumstances legislative committees may ask administrative agencies to work closely with them in deciding governmental objectives and procedures. Administrative agencies may even do much of the actual drafting of legislative language.

If administrative agencies thus participate to a very real degree in the formulation of public policy and its enactment into law—a situation today regarded as indispensable to the functioning of our government—is the legislature then to be thought of as removed from any direct interest in the administration of this public policy? Just as administrative agencies must necessarily play a part in the formulation of public policy, legislative bodies must play a part in the administration of public policy. This is true in a purely legal sense in terms of appropriations. It is true in terms also of possible legislative inquiry at any time into the administration of law prompted by a desire to consider possible modifications. But just how far can and should this legislative participation in administration extend? This is the crucial question which is by no means easy to answer.

The legislative power is extremely important in our government. It is essential to the performance of any governmental activity. It provides the foundation for all administrative endeavor. But the legislative power is not omnipotent. It is not synonymous with governmental power. Rather it is only one part of the totality of governmental power as exercised in our society. The legislative power is not limited just by certain constitutional prescriptions, such as the provision that it shall pass no bills of attainder or ex post facto laws. The legislative power is limited to matters legislative as distinct from matters executive and judicial. This indeed is the fundamental limitation upon legislative authority.

In relation to administrative agencies the legislature exercises such extensive power that on occasion it comes to consider its authority as all-pervasive. The power the legislature does possess is so great that legislators perceive few if any limits to its scope. Moreover, in an era when large-scale bureaucracy is the order of the day, the legislature often senses that it alone stands guardian over the liberties of the citizen and the freedom of the Republic. To suggest limitations to legislative jurisdiction is, it appears, to suggest a higher regard for bureaucracy than for supremacy of the law in our system of government. Many commentators about the legislature in recent years have encouraged this attitude.

For example, one acute observer of legislative operations has declared: "Most Congressmen are frustrated. . . . They are frustrated because, to paraphrase Browning, their reach for power exceeds their grasp. . . . President and department heads are beyond their control. There is a gap between what Congress actually does and what it wishes it could do."[1] Another spokesman for the legislative point of view has said of Congress, "It faces the problem of holding responsible the technically competent bureaucracy which in its growing strength unwittingly threatens to throw our representative government off balance."[2]

Still a third student of the legislature has written:[3]

> Many members of Congress spend more time overseeing the departments and bureaus than writing or debating laws. [He further remarks:[4]] The Congressman distrusts the bureaucrats as a group. They are experts in their fields,

---

[1] Roland Young, *This Is Congress* (New York: Alfred A. Knopf, Inc., 1943), p. 28.

[2] Ernest S. Griffith, *Congress: Its Contemporary Role* (New York: New York University Press, 1951), p. 1.

[3] James Macgregor Burns, *Congress on Trial: The Legislative Process and the Administrative State* (New York: Harper & Brothers, 1949), p. 98.

[4] *Ibid.*, p. 7.

while he must be a political jack-of-all-trades. They are theorists and technicians, while he would like to see more "practical" people in government, like himself. Worst of all, they exercise power without having earned the right to do so, he feels. He complains that none of them "could get elected dog-catcher in his home town."

It is fair to say that most legislators are inclined to believe that there are, or at least ought to be, no limits to the extent to which the legislature should direct, supervise, and control the work of the administrative agencies of government. And on occasion individual legislators, usually through a committee chairmanship, have played a dominant part in administrative activity. An interesting example extending over a more than twenty-year period was the chairman of the House Committee on Naval Affairs and subsequently chairman of the House Committee on Armed Services, Representative Carl Vinson of Georgia.[5] Indeed, when the late James V. Forrestal retired as Secretary of Defense in the President's Cabinet on March 28, 1949, a most unusual event occurred. The House Committee on Armed Services held a special meeting to pay tribute to the work of the Secretary beginning with his assumption of the position of Assistant Secretary of the Navy on August 20, 1940.[6] Chairman Vinson reviewed the story of naval affairs from that time until the creation of the Department of Defense in 1947 and the work of that agency thereafter. In closing the chairman said:

> In view of all of these significant events in which you have played so commanding a role, we want it long remembered and permanently recorded here that your outstanding talents and accomplishments on the highest levels of our Government have been appreciated and valued highly by this committee and the Congress.
>
> Your wise counsel and devoted service have been a tower of strength in aiding the old Naval Affairs Committee and this committee in the discharge of its responsibilities.

In and of themselves these words may seem simple enough, and Forrestal's response in which he turned the praise to the chairman and members of the committee might be regarded as polite self-effacement. But those who had followed naval affairs throughout the decades of the 1930s and 1940s knew better. There was even a story whispered throughout the corridors of Washington that on one occasion Vinson had said of Forrestal, "He was the best Secretary of the Navy I ever had." There was another piece of wartime gossip during the 1940s to the effect that President Roosevelt and Chairman Vinson had reached an understanding, or modus vivendi. The President as Commander in Chief would control naval

---

[5] Cf. Eliot Janeway, "The Man Who Owns the Navy," *Saturday Evening Post,* Dec. 15, 1945.

[6] The proceedings were published as an appendix to the *Congressional Record,* Mar. 30, 1949.

strategy as formulated and recommended by the Navy staff; Chairman Vinson would control the naval establishment, that is, the program for shipbuilding, procurement, personnel, and navy yards. It was even said that when Navy officers approached Vinson about the possibility of a building comparable to the Army's Pentagon, the chairman offered them the alternative of a building or a battleship. The officers decided to take the battleship.

All these stories may be exaggerated. But they are illustrative of the kind of relationship which may arise between a powerful legislative leader and an administrative agency of the government. This relationship, as has been pointed out before, may be very close indeed, many administrative policies being developed and put into effect after careful consultation with the appropriate legislative committee. The power of the committee may not be so great as the close relationship would suggest, but for various reasons it may seem advantageous to both parties to develop a mutual understanding. The extent of this relationship may almost appear to be one of legislative direction and control over administrative enterprise.[7]

Yet powerful as the legislature is and has been, dissatisfaction about its role has been substantial. Several suggestions have been put forth from time to time for a clearer, more precise working relationship between legislature and administrative agencies. These proposals have acknowledged two situations. One is that the legislature does and of right ought to have a major voice in the determination of policy and program to be carried out by administrative agencies. The other situation is that under existing arrangements the legislature lacks adequate machinery or devices for making its authority effective.

For example, the legislature may not dismiss an administrative officer. The legislature may criticize, may bring considerable public pressure to bear upon an administrative official, but only the President or a department head may actually exercise the authority to dismiss a public employee who does not voluntarily resign. The legislature may place certain safeguards about this removal power, and has in fact done so. The legislature still may not take the initiative in demanding a change in administrative personnel, except through the complicated process of impeachment.

Another complaint has been the inadequacy of direct communication between legislature and administrative officials. Department and agency heads, bureau chiefs, and other important administrative officers may and do make frequent appearances before individual legislative committees. Here the contact is between a representative group of legislators and an administrative agency; this does not afford a means of direct communica-

---

[7] George B. Galloway has declared that this particular form of legislative "oversight of administration" has expanded substantially since 1946. See his "The Operation of the Legislative Reorganization Act of 1946," *American Political Science Review,* vol. 45 (March, 1951), p. 41.

tion or access between the legislature as a whole and an administrative agency.

Still another complaint is that the legislature lacks its own body of experts to assist it in dealing with administrative matters. The chief executive in most governmental jurisdictions today has a more or less elaborate staff of assistants to help him in his analysis and control of administrative activities. The legislature, it is said, does not have similar assistance and cannot make its supervisory role effective without an extensive staff of its own.

These complaints in turn have led to various proposals for change. The most common of these are two: (1) that department and agency heads be requested or required to sit with the legislative assembly as a whole, and (2) that legislatures develop large-scale staff units responsible directly and solely to the legislature. Both these suggestions deserve some comment.

THE LEGISLATURE AND DEPARTMENT HEADS

Most proposals for some change in the relationship of department heads to the legislature draw upon the precedent of the parliamentary system of government in Great Britain. To be sure, there is a great gulf between the form of government as prescribed by the federal Constitution and the form of government which has evolved from practice in the United Kingdom. This gulf is usually ignored when the suggestion is made that we might well introduce certain features of the British system into our own scheme of operation.

It is often pointed out, for example, that in the British House of Commons all administrative agencies are represented by their heads or deputy heads who are available during a daily question period to answer any queries which may be raised about the work of their agencies. This practice of members of Parliament putting questions to ministers appears to have originated in the House of Lords about 1721. One hundred years later the custom had developed to the point where in the House of Commons a more or less fixed procedure for questions and answers was put into effect. Today, on four days a week the daily session of the House of Commons begins with approximately an hour devoted to answers from ministers. Questions are ordinarily submitted in writing and are printed in the order of the day when the minister is prepared to give his reply. A supplemental question or two may be asked orally, but usually a minister answers only those questions of which he has had advance notice. Questions which are not reached during the answer period may be handled simply as a part of the written proceedings of the day.

With this governmental practice to be observed in a fellow English-speaking nation, various Americans have asked why would not a similar arrangement be desirable in the United States. In 1789 the law establishing the Treasury Department provided that the Secretary "shall make report and give information to either branch of the legislature in person, or in writing, as may be required, respecting all matters referred to him by the Senate or House of Representatives or which shall appertain to his office." Apparently, however, Congress was not too enthusiastic about this possible arrangement. In 1790 Hamilton requested the privilege of presenting his report on public credit in person to both houses; the request was refused. Again in 1792 Hamilton and the Secretary of War wished to appear to explain the military defeats suffered by General St. Clair in the Ohio country; once more the request was turned down. At this time members of the legislature seemed to fear that personal appearances by officers who were appointed by the Chief Executive would lead to executive domination of the legislative branch. The whole early idea that heads of departments might appear in person at meetings of the legislature was thus allowed to wither.[8]

The matter of permitting department heads to participate in legislative sessions was raised again during the Civil War. A resolution on the subject was referred to a select committee, which reported favorably. The report declared that it was desirable to have "free, open, candid consultation" between the representatives of the people and members of the Cabinet. It even stated that the rules recommended for such appearances were "almost identical with those of the British House of Commons." The committee report acknowledged the fear that the new arrangement might "tend to increase the power of the executive department at the expense of the legislative," but went on to argue that it was better to have executive power exercised openly than secretly. The committee believed that the advantages gained in advancing congressional control over administration would far outweigh any possible dangers in the arrangement. The resolution seems to have been the personal idea largely of Representative George H. Pendleton of Ohio, an antiwar Democrat who later in the year was to be the running mate of General McClellan in his presidential campaign against Abraham Lincoln. Needless to say, the House of Representatives defeated the Pendleton resolution. In 1881 Pendleton, now a Senator from Ohio, again proposed such an arrangement. Once again the resolution he introduced was defeated.[9]

In 1912, interestingly enough, the idea that department heads should sit in Congress and participate in legislative debate was taken up by the Chief Executive, William Howard Taft. On December 19, the President sent a special message to Congress urging adoption of the practice. In this message he declared: "The rigid holding apart of the executive and legisla-

---

[8] Cf. W. F. Willoughby, *Principles of Legislative Organization and Administration* (Washington, D.C.: Brookings Institution, 1934), chap. 13.
[9] *Ibid.*

tive branches of this government has not worked for the great advantage of either." Although he recognized that the legislative and executive perform each its own "appropriate function," he argued that "these functions must be coordinated." He felt that information known to department heads would be helpful to members of Congress and would "contribute to the enactment of beneficial legislation." He felt further that such an arrangement would "spur each member of the cabinet to closer attention to the details of his department, to greater familiarity with its needs, and to greater care to avoid the just criticism which the answers brought out in questions put and discussions arising between the members of either house and the members of the cabinet may properly evoke."[10] But Taft was speaking as a Chief Executive whose bid for reelection had just been defeated. The suggestion was given little attention.

Ten years later, in 1922, President Warren G. Harding endorsed another resolution on the matter introduced in the House of Representatives. Further resolutions were put forth in 1925. Since that time the proposal has periodically reappeared. For example, in 1943 then Representative, later Senator, Estes Kefauver of Tennessee proposed that the House of Representatives establish a question period of two hours once a week when heads of departments and of independent agencies would be requested to answer written and oral questions propounded by members of the House. He suggested further that a copy of each written question go to the appropriate House committee and then, if approved by the committee, be forwarded to the proper administrative officer. The second half of each question period would be reserved for oral questions, the questioning to be controlled by the chairman and ranking minority member of each committee.[11]

As has already been indicated, a major argument on behalf of some procedure whereby administrative officers might appear personally before Congress is to provide all members with direct knowledge about administrative policies and programs. It is often pointed out that administrative contact with the legislature channeled through committees reaches only a small part of the membership. The result is that the bulk of the legislature must usually follow the decisions made by committees and the leadership, unless some independent source of information is utilized, and this may not always be reliable or unbiased.

The arguments against such a plan are usually twofold. One is that the existing arrangements for legislative-administrative contact are adequate, and the other is that a change along the lines just mentioned might bring about some undesirable consequences. It is pointed out that the com-

[10] *Ibid.*, pp. 189–190.

[11] See *Congressional Record*, Nov. 12, 1943. See also Estes Kefauver and Jack Levin, *A Twentieth-century Congress* (New York: Duell, Sloan & Pearce, Inc., 1947).

mittees of the legislature may now obtain all the information from administrative officers which they want or need. Oftentimes these existing relationships are quite informal and so result in a fuller mutual exchange of points of view than would otherwise be the case. Furthermore, committee hearings in the national legislature are all published and made available to the entire membership. Whereas state legislatures do not ordinarily publish committee hearings, some kind of record is available for use if desired. Moreover, administrative officers usually resort to various public appearances as an opportunity to propound or defend administrative policies; these public appearances are often fully reported and can be used by legislators for their information. In the federal government, most such public addresses are published in the *Congressional Record*. Any individual legislator is free at any time to write a direct inquiry to an administrative officer, and a response to these questions is almost always given prompt and courteous attention by administrative agencies.

A good deal of concern has also been expressed lest the proposed change bring in its wake a number of undesirable results. Some fear has been voiced that direct contact on the floor of the legislature might undermine the work done by committees, and it is argued that the real consideration of measures must occur within committees. It is also pointed out that the committee system enables legislators to hear not just department heads but also their chief subordinates as well. This might not be the case if the legislature relied upon a formal questioning period for its principal source of information. If the formal question period were simply added on to the existing practice of committee consideration of administrative matters, it would be an additional burden upon legislative time with few if any additional benefits. Then there has also been some question whether formal appearances of administrative officers before the legislature might undermine the authority of the chief executive. This may be a vague fear at best, but conceivably an individual administrative officer who appeared successfully before the legislative body as a whole in defense of administrative policies might come to overshadow the chief executive in influence and prestige.

In any event, there has been little disposition to adopt any proposal for administrative officials personally to appear before the legislature. It must be concluded, I believe, that legislators by and large are satisfied with existing arrangements and see no compelling reason for a change. Perhaps legislative control over the bureaucracy is now exercised in piecemeal or fragmentary fashion. Yet the fact of legislative control does still exist and operate. It may not be the most satisfactory form of legislative control; it is nonetheless control. Administrative officials who appeared before the whole membership of a legislative assembly might reach more individual legislators with a personal message. To legislators it would still be an unsatisfactory device unless they could probe at will with questions, listen to other points of view, and study problems. The committee system is necessary for such procedure, and the committee system appears to block a different procedure from the one now practiced.

LEGISLATIVE-EXECUTIVE RELATIONSHIPS

The proposal just examined contemplated no more than that department and agency heads should personally appear before either or both houses of a legislative assembly in order to explain administrative policies or to answer questions about policies and administrative details. Still a different kind of change has been urged on a few occasions, although not so frequently or so generally as the one mentioned above. This is the suggestion that heads of administrative agencies should actually be members of the legislature.

This proposal has been put forth by those who have been alarmed by the frequent clash of Congress and President. Even when the same political party affiliation is claimed by a majority of the legislature and the Chief Executive, the course of legislative-executive relationships does not necessarily run smoothly. When legislature and executive are of different parties, conflicts may be extensive and exacerbating. From time to time some way of diminishing this legislative-executive conflict has been sought.

Here again, it has been natural for our political observers to note the contrast which has generally prevailed over the past two hundred years in Great Britain. There, under the parliamentary system of government, there is little if any legislative-executive conflict. The reason is, of course, simple. In a parliamentary system of government the executive power is not only directly responsible to the legislature but also serves at the pleasure of the legislature. In Great Britain, furthermore, through control of party machinery and the authority to dissolve Parliament at its pleasure, the ministry of the day in effect dominates the work of the legislature in the period between general elections. There is no legislative-executive conflict in Great Britain because in theory the legislature controls the executive whereas in practice the executive controls the legislature.

Some political observers have accordingly speculated whether some such system as this, or a modified version thereof, might be preferable to our own arrangement. For example, one distinguished American scholar of constitutional law has suggested that the President's Cabinet should be composed of legislative leaders.[12] These leaders would not be heads of administrative agencies, however. They would be members of the legislature drawn from both the House of Representatives and the Senate who

[12] Edward S. Corwin, *The President: Office and Powers,* 3d ed. (New York: New York University Press, 1948), pp. 358–364.

would advise the President about legislative matters, including presumably current criticism of administrative behavior.

A somewhat similar idea has been put forth by another scholar. The desirability of a central council has been suggested wherein both legislative leaders and administrative officials would meet formally to advise the President.[13] This council would take the leadership in formulating a legislative program which would be acceptable to the legislature and assured of passage. This council would also advise the President about major matters of administrative policy, and through its legislative members assure the legislature, or a majority of it, that administrative agencies were functioning satisfactorily. Much the same kind of proposal, termed a "Joint Executive-Legislative Cabinet," has been advocated by Thomas K. Finletter.[14] He has even proposed that the terms of executive and legislature be made the same, six years, and that the President be able to call a general election between times in case of deadlock when he and a new Congress would both stand for reelection.[15]

At the other extreme, it has been proposed that the legislature should organize its own "council" of leaders who would determine legislative policy and supervise administrative agencies without paying any attention to the Chief Executive. It has even been said that this kind of development could occur within the framework of the existing Constitution.[16] Under such an arrangement the President would become little more than a ceremonial figurehead for the nation.

There is little need to explore these and similar suggestions at any length.[17] All such ideas have as their focus of attention some alteration in the existing scheme of legislative-executive relationships in our system of government. Exactly how such changes would affect the supervision and control of administrative agencies has not usually been explored in any detail. Presumably, some change would occur.

It seems adequate for the present simply to observe that the legislature now exercises a substantial degree of supervisory authority over administrative agencies as a part of its power to enact law. This supervisory authority is limited by the extent of supervisory authority enjoyed by the executive. The nature of this executive authority will be considered in the next part of this volume. If any fundamental change were to occur in

[13] Charles S. Hyneman, *op. cit.,* pp. 571–576.

[14] Thomas K. Finletter, *Can Representative Government Do the Job?* (New York: Reynal & Hitchcock, Inc., 1945), chaps. 11–13.

[15] This idea of dissolution will also be found in William Y. Elliott, *The Need for Constitutional Reform* (New York: McGraw-Hill Book Company, Inc., 1935).

[16] C. Perry Patterson, *Presidential Government in the United States* (Chapel Hill, N.C.: The University of North Carolina Press, 1947).

[17] For a convenient, brief summary of proposals for change, see Bertram M. Gross, *The Legislative Struggle* (New York: McGraw-Hill Book Company, Inc., 1953), pp. 121–129.

legislative-executive relationships under our system of government, then some change in the relations of both legislative and executive to administrative agencies would of necessity result.

Most proposals for legislative-executive change arise from the proposition, as we have said, that there does now exist a conflict between legislature and executive, and that this conflict is *bad*. The conflict is bad presumably because it results in a paralysis of governmental power in a period of national crisis. As an example of the consequence of such paralysis, the failure of the United States to join the League of Nations in 1919 is often cited, along with the implicit assumption that if the United States had belonged to the League of Nations, World War II would not have occurred in 1939.

All of this is at best debatable; as history it is beyond the power of man to alter. Questions of first importance to us for the moment are whether a change in legislative-executive relationships would result in the formulation of more effective public policy to be administered by administrative agencies and whether such change would ensure more effective supervision of administrative agencies carrying out such policies.

These are questions which it is practically impossible to answer. Supposing that there were acceptable standards about what constitutes "effective public policy" and "effective supervision," we cannot experiment with governmental institutions simply in order to answer an argument about preferable forms of procedure. Government is too important a social arrangement for mere tampering.

Actually, in practical terms an answer is readily available. Governmental practices will not ordinarily be changed in a society unless there is some widespread evidence and conviction of a breakdown or failure. Thus the burden of proof is always on those who urge change; they must present evidence that there is a serious failure in the functioning of an existing governmental system. And if such failure does in reality exist, opportunity for change may be at hand.

This author's observation would be that for the present there is no evidence of any serious breakdown of legislative-executive relationships as they affect the formulation and administration of public policy. To be sure, the legislature often appears to be stretching forth its authority to embrace more and more control of administrative agencies. Such efforts are resisted by the chief executive and even occasionally rebuked by the judiciary. Certainly, there is evidence of struggle and of conflict in the American system of government. But to confuse conflict with collapse is an unwarranted act of judgment. American political history is replete with accounts of legislative-executive conflict. Can anyone maintain that these conflicts have resulted in a breakdown of government?

It is therefore sufficient for us to note that some individuals have urged different governmental arrangements in order to lessen legislative-executive conflict. There is little reason to believe that any of these suggestions will be given serious attention in the absence of a serious breakdown in existing governmental practices.

INCREASED LEGISLATIVE STAFFING

Still a different kind of prosposal for more extensive congressional supervision of administration has been put forth from time to time. This has been the proposition to increase the staff facilities available to Congress, and especially the congressional committees. To some extent this proposal has been based upon the analogy of developments taking place in the executive branch. As we shall observe in the next part, the past twenty years have witnessed the institutionalization of the Presidency. No longer is the Chief Executive an individual; the Executive Office of the President has become an institution. Now, so the argument goes, if the executive needs "modern tools" of management and "up-to-date organization," then the legislature faces a similar necessity. The answer therefore is to institutionalize the legislature by providing it with larger and better staff assistance.[18]

In actual fact, Congress does have a fairly substantial staff organization, and this staff assistance has increased somewhat in recent years. Early in the 1800s congressional committees began to supply themselves with clerks; full-time clerks were common for all major committees by 1858 in the House of Representatives and by 1861 in the Senate. These staffs were small. As late as 1940 the largest staff of clerks in the House numbered thirteen for the Committee on Appropriations; most committees had simply a clerk and an assistant clerk. In the Senate the largest staff, nine persons, was possessed by the Committee on Finance, but the Committee on Appropriations had eight, the Committee on Post Offices and Post Roads had seven, six others had six persons, eleven had five, and thirteen had four. Then the Legislative Reorganization Act of 1946, in section 203, authorized each standing committee of the senate and the House of Representatives to appoint not more than "four professional staff members in addition to the clerical staffs on a permanent basis without regard to political affiliations and solely on the basis of fitness to perform the duties of the office." Most committees quickly took advantage of this arrangement, and chiefs of staff have been paid as much as $14,680 a year for their services. This law further limited the number of clerks for each committee to six. In this way, congressional committees have had the opportunity to utilize some minimum professional service in the regular discharge of their duties, including supervision of the work being

---

[18] Cf. Lindsay Rogers, "The Staffing of Congress," *Political Science Quarterly,* vol. 56 (March, 1941), p. 1.

done by administrative agencies.[19] As of 1953 the committees of Congress employed some eight hundred persons in professional, clerical, and stenographic positions.[20]

In addition, each individual senator and representative is entitled to a personal staff. For many years representatives were each given a fixed sum of money with which they might hire one, two, or three persons to assist them. Senators who were not chairmen of committees might have six or seven assistants. A provision in the legislative reorganization bill for an additional assistant to each member of Congress was stricken from the bill, but in 1947 by insertion of a clause in the legislative appropriation measure Congress provided that each of its members might have an administrative assistant to be paid $10,000 a year. As of 1953 the administrative, clerical, and stenographic staffs of individual members of Congress came to a total of some 2,700 persons.[21]

During World War II the Library of Congress began to seek a more active role in providing informational assistance to congressional committees. A reorganization of the Legislative Reference Service, first created in 1916, introduced four subject-matter specialists and a director for the purpose of providing professional services to the legislature. The Legislative Reorganization Act of 1946 went further and provided a specific statutory basis for the Legislative Reference Service, directing it to advise and assist committees in the appraisal of pending legislation and to collect data bearing on legislation "without partisan bias in selection or presentation." The service was authorized to employ specialists in agriculture, public administration, conservation, education, public works, housing, industrial organization and finance, international trade, money and banking, social welfare, transportation and communications, and veterans' affairs. The director of the service has reported that as a result of this expansion questions answered by the Legislative Reference Service increased from 300 to 3,000 a month.[22] As of 1953 the service numbered 160 persons.

In 1918 an Office of Legislative Counsel was created to serve both the Senate and House of Representatives by providing the leadership and committee chairmen with expert legal advice in drafting new laws. Before that time individual members of Congress prepared their own bills for introduction. The result was often the inclusion of language which meant something very different from that intended by the author. Because statutory construction became so important in subsequent litigation before the

---

[19] See Gladys Kammerer, *The Staffing of the Committees of Congress* (Lexington, Ky.: University of Kentucky Bureau of Government Research, 1949).

[20] George B. Galloway, *The Legislative Process in Congress* (New York: Thomas Y. Crowell Company, 1953), p. 42.

[21] *Ibid.*

[22] Ernest S. Griffith, *op. cit.*, p. 58.

courts, it was all the more important to draft laws with a careful regard for legal meaning and interpretation. For this reason bill drafting has become something of a special kind of legal service. As of 1953 there were twenty-eight persons employed by the Office of Legislative Counsel to render this assistance.

Finally, it should be noted again that the General Accounting Office is an agency of the legislature. The Legislative Reorganization Act of 1946 strengthened the statutory provisions affecting this office by directing the Comptroller General to make an "expenditure analysis" of each agency in the executive branch of the government and so help Congress "to determine whether public funds have been economically and efficiently administered and expended." This is a broad charter of authority indeed. This agency numbered nearly 6,000 employees in 1955.

In the light of all this array of staff, it can scarcely be said that the legislature is without assistance. The total number of persons of all grades and types involved in providing staff services to Congress as of 1955 was in the neighborhood of 11,500 individuals. This is not necessarily an excessive number, but it surely is an impressive one. It may be contrasted with some 1,200 persons employed in the Executive Office of the President. This latter number would be considerably larger if the size of the Central Intelligence Agency were a matter of public information.

Although not on the same elaborate scale, many states have also built up some kind of staff service for their legislatures. The common form for this development has been a legislative council composed of members of both houses. There is usually an executive director or secretary for the council who heads a small staff of investigators and clerks. The council is ordinarily busy between sessions of the legislature in prosecuting various studies deemed helpful for the next session. In addition, the staff may carry on such other activities as the council or legislature may authorize. For example, the staff may be instructed to obtain reports on the construction progress of public works projects, or to collect personnel data from various agencies. During a legislative session the staff of the legislative council may render such informational, investigative, and bill-drafting services as may be requested.

Over half of the state legislatures have now organized such legislative councils. Almost all the states have also a legislative reference service in connection with a state library or similar agency. In some instances there are also bill-drafting services available to a state legislature.

The key question, of course, in all this development is whether a legislature can make its role of supervision over administrative agencies more effective by the use of these and similar staff agencies. This is another question which cannot be answered with any definite assurance. But at least two aspects of the problem deserve careful attention.

One is the danger which may be inherent in the growing reliance of legislatures upon staff assistance in order to perform the legislative function. The larger staff operations become, the more likely it is that the staff personnel will become separated from legislative leadership and direction and become a kind of free-wheeling bureaucracy of its own. The very fact that a legislature does not speak with one voice but rather with many tongues encourages staff aides to go their own way. If it were possible to provide strong central direction to a large staff, the danger of irresponsible or individual action might be lessened. But this kind of leadership is almost by definition foreign to the fundamental character of a legislative assembly.

There is then the danger that in the growth of legislative staff we may simply be encouraging the creation of a new bureaucracy all the more dangerous because it may not be subject to effective leadership and restraint. Nor is this an entirely idle fear. If a full account of the activities of congressional committee staffs since 1946 were available, and if administrative officers felt free to talk without fear of legislative reprisal, much evidence would probably be accumulated of administrative difficulty. Legislative staffs have no responsibility for action, for administrative results. They have only the task of finding out what is happening and of criticizing. This is important, but the very nature of the assignment is a delicate one at best. It calls for subtle exercise, and legislative staffs, like other staffs, do not always measure up to the need. The danger then is of building a professional corps of critics who become expert in faultfinding but little versed in the exacting task of achieving administrative results from limited resources amid conflicting pressures.

There is a second factor to consider. The value of a legislature in our society lies especially in its individually representative character. Each member of a legislative assembly has been elected by a particular constituency to represent its political interests. Often, these particular constituencies will have varying needs and different interests. Individual legislators, moreover, will vary in the way in which they interpret these different needs and interests. The legislative assembly proceeds to develop public policy by a process of consensus and compromise achieved among individual legislators. This is the essence of the democratic process in enacting law.

Surely then the value of a legislature in supervising the administration of public policy lies in much the same kind of process. Consensus and compromise among individual legislators must produce a general conception of desirable administrative behavior as well as of administrative conduct which should be criticized. The existence of large legislative staffs made up of persons who have not run for public office but have been appointed to specialized duties may well become an obstacle rather than an aid to this process of legislative consensus and compromise. The legislative staff can scarcely substitute an independent judgment for that which is arrived at in the committee room or in the assembly chamber.

None of these comments is intended to question the need for legislators to have assistants. Legislators are among the hardest-working people in our society. They spend many hours a day performing a bewildering array of duties, from visiting with voters, writing letters, and making speeches to studying the intricacies of vital measures affecting the public interest. Legislators must have help in doing all this work, especially in a society of increasing complexity. But the help must always be kept helpful. There is a great danger in the legislative process that too much bureaucratization in this branch of government may be even more dangerous to a free society than the growth of large-scale organization among administrative agencies. Legislators should have help, not substitutes.

ADMINISTRATIVE INTERFERENCE

It is altogether possible that legislative supervision of administrative agencies may go so far as to render administrative performance ineffective. The legislature may surround the administrative process in general or particular administrative agencies with so many legally enacted details of procedure as to make administrative work one morass of red tape. Administrative performance may be slowed to a walk by legislative prescription of minute details of operation on such matters as organization, appointment of personnel, purchase of supplies, conduct of hearings, adoption of policies, and other items. Or the legislature may spend so much time carrying on an investigation of an agency as to prevent top administrators from giving adequate attention to operating problems. Sometimes it may happen that criticism of an agency by some legislative committee may go so far as to impair the morale of the personnel of an agency and result in an attitude of indifference toward work accomplishment.

Those who have studied the work of administrative agencies in our government in some detail and who have a basic sympathy with administrators have been aware how legislatures may harass and even interfere with administrative operations. In fairness, it must also be said that on occasion legislators more than executives have discovered administrative dry rot and have done much to improve inefficient or troublesome features of administrative activity. Moreover, legislatures often take the lead in developing new programs for administrative operation, the need for which has escaped administrative attention.

It is not easy to prescribe an ideal legislative-administrative relationship. It is customary to say that the legislature ought to confine its attention to broad aspects of public policy and leave details of operation to administrative discretion. This is a formula which is simple to suggest and difficult indeed to apply. Just how is a policy matter to be defined? Is the question whether atomic energy shall be developed under military or civilian direction a matter of policy? Is the question whether all purchases for supplies over $3,000 in amount shall be bought only through competitive bidding a matter of policy? Is the question whether the head of a department shall be paid $12,000 a year or $18,000 a year a matter of policy? Most persons would agree that all these items entail policy. But at what point then do details of organization, of procedure, and of personnel become no longer matters of policy? There is no simple answer.

Certainly it is possible for a legislature in the course of enacting laws or of pursuing investigations to interfere with administrative operations to an undesirable degree, that is, to a degree where administrative ineffectiveness in performance results. How can the legislature be restrained from such interference? One answer is for administrative personnel by concrete fact to demonstrate the results of such interference, to point to actual costs and other evidences of breakdown resulting from legislative interference. Since most public services arise from popular demand for action, any breakdown attributable to legislative interference will soon result in legislative unpopularity. The second answer is executive defense of administrative performance. The executive is expected to remind the legislature when its role of supervision is tending toward performance of the executive's role of supervision. This reminder may be sufficient to cause a legislature to reconsider its action.

Legislative direction and supervision are essential to our democratic system of government. But this power can be pushed to extremes. In the last analysis it is the legislature itself which must perceive this fact.

CONCLUSION

Law provides the basis of administrative authority in the United States. And it is the legislative branch which possesses the power to enact law. Through this process of enacting law the legislature gives direction to administrative effort, specifies the framework of administrative organization, and provides the funds for administrative activity. Incidental to these essential ingredients of public administration, the legislature may through an agency of its own creation watch over the expenditure of funds and through its committees may observe various elements of administrative practice.[23]

[23] W. F. Willoughby identified the elements of legislative supervision and control over administration as follows: (1) the requirement that administrative officers keep records of their official acts; (2) the requirement that administrative officers submit at least an annual report of their work; (3) the requirement that administrative agencies keep an accurate and full account of their financial transactions; (4)

Yet all these phases of the legislative process have limits. These limits are set primarily by a proper regard for the scope of authority which belongs to the executive and to the courts. The authority of the legislature is substantial. It is not all-powerful. Individual legislators are sometimes prone to believe that the supremacy of the law in our system of government means supremacy of the legislature. But the law of the land also provides for an executive power and a judicial power. The legislature is not an exclusive branch of government; it shares its power with other branches.

It is customary to speak of the American system of government as one of checks and balances. It would be more appropriate and more exact to speak of our structure of separated power as one requiring mutual consideration and collaboration. It may well be as one scholar has said about legislative-executive relationships in foreign policy, that collaboration is "irksome, time-consuming, and tiring."[24] And no doubt many difficulties do arise between the legislature and the executive because honest differences arise between what shall be regarded as collaboration in the formulation of public policy and what shall be regarded as interference in supervision of administration. Yet it still remains that not a checkmate but necessary collaboration is essential between the branches of government in order to operate the American political system.

A prime necessity in our scheme of governmental authority is legislative respect for the other branches of government just as the others must in turn respect the authority of the legislature. The legislature's own sense of self-restraint is the finest evidence of the existence of this respect. The executive is constitutionally bound to resist any encroachment upon his power. The judiciary is equally obligated to exercise its power with care and a proper regard for the niceties of constitutional distinction. The legislature can do much to make this concern of the executive and the judiciary a minor one.

The American scheme of government is not well served by legislators who see no limits to the legislative power. Legislative self-restraint remains as a most important guarantee of constitutional government. Executive and judiciary may from time to time remind the legislature of its proper role, especially in relation to administrative agencies. Yet it is the

---

provision for a system of examining or auditing these financial accounts; (5) provision for legislative committees to consider the results of this examination of financial transactions; (6) the requirement that administrative officers provide information to the legislature when called upon to do so; (7) provision for special investigation of the conduct of an administrative agency; and (8) provision for impeachment of a principal administrative officer guilty of treason, bribery, or other high crimes and misdemeanors, W. F. Willoughby, *op. cit.*, pp. 158ff.

[24] Robert A. Dahl, *Congress and Foreign Policy* (New York: Harcourt, Brace and Company, Inc., 1950), p. 212.

legislature itself which most, if not all, of the time must manifest a clear understanding of the scope and limits of the legislative power, and must scrupulously observe its proper role.

This proper role is by no means negligible in relation to public administration. The task of the legislature is to help ensure that the administrative agencies of government remain responsible to the leadership of the governmental institutions of a free society and of a democratic polity. This can be achieved only if the legislature performs effectively the various duties enumerated in the preceding chapters. It cannot be effectively performed if the legislature endeavors to move beyond its proper sphere of competence by encroaching upon the role of the executive or the role of the judiciary. The legislature has heavy responsibilities to perform, responsibilities of vital importance to the public welfare. The legislative role cannot be minimized. The legislature provides a major institutional device for realizing responsible bureaucracy in the American system of government.

PART THREE

The Executive

Chapter 13

The Executive Power

The second division of governmental power in the United States is that of the executive. Yet interestingly enough, our constitutions have not thought it necessary to define the executive power with any fine degree of precision. Rather executive power has developed more from custom, usage, and law than from constitutional prescription. Yet necessarily it is the constitution in our federal government and in our state governments which is the foundation of the executive power.

Article II of the federal Constitution begins with the simple words that "the executive power shall be vested in a President of the United States." Far more words are then devoted to how this executive is to be elected than to what he is expected to do. Presidential authority is set forth in a few brief phrases. The President is to be Commander in Chief of the armed forces; he is to make treaties, by and with the advice and consent of the Senate; he is to receive ambassadors and other public ministers; he is to nominate, and with the consent of the Senate, to appoint ambassadors, other public ministers and consuls, judges, and other officials as designated by law; he is to appoint without senatorial approval other positions in so far as authorized by law; he is to "commission" all officers of the United States; and he may grant reprieves and pardons for offenses against the United States except in cases of impeachment. The federal Constitution also declares that the President may require "the principal officer in each of the executive departments" to set forth his opinion in writing on any subject. And the President is to "take care that the laws be faithfully executed."

In addition, the President has certain legislative authority which is set forth in Article I of the federal Constitution. Annually he is to present a message on the "State of the Union" and from time to time is to recommend various measures for legislative consideration. He may summon the legislature into extraordinary session. If the two houses are in disagreement about adjournment, he may adjourn a session of Congress. He may disapprove legislation, which in turn may be passed over his objection by a two-thirds vote. Thus the President is given an important role in legislative matters.

To some extent the power of the governor has been stated in much the same kind of terms. He is commander in chief of the state militia (National Guard), which involves in practice the summoning of the militia to service and assignment in some location of the state where violence and disorder occur. He appoints such officers as are not independently elected or whose appointment is not otherwise provided for by law. He may grant reprieves and pardons. He has similar legislative authority to that possessed by the President.

There are also certain limitations upon the governor's authority not found in the case of his federal counterpart. The governor has no power to conduct foreign affairs since this is an exclusive federal function. Furthermore, and more importantly, the governor under terms of many state constitutions exercises the "principal" or "chief" executive power. Most state constitutions provide for the direct election by the people of such administrative officials as a secretary of state, an attorney general, a treasurer of state, an auditor of state, and a state board of education or a superintendent of public instruction. The governor is a "chief" executive then only in the sense that he is first among a number of persons who share the administrative authority of the executive. The governor has no power directly to supervise or control these officials in the exercise of their offices. Certainly, he cannot dismiss them, since they are responsible to the electorate rather than to him.[1]

From the rather sketchy provisions set forth in our constitutions the executive power has developed as we know it today. To some extent the basic constitutional conception of the position has changed to the extent that state constitutions have been amended or rewritten in order to increase executive authority over administrative agencies or in budget and appropriation matters. To some extent the executive power has responded to changing governmental needs in a highly industrialized society. To some extent the nature of the executive power has had to adjust itself to meet the requirements of our governmental system in practice, especially the requirement that there be some center for the formulation and advocacy of desirable public policy. And to a very considerable degree the executive power has responded to the impact of particular personalities who have been elected to hold the position of President or governor in our country.[2] It may well be, as one writer has declared: "The presidency

[1] Cf. Coleman B. Ransone, Jr., *The Office of Governor in the United States* (University, Ala.: University of Alabama Press, 1956), pp. 222ff.

[2] As an illustration of how one man affected the Presidency, see Arthur W. Macmahon, "Woodrow Wilson as Legislative Leader and Administrator," *American Political Science Review,* vol. 50 (September, 1956), p. 641.

itself has come to be our leading social invention and our main contribution to democratic government."[3]

Today it is realized that the Presidency is a position of many different responsibilities.[4] The President is ceremonial chief of state. He is the leader of a national political party. He is a legislative leader in the sense of formulating and presenting desirable public policy for statutory enactment. To this end he commands public attention through the media of mass communication.[5] He is Commander in Chief of the Armed Forces. He conducts the foreign relations of the United States. And he exercises extensive supervision over the administrative activities of government.

In a somewhat different way a recent study of the position of governor has suggested a threefold classification of responsibilities. First, the governor carries the burden of policy formulation for legislative consideration. Secondly, he exercises supervision over the administrative work of state government. And thirdly, he is the leader of partisan politics within his state.[6]

Our interest here is focused not upon the whole range of executive authority but more narrowly upon its role in directing and controlling the bureaucracy. Yet it is not easy, or realistic, to draw any sharp distinctions in the nature of the executive power. In the federal government, for instance, the Presidency is an office held by a single individual and all elements of the executive power are fused in one person; each particular element reinforces another. The legislative and partisan roles of the Chief Executive cannot be clearly differentiated from his administrative role. The legislative role is vastly important in providing a leverage for administrative supervision, since administrative agencies realize that if they are to obtain desired legislation they will be greatly aided by executive endorsement. Similarly, the role of an executive in partisan politics will do much to enhance his legislative leadership and his administrative influence.

One other aspect of the executive position must be emphasized at the outset of any discussion. The executive is a popularly elected official. He is politically responsible to the people. In the United States the President and the Vice President are the only two officials elected by all the voters

---

[3] Sidney Hyman, *The American President* (New York: Harper & Brothers, 1954), p. 4.

[4] For a general discussion, see Louis Brownlow, *The President and the Presidency* (Chicago: Public Administration Service, 1949); Hyman, *op. cit.;* W. E. Binkley, *President and Congress* (New York: Alfred A. Knopf, Inc., 1947); George Fort Milton, *The Use of Presidential Power* (Boston: Little, Brown & Company, 1944); Pendleton Herring, *Presidential Leadership* (New York: Rinehart & Company, Inc., 1940); Harold J. Laski, *The American Presidency* (New York: Harper & Brothers, 1940); and Clinton Rossiter, *The American Presidency* (New York: Harcourt, Brace and Company, Inc., 1956).

[5] Cf. James E. Pollard, *The Presidents and the Press* (New York: The Macmillan Company, 1947).

[6] Ransone, *op. cit.,* chap. 6.

of the nation. The executive is not selected by one state or one county. He is executive for the nation or state as a whole. He thus speaks for a nationwide or state-wide interest. The executive, moreover, is not selected by the bureaucracy. Rather, he is elected by the people to help direct and control the bureaucracy.

This point requires attention because at times in the acrimony of legislative-executive conflict legislators seem to assume that executive and bureaucracy are identical, and that only the legislature speaks for the interest of the citizen in his relations to government. This is not true. The executive, as we have said before, is a coordinate branch of government, sharing power with legislature and judiciary. The executive derives his power from constitutional prescription and constitutional usage. He obtains his position by vote of the people.[7] The executive is a part of the basic structure of government. He, too, is an instrument, a vital, indispensable instrument, in the quest for responsible direction of the bureaucracy.

THE PRESIDENT AS GENERAL MANAGER

Apart from a concern with national defense and foreign affairs which we shall consider in subsequent chapters, the President's authority as a general manager of administrative activities rests upon three particular provisions of the federal Constitution. The President may "require the opinion, in writing, of the principal officer in each of the executive departments, upon any subject relating to the duties of their respective offices." The President, with the consent of the Senate, appoints all the major administrative officers of the United States as determined by law. And the power of removal has been implied by this authority to appoint. Thirdly, as we have said, the President is to "take care that the laws be faithfully executed." Supplemented by certain statutory provisions, such as those of the Budget and Accounting Act of 1921, these words of the Constitution have enabled the President to become in fact the continuing general "overseer" or "manager" of all administrative activities. To the extent that there is any one person who can under the federal Constitution exercise a constant watchfulness over the national bureaucracy, that individual is the President of the United States.

The Supreme Court has never had any occasion to consider the language of the Constitution relating to executive departments. Court interpretations about the "faithful execution" of the laws of the land have had to do mainly with the guarding of a Supreme Court justice whose life

[7] In the case of the federal government the President may be elected by the House of Representatives if there is no absolute majority of electoral college votes. This has not happened since 1825.

has been threatened,[8] with the use of troops to prevent a rail strike from interfering with the dispatch of the mails,[9] and with other action involving strikes.[10] In its broad administrative implications, the language of the Constitution has not been brought before the Supreme Court for interpretation and decision.

It is not easy to know exactly what these words of the Constitution in practice actually mean. The President may require the head of an executive department to present opinions to him in writing. Just what is the importance of the authority to ask for opinions in writing from heads of administrative agencies? On the surface, the authority does not seem too important. It suggests only that the President may obtain any information he may want from administrative agencies and that such agencies have a constitutional obligation to respond to any Presidential request for information or advice.

Perhaps the injunction that the President shall see to it that the laws are faithfully executed is somewhat more concrete. At least there is a standard here for the guidance of the Chief Executive—the execution of existing law. In any event, within the limits of the law as enacted by the legislature the President is expected to make sure that administrative agencies perform their responsibilities. If the President were convinced that some agency or official was not faithfully carrying out the provisions of law, he would be expected to take corrective action. Here again the question arises about the situation where a department head may have one idea about what constitutes faithful execution of the law and the President has a different interpretation. Whose idea shall prevail? The answer of history is that the President's idea must prevail. The same answer must be given in terms of political theory, since the President is an elected official and the department head an appointed one.

Certainly the power of the President to request opinions and advice in writing from department heads and the power to see that the laws are faithfully executed carry with them a vital implication. They suggest that the President is expected to maintain a fairly close scrutiny over the work of administrative agencies. Moreover, this is a continuing responsibility, one which goes on every day of the year, contrasted with the more limited sessions of a legislative body. In order to fulfill his duty the President must be adequately informed about the policies and programs of administrative agencies and must be generally satisfied that the purposes of law are being observed. To the extent that he may so desire this provides a broad basis of supervision over administrative activities, since most laws usually afford some leeway for interpretation of policy in terms of what may be politically desirable and defensible. When this general power of

[8] *In re Neagle,* 135 U.S. 1 (1890).
[9] *In re Debs,* 158 U.S. 564 (1895).
[10] Cf. *United States v. United Mine Workers,* 330 U.S. 258 (1947); and *Youngstown Sheet and Tube Co. v. Sawyer,* 343 U.S. 937 (1952).

supervision is then further enforced by the power to appoint and remove key administrative personnel—a power to be discussed in more detail later—then the authority of the President to direct administrative operations is substantial indeed.

Historically, perhaps the most famous incident involving the power of the President was that concerning the handling of government bank deposits during the time of President Jackson. Soon after his reelection in 1832, in which his veto of the bill to extend the charter of the United States Bank, a private corporation, was a principal issue, President Jackson determined to remove government deposits from the bank. Jackson transferred one Secretary of the Treasury and removed another before he found in Roger B. Taney of Maryland a man willing to carry out his order. The government deposits were removed from the United States Bank and the bank itself passed out of existence as a federally chartered corporation in 1836.

In the bank case President Jackson insisted upon his own interpretation of what he considered desirable public policy in administrative operations. He had asked the Congress for authority to remove the federal government's deposits from the United States Bank and the Congress refused to grant such authority. After the election of 1832 the President felt that his interpretation of what should be done ought to prevail, and he insisted upon administrative action accordingly. Obviously, he believed such action to fall within the realm of his executive authority over administration.

Similar instances have occurred at other times in American history. President Theodore Roosevelt asked the Congress to withdraw from right of individual entry certain public lands containing mineral deposits. The President was concerned about large business interests arranging to acquire coal lands at the low prices fixed under the Homestead Act. When the Congress did not act, President Roosevelt proceeded on his own authority to issue a series of proclamations withdrawing large tracts of land from public entry and setting them aside as national forest reserves. The President considered such action as proper under his executive authority.

President Woodrow Wilson asked the Congress to authorize him to arm merchant vessels for their own protection against German submarines prior to American entry into World War I. A filibuster by a group of eleven Senators prevented passage of such a measure. The President then proceeded to direct administrative agencies to arm merchant vessels, relying upon his constitutional authority and the terms of an obsolete statute of 1819. Since the Congress did not then repeal the old law, the President could further claim legal sanction for his action.

In December, 1921, President Warren G. Harding informed the Congress in his annual message that he had no intention at that time of carrying out the provision of a law passed by the previous Congress. Under this law the Chief Executive was directed to terminate all existing commercial treaties in order to encourage the greater use of American ships in carrying both imports and exports. The President expressed his belief that the action would not realize its expressed purpose, that it would create a chaotic trade situation, and that it would invite international retaliation.

The constitutional role of the President in substance then is one of exercising his power in such a way as to ensure what he considers to be the proper behavior of administrative agencies. Proper behavior is essentially a twofold matter. It is legal behavior, behavior which satisfies the criteria of law as enacted by the legislative process of our government. It is also politically responsible behavior, behavior which meets the general political consensus of society as interpreted by the President.

In practical terms, especially in a time of large-scale activity, no Chief Executive can hope to be conversant all the time with all the work being done by the administrative agencies of government. The President is expected to intervene in those areas of administrative operation where some reason for his attention arises. Apart from foreign affairs and the national defense, the Chief Executive usually has his administrative interest aroused by the circumstances of the time. There may be public charges of maladministration in some field of activity, such as the delivery of rural mail, the issuance of grazing and mining rights on the public domain, the handling of oil rights, the operation of work relief, or the collection of taxes. When widespread criticism and a general breakdown in public confidence occur in any field of administrative activity, the Chief Executive is expected to take vigorous corrective action. Or a Chief Executive is confronted with some general social or economic need, such as large-scale unemployment, declining farm prices, or a collapse of the banking system. Or a President may have some particular policy point of view arising from his own political faith which he wishes to carry out, whether it be the advancement of internal improvements, the settlement of the public land, the preservation of the Union, the control of trusts, the conservation of natural resources, the readjustment of economic power, or the promotion of private rather than public development of resources. Presidents are usually persons with a good deal of experience in public life, persons who do have a point of view and a "program" to advance. In any event in these various ways the attention of a Chief Executive is directed to those aspects of governmental administration in which he has some definite interest.

The administrative work of the chief executive is part of his responsibility as holder of the executive power. The President of the nation and the governor of a state are political figures who achieve their vital position through the political processes of our society and who are entrusted with the exercise of essential political power. Their approach to administrative problems is therefore primarily political, and the very essence of this political interest is to ensure that administrative agencies carry out the policies which the chief executive sees and defines as in the public interest.

The President can use the sum total of all executive power to direct and control administrative activities to the extent he deems desirable and politically feasible. The President's approach to his role as general manager is essentially that of a concern that administrative agencies shall behave politically as he interprets the public interest of a particular time.

THE GOVERNOR AS GENERAL MANAGER

The authority of a governor as general manager is comparable in many essentials to that of the President.[11] His role is different in so far as other separately elected public officials exercise both executive and administrative duties. These other officials are administrative officers in so far as the actual work for which they are responsible is concerned; they share the executive power in so far as they are responsible to the electorate rather than to the governor. The importance of the position of governor differs a good deal among states because of differences in the size of the job as measured by the population, the territorial magnitude, and the total appropriations of the state. The expense entailed in holding the position of governor and the short duration of his term of office have also had some impact in limiting the development of the governor's administrative role. Furthermore, most governors see their administrative duties as second in importance to their role as legislative leaders.

In many instances a governor is restricted by law from removing administrative officials who head major activities. It is not unusual for statutes to specify that a director of public works, a superintendent of banks, a commissioner of health, among others, are to be appointed for a stated number of years. This has generally been interpreted as preventing a governor from removing these officials and appointing his own selections. Rather, the governor must await the expiration of the statutory term of office before he can make his own appointments. This situation curtails the governor's role as a general manager.

Furthermore, the large number of administrative agencies and the limited personal staff available to the governor have frustrated any inclination on the part of the chief executive of a state to keep in close touch with administrative activities. It is the budget power more than any other single tool which has given the governor some real influence in state administration.

To a considerable degree the governor's success in supervising state ad-

[11] This section has been written from the discussion contained in Ransone, *op. cit.,* chaps. 8 and 9.

ministrative activities depends upon persuasion. If the governor is recognized as having a good deal of personal popularity with voters and with
legislators, then administrators tend to be responsive to efforts by the
governor to provide administrative leadership. Some governors have been
successful in utilizing a "cabinet" or "council" of chief administrative
officials as a device for expressing their own points of view. The difficulty
has been of knowing whom to include in a governor's council. There are
so many administrative agencies that to have each represented may result
in almost a mass meeting. Like Presidents, governors have found that for
counsel on general legislative and administrative policies, they cannot depend upon a cabinet but must have their own small group of intimate and
completely loyal advisers.

There are many obstacles in the path of a governor who seeks to become general manager of administrative activities. In some states the
governor has become such in reality, especially in some of the larger states
with large annual expenditure budgets. In other states the executive power
is still much diffused and little in the way of constitutional or statutory
provision has enabled the governor to assert an active role of administrative leadership.

THE SOURCE OF EXECUTIVE POWER

As we have pointed out, it is the Constitution, federal or state, where
one must first seek the source of executive power. There are two legal
aspects of this situation which require some further elaboration. Both in
a sense are constitutional questions of great importance. The first of these
questions is whether there is a "general" executive power apart from the
more specific enumeration of executive authority, such as the power to
appoint, the power to conduct foreign relations, and the power to see
that the laws are faithfully executed? The other question is how far can
a legislature constitutionally go in defining executive power; can the legislature, if it so desires, remove as well as implement executive power?
These questions have especially attracted attention in our federal government.

As we have already observed, Article II of the federal Constitution
opens with the words: "The executive power shall be vested in a President of the United States of America." The Constitution then specifies
certain actions which the Chief Executive may take, or certain authority
which he may exercise. Does this specific enumeration that follows constitute the whole definition of executive power? Or is there a general executive power which is more than the sum total of this enumerated authority?

The classic formulations of position on this question were made in
American political history by President Theodore Roosevelt and by Presi-

dent William Howard Taft. In his autobiography President Theodore Roosevelt summarized his point of view in these words:[12]

> The most important factor in getting the right spirit in my Administration, next to insistence upon courage, honesty, and a genuine democracy of desire to serve the people, was my insistence upon the theory that the executive power was limited only by specific restrictions and prohibitions appearing in the Constitution or imposed by the Congress under its Constitutional powers. My view was that every executive officer, and above all every executive officer in high position, was a steward of the people, and not to content himself with the negative merit of keeping his talents undamaged in a napkin. I declined to adopt the view that what was imperatively necessary for the Nation could not be done by the President unless he could find some specific authorization to do it. My belief was that it was not only his right but his duty to do anything that the needs of the Nation demanded unless such action was forbidden by the Constitution or by the laws. Under this interpretation of executive power I did and caused to be done many things not previously done by the President and the heads of the Departments. I did not usurp power, but I did greatly broaden the use of executive power. In other words, I acted for the public welfare, I acted for the common well-being of all our people, whenever and in whatever manner was necessary, unless prevented by direct constitutional or legislative prohibitions. I did not care a rap for the mere form and show of power; I cared immensely for the use that could be made of the substance.

President Roosevelt's one-time colleague and his successor in the Presidency, William Howard Taft, was equally certain that Roosevelt was entirely wrong. In a series of lectures after he had left the White House, Taft presented his point of view in these words: "The true view of the executive function is, as I conceive it, that the President can exercise no power which cannot be fairly and reasonably traced to some specific grant of power or justly implied and included within such express grant as proper and necessary."[13]

Theodore Roosevelt thought that all Presidents in American history could be classified into two groups, the Lincoln group and the Buchanan group. The former consisted of those Presidents who conceived their responsibility in broad terms to exercise the executive power for the public welfare as they understood it. The latter group comprised those Presidents who saw executive power in the narrow sense of activity limited to the particular duties mentioned in the Constitution. Probably the real conflict here is not one of law but one of attitude and temperament.

The position of Theodore Roosevelt is sometimes referred to as the

[12] Theodore Roosevelt, *An Autobiography* (New York: The Macmillan Company, 1913), pp. 388–389.

[13] William Howard Taft, *Our Chief Magistrate and His Powers* (New York: Columbia University Press, 1916), p. 139.

"stewardship theory" of executive power. The position of William Howard Taft may be labeled the "limited theory" of executive power. It is no simple matter to say that one theory is right and the other wrong. The historical fact is that Presidents as persons have conceived their position in different ways and have behaved differently in office. The American structure of government has been sufficiently elastic to accommodate both points of view at varying times, and the citizenry of our Republic in various general elections have given their apparent stamp of approval to both attitudes.

It is important to emphasize, however, that there is a difference between the "stewardship theory," or what I would prefer to designate the concept of "general executive power," and the theory of inherent executive power. The latter position would seem to suggest that the executive power is some vast reservoir of authority of almost unlimited scope which may be called upon by a President when he sees fit.

The most important constitutional case to date involving the question of the President's inherent executive power occurred in 1952. During the last three months of 1951 a prolonged series of negotiations between the major steel companies of the nation and the United Steel Workers of America failed to produce a wage agreement. On December 18 the union gave notice of its intention to call a strike effective January 1, 1952. Presidential intervention in accordance with the terms of the Defense Production Act of 1950 delayed the strike but again failed to obtain an agreement. A nationwide strike was then called to begin on April 9. A few hours before the strike was scheduled to start, the President ordered the Secretary of Commerce to seize the major steel mills in the name of the government of the United States and to keep them in operation. The Secretary of Commerce proceeded to carry out these orders. The President gave as reason for his action the fact that steel production was essential to the national defense of the nation, and that although the nation was not at war it was in a state of "national emergency" arising from the fact of military action in Korea. On April 10 the President reported his action to Congress, and on April 22 sent a second message on the subject. The legislature gave no indication of taking any action.

In the meantime the steel companies took steps to obtain a judicial restraint upon the Secretary of Commerce for an illegal exercise of administrative power. On April 30 the federal district court for the District of Columbia issued a preliminary injunction against the Secretary. On petition of the Attorney General, the Court of Appeals issued a stay. On May 3 the Supreme Court of the United States agreed to hear the entire matter. Oral argument was heard on May 12 and the Court announced its decision on June 2, 1952.[14] By a six-to-three vote the Court upheld the injunction issued by the district court and ruled that the Secretary of

[14] *Sawyer v. Youngstown Sheet and Tube Co.*, 343 U.S. 937 (1952).

Commerce was without any authority to seize private property and operate it in the name of the government.

The sole justification which could be claimed on behalf of the Secretary's action was that he was carrying out instructions which he had received from the President. The question before the Court accordingly was whether the President had the power to issue such an order. The Solicitor General, presenting the argument on behalf of the President, did not claim any legal authority for his action, even though there were possibly two laws which might have been put forward in justification. Rather, the argument was solely that in time of national emergency the President had inherent power to take any action necessary to ensure the national defense. A majority of the Court refused to accept this position. Rather, the Court insisted that the President's power as Commander in Chief did not justify the seizure order. And in so far as the claim was made that the aggregate of presidential power justified the action, the Court declared that the executive power was to enforce law, not to enact it. The Court was satisfied that the legislature could have authorized the seizure; it was equally satisfied that the President had no power to direct such action. Thus the Court rejected any conception of an inherent executive power which would permit the President to issue orders for administrative agencies to carry out action not previously authorized by law, especially if such action involved a seizure of private property.[15]

As a question of interpretation, there was disagreement within the Court whether the President had issued his seizure order in the process of carrying out existing statutes or had issued his order without legal justification. With perhaps one exception the Court appeared to say that the President could not in effect write new statutory enactment. In the absence of further judicial elaboration on some other occasion, we may conclude for the moment that the doctrine of inherent executive power has been rejected, in part if not *in toto*.

It seems to this author, however, that the Youngstown case does not at this time justify the conclusion that the Supreme Court has accepted the Taft version of presidential power and rejected the Theodore Roosevelt version. The Court has simply rejected the idea that the President may in effect write statutory law. If in the Court's eyes a particular administrative action requires statutory authorization, then only legislative enactment can make such action legal. If on the other hand some line of action appears to be within the discretion of an administrative agency, then the exercise of that discretion may fall under executive scrutiny in so far as the President sees fit. We shall consider later some of the limitations which may arise in the exercise of this presidential oversight. More-

---

[15] For a good discussion of the constitutional aspects of the case and an elaboration of the Court's opinion, see David Fellman, "Constitutional Law in 1951–1952," *American Political Science Review,* vol. 47 (March, 1953), pp. 128–133.

over, as we shall discover later, many orders a President might issue could conceivably occur in areas of administrative action where private parties would find it difficult to obtain judicial review.

If there be an aggregate of executive authority, it lies in some vague, ill-defined area in which the President may set forth desirable policy and practice for administrative agencies to follow when carrying out existing statutory instructions. Beyond this, the President, of course, is free to use his influence in any way possible to persuade the legislature to provide different legal authority upon which administrative action shall be based. The executive authority falls in the broad realm of supervision and direction of administration, not in the realm of writing new legislation for administrative agencies to carry out.

This brings us to the second question concerning executive authority. To what extent is the power of the President derived from law rather than from the Constitution? As we shall observe in later chapters, the actual mechanics of presidential supervision over administrative agencies are today provided by statutes, such as the Budget and Accounting Act of 1921, the Employment Act of 1946, the National Security Act of 1947, among others. The power of the President in matters of administrative reorganization is based exclusively upon statute, as we have recounted earlier. Indeed, in matters of administrative reorganization it is not too much to say that the President serves simply as a legislative agent.

Unquestionably, much of what the President now does in the American scheme of government results from authority vested in him by statute. Yet as a general proposition it seems also proper to declare that such authority has been conferred upon the Chief Executive in the first place because of the fundamental nature of his executive power. Often the statute simply expresses *how,* or by what means, executive power shall be exercised. Statutes have not called executive power into existence but rather have regularized or institutionalized its exercise.

Here it is important once more to remind ourselves about a major aspect of the American system of government. Our government does not engage in any administrative activity just on whim. Political processes in which interest groups, individual citizens, business enterprises, other private bodies, legislators, administrators, and chief executives combine their efforts result in statutes specifying what administrative action government shall undertake and how government shall undertake it. The executive power to supervise administrative activity comes into play *after* this statutory direction has been provided. In some circumstances, as we shall observe, the legislature may circumscribe this executive power; it cannot eliminate or fundamentally change that power.

When the legislature by statute provides ways and means by which the chief executive shall carry out his power, it is not creating that power. The legislature is only implementing executive power. This is an important distinction to make. It is sound constitutional doctrine to maintain that the legislature cannot create executive power. There seem to be no constitutional grounds for declaring that the legislature may not implement executive power—that is, provide the means and set up the ways in which executive power shall be exercised.

There is yet a third aspect of executive power to consider. Is executive power created by crisis, by emergency? The attitude of the Supreme Court on this subject in so far as the exercise of legislative power is concerned was spoken in 1934.[16] The Court declared emphatically that an emergency did not create power. Rather, it might create the occasion for the exercise of power. This is a subtle distinction; it is nonetheless now an item of constitutional doctrine in our country. An emergency does not vest new power in the legislature, or the executive for that matter, and an emergency does not alter the distribution of power within our governmental system, nor does it remove the limitations upon power. Rather, the Supreme Court appeared to recognize that under extraordinary circumstances the legislature, and presumably the executive, may do extraordinary things, but only if they come within the general concept of legislative or executive power. When one studies the action of a chief executive in a time of crisis, one finds that he has greater scope to exercise his power than under ordinary circumstances, and that he may command a more ready response from legislature and public.[17] In a time of emergency, presidential leadership may be vigorous, urgent, and extensive. So long as the legislature and the public at large are willing to sustain this leadership, the President may enjoy a success and prestige which in less troublesome times may not be realized. Crisis alters the environment in which presidential power is exercised; it does not alter the nature of the executive power in our scheme of government.

THE EXECUTIVE AND ADMINISTRATION

At this point we must refer once again to a troublesome constitutional problem, one which is by no means yet resolved in terms of constitutional interpretation or prevailing political theory. The question is this: do all the administrative activities of government constitute a part of the executive branch of government? If one endeavors to answer this question from a doctrinaire point of view which begins with the assumption that under our scheme of government there are only three branches, the temptation is great to say conclusively: all administrative agencies are a part of the executive branch. Certainly one cannot say that administrative agencies are a part of the legislative or judicial branch. Therefore, since we recog-

---

[16] *Home Building and Loan Association v. Blaisdell,* 290 U.S. 398 (1934).

[17] Cf. Louis William Koenig, *The Presidency and the Crisis* (New York: King's Crown Press, 1944).

nize only three branches to our governmental structure, administrative agencies must necessarily be a part of the executive branch.

A realistic examination of the operation of our government suggests a different answer. It is of little importance that administrative agencies are described constitutionally as a part of the executive branch of government if one has a clear understanding of what the resulting executive branch really means. Suppose for the sake of discussion we assume that all administrative agencies of government comprise a part of the executive branch. If we accept this proposition, then the executive branch has certain particular characteristics.

In the first place, an executive branch which encompasses the sum total of the administrative work of government is different from the executive power set forth in our constitutions. It becomes necessary indeed to speak of the executive branch as having two distinct parts: the chief executive and all administrative agencies. The chief executive enjoys certain constitutional authority. Unless created by the constitution as is done for certain state activities, administrative agencies enjoy only a statutory existence and a statutory authority.

In other words, the chief executive is created by a constitution. Administrative agencies are created by law. This is a fundamental difference. Administrative agencies created by law may be changed by law, their powers increased, diminished, or ended. Administrative agencies must answer to the legislature for how their legal authority is exercised, at least to the extent of facing the possibility that their legal power may be changed. Administrative agencies must constantly justify their existence.

There is a second fundamental difference. Administrative agencies are created in order to carry out the operating tasks of government. The executive has been created to exercise the fundamental power of government. The two roles are different. The one involves the assignment of activities to be performed in accordance with the instructions of the legislature and the executive. The other, the executive, is charged with the exercise of the supreme governmental power, along with the legislature and the judiciary, of directing what administrative agencies shall do.

There is still another difference. The executive is a formal participant in the legislative process. Administrative agencies do not have such power. The executive is formally empowered by the constitutions of our federal and state governments to recommend desirable legislation and to veto measures which he considers undesirable. Administrative agencies may suggest desirable legislation only informally, that is, through individual legislators friendly to an agency. Nor can administrative agencies prevent the enactment of any legislation. Yet administrative officials must deal directly with legislative committees in seeking appropriations and in advocating particular statutory changes. Administrative relations with the legislature are not channeled exclusively through the executive. Administrative agencies, for example, obtain their appropriations directly from the legislature, not through the executive. The executive is not in practice the exclusive spokesman for the vast range of all administrative activities of government.

If we think of administrative agencies as a part of the executive branch of government, then we must at least draw a distinction between executive power which is derived primarily from our constitutions and administrative authority which is drawn from statutes. To be sure, the executive provides a continuing supervision of administrative agencies, a kind of general management, but he cannot provide an exclusive supervision. In supervising administration, as in exercising the power of governance, the executive must share his activity with the legislature and the judiciary. The executive branch, if it includes administrative agencies, is not the exclusive province of the executive. Nor can it be under the American system of constitutional government.

THE EXECUTIVE AND ADMINISTRATIVE ORGANIZATION

In discussing the legislative power we have already spoken of the legislature as the architect of administrative organization. This situation has not been altered in its basic constitutional status by the device of authorizing the executive in the federal government to prepare reorganization plans subject to legislative veto. We may note, however, that state governments have not seen fit to follow the federal precedent in arranging for administrative reorganization.

There are circumstances, however, in which the executive may exercise some authority in the establishment or alteration of administrative organization. Such circumstances have been exemplified a number of times, especially in the federal government, under emergency or other unusual conditions. When it is disposed to do so, the legislature may enact statutes setting forth broad purposes to be accomplished by administrative action but providing no specific administrative machinery. The establishment of appropriate administrative agencies is then left to executive action.

This was done, for example, in 1933 in the passage of the National Industrial Recovery Act. It was done again in 1935 in the passage of the Federal Emergency Relief Appropriation Act. In May, 1940, President Roosevelt used the authority of a 1916 defense law (the Army Appropriation Act of August 29) to create an Advisory Commission to the Council for National Defense. In turn, the statute permitted the Council to set up certain subordinate bodies, and in this way a variety of agencies came into existence. Subsequent legislation, such as the Priorities Act of June 28, 1940, conferred administrative power upon the President which he in turn delegated to the new defense agencies in process of development. The Defense Production Act of September 8, 1950, conferred broad administrative authority upon the President and included in section 304 these words: "For the purposes of sections 302 and 303, the President in hereby authorized to utilize such existing departments, agencies, officials, or corporations of the Government as he may deem appropriate, or to create new agencies (other than corporations)." Thus, at various times the President has been given a statutory authority to establish administrative agencies.

In addition, under certain circumstances the President may establish administrative devices without explicit statutory authorization. In general, I am inclined to believe that this power extends only to the Presidency itself; that is, to arrangements which may be set up to help the President in the exercise of his own executive power. The Cabinet is not exactly an administrative agency, but its existence is a matter of custom rather than of either legislative or executive prescription. A very important piece of administrative machinery, the Joint Chiefs of Staff, developed during World War II without any formal order from the President but functioned certainly with his approval and encouragement. This agency did not receive statutory sanction until 1947. From time to time the President creates study boards and commissions to investigate special problems for him. Sometimes these receive statutory approval or at least the sanction of an appropriation; sometimes these bodies operate without any such authorization. There have been many such bodies in the past thirty years, from the Air Policies Review Board (Morrow Board) in 1925 and the Commission on Recent Social Trends (1930–1932) to the President's Commission on Higher Education (1946), the President's Materials Policy Commission (1952), and the President's Committee on Education beyond the High School (1956). Thus the President may certainly set up temporary, and even continuing, units to help him in the performance of his immediate executive responsibilities. Usually, when needed on a continuing basis, the Congress has been willing to authorize such agencies upon request of the President.[18]

When full allowance is made for all these ways in which the President may influence or determine administrative organization, it is still constitutionally and legally correct to say that the President does not have any inherent power to create or alter administrative agencies to carry on the work of government. As we have said before, governmental policy and program to be accomplished by administrative agencies and the broad outlines of administrative structure itself are determined by law. The President may play a part in the preparation and approval of such law, but this is the extent of his basic power in matters of governmental administrative organization.

[18] Cf. Carl Marcy, *Presidential Commissions* (New York: King's Crown Press, 1945).

LIMITATIONS UPON EXECUTIVE POWER

As is the case with the other branches of government, the executive power is limited. It is limited by the specifications of the Constitution. It is constitutional doctrine that a branch of government possesses only those powers which are conferred upon it and which may be reasonably implied by the terms of the Constitution. As we have pointed out earlier, our courts have not looked with favor upon the idea of an inherent executive power. In the second place, the executive power is limited by the extent to which the legislature has seen fit to implement that power through legislation. We shall discuss the institutional aspects of the Presidency in the next chapter. We may note here that the President obtains such assistance in the performance of his duties as the legislature may be persuaded to provide. This necessarily enforces some limitation upon executive power.

In the third place, the executive power is limited by public opinion and popular accountability. The President or any chief executive is a popularly elected official. Under some state constitutions he may not seek reelection. Now under the provisions of the Twenty-second Amendment to the federal Constitution, no President may be elected to that office more than twice, and a President succeeding to office in the first two years of a term may be elected only once. Even though the two-term tradition was strong in American political usage until the time of Franklin D. Roosevelt, there was always the possibility that a President in the second term of office might still seek a third period of service. This probably made Presidents continually alert to public reaction on their policies and proposals. Now that this possibility has been removed, there is some doubt just what impact it will have upon presidential behavior during a second term. Conceivably the removal of the third-term possibility might make a President more independent and even decided in his own attitudes, and so reduce the restraint which might arise from a concern for popular approval. On the other hand, a President who may wish to have some voice in the selection of a successor and who may wish to ensure some continuity in party control of the Presidency will undoubtedly continue to be alert to public opinion during his second term. In any event, a concern for popular reaction is a restraint upon the exercise of executive power.

Finally, the judiciary should be mentioned as another limiting factor. In practice, this has not been too important because it is not ordinarily easy to test the exercise of executive power in the courts. But certainly the judiciary remains at all times an important potential force in limiting executive activity.

Executive power accordingly is not some vast range of authority without limits. The chief executive in our system of government is powerful. But he is not all-powerful. His power is subject to restraint in accordance with constitutional doctrine of limited and separated power. The executive has power to control the bureaucracy. He does not exercise an exclusive control over the bureaucracy.

CONCLUSION

The executive power is another element in the constitutional system for conducting the work of government in our society. The executive possesses considerable authority to keep the administrative agencies of government under continuing surveillance, especially to make sure that such agencies abide by the purpose of the law and perform their work as desired within a free society. Certain powers vested in the executive are administrative in nature, having to do with the appointment of administrative personnel, and general oversight of administrative operations. The political, legislative, and ceremonial duties of a chief executive serve to reinforce these administrative powers, and together combine to make the chief executive the vital figure which he is in our scheme of government.

The chief executive derives his power from the individual specification of authority and from the total implication of authority vested in him. But the constitutions of our government do not confer unlimited power upon the executive; nor is there some vague reservoir known as inherent power. The chief executive is a constitutional executive.

To some extent there has been a good deal of confusion in American government about the status of administrative agencies in our tripartite scheme. It has been assumed that administrative agencies had to be a part of one branch or another of the three, and that accordingly they must be a part of the executive branch. Such an interpretation must not blind us to the extensive part played by the legislature in the direction and supervision of administrative agencies. But neither should the role of the chief executive be thought of as dependent upon legislative permission. The chief executive is an independent branch of government, enjoying a status equal to that of the legislature and the judiciary and today often enjoying a prestige greater than the other two. With these two branches, in his own way, the executive has his role to fulfill in helping ensure that bureaucratic behavior shall be politically responsible.

Chapter 14

The Executive as an Institution

The executive power is vested primarily in a single individual. The incumbent of the position of chief executive is elected in accordance with the provisions of the Constitution of the federal government or of a state government. But at both the federal level and the state level the position of chief executive has become more than the office held by a single person. The executive power has become an institution.

This development of a position vested in a single person into an office of institutional proportions did not occur overnight. Within state government, moreover, the development has been uneven, proceeding more rapidly in some states than in others. The course of events has been especially noteworthy in the federal government, and for that reason we can well afford to concentrate our attention upon the Presidency of the United States.

The President today finds himself the center of a considerable apparatus to assist him in the exercise of the executive power. It has become literally true that the Presidency is now a position too big and too complicated for one person. The Presidency is an office with extensive work to perform involving specialized abilities and techniques. In performing this work many persons are necessarily engaged. In this sense the Presidency has become an institution. But this development should not blind anyone to the fact that the President is still an individual, and the vitality of the Presidency must necessarily depend upon the personality of the President.

HISTORICAL BEGINNINGS

No President has found it possible or desirable to serve alone. He has necessarily sought advice in the exercise of his high office. President Washington soon turned to his four department heads for continuing assistance and suggestion in the formulation of national policy.[1] Washington particularly invited Hamilton and Jefferson to meet with him often, and he in turn visited the secretaries in their own offices. In addition, a constant stream of correspondence arose between the President and his department heads. Sometimes the President referred matters to the secretaries and to the Attorney General requesting their opinion; even more often they in turn sought his guidance on matters requiring departmental decision. From these origins developed the extralegal device which has come to be known as the President's Cabinet.[2] By the end of Washington's two terms in office, the concept of the Cabinet was fairly well established and has survived to this day.

In Jackson's time, still another avenue of Presidential assistance became prominent, the "Kitchen Cabinet." There were at least four men, of whom Amos Kendall was most prominent, who held no official position with the federal government, but who became influential advisers to the President. Finally, in 1835, just about two years before his eight-year term of office expired, Jackson brought Kendall into his Cabinet as Postmaster General. But the idea of the unofficial adviser thus came into prominence and has continued down to the present day. President Theodore Roosevelt had his "Tennis Cabinet." Woodrow Wilson made extensive use of a personal friend and confidant, Colonel E. M. House. During World War II much the same sort of relationship to President Franklin D. Roosevelt was enjoyed by Harry Hopkins.

In the third place, at some time in the first half of the nineteenth century it was recognized that the President had to have some clerical assistance of his own. Probably during the period when Jefferson was President, Congress began to appropriate funds for the President to hire a single clerk. President Monroe is said to have used his brother as a secretary and President John Quincy Adams employed his son.[3] President Jackson used a nephew who officially held a clerkship in the General Land Office. President Tyler had a son to help him; Presidents Polk and Buchanan again had nephews. Finally, in 1857 Congress recognized that the time had come when the President must have some kind of personal staff, and provided funds for a private secretary, a steward to take charge

---

[1] Actually, originally there were only three executive departments: State, Treasury, and War. The Congress in 1789 also created the position of Attorney General (the Department of Justice did not become an executive department until 1870) and the position of Postmaster General. Washington considered the Attorney General a close adviser from an early period in his administration; the Postmaster General was invited to join the President's Cabinet by Jackson in 1829. See Lloyd M. Short, *The Development of National Administrative Organization in the United States* (Baltimore: Johns Hopkins Press, 1923), pp. 101–103.

[2] See Leonard D. White, *The Federalists: A Study in Administrative History* (New York: The Macmillan Company, 1948), especially chaps. 3 and 4.

[3] Leonard D. White, *The Jeffersonians: A Study in Administrative History, 1801–1829* (New York: The Macmillan Company, 1951), p. 75.

of the White House, and a messenger. Thus was begun the President's "official household."[4] President Lincoln had both a secretary and an assistant secretary, John G. Nicolay and John Hay, well-known subsequently for their ten-volume biography of the President. Henceforth, most Presidents had two secretaries; eventually President Hoover had three. The idea of a personal White House staff had now come into existence.

A fourth element was added when the Bureau of the Budget was authorized by the Budgeting and Accounting Act of 1921. Although nominally a part of the Department of the Treasury, the first Director (General Charles G. Dawes) successfully established the proposition that the Director of the Budget worked directly for the President and helped him in exercising some oversight of administrative agencies. Thus the President had a new kind of assistance, an organized agency with a number of specialized personnel working to implement his leadership.

By the time of President Franklin D. Roosevelt there were accordingly four constituent elements in the emergence of an institutionalized Presidency. These were the Cabinet, or council of official advisers; the personal associate or assistant available for a "roving assignment" on matters of immediate importance to the President; personal secretaries to take care of such matters as appointments, press relations, party relations; and an organized office, the Bureau of the Budget.

During the first four years of his administration, Franklin Roosevelt extended but did not fundamentally alter the pattern of White House organization which he found in existence in 1933. The Cabinet was supplemented by the creation of a National Emergency Council; the Council was different in that it had a staff. Indeed, the executive director on occasion was called an "Assistant President" by the press. The work of the Budget Bureau was supplemented by the creation of a National Resources Committee and a Central Statistical Board. Moreover, the wing of the White House which accommodated the immediate staff for the President was enlarged and rebuilt. But this by no means could house the staff which now surrounded the President himself. By 1936 the Presidency had been institutionalized on a sizable scale.

THE PRESIDENT'S COMMITTEE ON ADMINISTRATIVE MANAGEMENT

As we have noted in an earlier chapter, in the spring of 1936 President Roosevelt set up a study group known as the President's Committee on Administrative Management. Its report, released in January, 1937, was a landmark among public documents on the subject of government organization. Especially notable was the concentration of attention upon

[4] Leonard D. White, *The Jacksonians: A Study in Administrative History, 1829–1861* (New York: The Macmillan Company, 1954), pp. 82–84.

the Presidency itself. The keynote of the report was a single sentence: "The President needs help."[5]

The report began with a discussion of the White House staff itself and declared that the assistance available to the President was inadequate. It did not present any factual information about the existing White House staff, although it did say that the President had been compelled "in the past" to use personnel carried on the payroll of administrative departments. The Committee contented itself with advocating that a small number of executive assistants, not to exceed six in number, should be added to the three secretaries. The report left the nature of their duties to the President for determination; it said only that "they would not be interposed between the President and the heads of his departments" nor were they to be "assistant presidents in any sense." The report went on to declare:[6]

> Their effectiveness in assisting the President will, we think, be directly proportional to their ability to discharge their functions with restraint. They would remain in the background, issue no orders, make no decisions, emit no public statements. Men for these positions should be carefully chosen by the President from within and without the government. They should be men in whom the President has personal confidence and whose character and attitude is such that they would not attempt to exercise power on their own account. They should be possessed of high competence, great physical vigor, and a passion for anonymity. They should be installed in the White House itself, directly accessible to the President.

The President's Committee added that this step alone would not be enough.[7]

> The President must be given direct control over and be charged with immediate responsibility for the great managerial functions of the government which affect all of the administrative departments. . . . These functions are personnel management, fiscal and organizational management, and planning management. Within these groups may be comprehended all of the essential elements of business management. [The report asserted that the] three managerial agencies, the Civil Service Administration, the Bureau of the Budget, and the National Resources Board should be a part and parcel of the Executive Office.

Subsequent sections of the report of the President's Committee were entitled "Personnel Management," "Fiscal Management," and "Planning Management." Both the substance of government policy in these fields as advocated by the Committee and the organizational arrangements suggested were precedent-making. More than this, in the subsequent discus-

---

[5] President's Committee on Administrative Management, *Report,* p. 5.
[6] *Ibid.*   [7] *Ibid.,* p. 6.

sion of the proposals it was inevitable that the personality of the then incumbent of the White House should color all consideration of the ideas themselves.

The proposals on fiscal management were perhaps the most acceptable, at least in so far as they dealt with the Bureau of the Budget and with the strengthening of its staff, especially in the field of management analysis. In so far as the report advocated the transfer of certain functions of the Comptroller General to the Secretary of the Treasury, the recommendations were not destined to receive favorable action by the Congress. The subjects of personnel and of planning, however, aroused the most concern.

When the Pendleton Act was passed in 1883 and the Civil Service Commission created, the President had been given extensive authority in government personnel administration. Within the limits of exemption by law, the President was to determine the positions in administrative agencies which were to be filled by competitive examination. In addition, not only was the President given the authority to appoint three Civil Service Commissioners, but also the law said nothing about any limitation upon the President's authority to remove these commissioners at will. Nonetheless, the idea that the President himself should be thought of as directing the government's personnel system as a whole was new. Moreover, the recommendation that a single Civil Service Administrator be appointed to serve at the President's pleasure, aided by a Civil Service Board of an advisory nature, was a considerable departure from existing organizational practice. At a time when the government service had grown so greatly in numbers as it had since 1933, and in the light of the known importance of personnel administration as a leverage in executive-legislative relations, the Congress was not disposed to change the pattern of personnel administration in the federal government.

The idea of planning management was even more novel, and its implications even more far-reaching. The President's Committee realized this and handled the whole matter with some caution. It pointed out that 47 states now had planning boards and that over 1,100 municipalities had such agencies. The Committee called attention to the creation of the National Resources Committee as a part of the machinery under the public works title of the National Industrial Recovery Act of 1933. It then advocated a permanent National Resources Board of five members to serve without salary and to have a continuing staff. Such an agency was to serve as a "clearinghouse" of planning information and to keep in touch with the planning activities of departmental, state, and local agencies. In addition, the Board was to collect and analyze data "relating to our national resources, both human and physical," and also was to have the function of "shaping up advisory plans for the better use of these resources."[8] Thus

[8] *Ibid.*, p. 28.

the Committee called attention to the essential public works context of most governmental planning activity in the United States and then moving beyond this spoke only of "advisory plans." Yet the implications were obvious.

An outstanding American economist wrote in 1945: "Within little more than fifteen years, this country has witnessed two momentous revolutions: one in economic thinking and the other in the economic functions of government."[9] The report of the President's Committee on Administrative Management appeared in the midst of this so-called revolution. At that time, the Congress and certainly large segments of the American public were not yet ready to accept the proposition that the federal government should assume responsibility for the functioning of the American economy. If the President were to have as a permanent agency a National Resources Board to assist him, then economic depression or government intervention in economic affairs were to be considered permanent features of American society. In 1937 this was too far-reaching a suggestion for ready acceptance.

In any event, the report of the President's Committee on Administrative Management was a major step in urging the institutionalization of the Presidency. Its thinking was to be a guiding light in subsequent developments and to influence action for many years to come.

THE EXECUTIVE OFFICE OF THE PRESIDENT

The Reorganization Act of 1939 took two steps along the lines recommended by the President's Committee on Administrative Management. Title 3 of the law authorized the President to appoint up to six administrative assistants to perform such duties "as the President may prescribe." In this way the White House Office itself was enlarged. In the second place, as recounted earlier, the new law set up a procedure for administrative reorganization through reorganization plans subject to legislative disapproval.

Under the terms of this act President Roosevelt immediately took action in accordance with the recommendations of the 1937 report. Reorganization Plan I of 1939 transferred the Bureau of the Budget from the Treasury Department to an "Executive Office of the President." In addition, the designation of the National Resources Committee was changed to National Resources Planning Board, and it likewise was attached to the Executive Office of the President. One of the provisions of Reorganization Plan II of 1939 abolished the National Emergency Council and created in its place an Office of Government Reports. The plans were permitted

[9] John Maurice Clark, "Financing High-level Employment," in Paul T. Homan and Fritz Machlup (eds.), *Financing American Prosperity* (New York: The Twentieth Century Fund, Inc., 1945), p. 71.

to become effective by the failure of Congress to pass a concurrent resolution of disapproval; indeed, by terms of a joint resolution approved June 7, 1939, the effective date for the reorganization plans was fixed as July 1.

It is a nice constitutional and legal question whether Reorganization Plan I of 1939 created the Executive Office of the President as an institutional device. Certainly here is the first mention of the concept of an organizational entity entitled the Executive Office of the President. Yet the Reorganization Plan did not specifically say that it was creating a new agency; rather it seemed to assume that there already was in existence such an Executive Office of the President.

Subsequently, by Executive Order No. 8248 issued on September 8, 1939, President Roosevelt proceeded to organize the Executive Office of the President. Here again the order itself took care not to say anything about the actual creation of the new device. Instead the preamble recited that by virtue of the authority vested in him by the Constitution and by various statutes, and in order to carry out the purposes of the Reorganization Act of 1939 and of the two plans submitted to Congress, the executive order was being issued for the purpose of "organizing the Executive Office of the President with functions and duties so prescribed and responsibilities so fixed that the President will have adequate machinery for the administrative management of the executive branch of the government."

The executive order of September 8, 1939, thus made no pretense of *creating* the Executive Office of the President. It provided merely for its organization. We may conclude then that President Roosevelt and his advisers in 1939 conceived of the Executive Office of the President as an incipient arrangement which had existed since the federal Constitution went into effect in 1789. They apparently were careful not to *create* a new organizational device but only to call it into being. This may seem a subtle distinction, and perhaps no such intention as is here ascribed actually existed in the minds of President Roosevelt and his advisers.

In any event, the Executive Office of the President officially and formally came into existence in 1939. Executive Order No. 8248 went ahead to specify that the Executive Office of the President should have "six principal divisions": the White House Office, the Bureau of the Budget, the National Resources Planning Board, the Liaison Office for Personnel Management, the Office of Government Reports, and an Office for Emergency Management. The activities of the White House Office as specified by the order were "to serve the President in an intimate capacity in the performance of the many detailed activities incident to his immediate office." The office was to include the secretaries to the President, the executive clerk, and the administrative assistants to the President. The Budget Bureau was to assist the President in preparing the annual budget for transmission to the Congress and was to perform certain other activities. The National Resources Planning Board was to collect data and analyze problems pertaining to national resources and to recommend to the President and to the Congress "long-time plans and programs for the wise use and fullest development of such resources." In addition, it was to develop "orderly programs of public works and to list projects in the order of their relative importance," and it was to inform the President "of the general trend of economic conditions and to recommend measures leading to their improvement or stabilization." The Office of Government Reports was to provide a "central clearinghouse" on government information and to keep the President informed about citizen and group interests.

The creation of the Liaison Office for Personnel Management was a step toward the performance of the personnel functions recommended by the President's Committee in 1937. One of the administrative assistants was designated to fill this office and was directed to help the President in performing his duties under civil service laws. In a sense the new office was to be a kind of mediation agency between the Civil Service Commission and the personnel interests of operating departments and other units. It foreshadowed the development of a more vigorous and positive program of personnel management throughout the federal government.

Finally, the Office for Emergency Management was in 1939 no more than an office in embryo, or a declaration of intention. The Executive Order said only that "in the event of a national emergency, or threat of national emergency" such an office was intended to come into existence. Since the order was issued only a week after Hitler's invasion of Poland, it suggested the possibility of increased Presidential concern with national defense. Actually, the Liaison Office for Emergency Management was activated in May, 1940, when the appointment of the Advisory Commission to the Council of National Defense was announced. The Office for Emergency Management at that time provided a kind of organizational "tent" for the various component elements of the Advisory Commission. In 1941 as new operating agencies concerned with national defense production began to appear created by executive order—agencies such as the Office of Production Management, the Office of Price Administration and Civilian Supply, and the Office of Defense Transportation—the Office for Emergency Management became less important. The office finally came to an end in 1943.

One other important feature of Executive Order No. 8248 should be noted. The order directed that the Bureau of the Budget should be physically moved from the Treasury Building to the old State, War, and Navy Building immediately to the west of the White House. Offices for the administrative assistants and for the top personnel of the National Resources Planning Board were also provided in this building. Eventually, the entire building became an Executive Office Building. The concept of an institutionalized Presidency was to endure the vicissitudes of war, demobilization, and cold war and to become a permanent addition to the machinery of American government.

WAR AND POSTWAR DEVELOPMENTS

There is no need here to trace in detail the various changes in the organization or functioning of the Executive Office of the President which occurred from 1940 to 1949. It will be sufficient to sketch simply major elements of change in the structure of the Office.

It may be well to begin with the Office of Government Reports, since this unit of the Executive Office was to prove the least durable of any as originally established in 1939. The very origin of this element of the Executive Office may have prejudiced its history. It gave continued existence to what remained by 1939 of the old staff of the National Emergency Council. This office tried to perform two major functions. It endeavored to provide a central information office in Washington about government activities. The most tangible result of this effort was the publication of a government manual describing the function and organization of various administrative agencies. Eventually this function was to find a permanent home in the Federal Register Division of the National Archives. Otherwise, the informational effort of the office was only of slight importance; the unit could only refer inquiries or complaints to the agency involved and most people, certainly those with any knowledge of Washington (including the staffs of trade associations and other organizations), were able to make their own direct contacts with the administrative personnel competent to handle their concerns. The second function of the office as originally contemplated was to provide a kind of gigantic "weather vane" for the political climate of the nation. By newspaper clippings, by interview, and by other avenues of information, the office was to inform the President about political attitudes throughout the country. The function was on the one hand too "subjective" and too "political" to command much enthusiasm from Congress; on the other hand it was too remote and too impersonal to be of much tangible usefulness to the President himself.

In any event, the Office of Government Reports was absorbed into a newly created Office of War Information in June, 1942. In this setting the work of the agency concentrated in large part upon war propaganda overseas, both among our allies and against our enemies. For a time certain activities involving government liaison with the advertising industry and the motion picture business were continued after the war, but in 1947 Congress directed the liquidation of all such work not later than June 30, 1948. Thus this particular institutional experimentation in a central government information agency under the aegis of the President came to an end.

The Liaison Office for Personnel Management had considerable vitality for nearly two years after it was created. The veteran and able civil servant who filled the post of administrative assistant assigned to this work in 1940 became also the head of the Office of Emergency Management and was drawn heavily into the work of helping the new national defense agencies organize their activities. To a considerable degree after 1943 the work started by this office fell to the Civil Service Commission (and to one commissioner, Arthur S. Flemming, who for all practical purposes became the civil service administrator during these years) and to the chairman of the War Manpower Commission set up in 1942. After the war the practice of assigning one administrative assistant in the President's Office to concentrate upon personnel matters was revived. To some extent this interest was political, involving the recruitment of individuals to serve in major administrative posts; to some extent this interest was managerial, involving matters of general government personnel policy which needed presidential attention. Eventually, the office was officially abolished on May 1, 1953, shortly after the inauguration of President Eisenhower.

For a time after 1939 the National Resources Planning Board (NRPB) continued to perform the same kind of work previously undertaken by the National Resources Committee. A staff unit on programing public works was created, as well as another division on economic trends. Studies of long-range government policies continued to occupy Board attention, such as a review of security, work and relief policy, an analysis of national transportation policy, and a careful collection of data on trends in industrial location. As the crisis of national defense deepened in 1941 the Board turned a major part of its attention to the problems of postdefense economic readjustment. In 1942, with the United States at war, the Congress became more and more restive about government activities not immediately concerned with the war effort itself. This attitude was all the more understandable with the prospect of prolonged conflict before the tide of battle might be expected to turn in favor of the Allied Powers. In 1943 by an appropriation act approved June 26, the legislature directed that the NRPB was to be abolished by August 31, 1943. In this way an agency which had accumulated various hostilities and which symbolized the rationalization of the economic endeavors of the 1930s came to an end.[10]

In October, 1942, the President created an Office of Economic Stabilization to exercise a general oversight of the anti-inflationary policies and programs of the government during World War II. This office had been nominally established within the Office for Emergency Management, so that in effect, it too was a part of the Executive Office of the President. Thus one element of the work of the NRPB, the analysis of economic

[10] Cf. John D. Millett, *The Process and Organization of Government Planning* (New York: Columbia University Press, 1947).

trends, had already been lodged in another unit of the Executive Office when the NRPB was abolished. The Office of Economic Stabilization was indeed a powerful agency, far more powerful an influence in directing government administration than the NRPB had ever been.

Then in May, 1943, the President made an additional move. He created still a new agency, the Office of War Mobilization, which was located directly in the Executive Office of the President. Although the Office of Economic Stabilization was not officially abolished, the director of this office, Justice James F. Byrnes, was moved up to become director of War Mobilization. Thenceforth, for all practical purposes, the OES tended to function as a kind of subordinate part of the Office of War Mobilization. In October, 1944, the Congress by legislative enactment gave a statutory basis for the work of the Office of War Mobilization and Reconversion as it was thereafter designated. Throughout the war from 1943 on the OWMR was the top agency of government under the President supervising the mobilization of war resources and planning government policies for the postwar period of readjustment.[11] The OWMR and OES were finally officially merged by executive order in July, 1946, and then in December the designation was changed to Office of Temporary Controls. This agency, in turn, was liquidated effective July 1, 1947.

In the meantime still another agency in the field of economic planning had been created by an act of Congress, the Council of Economic Advisers, set up by the Employment Act of February 20, 1946.[12] This time the Congress in so many words provided that the Council of Economic Advisers was to be a continuing part of the Executive Office of the President. The implications of the Employment Act of 1946 are so sweeping, and the responsibilities thereby imposed upon the President are so great, that we shall consider this whole subject further in a subsequent chapter.

One other development needs to be noted. As we have remarked earlier, the Joint Chiefs of Staff came into existence in 1942 as a major element in assisting the President to perform his duties as Commander in Chief. Although never formally designated as such, the Joint Chiefs of Staff in effect functioned as an advisory arm of the President in directing the military strategy of World War II and in ordering the necessary logistical support. The whole subject of postwar military organization and defense planning became a vital matter of legislative concern even before World War II came to an end. For nearly two years thereafter, the Congress continued to consider the subject. Finally, the National Security Act of July 26, 1947, was passed and approved. In addition to creating the National Military Establishment, this legislation set up two new agencies. The

[11] Cf. Herman Miles Somers, *Presidential Agency: The Office of War Mobilization and Reconversion* (Cambridge, Mass.: Harvard University Press, 1950).
[12] Cf. Stephen Kemp Bailey, *Congress Makes a Law: The Story Behind the Employment Act of 1946* (New York: Columbia University Press, 1950).

first was designated the National Security Council, with the President as chairman and with certain department heads as members. This Council was a statutory cabinet for national defense planning and operation, with a staff secretariat. In addition, a Central Intelligence Agency was made a subordinate office for the National Security Council. In the second place, the law established a National Security Resources Board with a civilian chairman to be appointed by the President and with members drawn from various departments as determined by the President. This Board was to serve primarily as a planning agency in developing policies and programs for national economic mobilization in the event of another world conflict. In effect, although not so stated by law, the staff of the National Security Council and the chairman and staff of the National Security Resources Board were part of the President's Executive Office. Although now giving a statutory basis to its activities, the National Security Act of 1947 made the Joint Chiefs of Staff an advisory body to the Secretary of Defense rather than to the President as Commander in Chief.

The foregoing paragraphs sketch in broad outline the institutional developments in the Office of the President from 1939 to 1949. Although the pattern of organization changed in a number of ways during these years of defense planning, war, and demobilization, nonetheless the Executive Office of the President was well established and the Presidency had become an institutionalized branch of our national government by 1950.

THE FIRST HOOVER COMMISSION

It was understandable indeed that the first Commission on Organization of the Executive Branch of the Government as set up in 1947 should give a good deal of attention to the new phenomenon, the Executive Office of the President. The very first report of the Commission released in February, 1949, was entitled "General Management of the Executive Branch." In this report the Hoover Commission declared:[13]

> No executive, public or private, can manage a large and complex establishment without staff assistance. Staff agencies must keep the President informed on the way in which the various departmental programs are related to each other, assist in defining specific programs pursuant to the instructions of the Congress, and help him supervise the execution of these programs.
>
> Staff agencies do this by helping the President control the common requirements of all government programs—funds spent, legislation requested, personnel required, the relation of each program to others and to the national interest. The President's staff agencies can best help him by keeping in close touch with their counterparts in the departments.

[13] Commission on Organization of the Executive Branch of the Government, *General Management of the Executive Branch* (Washington: Government Printing Office, 1949), p. 5.

Here was complete acceptance of the concept of an institutionalized Presidency. The first Hoover Commission of 1949 recognized that under modern circumstances the President must have the assistance of staff agencies. The only criticism of the Commission was that "despite improvements during the past decade, these staff agencies are still less effective than they should be."

As of 1948 the Hoover Commission recognized five component parts to the President's executive staff: the White House Office, the Bureau of the Budget, the Council of Economic Advisers, the National Security Council, and the National Security Resources Board. The White House Office itself included three secretaries, an assistant to the President, six administrative assistants, a special counsel to the President, an executive clerk, and military aides assigned from the Army, Navy, and Air Force.

The Commission then recommended two additions to this staff: an Office of Personnel headed by a director who should also serve as chairman of the Civil Service Commission, and a "staff secretary" to assist the President "by clearing information on the major problems on which staff work is being done within the President's Office, or by Cabinet or interdepartmental committees." What the Commission seems especially to have had in mind was the creation of a secretariat which might help improve the advisory work of the Cabinet and also help in clearing reports made for the President's advice and guidance. The Hoover Commission also recommended that formally, as well as in practice, the National Security Council be made a part of the Executive Office of the President. It wanted the Council of Economic Advisers replaced by a single Economic Adviser. And the Commission urged that the President not be prevented by statute from organizing his office as he should see fit, and that the President be authorized to appoint heads of Executive Office units without the requirement of Senate approval.

The major change resulting from these recommendations was the formal incorporation of the National Security Council and the National Security Resources Board into the Executive Office of the President by Reorganization Plan 4 of 1949. The President did not see fit to carry out the recommendations involving the Council of Economic Advisers, personnel, or the Cabinet secretariat.

The impact of the undeclared war in Korea beginning in 1950 had its effect, however, upon the structure of the Executive Office of the President. On December 13, 1950, by Executive Order No. 10193 the President recreated an Office of Defense Mobilization in the Executive Office. The purpose of this order was to provide the President with an immediate assistant in directing the partial mobilization of economic resources occasioned by the military action in the Far East. Still another step was taken the next year. The program of international economic assistance begun in 1948 under the Economic Cooperation Act of April 3 of that year was altered by terms of the Mutual Security Act of October 12, 1951, into a program of essentially economic aid for military purposes. The act authorized the President to name a Director for Mutual Security in the Executive Office of the President to give continuing direction to the activities authorized by the legislation. The Economic Cooperation Administration was abolished and its place taken by a new agency called the Mutual Security Agency. This agency was to be headed by the Director of Mutual Security in the Executive Office.

Thus there came into existence a peculiar organizational arrangement whereby an operating agency was headed by a presidential staff assistant. This pattern seemed to emphasize the close personal relationship which the President himself was to have to the program, and at the same time expressed a legislative desire to avoid a situation where policy conflicts might arise between the head of an administrative agency and a staff adviser to the President. In any event, this particular device was to remain for the duration of the Truman administration.

In skeleton form, therefore, the Executive Office of 1952 included the White House staff, the Bureau of the Budget, the Council of Economic Advisers, the National Security Council and its Central Intelligence Agency, the National Security Resources Board, the Office of Mutual Security, and the Office of Defense Mobilization. It was a sizable array.[14]

THE EISENHOWER ADMINISTRATION

President Dwight D. Eisenhower brought to the position of the Presidency in 1953 the background of a life spent in the military service of the nation. He had held high command, including that of supreme command, Allied Expeditionary Forces in Europe, in 1944 and 1945, Chief of Staff of the United States Army, and the initial command of the Allied Powers in Europe, 1951 and 1952. As a result, he was familiar with large-scale organization and with the concept of staff operation necessary to the exercise of command.

To what extent such a background is the best possible preparation for the exercise of the varied duties of the Presidency is too large a subject for exploration here. It is fair to say, however, that President Eisenhower probably possessed in 1953 more experience with and appreciation of organizational concepts current both in the military and in large American business enterprise than any other President of the twentieth century. In this sense he was well equipped to cope with some of the basic features of handling the Presidency as an administrative institution.

Furthermore, after many years there was still a good deal of dissatisfaction in some quarters about the existing arrangements in the Executive Office of the President. A report published in December, 1952, identified

[14] On the historical development of the Executive Office, see Edward H. Hobbs, *Behind the President: A Study of Executive Office Agencies* (Washington, D.C.: Public Affairs Press, 1954).

this dissatisfaction as twofold: faulty organization and limited capacity to control, guide, and direct the work of the great administrative agencies of government.[15] Organizationally, this report criticized the large number of high-ranking aides each having access to the President, the informality of Cabinet meetings, and the large number of units making up the Executive Office. The report declared: "There is inadequate coordination between the units of the Office, and there are too many of them for constant Presidential supervision."[16] One consequence of these deficiencies was a failure on the part of the Executive Office to provide the President with some continuing review of governmental policy and performance in broad areas of administrative endeavor. These criticisms were repeated by others who were concerned with improving the operations of the Executive Office.[17]

During the first administration of President Eisenhower, certain important structural changes were made in the Executive Office. First, the President changed the relationship of the Civil Service Commission to the Executive Office by making the chairman of the Commission his immediate adviser on personnel matters. In the second place, although the Council of Economic Advisers was retained as a collegial body, the chairman of this Council was recognized in effect as principal economic adviser to the President. In the third place, the National Security Resources Board was abolished and its duties consolidated with those of the Director of Defense Mobilization. In the fourth place, the office of Director of Mutual Security was dropped with the creation of a consolidated operating agency, the Economic Cooperation Administration. In the fifth place, the President established a secretariat for the Cabinet. All of these were substantial adjustments which appeared to represent definite improvements over previous arrangements. In 1958 by terms of Reorganization Plan No. 1 submitted on April 24, the President consolidated the Office of Defense Mobilization and Federal Civil Defense Administration into a single Office of Defense and Civilian Mobilization. By terms of a statute approved August 26, 1958, this plan was amended to change the name to Office of Civil and Defense Mobilization in the Executive Office of the President.

The most important change of all, however, was the creation in effect of the position of Chief of Staff to the President. President Eisenhower made the post of The Assistant to the President in reality a position of head of the entire White House staff. To this position the President appointed an early political associate of the 1952 campaign, former Gover-

[15] Bradley D. Nash, *Staffing the Presidency*, Planning Pamphlet no. 80 (Washington, D.C.: National Planning Association, 1952).
[16] *Ibid.*, p. 24.
[17] Cf., for example, Herman Miles Somers, "The President as Administrator," *The Annals of the American Academy of Political and Social Science,* vol. 283 (September, 1952), p. 104.

nor Sherman Adams of New Hampshire. Although some criticism from time to time was directed at Governor Adams from political opponents, there was also agreement on two or three essential characteristics of the Executive Office under his direction. First, the Assistant to the President provided a degree of central direction and leadership for the Presidential staff never before realized. As a result, the various persons in the staff worked together more effectively than under previous administrations. In the second place, it was commonly agreed that Governor Adams had greatly reduced the immediate administrative burden of the President. Some declared that Adams was more than an assistant to the President; they declared he was assistant president and at times the actual formulator of policy for the President. Regardless of these criticisms, it was nonetheless evident that the President did obtain a lessening rather than an increased demand upon his own time by the work of the White House staff under Adams' direction. In the third place, Governor Adams remained in the background and subordinated his personality to the best interests of the Eisenhower administration. Obviously, Adams did not use his high position to advance his own political career. Instead, he shunned the limelight, made no public speeches, stayed away from newspaper men, devoted himself to his administrative duties, and claimed no prestige or status for himself. In consequence, he not only evidenced that "passion for anonymity" prescribed by the President's Committee on Administrative Management in 1937, but also represented a model for a presidential chief of staff. Because of criticism arising from the acceptance of gifts by him from a New England businessman, Governor Adams resigned his position in September, 1958. He was succeeded by his associate, a retired Army officer, Wilton B. Persons. The idea of a presidential chief of staff was thus continued, although General Persons had a more affable personality than Governor Adams.

To some extent the immediate White House staff under President Eisenhower included persons assigned to help keep the President informed about special programs of the government. These persons were designated "special assistants." For example, one was charged with coordinating government policies and programs in the field of foreign economic policies; another was a consultant on public works; one on disarmament; another on tariff and trade policy; still another on government reorganization and federal-state relations. The chairman of the Atomic Energy Commission was also listed as a White House adviser on atomic matters. These men were in addition to the usual Presidential secretaries and to the assistants for such matters as legislative relations, legal affairs, economic affairs, and reports.[18]

[18] For accounts of the White House staff, see Cobell Phillips, "Executives for the Chief Executive," *The New York Times Magazine*, June 5, 1955; *Time*, Jan. 9, 1956; and Gabriel Hauge, "White House Staff Work," *Looking Ahead*, a monthly report of the National Planning Association, Supplement No. 2, December, 1955.

In short, we may say that the Executive Office of the President under the Eisenhower administration had three major characteristics. First, it was a large staff, bringing together a greater number of persons with varied assignments than ever before had been used personally to aid the President. Secondly, the staff combined old-established administrative units such as the Bureau of the Budget and the Civil Service Commission, newer administrative offices such as the Council of Economic Advisers and the Office of Defense Mobilization, and individuals with no immediate staffs of their own. Thirdly, the staff was more closely integrated under central direction of an individual other than the President himself. The Executive Office of the President from 1953 to 1958 reflected how substantially the task of the President had expanded in supervising the administrative agencies of government.

THE CABINET

As we have commented earlier, the idea of a President's Cabinet developed during the time of President Washington.[19] The practice of using department heads as individual and collective advisers was strengthened during the administration of Thomas Jefferson. Indeed, throughout most of the nineteenth century the work of the federal government was relatively simple and there was little administrative reason why the heads of executive departments and even of other agencies could not be brought into close personal relationship with the President.

Administratively, this situation changed during the twentieth century. Heads of executive departments preside over large administrative units whose work is extensive and complex. The burden of their own administrative responsibility is heavy, and the problem of obtaining their own necessary staff assistance has not been easy to resolve. Furthermore, at no time in the past fifty years have the heads of executive departments encompassed the entire range of governmental administrative operations. The many separate agencies made a Cabinet of heads of executive departments simply a partial body in so far as its representative character was concerned.

But there have been other more fundamental reasons than administrative change which have made the early concept of the Cabinet unusable in more recent years. After his election to the Presidency by the House of Representatives in 1825, John Quincy Adams appointed Henry Clay as Secretary of State. Critical though the Jackson group was of an arrangement which smacked of "barter and sale," yet President Jackson in 1829 brought into his Cabinet three persons who were political friends of John C. Calhoun. Thus began the practice for Presidents to fill the

[19] Cf. Henry B. Learned, *The President's Cabinet* (New Haven, Conn.: Yale University Press, 1921).

posts of department heads with persons who represented various factions in the political alignment which had elected him President. The Lincoln Cabinet of 1861 included all his chief rivals for the Republican nomination of 1860. It became a kind of political tradition that an incoming President should placate party opponents and reward political allies by appointment to high governmental position without consideration for personal loyalty or policy agreement.

Such circumstances tended to make the Cabinet less and less influential as a group of advisers to the President. It was difficult for a President to work closely and confidentially with men who themselves had been influential party leaders and whose political ambition might flare again at any time. Memoirs of Cabinet officers, even those before 1933, frequently revealed that discussions at Cabinet meetings tended to be discursive and general, often dealing with the trivia of governmental operations rather than with fundamentals of high policy. The characteristic political mode of selecting heads of executive departments has done much to ensure the futility of Cabinet meetings. Presidents have preferred to deal with department heads individually and on specific subjects.

Under President Eisenhower there may have been some degree of change in this situation. A Cabinet secretariat was created to bring some element of precision into Cabinet meetings. To a greater degree than in previous administrations there tended to be more personal loyalty to the President among heads of departments. Yet even these circumstances were probably not sufficient to revive the Cabinet as an instrument of policy discussion and formulation for the President.

The Executive Office of the President rather than the Cabinet has tended to become the means for assisting the President in directing and supervising the work of the administrative agencies of government. The Executive Office has at least the twin advantages of a point of view that encompasses the government as a whole and of being headed by persons completely devoted to advancing the basic purposes of the Presidency. An institutionalized Presidency is the twentieth century's contribution to our scheme of government in making the President an effective element of political power.

INSTITUTIONALIZING THE GOVERNORSHIP

To some extent much the same kind of development has occurred at the level of the state governor in recent years.[20] Including professional and clerical personnel, the staffs of both the Governor of New York and the Governor of California included over forty persons as of 1951.[21] In sev-

---

[20] Cf. Coleman B. Ransone, Jr., *The Office of Governor in the United States* (University, Ala.: University of Alabama Press, 1956), chap. 10.

[21] *Ibid.*, p. 344.

eral other states the number varied from ten to twenty. And this was the purely personal staff, which did not include the budget office or the personnel of other agencies who might spend a good deal of time working on matters for the governor.

It has been suggested by one study that as a personal staff a governor needs three secretaries, one for policy matters, one for administrative management, and one for public relations.[22] In addition, he requires a legal secretary, perhaps an appointments secretary, and a personal secretary. Although some might debate whether this division of duties is the most desirable arrangement, none can deny that even in a small state the governor must have help. He needs assistance in developing the details of his legislative program. He needs help in preparing the executive budget and watching over its execution. He needs help in keeping in touch with political leaders, in carrying on his relations with the press, in his speech-making, and his numerous other duties. He must have help in running his own personal office.

It takes more than a secretary to do most of these chores. One person alone in each of these fields of interest is not enough. A governor needs a staff in studying many complicated problems, such as revision of a state tax structure, the long-range planning of needed public works, the analysis of expenditure trends, and the review of operating plans in such fields as mental health. To some degree a legislature, too, wishes to study these problems, and some degree of common effort between legislative committees and their staffs and the staff of the governor may be desirable.

In any event it is clear that a governor with one or two personal aides is no longer equipped adequately to handle the many burdens of his office. If a governor is to have any impact upon state government at all, and if that impact is to be more than casual and fortuitous, the governor must have an adequate staff to help him.

CONCLUSION

It must not be supposed that this development of an institutionalized executive office at the federal level or the state level has gone unopposed. Legislators have looked with some worry and even fear upon the emergence of an executive office of some size and complexity. One reason for this concern is that the executive may thus be enabled to augment his power and become even stronger as a legislative and political leader. Even as an administrative manager legislators are not enthusiastic about an institutionalized executive. If the executive is to become more effective in supervising administrative agencies, the influence of legislators may diminish. Then, of course, the element of cost in building up an executive staff does not appeal to a legislature.

[22] *Ibid.,* p. 318.

Other fears have been voiced from time to time. Chief among these is that an executive staff will become so large, so specialized, and so competent that the executive himself will have little personal impact upon his own office. It is a common practice for critics often to direct their attack upon the individuals around the executive. Legislators, party officials, leading citizens, and others who have been rebuffed by the executive often seek consolation by claiming that the executive has been misinformed, that his staff has given him incorrect information, or that his advisers have exerted an undue influence upon the executive.

A staff may on occasion appear to isolate an executive, to separate him from prominent persons who wish to speak with the chief executive and to convince him of the rightness of their case. Just because a governor does not have the time to consult personally with all the citizens who seek an appointment, the substitution of staff assistants to help carry the burden is regarded with suspicion. There is always the conviction in the minds of many that it is easier to convince the executive than his staff.

Regardless of these and similar worries, the institutionalized executive is with us to stay. The executive power can no longer be exercised by a single individual. It requires a staff of loyal, devoted, and competent aides to enable a President or governor today to meet the political, policy, and administrative load of his job.

Chapter 15

The President and Foreign Affairs

There are two parts of the executive power in the federal government which do not rest upon general but rather upon specific authority. One of these is the conduct of foreign affairs and the other is direction of our national defense. Any discussion of the relationship of the executive to the administrative agencies of the federal government is incomplete which does not acknowledge the peculiar position of the President in these two major fields of national concern. We shall deal with one of these in this chapter, and the other in the next.

As we have noted earlier, the role of the President in the field of foreign relations depends upon three different provisions of the Constitution. In enumerating the officials to be appointed by the President, by and with the advice and consent of the Senate, the Constitution specifically mentions "ambassadors" and "other public ministers and consuls." In the next section of Article II the Constitution provides that the chief executive "shall receive ambassadors and other public ministers." The most important provision, however, is the wording earlier in Article II which declares: "He shall have power, by and with the advice and consent of the Senate, to make treaties, provided two-thirds of the Senators present concur." Upon these few words has been built the crucial role of the President in the conduct of foreign relations.

It is not our purpose in this chapter to discuss the history of American foreign policy nor to analyze the various component elements of foreign policy today as these are evident in the conduct of the foreign relations of the United States. Both of these are matters of great importance to the student of American government. Our interest here, however, is more narrowly focused. Our concern is to observe that in the field of foreign relations the President's position is not simply one of supervising administrative agencies in a generalized way. Rather, under the Constitution the President personally is the principal instrument of the federal government in the conduct of foreign relations. To be sure, administrative machinery is necessary in carrying on relations with other nations. Yet this administrative machinery is peculiarly the personal agency of the President, subject at all times to the Chief Executive's own decision about the essential elements of foreign policy.

There is a role for the legislature also to fulfill in the formulation and administration of foreign relations. Not only is the Senate required to consent to the appointment of ambassadors and ministers and to ratify treaties by a two-thirds vote, but also both houses must provide by law for administrative agencies and must furnish the funds to be expended in the conduct of foreign relations. In a day when our foreign policy is so particularly oriented to the provision of economic assistance to other countries, the legislative control of the purse strings is especially crucial. Legislative authority in foreign relations certainly cannot be ignored.

Nonetheless, the President's power in the field of foreign affairs is unique in its relationship to administrative agencies. It is this element of uniqueness which we are concerned to explore in the present chapter.

THE INTENT OF THE FOUNDING FATHERS

The commentary contained in *The Federalist* leaves little doubt but that the conduct of foreign relations was a major concern to the men who wrote the federal Constitution. In *The Federalist,* no. 15, with bitter irony Hamilton enumerated some of the weaknesses of government under the Articles of Confederation. Among other items he inquired rhetorically: "Is respectability in the eyes of foreign powers a safeguard against foreign encroachments? The imbecility of our government even forbids them to treat with us. Our ambassadors abroad are the mere pageants of mimic sovereignty." Later, in no. 69, Hamilton compared the power of the President to make treaties with the authority of the King of Great Britain. He pointed out that the monarch was the "sole and absolute representative of the nation in all foreign transactions." Hamilton then noted that at least the treaty-making power of the Chief Executive was subject to the concurrence of the Senate.

Subsequently, in no. 75, Hamilton declared that the treaty-making power of the President was "one of the best digested and most unexceptional parts" of the proposed Constitution. He suggested that the essence of the legislative authority was to enact laws, that is, to prescribe rules for the regulation of society. The essence of the executive authority was to execute these laws, employing the common strength for this purpose and for the common defense. To Hamilton the power to make treaties did not belong clearly in either of these categories. Treaties were contracts with foreign nations, agreements of sovereign with sovereign. He then argued that the Constitution had solved this issue with admirable facility, since treaties would be made by the Chief Executive but would be valid only with the ratification of a two-thirds vote in the Senate. Hamilton quickly rejected the idea that the treaty-making power might have been vested in the Senate. To have done so, he declared, "would have been to relinquish the constitutional agency of the President in the conduct of foreign negotiations."

The various allusions to the position of the President in foreign affairs as set forth in *The Federalist* suggest several concerns. The power of making treaties loomed large in the eyes of the Founding Fathers. That foreign affairs might involve an intricate network of relationships beyond the formal provisions of a treaty did not seem to have occurred to their thinking. In the light of the experience and conditions of the infant republic in 1787 and 1788, this particular oversight is readily understandable. To persons like Hamilton the machinery for conducting foreign relations under the Confederation was quite faulty. Lacking any executive agency as such, government under the Congress carried on foreign negotiations through ministers accredited by it and supervised by a committee. There were two or three difficulties with this situation. Congress had so many committees—the number rose to ninty-nine in 1781—that jurisdictional lines were confused and policy making was diffused among many groups. Another problem was that within the committee on foreign affairs, for example, not one member but the group as a whole was responsible for formulating and carrying out policy. To be sure, to some extent these particular deficiencies were remedied by a reorganization of committees in 1781, the creation of administrative departments, and in 1784 the development of a central steering committee.[1]

Perhaps in time the confusion of multiple avenues for the exercise of authority might have been remedied. The Articles of Confederation nonetheless suffered from still a third and fatal defect. Once a treaty was negotiated with a foreign power, there was no way for the Congress to ensure its observance by the thirteen states. On one occasion the British Foreign Secretary suggested to John Adams, the American Minister in London, that the thirteen states send ambassadors to negotiate a commercial treaty, since obviously the Congress would never be able to enforce one if Britain should be willing to make such an agreement.[2]

The necessity to give a central government the means to carry out its delegated duties was a principal reason for writing a federal Constitution. In the process of formulating a new document the Founding Fathers decided to establish a separate executive power, and upon this power was conferred the major responsibility for conducting foreign relations. In the field of foreign relations, the concept of executive power was fairly definite

[1] Alfred H. Kelly and Winfred A. Harbison, *The American Constitution: Its Origins and Development* (New York: W. W. Norton & Company, Inc., 1948), vol. 1, p. 102.
[2] *Ibid.*, p. 108.

and specific. Not only were foreign affairs expected to command a major part of the attention of the Chief Executive, but also by constitutional prescription the Chief Executive became the instrument of government for handling foreign relations.

THE DEPARTMENT OF STATE

The Department of Foreign Affairs which had been established by the Congress in 1781 was entirely and exclusively an agency of the legislature. The department was headed by a secretary empowered to correspond with United States representatives abroad, to communicate the instructions of Congress to American ministers, and to send the advice of representatives to the Congress. Interestingly enough, the secretary was permitted to attend the sessions of Congress, but not to speak or vote.[3]

As soon as the new government under the federal Constitution began to function in 1789, the Congress quickly turned its attention to the creation of a new agency for foreign affairs. By an act approved July 27, 1789, the Department of Foreign Affairs was established as the first executive department. The law reflected the new concept of government. The Secretary as head of the department was to conduct its business "in such manner as the President shall from time to time order or instruct." The designation was legally changed to Department of State in September, 1789, and by that title it has been known ever since.

The nature of the new arrangements was to be tested very quickly. In 1793 the republic of France went to war with England and Spain. The young American government now had to decide whether under the Treaty of Alliance of 1778 it was bound to aid in this military activity. The French representative to the United States, Citizen Edmond Genêt, disliked the neutrality predilections of President Washington and endeavored to address his case directly to the Congress. This led Secretary of State Jefferson to declare in emphatic terms that the President was "the only channel of communication between this country and foreign nations, and it is from him alone that foreign nations or their agents are to learn what is or has been the will of the nation."[4] More than this, both President Washington and his successor, President Adams, gave a great deal of personal supervision and direction to foreign affairs.[5]

Thus a pattern was established which was to endure throughout subsequent decades down to the present. The authority vested in the Secretary of State by law was made exercisable only upon the order or instruction of the President. This was very different from the power conferred upon

[3] Graham H. Stuart, *The Department of State* (New York: The Macmillan Company, 1949), p. 3.

[4] *Ibid.*, p. 19.

[5] Leonard D. White, *The Federalists* (New York: The Macmillan Company, 1948), p. 131.

other department heads. In addition, it was established that the President and the President alone was the official and only channel of communication between the government of the United States and foreign governments. The primacy of the President in the conduct of foreign affairs was thus asserted and maintained as a basic feature of government under the federal Constitution.

In subsequent years, as the Congress passed legislation involving foreign relations, the President's special position was almost always recognized. Two illustrations will suffice. On June 12, 1934, the President approved the original Trade Agreements Act, legislation which in various guises has been extended from time to time since then. Under this law the President was empowered to negotiate trade agreements with other nations in which, in return for trade concessions, he might reduce tariff rates fixed by law on various commodities up to 50 per cent. Since 1945 a further reduction up to 50 per cent in the tariff rates in effect at the beginning of that year has been possible.

Ostensibly, it is the President who negotiates such trade agreements. In reality, of course, it has been the diplomatic machinery of the federal government which has carried on the task. Moreover, the condition that no agreement may be negotiated without advance notice and an opportunity for interested parties to be heard has been met through establishment of an Interdepartmental Committee on Trade Agreements. This Committee contains representatives from numerous government agencies, such as the Departments of Treasury, Defense, Agriculture, Interior, Commerce, and Labor, as well as the Tariff Commission. Through various subcommittees actual hearings have been held on proposed tariff reductions on commodities imported from some foreign nation. Drafts of an agreement have then been prepared within the State Department, and eventually submitted to the President for routine approval.[6]

All this procedure illustrates the complexity of carrying out a general policy, such as that of tariff reduction, under present-day conditions. Certainly, the President alone could not execute such a program. Administrative machinery of considerable scope is essential for such a task. But such administrative machinery in the field of foreign relations, we repeat, operates directly and entirely under such personal instruction and supervision as the President may choose to provide.

A second illustration is the Economic Cooperation Act, approved April 3, 1948. After reciting the various findings which justify the legislation, and after declaring it shall be the policy of the people of the United States to encourage and sustain economic development and improvement among the nations of Europe, the law established a new administrative agency

[6] For a brief general discussion of the program see Hollis W. Barber, *Foreign Policies of the United States* (New York: The Dryden Press, Inc., 1953), pp. 198–204.

to be known as the Economic Cooperation Administration. The legislation then asserted that the functions vested in the administrator were to be performed "under the control of the President." Subsequently, in various parts of the law the phrase "under the control of the President" recurs two or three times. In this way the special interest of the President was fully recognized in a major piece of legislation announcing a new policy and creating new administrative machinery.

Thus it is fair to say that the Department of State and other administrative agencies which may be set up in the field of foreign relations function peculiarly under the personal oversight of the President. To be sure, the administrative agencies themselves have been created by law. Their operation depends upon the necessary appropriations. Yet in this instance the authority of the President is not the generalized power of the executive; it is the specific authority to conduct the foreign relations of the United States. All administrative arrangements must necessarily acknowledge the President's unique status in this particular field of federal governmental activity.

THE RECOGNITION OF FOREIGN GOVERNMENTS

As we have noted, the Constitution simply states that the President "shall receive ambassadors and other public ministers." In effect, these words confer upon the President the power to determine with what nations the United States shall choose to maintain diplomatic relations and to determine what government of a nation shall be considered the proper government. These are important political questions, and questions which the President alone decides. He may have advice from the State Department; he may have advice from other sources. The point is that neither the State Department nor any other administrative body may decide this question. Administrative agencies in the field of foreign affairs maintain relations with those nations and with those governments which the President has decided to recognize.

During the administration of George Washington the question arose whether the United States government should recognize the revolutionary government of the Republic of France which had just put the King to death. Washington decided to recognize the government, suggesting that the determination of a people about the form of government it desired was sufficient guide to his own action. The rule has had to be modified, or reinterpreted in the light of subsequent circumstances.

The revolutionary governments of Latin America were recognized by President Monroe, although not before there had been some attempt in Congress to speed up such recognition. The recognition of Cuban independence in 1898 brought in its wake a declaration of war by Spain. Yet President Wilson refused in 1915 to recognize the Huerta government in Mexico, suggesting that a regime born of bloodshed and strife should not be acknowledged by the United States. Wilson and three subsequent Republican Presidents refused to recognize the Communist government of Russia. President Hoover upon the advice of Secretary Stimson in 1931 refused to recognize the Japanese conquest of Manchuria. After 1949 President Truman and then President Eisenhower refused to recognize the Communist government of China as the legitimate government of that country.

This record could be elaborated by still further episodes. Moreover, there is a considerable history of legislative attempts by various devices to hasten the act of recognition by the President in some cases and to retard a possible act of recognition in other cases.[7] These political controversies are not our immediate concern here. It is enough to note that legislative effort to assert primacy in this realm of government action has not succeeded and that the discretion of the President to formulate such doctrine of recognition as he may see fit remains unfettered.

To be sure, the legislature may refuse to appropriate funds for the maintenance of an ambassador or minister in a particular foreign country. This would prevent the President from sending a representative unless that representative paid his own expenses. The Senate may refuse to confirm the appointment of an ambassador and so hamper diplomatic relations. Both President Franklin D. Roosevelt and President Truman resorted to the device of appointing an unpaid "personal" representative to the Vatican, thus giving a form of political recognition to the separate existence of the Vatican state. Moreover there is no way presumably by which the President may be prevented from receiving the ambassador or minister of a foreign government, even though an American ambassador or minister may not be dispatched to that nation.

We repeat the basic point of emphasis here. Administrative agencies maintain day-to-day relationships with those foreign governments which the President chooses to recognize. The task of the Department of State or any other administrative agency is only to perform such duties as may be authorized by law or by the Chief Executive in relationship with those other governments which the President has recognized. The act of recognition is an important political act. It is an indispensable precondition for the work of administrative agencies concerned with foreign affairs.

THE TREATY-MAKING POWER

Most discussions of the treaty-making authority of the President focus attention upon presidential-senatorial relationships. It is generally under-

---

[7] Some of these episodes are recounted in Edward S. Corwin, *The President: Office and Powers,* 3d ed. (New York: New York University Press, 1948), pp. 226–235.

stood today that the treaty-making power is divided into two parts; first is the power to negotiate and to agree upon the terms of a treaty between the United States and a foreign nation. The second part of the power is that of ratifying a treaty. In practice, the first step tends to fall largely in the purview of the Chief Executive, although a cautious concern for ratification often has led a President to associate one or more key members of the Senate in the negotiation process. The second step, that of official ratification of a treaty, is accomplished by the President only after a two-thirds vote in the Senate has given approval to the terms of the treaty.

Perhaps because of this requirement of senatorial approval for treaties, a different class of international understanding has developed known as an executive agreement. An executive agreement is not submitted to the Senate for approval. The exact nature of an executive agreement is not easy to characterize. It might be said that an executive agreement regularizes relationships which may be placed into effect by administrative agencies of both governments. Thus, a President might agree to make certain administrative services available to a foreign government. Sometimes, an executive agreement is in the nature of a joint declaration of future policy. Sometimes, an executive agreement may extend military assistance to a foreign government. Sometimes, an executive agreement is made in execution of a law passed by the Congress.

For example, Theodore Roosevelt entered into an executive agreement with Santo Domingo whereby United States officials took over administration of that country's customhouses. President McKinley entered into an agreement with other countries to contribute American forces to the relief of the legations in Peking besieged by the Boxer revolutionaries. In 1940 President Franklin Roosevelt entered into an agreement with the British government whereby fifty "overaged" navy destroyers were given to that government in exchange for certain naval base privileges in the Caribbean. On the other hand, international postal agreements, trade agreements, lend-lease agreements, economic cooperation agreements, and mutual security agreements have all been made in accordance with authorization conferred upon the President by law. Undoubtedly, the largest single category of executive agreement is the number negotiated as a result of some law passed by Congress.

Our concern here again is not with the intricacies of presidential-legislative relations. Undoubtedly, a President may on occasion be guided in his determination whether to enter into a treaty or an agreement with another nation by his estimate of the chances for senatorial approval. It seems equally evident that any major understanding with a foreign nation must be embodied either in a treaty or in an executive agreement made in accordance with law. Otherwise, the prospect of legislative appropriation or other necessary action to carry out the terms of the understanding may be uncertain. The exception here would seem especially to embrace military agreements.

The important consideration for our attention is the power of the President to make treaties or agreements with foreign nations. The Department of State may do much of the work involved in negotiating the terms of a treaty or agreement. Yet it is the President who must in the end indicate approval. More than this, the President may take such initiative as he may deem desirable in stating the objectives of negotiation with another nation, or in setting forth conditions for an understanding, or in urging exploration of possible areas of understanding. The State Department, or a personal adviser, or any other administrative organization simply serves as the agent of the President when treaty or executive agreements are negotiated with another nation.

Similarly, American representatives in the United Nations or in any of the UN specialized agencies such as the International Labor Office or the United Nations Educational, Scientific, and Cultural Organization are personal representatives of the President. Here again a considerable administrative apparatus has become necessary because of the extensive character of the various phases of UN activities. But all this apparatus exists simply to enable the President to carry out his constitutional responsibility for formulating foreign policy and for conducting foreign relations.

EFFECTING PRESIDENTIAL LEADERSHIP

There are many different aspects to presidential leadership in foreign affairs. One necessarily is the President's own personal interest in and concern with foreign relations. Some Presidents have lacked any real concern with foreign affairs, partly because they had no background of experience in or knowledge about foreign nations. Such Presidents have been guided, if not dominated, by the personality of their Secretaries of State. Other Presidents have evidenced an intense personal interest in foreign affairs, sometimes almost to the point where the Secretary of State was expected to be little other than a chief clerk. There can be little doubt but that when a President does wish to exert personal direction of foreign affairs, the means at his command for doing so are substantial indeed.[8]

To be sure, there are limitations. The President is only a single person. He cannot give all his time and attention to foreign affairs. He has responsibilities of political leadership in domestic affairs and in other matters to which he must give a just share of concern. This means that to a con-

[8] Cf. the conclusion in James L. McCamy, *The Administration of American Foreign Affairs* (New York: Alfred A. Knopf, Inc., 1950), p. 137.

siderable degree the President's role in foreign affairs must be general, or in specific matters occasional.

The growth of agencies other than the Department of State vitally concerned with foreign affairs has presented another problem. Today, such executive departments as the Treasury, Defense, Agriculture, Commerce, and Labor have their own special interests in foreign affairs. The same is true of separate agencies, such as the U.S. Tariff Commission, the Atomic Energy Commission, and the Federal Communications Commission. This has placed a special burden upon the President. He must find a way, personally or institutionally, to provide a common sense of purpose and direction for all these agencies. If he fails to do so, conflict and even contradictory administrative effort may well result.

In foreign affairs, as in other fields of government policy, various devices for coordinated action are available. First, the President may use members of his personal White House staff to clear common interests among administrative agencies on his behalf. In the second place, he may use Cabinet meetings to discuss common concerns or at least to indicate his own personal wishes. Thirdly, he may ask some one administrative agency to take the leadership in developing or implementing policy in some area of foreign affairs in which several agencies have an interest. Fourthly, he may appoint an interdepartmental committee to study and recommend policy or program. Finally, he may ask one of the Executive Office agencies, such as the Bureau of the Budget, to assume leadership in some area of administrative concern.[9] All of these devices, of course, leave the President dependent upon the quality of work performed by his administrative associates.

These various devices have also frequently been criticized as inadequate. The need still exists, many have insisted, for some other kind of administrative arrangement which would make the President's role of leadership effective in fact as well as in constitutional status. For the most part, two alternative arrangements have been discussed. One has been to give a definite role of leadership in all foreign affairs to the Secretary of State. The other proposal has been to build a new staff within the framework of the Executive Office of the President to perform the leadership role on the President's behalf.

Interestingly enough, there has been general agreement among many commentators that the Department of State cannot be made into a supra-administrative agency directing foreign policy activities as a whole on behalf of the President. Some seem to have felt that the Department was too diffuse, too dominated by career Foreign Service officers, too bound by tradition and past experience, too immune to the policy guidance of both the Secretary of State and the President to be a satisfactory device

[9] *Ibid.,* pp. 141–145.

for presidential assistance.[10] Others have suggested that the Department of State has become a kind of whipping boy in the period when the nation has had to turn from the comfortable isolationism of the nineteenth century to the uncomfortable leadership of the Free World in the twentieth century. The State Department works with other nations, not with interest groups and voters at home. It appears to advocate the point of view and needs of foreigners. It tends to wrap some of its decisions in the cloak of secrecy because of a concern for "national security." The staff of the Department is thought to be mostly graduates of Eastern universities. For these and other reasons the Department is often mistrusted by legislators and others who fail to probe beyond these externals into the reality of their fears.[11] Whatever the reasons given, the State Department as an existing entity seems unlikely to become the top agency in foreign policy matters, even if reorganized for that purpose.[12]

The other alternative is to create in the Executive Office of the President some special staff organization giving exclusive attention to foreign affairs. In the last ten years this has been done several times on specific as distinguished from general matters of foreign relations. President Roosevelt used Harry Hopkins as a roving assistant on matters concerned with our military alliances during World War II. President Truman used a special assistant, Averell Harriman, on matters concerned with mutual security from 1950 to 1953. President Eisenhower used a special assistant, Harold Stassen, on matters concerned with disarmament between 1955 and 1958. In each of these instances the White House staff itself provided a base of operations for an individual whose subject-matter interest cut across the concerns of several executive departments and other administrative agencies. In none of these cases, however, was the assignment a general one of foreign policy oversight.

Whether a general staff unit on foreign policy questions is the answer to the President's need or not, no one can say. In any event, no such staff unit has as yet been created. It may well be that the answer lies in a more effective utilization of the devices already available within the Executive Office of the President rather than in a reorganized and concentrated staff agency. This appeared to be the opinion of a study group who examined this subject in 1951. The group pointed out that the opportunity was available now within the White House staff for the President to obtain the aid of men "of great ability and influence" to help him in

---

[10] *Ibid.*, esp. chaps. 3, 4, 8.

[11] Cf. Daniel S. Cheever and H. Field Haviland, Jr., *American Foreign Policy and the Separation of Powers* (Cambridge, Mass.: Harvard University Press, 1952), pp. 195ff.

[12] For one scheme of reorganization in this direction, see William Yandell Elliott (ed.), *United States Foreign Policy: Its Organization and Control, Report of a Study Group for the Woodrow Wilson Foundation* (New York: Columbia University Press, 1952), pp. 101ff.

foreign affairs. It admitted that with the array of agencies now making up the Executive Office of the President there was a need for "considerably greater unity." It is this need which to a substantial degree was realized under President Eisenhower. The study group also mentioned the continued availability of interdepartmental committees when there were common concerns to define or when there was a consensus to develop. In addition, the increasingly important role of the National Security Council in coordinating foreign policy matters was mentioned. In any event, here was the point of view that existing machinery was generally adequate. The problem was one of personality and motivation to make the machinery effective.[13]

There are, of course, institutional as well as personal limitations to the work in foreign affairs which a President may individually handle. American representatives abroad, the personnel of the State Department, officials in other government agencies—all develop or acquire definite knowledge and attitudes on foreign relations. It is characteristic of any bureaucracy that it should have a sense of corporate identity and hence expect some recognition of its existence. If the usual status and prestige important to a bureaucracy are to be maintained, then a President must indicate some confidence in the organized group. A President has then at least the obligation to listen and consider; he may not necessarily always agree.

It is not easy to draw a line between reliance upon a bureaucracy and capitulation to it. It is not easy to prescribe when a political leader should follow the advice of the expert and when he should be willing to venture upon his own program. The usual characteristics of a bureaucracy are caution, a tendency to be satisfied with arrangements as they are, fear of the unknown, inflexibility, intolerance of new ideas, and unwillingness to experiment. There are times and circumstances when these attitudes may all be useful. There are other conditions when change may be essential but the need may be little heeded by top leadership of the bureaucracy. The political leader with a sensitivity to great movements of mass life and thinking will generally be aware of the demands of the time. It seems likely that a President accordingly may resort to those administrative devices which he believes best calculated to obtain the results he wants: continued caution or rapid innovation.

CONCLUSION

The President is our nation's key figure in foreign relations. The constitutional powers vested in him personally are substantial. Foreign affairs are matters of major political concern. The President is expected to take the leadership in formulating foreign policy and in seeing to its execution.

To be sure, the President, as in other fields, is not omnipotent. Treaties

[13] *Ibid.,* pp. 74–101.

must be approved by a two-thirds vote of the Senate. Other policies may require the sanction of law. Certainly little can be done in foreign affairs without legislative appropriation.

More than this, the extent of our foreign relations concerns today is such that a sizable bureaucracy is required in order to handle the various details. Presidential leadership must be exercised within the context of this bureaucratic organization and operation.

The President today has resources within the Executive Office of the President to aid him in dealing with the various administrative agencies having an interest in matters of foreign affairs. This staff assistance may be used to the degree and in ways which the President may personally desire. Certainly the present staff resources can render a great deal of assistance.

The vital aspect of the matter is that in so far as all bureaucratic organization in the field of foreign affairs is concerned, its function is to advise the President and carry out his policies. There is no question in our system of government in so far as the field of foreign affairs is concerned but that the President makes policy. Administrative agencies can scarcely claim any legal authority which would transcend the constitutional authority of the President. The position in foreign affairs of the President is not just one of seeing that the laws are faithfully executed. He is rather the fount of most policy as it exists in the realm of foreign affairs. In this field of administration the President leads and directs; he does more than exercise a general oversight.

Chapter 16

The President and National Defense

The Constitution of the United States simply says: "The President shall be Commander in Chief of the Army and Navy of the United States, and of the militia of the several States when called into the actual service of the United States." With these few words the Constitution established a principle of absolute importance to the new Republic: the principle of civilian control over the armed forces of the nation. At the same time the Constitution vested in the President authority over a major segment of the administrative machinery of the federal government.

There can be no doubt that military considerations were much in the mind of the men who wrote the federal Constitution in 1787. The infant nation had just won its independence through military action aided by the substantial power of the Kingdom of France. Among the initial arguments presented in *The Federalist* in favor of the new Constitution was the case for a strong military position. Jay asserted that a united nation would be respected abroad, and hence less likely to be provoked into war. He pointed out as potential enemies England, France, and Spain. He said of foreign nations: "If they see that our national government is efficient and well administered, our trade prudently regulated, our militia properly organized and disciplined, our resources and finances discreetly managed, our credit re-established, our people free, contented, and united, they will be much more disposed to cultivate our friendship than provoke our resentment" (*The Federalist*, no. 4). And Hamilton summoned the testimony of history to bear witness that republics were not less immune to war than other forms of government. He declared: "There have been, if I may so express it, almost as many popular as royal wars" (*The Federalist*, no. 6). The preamble of the Constitution listed the common defense as one among several objectives; Hamilton went so far as to place it first (*The Federalist*, no. 23).

Concerned as they were with a framework of government adequate to provide for the common defense, the authors of *The Federalist* gave only slight attention to the actual military power vested in the Chief Executive. In two papers (*The Federalist,* nos. 69 and 74) Hamilton spoke of the authority of the President as Commander in Chief in language with which the states were already generally familiar from their own separate constitutions. It was scarcely necessary in eighteenth-century America to argue on behalf of a proper dependence of military authority upon civilian authority. This, like the propositions of the Declaration of Independence, was self-evident.

Yet the problem of military leadership in government has been a continuing concern of political society in Western history. Greek political thinkers were aware of the danger that military adventurers might seize and maintain power through armed force; their fears were well illustrated by the careers of King Philip of Macedon and his son, Alexander. The early Roman republic devised several ingenious arrangements for subordinating military enterprise to the Senate, until Caesar made himself master of both the military and the state, setting a pattern which was to characterize the empire for nearly four hundred years. Henceforth in Western Europe military and civil power were generally synonymous.

In enumerating the specific complaints of the American colonies against their duly constituted kingly authority, Jefferson in the Declaration of Independence pointed out: "He has affected to render the Military independent of and superior to the Civil Power." In these words Jefferson spoke a common point of view among the enlightened thinkers of his day. The American Revolution was won by an army of citizens; the military heroes of the day were planters, farmers, lawyers. With the cessation of actual hostilities against the British, the American army, such as it was, vanished almost overnight. It was this loss of military strength which constituted one of the pressing reasons for abandoning the Articles of Confederation in favor of a new form of government.[1] But in seeking to rebuild a needed military strength, the Founding Fathers were equally concerned to achieve civilian control of military power.

The legislature as well as the executive participated in the military provisions written into the federal Constitution. Only the Congress was to possess the power to declare war. Moreover, the Congress was not to appropriate any money for the support of a military establishment for a longer term than two years. Indeed, of the eighteen clauses included in Section 8 of Article I where the legislative power of the federal government was provided for, eight dealt in part or in whole with military matters. The legislature was expected to exercise its share of responsibility in ensuring civilian dominance of military power.

But the President was expected to have the principal role in directing the military affairs of the new Republic. This was the reason for the succinct language included in Article II. The writings of such political

---

[1] See Louis Smith, *American Democracy and Military Power* (Chicago: University of Chicago Press, 1951), chap. 2.

theorists as John Locke, Coke, Blackstone, and Montesquieu—the writings with which the Founding Fathers were especially familiar—had stressed the dangers of military despotism; they saw the solution in terms of a proper subservience of military to civilian authority. Hence it seemed altogether desirable and even essential to declare that the President was to be Commander in Chief of the armed forces of the United States.

In the political history of the United States the desirable size of the military establishment has been a continuing issue. Those persons who have most feared the menace of military power have usually advocated a small standing army. From 1789 until 1945 the United States provided only the most meager land and sea force for its protection except during actual periods of conflict. The practice of the Republic was to ensure civilian as opposed to military domination of political life by eliminating any military establishment. And even though the nineteenth century witnessed a number of major and minor military conflicts, not to mention various Indian campaigns, the United States generally enjoyed political circumstances which made unnecessary the maintenance of a substantial military force on a continuing basis.

The twentieth century has brought a change in this situation. The military participation of the United States in World War I was intensive but nonetheless of relatively short duration, from April, 1917, to November, 1918. In this time the United States mobilized 2½ million men and transported over a million of them to France. It took longer to mobilize the nation's economic resources and to transport military supplies overseas. The American Expeditionary Force was mostly equipped by England and France, especially in so far as artillery and airplanes were concerned. In the interval between 1919 and 1939 a handful of military personnel kept alive the idea of national economic mobilization as a vital factor in national defense. America's participation in World War II continued from December, 1941, until the official Japanese surrender on September 2, 1945. Moreover, the manpower mobilization of more than eleven million men at one time was accompanied by an even greater mobilization of economic resources; military supplies manufactured in the United States and other goods were shared substantially with England, France, Russia, and others.

After World War II it quickly became apparent that the United States had to assume leadership in opposition to Russia's efforts to spread its control over many nations. Moreover, if the United States was to be prepared to resist force with force, it had to have substantial armed forces in a continuing state of readiness, adequately equipped with the latest available implements of defense. Thus, a sizable standing military force and a large-scale continuing program of military procurement had to be introduced for the first time during a so-called peace. As a world power it was essential for the United States to be not a potential military power, but an actual, current military power. This status was tested by the sudden outbreak of hostilities in Korea in 1950, hostilities which continued, without a formal declaration of war, until 1953, to be followed by an uneasy armistice. In the years after World War II, the United States had to adopt various laws and to administer programs designed to ensure continuing military strength.[2]

These altered circumstances of the twentieth century have necessarily altered the actual position of the President. The Chief Executive as Commander in Chief of the military services has had to make vital decisions affecting the national security of the United States. The determination to support the Republic of Korea by military intervention is a single striking illustration. Perhaps more important, it has been the President who has had to decide in the first instance the basic strategic and tactical state of preparedness to be maintained by our national defense. These decisions, at least to some degree, may be reviewed by the Congress and even modified, primarily through the appropriation process. Yet it is the President who has had to carry the heavy burden of major responsibility for ensuring an adequate national defense.

In political terms, the primacy of national defense as the principal concern of our federal government has provided the President with enhanced status as a political leader. Since the federal Constitution recognizes the President as Commander in Chief of the armed forces, the legislature and the public have looked to the Chief Executive for leadership in formulating as well as in supervising national defense policies. In the absence of definite presidential leadership in this area, the very existence of our Republic could be jeopardized and lost. A general realization of this fact has given the President a basis for political influence and decision making which under other circumstances might not exist.

In administrative terms, the President's position as Commander in Chief has given him a major responsibility in the determination of policies and programs to be carried out by the nation's Armed Forces. The President is something more than a supervisor of the administrative performance of the Army, Navy, and Air Force. He is by constitutional prescription their Commander in Chief. The very administrative titles conferred upon the recognized professional heads of the armed services—that of Chief of Staff and Chief of Naval Operations—recognize a status subordinate to the Secretary of Defense and the President. The phrase "Commander in Chief" in military usage implies the authority of final decision in military matters. And this authority resides not in any career military officer, but in the political office of the President. Thus the administrative status of the Chief Executive rests upon very solid constitutional mandate, reinforced by political and military tradition.[3]

[2] Cf. Henry A. Kissinger, *Nuclear Weapons and Foreign Policy* (New York: Harper & Brothers, 1957).

[3] Cf. Samuel P. Huntington, *The Soldier and the State: The Theory and Politics of Civil-Military Relations* (Cambridge, Mass.: Harvard University Press, 1957).

PRESIDENTS AS COMMANDERS IN CHIEF

Just what is meant by the constitutional provision that the President shall be Commander in Chief of the Army and Navy? This question may be answered in part by reviewing the interpretation given the phrase by various Presidents.

Naturally, the first possible meaning is that of actual military command when the nation is involved in conflict. Certainly no one doubts that the President has constitutional authority to decide military objectives for the Armed Forces and to order their realization. President Polk in 1846 decided that American military forces should occupy the disputed area in Texas all the way to the Rio Grande River and ordered General Taylor to act accordingly. The decision brought about the expected Mexican reaction and a declaration of war followed. In 1861 after the firing upon Fort Sumter, President Lincoln issued a call for 75,000 troops to be provided by the states on a volunteer basis. President McKinley decided upon armed intervention in Cuba without an actual declaration of war in 1898. President Wilson dispatched a punitive expedition to Mexico to halt bandit raids into American territory. President Franklin Roosevelt made a number of decisions in 1941 involving military preparation for national defense before the Japanese attack at Pearl Harbor. President Truman in 1950 decided to order military intervention in Korea as a means of strengthening the Republic of Korea.

Moreover, once armed conflict begins the President becomes the final point of decision in determining the basic strategy of our war effort. President Lincoln had to make a number of decisions concerning the war effort along the Potomac and into Virginia in contrast with the war along the Mississippi and into Tennessee. In the end it was the action in the West which produced the two generals, Grant and Sherman, who were the key military leaders in the final defeat of the Confederacy.[4] President McKinley had to decide upon naval and military action in the Philippines as well as in Cuba during the Spanish-American War.

President Wilson had to decide the question whether American participation in World War I was to be undertaken as a full partner of the joint Allied Command in France. It was apparently General Pershing himself who was steadfastly determined to create an American Expeditionary Force which should be a full-fledged command assuming its proper share of a common military task. He was opposed to any proposal to integrate American divisions or even corps under French and English field commanders. This position could be maintained only with the complete concurrence of the President.

During World War II, perhaps as good an illustration of basic strategy

[4] For a very good account of presidential military leadership, see Colin R. Ballard, *The Military Genius of Abraham Lincoln* (Cleveland: The World Publishing Company, 1952).

occurred as has ever been provided in our history. The United States was first attacked by Japan and the Congress responded with a declaration of war against that nation. Two days later in fulfillment of their treaty obligations, Germany and Italy declared war on the United States, and Congress immediately in turn recognized a state of war with these two countries. Yet in organizing American military resources for war, the United States determined that first attention should be given to the defeat of Germany while endeavoring to contain Japanese military expansion in the Far East. There were many reasons for this decision which need not be discussed here. It is sufficient simply to note that this was a decision, in the last analysis, made by President Roosevelt.

The episodes just mentioned illustrate a kind of basic military decision which is made by the President of the United States. Such a decision is as much political as military, or perhaps it would be better to say that the highest or most fundamental questions of military strategy cannot be labeled exclusively as military. War, or any kind of military action, is an extension of national policy, and the President is a key figure in the determination of such policy. It is because military decisions are so important in the realization of national political objectives that they must be made by the highest political authority in our scheme of government.

An important element of military strategy is to decide whether the United States shall fight alone or enter into military alliance with other powers. Essentially, it is the President who determines what powers the United States shall join in concerted military endeavor. This problem arose in World War I and II and again in the Korean conflict. Agreements for joint command, such as that for the Allied Expeditionary Force which invaded France in 1944, were made exclusively by the President.

We may agree therefore that the President's role as Commander in Chief places upon the Chief Executive the final responsibility for fixing the basic objectives of military action; in other words, we may say that the President is the final authority in matters of high strategy. Moreover, we must realize that such decisions involving grand strategy are not necessarily confined to the formal stages of a conflict characterized by an actual declaration of war. A President may order military action which may influence another nation to declare war upon the United States. Or in the absence of any declaration of war at all, as in Korea from 1950 to 1953, the President may order military forces to engage in military action. All this is within the constitutional authority of the President as Commander in Chief.

But these words do not suggest that the President is to be an actual field commander. James Madison is said personally to have tried to organize troops for the defense of Washington against the British in 1814. In despair in 1862 President Lincoln for a time assumed actual direction of both Naval and Army forces in the successful assault upon Norfolk.[5]

[5] Smith, *op. cit.*, p. 48.

These are exceptions rather than a common practice. Presidents have given their attention primarily to broad matters of military strategy and political objectives in the use of military power. To be Commander in Chief has not meant that the President was the actual commander of military forces in the field engaging the enemy.

In the second place, the authority of the Chief Executive as Commander in Chief has placed upon him individually the responsibility to select field commanders for the military forces of the United States. To be sure, as we shall examine further in a subsequent chapter, the President enjoys a general power to appoint the key administrative personnel of the federal government. This alone might be sufficient to confer upon the President the authority to appoint key military personnel. But this general power of appointment is supplemented in the military field by the President's position as Commander in Chief. In consequence, the President must determine who among the professional personnel of the Armed Forces shall be entrusted with particular command assignments. In turn, the President must bear responsibility for their performance.

The story of President Lincoln's difficulty in finding a satisfactory commanding officer for the Union forces during the Civil War is familiar to all who have studied American history.[6] Lincoln was compelled to appoint one person after another in his effort to find a leader for the Army of the Potomac who would carry out military operations with care and dispatch. In the end, General Grant was given the supreme command and Lincoln remained patient while superior manpower, supplies, and time wore out the Confederate Army under General Lee.

In World War I President Wilson conferred the command of the American Expeditionary Force upon General John J. Pershing, although he was not at that time the ranking officer in seniority of service. Apparently, Secretary of War Newton D. Baker was instrumental in making this selection, although the responsibility for the choice rested upon Wilson. General Pershing considered his only superior to be the President and was quite critical of the effort of the Army Chief of Staff in Washington to assert command authority over his activities.[7] There is no evidence that President Wilson himself was aware of this conflict at the time it occurred. Unquestionably, he could have settled it if he had desired to do so.

During World War II another weighty problem of choice for command confronted President Franklin Roosevelt. It was well known that General George C. Marshall was interested in assuming field command of the American and Allied forces scheduled to invade France in June, 1944. As of early September, 1943, Secretary of War Henry L. Stimson and others assumed that the President would designate Marshall to assume the com-

---

[6] Cf. for example, T. Harry Williams, *Lincoln and His Generals* (New York: Alfred A. Knopf, Inc., 1952).

[7] See John J. Pershing, *My Experiences in the World War*, 2 vols. (Philadelphia: Frederick A. Stokes Company, 1931).

mand. Stimson, indeed, recommended Marshall for the position.[8] President Roosevelt asked Marshall whether he preferred the field command or his position as Chief of Staff; Marshall refused to express a preference, declaring that he would serve in either post as the President might wish. In fact, Marshall appears to have said that the matter was one the President himself would have to settle.[9] In the end, the President asked General Marshall to remain as Chief of Staff and the field command was given to General Eisenhower. In a sense, General Marshall carried the heavier responsibility and was the professional head of the Army on a world-wide basis. But the excitement and public acclaim of actual field command were thus denied him.

The authority to select military commanders is accompanied by the authority to dismiss them as well. As we have noted, President Lincoln dismissed a number of generals from command of the Army of the Potomac. Indeed, General George B. McClellan was dismissed from the command twice. No such necessity occurred in any major field command during World War II, although President Roosevelt approved the relief of both the Army and the Navy commander in Hawaii after the Pearl Harbor attack, as well as the dismissal of the Chief of Naval Operations. In 1952, President Truman dismissed General Douglas MacArthur as commander of American Forces in the Far East, which likewise terminated his position as Allied Commander in the same area. There was a good deal of controversy subsequently about the military and political reasons for this action, but no one could question the President's constitutional authority to act as he did, however much one might disagree on the desirability of the dismissal.

The President as Commander in Chief is thus the final arbiter in matters of military policy and strategy and in the selection of military advisers and field commanders. Today, and throughout most of our history, the military forces have been led by officers professionally trained for their tasks. Often they have been educated in the Military or Naval Academy (soon to include graduates of an air academy), have received other education both within and without the services themselves, and have served in a variety of command, staff, and administrative assignments. To some extent high position has been reached by men who came into the regular military forces other than through a service academy. Sometimes civilians have been appointed as officers to perform important military duties but ordinarily such persons have not held field commands or top advisory positions.

Accordingly, there is today a professional military officer corps in the United States as in other nations which fills the top field command and

[8] Henry L. Stimson and McGeorge Bundy, *On Active Service in Peace and War*

(New York: Harper & Brothers, 1948), p. 437.

[9] *Ibid.*, pp. 440–443.

staff positions. Yet by tradition this officer corps recognizes its political subordination to civilian authority exercised first of all by the President as Commander in Chief. To be sure, a President is expected to listen to the military advice of his professional staff, but the final decisions must be those of the Commander in Chief himself. This fact is now an accepted feature in the operation of American government.

Yet a third military power of the Chief Executive is to declare martial law in American territory subject to actual or threatened invasion and to establish military government in hostile areas occupied by United States forces. Immediately after the attack on Pearl Harbor, President Roosevelt declared martial law in Hawaii. After the war the Supreme Court declared this action unconstitutional.[10] But a distinguished authority on constitutional law has asserted that "the opinions which support the decision are not persuasive."[11] The President also ordered the evacuation of Japanese-descended persons from the West Coast, and in two cases in 1943 and 1944 the Supreme Court upheld this action.[12] The President established a military commission to try German saboteurs landed in this country; here again the Supreme Court upheld the action of the President.[13] It was Presidential action which led to the international trial of war criminals at the end of World War II. As dramatic action as was ever taken under the authority of military government was President Lincoln's Emancipation Proclamation of 1862, applicable only to occupied territory but made effective throughout the United States by the Thirteenth Amendment.

Finally, we may note that as Commander in Chief a President may terminate hostilities at any time by entering into an armistice with a belligerent power. Such an armistic is not a treaty requiring senatorial approval. It is simply an agreement not to fight. President McKinley thus terminated the Spanish-American War in 1898, President Wilson World War I in 1918, President Roosevelt World War II in 1945, and President Eisenhower the Korean conflict in 1953.

WAR AND THE HOME FRONT

Thus far, we have concerned ourselves with the more strictly military aspects of the President's role as Commander in Chief. We have learned in the past one hundred years, however, that national defense is more than just the organization and training of military forces themselves. Such forces must be supplied with all kinds of military weapons and equipment, they must be transported to areas of existing or potential military

---

[10] *Duncan v. Kahanamoku,* 327 U.S. 304 (1946).
[11] Edward S. Corwin, *The President: Office and Powers,* 3d ed. (New York: New York University Press, 1948), p. 307.
[12] *Hirabayishi v. United States,* 320 U.S. 18 (1943); and *Korematsu v. United States,* 323 U.S. 214 (1944).
[13] *Ex parte Quirin,* 317 U.S. 1 (1942).

conflict, and they must be serviced in many ways from communication to medical care. All these activities raise many problems in the operation and control of civilian manpower and the civilian economy. Total war involves the total nation. Does the position of the President as Commander in Chief then extend to this entire realm of military support and service? This problem has been raised in various ways at different times in our recent history. But no conclusive answer seems possible at present.

After the Fort Sumter incident, President Lincoln proceeded to mobilize military forces without any legislative authorization to do so. Subsequently, the Congress ratified the President's action and provided all the funds necessary. And in 1863, the legislature passed a draft law for compulsory military service. In World War I, before and during World War II, and in the years since, the legislature has enacted laws necessary to provide military manpower for national defense.

During the Civil War a major problem confronting President Lincoln was the existence of large numbers of sympathizers with the Confederate cause behind the actual Northern battle lines. In order to ensure public order and to suppress both espionage and sabotage of the Northern war effort, President Lincoln found it necessary to suspend the writ of habeas corpus. In this way he authorized military commanders to arrest citizens suspected of interference with the war effort and to hold them in custody without filing any specific charges or bringing the individuals before courts of law. Later, in 1863 Congress passed legislation stating simply that the President was authorized to suspend the writ.

In 1866, after the end of the war and after Lincoln's death, the Supreme Court in the famous Milligan case decided that in those areas where the "courts are open and their process unobstructed" the President could not suspend the regular judicial liberties of American citizens.[14] Although four justices made a somewhat different statement, the case appeared to say that, at least in the instance of Milligan, the military commander who had arrested and imprisoned him had acted beyond his authority and that the orders of the President were illegal.

During World War I Congress was induced to pass almost all legislation thought desirable by the President for the prosecution of the war effort. The questions ultimately presented to the Supreme Court thus concerned the joint war powers of Congress and Chief Executive; in this setting the constitutionality of all the legislation was sustained.[15]

During World War II a curious episode occurred in connection with the Emergency Price Control Act of 1942. This statute prohibited any price control on agricultural products until the price received by farmers should

---

[14] *Ex parte Milligan*, 4 Wall. 2 (1866).
[15] *Hamilton v. Distillers and Warehouse Co.*, 251 U.S. 146 (1919); *Schenck v. United States*, 249 U.S. 47 (1919); *Selective Draft Cases*, 245 U.S. 366 (1918); and *Block v. Hirsch*, 256 U.S. 135 (1921).

rise to 110 per cent of the parity price. President Roosevelt in April, 1942, asked the Congress to repeal the section of the law dealing with agricultural prices in order to permit price control at 100 per cent of parity. When four months later there had still been no action by the Congress, President Roosevelt on September 7 sent a message declaring that wage stabilization was impossible without control of agricultural prices. He, therefore, asked Congress to take repeal action by October 1. He added:

> In the event that the Congress should fail to act, and act adequately, I shall accept the responsibility, and I will act. . . . The President has the powers, under the Constitution and under Congressional Acts, to take measures necessary to avert a disaster which would interfere with the winning of war. . . . The American people can be sure that I will use my powers with a full sense of my responsibility to the Constitution and to my country. The American people can also be sure that I shall not hesitate to use every power vested in me to accomplish the defeat of our enemies in any part of the world where our own safety demands such defeat. When the war is won, the powers under which I act automatically revert to the people—to whom they belong.

This was a unique enunciation of Presidential power. President Roosevelt claimed power as Commander in Chief to repeal a provision of law which he held was jeopardizing the entire economic stabilization program in support of the military forces. At the same time, he indicated that such power was his only in time of actual war; he spoke of his power as reverting in peacetime to the people. Whether such a claim to power would have been sustained by the Supreme Court or not, it is impossible to say. In early October the Congress saw fit to avoid a bitter conflict about legislative-executive power in the midst of war by passing the necessary repeal legislation. At no other time during World War II did the President threaten to suspend legislative authority because of the necessities of war.

We have already mentioned in an earlier chapter the action of President Truman in directing the Secretary of Commerce to operate the private steel companies threatened with a strike during the Korean hostilities. In this instance a majority of the Supreme Court ruled that the President had exceeded his constitutional authority. In the absence of an actual declaration of war, the argument of the Solicitor General of the United States on behalf of the President's action said little about his role as Commander in Chief. Certainly during and even immediately before World War II, President Roosevelt had taken similar action which had not been overthrown in the courts.

Unquestionably, the President faces a difficult task today in endeavoring to balance the claims of the military and of the civilian population upon the economy in time of war. During World War II the problem of such balance fell almost entirely upon the President, since the Congress appropriated funds to the Armed Forces far in excess of their capacity to purchase supplies in any given year. The President established a special agency, the Office of War Mobilization, to assist him in the performance of this task. In this way the President in his capacity as a civilian political leader must determine the extent to which civilian production shall be limited during wartime in order to provide necessary military supplies. Under modern conditions of warfare in which complex military weapons and equipment play so essential a part in determining military success or failure, no other power of the President may be more important in time of war.

The President is thus as much concerned with the home front as with the war front in his capacity as chief executive. War is as much a matter of economics as of manpower and strategy. For this reason the President in his person combines direction of both phases of modern war.[16]

DEFENSE ORGANIZATION

The framework for organization of the Armed Forces of the United States has been provided by the National Security Act of July 26, 1947, the National Security Act amendments of August 10, 1949, and the Department of Defense Reorganization Act of August 6, 1958. These statutes have created the basic structure through which the President exercises his more important powers as Commander in Chief. These laws are notable, not because they confer new substantive authority upon the President, but because they provide administrative assistance in the performance of his constitutional duties.

Defense organization problems since the end of World War II have centered in two major areas. One problem has been to provide the President with an organizational structure within the Executive Office itself to perform certain important policy-making functions involving national security. The other problem has been to provide a desirable degree of unified direction over the Armed Forces short of the President himself. We may begin with this second problem.

It is not necessary to trace in detail the development of the legislative language which has gradually, but steadily, made the executive Department of Defense and the Secretary of Defense a command structure for direction of the Armed Forces of the United States. The 1949 law changed the status of the Departments of the Army, Navy, and Air Force from that of executive departments to a new type of agency, military depart-

---

[16] Cf. Dorothy Schaffter and Dorothy M. Mathews, *The Powers of the President as Commander in Chief of the Army and Navy of the United States*, HR Doc. 443, 84th Cong., 2d Sess. (1956).

ments. The 1958 law specified that each military department was to be separately organized under its own secretary and was to function under the "direction, authority, and control" of the Secretary of Defense. The new law then added the words: "The Secretary of a military department shall be responsible to the Secretary of Defense for the operation of such department as well as its efficiency."

The 1958 legislation directed the Secretary of Defense to provide a more "effective, efficient, and economical administration and operation" of the Department and "to eliminate duplication." In carrying out this injunction, the Secretary of Defense might transfer, reassign, abolish, and consolidate functions within the department and its constituent military departments. If his action extended to a function established by law, he was required to delay his orders until thirty calendar days of "continuous session of the Congress" after he had reported his intention to the Armed Services Committees of the Senate and the House of Representatives. If either committee reported to the parent body a resolution of disapproval upon the grounds that the proposed action of the Secretary involved a "major combatant function" established by law or might impair the defense of the United States, then another forty days of continuous session must elapse. During this period, either house of the Congress might adopt a resolution of disapproval and so veto the Secretary's internal reorganization order.

In addition, the 1958 statute authorized the President, with the advice of the Joint Chiefs of Staff and through the Secretary of Defense, to establish unified "combatant commands for the performance of military missions" and to determine the "force structure" of such commands. It was then the responsibility of the three military departments to provide the necessary administrative support of such combatant commands. This part of the law meant that field commands might be organized on a unified basis and would report to the President through the Secretary of Defense and the Joint Chiefs of Staff rather than through the command structure of the three military departments.

Without considering further details of the defense statutes, we may observe that these laws in effect provide the President of the United States with a deputy commander in chief of the Armed Forces in the person of the civilian Secretary of Defense. The Secretary, in addition to a Deputy Secretary, and seven Assistant Secretaries, is aided by a director of defense research and engineering, and by the Joint Chiefs of Staff. The Secretary has substantial power over internal organization, but must operate through the three military departments and the unified combatant commands. As a result, the President can look to the Secretary of Defense as a single avenue of action in matters involving the deployment of the Armed Forces and their necessary personnel and logistical support. The burden of command effectiveness for the President has been substantially lightened by the gradual evolution of defense organization since the end of World War II.

The National Security legislation also gave a statutory basis for the Joint Chiefs of Staff. The Joint Chiefs of Staff, with a chairman who becomes thereby the principal professional military leader in the Armed Forces and with the three professional heads of the military services, are presumably part of the Department of Defense. It seems obvious that the Joint Chiefs of Staff may serve as the principal agency of military advice and leadership for both the Secretary of Defense and the President. In practice, on most matters of continuing military policy and operations the Joint Chiefs of Staff have served as adviser to the Secretary of Defense. But when matters of great moment arise, it is the President directly who, through the chairman or through the body as a whole, seeks military advice and assistance. Accordingly, the Joint Chiefs of Staff must be thought of as an agency both of the Department of Defense and of the President.

In so far as the Executive Office itself is concerned, the National Security legislation established three new agencies for the assistance of the President: the National Security Council, the Central Intelligence Agency, and the Office of Civil and Defense Mobilization.[17] The National Security Council is in effect a statutory Cabinet to advise the President "in respect to the integration of domestic, foreign, and military policies relating to the national security so as to enable the military services and the other departments and agencies of the government to cooperate more effectively in matters involving the national security."

Beyond this general statement of purpose the law says that the National Security Council, subject to the direction of the President, shall assess and appraise the objectives, risks, and commitments of the United States as these affect our national security and as they are related to actual and potential military strength. In addition, the Council is supposed to consider all major policy questions concerned with national security. The law also provided that the Council should have an executive secretary who is a part of the President's staff. The National Security Council is supposed to be presided over by the President, and its membership includes the Vice President, the Secretary of State, the Secretary of Defense, the director of the Office of Civil and Defense Mobilization, and such other department and agency heads as the President may designate.

The Central Intelligence Agency was established "under the National

---

[17] The 1947 law actually created a National Security Resources Board, but Reorganization Plan 3 of 1953 abolished the NSRB and replaced it with the Office of Defense Mobilization. Reorganization Plan 1 of 1958 merged the ODM with the Federal Civil Defense Administration.

Security Council" but is headed by a director appointed by the President "by and with the advice and consent of the Senate." The director may be either a civilian or a military official. Although the statute is worded so as to suggest that the Agency is primarily one for coordinating intelligence collection and for assessing intelligence information, actually the CIA has to some extent also been engaged in the actual collection of intelligence. The very secrecy which must necessarily surround intelligence endeavor has meant that very little is known about the work of the CIA. It is apparent, however, that the Executive Office of the President is now provided with its own direct service in collecting, coordinating, and evaluating intelligence data. This fact attests the preponderant concern of the President and of our government with matters of national security.

In the third place, the Office of Civil and Defense Mobilization is an agency for advising the President on policies concerning mobilization of the nation's manpower, industrial, and agricultural resources in support of the Armed Forces. In peacetime such an agency is concerned with the current impact of military procurement upon economic resources as well as with plans for government policies and operations in the event of hostilities which increase military demand for supplies and service (such as transportation and communication). Between World War I and World War II such planning was carried on within the War and Navy Departments through an agency known as the Army-Navy Munitions Board. Since World War II, such planning has been removed from the military services themselves and assigned directly to the Executive Office of the President. The essentially political nature of the task made the rearrangement eminently desirable.

In a day and age when military strength is vital to survival of the Free World, and when that military strength depends in large measure upon the concept of "steady build-up"—that is, continued large-scale military development and procurement of improved weapons—the economic aspects of national security are of fundamental importance. To a substantial degree the research and development talent of the nation must be devoted to such matters as supersonic speed, jet and atomic propulsion, nuclear and thermonuclear explosion, guided missiles, electronic navigation and warning systems, and other ideas for military force. Research and development alone is not enough. At any one time the Armed Forces must have an adequate supply of the latest and best types of military equipment. The budgetary size of national defense operations is but an indication of manpower and economic resources devoted to national security. The planning of this operation in terms of available resources is consequently an indispensable activity of government. Today it is another part of the job of the Commander in Chief.

In practice, we are told that the Secretary of the Treasury, the Chair-

man of the Joint Chiefs of Staff, and the director of the CIA usually attend
the meetings of the National Security Council.[18] The director of the
Bureau of the Budget also attends. Other department and agency heads
are present when items on the agenda require their presence. The Council
has created a subcommittee, which is known as the Planning Board, consisting of assistant secretaries of departments and other staff officials.
Most studies, special reports, and policy recommendations clear through
this subcommittee before they are considered by the Council itself. The
staff of the Council apparently keeps in close touch with the prosecution
of all studies and reports. In addition, President Eisenhower added another group to function under the aegis of the National Security Council:
an Operations Coordinating Board. The Board consists of the Under
Secretary of State, the Deputy Secretary of Defense, and other departmental representatives. Meeting regularly once a week, the Board is supposed to ensure that the various international assistance programs concerned with national security are functioning properly and harmoniously.
This Board likewise is staffed from the White House.

The National Security Council has met regularly in the Cabinet room
of the White House every Thursday morning.[19] The meetings usually take
2½ hours. There is a prepared agenda, and each item is introduced by
the Special Assistant to the President for National Security Affairs. This
assistant explains whether the matter is new or a revision of previous
action, points to the recommendations of the Planning Board, and endeavors to sharpen the issues to be decided. The President has usually
been over most of the matters with the Special Assistant before the meeting begins. Discussion then follows on the basis of a free exchange of
points of view. No record is kept of this discussion; there is only a record
of action taken. In the end it is the President who decides what is to be
done. His is the authority and the responsibility.

In the period from 1947 to January, 1956, the National Security Council held 273 meetings and had adopted over 1,500 separate policy actions.[20] Some 128 meetings and 699 actions occurred during a little over
five years during which Truman was President, and 145 meetings and
809 actions took place in three years while Eisenhower was President.
The Council has met more frequently than the Cabinet during the Eisenhower administration. It appears that President Eisenhower has looked
upon the Council as a major means for arriving at national security policy
and has expected the members of the Council to reach agreement which
he in turn may endorse. In this way he made policy determination a col-

[18] Dillon Anderson, "The President and National Security," *The Atlantic Monthly,*
vol. 197 (January, 1956), p. 42.
[19] *Ibid.*
[20] Robert Cutler, "The Development of the National Security Council," *Foreign
Affairs,* vol. 34 (April, 1956), p. 441.

lective task. Yet a President obviously may make such use of the National Security Council as he sees fit. He may find aid and comfort in the advice generated by Council discussion and consensus. No President can shift responsibility for final decision.

It has been suggested that the membership of the National Security Council should be enlarged and that the President should take into the group certain "elder statesmen" to help in recommending policy. A former Special Assistant to President Eisenhower on national security matters has written: "It [the essential virtue of the Security Council] is that this procedure brings to the President the views of the very officials upon whom he will later rely to carry out his national security policy decisions."[21] The time consumed in informing such civilians on the questions at issue, the danger that outside consultants may become rivals of department executives, and the likelihood that persons without responsibility for administrative results may indulge in fanciful thinking are all considerations which suggest the inadvisability of the "elder statesmen" approach. Where the civilian outsider is an expert in some particular field of consideration, where he has some special knowledge or background on a problem, he can always be called in as a special consultant if the President or a department head desires to obtain his views.

In so far as staff is concerned, in practice the National Security Council has developed a twofold arrangement. The executive secretary and a small group of twenty-seven persons serve as a permanent staff; President Eisenhower continued in the post the individual earlier appointed by President Truman. The permanent staff is nonpartisan and provides continuity in the work of the Council. On the other hand, President Eisenhower introduced the practice of designating one of his administrative assistants as Special Assistant for National Security Affairs. This individual is a personal appointee enjoying the full confidence of the Chief Executive and in turn he must be personally and completely loyal to the President. The Special Assistant has served as chairman of the Planning Board and has made sure that appropriate instructions were issued after a matter had been decided by the President. The staff has not endeavored to take over the basic responsibilities for planning which are vested in the operating agencies themselves. Rather, the staff has endeavored to make sure that policy matters were properly cleared among all interested departments and agencies, and that matters of first importance came before the President, with the benefit of any ideas or proposals from department heads. Thus the staff is not thought of as an instrument for formulating national security policy but rather as an agency for ensuring the coordination and discussion of policy questions at the level of the Chief Executive himself.[22]

[21] *Ibid.*, p. 453.   [22] *Ibid.*

SUMMARY

Our attention here has been directed to the role of the Chief Executive as Commander in Chief of the Armed Forces of the United States. In the individual states the governor is similarly the commander in chief of the state militia or National Guard. Since national defense is primarily a matter of federal interest, the governor's importance as commander in chief is not so important.

To be sure, the Congress, too, has its part in the direction and control of the Armed Forces, such as the determination of the basic organization of the services, the appropriation of funds including levels of compensation for all personnel, the specification of the terms and obligations of military service, the enactment of laws giving priority to military procurement, the investigation of military performance in all its aspects, and the declaration of war. This is a formidable array of authority.

But the President's status as Commander in Chief is likewise a position of vital importance in providing for the national security of the United States. The President is the focal point for determining the strategic objectives of our national defense and for directing the commitments necessary to the realization of those objectives. He is in a very real sense the supreme commander of American military might.

This status has two broad implications for the operation of our system of government in so far as the national defense is concerned. In the first place, the President's relation to the Armed Forces is different from his relation to the other administrative agencies of government, even including the field of foreign affairs. The President's executive power in the field of national defense includes the power of being Commander in Chief. His is the top voice in the administrative direction of the Armed Forces. The Secretary of Defense and all the Secretary's staff are only assistants to the President. The President's authority is final and complete, within the realm of administrative operation.

In the second place, this different status which the President enjoys in the field of national defense serves a very definite purpose. The President as Commander in Chief is expected to provide the means whereby military power is always kept subordinate to civil power. The President is a political leader; the military power is expected to serve the needs of our society as defined by the legislature and the executive. Such has always been the case throughout our history. Such will continue to be the case while the President's superior position is clearly understood and sustained.

Chapter 17

The Executive and Administrative Personnel

We have already observed that our constitutions vest the power of appointment in the executive but that the actual extent of this authority is left for statutory determination—that is, decision through the legislative process. Thus the appointing power is a matter of legislative-executive relations, at least in so far as the types and numbers of positions to which it applies are concerned.

We have noted also that there is a disposition on the part of the legislature, or at least on the part of the upper chamber of the legislature, to have a goodly number of positions filled by executive appointment and senatorial confirmation. This arrangement guarantees to the members of the upper chamber at least some part in the selection of administrative personnel. Senators may even be able to exercise the initiative in proposing individuals to be nominated by the executive.

It needs to be understood that from the point of view of the executive himself this legislative interest in the selection of administrative personnel is not necessarily undesirable. The executive is more than an administrative overseer. An even more vital role under present-day conditions is his position as a legislative leader. And lacking formal sanctions to a considerable degree which may reinforce his leadership position, the executive must rely upon other means. In the past and to some degree today, patronage—the executive appointment of personnel upon proposal or endorsement by legislators and local political organizations—has done its bit to encourage legislative cooperation with the executive.

From a strictly administrative point of view the patronage practice has on many occasions brought men to important positions who were not sympathetic personally with an executive's point of view. Such men may pursue policies at variance from the executive's own desires. The only recourse an executive has in these circumstances is to dismiss the administrator, and this may mean embarrassment for the executive in his relations to the administrator's legislative sponsor.

It is not unusual at any one time under a President or a governor to find the head of an important administrative agency who does not share the executive's attitude on important issues of public policy. Some executives willingly tolerate a wide divergence of opinion among the heads of principal administrative agencies because they find it useful to appeal to various segments of the population in this way. But occasionally executives are forced to endure the presence of persons in high administrative position simply because dismissal would jeopardize necessary collaboration with key figures in the legislature.

The requirements of the executive's legislative and political roles frequently interfere with any desire the executive may have to impose close supervision upon administrative activities. Here again is an illustration of how the position of chief executive embodies many different parts. Then it is the composite which must be understood and evaluated rather than any one component. From a strictly administrative point of view an executive may wish to appoint as heads of administrative agencies persons who have a reputation as good administrators and who have a basic loyalty to him. But in his legislative and political roles the executive may have to select individuals for key administrative positions for other than their administrative qualifications. No executive can afford to think of himself solely as a general manager.

THE OBJECTIVE OF EXECUTIVE APPOINTMENT

Executive appointment of the heads of administrative agencies serves a basic purpose. Thereby persons are designated to assume responsibility for the conduct of governmental activities who represent the executive and his point of view. Ordinarily, an executive is expected to seek out and appoint persons who will have a general sympathy or loyalty to him. In this way he achieves some degree of administrative supervision over the work of various agencies. In this way he can ensure that administrative policies will follow his instructions. In this way administrative agencies receive their political direction.

To be sure, an executive may on occasion select men for administrative positions in terms of their general ability, rather than in terms of any specific point of view they may possess. And in some instances, an executive will have no specific instructions he wishes to be carried out other than a "good job." To some extent, after an appointee has taken over direction of an agency, the new head will be expected to consult with the executive on any major problems which arise. The usual assumption is that men selected by the executive to head an agency will be more likely to keep in close touch with the executive than permanent civil servants or administrators appointed by a prior executive.

In defending the appointing power of the President, Hamilton argued

(*The Federalist,* no. 76) that executive selection was essential in order to recruit able men to work for the government. Hamilton thought that the executive as a single individual would seek out the best persons available for government work, would investigate qualifications carefully, and would have few "personal attachments to gratify." Obviously Hamilton thought of executive appointment as superior to legislative appointment and saw in the executive the way to selection of better administrative officials. If the legislature undertook to select heads of administrative agencies, Hamilton implied that selections would be made on a logrolling basis in order to satisfy many individual legislators.

This concern of Hamilton is no longer thought of as the major objective in executive appointment of administrative personnel. Rather, executive selection is now thought of primarily as a means to the end of providing appropriate and responsible political direction to administrative agencies. To a substantial degree citizens and legislators now accept the proposition that most of the actual everyday work of government must be done by professionally and technically trained personnel. The purpose in executive appointment of top administrative personnel is to provide an element in every agency which politically will speak the point of view of the "consumer" of an agency, or at least the point of view of the lay, interested citizen. Executive-selected administrators are intended to provide the channel of communication whereby executive desires are transmitted to the permanent officials of an agency. Both politically and personally, an element of administrative authority in an agency responsible to the executive is essential in order to maintain balance between the public interest and the professional interest.

This theory in turn raises the problem of relationship between the politically selected head of an administrative agency and the professionally competent staff. In so far as the theory of democratic organization of administrative activities is concerned, the top command selected by the executive is expected to have final authority short of the executive and the legislature in making all major decisions. On the other hand, professional leadership in administrative agencies is becoming more and more important as the work of government becomes more highly specialized and technical. Professional leadership enjoys the advantage of careful preparation through education and experience to handle the particular programs of an agency. Professional leadership usually enjoys also the advantage of long familiarity with the work of an agency. This kind of *expertise* and long-term experience is essential to political leadership. Indeed, those appointed to provide the element of public interest in the conduct of an agency must depend upon the professional element both for counsel and for execution.

Prevailing democratic theory requires that professional leadership shall give its complete political loyalty to those persons selected by the executive to assume political responsibility for the work of the agency. This loyalty has a dual nature. One is to provide the best professional advice possible to one's political superiors. The other is to accept the political judgment of the head of an agency and to do one's best in carrying out these directives. Yet this theoretical relationship is not always simple to realize in practice.

Political leadership at certain times and in certain conditions can be inept, confused, and even harmful. It is not easy for professional leadership to follow political leadership under these circumstances. Furthermore, the judgment of professional personnel may suggest that the points of view of political personnel are uninformed and in the long run dangerous for the public interest. And sometimes political judgment may look upon the professional point of view as too protective of a vested interest, too unimaginative, too out-dated, and too out-of-touch with popular aspirations.

There is no ready solution to this kind of conflict. It occurs with more frequency than is sometimes realized. Differences in matters of public policy may arise between lay and professional leaders, between political and permanent elements in administrative organization, in such diverse fields of governmental activity as education, public health and mental hygiene, public works, foreign policy, and national defense. Sometimes such conflict may reach the public notice and result in legislative hearings, public debate, and even electoral controversy.

The best that present-day theory can do is to lay down certain guidelines for conduct in those instances where conflict between political and permanent officials occurs. First of all, permanent leaders have the obligation to express their professional judgment to political leaders as forcefully, clearly, and reasonably as possible. They must marshal all the necessary facts and conclusions in such a way as to make the issues entirely understandable. In the second place, political leaders have the obligation to consider the points of view of the permanent leaders courteously and fully. They may, of course, consult outside advisers as well if they wish to do so. They must make their own concern with a problem and their own point of view entirely clear to their permanent associates. In the third place, when a resolution of differences on a mutually satisfactory basis is not possible, then the decision of the political leaders must be final. In the fourth place, permanent officials have an obligation to accept the decisions of the political leaders without rancor and faithfully to do their best to carry them out effectively. Or, in the fifth place, if a permanent official believes very strongly as an individual that the wrong decision has been made, he should resign his position. He then is at complete liberty "to take his case to the country"—to write, discuss, and agitate in all legal ways in order to encourage a different political decision, if necessary under a different set of political leaders.

Any prescription of proper behavior other than the one just outlined could only be destructive of the ends of democratic government. Any other theory would uphold the status of a permanent bureaucracy against the elected and appointed representatives of the people and would uphold the wisdom of a few against the wisdom of the many. Such a theory may be reasonable, but by definition it cannot be democratic.

As an illustration of conflict between political and professional leadership in a bureaucracy, we may cite the recent controversies about the size and composition of our Armed Forces. The professional heads of the three Armed Forces of the United States have set forth competing claims of air, sea, and land power for the allocation of procurement and manpower resources. When there is only a limited amount to be expected from legislative appropriations, then the civilian element in the Department of Defense, the Executive Office of the President, and finally the legislature must decide the proportions which shall go to air, sea, and land components of the Armed Forces. Similar decisions must be made between nuclear and conventional weapons, and between guided missiles and other firing devices. These decisions may be protested, as indeed they have been, by professional military leaders who believe that the needs of one particular service or weapon are being neglected. In such circumstances it is not easy to determine when professional leadership possesses a clear insight which should be heeded.[1] In our scheme of government the politically elected and appointed officials must make the final judgment.

The extent of actual conflict which does arise between political and professional leadership in our administrative agencies should not be exaggerated. Such conflict tends to be the exception rather than the rule. For the most part, political and permanent officials find a common basis of operation. Mutual adjustment usually occurs. Sometimes the political leadership defers to the judgment of the professional leadership in most issues where there is clear evidence that expert knowledge is necessary to a decision. Sometimes there is a full and frank meeting of minds between political and professional leadership. Sometimes particularly able political leadership may become dominant and succeed in winning both the confidence and the support of professional leadership. Sometimes, for all practical purposes, the political leadership is content with the outward trappings of power and leaves actual decision making to the professional element of an administrative agency. There may even be a cycle of these different leadership situations in the life of a single administrative agency. Some degree of accommodation between political and professional leadership is the usual pattern of administrative behavior rather than open and bitter conflict.

The second Hoover Commission was aware of this potentiality of con-

[1] Cf. Henry A. Kissinger, "Strategy and Organization," *Foreign Affairs*, vol. 35 (April, 1957), p. 379.

flict between political and professional leadership although it failed to make clear the exact nature of its concern. In 1955 the Commission proposed that there should be established a body of career administrators to be known as the "Senior Civil Service."[2] It was suggested that individuals would be nominated to this rank by department and agency heads and would be appointed by a Senior Civil Service Board with the consent of the President. Such appointment would carry with it status, rank, and salary for the individual regardless of the particular post he might be assigned to fill. The Commission said:[3]

> The primary objective is to have always at hand in the government a designated group of highly qualified administrators whose competence, integrity, and faithfulness have been amply demonstrated; who will make it easier for non-career executives to discharge their responsibilities; and who will add to the smoothness, effectiveness and economy of governmental operations. A secondary but related objective is to make the civil service more attractive as a career to able men and women.

The Commission made it appear that it was primarily concerned with improving administrative performance through providing career opportunities at the highest level of the public service. What the Commission did not make clear was that various high positions in the federal service had already been designated to be filled by career or professional personnel, including administrative assistant secretaries in a number of departments. The real problem is how to achieve some degree of flexibility in filling these positions, so that any particular politically appointed department head might exercise some judgment in selecting the professional personnel to be associated with him in the leadership of an agency.

When a career professional civil servant is promoted to a high post, he enjoys the prestige and salary which attach to that particular post. If he is shifted, he may have to be located in some other position with less salary and reduced prestige. Such action is regarded as a demotion, and may well embitter the individual toward public service. Furthermore, fearing that his tenure in a top position may be a short one, a civil servant may be reluctant to accept promotion to a high career position. The public service in America is organized largely in terms of positions, and the individual has only such rank and salary as the position he holds may carry with it.

The second Hoover Commission in effect proposed that there be a top civil service "class" all the members of which would have comparable rank and salary. The persons appointed to this group might have varied

[2] Commission on Organization of the Executive Branch of the Government, *Personnel and Civil Service: A report to the Congress* (Washington: Government Printing Office, 1955), pp. 37ff.

[3] *Ibid.*, p. 39.

assignments and could be transferred to different posts. Once selected to membership in this class, the individual would always have approximately the same salary and prestige even though he filled different posts. In this way it would be possible for a department or agency head to shift his permanent professional advisers without their suffering too severe a setback in salary or prestige. Such an arrangement would have the advantage of permitting an adjustment between the political and permanent elements of leadership in favor of the political element.

The difficulty with the proposal, apart from its novelty, is that it would introduce a general group in the Civil Service which would not be too easy to define. For example, would the head of a scientific bureau or the head of the forestry service or the head of a public works agency be eligible for selection to the Senior Civil Service? Would it then be possible for an engineer to be shifted to a welfare agency and a lawyer made head of a scientific bureau? Or is the Senior Civil Service to be made up of men and women who have come up through staff services such as budgeting, personnel, and supply, and would only persons with such experience rise to top administrative position?

The public service in America is position-oriented because of the variety of activities performed by government and because this variety requires a wide diversity of professional competencies. Should an individual with education and experience as a doctor, botanist, physicist, accountant, lawyer, nurse, engineer, forester, social worker, teacher, psychologist, or statistician be selected for high position on the basis of some indefinite quality termed "administrative ability" and then be assigned to a top administrative post regardless of its particular technical requirement? There are many persons familiar with the public service who are not yet ready to answer this question in the affirmative.

Undoubtedly the Hoover Commission sensed a very real problem. Studying the public service as it did soon after the shift from Democratic to Republican control of the Presidency, the Commission was aware of the fear on the part of many new department and agency heads that their professional colleagues were not entirely sympathetic or loyal to them. The idea of the Senior Civil Service seemed a partial solution to this problem. But the proposed solution could be harmful as well. For this reason little had been done through 1958 to put the proposal into effect. Rather, the Eisenhower administration appeared to be moving toward a general program of career development for executives in the federal service.[3a]

The more promising solution appears to be the development of traditions of political neutrality on the part of high civil servants who can serve political leadership loyally regardless of policy differences. Moreover, the fact that policy shifts tend to be slight in America when first the

[3a] See Paul P. Van Riper, "The Senior Civil Service and the Career System," *Public Administration Review,* vol. 18 (Summer, 1958), p. 189.

Republicans and then the Democrats assume power favors this kind of solution.

The Eisenhower administration sought its own answer to the problem of political versus professional leadership by enlarging the scope of political leadership in departments and agencies. The particular device employed was called Schedule C to the Civil Service Rules and Regulations. Beginning in 1903 Presidents of the United States in the process of extending civil service requirements to various types of positions in the federal service had found reason to make certain exemptions. After 1910 these exemptions were known as Schedule A and Schedule B. Schedule A included positions to which appointments might be made without examination and Schedule B listed positions to be filled by noncompetitive examination. It was expected, however, that these positions would be a part of the "classified service." Schedule A applied to attorneys, employees in foreign countries, confidential secretaries, and certain patronage posts such as deputy collectors of customs and assistant postmasters. Schedule B was never very long and included positions such as chief engineer or comptroller of an agency. In 1938 the idea of adding "policy-determining" positions to Schedule A was included in an executive order, and some departments made several proposals for inclusion under this category.[4]

In March, 1953, the Eisenhower administration announced that certain changes would be made in the civil service rules, and on March 31, Executive Order No. 10440 created a new Schedule C which was to be made up entirely of positions exempted from civil service regulations because they were decided to be of a "policy-determining nature." Positions placed on this schedule were to be filled by the head of an agency entirely on his own discretion. Some positions were transferred from Schedule A to Schedule C; in addition, departments requested and obtained approval to add to Schedule C a number of posts including chiefs and assistant chiefs of bureaus, departmental directors of information, general counsels, heads of departmental planning units, and special assistants to departmental heads. As of September, 1954, about 1,100 positions had been placed under Schedule C.[5] The number grew only slowly after that time.

Any large organization such as a government department or separate agency requires a top-management staff.[6] For 47 larger agencies in 1954 a study group for the second Hoover Commission enumerated some 1,255 posts which it labeled "top-management positions," including heads of agencies, under secretaries, deputy agency heads, assistant heads, special aides, and major bureau or staff office heads. The President appointed

[4] Cf. Commission on Organization of the Executive Branch of the Government, *Task Force Report on Personnel and Civil Service* (Washington: Government Printing Office, 1955), pp. 186–190.

[5] *Ibid.*, pp. 191–192.

[6] For recent developments here see *ibid.*, pp. 199–209.

249 of these subject to senatorial confirmation and 22 others without Senate approval. Some 374 were filled by competitive requirements of the civil service rules, whereas 178 were exempted by statute; 76 were under Schedule A, 7 under Schedule B, and 294 under Schedule C. Another 100 posts were filled by professional men of the Armed Forces.[7] These were the key positions in the management of various agencies. They combined posts held under political appointment and under professional appointment. It takes both kinds in order to develop a top-management staff.

If top management were exclusively political, its impact upon departmental operations would be small. Here is one of the paradoxes of public administration. It is not easy to get "good" men into the top positions of the public service. If all top-management posts were declared to be political, it would be easy to fill them with loyal party workers. But it would not be easy to find men and women with the background, experience, and intelligence required to provide positive direction of the large and complicated tasks of government. Recent experience has demonstrated continued difficulty for Presidents and department heads in obtaining the quality of personnel they need if top management is in reality to assume direction of governmental agencies.[8] The need in order to ensure presidential supervision and control of administrative agencies is for top-management staffs which will combine political and professional competency.

This leads to one other observation which must be made in connection with executive selection of administrative personnel. In substantial part the reputation of a President or governor today depends upon the satisfactory performance of public service. An executive's political career can be broken by a failure or by a major breakdown in the performance of governmental administrative activities. Furthermore, tax and budget pressures are such that waste in the operation of the public service becomes more and more intolerable. It is no longer a relatively simple matter in many levels of government to have numerous employees on the public payroll who perform little if any public service or who perform public service at a relatively low level of competence. The public service has become too important for this. An executive today has as a major political concern the need to advance the professional competence of all public service.

Heads of government agencies and their staffs are an outpost for the executive, on the one hand advising him in the formulation of his own policy objectives and on the other hand serving as a conveyor belt for transmitting executive purposes to the administrative agency. The execu-

[7] *Ibid.*, p. 213.

[8] Cf. John J. Corson, *Executives for the Federal Service* (New York: Columbia University Press, 1952); John A. Perkins, "Staffing Democracy's Top Side," *Public Administration Review*, vol. 17 (Winter, 1957), p. 1; and Paul T. David and Ross Pollock, *Executives for Government* (Washington, D.C.: Brookings Institution, 1957).

tive's power to appoint key personnel in departments and agencies is a major instrument for enabling him to exercise popular direction and control over administration.

THE POWER OF REMOVAL

A concomitant of the power to appoint is the power to remove. The appointive power may be successful as a device for transmitting presidential purposes to the bureaucracy if the President is satisfied in advance that the person selected by him will perform as he desires. If this expectation or hope is not fulfilled, the power of removal may be necessary in order to permit another, and from the President's point of view, "better," choice.

The federal Constitution, however, is silent on the matter of removal. So also are many state constitutions. It was left for constitutional usage and court interpretation to settle the question. The matter of the President's power to remove heads of executive departments on his own discretion was debated during the very first Congress in 1789. In the end laws were passed employing language which suggested that the power of removal was vested in the President by the Constitution itself.[9] Even so, there was some doubt still whether Congress might fix a period of time as the tenure of an officer appointed by the President, and also whether the President should in some way consult with the Senate about the removal of officers appointed with the consent of that body.[10]

In 1867 Congress passed a Tenure of Office Act which declared that the President would be guilty of a "high misdemeanor" if he removed an officeholder without the consent of the Senate. The act, passed over the veto of the President, specifically included the heads of executive departments. In disapproving the measure the President declared that the statute was unconstitutional and violated previous usage. Then in February, 1868, President Johnson removed the Secretary of War, Edwin M. Stanton, from office. This action was made a major item in impeachment proceedings brought immediately against the President. In the end this particular charge was not pressed, and when by the narrow margin of one vote the President was acquitted, little further attention was given to the provisions of the 1867 statute. It was formally repealed in 1887.

In the meantime Congress by statute in 1876 provided that postmasters of the first, second, and third classes "shall be appointed and may be removed by the President by and with the advice and consent of the Senate, and shall hold their offices for four years unless sooner removed or suspended according to law." Here the implication was clear that a postmaster was not to be removed by the President without the consent of the

---

[9] Edward S. Corwin, *The President: Office and Powers*, 3d ed. (New York: New York University Press, 1948), pp. 103–105.

[10] *Ibid.*, pp. 105–106.

Senate. The validity of the law was not tested in the courts, however, until the 1920s.

In July, 1917, a man named Myers was appointed to be postmaster at Portland, Oregon, for a term of four years. In January, 1920, President Wilson asked for his resignation. Myers refused the demand. A month later the Postmaster General issued an order removing Myers from office, saying that he was acting under orders of the President. Myers protested this action and subsequently brought a suit in the Court of Claims to recover his salary for the remainder of his term of office. The court gave judgment against Myers and the case was then appealed to the Supreme Court. In 1926 Chief Justice Taft, a former President, rendered the decision and opinion on behalf of a majority of the Supreme Court. The Court held that any legal limitation upon the power of the President to remove an appointee was unconstitutional.[11]

In this famous Myers case Chief Justice Taft declared that the provision for senatorial consent to Presidential appointments was to be strictly construed. He asserted: " . . . the fact that no express limit was placed on the power of removal by the executive was convincing indication that none was intended." He referred to debate on this matter in 1789 and spoke of a "legislative decision" at that time in favor of an unlimited presidential authority to remove administrative officers. Taft pointed out that the power of the Senate to disapprove removals would be a much greater limitation upon the Chief Executive than the power to approve appointments. He refused to read such a power into the Constitution by implication. The legal provision requiring Senate approval of presidential removals was therefore declared unconstitutional. The Myers decision has stood as the supreme law on this subject for the past thirty years.

In the meantime, another situation arose. As we have mentioned earlier, Congress in 1887 began the practice of creating a new kind of administrative agency, the so-called independent regulatory commission. First, there was the Interstate Commerce Commission in 1887, followed by the Federal Trade Commission (1914), the Federal Tariff Commission (1916), the Federal Power Commission (1920 and 1930), the Federal Communications Commission (1934), the Securities and Exchange Commission (1934), and the National Labor Relations Board (1935). In every one of these instances the law specified a statutory term of office for the board members appointed by the President and confirmed by the Senate. This fixed term was an essential part of the concept of these agencies. Furthermore, in the first three instances the law specified that the President might remove these commission members only for "inefficiency, neglect of duty, or malfeasance in office." After the Myers case there was some uncertainty whether this kind of restriction upon the President's removal power was constitutional or not.

In 1935 the Supreme Court had a case before it involving this very set

[11] *Myers v. United States,* 272 U.S. 52 (1926).

of circumstances. In 1931 a man named Humphrey was appointed to a seven-year term as a member of the Federal Trade Commission by President Hoover, with the consent of the Senate. In July and again in August, 1933, President Roosevelt wrote to Humphrey requesting his resignation. The second letter declared: "I do not feel that your mind and my mind go along together on either the policies or the administering of the Federal Trade Commission." When Humphrey still refused to resign, the President notified him in October that he had been removed from office. In due course, Humphrey brought suit in the Court of Claims for back salary. When the case reached the Supreme Court on appeal that body unanimously decided that the President had acted illegally.[12] In the Humphrey case the Court declared that the Myers case did not

> . . . include an officer who occupies no place in the executive department and who exercises no part of the executive power vested by the Constitution in the President. [The Court spoke of the Commission as] . . . an administrative body created by Congress to carry into effect legislative policies embodied in the statute. [It went on to say] The authority of Congress in creating quasi-legislative or quasi-judicial agencies, to require them to discharge their duties independently of executive control, cannot be well doubted; and that authority includes, as an appropriate incident, power to forbid their removal except for cause in the meantime. For it is quite evident that one who holds his office only during the pleasure of another cannot be depended upon to maintain an attitude of independence against the latter's will.

One other case involving removal should be mentioned. In 1938, President Roosevelt removed Dr. Arthur E. Morgan from the chairmanship of the Tennessee Valley Authority on the grounds of "contumacy." The 1933 statute establishing the TVA specified that the three directors should be appointed each for a term of nine years. The law went on to say that any member of the Board might be removed at any time by a concurrent resolution of the Senate and House of Representatives. In addition, the statute declared that any member of the board found guilty of applying a "political test" in the selection or promotion of TVA employees "shall be removed from office by the President of the United States." At an early stage in the agency's history, antagonism developed between the members of the TVA board. In 1936, Dr. Morgan protested to President Roosevelt against the reappointment of David E. Lilienthal as a board member. The President did not heed the protest. Thereafter an open break occurred between the chairman and his two colleagues. The chairman began to make public charges which reflected upon the integrity and conduct of his fellow directors.[13]

The situation reached the point where in January, 1938, the two di-

---

[12] *Humphrey v. United States,* 295 U.S. 602 (1935).
[13] See C. Herman Pritchett, *The Tennessee Valley Authority* (Chapel Hill, N.C.: The University of North Carolina Press, 1943), pp. 186–211.

rectors wrote a letter of protest to the President about the behavior of the chairman. Finally, after another public statement by Dr. Morgan about his colleagues, President Roosevelt in March, 1938, asked the three directors to meet with him at the White House to discuss their differences. Dr. Morgan at first refused to attend. When the conference was finally held, the President asked Dr. Morgan what evidence he had of misconduct on the part of the other two directors. The chairman refused to answer. A week later the chairman still refused, declaring that only a congressional investigation was competent to handle the issues involved. When at a third meeting the chairman still refused to cooperate, the President removed him from office. Subsequently Dr. Morgan brought suit in a Tennessee court asking for back salary. The case was transferred to a federal district court which held against Dr. Morgan. On appeal the Circuit Court of Appeals upheld the district court.[14] In March, 1941, the Supreme Court refused to review the opinion of the circuit court, thus in effect affirming the judgment of that court.

The contention in the Morgan case was that the law had provided for a power of general removal only by a concurrent resolution of Congress. The power of the President was limited to removal in cases involving the political appointment of employees. The district and circuit courts rejected this line of argument and insisted that no limitation upon the President's power to remove had been specified in the statute, and in the absence of some such definite limitation the President's authority to act as he did could not be questioned.

In the light of these three cases of recent years, two generalizations about the President's power of removal seem possible. One is that the legislature cannot constitutionally subject the President's power of removal of administrative officers to legislative or senatorial approval. But the Congress by law may set up standards to guide the President in exercising the power of removal, so that he is to act only in case of inefficiency, neglect of duty, or malfeasance in office. Who is to say when these standards have been met? Presumably, the President is the sole judge, unless the Supreme Court should at some later date decide to interpose its own judgment.

The opinions of the justices in the Myers case and the Humphrey case appear to suggest another distinction, a distinction between "executive officers" and "administrative officers." It is important to observe that in not a single one of the three cases discussed here did the Supreme Court uphold the idea that Congress could subject presidential removal to legislative approval. The Myers case seems rather to make it clear that any such attempt would be regarded as unconstitutional by the Supreme Court. The Humphrey case upheld only the legislative power to establish

---

[14] *Morgan v. Tennessee Valley Authority*, 115 Fd. 2d 990 (1940).

certain standards for presidential action. And this power was recognized only in cases of so-called quasi-legislative or quasi-judicial agencies.

To suggest that there is a constitutional distinction between "executive" agencies and "administrative" agencies appears to be questionable. To be sure, the Supreme Court in the Humphrey case felt that there was a difference between removal of a postmaster in Portland, Oregon, and the removal from office of a member of the Federal Trade Commission. The problem facing the Court was how to describe or how to recognize this distinction. This author believes that there is a difference, but that the difference cannot be described in terms of executive versus administrative agencies. An executive department is an administrative agency. The Supreme Court tried also to apply the terms "quasi-legislative" and "quasi-judicial" as the characteristics of the Federal Trade Commission. The Court in effect said that when the Congress creates an agency which possesses "quasi-judicial" and "quasi-legislative" authority, it may limit the power of the President to remove an officer by requiring that such removal shall be only for neglect of duty, inefficiency, or malfeasance in office. The difficulty with this distinction is that a great deal of administrative authority may at times appear to have the nature of action akin to the enactment of laws by the legislature or akin to the adjudicative power of the courts. Moreover, the source of administrative authority of all kinds is the law as enacted by the legislature. There is little distinction between administrative agencies in so far as obtaining authority from the legislature is concerned.

There does seem to be a difference between an agency whose administrative duties are primarily regulative in character and an agency whose administrative duties are primarily of a service or positive character. For example, in local government there is a difference between the work of paving a street and the revocation of a street vendor's license, or between operating a school system and the inspection of restaurants for compliance with health orders. If a state legislature wishes to establish certain procedures whereby local government shall perform these latter duties, and to restrict the authority of a mayor to remove board members who decide violations of the law, this would presumably be a constitutional exercise of legislative authority. Or, at the federal level, there is a difference between an administrative agency set up to deliver the mails or to manage national forests and an agency set up to issue licenses for radio broadcasting or an agency set up to determine when an airplane company is violating safety regulations. If the Congress in these latter instances wishes to fix tenure for board members and make them removable by the President only for specified causes, then this is presumably a constitutional exercise of legislative power.

It is important to emphasize that not all regulatory duties may require exercise by a board or by officers whom the Chief Executive can remove only for cause. The Forest Service is expected primarily to manage forests and prevent fires, but it exercises a regulatory power when it licenses certain persons to graze cattle in the forests. The State Department is expected primarily to carry on relations with foreign governments, but it exercises a regulatory power when it decides whether to issue a passport to an American citizen or not. This incidental regulatory activity does not necessarily confer some special status upon administrative officers subject to the President's power to remove.

We may summarize the power of the Chief Executive to remove administrative officers in this way. Within the limits of the Constitution the legislature decides what officers in an administrative agency shall be appointed by the Chief Executive. The legislature may decide that these officers shall serve for a fixed period of time or shall serve at the pleasure of the Chief Executive. The legislature may also specify that officers appointed by the Chief Executive shall be removed by him only for some specified cause, and this restriction upon the executive's removal power is constitutional when the nature of the work performed by the officer is primarily of a regulatory nature.

THE PRESIDENT AND CIVIL SERVICE

The Pendleton Act of 1883 which created a civil service system in the federal government left it to the discretion of the President largely to determine the extent of civil service coverage among federal personnel. Thus the President of the United States exercises a peculiar personnel authority: the authority to decide what administrative employees shall be subject to appointment and removal under civil service rules and regulations. An incidental implication of this authority is to give the President responsibility for exercising general oversight of the satisfactory performance of the entire civil service system of personnel management. Incidentally, this same authority is not ordinarily exercised by governors of the several states, since the state legislatures themselves have determined by law the extent of the application of civil service practices to administrative personnel.

It is not necessary here to trace the history of civil service management in the federal government. It is sufficient to observe two major trends. One is the steady expansion of the civil service system since the time of President Arthur. The other development has been the growing concern of the President in exercising a positive leadership in personnel management.

The Civil Service Act as passed in 1883 applied to all persons employed by administrative agencies unless they were day laborers or unless they were appointed by the President with senatorial confirmation. From time to time as new agencies were created by Congress the personnel to be appointed might be exempted from the civil service regulations. This was especially true of so-called emergency agencies set up during World

War I, during the Depression of 1930 to 1939, and during the defense crisis and World War II. But the actual extent of the positions within this broad category brought under civil service jurisdiction depended upon executive orders issued by various Presidents.

In the first year the law was applied so as to provide for competitive examination in about 10 per cent of all possible positions. The proportion had risen to 25 per cent ten years later, by 1894, while Cleveland was serving his second term as President. President McKinley extended the coverage substantially, as did President Theodore Roosevelt, so that by 1904 slightly over half of all possible positions were brought under competitive examination. By 1914 under President Wilson the proportion reached 67 per cent. Under President Coolidge and President Hoover the proportion reached 80 per cent. Under the impact of New Deal legislation this percentage dropped back to 60, but after 1936 President Franklin Roosevelt brought additional positions under civil service regulation until once again it covered two-thirds of all administrative employees.[15] By 1955 under President Eisenhower it was estimated that 90 per cent of all civilian employees of the federal government working within the United States are subject to the civil service law and 84 per cent of all civilian employees abroad.[16] Thus, there has been steady expansion in civil service coverage under presidential leadership.

In 1937 the President's Committee on Administrative Management urged a reorganization of personnel administration in the federal government. The major action proposed was to create a single official under the President to be known as the Civil Service Administrator. The President's Committee said that this administrator[17]

> . . . would act as the direct adviser to the President upon all personnel matters and would be responsible to the President upon all personnel matters and would be responsible to the President for the development of improved personnel policies and practices throughout the service. From time to time he would propose to the President needed amendments to the civil-service rules and regulations. He would suggest to the President recommendations for civil-service legislation and would assume initiative and leadership in personnel management.

Although this particular organizational arrangement was not put into effect, the proposal of the President's Committee called attention to a vital matter. Under the civil service law of the United States the President must assume leadership in determining the extent of civil service coverage and must furthermore issue all civil service rules and regulations. In our time

---

[15] Cf. Table in William E. Mosher and J. Donald Kingsley, *Public Personnel Administration* (New York: Harper & Brothers, 1941), p. 26.

[16] U.S. Civil Service Commission, *1955 Annual Report* (Washington: Government Printing Office, 1955), p. 158.

[17] President's Committee on Administrative Management, *Report with Special Studies* (Washington: Government Printing Office, 1937), p. 10.

the problem of civil service management is not so much the prevention of political favoritism in administrative appointments as it is the recruitment, appointment, promotion, and retention of capable personnel in all positions. In other words, the task of personnel management is less "keeping the rascals out" than getting and keeping the best available individuals in government employment.

Because only the President can exercise leadership in the area of modern personnel management within the federal government, he must have assistance in performing this vital task. For this reason during the past twenty years the President has had as a part of the Executive Office some person serving him in directing and handling personnel matters.

The extent of presidential interest in personnel matters can be illustrated by enumerating the civilian personnel legislation which was enacted by the Congress in the single year 1955. These laws included five measures on salary compensation, two measures on travel allowances, two on retirement, three on extension of the civil service, a law on group life insurance, and two other measures on employee benefits. This listing does not include certain other laws indirectly affecting conditions of federal employment.[18] Other measures were recommended for consideration in 1956. In addition to legislative matters requiring Presidential attention, President Eisenhower in 1955 issued a directive on federal training policy to all agencies, established a President's Committee on Employment Policy, and issued eight other executive orders affecting government personnel administration.

The question may well be asked: just what is the President's direct and personal interest in civil service management? It is easy to see why a President, as so many if not all of them have been, should be interested in appointing personnel to government positions who might strengthen his political or party role in our scheme of government. But does a President have any real interest in trying to ensure the recruitment and retention of personnel selected solely upon the basis of individual merit? Perhaps the best answer to this question has been provided by one of our Presidents himself. In his last annual message to Congress, President Ulysses S. Grant felt it necessary to comment about the scandals which had continually beset his administration. In forlorn and almost bitter terms the President admitted that "mistakes have been made, as all can see." But he went on to say that the "failures have been errors of judgment, not of intent." Grant identified his errors as involving "the selections made of the assistants appointed to aid in carrying out the various duties of administering the government, in nearly every case selected without personal acquaintance with the appointee, but upon the recommendations of the representatives chosen directly by the people."[19]

[18] U.S. Civil Service Commission, op. cit., pp. 10–13.
[19] Quoted in Sidney Hyman, The American President (New York: Harper & Brothers, 1954), p. 87.

President Grant discovered two tragic truths, much to his regret. He learned that in recommending individuals for administrative positions, legislators were not necessarily concerned with finding the best available persons. Secondly, he learned that the public expected him to assume full responsibility for the satisfactory—that is, the honest and competent— performance of the public service. Other Chief Executives have discovered these same truths if they were not fully aware of them at the time they assumed their high office.

The President of the United States must take an active role in civil service management because much of his own personal success as Chief Executive depends upon how the administrative work of government is performed. The assurance of an adequate and able personnel system is part of the President's task in supervising the administrative agencies of government.

LOYALTY AND SECURITY

In recent years the President has assumed a new responsibility in the personnel management of the federal government. He has undertaken to ensure that personnel are loyal to the United States of America and that no employee by his action shall undermine the national security.

In the aftermath of World War II it was revealed that certain administrative employees of the United States had been members of the Communist Party and that in this capacity had engaged in espionage on behalf of the Russian government. The problem was how best to handle such a situation. As early as 1939 the Hatch Act had declared that it should be unlawful for any person employed by an agency of the federal government to belong to a political party or organization which advocated the overthrow of "our Constitutional form of government in the United States." The difficulty was that this law was not self-enforcing. There remained the problem of identifying individuals who might belong to such an organization and of removing them from public employment.

In the light of various revelations made in the first few years after the war, and in the face of a general expectation that some action should be taken to make certain that public employees were loyal to the United States, President Truman on March 21, 1947, issued an Executive Order (No. 9835) prescribing "procedures for the administration of an employees loyalty program in the Executive Branch of the Government." The order provided first for a loyalty investigation of every employee entering the civilian employment of an administrative agency. This investigation was to be undertaken by the Civil Service Commission. In the second place, the head of each department and agency was made responsible for "an effective program" to assure that disloyal civilian employees were not retained in employment. A department head was to carry on such investigation as he might deem necessary, and he was to appoint one or more loyalty boards to hear loyalty cases which might arise. An employee charged with disloyalty was to have the right of an "administrative hearing" before such a board.

In the third place, the order established a Loyalty Review Board within the Civil Service Commission with authority to review departmental decisions for dismissal of an employee and to make an advisory recommendation to the head of the department. In the fourth place, the order directed "an investigative agency"—presumably the Federal Bureau of Investigation—to make available to the head of a department or agency all material and information collected about an employee or prospective employee. The investigative agency, however, might refuse to disclose the names of confidential informants.

In the fifth place, Executive Order No. 9835 established certain standards for the determination of whether a person should be removed from employment because "reasonable grounds exist for belief that the person involved is disloyal to the Government of the United States." The activities and associations to be considered included: sabotage and espionage; treason or the advocacy of treason; advocacy of revolution or force to alter the constitutional form of government of the United States; intentional disclosure of documents or information of a confidential or non-public character under circumstances indicating disloyalty; performing duties so as to serve the interests of another government in preference to the interests of the United States; and membership in or "sympathetic association" with any group designated by the Attorney General as totalitarian, communist, fascist, or subversive.

Executive Order No. 9835 inaugurated a program of immense scope. It has been estimated that under this order over 4,750,000 persons were covered by some form of check or investigation. Of these 26,236 persons were referred to agency loyalty boards for consideration; in turn 16,503 of these were cleared. Only some 560 persons were removed from employment or denied employment, although another 6,828 cases were discontinued because the individuals involved left the service or withdrew their application for employment.[20]

What is important to notice about this program is that it was inaugurated by the President without any legislative authorization to do so. Professor Edward S. Corwin has expressed his view of the President's power to take such action in these words:[21]

That, on the other hand, the President had, in the absence of any conflicting expression of policy by Congress, the power to issue the order seems to me indubitable, in view of his duty to "take care that the laws be faithfully

[20] These statistics are to be found in appendix A, *Report of the Special Committee on the Federal Loyalty-Security Program of the Association of the Bar of the City of New York* (New York: Dodd, Mead & Company, Inc., 1956), pp. 219–220.

[21] Edward S. Corwin, *op. cit.*, pp. 125–126. Italics in original.

executed," which embraces not only such legislative provisions as those reviewed above, which voice Congress's apprehensions of loyalty, but any and all laws for the enforcement of which loyalty may be reasonably deemed a necessary prerequisite—in short, *the laws in general*. That the President is entitled to claim broad powers under his duty to take care "that the laws be faithfully executed" has been demonstrated many times in our history.

It is not our task here to review the criticisms which have been made about either the provisions of Executive Order No. 9835 or the administration of that program. It is enough to observe that questions have been raised about the adequacy of the standards for determining "reasonable grounds" for believing that a person may be disloyal, about the fairness of the hearings, about a tendency to raise questionable charges of a harassing nature against some employees, and about the use to be made of the Attorney General's list of subversive organizations.

In 1950 Congress by statute provided that the heads of certain "sensitive agencies"—the Secretary of State, the Secretary of Defense, the secretaries of the military departments, the Secretary of the Treasury, the Atomic Energy Commission, and one or two others—might, when they deemed it necessary in the interest of national security, suspend any person from employment. Following such investigation and review as the department head might think necessary, he might then terminate the employment of any person. For an employee on indefinite appointment, privileges of a statement of charges, a hearing, and a review were included in the statute. The provisions of this act might be extended to other agencies, as the President might determine.

On April 27, 1953, President Eisenhower issued a new Executive Order, No. 10450, setting up a general program of government security. In the first place, he directed that the provisions of the Act of August 26, 1950, should apply to all departments and agencies of the federal government. Secondly, all department and agency heads were made responsible for establishing and maintaining a program which would ensure that the employment and retention of any civilian employee was "clearly consistent with the interests of national security." In the third place, the appointment of every employee was made subject to investigation, the scope of this investigation to depend upon the nature of the position to be filled. In the case of positions determined to be "sensitive," a full field investigation was required. In the fourth place, department heads were instructed to review all cases in which a full field investigation had been made under the 1947 executive order. Whenever any new information might arise about an employee, the department head was to review the case. In the fifth place, any person whose employment was suspended or terminated was not to be reinstated without a positive finding by the agency head that such action was clearly consistent with the interests of national security. In the sixth place, Executive Order No. 10450 set up eight different categories of information which should be developed in an investigation. These included personal characteristics such as immoral behavior, habitual use of intoxicants to excess, or circumstances which might subject an individual to coercion or pressure; commission of espionage or sedition; sympathetic association with persons who have committed espionage or sedition or with persons who advocate the use of force or violence to overthrow the government of the United States; advocacy of force or violence; membership in or sympathetic association with groups of a totalitarian, fascist, communist, or subversive character; unauthorized disclosure of security information; acting to serve the interests of another government in preference to the interests of the United States; and refusal on the grounds of self-incrimination to testify before a congressional committee regarding charges of alleged disloyalty or other misconduct.

The executive order of President Eisenhower differed from that of President Truman in several important respects. First of all, it was based upon the 1950 statute and so could be interpreted as an extension of that legislation rather than as a general exercise of executive power. In the second place, it changed the basis of personnel action. Under the Truman order a department or agency was expected to make a positive finding of disloyalty to the United States as indicated by one of the standards of conduct enumerated in the order. Under the Eisenhower order a department or agency was expected to establish that employment or retention of an employee was "clearly consistent with the interests of national security." And in some particulars the standards of acceptable behavior were made more rigorous, being extended to such matters as any immoral action. Finally, the decision of a department or agency head was final, without any right of appeal to a higher body.

It has been estimated that the total civilian employment subject to Executive Order No. 10450 was in the neighborhood of 2½ million persons. Between July 1, 1953, and June 30, 1955, some 727,000 of these were subjected to a security check. In the two-year period ending September 30, 1955, there were 1,016 suspensions and 342 terminations of employment. In addition, of some 37,000 discharges from federal service, some 3,200 were said by department and agency heads to involve security questions. Of nearly a half-million resignations, there were said to be some 5,684 resignations where adverse security information was contained in the files of the persons leaving federal employment.[22]

For our purposes here it is especially important to note that under President Eisenhower as under President Truman, it is the Chief Executive who has assumed responsibility for the general operation of a personnel security system in the United States. Among recommendations for improvement in the program proposed by a special committee of the As-

[22] *Report of the Special Committee on the Federal Loyalty-Security Program*, p. 220.

sociation of the Bar of the City of New York was one for the creation of
an Office of Director of Personnel and Information Security in the Executive Office of the President. The Director was to maintain continuous review and supervision over the personnel security programs as operated
by the various departments and agencies.[23] Other recommendations of the
bar committee had to do with limiting the scope of the system to "sensitive positions," with simplifying the standards for determining whether a
person should be employed in a sensitive position, with training of security
personnel, and with revised procedures in bringing and hearing security
charges.

In 1955 Congress established by law a Commission on Government
Security composed of twelve persons, four named by the President, four
by the Speaker of the House of Representatives, and four by the President
of the Senate. The Commission was directed to make a careful study of
the government security program and to suggest desirable changes needed
to protect both the national security and "basic American rights." The
Commission reported on June 21, 1957.

The Commission proposed the creation of a Central Security Office
which would assist departmental security activities, provide hearing examiners for loyalty cases, and establish a central review board to review
various cases. The other recommendations looked to certain refinements
in the processes for handling cases. One suggestion was to separate security cases from loyalty cases and to recognize that different standards
might govern the two types of action. Thus a finding that a person was
a security risk would be possible without implying that the individual
was or had been disloyal. The Commission advocated fair hearings in
loyalty investigations, and the right of an individual to know and to challenge a witness presenting derogatory information other than a confidential
informant engaged in intelligence work. The Commission also considered
various improvements in industrial security, port security, air transport
security, passport security, and transfer of the issuance of visas from the
State Department to the Justice Department. The Commission proposed
the enactment of legislation making admissible in court evidence of subversion obtained by wiretapping by authorized investigative agencies, and
providing penalties for the unlawful disclosure of classified information
by any person outside as well as within the government service.[24]

In some respects the Commission anticipated a more rigorous security
program than then existed; in other respects it proposed more careful observation of procedural safeguards for the affected individual. As of
1958, however, neither the President nor the legislature was inclined to

[23] *Ibid.,* p. 7.
[24] *Report of the Commission on Government Security* (Washington: Government
Printing Office, 1957).

take any additional action to strengthen or to restrict the government's loyalty program.

In 1956 in a major case, the Supreme Court of the United States held that the action of President Eisenhower in extending the provisions of the Summary Suspension Act of 1950 to all governmental agencies was illegal, and that summary dismissal under terms of the law should be confined to positions within "sensitive agencies" where the interests of national security were paramount.[25]

There has been a good deal of criticism of loyalty programs in actual practice. It has been said that government employees have been harassed by questionnaires and investigations, and that actual standards of disloyal conduct have been vague. It would appear that on occasion inquiries have been started which arose from personal jealousies or animosities rather than from any real evidence of subversive behavior. At the same time it is important to recognize that loyalty is an essential requirement of the public service. The solution has not been to abandon loyalty investigation and review but to make the procedure careful and fair.[26]

SUMMARY

The executive in our system of government has substantial personnel responsibilities. Here again the President carries heavier burdens than the governors of states, since personnel laws tend to confer more discretion upon the federal executive than the state executive. For example, it is by statute rather than by executive action that the extent of the civil service system is determined for state agencies and employees.

By his appointment authority the executive is expected to provide political leadership of the bureaucracy. This appointment authority is reinforced by the power to dismiss. This removal power may be circumscribed, however, by statute, as has been done in the federal government and in state governments.

The executive responsibility goes beyond appointment and removal, however. He has the broader task of watching over the personnel system of government as a whole to ensure that there shall be satisfactory performance of the public service.

[25] *Cole v. Young,* 351 U.S. 536 (1956).
[26] In *Service v. Dulles,* 354 U.S. 363 (1957), the Supreme Court insisted that, even though he had broad discretionary authority to dismiss employees, the Secretary of State was expected to observe the general procedures for such action established by departmental regulations.

Chapter 18

The Executive and the Budget

In most units of government today the executive has been made responsible for preparing a comprehensive and detailed set of budget estimates setting forth administrative needs for funds with which to operate in an ensuing fiscal period. This is known as the executive budget. The executive does more than simply collect estimates of financial requirements from administrative agencies. He is expected to review these requirements and submit his own independent recommendations to the legislature. He is expected to express his judgment about the relative merits of various administrative activities and to present a total budget program which will fit into a particular fiscal policy of tax and other resources for meeting recommended appropriations.

The executive budget is a development largely of the first half of the twentieth century. It was intended to strengthen the position of the chief executive as an administrative overseer. More than this, it was intended to provide the legislature with a budget program which could be examined in its component parts but still remain a general scheme of operation. Both of these objectives have been realized in considerable degree by the executive budget. The story of developments within the federal government will in large part indicate the kind of change which has also been introduced in most state governments.

THE BUDGET AND ACCOUNTING ACT OF 1921

The executive budget system as such was inaugurated in the federal government by the Budget and Accounting Act of June 10, 1921. With the addition of only a few amplifying phrases added in legislation approved September 12, 1950, August 1, 1956, and August 25, 1958, this statute has provided the basis for the creation of machinery and procedures which have greatly enhanced the administrative role of the President. It is no exaggeration to say that no single other event has done so much as the 1921 law in providing the executive with an effective technique for supervising and controlling the administrative activities of the federal government.

Behind the statute of 1921 lay ten years of continuous effort to persuade the Congress to enact legislation providing for an executive budget system in the federal government. And behind this effort in turn was a larger movement sometimes referred to as scientific management. It is not necessary here to trace the entire story of the ideas which eventually resulted in passage of the 1921 law. It is sufficient briefly to note two particular aspects in the historical development of governmental budgeting.

In the first place, from the very beginning of federal government administration in 1789, there were at least the major elements of a budget system. Budgeting as a general governmental practice did not suddenly burst into life in 1921. Actually, the Congress in 1789 in creating the Treasury Department provided that the Secretary was to "digest plans for the improvement of the revenue, and for the support of the public credit" and was to "prepare and report estimates of the public revenue, and the public expenditure." More specific legislation was passed in 1800 requiring the Secretary of the Treasury at the beginning of each session of the legislature to prepare and present a report on governmental finances, "containing estimates of the public revenue and public expenditures. . . . " Another law passed in 1820 required the Secretary of the Treasury to present information about continuing appropriations and unexpended balances from previous appropriations.

These various laws made it possible for the Secretary of the Treasury to exercise a general oversight of budget preparation by all administrative agencies. Men like Hamilton and Gallatin were more than willing to assert governmental leadership in all fiscal matters, including budgeting. Yet with time, the beginnings thus made largely disappeared. Various Presidents were little interested in the budget as a technique of administrative supervision. And the Congress encouraged heads of departments and other agencies to come directly to the legislature with their expenditure estimates. Little by little department heads were instructed by law to submit their budgets directly to the legislature rather than through the Secretary of the Treasury. By 1878, the Treasury had become merely a routine channel for presenting budget requirements to Congress. By 1900, administrative agencies prepared budget estimates but only the legislature undertook to review and revise them.[1]

Secondly, we should note the broad purposes behind the new ideas about budgeting which were developed early in the twentieth century. The scientific management movement was dedicated to improvement in work

[1] Cf. Daniel T. Selko, *The Federal Financial System* (Washington, D.C.: Brookings Institution, 1940), chap. 4.

methods, first in industry, and subsequently in government. Efficiency was the new watchword in industry in order to increase output and to advance the material well-being of owners, labor, and consumers. Economy became the watchword for government upon the general assumption that careful control of governmental expenditures left more of the national output for the satisfaction of individual and business needs. Two legislative agencies, the Cockrell Committee from 1887 to 1889 and the Dockery Commission from 1893 to 1895, studied federal governmental budget and accounting practices. Their recommendations reflected a growing dissatisfaction with existing arrangements for handling governmental expenditures.

In 1905, Theodore Roosevelt became the first Chief Executive to give recognition to the concern for scientific management. In that year he appointed the Keep Committee to study departmental operating practices. Some improvements followed from this effort. When President Taft obtained legislative approval for the creation of a Commission on Economy and Efficiency, the attention of this body immediately turned to the need for budgetary reform in the federal government. A principal report of the Commission was published in 1912 under the title, *The Need for a National Budget*. Two aspects of existing practice were especially singled out for criticism. One was the lack of any orderly, systematic plan for presenting appropriation estimates to the Congress. Supposedly, the Treasury Department was expected to bring estimates of expenditure requirements and of prospective revenue together for transmission to the legislature. In practice, departments and other agencies presented their needs directly to various committees of the Congress. A balance between outlay and income was fortuitous. Each agency sought to obtain all that it could extract from the legislative committees. The other defect was the absence of any single critical review of the appropriation estimates prepared by these administrative agencies. Presumably this function was being performed by the Congress as a whole, but actually no such central critical examination was made in order to make certain that administrative budget programs did not compete with or duplicate each other.

The solution to these deficiencies called for changes in practice at the level both of the Chief Executive and of the legislature. The President should be made responsible for preparing an executive budget which he would transmit to the Congress. This budget would bring together the expenditure requests of all administrative agencies. It would present them in an orderly, comparable, and systematic fashion. More than this, the President should have a staff to assist him not just in the collection of these requests but also in the critical analysis of each. The Taft Commission on Economy and Efficiency even prepared such a budget for the entire federal government for the fiscal year 1914 which the President sent to Congress in February, 1913. The other reform was needed in the Congress itself, where the Commission urged that a single committee on appropriations in each house be vested with the responsibility for reviewing appropriation requests.

The budget reforms advocated by President Taft and his Commission on Economy and Efficiency were not immediately acceptable to the legislature. President Taft was convinced that new legislation was needed in order to accomplish the necessary reforms. After all, the statute books contained over a century of legislative enactment on budgeting, appropriation, and accounting matters—laws which were not always consistent one with the other. The President was doubtful whether an executive budget system could be installed in the federal government by action of the Chief Executive alone. In the meantime, political developments during 1912, coupled with Democratic party control of the House of Representatives after the election of 1910, undermined Taft's executive leadership. Congress and national political attention were turned to public issues more exciting than a question of administrative reform. Moreover, President Wilson, inaugurated in March, 1913, was primarily concerned to assert his leadership in legislation looking to new tariff, antitrust, and banking policies, among others. He was not much concerned with lesser matters of governmental practices. Moreover, the advent of World War I served also to distract attention from the proposals made by Taft's Commission.

In 1916 Congress took a first step toward change by establishing a Bureau of Efficiency as an independent agency under the Chief Executive. The bureau was given no specific budgetary authority but was expected to serve the President by studying problems of organization and business methods in the departments and other agencies of the federal government. This was the first time in American history that an administrative agency had been established simply to serve the President, that is, to assist him in carrying out his executive duties. Eventually, in 1933, this bureau was to be merged with the Bureau of the Budget. Then, in 1919, Congress passed legislation setting up a budget system. President Wilson vetoed the bill, objecting on constitutional grounds to the provision making the incumbent of the new position of Comptroller General removable only by concurrent resolution of the Congress. Finally, under President Harding, the Budget and Accounting Act of 1921 was passed and approved.

EXECUTIVE BUDGET BY LAW

A few words are necessary about the fact that the budget practice established within the federal government in 1921 was set up by legislation. As we shall note in a moment, the Budget and Accounting Act confers broad and substantial authority upon the President in his relations to the administrative agencies of government. The question naturally arises whether this authority could exist apart from such statutory enactment. In budgetary matters, is the President simply an agent of the Congress? Could his authority be changed at any time? Is the so-called executive budget system only a matter of authority delegated to the Chief Executive by the legislature?

Before we discuss this question, it is interesting to note that the movement for budgetary reform in the federal government was accompanied by a like movement at the level of state and local governments.[2] Yet in most instances state government changes were introduced by constitutional amendment or constitutional revision rather than by legislative enactment. This fact recognized that budgetary procedures intimately involved the work of both executive and legislature. Constitutional prescription seemed then the appropriate method of setting forth the desired budgetary practice.

There appear to be two major elements of an answer to the constitutional status of the budget system which now exists in the federal government. It seems evident that the authority to prepare and submit a budget to the legislature could not be vested by law in any other official except the Chief Executive, unless it were vested in a committee of the legislature itself. More than this, it probably would be accurate to say that a President could establish an executive budget system without statutory enactment if he were disposed to do so. On the other hand, a budget system is something more than the preparation of appropriation requests and of revenue estimates. It involves also the actual appropriation process itself. And only the legislature can enact appropriation measures.

The virtue of the Budget and Accounting Act of 1921 is that it acknowledges a joint interest between the executive and legislature in an orderly and systematic procedure for preparing appropriation requests and for considering them. Certainly the legislature is vitally interested in how appropriation requests come to it for attention. The executive is much interested in budget requests and their relation to income, since budgetary policy has become today a major political issue.[3] More than this, budgetary policy is only a part of a broader matter of governmental fiscal policy, and this in turn intimately affects employment, production, and the distribution of income within society. In terms of his role as a political leader the President of the United States today must give careful attention to budgetary policy in its many ramifications.

This author would question whether it would be entirely accurate to say that the Budget and Accounting Act of 1921 created an executive budget system in the federal government. It might be more appropriate to the niceties of constitutional distinction to say that the 1921 legislation simply recognized the need for an executive budget system and created

[2] See, for example, W. F. Willoughby, *The Movement for Budgetary Reform in the States* (New York: D. Appleton & Company, Inc., 1918).

[3] Cf. A. E. Buck, *The Budget in Governments of Today* (New York: The Macmillan Company, 1934).

the machinery and regularized the procedure for its operation. Nonetheless, it is certainly evident that the Budget and Accounting Act of 1921 is an impressive illustration of how, in our federal government especially, the essential framework of governmental operation has been elaborated by law.

PROVISIONS OF THE BUDGET AND ACCOUNTING ACT

The Budget and Accounting Act of 1921, as its title suggests, is concerned with two subjects, budgeting and accounting. For the present, it is the first of these in which we are interested. The law specifies that within fifteen days of the opening of a regular session of the Congress in January of each year the President shall transmit to the legislature *The Budget,* which shall consist of a budget message, summary data, and supporting detail on proposed appropriations "necessary in his judgment for the support of the government for the ensuing fiscal year. . . . " The law exempts from the exercise of this executive judgment the appropriation requests of the legislative and judicial branches. For these branches the President simply collects the necessary information in order to present the Congress with a comprehensive statement of expenditure needs. Section 206 of the 1921 statute went on to say that no officer or employee of any administrative agency was to submit to the legislature any appropriation request other than that recommended by the President except as he might be asked to do so by either house of the Congress.

In addition to expenditure detail, the President was to recommend in his budget message any new taxes, loans, or other appropriate action to meet the difference between proposed outlays and estimated income. This meant that the President was expected to "balance" income and outgo in the financial transactions of the federal government by proposing appropriate fiscal measures, be those taxation, borrowing, currency expansion, or any combination thereof.

To assist the President in the performance of this sizable task of budget collection and review the law created a Bureau of the Budget headed by a director appointed by the President but not subject to senatorial confirmation. Originally, in 1921 this Budget Bureau was "located" within the Treasury Department, partly in acknowledgment of the long role of that department in routine budget operations. Actually, this so-called location made little difference, since the first director in 1921, General Charles G. Dawes, firmly established the idea that the director worked exclusively for the President.[4] Finally in 1939, the Bureau of the Budget became officially a part of the Executive Office of the President. Under

---

[4] Charles G. Dawes, *The First Year of the Budget in the United States* (New York: Harper & Brothers, 1923).

regulations approved by the President, every department and other administrative establishment was directed by the statute to provide the Budget Bureau with any and all information that agency might require.

Section 209 of the original law stated that the Budget Bureau, when directed to do so by the President, should make detailed studies of department and other agencies for the purpose of enabling the President to determine desirable changes in existing organization, activities, or methods of business of governmental agencies, the necessity for appropriations, the assignment of operating activities, and the possible regrouping of activities and services. But the law did not give the President authority to accomplish such changes; it directed him only to submit his recommendations on these matters to the Congress for its consideration. Section 104 of the legislation enacted in 1950 amplified this provision somewhat by saying that the President, through the director of the Bureau of the Budget, was authorized and directed "to evaluate and develop improved plans for the organization, coordination, and management of the executive branch of the government with a view to efficient and economical service." We may note in passing that the 1950 law also approved a function exercised through the Budget Bureau since 1939, that of improving and controlling the gathering, analysis, publication, and dissemination of statistical information by all administrative agencies.

Upon the foundation of these essential provisions of the Budget and Accounting Act of 1921, has been constructed the executive budget system of the federal government.

THE CONCEPT OF EXECUTIVE BUDGETING

The system of executive budgeting entails first of all the authority of the President to review the expenditure requests of every administrative agency. This means an annual examination of the work of an agency and what it costs to perform that work. Thus, every program of an agency, its work procedures, and its management practices may come under such review as the Chief Executive desires to exercise, through the instrument of the Bureau of the Budget. The only limits to this power of review are those of time, personnel, and technique. It is inevitable that presidential attention itself should concentrate upon the major areas of governmental expenditure in which there is a good deal of public interest for one reason or another.

The sanction of this presidential review of expenditure requests is the power to recommend action to the Congress. This is, of course, only the power to recommend. There is no obligation on the part of the legislature to accept the executive proposal. Yet the fact is that the legislature only occasionally undertakes any substantial alteration in the budget estimates submitted by the President. Once expenditure plans have been put together and the whole set forth in the context of a particular set of taxation and other fiscal policies, there are powerful incentives to leave the entire structure unchanged. If legislative committees undertake to review all needs, then they must consider each agency on its merits. Pressures arise for increases, and if a few increases are made it is difficult to resist others. Sometimes the legislature may undertake to reduce the appropriation requests of the executive, but except in unusual circumstances reductions create opposition from those who are interested in the work of an agency.

Furthermore, if a legislature departs too far from executive recommendations, it invites the possibility of executive veto of the appropriation measure. It is difficult for the Chief Executive in the federal government to disapprove an appropriation measure, since he must return the entire measure to the legislature and face the possibility of delay in obtaining any funds for administrative operations. In several states the executive enjoys the authority of "item" veto on appropriation measures and hence may disapprove any individual item without acting upon the whole. This gives the executive a good deal of leverage in his relationship with the legislature on budget matters.

The provisions of the 1921 law, as well as those of the 1950 amendment, make it clear that the President is expected to give particular attention to the "how" of administrative operations. He is expected not alone to review the proposed magnitude and scope of governmental activities; he is expected also to review the way in which these activities are being carried out. Could the same results be achieved with a lesser expenditure of funds? Could greater results be obtained if work methods were simplified or otherwise improved? These are continuing challenges to the management of all administrative agencies. Through the budget operation the President is supposed to encourage and assist active efforts to improve management practices within government.

There can be no doubt but that the budget power is a substantial power. In it the President, or any chief executive, possesses a vital tool for supervising both the substance and the process of administrative endeavor. Furthermore, this review is continuing. In the federal government it must be performed every year. In most state governments it is undertaken every two years. But upon either an annual or biennial basis the entire range of the administrative work of government must come under executive review. No administrative agency can afford to be indifferent to or careless about this executive authority. It is the budget power of the chief executive which is his chief basis of concern with most administrative agencies most of the time.

In the very early days of the movement for budget reform, it was pointed out that an executive budget system would lodge immense authority in the hands of the President.[5] The power to appropriate funds for the operations of government had been vested by the Constitution in the hands of the legislature. For over a century in practice the actual process of budget making had been performed by the Congress. To change this arrangement and to vest authority in the hands of the Chief Executive would be to transfer power of the legislature to the executive. Thus the argument was presented.

In defense of the proposal to provide the President with the power to prepare budgets, two major propositions were put forth.[6] The first was a denial that any change in constitutional authority as between the two branches of government was involved. The Congress would continue to appropriate funds as in the past. The authority of the President to present a budget was no more than the authority to recommend measures for the public good which was a part of the executive power. It would still remain for the legislature to consider, accept, or modify these recommendations. Secondly, it was suggested that the objective was to strengthen supervision over the growing administrative activities of government and that this power of supervision was a part of the executive authority under the Constitution.

There was much experience at the time to suggest in fact that the budget supervision exercised by the legislature was a good deal more lax than that which would be exercised by the executive. Administrative agencies presenting their requests for appropriations to the legislature naturally pressed for all that they thought they might obtain. In turn, interest groups concerned with particular administrative activities importuned the legislature to grant these requests. Individual legislators and legislative committees developed a substantial interest in the work of particular agencies. Often the process of legislative budget making was little more than a process of compromising these competing interests at or near the level of the original budgetary request. In this way administrative expenditures continued to rise, perhaps more rapidly than was essential.

Executive budget making would be different, it was asserted. For one thing, the executive elected to represent the nation as a whole might be expected to review needs in terms of the general welfare. Being a single person and so capable of decisive action by himself, the executive could better resist individual pressures and seek the welfare of the whole as a gauge of his budget recommendations. Moreover, having institutional assistance in conducting his review of budget requests by administrative agencies, the chief executive could exercise a continuing, informed scrutiny

---

[5] Edward A. Fitzpatrick, *Budget Making in a Democracy* (New York: The Macmillan Company, 1918).

[6] Frederick A. Cleveland and A. E. Buck, *Budget and Responsible Government,* with an introduction by William Howard Taft (New York: The Macmillan Company, 1920).

of administrative needs. In this way the executive could balance various requirements and so arrive at budget recommendations which would involve the best interests of the government in general.

It has even been suggested by one student reviewing the early story of the executive budget movement in this country that the advocates of the new system were motivated by a desire to reduce governmental expenditures and to assure balance of taxation and administrative outlay at a level ensuring maximum private enterprise. Such advocates had despaired of any such interest within the legislature and sought an executive budget as a means for realizing broad fiscal and economic objectives.[7] Certainly the watchwords of "economy" and "efficiency" which accompanied the movement for executive budgeting might have had such meanings in the context of the day.

At present we realize that a budget system does not in and of itself necessarily imply any particular fiscal or economic policy on the part of government. What a budget system does do is to help a chief executive in giving expression to whatever public policy he wishes to frame and advocate. It enables him to give more effective implementation to such fiscal policy goals as he may advocate.

The politics of executive budget making nonetheless implies that executive scrutiny will result in a reduction of the requests submitted by administrative agencies. Many budget presentations in state and local government show what the agency requested and what the executive recommended. Where this practice exists, it is a direct invitation to administrative agencies to present their needs to the fullest extent because they may confidently expect that the executive will have to make reductions. How else can the executive's budget authority be defended in political terms? In the federal government, the budget as presented by the President to the Congress does not show the departmental or agency request. Yet some question about the size of the original request is often asked by legislators when administrative spokesmen appear before the appropriations committees. The executive may reasonably anticipate that such queries will be made. Here again, except in special circumstances, the political assumption appears to be that the executive budget system is not functioning properly unless it results in a reduction of the operating funds sought by administrative agencies.

About one aspect of the executive budget system, there is little doubt. The system has certainly strengthened the means available to the chief executive for supervising the work of administrative agencies. Perhaps more even than the appointing power, the budget authority of the executive has made administrative agencies "executive-conscious." In this sense

---

[7] Harvey S. Perloff, "Budgetary Symbolism and Fiscal Planning," in C. J. Friedrich and E. S. Mason (eds.), *Public Policy*, vol. II (Cambridge, Mass.: Harvard University Press, 1941).

the authority of the chief executive over administrative agencies has been greatly increased. Administrative behavior has consequently become more responsible to the public policy purposes of the chief executive. To some degree this strengthening of executive authority has resulted in a diminution of legislative authority, not in theory or in constitutional status, but in actual practice. It may be argued, however, that legislative budget making tended to diffuse and scatter administrative supervision and was at best of dubious effectiveness. We may safely say also that the executive budget system is now an accepted element of American government.

THE BUDGET AS PUBLIC POLICY

The process of budget making presents a basic question. It is this: shall a particular program or activity of government be expanded, supported as at present, or curtailed? For example, at the level of the federal government in any year such questions must be answered as shall procurement of military aircraft be expanded, shall foreign economic assistance be curtailed, shall research in nuclear physics be continued on the present scale? In a state government the subjects are somewhat different but the questions are the same: shall more money be spent on support of higher education, shall less be spent on the operation of mental health facilities, shall old-age assistance grants be continued at existing levels? Within a municipal government the questions are: shall more be spent on public health, shall less be spent on fire protection, shall street maintenance be continued on its current basis?

Such questions must be analyzed in terms of two important considerations. One is the social desirability of a particular level of activity for any government service or control. In other words, the President or other chief executive in our system of government must initially place some evaluation upon the various programs of government. He must express some judgment about the magnitude of each major segment of governmental endeavor. The other consideration is one of expressing a judgment about the relative merits of all the administrative undertakings of government. Budget policy is not simply a matter of decision making about individual activities; it is equally decision making about the sum total of all the work of government and the relative merits of each component element.

The problems of public policy involved in budget making are both economic and political in character. Indeed, it is doubtful if any sharp distinction can be made between factors of economic and political judgment in the budget-making process. The chief executive is a political leader, as we have emphasized many times. He is not necessarily a trained economist, nor can economic knowledge offer sure and final answers to the types of questions enumerated above. In the end, the chief executive must make such decisions as he believes to be most conducive to the general welfare and to be politically defensible.

For example, let us return to the particular illustration of the amount to be budgeted in an ensuing year for support of air power as a constituent part of our system of national defense. The questions to be answered by the President involve desirable size of the Air Force and its distribution among strategic, tactical, defense, and support operations; the personnel required to man such a force; the scope of training to be undertaken; the volume of maintenance required; the procurement needed of new types of aircraft and other supplies; the research and development to be undertaken, and the general support and administration necessitated.[8] How are these questions to be answered? No economic solution is possible to these problems. The answers must depend upon a careful study of air power: its potential achievements and its relation to the defense needs required in a troubled world.

Then a second set of questions arises involving the relationship of the Air Force to the Army and Navy. If we assume that the needs as formulated by the specialists in each kind of defense element cannot all be satisfied, then some basis of choice must be found. The economist has an answer to this problem. It is the doctrine of marginal utility. The degree of national defense obtained by an additional expenditure for air power as against a similar additional expenditure for land or sea forces—this should be the determining factor in analyzing the relative merits of the claims for additional levels of expenditure. As a standard for the general guidance of the budget maker, this doctrine of marginal utility has its place. But the application of the concept—the precise measurement of the defense results to be obtained from expenditure of additional funds for various purposes—is by no means a simple matter. There are too many variables and too many differences of opinion to be able to measure marginal utility with any definite finality.

In the third place, there is a set of questions involving the total size of the outlay for public purposes and the ways in which this total size shall be financed. It is no easy matter to decide just how much of the total economic endeavor of the country shall be devoted to governmental purposes. In our society no one group of persons makes any such decision. The President is responsible for preparing the budget of the federal government, but large as this is, it is by no means the total of governmental activity in the United States. In the calendar year 1957 the total gross national product of the United States was estimated at 434 billion dollars. From this total 86.6 billion dollars, or almost 20 per cent, went for governmental purchases of goods and services. In turn, of this 86.6 billion

[8] See the suggested elements of a performance budget for the Air Force in Arthur Smithies, *The Budgetary Process in the United States* (New York: McGraw-Hill Book Company, Inc., 1955), p. 267.

dollars, 50.5 billion represented the share commanded by the federal government; 36 billion dollars went for state and local governmental activities.[9] The 36 billion dollars of state and local governmental expenditure represented decisions made by some 102,000 different units of government. There is thus no one point in our economy where a single decision can be made about the size of the public sector of our economy.

Nonetheless, certain prevailing attitudes tend to guide and influence these decisions. There is a general public disposition in this country to believe that governmental activity should be confined to certain types of work generally of a "nonbusiness" character. There is another popular attitude often expressed to the effect that private business activity should be encouraged over and above public services. In spite of these general guidelines for public policy, governmental expenditures have steadily increased in the United States and a substantial proportion of total economic endeavor has been required for support of governmental activities. This is understandable in the light of our national defense situation, our increasing population, the growing industrialization and urbanization of our society, and the increasing concern of government with the economic welfare of the nation.[10]

This outline of fundamental issues in budget making indicates the range of public problems to which a chief executive must address his attention. Obviously all these questions are matters of major public importance, all are matters of grave public policy. The budget of government is a compilation of public policy decisions of great complexity and of far-reaching effect upon the national welfare in terms of total outlay, in terms of the proposed allocation of that outlay among various activities or programs, and in terms of the amount available for any one particular endeavor.

Unfortunately, most budget presentations do not clearly focus attention upon these basic issues. Budget details swamp the broad recommendations of public policy in a welter of salary schedules and proposed expenditures for fuel, transportation, communication, travel, supplies, and similar items. Presentation of estimates in accordance with detailed units of organizational structure obscures program objectives. Although much has been said about "program budgeting" in recent years, much still remains to be done to make the idea real and meaningful in the actual budget process.[11]

[9] *Economic Report of the President,* January, 1958 (Washington: Government Printing Office, 1958), p. 165.

[10] For a further discussion of this problem, see Jesse Burkhead, *Government Budgeting* (New York: John Wiley & Sons, Inc., 1956), pp. 38–44. See also Solomon Fabricant, *The Trend in Government Activity in the United States since 1900* (New York: National Bureau of Economic Research, Inc., 1952).

[11] Cf. Arthur Smithies, *op. cit.,* parts 4 and 5; and Jesse Burkhead, *op. cit.,* chaps. 6 and 7.

In recent years the Executive Office of the President has made definite efforts to provide summary information about budget proposals which will indicate the program purposes of the Administration. In 1958, for example, the Bureau of the Budget prepared a document for popular consumption which set forth broad classifications of expenditures recommended by the President for the fiscal year 1959, and within these broad classifications set forth component program parts.[12] This summary was perhaps too brief, and too general, in its program descriptions to be of much value. It certainly was a step in the right direction. Intended for the interested general public, it contained useful information. It needed to be more specific in setting forth program objectives.

Yet this 1958 *The Federal Budget in Brief* was a document for popular use, not one for legislative action. The faults of public budgeting are perhaps more attributable to legislative than to executive reluctance to change. Legislators fear lest some so-called budget improvements will actually turn out to be devices for weakening that legislative control over expenditure which they have become accustomed to exercise. Under these circumstances improvements come slowly.[13]

BUDGET EXECUTION

Budget preparation is only one essential step in the process of public budgeting. The actual work of preparing budget requests falls upon administrative agencies. The review of these requests and their adjustment into a total pattern of proposed governmental expenditures are left to the chief executive. The legislature enacts the actual appropriations for performance of administrative tasks. There remains the expenditure of the funds appropriated, or budget execution.

In substantial measure the responsibility for budget expenditure rests with the management of administrative agencies. The role of the chief executive in this phase of the budget process is by no means so clearly prescribed as his part in budget preparation. The chief executive may enjoy some degree of supervision through a treasury or finance department which keeps records of administrative expenditures. But this control tends to be routine; it is concerned with correct procedure and with observation of legislative limitations rather than with program objectives.

[12] *The Federal Budget in Brief, Fiscal Year 1959* (Washington: Government Printing Office, 1958).

[13] For two very useful accounts of problems in budget preparation and presentation, see Sidney G. Tickton, *The Budget in Transition,* Planning Pamphlet no. 89; and *The Need for Further Budget Reform,* (a Joint NPA Statement together with Gerhard Colm and Marilyn Young, *The Federal Budget and the National Economy*), Planning Pamphlet no. 90 (Washington, D.C.: National Planning Association, 1955).

Beyond this degree of expenditure supervision, it is by no means clear just what the extent of executive authority may be.

Two basic questions about executive participation in budget expenditure have arisen over the years. One involves administrative desire to transfer funds from one purpose to another. The other involves the adjustment, or reduction, of program objectives during a fiscal year. In so far as transfers from one category of expenditure to another are concerned, the chief executive exercises only such authority as may be conferred upon him by appropriation or other legislation. Sometimes the legislature is willing to permit the chief executive to make adjustments within percentage limits (10 per cent is not infrequent) among detailed appropriation items. Almost always the power to transfer specifically forbids any increase in the total appropriation for a particular administrative agency. In some state governments the chief executive, along with certain legislators and others, enjoys a collegial authority to approve transfers.

In the federal government the President must approve any departmental requests for supplementary or deficiency appropriations before these can go to the legislature. Administrative agencies, therefore, are careful to obtain presidential approval before overcommitting the funds appropriated by the Congress. Thus the President has obtained an additional means for supervising actual budget expenditure.

Departments and other agencies ordinarily look upon the legislative appropriation as a mandate to spend government funds up to the full amount authorized. Since agency requests are almost always greater than the recommendations of the chief executive and the appropriations of the legislature, it is natural for administrators to take this attitude. Moreover, when a legislature approves a particular level of activity, is not this a declaration of legislative intent which the chief executive should honor, not ignore?

This question of executive authority to reduce legislative appropriations has arisen at different times since 1921 in the federal government. As first Director of the Budget, General Dawes insisted that appropriations by Congress were an upper ceiling for administrative operations, not a direct command to spend no less than the authorized amount. In practice, however, Presidents have found it generally desirable to accept appropriations as a kind of mandate. After World War II, in 1948, a dramatic episode occurred when President Truman impounded funds beyond the amount recommended by him for the procurement build-up of the Air Force. Although there was much grumbling about action reversing the intent of the Congress, the President was able to make his cut stick. This was an unusual rather than a customary situation.

In 1950 the Congress in the general appropriation law provided that the President might establish reserves for contingencies in an appropriation item, or set up reserves to effect savings realizable through changes in requirements, improved efficiency of operations, or other developments subsequent to the effective date of the appropriation. This provision appeared to make it quite clear that the President, through the Bureau of the Budget, might establish reserve funds in appropriation items and thus in effect reduce an appropriation made by the Congress.

In 1956 again the legislature enacted appropriations providing larger outlays for the United States Air Force than had been recommended by the President. In making these appropriations, the committees of Congress pressed the Secretary of Defense to indicate whether he would order expenditure at the higher level desired by the legislature or would seek through Presidential action to reverse the legislative intent. The Secretary promised that the increased appropriation would be committed. No doubt such a promise was necessary in order to avoid repeal of the general provision for setting up reserve funds.

To a considerable degree the President's desire to reduce a legislative appropriation will depend upon the extent to which his original recommendation was altered. Since in most instances the legislature makes only slight adjustments in the President's budget proposals and since most of these adjustments are downward rather than upward, the President has little incentive to reduce appropriations. To curtail outlays below his original recommendation is to admit that something was wrong with the initial proposal. Presidential interest in reduction of an appropriation item arises only when the legislature provides substantially more than the original recommendation. In such instances the President must determine the political repercussions which may arise among interest groups and within the legislature if he undertakes to alter the legislative judgment. This judgment of political consequences imposes a limitation which has to this point provided the only answer to the question how far the President may go in altering legislative appropriations.

THE BUDGET AND MANAGEMENT EFFICIENCY

The budget prepared by the President and presented to the Congress is more than a series of policy decisions about the scope of proposed administrative activity in an ensuing fiscal period. The budget is also a promise of administrative performance. It is a pledge that resources requested will realize promised goals. It is also an implied statement that these goals cannot be realized with any lesser expenditure. This is one of the great challenges of budget administration: could the same policy and service goals actually be achieved with a lesser use of resources? Or to state the challenge in a different way: could the same input of resources result in a greater output of activity?

Properly, this matter of administrative efficiency is the primary responsibility of management in the various administrative agencies of government. Management has the actual task of performing the operations authorized by law. It commands the resources of personnel, facilities, and supplies provided for any task. It fixes policies and programs. It checks results. No amount of criticism, suggestion, or assistance from outside an agency can ever compensate entirely for internal management deficiencies which result in work inefficiency.

The problem in executive budget making and control has been just how far to go in an effort to improve management performance at the departmental and other agency level. Different answers have been attempted at different times. In 1921, General Dawes set about creating a number of committees and boards to promote economy in printing, transportation, purchasing, office facilities, and office practice. There were even regional bodies to help encourage an interest in these subjects. In part, these coordinating committees were for the exchange of information, in part they actually began to perform certain central services. All were concerned with administrative "housekeeping." By the end of the Coolidge administration in 1929, much of the enthusiasm for this kind of efficiency had begun to wane.

Early in the Roosevelt administration in 1933 a central procurement agency was created in the federal government as well as a strengthened public buildings agency and a central statistical board. Eventually in 1949 a General Services Administration was created as a government agency to perform various central services for the operating departments and other establishments; these central services include the purchase of supplies and the disposal of excess property, central records storage, and the construction and operation of public buildings. Thus, budget administration under the President led to the creation of a central service agency for the government as a whole, and the President, among his many other duties, acquired supervisory responsibility for its satisfactory performance in servicing operating agencies.

In 1939, as a result of the report of the President's Committee on Administrative Management in 1937, the Budget Bureau enlarged its staff and created a Division of Administrative Management. Almost at once this division became involved in helping to establish and organize the emergency agencies required by the growing defense crisis and then by the actual advent of war. After the war a good deal of attention was absorbed by the changing organizational needs arising from this country's new role of leadership in international affairs. Some effort was devoted to improving procurement, personnel, and accounting procedures in the government. Training programs were also established to stimulate increased attention to work efficiency within the management of operating agencies.

In 1949 the first Hoover Commission called attention to the fact that in ten years of existence the work of management appraisal had not been integrated with the work of reviewing budget estimates or with the work of checking subsequent performance. The tasks undertaken by the division of administrative management had all been worthwhile and necessary, but the job of ensuring management efficiency by operating agencies still remained to be done. The result of this comment was that before the end of the Truman administration in 1953, the work of budget preparation was reorganized in an effort to give more attention to problems of how well the operations of administrative agencies were being conducted.

In addition, in 1949 President Truman created an Advisory Committee on Management composed of certain department heads and citizens prominent in the field of management. This body was staffed by personnel from the Bureau of the Budget. The committee met from time to time with Cabinet members and heads of other agencies in order to stimulate their interest in management improvement and to acquaint them with the resources available for this purpose. When reporting in 1952 the committee enumerated current management goals as: (1) improvements in organizational framework; (2) strengthening the position of top executives by redefining their powers and furnishing them adequate staff support; (3) improvement in such government-wide processes as budgeting, accounting, personnel, and other procedures; and (4) stimulation of interest in management improvement through employee suggestions and top leadership.[14] This particular method of encouraging management improvement was not continued during the first Eisenhower administration; during this period, however, a President's Advisory Committee on Government Organization helped to review and advise on broad organizational problems of the government.

Administrative efficiency depends upon a number of factors which need continuing attention. These include such questions as whether an agency is overcentralized, with too many details of operation concentrated in the nation's capital, whether an agency is overstaffed in terms of its essential goals, and whether management is alert to possibilities of work improvement and endeavors to achieve greater efficiency in its activities. Certainly management needs constant encouragement to improve its operations; such encouragement is not realized by cutting appropriations but must be promoted by public appreciation, by increased compensation, and even by assignment of additional appropriate duties.

Recently, one writer has suggested that the President should transmit to Congress each year a Report on Executive Performance in addition to his budget message. This report, it is proposed, would give particular attention to action taken by the Chief Executive to improve the organization and work process of administrative agencies. The President might transmit his reorganization plans in connection with this report and call attention to restrictive legislation which might affect the efficient use of

[14] President's Advisory Committee on Management, *Report to the President* (Washington: Government Printing Office, 1952).

personnel or other administrative resources. To some limited extent steps in the direction of such a report have been taken in the present annual budget message.[15]

The idea of a President's Report on Executive Performance certainly has merit. The principal defect of such a practice would be the tendency for a President to picture current operations as satisfactory; at the least any chief executive would be unlikely to express any major criticism of the work of an executive department or other administrative agency. If a President were to make public various criticisms which his office had accumulated about any particular agency, legislators and others would immediately want to know what he intended to do about them. After all, the President must bear the major responsibility for the performance of administrative bodies. If a President has any particular ideas about management improvement needs in any given agency, he is more likely to achieve some progress through direct personal insistence rather than through public comment. It may be possible to prepare a report on executive performance which will avoid these dangers and still have meaning. The innovation might well be tried, at least as an experiment.

THE BUDGET AS AN INSTITUTION

It must be evident from this brief summary of a chief executive's role in governmental budgeting that such onerous duties cannot be performed without assistance. Throughout this discussion we have referred to the President and the Bureau of the Budget interchangeably. In theory, they are one and the same. The Budget Bureau as a part of the Executive Office of the President is an instrument of the Chief Executive. It is his tool to use as he may wish. This fact is underlined by the legal provision which gives the President authority to appoint the director of the budget without senatorial confirmation. The President can make of the Budget Bureau what he wishes, depending upon his interest in budget matters and his appreciation of how budget administration can help him.

Obviously, a chief executive has other worries besides budget matters. To be sure, financial considerations will sooner or later arise to plague almost all governmental problems. Nonetheless, a chief executive in his political and party roles has many concerns which will ordinarily not begin with budget pressures, or in which the budget office as such will not be at first interested. And a chief executive will not necessarily have a firm grasp of all the potential use which he may make of a budget office.

At the same time, it must be recognized that the Budget Bureau has had and does have its own institutional role.[16] An immense amount of

[15] Arthur Smithies, op. cit., pp. 212–213.
[16] For a brief survey of the Bureau's history, see Jesse Burkhead, op. cit., pp. 228–296.

routine work must be accomplished each year in preparing budget estimates, in reviewing legislative proposals, in processing enrolled legislation, in exerting an oversight of statistical activities, and in watching over many other aspects of government operations. Today, the President's budget is an institution, not a personal state paper, and the Bureau of the Budget is an indispensable element of the Executive Office of the President. Budget activities go on whatever may be the personal interests of the President himself.

Nonetheless, it is evident from past experience that the budget, as an instrument of executive direction and supervision, takes on real vitality when a President appreciates the budget function and uses the budget office to its fullest potentiality. The same thing is true in state and local government, even though budget work is not always so well organized and staffed as it is in the federal government. Budgeting is now a well-established part of the executive process in American government.

Chapter 19

The President and Economic Development

Article II of the federal Constitution provides that the President "shall from time to time give to the Congress information of the State of the Union, and recommend to their consideration such measures as he shall judge necessary and expedient. . . . " Thus developed the custom whereby the Chief Executive has sent to the opening of each annual session of the legislature a message on the "State of the Union." This is an occasion for enunciating such continuing and current policy goals as a President deems desirable and wishes to present. The content of the message has thus been left entirely to the discretion of the President.

The economic well-being of the nation has been a major concern of every administration since that of President Washington. As Secretary of the Treasury, Alexander Hamilton was especially active at the very beginning of our federal government in pushing the adoption of economic policies and programs which he conceived to be in the best interest of the new nation. In major degree his proposals were written into law. In subsequent years, such economic matters as tariffs, banking, the promotion of transportation, currency, and public works have been in the forefront of political controversy in our country. Governmental concern with economic problems is as old as government itself.

In the 1920s as an aftermath of World War I, the condition of the farm segment of the economy became a special political issue. Then in 1929 general economic depression began, resulting in a decade of sizable levels of unemployment and of curtailed industrial production. The Roosevelt administration in 1933 introduced a series of governmental experiments in an effort to encourage increased industrial production and higher prices for farmers. These programs included banking reforms, currency adjustments, reduced tariffs, the control of security markets, the protection of collective bargaining for labor organizations, the enforcement of minimum wages, an abortive effort at codes of "fair practice" for industrial production, the encouragement of home financing and of farm credit, the

366

promotion of public housing and slum clearance, the development of compulsory old-age insurance, federal participation in public relief to the poor and various categories of unfortunate persons, and large-scale public works and work-relief projects, including river development, public roads, and public buildings.

As might well be expected, there was a good deal of political controversy involved in the formulation and execution of these various policies and programs. Certainly, there was little in the way of consistent, carefully formulated planning by government to meet the conditions of industrial employment existing during the decade of the 1930s. For one thing, there was little if any economic knowledge to explain the extent and duration of so severe a curtailment in business activity, and accordingly little to guide governmental action. In addition, government intervention tended to follow avenues of action about which there had been a good deal of previous discussion. Most New Deal programs had been advocated by some group of citizens and legislators during the 1920s or earlier. In a democracy such as ours, this slow development of public policy and its continuity over a period of many years is a source of strength and unity.

There was also a good deal of public controversy about just how much effect these various policies and programs had upon economic recovery, ostensibly the principal objective. Between 1929 and 1933 gross national product declined about 45 per cent. By the end of 1939 national product had risen from the low point of 56 billion dollars in 1933 to over 91 billion dollars, an increase of 62 per cent, yet gross national product was still nearly 13 per cent under the 1929 level. Unquestionably, there was substantial economic recovery between 1933 and 1939; it is equally clear that this recovery was by no means full or complete. There was even a fairly severe economic recession in 1938. It would be difficult, moreover, to point to any one program of government as exerting a decisive influence in promoting such economic recovery as did occur in these years. It has been assumed by some that the principal program was that of "deficit spending" for public works.

The advent of World War II brought a complete change in the economic condition of the nation. Unemployment, which had been 25 per cent of the labor force in 1933 and was still 17 per cent in 1939, dropped to 1.2 per cent in 1944. National product climbed from 100 billion dollars in 1940 to 215 billion dollars in 1945. Although some of this advance reflected price increases rather than actual growth of economic output, even in terms of stable price levels the advance of 55 per cent was a substantial achievement.

Under these circumstances, it was natural that a good deal of popular concern should have been directed even before the end of World War II to the question of postwar economic expectations. Some feared substantial curtailment of economic activity and a return to the conditions of unemployment and underproduction which had prevailed during the 1930s. Others believed that adequate preparation by government for stimulation and direction of the economy could forestall such dire possibilities. Only a few dared to forecast or expect continued large-scale economic development once the war ended. Before the conclusion of World War II several legislators in the Congress were interested in some positive steps to ensure continued high levels of employment and production; working at the behest of Senator James E. Murray of Montana, a group of government officials undertook to draft a "full employment" bill. Subsequently a number of interest groups became concerned in the matter and pushed for congressional action. From all this effort emerged the Employment Act of 1946, approved by the President on February 20 of that year.[1]

THE EMPLOYMENT ACT OF 1946

The Employment Act begins with a declaration of the Congress "that it is the continuing policy and responsibility of the Federal government to use all practicable means . . . to promote maximum employment, production, and purchasing power." Various conditions were attached to this declaration of purpose. The goal was to be achieved "with the assistance and cooperation of industry, agriculture, labor, and State and local governments." Government activity designed to promote maximum employment was to be undertaken "in a manner calculated to foster and promote free competitive enterprise and the general welfare."

The act went on to provide that the President should transmit to the Congress at the beginning of each regular session an economic report setting forth: (1) current levels of employment, production, and purchasing power in the United States, (2) foreseeable trends in these levels, (3) a review of the economic program of the government and of economic conditions affecting employment and production, and (4) a program for achieving maximum employment, production, and purchasing power. To assist the President in this task the law established a Council of Economic Advisers in the Executive Office of the President. Among other things this Council was directed to "appraise the various programs and activities of the Federal Government" in the light of the general policy objectives set forth in the act. In addition, the Council was to develop and recommend to the President "national economic policies to foster and promote free competitive enterprise, to avoid economic fluctuations or to diminish the effects thereof, and to maintain employment, production, and purchasing power."

Several features of this Employment Act of 1946 deserve special atten-

---

[1] Cf. Stephen K. Bailey, *Congress Makes a Law: The Story Behind the Employment Act of 1946* (New York: Columbia University Press, 1950).

tion. The law expressed a general goal; more than this, it committed the federal government to the broad purpose of promoting high levels of employment and production in the American economy. But the law did not indicate how this general goal was to be achieved. It suggested no new or unusual programs of government activity in the economic field. Rather, the implication was present that the existing array of governmental policies and programs could be so coordinated, and their scope or magnitude so adjusted, as to have a considerable impact upon general levels of economic activity and so help to promote maximum employment and production.

It was left for the President to assume two major tasks. One was to review and appraise the various governmental policies and programs which might have some major impact upon the national economy. The other responsibility of the Chief Executive was to recommend such changes in these policies and programs as he might deem necessary in order that they should better stimulate maximum employment and production. The President was thus directed to supervise the administrative activities of the government in a new light, in the light of their importance in contributing to a coherent pattern of governmental endeavor calculated to promote employment, production, and purchasing power.

The incidental aspects of the law involving economic reporting need not detain us here. It was assumed that techniques were available, or could be developed, which would provide the President with the full range of economic data he would need in fufilling his responsibility under the law. It was left to the Council of Economic Advisers to do this work for the President. It was also assumed that the impact of governmental policies and programs upon the nation's economy could be determined with at least an adequate degree of precision to permit desired policy decisions. In other words, a far greater degree of economic knowledge than had existed in the early 1930s was now assumed to exist, or to be on the verge of discovery.

Perhaps it should be said again that the Employment Act of 1946 was not so different or far-reaching as some have suggested. Governmental concern with the functioning of our national economy was not new. Presidential recommendations on economic policies and programs were not new. Large-scale governmental intervention in economic affairs had occurred during the 1930s—as well as earlier—and some degree of government responsibility for the satisfactory performance of the nation's economy was generally acknowledged by the early 1940s. The Employment Act sought primarily to place all these circumstances into some kind of ordered procedure, one vehicle of which henceforth was to be an annual economic report by the President. The result was a greater degree of executive authority to review and appraise the economic activities of all agencies of the federal government.

ECONOMIC POLICY AND ECONOMIC DEVELOPMENT

Behind the Employment Act of 1946 were two basic ideas of far-reaching importance. The first was that government, meaning in this instance the federal government, could and should take positive action to prevent, or at least to ameliorate, any severe recession in levels of employment, production, and purchasing power in the American economy. The second, and equally fundamental idea, was that this governmental action need not and should not be socialistic in nature. Socialism means government ownership and operation of all major fields of economic activity. Few persons in the United States have ever embraced socialism in this doctrinaire sense. Rather, the belief has prevailed that government can by the proper formulation of economic policy stimulate and influence the operation of the American economy while most major fields of activity remain under private ownership and direction.

Classical economic theory, largely formulated by several English thinkers and widely held by economists and businessmen in this country, held that depressions—a substantial decline in employment and production —represented a state of disequilibrium between the various factors of production. In a free economy this situation would be automatically adjusted by a number of actions which would shortly produce a new equilibrium in which productive resources would be fully utilized. Prices of commodities would be reduced until purchasing began to create new demands for goods. Wage rates would be cut until most unemployed persons could find jobs, thus reducing costs of production and encouraging a greater output. Interest rates would fall, thus encouraging investment. In this situation, all government need do was to curtail its own expenditures, reduce taxes, maintain a stable monetary system, and otherwise not hamper the economic adjustments necessary to restore conditions of full business activity.

Whether classical economic theory was an adequate government policy for the Depression of 1929 has been much debated. There was some evidence that industrial management decided to curtail production rather than to cut prices substantially. Labor leaders were unalterably opposed to any reduction in prevailing wage rates. And governments found revenue declining more rapidly than they could cut expenditures—indeed, with mounting unemployment there were increased demands for many government services, especially in the fields of welfare, health, and education.

In any event political events did not await the unfolding of classical economic theory. The Hoover administration in 1931 and 1932 began partial action to stem the ravages of depression. The Roosevelt administration in 1933 quickly committed itself to large-scale governmental action. Economic policy was thus born of events; it was not based upon any systematic economic theory. But the theory was subsequently provided by another English economist, John Maynard Keynes, later Lord Keynes, in a book published in London in 1936 and entitled *The General Theory of Employment, Interest, and Money.* Subsequently, Keynes's analysis was extended and given specific application to circumstances in the United States by a number of American economists.[2]

In its essence Keynesian theory put forth a new approach to employment in a capitalist, or nonsocialist, economy. Employment at any given time depends upon the volume of spending in an economy. This spending is of three basic types: individual or personal expenditures for consumer goods and services, governmental expenditures for social goods and services, and capital investment (the addition to physical plant for productive purposes). Unless the combination of spending for these three types of outlay is at a level sufficient to achieve full employment and full use of productive resources, an economy is not operating at its potential. The possibility of mass unemployment arises because decisions to spend are made by millions of people, and they may not decide to spend at the levels required to produce full use of productive resources. An individual or a corporation may decide to spend or save available income. The funds which are saved do not flow into expenditure channels unless they are actually used for investment purposes, that is, for an increase of productive facilities. Savings which are hoarded rather than invested result in a curtailment of the total volume of expenditure in an economy, and this may in turn result in a reduction of production and a rise in unemployment.

Obviously, this is at best an inadequate summary of a complicated theory of economic operation. It is enough for us here to recognize that there is an analysis of economic activity which presupposes the possibility of continued low level of production and mass unemployment without any "automatic" adjustment taking place. This theory also presupposes that certain economic policies of government may alter expenditure patterns in the economy so that production and employment do increase.

Government economic policies are of several different kinds. In part they embrace fiscal policies, that is, policies involving the magnitude and purpose of government spending and financing. An increase in government expenditures may bring about an increase in total expenditure levels of the economy and so increase production and employment. In part, the impact of government expenditures upon the economy will depend upon the general magnitude of these expenditures and upon the purposes for which the expenditures are made, such as an undergirding of consumer spending, the construction of public works, and the provision of social services. In turn, the impact of government fiscal policy will depend upon

[2] Cf., for example, Alvin H. Hansen, *Fiscal Policy and Business Cycles* (New York: W. W. Norton & Company, Inc., 1941).

how any given level of expenditure is financed, that is, the magnitude and characteristics of the tax system and the magnitude and characteristics of borrowing. The way in which the currency supply is managed also influences the operation of the economy. These various elements of fiscal policy are important component elements of government economic policy.

But economic policy moves beyond these particular fiscal matters, important though they are. The government may endeavor to encourage an expansion of capital facilities—that is, an increased expenditure for investment purposes—by various devices for lower rates of interest on private, or non-federal government, borrowing. The federal government may create lending facilities of its own, or it may stimulate increased risk-taking by a system of guaranteeing loans made by private investors. The government may endeavor to influence business organization and price policy by its attitude on the enforcement of antitrust laws and laws for so-called fair competition. The government may influence labor-management relations by its policy toward collective bargaining and the settlement of economic strife. The whole area of farm programs is an immense concern of economic policy. The extent to which foreign policy and national defense objectives may be and should be realized through economic assistance to other nations is yet another broad area of economic policy. Government action may be taken to encourage small business enterprises through low interest rates or by governmental purchasing policy. The federal government may even encourage economic expansion in some particular region of the nation through direct provision of cheap electric or other power. Government may undertake research and technical development projects to help business expansion into new types of products, or it may provide various statistical and other advisory services. There is, in other words, a vast range of governmental programs involving fundamentals of economic policy but only to a limited degree involving matters of fiscal policy.[3]

The extent of governmental concern with economic affairs is great indeed. Nor is this concern confined solely to the federal government. Both state and local governments participate in the regulation of public utilities, in the licensing of professions and occupations, in the control of conditions of employment, and in the stimulation of business expansion through community development and other inducements. The federal government plays a major role in economic affairs because ours is a national economy and because in such matters as currency, banking, transportation, communication, and business regulation, central influence is determinative. The nation's economy today is perhaps best described as a "mixed economy"; that is, one in which economic activity is influenced by

[3] For a discussion of alternatives and techniques in achieving "high resource output and development" in a democratic society, see Robert A. Dahl and Charles E. Lindbloom, *Politics, Economics, and Welfare* (New York: Harper & Brothers, 1953).

a combination of both private and public economic decisions.[4] In all, fourteen different major kinds of governmental economic action have been identified, from services such as aids to navigation and transportation and the regulation of prices charged by public utilities to direct economic enterprise (the postal service and the generation of hydroelectric power) and control of the distribution of raw materials in wartime.[5]

The governmental implication of present-day concern with economic policies and programs is staggering. The implication simply is that all these policies and programs can be geared to a single overriding objective: the realization of a high level of productive output and resource development within the context of a democratic political system. Moreover, it is a fundamental commitment of this implication that government's role in the economy can be performed principally through the work of the President. It is the President who is expected to identify and evaluate all existing governmental policies and programs with an important economic impact. It is the President who is expected to see these policies and programs as a coherent whole. It is the President who is expected to watch the performance of the nation's economy with precise instruments of observation and calculation. It is the President who is expected to decide what alterations in individual policies and programs can best be calculated to realize maximum production, employment, and purchasing power.

To be sure, the President's responsibility is not final. He can but recommend certain kinds of action for legislative enactment. Other action may be provided through administrative direction to the operating agencies of government. But even if not always final, the President's determinations are certain to be influential.

The President must today necessarily concern himself to a fine degree with the functioning of the American economy. He has both a political responsibility and a legal directive to do so.

Whether the knowledge of economics has now advanced to the point where it can adequately guide the President in formulating and recommending desirable economic policy is still an uncertain question. One outstanding scholar has presented the role of the economist today in these terms:[6]

> It is the peculiar skill of the economist to bring to government a clear image of its function as a *governor,* or control mechanism. He sees government's task, for instance, as that of stabilizing the wild gyrations of the free market without destroying its essential freedom. He sees it as promoting economic progress, correcting economic injustices, and defending personal liberties

[4] Cf. George A. Steiner, *Government's Role in Economic Life* (New York: McGraw-Hill Book Company, Inc., 1953), especially chap. 9.

[5] *Ibid.*

[6] Kenneth E. Boulding, *The Skills of the Economist* (Cleveland, Ohio: Howard Allen, Inc., 1958), pp. 128–129. Chapter 4, "The Economist's Vision of the Economy," is an excellent short summary of the knowledge of the professional economist in guiding governmental economic policy.

where there is a perceived divergence between the image of the ideal and the perception of the real. To these ends the economist develops an information system—price levels, national income statistics, and so on—by which the mind of the decision maker can grasp the essential dimensions of the social and economic scene. This information system is like the thermometer of a thermostat or the dials and instruments of the aviator, without which control systems would not be possible. The theoretical system of the economist then points to the *effects* of government action and gives at least qualitative clues as to what actions produce what effects.

The President of the United States must today accept a responsibility of far-reaching scope. He must understand the economic aspects of governmental operation in considerable detail. He must be prepared to recommend changes in governmental fiscal and economic policies if he believes these changes will advance the economic development of the nation, or otherwise contribute to the economic well-being of the citizenry. He must seek to guide administrative action in accordance with legal requirements and the fundamental policies which will tend to achieve his desired economic goals. Because of the concern of government with economic well-being on a scale never before acknowledged, the President has new authority to watch over and direct the administrative activities of the federal government.

ECONOMIC DEVELOPMENTS SINCE WORLD WAR II

The major economic problem of the federal government in the years after World War II proved initially to be inflation. Gross national product dropped slightly from 214 billion dollars in 1945 to 209 billion dollars in 1946. Thereafter it rose steadily to 285 billion dollars in 1950, to 415 billion dollars in 1956, and to 434 billion dollars in 1957. To be sure, some of this increase was accounted for by price increases rather than productive output. But even in terms of dollars of constant purchasing power, gross national product, in terms of 1957 price levels, had increased from 340 billion dollars in 1945 to 397 billion dollars in 1953 and to 434 billion dollars in 1957. With a total labor force which grew from 65 million persons in 1945 to nearly 71 million persons in 1957, unemployment was never more than 5.5 per cent of the total civilian labor force during these years.[7]

In the years after the end of World War II commodity prices continually rose. The index number of wholesale prices, with the average price of 1947–1949 as 100, rose from 69 in 1945 to nearly 118 in 1957.[8] This was an increase of 70 per cent. In the same period the index number for consumer prices rose from 77 to 120.[9] This was an increase of nearly 56 per cent in the general level of consumer prices. This meant in effect that one dollar in 1957 bought what 64 cents had been able to buy twelve

[7] These data are taken from *Economic Report of the President,* January, 1958 (Washington: Government Printing Office, 1958), pp. 117, 118, and 134.
[8] *Ibid.,* p. 156.   [9] *Ibid.,* p. 160.

years before. A substantial part of this price increase occurred between 1950 and 1951, when the index of consumer prices advanced nearly nine points shortly after the outbreak of the Korean conflict. In terms of the experience of some other nations, however, the United States did not have nearly so rapid a rise in general price levels.

At the same time that a general trend toward rising prices became evident in the American economy, it also became apparent that some fluctuations in productive output and employment continued. In terms of 1957 price levels, gross national product rose substantially in 1948 and then fell back slightly in 1949. Large increases occurred in the four years 1950 through 1953, with a fairly substantial drop in 1954. A large increase in output took place again in 1955, a somewhat smaller increase in 1956, and then only a slight increase in 1957. By mid-1958 it was evident that productive levels for the year would probably be below those of 1957. Unemployment tended to fluctuate with these changing levels of national productive output. The number of jobless in the civilian labor force in 1948 came to about 2 million persons, and then rose to nearly 3.4 million persons in 1949. The number was under 2 million in the years 1951 through 1953, but was up to 3.2 million in 1954. The number dropped to 2.5 million in 1956 but was again over 3 million in 1958.[10]

Under these fluctuating circumstances, it was natural that the various economic reports of the President in the last half of the 1940s and in the decade of the 1950s should reflect the principal concern of the moment. Thus at times the major emphasis has been upon price stability, budget surplus, and control of credit. At other times the concern has been an increase in productive output, with an easing of credit controls, a budget deficit, and possible tax reduction. Throughout all the reports there is the common theme of economic growth and development and some alarm about the economic status of American agriculture.

The annual economic reports of the President clearly indicate the extent to which the national government has become concerned with economic problems. Next to national defense and foreign affairs, it is safe to say that no public issue requires more continuing concern on the part of the President than the well-being of the American economy. Indeed, the two are closely related, since national security is dependent in large measure upon national economic prosperity. This concern of the President with the state of the economy necessarily involves close working relationships between the Presidency and the administrative agencies of the government.

THE COUNCIL OF ECONOMIC ADVISERS

Just as the budget responsibilities of the President impose duties which can only be met by institutional assistance through a Bureau of the Budget,

[10] *Ibid.,* p. 134, except for the 1958 figure,

so the economic responsibilities of the President impose duties which can only be met through institutional assistance. We have noted already that the Employment Act of 1946 provided the President with a Council of Economic Advisers and that the National Security Act of 1947 established a National Security Resources Board. This latter agency was abolished by Reorganization Plan 3 of 1953 and its place taken by an Office of Defense Mobilization headed by a single individual located within the Executive Office of the President.

The Office of Defense Mobilization has had a dual task in which to assist the President. One was to prepare for the economic impact of all-out military mobilization to repulse aggression by Russia and any combination of other nations which might threaten our national security. The other was to watch over the economic impact of current defense activities, especially as these might affect supplies of raw materials, the numbers and utilization of manpower resources, and the growth of productive facilities. To a considerable degree this interest in the economic impact of current defense programs was shared with the Council of Economic Advisers. The tendency was for the Office of Defense Mobilization to concentrate its attention on particularly troublesome areas of the defense economy, such as the supply of raw materials and the availability of scientific manpower, leaving broader and more general concerns to the Council.

It is the Council of Economic Advisers which is of major interest to us here. The Employment Act of 1946 appears to have established a council to advise the President on the assumption that several heads would be better than one. The exact relationship which the Council was to have to the President was not set forth in the legislation. It was left for experience to afford some answer to this question. In general, there were two broad possibilities. One was for the Council to be an aloof, objective group of men professionally competent in the field of economic knowledge and expressing that knowledge as they might see fit. The other possibility was for a Council which would become an intimate associate of the President in the formulation, development, and advocacy of national economic policies and programs.

The first chairman of the Council of Economic Advisers appointed by President Truman in 1946 was Dr. Edwin G. Nourse, a distinguished professional economist and a vice-president of the Brookings Institution in Washington, D.C. Dr. Nourse had a very definite conception of the role which the Council should play in the Executive Office of the President. He felt strongly that "the economist as such is not the proper instrument for making actual policy for the nation."[11] He saw the purpose of the Employment Act of 1946 as that of invoking "the aid of professionally trained economists as technical advisers at the policy-making

[11] Edwin G. Nourse, *Economics in the Public Service* (New York: Harcourt, Brace and Company, Inc., 1953), p. 16.

level as a means of raising the quality of economic statesmanship, both in the executive office and in the Congress, in approaching the task of economic stabilization."[12] He did not want the Council to become involved in the advocacy of particular economic measures or to become a participant in political controversy. He thought of the Council as a "scientific agency" providing facts and analysis for the President but leaving decision making to him and other advisers.[13] Specifically, Dr. Nourse was determined that the Council should not appear before congressional committees in the role of defender for any particular economic policy or program which the President might advocate.[14] Certainly, behind the scenes Dr. Nourse was willing to be as helpful as possible in getting government officials together for discussion of economic matters. He was not willing to be the advocate of specific recommendations in the name of the President.

Eventually this attitude of the first chairman produced an irreconcilable cleavage within the membership of the Council of Economic Advisers. The other two members—Dr. John D. Clark, former businessman and later an economist, and Leon Keyserling, lawyer and protégé of Senator Robert Wagner of New York—wanted the Council to assert active leadership in reviewing agency activities, in formulating policies to be approved by the President, and in defending these policies before Congress and the general public. More than this, a strong difference arose in 1949 between the chairman and the other two members about a probable continued increase in price levels. The chairman felt that a halt might now be expected in the steady postwar increase of consumer prices. The others identified the control of inflation as the major economic problem of the day.[15] Furthermore, the chairman was not interested in the suggestion that the federal government should construct facilities to increase steel capacity in the country. In consequence, Dr. Nourse left the position of chairman of the Council on November 1, 1949.

As acting chairman, Leon Keyserling became thereafter the key figure in the work of the Council of Economic Advisers. In March, 1950, he was named chairman. A lawyer and not a professional economist, by disposition one who was eager to participate in the formulation of government policy, an individual who enjoyed the rough and tumble of political battle, Keyserling had no particular regard for caution. Soon Keyserling was attending conferences of Democratic party leaders to expand upon the particular economic ideas which were supposed to be guideposts of the current administration. More and more the Council, or at least its chairman, became identified as a policy spokesman for the Truman administration. Then, as economic mobilization became more and more important in support of American military action in Korea, the Council

[12] *Ibid.*, p. 67.   [13] *Ibid.*, p. 107.   [14] *Ibid.*, appendix C, p. 475.
[15] *Ibid.*, chap. 12.

of Economic Advisers tended to recede into the background, at least in so far as the determination of economic policy was concerned.

When General Eisenhower was inaugurated President in January, 1953, there was a good deal of uncertainty about the future of the Council. In 1949 the first Hoover Commission had suggested that the Council be replaced by a single individual serving as Economic Adviser. Disturbed by the apparent advocacy of large-scale governmental spending and of unbalanced federal budgets, the Congress evidenced a reluctance to continue to appropriate funds for the Council. Indeed, the funds voted in 1952 were sufficient to operate the Council only until March, 1953, in the expectation that the next President would wish to make some change, or at least would express some desire about the Council's future work. At first President Eisenhower indicated his intention to have only an Economic Adviser. He named Dr. Arthur F. Burns of Columbia University as both chairman of the Council and as Economic Adviser and announced his intention to name no other members. From April to July, 1953, the functions of the Council were actually vested in the Economic Adviser. Then by Reorganization Plan 9 of 1953 the Council was reconstituted and reorganized. The position of vice-chairman was abolished and the function of directing the staff and of reporting to the President was vested exclusively in the chairman of the Council. Dr. Burns became chairman of the revived Council, and President Eisenhower appointed as the other members, Dean Neil H. Jacoby of the School of Business Administration at the University of California at Los Angeles and Dr. Walter W. Stewart, professor emeritus of economics at Princeton University.

In addition, President Eisenhower established an Advisory Board on Economic Growth and Stability to work with the Council. Dr. Burns served as chairman of this board, whose members were under secretaries, assistant secretaries, and other major administrative officers in agencies having important economic activities to perform. An auxiliary staff committee composed of the heads of departmental and other staff units collecting and analyzing economic data was later appointed to assist the Advisory Board.[16]

Under Dr. Burns's direction the Council of Economic Advisers appeared to enter upon a period of some stability and general acceptance. Dr. Burns was a professional economist of moderate views. He was not interested in personal publicity; he had no desire to be in the limelight nor to become a public spokesman and defender of administration economic policy. At the same time he was active in the discussion and consideration of government economic policies. Always he had a strong sense of the intricacy of economic affairs and the limits of definite economic knowledge. Inclined to be somewhat cautious, he nonetheless recognized

[16] See *Economic Report of the President,* January, 1954 (Washington: Government Printing Office, 1954), pp. 119ff.

that governmental action was important, even vital, to the satisfactory future functioning of the economy.

From 1953 to 1956 the Economic Reports of the President tended to stress economic reporting and the identification of problem areas. Sometimes they also reported administrative action which was being taken to cope with a problem. The Council of Economic Advisers did not appear in the role of advocating general or specific economic goals or as instrumental in the determination of a particular economic policy or program. The members of the Council tended to become economic colleagues or associates of the chairman. In 1955, Dr. Raymond J. Saulnier, professor of economics at Barnard College, succeeded Dean Jacoby, and Joseph S. Davis, director emeritus of the Food Research Institute of Stanford University, succeeded Dr. Stewart. Dr. Burns retired in December, 1956, and was succeeded by Dr. Saulnier. As the new member of the Council, the President appointed Dr. Paul W. McCracken, a professor in the School of Business Administration at the University of Michigan.[17]

Two major problems have confronted the Council of Economic Advisers as an agency of the Executive Office of the President. The first has been the problem of economic reporting and analysis as against economic policy making. The second has been the problem of relationships to the President in defending administration economic policies. Granted that the President needs and must have economic assistance in the performance of his political duties, just what kind of assistance can and should the Council of Economic Advisers be expected to perform? After ten years of experience a tentative answer to this question is becoming apparent.[18]

The Employment Act of 1946 in and of itself is not a sufficient guide to provide any sure path of action for the Council. Obviously, in providing for a Council instead of a single Economic Adviser the Congress was suggesting the need for considered judgment by a group of presumably qualified persons upon the meaning or implication of economic events. Furthermore, a collegial body sitting in considered judgment could be expected to have a fairly formal rather than an intimate personal relationship to the President.

In emphasizing the importance of an annual economic report by the President, the act appeared to expect definite policy and program recommendation. In this respect, therefore, political action seemed to be expected.

In practice the Council of Economic Advisers has become the central body in the federal government bringing together those economic statistics and other data which report the general performance of the American economy. In preparing such a central report the Council must necessarily

---

[17] *Economic Report of the President,* January, 1957 (Washington: Government Printing Office, 1957), p. 82.

[18] Cf. Gerhard Colm (ed.), *The Employment Act: Past and Future,* Special Report no. 41 (Washington: National Planning Association, 1956).

collect those data which it believes most important in indicating trends, economic strengths, and economic weaknesses. Presumably, this calls for a professional, objective judgment. Yet obviously, the Council cannot be expected to be an agency for criticizing the policies and programs of the existing administration. Its role is to serve the President, not to hand ammunition to his political opponents.

At the same time the task of objective reporting on the state of the economy is an important one. Granted that statistical data may be interpreted in different ways, we may nonetheless reasonably expect statistical information to be collected and presented without political bias. Moreover, there is a considerable degree of general agreement about those statistical data which are meaningful in judging the satisfactory performance of the nation's economy. There is no reason why this task of economic reporting cannot be performed for the President without an obvious partisan slant. It may well be that the economic data available about our economy need constant review and expansion. It still does not seem too much to expect that the Economic Report of the President should become the single most authoritative presentation of economic data published in the United States.

Economic reporting is concerned with current events and the immediate past. What about economic forecasting? Can future events be reliably anticipated from past trends? Under present circumstances the only possible answer is that economic forecasting is an art, not a science. One might even say that forecasting is an exercise in guessing or gambling. There are predictions which may be made. If unemployment is increasing month by month, there is a reasonable likelihood that it will continue to rise unless some corrective actions take place. If price levels are advancing, there is a reasonable likelihood that inflationary pressures will continue to mount unless some corrective actions take place. Such qualified forecasts may well be all that present economic knowledge will justify.

Economic reporting is a first step. Facts require analysis, and the interpretation which is placed upon any given set of economic data may lead to certain policy conclusions. A steady rise in prices may suggest the desirability of "tightening" the credit markets. An increase in unemployment may suggest to some the desirability of increasing social security benefits; to others it may suggest the desirability of increasing government expenditures for public works; to some it may suggest the desirability of tax reduction; and to still others it may suggest the desirability of encouraging an expansion of private investment through credit guarantees or other devices. To what extent should the Council of Economic Advisers participate in making definite recommendations for economic action to the President?

Certainly the responsibility of decision on economic recommendations to the Congress or an action to be undertaken by administrative agencies rests upon the President and no one else. To be sure, the President needs advice, needs to consider various points of view. If economic knowledge were precise and adequate, a group of professional economists might be able to give fairly exact advice to the President. Or at least a Council of Economic Advisers might be able to predict fairly well the consequences likely to result from one given course of action as compared with another. The Council is surely obligated to provide the President with the best analysis it can present on any desired economic problem. In making a decision the President may wish to be guided by the judgment of department heads and other administrative officials. He may wish to consult other advisers, personal and legislative. In the end the decision remains that of the President alone.

In presenting its advice the Council of Economic Advisers occupies a confidential relationship to the President. There is no reason why the Council need publish its advice, or present its advice to the Congress. To do so would be to destroy any possibility of close working relationship with the President. The Council members and its staff may work closely with other presidential advisers and with heads of administrative agencies and their staffs. It may participate in all stages of the consideration of any particular economic problem. It may play the principal role in exploring various points of view on an economic policy or program and summarize a problem and proposed solutions for the consideration of the President. All of this is participation in policy formulation. In all such participation the Council is merely an instrument of the President. The decision belongs to the President.

It follows then that the Council of Economic Advisers may do well to avoid any appearance of serving as spokesman for the President's particular economic policies and programs. The President's chief administrative associates such as Cabinet officers are better cast in this position. If the Council becomes peculiarly a personal staff rather than a professional staff, there can be no hope of continuity in any of its work. The possibility of institutional assistance to the President is largely sacrificed. The hope that economic knowledge may be accumulated and extended so as to enable a President's decisions to be founded on as few elements of chance as possible can be realized only through a professional rather than a personal agency.

It seems to this writer that Reorganization Plan 9 of 1953 was an improvement over the original Employment Act of 1946. The Plan made the chairman of the Council the individual avenue of communication with the President. This has made possible the development of a close, confidential relationship between the Council and the President. When three persons were coequal in serving the President, there was a likelihood of personal jockeying for influence. This did indeed happen. The Council is still retained by the 1953 arrangement and can exert effort to improve its work of economic reporting and of economic advising based upon careful analysis.[19]

It must nonetheless remain true that the effectiveness of the Council of Economic Advisers as an institutional aid to the President will depend not merely upon the personality of the three persons comprising the Council but even more upon the personality of the President himself. If a President has some respect for the role of economics as a profession, the Council can become an institutional device of real assistance. If a President has little regard for economics or economists, then the utility of the Council is likely to be small. If the President knows how to work carefully and considerately with a group such as the Council, he may obtain real assistance in his heavy responsibilities.

CONCLUSION

A major preoccupation of the federal government has become the state of health of the American economy. Economic growth and widespread distribution of the benefits of material prosperity have become national economic goals. To some extent the economic policies and programs of the federal government are expected to contribute to these ends. The exact extent and the precise nature of this contribution are still matters of some political disagreement. Yet it is commonly accepted that in various ways the federal government can do its part in promoting the objective of an expanding economy.

In this expectation that the federal government will adapt its policies and programs to help realize economic development, the President occupies a crucial position. On the one hand, he is expected to exercise a careful oversight of the functioning of the economy, making use of the extensive fact-finding and analytical resources of federal administration. He is also expected to analyze the impact of current federal fiscal and economic policies and programs upon the performance of the economy. This calls for a continuing, informed supervision of the economic activities of administrative agencies.

On the other hand, the President is expected to make recommendations from time to time to the Congress for legislation which may modify, extend, or curtail existing policies and programs in the interest of promoting economic development. In addition, within the realm of his executive discretion, he may direct administrative agencies to adjust their policies and programs in ways which he believes will assist the continued growth and prosperity of the economy.

[19] For a more detailed discussion of these problems of relationship of the Council of Economic Advisers to the President, see Edwin G. Nourse, *op. cit.*, part 3.

Chapter 20

The Role of the Executive

It is significant of the role filled by the executive in the American scheme of government that we ordinarily refer to the term of a particular incumbent as an administration. Thus we customarily speak of the Washington administration, the Jackson administration, the Lincoln administration, the Wilson administration, or the Eisenhower administration. Similarly, at the level of state government it is not unusual for us to refer to the Dewey administration, the Warren administration, or the Lausche administration. Obviously, the executive incumbency is closely associated in our popular thinking with its administrative duties.

In one sense our customary practice is especially appropriate. As we have pointed out, the executive is more than a general manager of administrative activities. He is a political leader in terms of a national or state party organization, however loosely formed it may be. He is a legislative leader in terms of his advocacy of particular policies for statutory enactment. But today certainly much of public policy requiring executive and legislative attention arises from administrative activity. At the level of the executive we find a common focus of administrative, legislative, and party considerations.

As a supervisor of the administrative activity of government, the executive enjoys a unique position. First, we must emphasize again that the executive is a single individual exercising a continuing oversight of the work of government. The executive is a full-time official, contrasted with the legislature which is in session only a part of each year or each biennium. The judiciary, as we shall shortly observe, operates only on the basis of cases or controversies brought by others rather than initiated by itself. The executive is on duty three hundred sixty-five days a year fulfilling the responsibilities of his office. Furthermore, the executive represents all the people of the nation or of a state; his constituency is not a particular area or district. His point of view accordingly is expected to embrace the totality of the geographical interests of the government he serves.

In the second place, the executive is an active participant in the legislative and political processes of our government. He is not the spokesman just of an administrative point of view. He is not an advocate solely of policies which are developed within administrative agencies. The executive expects many ideas to come to his attention from the heads of departments and other agencies. To some extent, he looks upon some of these officials as his associates, or more accurately as his assistants, in the exercise of the executive power. But the executive's sources of policy formulation are not administrative only. He has legislative colleagues and political advisers as well. The executive necessarily thinks in terms of legislative acceptability and political expediency in addition to administrative advocacy. It is this combination of points of view, we repeat, which makes the executive so remarkable a governmental instrumentality.

In the third place, the executive's oversight of administrative agencies is not an exclusive prerogative. The executive shares his power of government with the legislature and the judiciary. And the power of government means the power to determine and to supervise the administrative tasks undertaken by government. The legislature is necessarily concerned with public administration, and cannot be expected to deal with administrative agencies only through the executive. Administration is subordinate to the legislature in those aspects of government which require the enactment of law. The executive is not subordinate to the legislature, and cannot be placed in any apparent position which implies such subordination. For this reason, the executive cannot claim that he alone is responsible for the administrative endeavors of government. He can claim only the exercise of that supervision of administration appropriate to his executive power.[1]

In and of itself, the constitutional basis of executive power over public administration is meager enough. In the federal government it consists of two general directives to obtain the opinion of department heads and to see that the laws are faithfully executed. More than this, the executive has the authority to appoint department and agency heads, along with other key administrative personnel, usually subject to senatorial approval. With the authority to appoint goes the implied authority to remove, subject to certain restrictions of procedure. The appointing power is vital to executive supervision, conferring as it does the means to obtain as heads of agencies those who share some common purpose with the executive. This is the extent of the executive power in relation to administrative activities as such.

To be sure, in the federal government the executive has more than a

---

[1] For a useful review of the subject, see "The Office of the American Presidency," *Annals of the American Academy of Political and Social Science*, vol. 307 (September, 1956).

general formal relationship to the administration of two major federal activities: the conduct of foreign relations and the provision of national defense. The President is principal diplomat of our nation, sending and receiving representatives to and from foreign countries. He is also Commander in Chief of our Armed Forces, exercising the power of supreme command in matters of grand strategy. No one can question the President's status as chief administrator as well as general overseer in matters of foreign affairs and national defense. Yet even here the President must depend upon legislative cooperation in providing the means for conducting our foreign relations and for supporting our armed might.

To a very substantial degree, the executive in our scheme of government is general manager of administrative activities because of his legislative role. The executive authority to recommend desirable legislation underlies the budget authority whereby he prepares each year or every two years an executive budget for legislative consideration. It is this budget authority which enables the executive to review the entire scope of the administrative work of government in such detail of policy, program, and procedure as he may desire—or have the assistance to perform. The importance of the budget as an executive instrument for administrative supervision cannot be overemphasized. Here is a ready reason to observe administrative operations in their full scope and in their relationship one agency to another. The executive is able to ask any question and obtain an answer. His own judgment may have great influence in persuading the legislature to provide a particular level of support.

In the federal government today the President finds his legislative role reinforced by provisions of the Employment Act of 1946, providing as it does for a careful review of the economic impact of administrative activities. Here again the whole range of administrative operations may pass in review before executive judgment. At the present time the tools of economic analysis are scarcely comparable in precision with the exact reality of a budget estimate. Yet the potentiality of the Economic Report of the President is more far-reaching in its administrative implications than the budget message. For the economic report seeks a standard of measurement—its impact upon employment, production, and purchasing power—for every administrative activity of the federal government.

In budget matters as in questions of economic policy the executive's position is one of adviser to and leader for the legislature. In rendering his advice the executive obtains information and recommendations from administrative agencies. No department or other agency can afford to ignore the executive's authority. Each must work with him, even though the final answer on governmental policies and appropriation resources must be obtained through the legislative process. The executive is so important a part of this legislative process in most circumstances that he builds his administrative status in large measure therefrom.

THE EXECUTIVE BRANCH

If all administrative agencies of government are to be thought of as part of the executive branch, then there are certain peculiar characteristics of the executive branch in this enlarged sense. First of all, it is the President or governor (plus other separately elected officials within a state) who exercises the executive power as set forth by our constitutions. Administrative agencies do not share in the exercise of executive power. Because administrative agencies are subject to executive supervision, they do not thereby acquire the same relationship to the legislature or judiciary as that enjoyed by the executive. The executive is a separate and independent element of political power. Administrative agencies do not constitute a part of that power.

Secondly, the executive is a general manager of public administration only in a limited sense. He is the only general manager possible·under our constitutional scheme of government, and his role as a general manager is a constitutional role, not one delegated by law. Yet as a general manager the executive is not head of a monolithic administrative structure. All administrative affairs do not come from the administrative agencies to the executive, then to be referred by him to either the legislative or judicial branch of government. Nor does the legislative branch enact laws for the executive to carry out; rather the legislature specifies usually what particular agencies shall do. Moreover, funds are appropriated directly to individual administrative agencies to spend. The judiciary, furthermore, entertains suits against particular administrative agencies; the executive is not necessarily a party to such legal controversies.

The executive exercises a general oversight of administrative activities, but he exercises only such oversight as he is empowered to assert through the constitution. We repeat that these powers include authority to appoint key personnel, and to remove them under certain legal restrictions. He is to see that the laws are faithfully executed. He may consult with administrative officials about the exercise of their legal authority. And in so far as the executive is an effective legislative and political leader, he may influence administrative affairs which depend upon legislative enactment.

The executive cannot alter the law which administrative agencies exist to carry out. The executive cannot create new administrative agencies or alter the organizational structure established by law. The executive cannot appropriate funds for the operation of administrative agencies. The executive cannot interpose his judgment in any administrative matters which are brought before the judiciary for consideration.

In 1949 the first Hoover Commission presented as its first two findings of fact the following statement:[2]

---

[2] The Commission on Organization of the Executive Branch of the Government, *General Management of the Executive Branch* (Washington: Government Printing Office, 1949), pp. 3–4.

The executive branch is not organized into a workable number of major departments and agencies which the President can effectively direct, but is cut up into a large number of agencies which divide responsibility and which are too great in number for effective direction from the top. . . .

The line of command and supervision from the President down through his department heads to every employee, and the line of responsibility from each employee of the executive branch up to the President, has been weakened, or actually broken, in many places and in many ways.

As statements of fact, no one can question these two observations of the Hoover Commission. These comments did not go far enough, however, in illuminating the problem which was involved. Unquestionably, executive oversight of administrative activities has been hampered by the large number of agencies created by law. Furthermore, control by department heads over administrative activities within their jurisdiction has been hampered by the appointment of personnel in supposedly subordinate positions who are actually selected by the executive for political rather than administrative reasons.

The executive by himself is powerless to rectify these conditions. Change must come through legislation, or in the federal government, through reorganization plans in which the legislature is willing to acquiesce. Yet these conditions have arisen in the first place because the legislature created them. The reasons were not necessarily to hamper the executive but to meet the demands of particular interest groups or of certain individuals who pushed for some particular legislation. Moreover, the legislature is not too much impressed by arguments involving the status and convenience of the executive. The general trend of American history has been one of enhancing the prestige and role of the executive. Increasingly aware of executive influence in both legislative and political matters, individual legislators may well have reason from their point of view to ask why they should seek further to advance executive power.

More than this, legislatures tend to see in more effective executive direction of administrative affairs two threats to their own legislative power. For one thing, if the executive gains closer supervision over administrative activities, then legislative influence in administrative matters may possibly be reduced. The legislature appears to believe that a multiplicity of administrative agencies of various types tends to increase legislative control over administration, regardless of what it may do to executive control. Not until the legislature sees its interest and executive interest in relationship to some administrative activity as identical is the legislature disposed to consent to some change. In the second place, the legislature has some reason to fear that a clear-cut system of executive control over administrative activities may make executive power so great that it would completely overshadow the legislature. Obviously, the legislature will be reluctant to pass legislation which might tend to make the executive an even more powerful participant in the political process.

A recent commentator has spoken of "administrative pluralism" as one of the factors in inhibiting executive direction of the federal bureaucracy by the President. He has defined his meaning in these words:[3]

> . . . Many agencies are rendered independent of the President's immediate supervision by statute; many more are exempt from his influence because of political and personal circumstances. The most usual circumstance, one that can frustrate any President, is that of an upright agency headed by a case-hardened chief who numbers more real friends among the leaders of Congress than any President who ever lived, not even excluding William G. McKinley. The Federal Bureau of Investigation under J. Edgar Hoover, the Passport Office under Mrs. Ruth Shipley and Miss Frances Knight, and the Corps of Engineers under almost anyone are examples of what I mean by "pluralism in fact." Although a President may count on these agencies to execute the law faithfully according to their own lights, he would invite disaster, both administrative and political, if he tried to alter the course that each has been following for these many years. Mr. Hoover has a kind of tenure that even the most carefully sheltered administrator would have reason to envy; his time-tested ability to outlast the President of the moment must always give that President pause. I cannot help wondering how often President Truman thought of relieving Mr. Hoover—and then thought a second time, sighed, and went about his business.

This description of the relationship of the President to certain administrative agencies is accurate in so far as it goes. What needs to be added is that over a period of time some divergence in executive and legislative point of view about the conduct of these particular activities has arisen. The legislature sees no reason why it should encourage executive control over these agencies when it is satisfied with their administrative performance. And whatever the outside observer may believe—and no matter how cogent his argument—legislators must first change their own attitude toward particular administrative activities before they will acquiesce in a change of administrative status or a greater degree of executive oversight.

THE EXECUTIVE POINT OF VIEW

As a general manager of administrative activities, the executive in our scheme of government is not simply an administrative officer taking policy direction from the legislature. The theory of much corporate organization is that all policy authority resides finally in a board of directors or a board of trustees. This board selects a president who becomes its chief administrative officer. He is delegated authority to direct all administrative activities of the enterprise. He may be delegated broad decision-making authority by the board. He may exercise a close, almost absolute control over all his subordinates. The president presents his recommenda-

[3] Clinton Rossiter, *The American Presidency* (New York: Harcourt, Brace and Company, Inc., 1956), pp. 42–43.

tions for new policies or modification in policies when and as he deems necessary.

Furthermore, we know that in practice a particular chief administrative officer in some enterprise may reach such a status of prestige and influence that he does in effect select his board members and dominate all board decisions. Thus a post of administrative subordination in theory may become in reality a position of administrative domination.

Many persons are so familiar with this corporate theory of organization and management that they come to believe that governmental organization and management does, or should, parallel it. Actually, there are such fundamental differences between the two that any resemblance between them is purely coincidental. Our understanding of government is hampered, rather than advanced, by any attempted analogy between corporate organization and governmental organization.

Many American students of government are so familiar with the parliamentary system of Great Britain that their understanding, or their evaluation, of American governmental practice is colored by this contrasting arrangement. Under the parliamentary system the executive is a committee of the legislature, and each department or agency (with a few exceptions) is headed by a member of Parliament. In theory, the executive is selected by the legislature and may be dismissed at any time by the legislature. In turn, the executive exercises certain controls over the legislature, determining the legislative timetable and calling a general election within a five-year time limit if the legislature disapproves its conduct. The executive exercises complete control of public administration, and the legislature deals with administrative agencies only through the executive. This is a satisfactory arrangement since the executive is a committee of the legislature and is subject to legislative control.

American political institutions do not resemble either the corporate practice with which we are familiar or the parliamentary political institutions such as those of Great Britain. Let us review again the fundamental differences. In the first place, the executive in our scheme of government is not selected by the legislature. He is independently elected. In the second place, the executive obtains his power from constitutional prescription, not by delegation from the legislature. Thirdly, the executive does not serve at the pleasure of the legislature; he serves an independent term of office. In the fourth place, the executive direction of administrative activities is limited in scope just because the executive is independent of the legislative power to select or dismiss. The legislative must exercise its own direct supervision over administrative activities because it cannot exercise any direct supervision over the executive.

We may then ask what is the executive point of view in relationship to administrative agencies. The answer involves a basic feature of the American scheme of government. The executive point of view is not confined to administrative management in any technical sense, that is, in terms of some effort to ensure economical and efficient performance of operations. Nor is the executive point of view confined to a concern to ensure political responsibility by bureaucracy. The executive does not worry exclusively about making sure that administrative agencies meet popular expectation. The executive point of view is first of all influenced by his role as a participant in the exercise of governmental power.

This means that the executive is above all else concerned with his role as a legislative and political leader. He is but incidentally concerned with general management as such. From time to time it is said that some particular executive is not a "good administrator." Such criticism implies that the administrative duties of the executive are his first and primary task. In practice the "great" Presidents as recorded in American history have been those who achieved substantial success in their political and legislative roles, Presidents such as Jefferson, Jackson, Lincoln, Theodore Roosevelt, Wilson, and Franklin Roosevelt. With the possible exception of Theodore Roosevelt, none of these men was ever accorded any special praise for being an outstanding general manager of the administrative activities of government. Instead their stature as Chief Executives is based upon their role as legislative and political leaders.

These comments are not intended to suggest that the administrative role of the executive is unimportant. The contrary is, of course, the case. The executive must necessarily give careful attention to any administrative problem which threatens to become a particular political or legislative problem. If public criticism arises about the conduct of any particular administrative agency, the executive cannot afford to ignore the situation. If some particularly influential legislator or legislative committee becomes concerned for some reason with the work of an administrative agency, the executive, too, must share the same concern. Otherwise, the executive surrenders his leadership position.

It is unrealistic to think of administrative problems as in some special category apart from political issues. There is a distinction to be drawn between administration and politics, but it is at best always a difficult distinction. And it is an accepted element of administrative theory that, at the level of the department or agency head, politics and administration must merge. For this reason, it is important to have politically selected officials as head of administrative agencies. But if there is a conjunction of politics and administration at the level of the department head, even more is such a joint point of view to be expected at the level of the executive.

If the executive is primarily a political and legislative figure, is it, therefore, unnecessary to equip him for his administrative tasks? Here again the answer seems obvious. If political issues have administrative aspects—as they almost always do—how is an executive to handle these problems without some assistance? Certainly no executive can by himself prepare a budget or study needed personnel problems. Furthermore, if many political issues arise within an administrative context—as indeed they do—then an executive must be enabled to identify such issues as they are thrown up out of the multitude of current administrative operations. Certainly no executive can by himself undertake to examine administrative details in order to determine what particular items require special political attention, such as the biological consequences of experimental explosion of nuclear weapons, or the economic consequences of a tightening in credit availability.

Moreover, almost every great public issue, once it is identified as such, raises administrative implications. For example, it has been a continuing policy of the federal government since the end of World War II to encourage scientific research and development, both by governmental agencies and by universities and industry.[4] The extent and the quality of American scientific progress have become a major public issue, a matter of grave importance to legislators and to political parties. In the midst of the discussion about our country's scientific practices, the criticism has been made that one fault is inadequate administrative organization for handling scientific problems.[5] It is said that the executive is adequately equipped to consider scientific questions, and it is suggested that he needs a new executive department of science, or at least a standing science commission within the Executive Office of the President.

For our purpose here, it is not important to consider the merits of the whole subject of the government's relationship to scientific research and development. It is sufficient to note two features of the discussion. One: the issue immediately raises questions about how to organize for administrative purposes the government's interest in this particular field of activity. Secondly, at the same time the question arises how is the executive to be equipped adequately to handle his policy-making role in this vital field of political and legislative concern.

We repeat that the executive's role is legislative, political, and administrative. At the level of the executive, these three interests merge into one, and it is this merger which makes the executive so unique a governmental institution and so vital an influence in the administrative affairs of our government.

ISSUES OF EXECUTIVE SUPERVISION

Two major problems arise in a discussion of the executive's relation to administrative activities. One is the adequacy of the constitutional power

[4] On this development see particularly Vannevar Bush, *Modern Arms and Free Men* (New York: Simon and Schuster, Inc., 1949); and Don K. Price, *Government and Science* (New York: New York University Press, 1954).

[5] Cf. Sidney Hyman, "Science: The President's New Power," *Saturday Review,* Feb. 2, 1957, p. 40.

possessed by the executive. The other is the adequacy of the institutional assistance provided the executive.

In so far as the adequacy of constitutional power is concerned, the answer seems fairly clear. Executive authority is extensive. Were it more extensive, there is some question whether an independent legislature and judiciary would be possible. Yet this answer is not sufficient to guide public policy in certain specific matters.

For example, is it desirable that a governor should share his executive power with an independently elected secretary of state, state treasurer, state auditor, and state attorney general? This is the age-old question of the strong versus the weak executive. In some states constitutional reform has undertaken to strengthen the executive role by eliminating these separately elected officers. There is much to be said for this change, since it lessens the diffusion of executive authority among different individuals. Yet when a governor is an influential political leader and when these other posts are held by members of the same political party, a governor is usually able to exercise some degree of broad supervision over these positions. An integrated executive power would still seem to be the preferable arrangement, as it is in the federal government.

Another issue is the extent to which the executive's power to remove heads of departments and agencies should be circumscribed by law. In the federal government it is recognized that in regulatory agencies the legislature may provide a statutory term of office and then prohibit executive removal except for cause, such as malfeasance in office. In many state governments certain administrative officials and members of boards are appointed for a fixed number of years. It is usually recognized that the governor may not, or should not, remove such persons before the expiration of their statutory term of office. The only real recourse is to seek legislative action in abolishing such positions, or the agencies of which they are part, and in re-creating new administrative devices. This may be done when an executive and legislature see eye to eye on some particular matter. Otherwise, the executive must restrain his impulse to rid himself of unwanted administrative officials.

Still another issue is whether the extent of the "political" element in an administrative agency is sufficient to ensure effective executive oversight. Tradition in our country emphasizes the subordinate role of the career or professional official. To decrease the number and prestige of such officials is not necessarily the solution to the issue of adequate political direction of administrative activities. An enlarged political element may only serve to bring about some breakdown in the performance of essential public service. The failure of political leadership is more apt to be caused by inept, faltering direction and supervision than by a lack of numbers.

The extent of the executive role in the legislative process is, as we have commented earlier, a sure guarantee that administrative officers cannot afford to ignore the executive. Executive endorsement may help achieve legislative action. Executive hostility, reinforced by the veto power, may serve to defeat legislative action. Administrative departments and agencies are therefore disposed to work closely with an executive in achieving their statutory objectives. This legislative influence of the executive extends to appropriation matters and to modification of the economic policies of government.

It is safe to conclude that executive power in relation to administrative agencies is in fact substantial. There are only sporadic movements at times to strengthen the constitutional status of the executive, and these movements are confined almost exclusively to state governments.

The other major problem in executive supervision is the extent of executive assistance in the performance of his authority. The idea of a cabinet or council to provide assistance to the executive has a firm hold in American governmental practice. But it seems fairly evident today that this device alone is not sufficient. The executive's associates in a cabinet or council are usually his own politically selected heads of departments and agencies. They can be effective as advisers only to the degree that they have an executive point of view which goes beyond the interests of the agency over which they preside. This point of view department heads ordinarily do not have and do not cultivate.

For this reason, an executive must have his own advisers, and in this day of complex administrative operations, his own machinery for budget preparation, for economic analysis, for administrative supervision in troublesome fields of activity requiring executive attention. To be sure, a legislature may be reluctant to provide this assistance on an institutional basis. Yet to provide no such assistance, or only the most limited kind of assistance, is to deny to the executive the means for the present-day performance of his job. The executive must have some help, and legislature and executive must find some common grounds for providing sufficient but not too much assistance.

All this array of executive authority and of institutional assistance has a basic purpose in our scheme of government. This is to enable the exercise of governmental power within our society, subject to some degree of restraint which will preserve for the individual a measure of political freedom. The purpose of American government is obviously government. But this purpose is expected to be realized within a context of considerable personal political freedom.

The executive is a vital element in the process of government. He has a key role in helping to make bureaucracy politically responsible. Yet at the same time the executive is not all-powerful. He shares governmental power. Hence his power in relation to administrative agencies is not all-inclusive, unlimited, or absolute. Rather, the executive exercises continuing oversight of public administration while sharing the power of government with legislature and judiciary.

PART FOUR

The Judiciary

Chapter 21

The Judicial Power

Article III of the federal Constitution completes the prescription for the triumvirate which exercises governmental power in our country. Similar provisions are to be found in the constitutions of state government. Article III declares: "The judicial power of the United States shall be vested in one Supreme Court, and in such inferior courts as the Congress may from time to time ordain and establish." Section 2 of the Article goes on to specify that "the judicial power shall extend to all cases, in law and equity, arising under this Constitution, the laws of the United States, and treaties made, or which shall be made, under their authority; to all cases affecting ambassadors, other public ministers, and consuls; to all cases of admiralty and maritime jurisdiction," and to controversies between specified parties, such as between citizens of different states.

The American legal tradition has been largely acquired from English antecedents; it has an Anglo-Saxon background. The early idea of law was that of an orderly relationship among individual persons. The alternative to law was private vengeance, wherein one person undertook on his own to remedy any wrong or damage which he believed he had suffered at the hands of another. Anglo-Saxon law recognized rights existing between individuals, rights of a minimum degree of security in person and property. These rights could be sustained in the courts of the land, which decided individual quarrels and which, on the basis of the evidence at hand, ordered one person to pay damages to another or to make restitution of property wrongfully seized.

In time this early Anglo-Saxon conception of law came to be modified in two particulars. The more important of these was the growth of criminal law. Now the state intervened as a third party in certain kinds of cases. The state, as represented by kingly authority, had always recognized as crime any action taken against the sovereign, such as treason, conspiracy, refusal to pay taxes, or refusal to perform feudal obligations of service.

Now, however, the sovereign recognized that for one man to kill another man, or for one man to rob another man on the king's highway was a breach of the king's peace and hence punishable by the state itself. The criminal law stepped in to place the power of the state behind the apprehension and punishment of those who harmed others through criminal action. In time, a crime became any offense which the legislative power so defined, and which occurred anywhere in the realm.

A second modification in the early idea of law came about through the development of the concept of equity. In some instances the appeal to a court of law to remedy an injustice through damages or punishment was insufficient. There was a need for action which would prevent an illegal action from being committed or which would order a person to perform a promised act. Equity was an appeal to the king's conscience for legal assistance; in time it became a fairly technical branch of law handled through the same courts as ordinary civil and criminal law.[1]

The common law—that is, the law common to all of England—was in large measure judge-made. This was the law which governed the relationship of individual to individual. The criminal law was enacted by the King in Parliament. To be sure the legislative power might modify civil law as well, but to a considerable degree England was content to recognize judges as having a special governmental role. In time the status of the judiciary became more than a structural part of English government; free access to the courts came to be regarded as one of the peculiar rights of English citizens. On occasion these courts even imposed standards of conduct upon the sovereign, insisting that property be taken from a citizen by governmental action only through a prescribed procedure, and that criminal punishment be exacted only upon indictment, the presentation of evidence, and a decision of guilt by a jury of one's peers.

It must not be supposed that these legal developments occurred all at once or that they applied equally to every citizen. English law was an accretion of several centuries of growth. Moreover, legal rights were first claimed by the nobility as a check upon an all-powerful king; later they were obtained by the leading burghers of a city when charters of local municipal government were granted. Often a king was persuaded to grant such charters by his need for money or for political support in his struggle with feudal lords. The idea that rights might be possessed by the common man—the worker in the field or the city—came only slowly; this was one of the revolutionary concepts, for example, of the Levelers during the seventeenth century.

The Tudor and Stuart dynasties of the sixteenth and seventeeth cen-

---

[1] These developments are sketched in John Dickinson, *Administrative Justice and the Supremacy of the Law* (Cambridge, Mass.: Harvard University Press, 1927), chap. 1.

turies were almost absolute in their exercise of political power. The Tudor monarchs brought order to a country devastated by the final gasp of feudalism in the War of the Roses. The Tudors, moreover, were astute political leaders, tending to favor the growing business and mercantile classes of the kingdom. For the most part the Tudors were careful to make their political power palatable to important elements of the citizenry. The Stuart kings of the seventeenth century lacked this ability; they loudly proclaimed their absolute power and then exercised it poorly. Thus one Stuart king, Charles I, brought on civil war, his own execution, and the abortive period of the Commonwealth. His son, James II, was directly responsible for the Glorious Revolution of 1688 which introduced into England the idea of constitutional monarchy.

Both the Tudors and the Stuarts found the judiciary an obstacle to the exercise of absolute power. Henry VII, founder of the Tudor dynasty in 1485, had established a Court of Star Chamber to enforce order by bringing the great nobles before his own judgment seat. He used the court especially to break up the practice whereby nobles in the past had maintained their own private armies. But the new court was an exception to the traditional judiciary, and the procedure was simpler. This particular court was readily converted by Henry VIII into an instrument of tyranny. Subsequently, another court of high prerogative, a Court of High Commission, was created. Although there may have been good reasons initially for these courts, in time they became symbols of kingly power, and in the Parliamentary struggles of the Stuart period, these prerogative courts were attacked as evidence of a usurpation of power. They were swept away with the last of the Stuart monarchs.

When Blackstone published his *Commentaries on the Laws of England* in the years 1765 to 1769, he wrote from the vantage point of nearly one hundred years after the Glorious Revolution. He laid great stress upon the English Constitution as a guarantor of individual freedoms, expressing the opinion that England was perhaps the only land in the world where "political or civil liberty is the very end and scope of the Constitution." To Blackstone the common law, the product of custom and tradition, had as its very purpose the protection of rights and liberties which, although some of them had been declared by Parliament, were rooted in the natural rights of man. Blackstone then went on to define the various rights which belonged to Englishmen and which it was the special province of the judiciary to preserve.

Blackstone made no claim that the rights of Englishmen were to be maintained against Parliament. Indeed, he specifically rejected this thesis on the grounds that any such claim "were to set the judicial power above that of the legislature, which would be subversive of our government." Rather, failing to comprehend the nature of the parliamentary system of government evolving before his eyes, Blackstone thought of the judicial power as a protection against monarch and administration.[2]

All four volumes of Blackstone were reprinted in Philadelphia in 1771; his ideas were well known to the lawyers and others who gave leadership to the American Revolution and who later participated in drafting the federal and state constitutions. It was understandable, too, that Blackstone's ideas should have influenced the opinions which early shaped the role of the judiciary in our scheme of government. It makes little difference that Blackstone but imperfectly understood the British Constitution. To a considerable degree his ideas suited the constitutional objectives of many Americans of the Revolutionary and post-Revolutionary era.

It is no exaggeration to say that American law carried over into its operation the general body of concepts and purposes which were thought to have grown up as a part of the common law. We cannot, of course, even begin here to explore the range of ideas which were thus introduced into American government. It is sufficient to observe one of the concepts in so far as it relates to the conduct of governmental administrative agencies.

We have mentioned that Blackstone thought of the courts as a bulwark of man's liberties. Although he did not suggest that the courts might become censors of the King in Parliament, American jurists early declared that the courts had an obligation to enforce the requirements of the Constitution against any invasion of power or violation of purpose by legislative enactment. The doctrine of judicial review was thus early written into the very structure of American government.

In practice, and perhaps almost without judicial understanding, this doctrine of judicial review eventually became less an instrument of judicial control of legislative policy than a mechanism of judicial supervision of public administration. Indeed, it may be asserted that the most profound consequence of the judicial power as it came to be exercised in the United States has been this element of judicial oversight of the conduct of administrative agencies. It is this particular phase of the doctrine of judicial review which is our special concern in this volume.

One other general feature of the American judicial system must be understood by way of background. A great English writer on the English Constitution, A. V. Dicey, in 1885 set forth as a cardinal element of the English system of government what he called the "Rule of Law." As he defined his proposition, Dicey declared that "no man is punishable or can be lawfully made to suffer in body or goods except for a distinct breach of the law established in the ordinary legal manner before the ordinary courts of the law. In this sense the rule of law is contrasted with every

[2] This interpretation of Blackstone has been drawn from Sir Ernest Barker, "Blackstone and the British Constitution," in *Essays on Government* (New York: Oxford University Press, 1945), p. 121.

system of government based on the exercise by persons in authority of wide, arbitrary, or discretionary powers of restraint."[3]

Just as Blackstone some one hundred years earlier had failed to understand the essential elements of a parliamentary system of government, so Dicey failed to understand the nature of modern administrative authority. If Dicey's proposition that every distinct breach of the law had to be established in the ordinary legal manner before the ordinary courts of law were accepted, then public administration would be slow, cumbersome, and even more expensive than it is. If Dicey's proposition were accepted, then there could be no such thing as administrative discretion. If Dicey's proposition were accepted, then all public administration would become fundamentally judicial administration.

Yet Dicey enunciated an idea of great importance. He saw that an essential element of the English Constitution was protection of the individual from unreasonable or arbitrary exercise of administrative authority. As the judiciary has struggled to give meaning to its role of supervisor over administrative agencies, it has endeavored to square the requirements of the modern administrative state with protection of the citizen from unreasonable or arbitrary exercise of administrative authority.[4]

Another element of Dicey's "Rule of Law" was his emphasis upon "the ordinary courts of law." Here Dicey had in mind the English legal system in contrast with the French system of *droit administratif*. The French legal system provides a special place for a structure of administrative courts. This system has become the model for legal practices in a number of other countries. The actual nature of these administrative courts has been frequently misunderstood by English and American writers. From the background of English history, with its story of a long struggle for parliamentary rights, some have assumed that "administrative courts" could mean only a lack of protection for the citizen against unreasonable or arbitrary administrative action.

Actually, a careful study of the French system of administrative law would probably reveal that the ordinary citizen does enjoy a good deal of protection by means of the administrative courts. Under a law of 1872, the structure of administrative courts is headed by the Council of State. In addition, there is a Tribunal of Conflicts which decides whether a matter should properly be heard by the civil or administrative courts. The administrative courts hear all claims against the state arising out of contracts with local or central government and all claims for damages arising out of the acts of a public corporation, a ministry, or local government. The court may award damage as it believes necessary; it does not order

[3] A. V. Dicey, *The Law of the Constitution*, 8th ed. (London: Macmillan & Co., Ltd., 1915), pp. 183–184.
[4] For a good discussion of this problem see Roland Pennock, *Administration and the Rule of Law* (New York: Rinehart & Company, Inc., 1941).

an administrative agency to cease from some operation. In addition, the courts may hold that an official of government exceeded his legal power; his act is then nullified and damages are payable by the state. Or the courts may hold that there was a misapplication of power, such as the performance of an act for a purpose other than what the law had intended. For example, a grain dealer brought suit against the War Minister on the grounds that he had been excluded from bidding on war contracts because the War Minister disliked his political and religious points of view. In the absence of any good reason offered by the Minister for his act, the Council of State on appeal held that such exclusion from bidding on war contracts was a misapplication of power. The French administrative law system has evolved a doctrine that it will not consider a case involving an "act of government"—these acts apparently revolve around the conduct of foreign relations, actions taken in time of war, and the relations of ministers and agencies to the National Assembly.[5]

The whole subject of French administrative law is too broad for discussion here. It is important for our purpose only to bear in mind that our American legal system does not have an exact counterpart to the French system of administrative law and that the French system is not necessarily inferior to our own. Our system developed from one particular set of historical circumstances, whereas the French system developed from another. Both systems recognize certain essential needs in the apparatus of the modern democratic state.

In any event, the ordinary court structure—the courts which hear civil and criminal cases—in the United States also hears cases against administrative agencies. In the federal government, this means that initially cases involving the validity of administrative decisions will be brought in the federal district court unless the Congress by law declares that enforcement of or appeal from an administrative decision shall begin with a Court of Appeals. Decisions of a district court may be appealed to the Court of Appeals for one of the eleven judicial circuits. Today the Supreme Court grants review of decisions by a Court of Appeals only if it believes such decisions involve some important constitutional or legal principle to which it should give attention. Within the states, initial action would ordinarily begin in a county court, whatever may be its designation, may be appealed to an appellate court if there be such, and then may be taken to the highest court of the state.

In 1955 the second Hoover Commission recommended the creation of an Administrative Court of the United States to be composed of three

---

[5] Cf. Georges Langrod, "The French Council of State: Its Role in the Formulation and Implementation of Administrative Law," *American Political Science Review*, vol. 49 (September, 1955), p. 673. See also, C. J. Hamson, *Executive Discretion and Judicial Control* (London: Stevens and Sons, 1954).

sections: a Tax Section, a Trade Section, and a Labor Section.[6] This recommendation appeared to be concerned with the performance of adjudicative functions by such agencies as the Tax Court, the Federal Trade Commission, the Federal Communications Commission, and the National Labor Relations Board rather than with a desire to create a new kind of court structure within the United States. Presumably, although here the Hoover Commission was not explicit, judicial review of the decisions of the Administrative Court would lie to the regular federal Courts of Appeals. As of 1958 no action had been taken on this recommendation of the Hoover Commission.

The basic concept of the judicial power in relation to administrative agencies in the United States is that the ordinary courts of law may examine the actions of administrative agencies in order to protect individual citizens and private bodies (such as corporations) from any illegal, unreasonable, or arbitrary exercise of administrative power. There are many qualifications to this general statement which we shall examine in the following pages. This statement, however, sets forth the fundamental proposition which we must proceed to examine.

ADMINISTRATIVE LAW

Before we proceed, however, it may be worthwhile to say a few words about the term administrative law in American usage. The first American scholar to give particular attention to the subject was Frank J. Goodnow. As early as 1893 he defined the phrase as meaning that part of law "which governs the relations of the executive and administrative authorities of the government."[7] He then broadened the definition to encompass "that part of the public law which fixes the organization and determines the competence of the administrative authorities, and indicates to the individual remedies for the violation of his rights."[8] Goodnow was concerned by the failure of English and American legal authorities to give what he considered proper attention to this broad subject. Common-law concepts, so largely concerned as they were with contractual relations and torts involving private persons, were inadequate for public law concerned with the authority and performance of administrative agencies. The particular subjects discussed by Goodnow included the legal status of administrative agencies under the system of a separation of power, the status

---

[6] Commission on Organization of the Executive Branch of the Government, *Legal Services and Procedures* (Washington: Government Printing Office, 1955), pp. 85–88.

[7] Frank J. Goodnow, *Comparative Administrative Law,* students' ed. (New York: G. P. Putnam's Sons, 1903), p. 7.

[8] *Ibid.,* pp. 8–9.

of the chief executive, the power of heads of departments, and laws establishing local units of government.[9]

For a time there was a disposition on the part of some law schools to define administrative law as the law promulgated by administrative agencies.[10] This idea of the term grew from the study of the regulation of utility rates, for example, by administrative agencies. Since it was an administrative agency—either a state public utility commission or the federal Interstate Commerce Commission—which had to define in the first instance what were "fair and reasonable rates," these determinations were thought to constitute administrative law. This definition has today virtually disappeared. Law schools and legal scholars recognize that utility rate law, or tax law, or fair-trade law, is a combination of what legislature, administrative agencies, and courts say it to be, and that any such given body of law must be sought from all three sources.

Today, accordingly, administrative law has come to have a more limited, specific meaning. In general, administrative law is that part of the law which establishes the procedure or methods by which administrative agencies conduct their business in their relations with private parties and interests and which provides for judicial restraint upon the exercise of administrative authority.[11] In this sense administrative law is not quite the same thing as the "law of public administration." We are not concerned now with that statutory enactment which creates administrative agencies, specifies whether they shall have a single head or a board, determines internal organization, sets forth personnel and budgeting and purchasing procedure, and establishes the goals of administrative endeavor. All such law is important; today it is quite voluminous. All such law is best defined as the "law of public administration."

Administrative law takes as its focus of concern a somewhat narrower scope, as the following discussion will indicate. Administrative law is concerned with the impact of administrative operations upon private parties and the circumstances and conditions under which the individual may ensure that administrative authority is legally and reasonably exercised.

ADMINISTRATIVE AUTHORITY

If we are to understand the role of the judiciary in supervising administrative agencies, we must again refer to the nature of the work done by public administration. One reason, of course, why judicial control of administration is a matter of great importance—not just to the individual as a person but also to the individual in society—is the scope of govern-

[9] Cf. also Frank Goodnow, *The Principles of the Administrative Law of the United States* (New York: G. P. Putnam's Sons, 1905).

[10] Cf., for example, Ernst Freund, *Administrative Powers over Persons and Property* (Chicago: University of Chicago Press, 1928).

[11] Cf. Ralph F. Fuchs, "An Approach to Administrative Law," *North Carolina Law Review,* vol. 18 (1940), p. 183.

mental administration today. The individual as a person has a stake in administrative legality; the individual in society has a stake in satisfactory performance of the public service. The judiciary cannot directly control satisfactory performance in the sense of ensuring that administrative policy and administrative activity shall be adequate to meet the grave social needs of the day. Rather, the judiciary can by its requirements of legal procedure in the interests of fairness to an individual almost guarantee a breakdown, or a major slowdown, of public service. The very extent and importance of public administration are, therefore, factors which the courts are compelled to recognize.

At the same time the extent of administrative activity makes the work of administrative agencies of concern to more and more people. The legality and fairness of administrative procedure therefore become all the more essential. Moreover, the variety of authority exercised by administrative agencies makes their operation a matter of concern to the courts if they are to fulfill the judiciary's historic task of helping to preserve individual liberty.

We have previously observed that the nature of administrative activity may be classified in various ways. The authority conferred upon an administrative agency may be described as service or as regulatory. The conduct of foreign relations, the provision of national defense, the operation of a school system, the construction and maintenance of roads, the promotion of soil conservation practices, the payment of benefits to veterans—these are broad positive undertakings oriented to rendering service to all or a considerable group of citizens. Except for the taxes needed to maintain these services, people who obtain no direct benefit from such activities are not usually disadvantaged or harmed personally by this omission.

Regulatory authority vested in an administrative agency is different. Regulation is aimed at requiring an individual person to observe certain legal standards in his own conduct. The individual is thus directly and personally concerned. A businessman has his place of business inspected to make certain that he is observing fire regulations, that the elevator in his office building functions properly, that the airplane he operates is carefully maintained, or that the wages he pays meet minimum legal standards. An architect, a lawyer, a physician, an engineer, a barber, and many other professional and business operators can conduct their affairs only if licensed to do so. A business corporation may be required by administrative order to charge fair prices, to refrain from unfair trade practices, or to engage in collective bargaining with a labor union. An individual may be required to keep his business accounts in a certain way and to produce them for examination when directed to do so.

Regulatory authority is therefore a matter of great individual concern to the person directly affected. Of course there is a public or social interest in regulation as well. Other individuals in goodly number will be harmed if they are charged too much for electric power or railroad transportation, if the airliner they are riding crashes because of motor defects, if the doctor who treats a disease is incompetent, if the architect who designs a building specifies a faulty wall, if one business corporation succeeds in eliminating all competition and obtains a monopoly, if an individual refuses to keep proper accounts and therefore escapes his fair share of a tax. But although a social interest justifies regulatory authority in the first place, it is this power to exact a certain standard of behavior from the individual which entails a vast power over the person. So long as this authority is exercised legally and fairly there is no reason for direct complaint. Of course, an individual may not approve of the public policy which the administrative agency enforces, but so long as he is treated equally with all others in like circumstances, he has no real basis for claiming he has been disadvantaged by administrative conduct as such.

It is here where the judiciary plays its particular role. The courts stand as guarantor of legal and fair behavior by administrative agencies in regulating the conduct of the individual. Here is a person who claims that he possesses all the proper qualifications for licensing as a doctor but that the state medical board refuses to grant him a license. Here is a public utility which claims that the electric rate it is directed to charge will actually bring in too little income to meet operating expenses and provide a reasonable return on investment. Here is a broadcasting company which claims that it has met all the legal standards of operation and that its license has been revoked. Here is a motion picture theater told to close because the building does not conform with fire regulations when the proprietor believes that he has reasonably complied with all such standards. The aggrieved individual or business may properly want some assurance that such vital authority over its welfare is not being exercised arbitrarily. It is the task of the judiciary to provide this assurance.

We do not wish to suggest that all judicial supervision of administrative activity is confined solely to the administrative exercise of regulatory authority and not to the exercise of service authority. The payment of benefits to veterans may involve the possibility of administrative favoritism or abuse, too, even if the usual avenues for redress of such grievances are legislative and executive rather than judicial. And there are many instances when it is not easy to draw the line between service authority and regulatory authority. A citizen denied the opportunity to seek public employment, or refused a visa in order to travel abroad, may have lost only a privilege, not a right. But both may be matters of vital privilege indeed to the individual concerned. We emphasize only the matter of regulatory authority here because it is the kind of administrative action which has raised the most problems in judicial supervision.[12]

[12] Cf. Walter Gellhorn, *Individual Freedom and Governmental Restraints* (Baton Rouge, La.: Louisiana State University Press, 1956).

THE SCOPE OF JUDICIAL CONTROL

One possible answer to the problem of ensuring the legal and reasonable exercise of administrative authority is to require that all action placing restraints upon the individual be taken only by courts. For instance, this is the process of criminal action. Police and other criminal investigative forces are organized as administrative agencies. They may apprehend a person caught in the act of violating a criminal statute, or by investigating the circumstances of a murder or robbery or other crime police agencies may gather evidence which suggests the guilt of a particular person or group of persons. The police force and the prosecuting attorney may not issue an administrative order finding that a named individual committed a stated robbery. Rather, after indictment or other preliminary action, the government, through police and prosecutor, must present its evidence in court, and judge and jury must decide the question of guilt or innocence. Why is not such a process as this desirable throughout the entire machinery of public administration?

The answer is simply that competent as the judicial process is in determining the guilt or innocence of an individual accused of crime, this same process is not readily adaptable to meet the public interest needs of *expertise* and timeliness in the performance of administrative activity. Let us look at certain examples.

A university supported by state government exists to provide educational opportunity to young men and young women at low cost to the individual student. Such a publicly supported university may open its doors to young persons of widely varying abilities and interests. In order to remain a student, however, the young person must meet certain minimum standards of academic performance as established by the faculty and administrative officers of the state university. A student who fails to meet these standards is suspended from attendance. Such action may make it difficult if not impossible for the student to obtain admission to another college or university and may prevent the student from obtaining a college degree. Thus the action of a state-supported university in suspending a student has an adverse effect upon that individual. Should such suspension be ordered only by a court of law and not by the staff of the university?

If a university suspension case had to go to a court of law a judge would be required to review the student's academic performance, the reasonableness of the standards established for continued study, and the record of the student in relation to these standards. The court would have to familiarize itself with academic tradition and procedure and with methods of student evaluation. It would have to decide whether the academic standards established by the state-supported university appeared to be reasonable in the light of educational objectives fixed by the university. And it would then have to decide whether the individual student failed to meet these standards. In the process of making such a decision a court of law would have in effect to substitute its judgment for the expert judgment of the university faculty.[13]

Or let us take another illustration. In order to protect the health of their inhabitants, state governments, through their own health departments or through county health agencies, regularly inspect the dairy herds supplying milk to city processors and distributors. If a herd of cattle is found to be diseased, a health inspector may order a farmer to kill the diseased cattle immediately. The reason for this is both to stop at once the shipment of bad milk for individual consumption and to prevent the spreading of infection to other cattle. The farmer who is thus directed to destroy one or more milk cows suffers a severe economic blow. Should such destruction be ordered only by a court of law?

If a court of law had to intervene in such a case, the element of timeliness in administrative operation might be sacrificed. Is diseased milk to be shipped to consumers while the court decides whether the cattle are diseased or not? Is the danger of the spread of infection to other cattle to be endured while the diseased condition of the particular cattle in question is decided to the satisfaction of a court of law? Great economic as well as health damage may be done to all concerned by any delay in the immediate destruction of cattle found to be diseased.

The relative merits of administrative and judicial process were considered nearly twenty years ago in the United States by a Committee on Administrative Procedure appointed by the Attorney General. This committee pointed out the various considerations which had led the Congress to vest authority in administrative agencies to decide how private persons should behave under certain circumstances, such as the fixing of transportation rates. First, there was the element of specialization, or *expertise*. Administrative agencies were able to hire accountants, engineers, and other professional personnel who could be used to inquire into and recommend to an administrative tribunal what was a reasonable transportation rate for a particular commodity. Specialization, furthermore, meant continued contact with a particular activity, so that an accumulation of experience would help to ensure proper action. Such continuity of attention was advantageous to the public interest. Secondly, an administrative agency may take preventive action, that is, it may order a railroad to charge a certain rate and so prevent unreasonable rates from being assessed against shippers. A court would ordinarily intervene only after some alleged damage has been suffered by the shipper. In the third place, the volume of cases to be handled may be such that some informal procedure is preferable in order to get the work done. In the fourth place,

---

[13] The illustration is not hypothetical. See, for example, *West v. The Board of Trustees of Miami University*, Court of Appeals, First Appellate District of Ohio, Dec. 1, 1931, 41 O. App. 367.

administrative agencies may have responsibility for a variety of related tasks and in the process of handling these various duties may make adjustments which consideration of just a single item might not suggest.[14]

It seems reasonable to declare that if all administrative action in the regulatory field were to proceed only by a process resembling criminal law, courts of law would be swamped, and administrative agencies would be frustrated in their effort to advance the public interest.

LIMITATIONS UPON JUDICIAL CONTROL

If we accept the proposition that the administrative process in government cannot be equated with the ordinary civil and criminal process of the judiciary, there remains the question how the courts shall themselves recognize their limitations. How can the judiciary decide when to intervene in the administrative process and when not to intervene? This has been a difficult question for courts themselves to answer. Judges have seen the complexity of the problems confronting them and have endeavored to develop a number of doctrines for their guidance. At the same time the judiciary has been concerned to preserve its conception of legal and reasonable administrative action. The consequence is that courts often find some reason in a particular case to depart from so-called doctrine. In the field of judicial supervision of administrative agencies, any generalization is almost certain not to be true in every instance.

The scope of judicial oversight of administrative agencies may be limited by statutory enactment itself. The second Hoover Commission in 1955 reported that at least six statutes concerning major administrative programs of the federal government specifically precluded any judicial review of administrative action. For example, the decisions of the Civil Aeronautics Board granting licenses for overseas air transport or any other orders affecting international air service are not reviewable in a court of law; such decisions are subject only to review by the President to make certain that the orders conform with the foreign policy of the United States. Similarly, decisions of the Secretary of Labor on allowances due federal employees for injuries sustained in the course of federal employment are not subject to judicial review. Determinations by the Administrator of Veterans' Affairs on pensions, benefits, hospital treatment, domiciliary care, and disability retirement are, under the statute, "final and conclusive on all questions of law and fact, and no other official or court of the United States shall have jurisdiction to review by mandamus or otherwise any such decision." Similarly, orders of the Department of Agriculture under the Packers and Stockyards Act and decisions of the

[14] *Administrative Procedure in Government Agencies,* Report of the Committee on Administrative Procedure appointed by the Attorney General, Sen. Doc. 8, 77th Cong., 1st Sess. (1941), pp. 7–21.

Foreign Claims Settlement Commission have been removed from judicial review by statute.[15] In these instances the Congress has felt that there was some special reason for precluding judicial review. The result has been to rule out any appeal to the courts in these particular instances.

Other statutes do not undertake to forbid judicial review but seek rather to limit the scope of judicial scrutiny of administrative action. For example, the Federal Trade Commission Act of 1914 provided that orders of the Commission requiring a business to cease and desist from "unfair methods of competition in commerce" might be appealed to a Court of Appeals. At the same time the law declared that the findings of fact by the Commission were to be final if supported by evidence. Similarly, other statutes have endeavored to limit the scope of judicial review by making administrative findings of fact binding upon the court. This kind of limitation is intended to prevent courts of law from undertaking to hear all over again the factual evidence previously considered by an administrative agency. Presumably, under this provision the court is expected to review the law applied to a given set of facts. Thus, for example, a Court of Appeals is not supposed to question the fact whether a distributor of steel ties for baling cotton refused to sell such ties unless the purchaser also bought jute bagging from that distributor. The question for the court was the legal one whether such "tie-in sales" constituted an unfair method of competition.[16]

We shall discuss some of the complexities in this matter of separating fact from law in a later chapter. We need note here only that the distinction is a difficult one to apply in practice, and that the courts themselves are inclined to recognize the difference only on occasion. Nonetheless, some effort has been made by legislatures to limit the scope of judicial review by placing administrative findings of fact when supported by substantial evidence beyond the purview of court examination.

Within the federal government the Administrative Procedure Act of June 11, 1946, endeavors to define relationships between administrative agencies and the courts. Section 10 of this statute declares that, except in so far as a statute precludes judicial review or the action of an agency is expressly committed to that agency's sole discretion, any person suffering a legal wrong or adversely affected by the action of some administrative agency shall be entitled to judicial review. This section then says that a court shall decide all relevant questions of law, interpret constitutional and statutory provisions, and determine the meaning or applicability of any administrative action. More specifically, the statute says that a court may compel administrative action which is unlawfully withheld or unreasonably delayed, and may set aside any agency action or findings

[15] Commission on Organization of the Executive Branch of the Government, *op. cit.,* pp. 73–74.
[16] Cf. *Federal Trade Commission v. Gratz,* 253 U.S. 421 (1920).

found to be (1) arbitrary, capricious, an abuse of discretion, or otherwise not in accordance with law; (2) contrary to constitutional right, power, or privilege; (3) in excess of statutory jurisdiction or authority; (4) without observance of legally prescribed procedure; (5) unsupported by substantial evidence; or (6) unwarranted by the facts to the extent that the facts are subject to the court's power to review.

There has been a good deal of debate among students of administrative law whether section 10 of the Administrative Procedure Act of 1946 enlarges the scope of judicial review in federal administration or restricts it. A careful consideration of the text and some ten years of experience would appear to suggest that section 10 was more a restatement of the basic law of judicial review than any considerable enlargement of it. For the most part, the statute tends to place judicial review within some legal restriction rather than to throw it wide open.

It is important to observe that legislation enacted by the Congress and approved by the President can place some checkrein upon judicial review of administrative agencies. The extent of such restriction is then a matter of public policy. It seems unlikely, however, that the Supreme Court would uphold the constitutionality of any legislation in the field of regulatory administration which would eliminate all possibility of judicial review.

Judicial review of public administration is not a cure-all, however. It is further limited by the court's conception of its function: to check an excess of power rather than to correct every possible administrative failure. This limitation of the judicial function and some perspective about its role in the general operation of government were well expressed by the Attorney General's Committee on Administrative Procedure in 1941:[17]

> Yet judicial review is rarely available, theoretically or practically, to compel effective enforcement of the law by administrators. It is adapted chiefly to curbing excess of power, not toward compelling its exercise. Constitutional limitations may in some cases forbid the use of judicial power to correct underenforcement. But constitutional difficulties aside, the courts cannot, as a practical matter, be effectively used for that purpose without being assimilated into the administrative structure and losing their independent organization. To assure enforcement of the laws by administrative agencies within the bounds of their authority, reliance must be placed on controls other than judicial review—internal controls in the agency, responsibility to the legislature or the executive, careful selection of personnel, pressure from interested parties, and professional or lay criticism of the agency's work.

CONCLUSION

The judicial power in our structure of government is substantial. The court system of the federal government and of state governments serves a

---

[17] *Administrative Procedure in Government Agencies,* p. 76.

dual purpose. On the one hand, the courts exist to settle the civil suits or controversies of one citizen versus another and to protect the public interest through the handling of criminal cases presented by law enforcement agencies. On the other hand, the courts serve also to protect and preserve the constitutional liberties of the individual citizen. This means careful watchfulness to make sure that law enforcement agencies do not violate the constitutional immunities of the citizen, such as the right of trial by jury, the right to know the charges against him, the right to be free from unlawful search or seizure, and the right not to be required to bear witness against himself. In addition, the citizen is entitled to be free from any unlawful or unreasonable action taken by administrative agencies.

An administrative agency which takes action beyond the legal competence or authority conferred upon it behaves unlawfully. An administrative agency which acts without observing certain standards of procedure or without giving careful attention to facts behaves unreasonably. The ordinary courts of law in our judicial system endeavor to ensure that public administration, especially administration of a regulatory nature, shall be both legal and reasonable.

Chapter 22

Special Problems of Constitutional Doctrine

In their supervision of administrative activities our courts have had to struggle with two troublesome issues of constitutional doctrine. One of these issues has been the doctrine of the nondelegation of power. The other has been the doctrine of governmental nonliability for torts, that is, for damages to person or property arising from the conduct of an administrative employee. Both of these doctrines have occasioned difficulties in reconciling the traditions of the common law with the realities of the administrative state.

THE DELEGATION OF GOVERNMENTAL POWER

In writing about the new Constitution of 1787, James Madison referred to a "political maxim, that the legislative, executive, and judiciary departments ought to be separate and distinct." He went on to declare: "The accumulation of all powers, legislative, executive, and judiciary, in the same hands, whether of one, a few, or many, and whether hereditary, self-appointed, or elective, may justly be pronounced the very definition of tyranny." In discussing his subject, Madison made mention of the "celebrated Montesquieu"—"the oracle who is always consulted and cited on this subject." (*The Federalist,* no. 47.) In elaborating his theme that the federal Constitution did preserve the principle of a separation of governmental power, Madison referred to the various state constitutions which had embodied a like arrangement. There can be no doubt that a separation of power into legislative, executive, and judicial components was a basic political conception of those who established the framework of American government.

The doctrine of separation of power implied a corollary concern: "that the powers properly belonging to one of the departments ought not to be directly and completely administered by either of the other departments." (*The Federalist,* no. 48) In developing this theme, Madison was concerned to point out the necessity for some means of preventing one branch of power from encroaching upon the other. He was not satisfied by "parchment barriers," as he termed the provisions of most state constitutions. He noted in particular: "The legislative department is everywhere extending the sphere of its activity, and drawing all power into its impetuous vortex." Madison answered his problem with a prescription: "But the great security against a gradual concentration of the several powers in the same department consists in giving to those who administer each department the necessary constitutional means and personal motive to resist encroachment of the other." (*The Federalist,* no. 51.)

Madison was concerned about the encroachment of one branch of power upon the other. He believed the federal Constitution had gone as far as an instrument of government might go in forestalling this danger. He did not anticipate that an equally fundamental issue might arise in the actual practice of government—the issue of a delegation of power from one branch to another. It seems not to have occurred to those who wrote the federal Constitution or the early constitutional commentaries that one branch of power might seek to confer its power upon another. Yet as the American government developed, this very issue did arise. And it arose primarily in the context of governmental administration.

We have had occasion at several different points to comment about the absence of any definite, coherent doctrine of constitutional status for the administrative work of government. This absence arose from the almost complete lack of attention to administrative matters in the federal Constitution and in the corresponding state constitutions. The only constitutional proposition which readily met the need was to consider all administrative agencies as a part of the executive branch and all administrative power, therefore, as executive power.

During the first half of the nineteenth century the problem of administrative power appears to have been of small if any concern.[1] The administrative apparatus of the federal government before the Civil War was still rudimentary, and administrative activities at all levels of government

---

[1] Actually, early in the history of our nation a case arose involving the question of delegating legislative power to the President. While Jefferson was President, the Congress in 1807 had enacted an embargo law prohibiting both exports and imports. This law had been repealed in 1809. In this same year Congress enacted a nonintercourse law which permitted commerce with all countries except England and France and authorized the President to suspend nonintercourse with either of these powers whenever one or the other withdrew its restrictions upon American trade. The act was extended in 1810. The constitutionality of the law was challenged later upon the grounds that it delegated power to the President to determine the effectiveness of a statute. Although announcing adherence to the doctrine that power could not be delegated by one branch of government to another, the Supreme Court upheld the constitutionality of this particular legislation. The Court held that the executive power to suspend operation of a law under definite standards fixed by the Congress was not an unconstitutional delegation of legislative power. *Brig Aurora v. United States,* 7 Cranch 382 (1813).

were limited. Only in the second half of the century did the judiciary, as guardian of the sanctity of the Constitution, suddenly become aware of a problem. This awareness coincided with the growth of administrative activity and especially of regulatory administration. Many of the cases arose in state courts and involved the constitutionality of state legislation.[2]

In 1892 the constitutionality of the federal Tariff Act of 1890 was questioned before the United States Supreme Court. A section of this law declared that in order to promote reciprocal trade with other countries the President might suspend the free importation into the United States of sugar, molasses, tea, coffee, and hides from countries imposing duties upon American agricultural products. This section was challenged as a delegation of legislative power to the President. The Supreme Court rejected this argument, declaring that the President had not been given the power to make law but simply to determine facts requiring a particular execution of the law.[3] A so-called flexible tariff provision in the Tariff Act of 1922 was similarly sustained; under this provision the President was authorized to increase tariff rates when he should find that the duties fixed by the law did not equalize differences in the "cost of production" between the United States and foreign countries.[4]

In the Hampton case, Chief Justice William Howard Taft reviewed the whole subject of the delegation of power. He pointed out that it was a well-known maxim of the common law that "delegated power cannot be delegated." This maxim had been applied to the operation of both federal and state constitutions. The Chief Justice declared:[5]

> The Federal Constitution and State Constitutions of this country divide the governmental power into three branches. The first is the legislative, the second is the executive, and the third is the judicial, and the rule is that in the actual administration of the government Congress or the Legislature should exercise the legislative power, the President or the State Executive, the Governor, the executive power, and the Courts or the judiciary the judicial power, and in carrying out that constitutional division into three branches it is a breach of the national fundamental law if Congress gives up its legislative power and transfers it to the President, or to the Judicial branch, or, if by

[2] See Frank E. Cooper, *Administrative Agencies and the Courts* (Ann Arbor, Mich.: University of Michigan Law School, 1951), pp. 28ff. For example, the Court of Appeals in New York as early as 1908 considered the constitutional question whether a regulatory commission might be empowered to fix the maximum rates to be charged by gas and electric light companies. Although the court agreed that the power to fix rates was legislative in character, it held that such power might be delegated to an administrative body, provided there was some legislative standard for guidance in the exercise of this rate-making power. *Village of Saratoga Springs v. Saratoga Gas, Electric Light and Power Company,* 83 N.E. 693 (1908).

[3] *Field v. Clark,* 143 U.S. 649 (1892).

[4] *J. W. Hampton, Jr., and Company v. United States,* 276 U.S. 394 (1928).

[5] *Ibid.*

law it attempts to invest itself or its members with either executive power or judicial power.

The Chief Justice then went on to assert that this doctrine of the non-delegability of power was not to be construed as preventing one branch from seeking the assistance of another branch. He proceeded to point out with some care:

> The field of Congress involves all and many varieties of legislative action, and Congress has found it frequently necessary to use officers of the Executive Branch, within defined limits, to secure the exact effect intended by its acts of legislation, by vesting discretion in such officers to make public regulations interpreting a statute and directing the details of its execution, even to the extent of providing for penalizing a breach of such regulations.

Chief Justice Taft mentioned that Congress might decide to leave the determination of future conditions when a law would be effective to the decision of the President. He also observed that the Supreme Court had upheld the constitutionality of legislation permitting the Interstate Commerce Commission to fix railroad rates within the limits of a general rule laid down by Congress that these rates were to be just and reasonable and not discriminatory.

In 1932 the Supreme Court of the United States considered a different kind of delegation. The Pure Food and Drug Act of 1906 made it unlawful to ship in interstate commerce any article of food or drugs which was misbranded. Under the law an article of food was misbranded if a package did not clearly indicate the quantity of the contents. One section of the law then provided that reasonable variations between quantity shown and actual quantity might be established by an administrative agency. The constitutionality of this law was challenged on the grounds that the administrative authority to prescribe rules and regulations was an exercise of legislative power. The Supreme Court rejected this contention. Once again the Court affirmed the general proposition that the legislative power of Congress could not be delegated. But said the Court: "Congress may declare its will, and after fixing a primary standard, devolve upon administrative officers 'the power to fill up the details' by prescribing administrative rules and regulations."[6]

During the New Deal the Supreme Court found two instances, however, in which statutes of Congress passed beyond approved limits. The first such instance was the "hot oil" case of 1935.[7] Under section 9(c) of the National Industrial Recovery Act of 1933 the President was authorized to prohibit the shipment in interstate commerce of any oil produced in excess of quotas fixed by state regulatory agencies. In July, 1933, the President issued an executive order prohibiting such shipments

[6] *United States v. Shreveport Grain and Elevator Company,* 287 U.S. 77 (1932).
[7] *Panama Refining Co, v, Ryan,* 293 U.S. 388 (1935).

and delegating enforcement authority to the Secretary of the Interior. In holding that section 9(c) was an unconstitutional delegation of power to the President, the Supreme Court pointed out that the statute failed to state any circumstances or conditions to govern the President's action in prohibiting or failing to prohibit the shipment of "hot oil." Speaking for the Court, Chief Justice Charles Evans Hughes said: "The Constitution has never been regarded as denying to the Congress the necessary resources of flexibility and practicality, which will enable it to perform its function in laying down policies and establishing standards, while leaving to selected instrumentalities the making of subordinate rules within prescribed limits and the determination of facts to which the policy as declared by the legislature is to apply." Because the law in this instance exceeded the "limits of delegation which there is no constitutional authority to transcend," the Court held this particular section of the law unconstitutional.

Later in the same year the Court considered the broader provisions of this same National Industrial Recovery Act of 1933. Under section 3(a) of the statute, the President was empowered to approve codes of fair competition for a particular trade or industry upon application by a trade association or group. The President was to approve such codes if he found (1) that an association or group preparing a code imposed no inequitable restriction on admission to membership and (2) that the code was not designed to promote monopoly or oppress small enterprises. The constitutionality of the statute was attacked in a case brought against a poultry dealer accused of violating a code of fair competition approved for the live poultry industry in the New York metropolitan area. Two constitutional questions were presented to the Supreme Court. Was the law, and the particular code under the law, a regulation of interstate commerce? Secondly, did the law constitute a valid delegation of power to the President? On this second point the Supreme Court declared that no standard had been established for guiding the President in approving a code of fair competition.[8] The statute gave no indication of what purposes were to be achieved by the codes of fair competition. Any purpose might be conceived as desirable within the provisions of the statute. As Justice Cardozo in a concurring opinion declared: "This is delegation running riot." The statute was held to be unconstitutional.

In 1939 the Supreme Court upheld the provisions of the Tobacco Inspection Act of 1935. The statute established federal regulation of tobacco auction markets and authorized the Secretary of Agriculture to establish standards for tobacco by type and grade. A system of tobacco inspection was then provided in order to make grading effective. The Secretary of Agriculture might designate an area as a tobacco market area in interstate commerce. If such a designation was approved in a referendum by

[8] *Schechter Poultry Corp. v. United States,* 295 U.S. 495 (1935).

two-thirds of the growers in the area, it became effective. When such a market area was officially designated, the law forbade the sale at auction of any tobacco in this market unless it had been inspected and met the standards of type and grade promulgated by the Secretary. This statute was attacked likewise as a delegation of legislative power. It was said that the legislature had delegated its proper authority to the Secretary of Agriculture in permitting him to fix standards of type and grade, and it had delegated to a private group, the growers, the authority to define a market area in interstate commerce. This time the Supreme Court rejected these contentions, declaring that the law established sufficient guides for the operation of the Secretary of Agriculture.[9]

Similarly, during World War II the Court upheld the Price Control Acts of 1941 and 1942. These acts set forth that their purpose was to stabilize prices in the interest of national security and to prevent profiteering and other undesirable practices caused by the national emergency. The Administrator was authorized to promulgate regulations fixing prices which in his judgment "will be generally fair and equitable." In establishing a maximum price the Administrator was to give "due consideration" to the prices prevailing between October 1 and October 15, 1941, and to make such adjustments as he might deem "to be of general applicability," such as increases in costs of production and general increases or decreases in profits earned by sellers. Under the 1942 amendment the law directed the President to stabilize prices, wages, and salaries "so far as practicable" at September 15, 1942, levels. In upholding the constitutionality of this statute, the Supreme Court declared:[10]

> The essentials of the legislative function are the determination of the legislative policy and its formulation and promulgation as a defined and binding rule of conduct. . . . These essentials are preserved when Congress has specified the basic conditions of fact upon whose existence or occurrence, ascertained from relevant data by a designated administrative agency, it directs that its statutory command shall be effective. It is no objection that the determination of facts and the inferences to be drawn from them in the light of the statutory standards and declaration of policy call for the exercise of judgment, and for the formulation of subsidiary administrative policy within the prescribed statutory framework. . . . Nor does the doctrine of separation of powers deny to Congress power to direct that an administrative officer properly designated for that purpose have ample latitude within which he is to ascertain the conditions which Congress has made prerequisite to the operation of its legislative command. . . . Acting within its constitutional power to fix prices it is for Congress to say whether the data on the basis of which prices are to be fixed are to be confined within a narrow or broad range. In either case the only concern of courts is to ascertain whether the will of Congress has been obeyed. This depends not upon the breadth of the

[9] *Currin v. Wallace,* 306 U.S. 1 (1939).
[10] *Yakus v. United States,* 321 U.S. 414 (1944).

definition of the facts or conditions which the administrative officer is to find but upon the determination whether the definition sufficiently marks the field within which the Administrator is to act so that it may be known whether he has kept within it in compliance with the legislative will. . . . Only if we could say that there is an absence of standards for the guidance of the Administrator's action, so that it would be impossible in a proper proceeding to ascertain whether the will of Congress has been obeyed, would we be justified in overriding its choice of means for effecting its declared purpose of preventing inflation. . . . The standards prescribed by the present Act, with the aid of the "statement of considerations" required to be made by the Administrator, are sufficiently definite and precise to enable Congress, the courts, and the public to ascertain whether the Administrator, in fixing the designated prices has conformed to those standards.

Enough has been said to point to the general nature of the doctrine of separation of powers in relation to public administration. The courts, both federal and state, have insisted that legislative power may not be delegated to the executive or the judiciary, and that in turn legislative and judicial power may not be delegated to administrative agencies. For example, a statute may not properly confer upon an administrative agency the authority to prescribe acts which shall constitute a crime and then to fix the penalties for violation of such acts.[11] At the same time this doctrine of the nondelegability of power does not mean that statutes are necessarily unconstitutional which vest considerable discretion in the hands of the executive or of an administrative agency.

The problem is one of proper safeguards to the exercise of administrative discretion and of adequate standards for the guidance of administrators in the exercise of discretion. Neither of these cornerstones of proper administrative authority can be described with finality. In the last analysis it remains for the courts to say in individual cases whether the safeguards have been sufficient and the standards are adequate. The court is thus concerned with keeping administration within bounds, not in supervising the legislature.

In general, the courts expect the scope of administrative authority to be as carefully defined as the circumstances seem to warrant. At the least the general policy or purpose to be realized by administrative action must be set forth. The administrative agency or official entrusted with the exercise of discretion must be indicated. The provision of standards for the guidance of administrative action is also essential. But what constitutes an adequate standard is difficult to say. Whenever a statute deals with some new and complex situation, it must almost always do so in general terms. The standards for the guidance of the administrator must usually be set forth in broad language. Some discretion must be left to administrative officials, as when the Secretary of Agriculture was authorized to make

[11] *People v. Grant,* Court of Appeals of New York, 196 N.E. 553 (1935).

rules and regulations governing grazing rights within a broad mandate to improve and protect the national forests.[12] In contrast with statutory law, administrative rules and regulations may be framed in considerable detail by drawing upon expert judgment. More than this, such rules may have considerable flexibility, being subject to change by administrative discretion.[13] It has remained then for the courts to decide whether the standards fixed by law appear to have sufficient meaning to serve as a guide to administrative action. One commentator has suggested that the principle might be stated in these terms: that one branch of government may delegate power to another branch "if only a sufficient number of strings are attached."[14]

Thus far we have spoken of the delegation of authority to administrative agencies to make rules and regulations which supplement statutory enactment. Regulatory authority involves a different kind of administrative action, action which is called adjudicative or quasi-judicial in character. When the Federal Trade Commission issues a "cease and desist" order in a particular controversy involving the specific action of an individual company accused of an unfair trade practice, the commission is in effect interpreting the applicability of a statute to an individual case. Is this not the exercise of a judicial function? Administrative adjudication does bear some resemblance to the judicial process. It is also quite different, in such matters as specialization, procedure, and responsibility for defining public policy through specific instances.

The courts have not been too much concerned with administrative adjudication as a possible delegation of judicial power to administrative agencies. Rather, the courts have accepted administrative adjudication as an essential element of the regulatory process. The courts have been primarily concerned with the procedure employed in the process of administrative adjudication and with the preservation of some degree of judicial review of administrative decisions.

It appears to be evident that the general effect of the doctrine of nondelegation of power is primarily to prevent a legislature from vesting uncontrolled or unlimited discretion in administrative hands. The courts must themselves determine when discretion is uncontrolled or unlimited. Certainly, at one extreme, it is easy to say that the courts will not tolerate a situation where administrative agencies undertake in effect to write statutory law. On the other hand, the courts will sustain broad language conferring administrative discretion if it appears to provide some degree of adequate standard for the guidance of administrative conduct.

[12] *United States v. Grimaud,* 220 U.S. 506 (1911).

[13] On the advantages and disadvantages of administrative rule making, see Frederick F. Blachly and Miriam E. Oatman, *Administrative Legislation and Adjudication* (Washington, D.C.: Brookings Institution, 1934), chap. 3.

[14] Oliver P. Field, "Separation and Delegation of Powers," *American Political Science Review,* vol. 41 (December, 1947), p. 1161.

Administrative realism dictates that administrative agencies must have a good deal of discretion in the pursuit of legislative policies and programs. Concern for the rights of the individual and for the preservation of limited government dictates that the courts shall review and halt any administrative action not properly guided by law. There is no general rule at present by which it is possible to determine in advance what is an adequate or sufficient standard for the guidance of administrative operations. The most that can be said is that various factors will influence the judiciary in this judgment: factors, such as the nature of the case (is the license to be revoked that of a doctor of medicine or of a saloon?), current economic and political thinking, attitude of the judiciary toward its role in relation to administrative agencies, administrative tradition, relationship of a standard to some prevailing legal concept, and the administrative observance of procedural safeguards.[15] But at the least we must observe that the judiciary may use the doctrine of nondelegation of government power as the basis for review of administrative activity.

GOVERNMENTAL TORTS

There is a second kind of problem in the relationship of the judiciary to administrative operation which we must note. This is the problem of torts. Under common law it has been possible for one citizen to sue another for damages arising out of any tort, such as trespass upon private property or carelessness or negligence resulting in damage to property or person. A considerable part of the work of the judiciary has arisen from tort law. Yet early in the development of the common law the courts enunciated the doctrine that the "king can do no wrong."

There were practical reasons why the courts of England should have taken this position. If private citizens were to be permitted to bring legal action against the sovereign and his administrative agencies, then much of the work of government could have been hampered by such attack. Moreover, since the early judges were engaged in dispensing the "king's justice," they were in a vulnerable position to begin to take judicial action against that same king. So for various reasons the courts early decided that they would not hear cases or assess damages against the king or the administrative agencies of government.

This same doctrine became a part of the legal tradition of the United States, although it had now to be set forth in the terms that "the state can do no wrong." As successors of the English government, first the state governments and then the federal government inherited the constitutional doctrine that they were free from suits for damages arising out of torts which might be committed by administrative agents. If the citizen were

[15] Frank E. Cooper, *op. cit.,* pp. 36–44.

to obtain redress for governmental torts, it had to be realized through administrative or legislative channels.

The difficulty with the doctrine that the state can do no wrong is quite evident. In the actual administration of their work, governmental servants may damage private citizens in property or person. This has been especially true in recent years with the advent of the automobile. If an unlighted hole is left in a street and a citizen damages his car, has he no recourse? If a police car is in an accident and damages the window of a retail shop, has the owner no legal recourse? The customary judicial answer has been that the wrong suffered by the individual simply had to be borne as an unfortunate event.

Actually, administrative officials may damage persons or property unintentionally and yet substantially. If the cost of this damage is to fall on the shoulders of the person harmed, he may suffer a sizable individual loss. To many persons it did not seem fair that the loss should be so heavy upon a single individual. Would it not be more fair for society to share these losses, since society as a whole is the beneficiary of administrative activity? For this reason there has been a good deal of dissatisfaction with the legal doctrine that the state can do no wrong.

Or, consider the situation of the person or company who does business with the government. An administrative agency contracts for services, such as electric power; for supplies, such as drugs and clothing; for equipment, such as airplanes; and for construction of physical facilities, such as roads and buildings. If an administrative agency refuses to pay the stated price, or if the administrative agency insists upon specifications or standards not set forth in the original contract, has the contractor no recourse for damages suffered under these circumstances? If the doctrine that the state can do no wrong is faithfully adhered to, then the contractor cannot sue for damages. In turn, why should any business enterprise wish to do work for the government under such conditions?

In practice, there have been three ways in which the doctrine that the state can do no wrong has been modified so as to reduce the cost burden upon the individual citizen or business that suffers loss at administrative hands. One remedy has been a modified judicial doctrine which developed in the law of municipal government corporations to the effect that when performing a proprietary function, city government was subject to a suit for damages. The second development was the custom of state legislatures and of the federal legislature to pass private bills compensating an individual for some damage suffered by administrative action. The third device has been for a government to consent voluntarily to be sued for damages, especially in the field of government contracts.

Since local government is the creation of state government, the immunity which attends the acts of the state has been extended in legal practice to the city or other unit of local government. At some early point in judicial concern with torts inflicted by administrative officials of government, state courts developed the doctrine that the functions of local government were of two kinds: governmental and proprietary. The basis of the distinction seems to have developed from the peculiar governmental terminology which grew up in England and the United States. City governments were spoken of as municipal corporations. A characteristic of a corporation is its capacity to sue and be sued in the courts of law. If a municipal corporation possessed characteristics of a corporation, then it could be sued for damages arising from any torts committed by its servants or agents. Some such reasoning as this resulted in the conclusion that municipal corporations could be sued for damages which might occur in the performance of corporate activities.

The difficulty was that of deciding just what were the corporate or proprietary functions of municipal government. In general, there has been a tendency for state courts to hold that the operation of municipal utilities, such as water and electric systems, was a corporate activity. Police and fire protection, health and welfare activities have been held to be governmental activities. Then there has been an area of confusion, such as the construction and operation of streets, sewers, walks, and parks. Some state courts have held these activities to be proprietary and others have held them to be governmental.[16]

There is general agreement among students of municipal government that the attempted distinction between proprietary and governmental functions is at best a questionable one. Indeed, the Supreme Court of the United States has observed: "The basis of distinction is difficult to state, and there is no established rule for the determination of what belongs to the one or the other."[17] Thus, if a person's car is hit by a fire truck, he would ordinarily have no recourse to recover damages; on the other hand, if his car is hit by a truck of the municipal water department, he may be able to obtain damages. Such a distinction is difficult for the ordinary citizen to grasp. In consequence, many states have tended to supersede the judge-made law on municipal tort liability by statutory enactments which have broadened the scope of city liability for torts. In some states even the courts themselves have abandoned the distinction. The result has been that municipal liability has been extended. Yet in some jurisdictions the citizen may still recover damages if he can claim he was harmed by municipal officials in the course of performing a proprietary function.

The second method of handling damages is through the legislative process. There is nothing to prevent the legislature from passing bills which compensate individuals for damages if the committees and then the

---

[16] Although now dated, the classical treatment of this subject is J. F. Dillon, *Commentaries on the Law of Municipal Corporations,* 5th ed., vol. IV (Boston: Little, Brown & Company, 1911), chap. 32.

[17] *City of Trenton v. New Jersey,* 262 U.S. 182 (1923).

legislature are satisfied that an individual has been harmed through no fault of his own. This process, of course, is not judicial and does not involve the judiciary in any review of administrative action. Indeed, in the federal government a rather elaborate procedure has been developed for handling private bills settling tort claims against the federal government.[18] An individual representative or senator may introduce a bill to satisfy the claim of some citizen. The measure is then referred to the Judiciary Committee. The claimant presents written evidence of his case. The administrative agency involved is asked to give its side of the story. Often this account is quite objective, and may recommend the payment of damages, as in the case of a Navy station wagon which struck a girl crossing the street to board a school bus in a Massachusetts town. In the House of Representatives the Judiciary Committee relies upon the judgment of a subcommittee; in the Senate the Committee relies heavily upon a staff of six attorneys. The recommendation of the full Committee is usually accepted by the House or Senate. To be sure, a claim bill passed by the Congress is subject to presidential veto, and often the Bureau of the Budget makes an independent examination of the facts in order to recommend either approval or veto of a private claim bill.

The difficulty with this procedure is simply the burden it places upon the legislature. Legislators are overworked in any event. Even the members of a committee cannot give full time and attention to the consideration of the merits of a claim for damages. Although usually the task is undertaken with proper caution and care, legislative determination of proper claims for government to accept is at best a time-consuming, uncertain process.

The third possibility in handling governmental torts is for the legislature to accept liability in various types of cases and to establish special courts or administrative tribunals to consider the merits of individual claims. Or general statutes may confer jurisdiction in tort or damage cases upon the regular courts. It is then necessary to appropriate funds by general or special legislation to meet the claims actually awarded by administrative bodies or by the courts, special or general.

As early as 1855 the Congress of the United States created the Court of Claims, early called a "legislative court."[19] The jurisdiction of this court was to consider claims against the United States arising out of contracts with the government. Any time a contractor felt he had not been fairly paid under the terms of a government contract, he might bring a suit in the Court of Claims. If he obtained a favorable judgment, the

---

[18] Walter Gellhorn and Louis Lauer, "Congressional Settlement of Tort Claims against the United States," *Columbia Law Review,* vol. 55 (January, 1955), p. 1.

[19] *Gordon v. United States,* 2 Wall. 561 (1865); *Williams v. United States,* 289 U.S. 553 (1933).

claim was referred to Congress for inclusion in an appropriation bill. Almost without exception Congress has honored the decisions of the Court of Claims. Today the Court of Claims is thought of as a specialized unit of the court system of the United States.

In 1946, as a part of the Legislative Reorganization Act of that year, Congress enacted the Federal Tort Claims Act. The statute appeared to extend federal government liability to any property damage or personal injury or death "caused by the negligent or wrongful act or omission of any employee of the government while acting within the scope of his office or employment, under circumstances where the United States, if a private person, would be liable. . . . " The consideration of such damage claims was assigned to federal district courts. The statute recognized that Congress would have to continue to consider claims which would arise out of certain kinds of circumstances, such as the exercise or failure to exercise a discretionary duty, or claims arising from false arrest, false imprisonment, assault, claims arising from regulation of monetary and fiscal affairs, claims from combatant service in the Armed Forces, or claims arising from carrying the mails.

Under the provisions of the Federal Tort Claims Act heads of administrative agencies may settle any tort claim up to $1,000. If the administrator's judgment does not satisfy the claimant, he may then institute a suit in a federal district court. Or if the claim is greater than $1,000, it must be brought originally in a district court. An appeal lies to the Court of Claims or a Court of Appeals. If the claimant is still not satisfied, he may, of course, seek direct legislative assistance. In construing the terms of the 1946 law, the courts have tended to limit governmental liability to a considerable degree.[20]

Many states have followed similar arrangements. Administrative officials are permitted to settle small claims, whereas special or regular courts review larger claims. When judgment is rendered in favor of the claimant, the legislature then includes the item in an appropriation measure.

Under the common law a number of standards were developed in fixing liability for damages done by one person to another. Thus from the "master-servant" rule, liability is usually not fixed unless the damage occurred during an act of employment, that is, while the administrative officer was actually on duty. The government does not accept liability if an employee commits some damage beyond the terms of his authority. Under these circumstances the individual may be sued in his personal capacity for an act *ultra vires*. Sometimes a government will not accept liability suffered by an employee in an especially hazardous occupation.

---

[20] Cf. Walter Gellhorn and Louis Lauer, "Federal Liability for Personal and Property Damage," *New York University Law Review,* vol. 29 (November, 1954), p. 1325.

And if there is some contributory negligence on the part of the individual suffering damage, or if the tort occurs during trespass upon governmental property, no damage may be allowed.

There can be no doubt but that both the law of governmental liability and the machinery for determining liability are something less than satisfactory in the United States. In general, there is no regular system for judicial determination of an injurious act on the part of administrative officials. Some torts are handled by courts, entailing a degree of judicial review of administrative behavior. To a considerable extent legislatures continue to handle many claims on an individual basis, opening the possibility that not all claims will receive an equal and fair consideration on their merits. More than this, both the statutory law and the judicial decisions on governmental tort liability are confused and generally inadequate.

Thus, within this field of torts inflicted by administrative officials, there is a limited degree of judicial review, depending upon the statutes enacted by the federal or state legislature. There is a limited degree of law covering acts which will be considered by the courts as imposing liability upon the government.

Much still remains to be done through statutory enactment and perhaps through enlarged jurisdiction conferred upon courts to create an adequate system of governmental tort liability. Under existing circumstances the citizen may expect only a limited extent of judicial protection from damages inflicted by an administrative employee or from chance circumstance involving a governmental activity. Some further degree of protection is afforded by the practice of direct legislative consideration of individual claims. All these arrangements leave a good deal of uncertainty about the actual recourse an individual may have when he has suffered a governmental tort.

Chapter 23

Due Process in Administrative Procedure

In recent years a good deal of attention has been focused upon two particular phases of administrative activity. One of these is the procedure employed in administrative rule making. The other is the procedure employed in administrative adjudication.

We have already noticed the role of the judiciary in erecting safeguards for the process of delegating so-called legislative power and judicial power to administrative agencies. Especially in the instance of the rule-making power the courts have insisted that adequate standards must be established to guide the administrative agency. In so far as adjudicative power is concerned, usually the courts have insisted upon an adequate scope of judicial review, a subject we shall consider in the next chapter.

Beyond this dual concern for adequate standards to guide administrative rule making and an adequate scope for judicial review of administrative adjudication, the courts have been concerned also that administrative agencies shall observe certain procedural safeguards in the exercise of this rule-making and this adjudicative function. These procedural safeguards constitute a kind of administrative "due process" which courts expect administrative agencies to observe.

The phrase "due process of law" first appeared in the Fifth Amendment to the Constitution of the United States adopted December 15, 1791. Among other things this amendment declared that no person should be "deprived of life, liberty, or property, without due process of law." This amendment was a restriction upon the federal government. Subsequently, the Fourteenth Amendment to the Federal Constitution adopted July 28, 1868, declared: "nor shall any State deprive any person of life, liberty, or property, without due process of law." Thus the same restriction previously placed upon the operation of the federal government was extended to the operation of each state government.

Edward S. Corwin has said of these two clauses that "from the point of view of constitutional limitations on power, and so from the point of view of the control exercised by the Supreme Court, through judicial review, upon the powers of government, whether state or national, in the United States . . . [they] are the most important clauses of the Constitution."[1] The phrase "due process of law" referred to a concept derived from the common law. It meant that in any trial at court where a person's life, liberty, or property was involved, certain definite procedures were to be followed. These procedures centered in such criminal law requirements as those of indictment, trial by jury, the right to summon witnesses on one's own behalf, the right not to be required to testify against oneself, the right to be represented by counsel, and the right to question witnesses against the individual. In civil trial where a person's property was at stake, many of these same procedural safeguards in the judicial process came to be recognized.

In the course of a long series of judicial decisions by state and federal courts, the constitutional provisions against depriving a person of his life, liberty, or property without due process of law have come to have three meanings. The first meaning has to do with the substance of legislation. The Supreme Court has several times held that legislation enacted by the Congress or by a state legislature must be *reasonable* in its substance if it is to pass the test of due process of law. Thus, a state law outlawing the yellow-dog contract—that is, outlawing the promise exacted from a worker that during the course of his employment he would not join a labor union—was once declared unconstitutional by the United States Supreme Court on the grounds that it deprived a person of his liberty without due process of law.[2] The difficulty with so-called substantive due process is that it substitutes the judgment of the court for that of the legislative body about what is reasonable public policy, especially in the field of economic regulation. Although in recent years the Supreme Court has tended to be cautious about exercising its public policy role, it continues to do so in various types of cases.

In the second place, due process of law sets up certain standards in the handling of civil and criminal proceedings by the courts. The Supreme Court often insists that lower federal courts and state courts shall make sure that all the requirements of due process are fully observed in judicial proceedings before them. And in the third place, there is a kind of "administrative due process" which the courts expect administrative agencies to observe in the exercise of their authority. It is this third aspect of due process of law which is our concern in the present chapter.

[1] Edward S. Corwin, *The Constitution and What It Means Today*, 10th ed. (Princeton, N.J.: Princeton University Press, 1948), p. 168.
[2] *Coppage v. Kansas*, 236 U.S. 1 (1915).

CONTROL OF RULE MAKING

At the end of the 1920s a Lord Chief Justice of Great Britain unleashed a vigorous attack upon what he termed the "New Despotism."[3] The object of his condemnation was the growing practice in Parliament of providing in statutes that Ministers might issue rules and regulations to carry out the purposes of law. To the Lord Chief Justice this practice was a violation of the "law of the land," of constitutional practice whereby statutes were to be written by the Parliament. The practice of ministerial "law-making," as well as that of administrative adjudication, was a new form of despotism contrary to British governmental tradition.

The result of this attack was the appointment in 1929 by the Lord High Chancellor of a Committee on Ministers' Powers. In 1932 this committee submitted its report to the Chancellor who in turn laid the document before Parliament.[4] The Committee acknowledged at the outset the criticism of those who considered the practice of administrative rule making "wholly bad," a practice which "should be forthwith abandoned." The Committee reported its general conclusion to be that the practice had "definite advantages, provided that the statutory powers are exercised and the statutory functions performed in the right way."[5] It then went on to declare that whether good or bad, "the development is inevitable." "It is a natural reflection, in the sphere of constitutional law, of changes in our ideas of government which have resulted from changes in political, social, and economic ideas, and of changes in the circumstances of our lives which have resulted from scientific discoveries."[6]

Much of the same kind of conclusion has been reached by those official bodies which have considered the same problem in this country.[7] For example, in 1955, the second Hoover Commission declared: "The administrative process has been developed and utilized by the Congress primarily because regulatory action requires attention to a multitude of details and situations which cannot be met by statutory enactment. Congress declares policy, prescribes standards defining agency action, and entrusts to the agencies of the executive branch the function of completing the process of control."[8]

[3] Lord Hewart of Bury, *The New Despotism* (London: Ernest Benn, Ltd., 1929).
[4] Committee on Ministers' Powers, *Report,* Cmd. 4060 (London: His Majesty's Stationery Office, 1932).
[5] *Ibid.,* pp. 4–5.   [6] *Ibid.,* p. 5.
[7] See in particular, Attorney General's Committee on Administrative Procedure, *Administrative Procedure in Government Agencies,* Sen. Doc. 8, 77th Cong., 1st Sess. (1940); and Robert M. Benjamin, Moreland Commissioner, *Administrative Adjudication in the State of New York,* Report to the Hon. Herbert H. Lehman, Governor (1942).
[8] Commission on Organization of the Executive Branch of the Government, *Legal Services and Procedures,* a report to the Congress (Washington: Government Printing Office, 1955), pp. 53–54.

If we accept the indispensability of administrative rule making—and legislatures, official inquiries, students of government, and courts have all reached this conclusion—the problem then is how to maintain some oversight of such rule making to ensure that administrative authority is exercised "in the right way." There are several broad answers to this problem. One is to make administrative rule making tentative only and to require some form of legislative approval before the rules become effective. Another is to establish broad statutory prescription over the exercise of administrative rule making. A third is for the courts to exercise a close control over administrative procedure in rule making. These three forms of control are not mutually exclusive.

The practice of legislative control over administrative rule making is not particularly well developed in the United States. Perhaps the best example of the practice is to be found in the field of handling the deportation of aliens. Under the Alien Registration Act of June 28, 1940, the Attorney General may issue an order suspending the deportation of an alien illegally resident in the United States under certain standards. Such orders must be reported to the Congress and both houses by concurrent resolution may disapprove any suspension. If a suspension order is not disapproved by the Congress at its next regular session, the alien is considered a legal resident.[9] This is not an exact illustration, since a suspension order is not a rule of general applicability but an exception to a statutory requirement. But in this instance each individual order does have to be submitted by a department head to the legislature for review.

In certain other instances from time to time Congress has required the head of a department to lay orders before the legislature for a period of time; such orders become effective only after a specified interval during which the legislature might take action to modify or override the order. Thus, under the Atomic Energy Act of 1946 the Atomic Energy Commission is forbidden to issue any license for the manufacture or export of equipment utilizing fissionable materials without first reporting the intention to issue such license or licenses to the Congress. The report must lie before Congress for ninety days while the legislature is in session before administrative action is taken. In this way the Congress tried to ensure an opportunity by law to prevent any licensing action to which it might object.[10]

It is conceivable that a legislature might require a wide variety of administrative rules and regulations to lie before that body for a stated period of time before becoming effective. There are certain disadvantages to any such general practice. The more rules and regulations which require legislative consideration, the greater becomes the burden upon the legislature.

[9] Harvey C. Mansfield, "The Legislative Veto and the Deportation of Aliens," *Public Administration Review,* vol. 1 (Spring, 1941), p. 281.
[10] Sec. 7(b), 60 Stat. 755.

Moreover, the legislature, or legislative committees, might have to give attention to a great many details which would take a considerable amount of time to master. In addition, the requirement of issuing rules which would become effective only at the end of the next session of the legislature would cause some delay in putting needed regulations into effect. The modification of such rules would also be time-consuming. In any event, legislatures have not seen fit to introduce any widespread practice of controlling administrative rules and regulations through a requirement of their specific review. This has made the other two types of control more important.

The Congress in enacting the Federal Administrative Procedure Act of June 11, 1946, included a section on rule making. There were three kinds of exceptions to the law's requirements: rules involving military, naval, or foreign affairs functions; rules relating to agency management or personnel; and rules concerning public property, loans, grants, benefits, or contracts. Otherwise, any administrative agency was required to issue general notice of a proposed rule or regulation, stating the authority under which the rule was to be issued, describing the rule-making procedure to be followed, and providing the terms or substance of the proposed rule. This provision for general notice did not apply, however, to any general declaration of policy, to an interpretative rule, to rules for agency organization or procedure, or to any situation where notice and hearing would be contrary to the public interest. Secondly, an agency was to afford interested persons an opportunity to submit written data and arguments. A public hearing might be held in the discretion of the agency. When the rules were issued, a general statement of their basis and purpose was to be incorporated within them. In the third place, a rule or regulation was to be published or served upon interested parties not less than thirty days prior to the effective date. Finally, an agency was to accord an interested person the right to petition for the issuance, repeal, or amendment of a rule. There has been a tendency in many states to enact similar requirements.[11]

When the legislature enacts a general statute setting forth procedures or due process to be observed in administrative rule making, the law has the effect of establishing general requirements. The enforcement of these general requirements must then fall upon the courts. It is interesting to note that federal and state administrative procedure laws have insisted upon certain procedural safeguards in the exercise of administrative authority to make rules. In the process of enforcing these requirements, the court may still be guided in its judgment by its own concept of what constitutes administrative due process. It is the judiciary, therefore, which

---

[11] See Ferrel Heady, *Administrative Procedure Legislation in the States,* Michigan Governmental Studies no. 24 (Ann Arbor, Mich.: University of Michigan Institute of Public Administration, 1952), chap. 3.

remains as the basic element of government in exercising some oversight of administrative rule making.

TYPES OF ADMINISTRATIVE RULES

Before we discuss further judicial concern with administrative rules, it is important to recognize that there is a great variety of administrative rule making. No two agencies may necessarily have the same problems with which to deal or the same kinds of activity to administer. For this reason there has to be some variety in the procedural safeguards which surround rule making. For example, many administrative agencies issue rules or regulations which establish their internal administrative organization, which define the authority of particular administrative officials within the agency, and which do not necessarily affect adversely the clientele of an agency or any other individual.

A second kind of rule or regulation may be a broad statement of policy. Usually policy declarations are not thought of as rules or regulations at all. For example, it was a broad matter of policy for the Veterans' Administration at the end of World War II to decide to locate new veterans' hospitals adjacent to existing medical schools and large medical centers. It is a matter of broad policy when a state university decides, within the limitations of state law, to charge students from outside the state larger fees than those charged students who are residents of the state. It is a matter of broad policy when a state highway department decides that new highways shall avoid congested urban areas and skirt small villages. Every administrative agency must make such policy decisions as these. And such policy decisions necessarily have some impact upon the liberty or property of individual citizens.

In the third place, an agency may issue interpretative rules. These rules set forth the meaning an agency proposes to give to the wording of a statute. A statute may apply to "small business" but fail to establish a definition of what constitutes smallness in business enterprise. A tax statute may make certain exceptions for the "self-employed" but fail to define the circumstances of such self-employment. In these situations the administrative agency is left to issue interpretative rules. These do not apply to any specific persons or any given set of circumstances. They are simply general statements of administrative purpose.

Then there are the actual substantive rules and regulations which an agency may issue in accordance with statutory authority. An agency is authorized to establish rules fixing standards of air safety, of meat or milk proper for public distribution, of grazing on the public domain, of discount requirements in banking operations, of reserves for insurance companies, etc. Such rules and regulations carry out the purpose of law, amplify or supplement its provisions, and in themselves have the force of law.

Then there are orders which apply to individual persons or objects. Such orders are usually thought of as adjudicative rather than rule making in character, but the distinction is not an easy one to make. Thus an order fixing the prices to be charged by a particular utility is often said to be legislative, or quasi-legislative, in character. Thus, it does in effect appear to be supplementary to legislative enactment. As a general proposition, however, it seems more satisfactory to think of rule making as the issuance of regulations of general applicability to persons in like circumstances, or the announcement of general purposes or procedures rather than the making of determinations which affect specific persons or situations.

There are still other distinctions to be made in administrative rule making. For procedural purposes much may depend upon the character of the parties affected, the nature of the problems dealt with, the character of the administrative determination, the type of administrative agency involved, and the kind of enforcement involved.[12] If the parties affected are easily and readily identified as having a definite interest or stake in administrative action, then one kind of procedure may be reasonable. If the parties affected have only a general stake in the rule or regulation, procedural requirements may not be so exact. If the administrative determination has to do with the hours when an office is open for the transaction of public business or with the location of a public office, then procedural safeguards for such decisions are not likely to be imposed. On the other hand, if the administrative regulation has to do with some definite economic practice or operation, then procedural requirements are apt to be more stringent. Where the standard to be imposed is fairly technical or clearly requires the use of expert judgment, then procedural requirements may be fairly broad. Such might be the case in the decision of a board of health or of a health department on how to combat a threatened epidemic. If an emergency exists, then the requirements may be less exact. Or if a considerable range of discretion has been left to an administrative agency, and there are definite choices to be made, the courts will often be reluctant to impose rigorous procedural standards. If the type of function involved has to do with the granting of loans or the payment of benefits or with other service operations, the procedural restrictions are not likely to be very precise. If the function is regulatory of a particular business enterprise, then the procedural restrictions are more precise. If the result of a rule is to cut an individual off from a government benefit, the courts are not apt to be too rigorous in the procedural standards they insist

[12] Cf. Ralph F. Fuchs, "Procedure in Administrative Rule-making," *Harvard Law Review,* vol. 52 (1938), p. 259.

upon; if the result of a rule is to deprive a person of some liberty or property now enjoyed, the courts are likely to be rigorous in establishing the standards they expect an agency to observe.

Moreover, rule making often is expected to be based upon an investigation of facts. The courts may then wish to know how extensive was the actual fact-finding process. Sometimes an agency is expected to issue rules only after a kind of adversary procedure has been observed, providing an opportunity for opposing interests to present different points of view. Such circumstances, for example, have arisen in the determination of the Federal Communications Commission about the number and type of channels which should be available for commercial television operations and those which should be reserved for nonprofit educational television. In such circumstances courts wish to be reassured that opposing interests were given a full and fair opportunity to present their differing positions.

Some of these distinctions were observed in the provisions of the Federal Administrative Procedure Act of 1946. Thus, military and foreign affairs functions were exempt from the act. Furthermore, matters of internal management and of administrative personnel were placed outside the purview of the law. So also were rules involving loans, grants, and benefits, and even general declarations of policy. Sometimes these distinctions and exemptions are questioned, although the need for emergency rules and for secrecy requirements in certain circumstances has been acknowledged. In 1955 the second Hoover Commission urged that except in matters requiring secrecy in the public interest, or in matters relating solely to internal management, public participation through submission of written data and arguments should be afforded in all rule-making activity.[13] The advisory group to the Hoover Commission would have gone even further, not exempting matters of internal management.[14] As a practical matter, however, the courts do recognize substantial differences in rule-making requirements. The outline of procedural standards which follows is necessarily general in scope. These standards are not rigorously applied in any and every kind of administrative circumstance.

DUE PROCESS IN RULE MAKING

Depending upon the kind of rule making involved and the interests concerned, the courts have outlined several requirements for reasonable exercise of rule-making authority. The first requirement is one of notice of the substance of a proposed rule and an invitation to present evidence. The second requirement may be that of a hearing or other device for con-

[13] Commission on Organization of the Executive Branch of the Government, *op. cit.,* p. 56.

[14] Commission on Organization of the Executive Branch of the Government, *Task Force Report on Legal Services and Procedure,* March, 1955 (Washington: Government Printing Office, 1955), pp. 157–164.

sidering the points of view of affected interests. A third requirement may be that of setting forth the findings which have resulted in the issuance of a particular rule or regulation. A fourth requirement is that of publication of a rule or regulation before it becomes effective. Not all these requirements may exist in every kind of administrative rule making. Yet these are the essential elements of due process in rule making as they have developed in legislative prescription and court decision.

Notice. The importance of notice is obvious. If an affected individual is to be asked to comment about a proposed rule, or if a person or group is to have an opportunity to present evidence about the effect of a proposed rule, then he must know in advance the substance of the proposed rule or regulation. Without such notice there can be no effective participation by any affected person in the consideration of pending regulations.

Yet in the absence of a specific or general statutory requirement of advance notice of a particular rule, the courts will not necessarily demand that an administrative agency give notice before exercising its rule-making authority. For example, the defense of a milk producer that it had not been given an opportunity to be heard on a milk-control-board order fixing *minimum* prices for the sale of milk was not allowed as a justification for violation of the order.[15] Prior to the enactment of the Federal Administrative Procedure Act, the Supreme Court had held that a regulatory agency did not need to hold one hearing to investigate a reasonable minimum wage in the cotton industry and then give notice of another hearing on the specific minimum price fixed.[16] But where notice is essential, that notice must be adequate to give affected parties full knowledge of the substance of the proposed regulation. And the notice must be communicated effectively, through some form of publication or service to interested parties.

Hearing. When a hearing is held, two conditions are necessary. One is that the affected parties be given a full opportunity to present the details of their position. If anything, hearings before an administrative agency sometimes tend to be more detailed than those before a legislative committee. It is, of course, not necessary that the opportunity to present evidence be before a formal tribunal which hears and considers only oral testimony. Much of the data provided may be submitted in writing. The other condition is the assurance that all relevant points of view are considered. This may mean the investigation and presentation of evidence by the staff of the administrative agency itself. Here is one of the great differences between an administrative agency and a legislative committee. The committee may rely upon an administrative agency to take one point

[15] *State Board of Milk Control v. Newark Milk Company,* 179 A.N.J. 116 (1935).
[16] *Opp Cotton Mills, Inc. v. Administrator of the Wage and Hour Division of the Department of Labor,* 312 U.S. 126 (1941).

of view about some desired legislation and upon affected interests to take the opposing position. This does not always happen, but legislative committees often expect their hearings to provide conflicting points of view. An administrative agency engaged in rule making may have to take its own action to ensure presentation of a complete record.

Findings. In some instances, it is legally necessary, or at least administratively desirable, for an agency to make findings of fact before a rule is promulgated. These findings present a summary of the evidence presented and recite the basic considerations which have led to a particular rule or regulation. Such findings may satisfy the court that the purposes and reasoning behind a rule accord with statutory authority. Such findings may also help to convince the affected parties that an agency has given consideration to their point of view and may even help to win compliance. Where a statute requires that rule-making authority shall become effective only where certain facts or conditions exist, a finding of such facts to exist is an important element in obtaining judicial approval of the exercise of the rule-making power.

Publication. Finally, the rules or regulations as drafted by the agency must be published for the information and guidance of the affected parties. Prior to 1935 there was no definite system in the federal government for the publication of rules and regulations made by administrative agencies. That year the Congress passed the Federal Register Act which established the *Federal Register* as the official means for publishing administrative rules. For the most part only substantive rules tend to be published; agencies neglect to send to the National Archives a vast array of informational material such as interpretations of rules, opinions or explanatory statements accompanying a rule, administrative orders on internal organization and procedure, announcements about the creation of field offices, and similar material.[17]

It has not been practicable to establish one authoritative source where an individual can go and find out everything he needs to know about administrative rules to which he is subject. In the first place, the number and variety of administrative agencies make this idea difficult if not impossible to realize. In the second place, the variety of published materials put out by an agency complicates the situation. And in the third place, administrative changes in policy and rules often create a lag between action and publication, or at least between action and widespread distribution of publications. It is no simple matter to provide an adequate system of publication, and the courts have been reluctant to press for any one kind of publication of administrative rules.

These then are the more or less definite standards of procedure which

[17] Cf. Frank C. Newman, "Government and Ignorance: A Progress Report on Publication of Federal Regulations," *Harvard Law Review,* vol. 63 (April, 1950), p. 929.

administrative agencies are expected to follow in the exercise of their rule-making authority. Not all agencies are subject to these same standards in exactly the same way. But in reviewing the procedural phases of rule making, the courts will usually desire some reassurance on these items if the exercise of authority is to be considered as reasonable and as meeting statutory requirements.

ADJUDICATION

Procedure is even more important in the case of adjudicative action undertaken by an administrative agency. Usually, adjudication occurs in the exercise of a regulatory authority establishing some norm of legal conduct for an individual or depriving a person of a license to do business. But not all adjudicative action is regulatory. It also occurs in workmen's compensation cases, in cases where benefits or privileges are sought by or denied to specific individuals, as in claims for veterans' disability pensions. In the exercise of regulatory authority over economic and certain other interests, the courts have insisted usually upon a fairly precise regard for procedural safeguards. This concern has been reinforced by statutory requirements. On the other hand, there is a great deal of administrative action which is adjudicative in nature but much more informal in practice. In some instances laws provide that the administrator's discretion shall be final, as in determining veterans' benefits or home relief payments. The process of determination may involve some internally established procedure for a hearing, especially if the initial determination is protested by the individual concerned. But the legislature and the courts have tended to consider adjudication of benefits and of so-called privileges (such as immigration and personnel matters) in a different light from adjudication of a strictly regulatory nature.

The requirements of due process in administrative adjudication are established by specific statute, by general statute, and by court decisions. In the federal government the Administrative Procedure Act of 1946 established certain general requirements. These will be noted in subsequent paragraphs. State administrative procedure laws contain similar provisions. The exceptions to the federal law once again extend to the conduct of military, naval, or foreign affairs functions, and to governmental personnel matters. In addition, several special types of situations were exempted. One was any matter subject to trial of both facts and law *de novo* in a court of law subsequent to the administrative action. A second exemption was any instance in which an administrative agency might serve as an agent for a court of law. A third was any proceeding in which decisions rested solely on inspections, tests, or elections. And a fourth was any proceeding involving the certification of employee representatives for collective bargaining purposes.

Notice. In adjudicative procedure the requirements of notice are more exact than in rule making. Under the Federal Administrative Procedure Act, in those instances where a formal hearing is required by statute or by court decision, the persons directly concerned or involved in administrative adjudication must receive notice which provides information about the time, place, and nature of a hearing, the legal authority and jurisdiction under which the hearing is to be held, and the "matters of fact and law asserted." The act further specifies that the time of a hearing shall be fixed with "due regard" for the convenience of the parties and their representatives.

The especial care to ensure adequacy of notice which the courts insist upon in administrative adjudication is understandable. In most such cases important property or personal rights are at stake, and the individual concerned is entitled to know specifically what the issues are and how and where a hearing will be conducted. Thus, the administrative agency must usually take steps to ensure that the individual parties receive direct notice of a hearing by personal service of papers or by registered mail. Furthermore, the notice must provide adequate information about the facts and law which are in controversy. If an agency does not provide adequate notice, its proceeding may subsequently be held to violate due process of law.

Yet it is up to the individual involved to make a point during an administrative hearing that he has not been given an adequate bill of particulars of the complaint against him. He cannot usually participate in a hearing and then subsequently complain that he was not provided adequate information about the charges against him. For example, if a hearing is called for one matter, such as excess use of power under terms of a radio license, and then broadens out into a hearing on other matters, the procedure is not necessarily invalid unless the applicant for renewal of a radio license actually complains during the hearing itself.[18] Similarly, if sufficient detail is not provided at the beginning of a hearing but develops during the course of a hearing which continues over a considerable period of time, then the proceeding may still meet the requirements of due process of law.[19]

The requirements of adequate notice, and even of hearing, cause particular difficulty in administrative action brought under the police power. Such power, of course, is the authority to act to protect public health, safety, and morals and is most frequently exercised by administrative agencies of state government. Where there are cases involving the destruction of dangerous or diseased food or liquids, the quarantining of persons having a contagious disease, or the confiscation of property in and of it-

[18] *Brahy v. Federal Radio Commission,* 59 F.2d 879 (1932).
[19] *National Labor Relations Board v. Remington Rand, Inc.,* 94 F.2d 862 (1938).

self illegal such as gambling equipment—in these cases most courts tend to agree that administrative action may proceed in summary fashion.

Moreover, the kind of action being taken by an administrative agency may make a difference. No formal notice and proceeding is ordinarily required in an application for a license when an agency undertakes an investigation and then decides to issue the requested permit. It is only in case of the revocation of a license, or instances where an agency is inclined not to issue the license, that formal practices of notice and of hearing are likely to be regarded as necessary by the courts.

Hearings. One of the important characteristics of administrative adjudication is that disposition of a case may be made without the formality of a hearing. The result of notice and preliminary investigation is not necessarily a hearing; the result even more often may be dismissal of the charge or an agreement to change behavior. Such an outcome speeds the administrative process, although it may also result in some abuse. The pressure upon the cited party to come to some agreement may be heavy; in other instances, the agreement may not be entirely in the public interest. Yet the fact remains that only in the most important conflicts involving substantial issues or an unreconcilable interpretation of facts and law does a formal hearing occur.

The hearing as used in administrative adjudication presents a number of special problems. For example, shall the agency allow other interested parties beyond the two immediately concerned to intervene in the proceeding? In the absence of statutory provision to the contrary, intervention is a privilege controlled by the discretion of the administrative agency. A more important question is that of compelling testimony. Many regulatory agencies have statutory authority to issue a subpoena directing a respondent to produce books and papers. Much of the prehearing preparation of a case may rest upon such an investigation. Agencies may also inspect the operations of a person or business corporation and may require the filing of reports. The courts usually insist that only the judiciary, not an administrative agency, may punish for contempt when a person refuses to produce papers and documents. Thus the courts obtain an opportunity to examine the legal validity of an inquiry and its reasonable conduct. But naturally the question arises of the extent to which the respondent should obtain administrative assistance in summoning witnesses and papers for his own defense. Section 6 of the Federal Administrative Procedure Act requires federal agencies to issue subpoenas to any party upon request and upon a showing of general relevance and reasonable scope of the evidence sought. An administrative agency may be understandably reluctant, however, to honor a demand

[20] Frank E. Cooper, *Administrative Agencies and the Courts* (Ann Arbor, Mich.: University of Michigan Law School, 1951), pp. 74–76.

to produce all its own records in a case other than those used in the actual hearing itself.

A major problem is the extent to which an administrative hearing must correspond to that of a court of law. Should a hearing be conducted with considerable informality rather than with the full formality of courtroom procedure? In some instances an informal arrangement may be justified and will be sustained by the courts. But administrative agencies have usually learned that in cases where vital personal and property rights are at stake, a considerable degree of formality is desirable in order to convince a court subsequently that the hearing was fair. The respondent may usually insist upon being represented by counsel; such a right is provided by the Federal Administrative Procedure Act. The respondent may claim prejudice on the part of an examiner or investigator, or charge that the orderly presentation of his evidence was interfered with. The respondent may expect that the place where a hearing is conducted will be convenient for him. He may expect that the agency's rules for conducting a hearing will be fairly observed. In cases where trade secrets are involved, a respondent may desire a private rather than a public hearing. The respondent may reasonably expect that all the evidence to be used in deciding his case will be presented at the hearing. But the evidence does not have to be oral; it may be documentary. Section 7 of the Federal Administrative Procedure Act permits a party in a hearing "to conduct such cross-examination as may be required for a full and true disclosure of the facts." And the right to a hearing implies the right to present all the evidence which is material and relevant to the issue. All these aspects of procedure may still be realized in an atmosphere less formal than that of a courtroom, but the courts can be expected to be concerned that the administrative proceeding was fairly conducted.

Then there is the question whether the common-law, or technical, rules of evidence shall apply in administrative hearings. Most administrative agencies do not use such rules, and the courts have not insisted upon such a practice. Yet the departure from these rules is not so great as some persons have supposed. Administrative agencies may insist that evidence be relevant and may protect themselves from the endless offering of repetitious, immaterial, or irrelevant evidence. Furthermore, an agency is expected to rely upon "substantial evidence" of probative value. In 1955 the second Hoover Commission recommended that in administrative adjudication "the rules of evidence and requirements of proof as found in civil non-jury cases in the United States district courts shall be applied, so far as practicable, except that the admission of evidence not admissible under such rules and requirements shall not be deemed ground for reversal."[21] The Supreme Court a number of years ago held that the mere admission by an administrative agency of evidence which in a judicial pro-

[21] Commission on Organization of the Executive Branch of the Government, *Legal Services and Procedures* (Washington: Government Printing Office, 1955), p. 72.

ceeding would be excluded did not invalidate a subsequent agency order.[22] An administrative agency may receive hearsay evidence. It may hear expressions of opinion from a witness. It may receive statements by expert witnesses whose technical competence is only sketchily established. But these practices are usually followed with some caution by administrative agencies. Moreover, agencies are expected to recognize that some communications, as between client and attorney or patient and physician, are privileged. The major problem is the extent of the right of cross-examination as a means of testing the value of evidence. The courts may not expect administrative agencies to observe strict judicial rules of evidence but they nonetheless expect the evidence used in an order to be "substantial," and this will usually mean that a good proportion of the testimony is technically competent by judicial standards.

One problem in administrative adjudication is the extent to which an agency shall utilize expert or technical knowledge acquired from long, specialized experience but which is not specifically introduced as evidence during the hearing. To be sure, an administrative agency may reasonably be expected to draw upon its accumulated expert knowledge in the process of making decisions. Since the burden of proof in administrative adjudication usually rests upon the party appearing before it, an agency does not specifically have to refute the evidence presented by that individual. Thus, for example, an agency need not accept the valuation of property claimed by the expert witness for the owner who testifies before the hearing, even though its own evidence of a different value is not specifically presented during the hearing. This kind of latitude permitted by the courts is applicable, however, only to generalized knowledge. If an agency has in its possession any detailed information gathered in connection with the particular controversy before it, then the agency is expected to present it. The doctrine of the legal right of an agency to give "official notice" to facts and knowledge acquired over a long period of time is limited to specialized circumstances, such as the general determinations of an industrial accident commission about what constitutes a traumatic injury. Section 7 of the Federal Administrative Procedure Act requires an agency proposing to base a decision on "official notice" of a material fact not incorporated into the specific record of an individual controversy to afford the other party an opportunity to show the contrary. If the agency fails to advise the party of the assumed facts which it proposes to notice, or fails to provide an opportunity to a party to refute or explain those facts, then there has been a denial of due process of law to the individual party.[23]

Administrative agencies with regulatory authority are usually headed by

---

[22] *Interstate Commerce Commission v. Abilene and Southern Railway Co.,* 265 U.S. 274 (1924).

[23] Cf. *Ohio Bell Telephone Company v. Public Utilities Commission of Ohio,* 301 U.S. 292 (1937).

a board or commission. The right to a hearing does not necessarily mean that the hearing must be conducted before the full board or commission. If this were necessary, the burden would prevent an agency from considering any but a few major controversies each year. Instead, the uniform practice is generally followed and recognized whereby an agency designates a hearing officer to take testimony. A great responsibility for the proper conduct of an administrative hearing thus falls upon this officer. Yet at the conclusion of the hearing the actual decision may not rest with the hearing officer. In 1936 the Supreme Court declared that one of the fundamentals of due process was that the one who decides must exercise a personal judgment concerning the matters he decides. It was not sufficient for an administrative officer simply to sign the papers.[24] Yet it has become evident from subsequent court decisions that it is not necessary for all the members of a board or commission personally to consider a matter; the board may divide itself into panels. Nor is it essential that a board or administrator must decide; a hearing officer may decide. The decision may be made by a board or commission after review of the record and after discussion of the findings with the hearing officer.

Section 8 of the Federal Administrative Procedure Act sets forth a standard of fair adjudicative practice. The hearing officer may make a decision upon the basis of the evidence presented to him; when he does so and in the absence of an appeal by the affected party or a motion to review by the agency itself, then his decision becomes the decision of the agency itself. If the agency asks the hearing officer to certify the record to it for initial decision, then the hearing officer is required to prepare a recommended decision. When an agency considers the hearing officer's decision on appeal or review, then the agency itself is expected to examine the issues over again except as it may limit the issues by order or rule.

The Administrative Procedure Act goes on to specify that before any initial, tentative, or review decision is made, the parties shall be given a reasonable opportunity to submit to the officer or officers concerned proposed findings and conclusion, exceptions to a recommended or tentative decision, and supporting reasons for such proposed findings and conclusion and for such exceptions. Finally, the act requires that all decisions shall include a statement of findings and conclusions, with reasons therefor, upon all the material facts, law, or discretion presented in the record, as well as a statement of the appropriate order, sanction, or relief which is granted or denied.

In outline, these are the principal areas of concern in administrative adjudication to which the courts have given attention and in which statutory enactment has provided some definite guides. An administrative agency engaged in an adjudicative activity is expected to observe these standards of fair practice if it is not later to encounter judicial criticism

[24] *Morgan v. United States*, 298 U.S. 468 (1936).

of having ignored statutory requirements or of having deprived a person of life, liberty, or property, without due process of law.

SEPARATION OF THE INVESTIGATIVE AND ADJUDICATIVE FUNCTIONS

As the practice of administrative adjudication has grown, some criticism has been directed at the regulatory agency upon the ground that it combines both the investigative function and the judicial function. It has been said that a combination of these functions in the hands of one agency must necessarily result in an unfair hearing for a private party. The same agency is both prosecutor and judge. Does this arrangement not violate the very fundamental conception of proper procedure under due process of law?

This question has aroused a good deal of concern in recent years. An essential element of the administrative process in dealing with complex economic problems is the utilization of a variety of procedures for carrying out a basic public policy. For example, the promotion of civilian aviation includes the licensing (or certificating) of commercial airline routes to avoid unnecessary or uneconomical duplication of service, the promulgation of air safety regulations, and the operation of air directional and landing systems. All these activities together—involving the regulation of competition, the issuance of rules, and the provision of service—are necessary to the basic public policy of encouraging a healthy commercial aviation business under private operation. Many other activities of government involve a similar combination of functions, from rule making to administrative adjudication. To suggest any clearly defined separation of these functions may divide the execution of public policy into confusing bits and pieces. More than this, often public policy is developed mainly through a consideration of specific problems. Both investigation and decision in an adjudicative procedure may be required to enable an agency to give concrete meaning to such concepts as "fair trade," "collective bargaining," "adequate service," and other broad declarations of public policy.[25]

In discussing this problem of the combination of the role of prosecutor and judge in a single administrative agency, the Attorney General's Committee on Administrative Procedure insisted that two points should be borne in mind. First, an administrative agency is composed of many persons, and although the agency may be entrusted with a variety or combination of functions, the internal administrative organization of that agency can achieve a considerable degree of separation among these activities. Secondly, the Committee pointed out that the actual functions combined within administrative agencies might vary a great deal from one

[25] For an early development of this thesis, see James M. Landis, *The Administrative Process* (New Haven, Conn.: Yale University Press, 1938).

agency to another. Generalizations about how these functions were exercised in practice were difficult to make. The Committee also pointed to the confusion and the lack of consistency in administrative action which might arise if two agencies were created where only one had existed before. The Committee concluded that impartiality in the conduct of administrative hearings could be achieved within the structure of regulatory agencies by an internal separation of investigative from adjudicative functions.[26]

Section 5 of the Federal Administrative Procedure Act of 1946 in general followed the proposal of the Attorney General's Committee. It specified that no official of an agency engaged in the performance of investigative or prosecuting functions should then participate in the decision of the subsequent hearing. This did not apply to actual members of an administrative board or commission but rather to the subordinate officials of an agency. Just how effective the 1946 legislation has been or will be is still difficult to determine. One commentator shortly after its enactment expressed the opinion that the statute had "crystallized some devices for the administrative adjudicative process which have undoubtedly attacked some of the evils apparent in that process, and it may be instrumental in developing public confidence in its fairness, which would be an accomplishment of no mean worth."[27]

In 1955 the second Hoover Commission went a step further. It recognized that a board or commission would have to assign the initiation of investigations and prosecutions to members of the staff. The Commission then suggested that there be no subsequent consultation between the members of the board or commission and the staff who carried on the inquiry. "The expert advice and help which the agency members then require can and should be furnished by special review staffs or assistants."[28] In other words, the Hoover Commission wanted these regulatory agencies to recognize an internal separation of investigative and adjudicative functions all the way to the very top, up to the agency members themselves.

It is uncertain just how far the courts may go in insisting upon the internal separation of the investigative or prosecuting function from the adjudicative function of administrative agencies. Certainly the courts are aware of the problem.[29] They may be expected to examine this aspect of administrative procedure from time to time in order to make certain that the fundamentals of due process have not been violated. But the courts have also been understandably reluctant to press their interest in separa-

---

[26] Attorney General's Committee on Administrative Procedure, *op. cit.*, pp. 55–60.
[27] Milton M. Carrow, *The Background of Administrative Law* (Newark, N.J.: Associated Lawyers Publishing Company, 1948), p. 111.
[28] Commission on Organization of the Executive Branch of the Government, *op. cit.*, p. 62.
[29] Cf. *Wong Yang Sung v. McGrath*, 339 U.S. 33 (1950).

tion of function too far lest they destroy the very effectiveness of the administrative process itself. To the extent that changes have been introduced in administrative organization in the direction of a greater separation of the investigative from the adjudicative function, this has been directed by the executive or the legislature rather than the courts.[30]

CONCLUSION

Administrative agencies which exercise far-reaching power over the life and property of the individual citizen or the private corporation must give careful attention to their internal procedures. The courts are much concerned to ensure that, in the process of supplementing legislative intent through rules and regulations and in the process of applying broad declarations of public policy to individual cases through adjudication, administrative agencies observe fundamentals of due process. This does not mean that an administrative agency must behave exactly like a legislature in enacting rules. It does not mean that an administrative agency must behave exactly like a court in hearing a case. It does mean essentially that administrative agencies must give the individual a fair opportunity to present his point of view and to offer his explanation or defense of any conduct which is called into question. An administrative agency disposed to arbitrary or unfair action in its rule-making and adjudicative functions is likely to encounter subsequent judicial disapproval.

Administrative agencies can do much to control the extent of judicial concern with their activities by a careful handling of their procedures in order to ensure due process of law in those sensitive areas of administrative activity involving the person and the property of private parties.

[30] See the discussion earlier in chaps. 5–7. See also Nathaniel L. Nathanson, "Central Issues of American Administrative Law," *American Political Science Review*, vol. 45 (June, 1951), p. 348.

Chapter 24

Judicial Review of Administrative Decisions

Judicial supervision of administrative activities involves a basic question which both legislatures and courts have endeavored to answer: under what circumstances and to what extent shall the judiciary review administrative decisions. Obviously there are two extreme positions which may be taken on this issue. One extreme is to insist that all administrative activity shall be subject to judicial review. Such an answer might well have far-reaching results. It might hamper or delay administrative action on the one hand and swamp the judiciary on the other. Indeed, the substitution of judicial decision for administrative decision might even mean the transfer of administrative power to the judicial branch of government. This in turn would probably lead to endless friction with the legislative and executive branches about the respective roles of each in supervising administrative activity. The other extreme would be for the judiciary to relinquish any power to supervise administrative agencies at all. To take this position might well be for the courts to acquiesce in the illegal exercise of authority by administrative officials and to deny citizens the basic protection of the American constitutional system. Few would be willing to contemplate such an eventuality.

Mindful of the undesirable consequences of adopting either extreme, statutory law and constitutional doctrine have sought to make the judicial power meaningful in terms of exercising a limited—or we might say an appropriately judicial—restraint upon administrative action. The scope of judicial supervision over administration has been well summarized in these fourfold terms: (1) checking any administrative exercise of authority beyond that conferred by law; (2) providing a final interpretation of statutory intention, until the legislature clarifies a situation by further enactment; (3) requiring fair procedure in administrative action; and (4) disapproving any arbitrary or unreasonable exercise of administrative

446

authority.[1] In large part the courts themselves have developed these basic doctrines as a means for guiding their own role in reviewing the work of administrative agencies.

Where statutory provisions are not clear-cut, the courts themselves have sought to put limits upon the circumstances and conditions under which they will review administrative decisions. These efforts have not always been successful in providing an adequate basis in legal doctrine or principle for both administrative and judicial guidance. Yet the history of the judiciary, and of administrative law, in our country is a story of the courts' attempt to place boundary lines around their role in relation to administrative agencies.

One effort has been to classify certain kinds of action as involving purely "administrative" questions not presenting a legal issue. Just as the courts early declined to become involved with so-called political matters,[2] so have they refused to review what are called questions of administrative discretion.[3] For example, the refusal of an administrative agency to make a loan or grant to a given individual will not ordinarily be reviewed by the courts unless a clear case of unreasonable administrative discrimination can be established. If it is evident that an agency has acted within the limits of discretion conferred upon it by law, the courts generally will not go farther into the matter.

Early in the nation's history, the Supreme Court declared on one occasion: "The interference of the courts with the performance of the ordinary duties of the executive departments of the government would be productive of nothing but mischief."[4] On still another occasion, the same tribunal commented: "It has been repeatedly adjudged that the courts have no general supervising power over the proceedings and actions of the various administrative departments."[5] Accordingly, it may be said that the courts have not claimed an unlimited power of judicial review over administrative action. They have themselves imposed limits of self-restraint. In general, the courts tend to recognize that administrative agencies develop policy. In reviewing the exercise of administrative discretion in fixing policy goals, the courts apply certain common-law doctrines for the safeguard of the individual and interpret statutory meaning.

Another effort to limit the scope of judicial review has been to separate questions of fact from questions of law. Sometimes statutes provide that findings of fact, if based upon substantial evidence, shall not be reviewed

[1] Frank E. Cooper, *Administrative Agencies and the Courts* (Ann Arbor, Mich.: University of Michigan Law School, 1951), p. 305.
[2] Cf. *Luther v. Borden*, 7 How. 1 (1848); *Mississippi v. Johnson*, 7 Wall. 475 (1867); *Pacific States Telephone and Telegraph Co. v. Oregon*, 223 U.S. 118 (1912); and *Oetjen v. Central Leather Co.*, 246 U.S. 297 (1918).
[3] *Williamsport Wire Rope Co. v. United States*, 277 U.S. 551 (1928).
[4] *Decatur v. Paulding*, 14 Pet. 497 (1840).
[5] *Keim v. United States*, 177 U.S. 290 (1900).

by the courts. Sometimes the courts themselves have endeavored to make this same distinction. In actual practice, the distinction is not too satisfactory. We shall discuss this further in a moment.

Another judicial limitation has been the development of the doctrine that an injured party must seek all possible administrative remedies for his situation before resorting to the courts. For example, there is the doctrine that courts will not entertain a suit in law if there is an administrative remedy available to the aggrieved individual.[6] When one steamship company sought to enjoin another one from engaging in unfair competition, the courts refused to take jurisdiction on the grounds that a remedy was available through an administrative agency.[7] In this way the courts have usually discouraged any inclination to "short-circuit" the administrative process. The courts have also insisted that aggrieved individuals must exhaust all possible administrative consideration before seeking judicial review. A person may not appeal for judicial review while his case is pending before an administrative body, and he may not ask for judicial review if further opportunity for administrative review of his case is available. The courts are not always uniform in their ideas of just what constitutes exhaustion of administrative remedies. Sometimes a court may permit the issue of constitutionality of a particular statute to be raised before an administrative appeal is taken. There is some confusion, too, on the question whether an appeal must be taken to the head of an agency, such as the board or department head, before asking for court review. The Supreme Court appears at present to expect such an effort before considering a case.[8] Yet if an administrative agency delays unreasonably in deciding a case or in acting on a motion for rehearing, then the courts may be willing to step in. There are even instances in which the courts have insisted that a person cannot be helped by the courts because he failed to exhaust his administrative remedies when those remedies were no longer available to him. This is a somewhat unusual situation, however. In any event, the citizen and his lawyer involved in administrative adjudication are well advised to know carefully the remedies available to them in the procedural practice of an agency for full agency consideration of a case before resorting to the judicial process.[9]

In general, the concept of judicial self-restraint in handling cases involves both matters of procedure and substance. These have been well summarized in these terms. Procedurally, courts may exercise some control over their dockets, encouraging settlement or adjustment outside the

[6] *Texas and Panhandle Railway Co. v. Abilene Cotton Oil Co.*, 204 U.S. 426 (1907).
[7] *United States Navigation Co. v. Cunard Steamship Co., Ltd.*, 284 U.S. 474 (1932).
[8] *Levers v. Anderson*, 326 U.S. 219 (1945).
[9] The intricacies of this subject are outlined and the leading cases cited in Cooper, *op. cit.*, chap. 17.

court; appellate bodies, especially the Supreme Court, may in many instances simply refuse to review lower courts. In so far as substance is concerned, the Supreme Court of the United States will not review a political question, will not review a matter until some person is adversely affected by administrative action, and may refuse to review on the grounds that the judgment of an administrative body is not to be overturned by the court.[10] Thus there are many ways in which the courts may limit their jurisdiction in relation to administrative bodies.

METHODS OF OBTAINING JUDICIAL REVIEW

The simplest method of obtaining judicial review of administrative action is where a statute itself provides for such action. This is done in many statutes creating regulatory agencies. Furthermore, the Federal Administrative Procedure Act of 1946 provides a general statutory basis for judicial review, but this law does not apply to any circumstance in which an existing or subsequent law precludes judicial review or where "agency action is by law committed to agency discretion." The 1946 law goes on to say that any person suffering legal wrong because of agency action, or adversely affected by such action "within the meaning of any relevant statute," shall be entitled to judicial review.

Apart from statutory provisions for review of administrative action, there are three common-law writs ordinarily available to the aggrieved individual as a means of seeking relief from administrative action or inaction. These are the writs of certiorari, mandamus, and prohibition. The writ of certiorari is little used by federal courts in reviewing administrative decisions but is commonly employed by state courts. A writ of certiorari issued by a court requires an administrative agency to transfer, or certify, the record of some action it has taken. The court may then review some question of law on the face of the record or consider the question whether the action is irregular or illegal. Moreover, the prevailing doctrine is that a court will issue such a writ only when the action of the agency is adjudicative in nature, not when rule making or the exercise of administrative discretion is involved. Furthermore, the writ tends to be used as a kind of last resort, when some other means of obtaining judicial review is not available.

The writ of mandamus is available as a means for the court to demand or order that an administrative agency take some action. It is employed only where an administrative agency has a clear, nondiscretionary duty to perform, sometimes called a ministerial act. If administrative refusal to act violates some clearly defined legal right, the writ may be issued; if an administrative agency refuses to accept jurisdiction of some case clearly

---

[10] Cf. John P. Rocke, "Judicial Self-restraint," *American Political Science Review,* vol. 49 (September, 1955), p. 762.

belonging within its competence, then the writ may be issued. Here again, if some other form of relief is available to an aggrieved individual, the courts will usually refuse to issue the writ of mandamus.

The third writ, the writ of prohibition, is a court order to an agency to refrain from handling some particular matter. It is issued only on the single legal ground that an administrative agency lacks any statutory authority to take the contemplated action.

Certain other extraordinary remedies are available to an individual. The writ of habeas corpus may be used to challenge any alleged unlawful detention of the person. It may be employed to question police action, and it has also been used on occasion in quarantine matters and in alien extradition cases. It has been used to challenge military jurisdiction over civilians arrested and held by military authority; it may even be used to challenge the authority of military officials to compel an individual to serve in the military forces. A writ of quo warranto may be used to determine the legal authority of a particular individual to exercise the duties of a public office. In common law the writ may be sought only in the name of the state by the attorney general, but the latter may proceed on the petition of a private citizen. If the court decides that the official does not have a legal claim to his office, such as proper election or appointment, then all the acts of that official are null and void.

The writ of injunction is not a common-law remedy; in the absence of statutory provision, it is a matter of equity. The rules of equity historically were quite different from the common law, but today a court assumes equity jurisdiction only in accordance with doctrine which is fairly narrowly prescribed. An injunction may be temporary, until a full court hearing on a question may be decided, or permanent. An injunction may be mandatory, requiring an administrative officer to take certain action, or it may be preventive, prohibiting an officer from taking certain action. Usually a court will assume equity jurisdiction only in the absence of any common-law or statutory remedy. It is especially employed to test the constitutionality of a statute under which an administrative agency is operating, but it is also sometimes issued on the ground that an official is exercising authority which he does not legally possess. An action in equity is a suit against the administrative official or tribunal in its personal or unofficial capacity and is not regarded as a suit against the agency or the government itself.

Historically, the basic remedy in the common law for protection of the individual was a private suit for damages against an administrative officer in his capacity as a person rather than in his capacity as an official. If the individual could show that the official had committed a private wrong—and any illegal act was a private wrong—then the plaintiff might recover damages. The issue in such cases was necessarily the question whether the official had acted within the limits of his legal authority. Today, the damage suit is occasionally used, as in suits for false arrest, but it is not common. If the courts were to hold administrative officials personally liable for wrongs arising out of misinterpretation of statutory authority, or from mistaken judgment of facts, then administrative action would generally be hampered. It would be difficult indeed to persuade any person to assume the risks of public administrative authority if he were to be regularly subjected to suits for private damages. The federal courts recognize as an adequate defense the declaration of the administrative official that he acted within his jurisdiction; in some instances, he may be expected to demonstrate good faith on his best understanding of the law and facts. In general, courts prefer to have an action brought against an administrative officer in his official capacity.[11]

In common law there was yet another kind of private action, a suit for restitution of money illegally taken by an administrative officer. Usually the claim had to be that the official had exacted funds beyond those permitted by law; it was not enough to claim just that the officer had made a factual error. Today, in tax matters especially, the suit for restitution is a statutory right and may be employed to question details of tax law and administration.

There are two methods of collateral attack upon the work of administrative agencies. One is the taxpayer's suit in which an individual brings action to prevent enforcement of a law on the ground that the law is unconstitutional and that as a taxpayer he has an interest in preventing such action. The Supreme Court of the United States has refused to recognize taxpayers' suits,[12] and the right exists in state jurisdictions only where it has been conferred by law. In addition, although the Supreme Court has refused to give advisory opinions, it has recognized the device of declaratory judgments.[13] When such jurisdiction is conferred by law, a petitioner who may be adversely affected by a statute or a rule promulgated under a statute may ask the courts to review the constitutional validity of the law or the legal authority of an agency's rule. In such instances the court may have occasion to review the work of an administrative body. The device of the declaratory judgment is carefully limited by most courts.

As we have indicated, many regulatory statutes contain a general provision of some sort for judicial enforcement. A cease and desist order issued, for example, by the Federal Trade Commission or the National Labor Relations Board, can be enforced only by order of a court of appeals. This act of judicial enforcement necessarily provides a basis for judicial review of the decision of the administrative agency. Or another enforcement device may be to permit a private individual to bring suit for

[11] Cf. Kenneth C. Davis, "Administrative Officer's Tort Liability," *Michigan Law Review*, vol. 55 (1956), p. 201.

[12] Cf. *Massachusetts v. Mellon*, and *Frothingham v. Mellon*, 262 U.S. 447 (1923).

[13] *Nashville, Cincinnati, and St. Louis Railway v. Wallace*, 288 U.S. 249 (1933).

damages—sometimes multiple damages—if, for example, he is charged utility rates in excess of the order of an administrative tribunal. Still another device is for a statute to authorize the government itself through its chief law enforcement officer, usually the attorney general, to bring civil or criminal action against the individual who fails to obey an administrative order. Such statutory provisions provide an opportunity for the courts to examine the legality of administrative behavior.

The Federal Administrative Procedure Act of 1946 and corresponding state statutes provide a generalized statutory basis for judicial review. The federal statute, for example, refers to the specific statutory arrangement for judicial review affecting specific agencies, and then says that "in the absence or inadequacy thereof, any applicable form of legal action (including actions for declaratory judgments or writs of prohibitory or mandatory injunction or habeas corpus) in any court of competent jurisdiction" may be utilized by an aggrieved individual. The statute goes on to say "agency action shall be subject to judicial review in civil or criminal proceedings for judicial enforcement except to the extent that prior, adequate, and exclusive opportunity for such review is provided by law." This provision would appear not so much to provide a new basis in statute for judicial review of administrative action as to codify the law on the subject already developed by the courts.

Thus we have a variety of ways to bring the rules and orders of administrative agencies under judicial scrutiny. There is no single or simple avenue for invoking judicial concern. The method appropriate to the individual circumstance and satisfactory to the court must be found and utilized.

SCOPE OF REVIEW: AGENCY FINDINGS OF FACT

Necessarily administrative action in both rule making and adjudication proceeds upon the basis of findings of fact. The tax agency finds that there has been a failure on the part of an individual correctly or fully to report his income. A health agency finds that an annual chest X ray of restaurant personnel for possible tuberculosis is necessary to protect the public. A workmen's compensation board finds that a man suffered an injury in the course of performing his occupational duties. A board finds that an airline has failed to observe air safety regulations. The very essence of administrative action of a rule-making or of an adjudicative nature is a finding of fact.

One troublesome issue the courts have faced in reviewing administrative action has been the question of the finality to accord these administrative findings of fact. Shall the court accept the agency's finding that a chest X ray is necessary for restaurant workers in order to protect the public health? Shall the court accept the agency's finding that an injury was suffered in the course of a man's occupational duties? Or shall the court review the facts *de novo,* from the beginning, demanding all the evidence and substituting its judgment about the meaning of that evidence?

Many statutes which provide for judicial review of administrative determinations state that findings of fact, if supported by substantial evidence, shall be conclusive upon the courts. For example, the National Labor Relations Act of 1935, as amended by the Taft-Hartley Act of 1947, says: "The findings of the Board with respect to questions of fact, if supported by substantial evidence on the record as a whole, shall be conclusive." The Federal Administrative Procedure Act of 1946 defines the scope of judicial review to include agency actions, findings, and conclusions "unsupported by substantial evidence." The problem left to the courts has, therefore, been the extent to which they shall inquire into the existence of substantial evidence and what they shall consider to be substantial evidence. There are no final answers to these questions. The point of view of courts has varied from time to time. Justice Brandeis in a concurring opinion in 1936 declared:[14]

> . . . in deciding when, and to what extent, finality may be given to an administrative finding of fact involving the taking of property, the court has refused to be governed by a rigid rule. It has weighed the relative values of constitutional rights, the essentials of powers conferred, and the need of protecting both. It has noted the distinction between informal, summary administrative action . . . and formal, deliberate, quasi-judicial decisions. . . . It has considered the nature of the facts in issue, the character of the relevant evidence, the need in the business of government for prompt final decision. . . . It has enquired into the character of the administrative tribunal provided and the incidents of its procedure.

There were two cases decided by the Supreme Court of the United States which appeared at the time greatly to broaden the scope of judicial reexamination of all the factual evidence. One of these was the Ben Avon Borough case.[15] In this instance, the Public Service Commission of Pennsylvania fixed a schedule of rates to be charged upon the basis of its findings of fact about what constituted the fair value of utility property. A state court reversed the order with instructions to the commission to revise in certain particulars its findings of fair value of the property. The state Supreme Court said that the lower court could not substitute its judgment for that of the commission. The Supreme Court of the United States ruled that where the facts involved the issue of depriving a person or corporation of property, the state must provide that person with a fair opportunity to submit that issue to a judicial tribunal "for determination

---

[14] In *St. Joseph Stock Yards Co. v. United States,* 298 U.S. 38 (1936), quoted in Cooper, *op. cit.,* pp. 340–341.

[15] *Ohio Valley Water Company v. Ben Avon Borough,* 212 U.S. 287 (1920).

upon its own independent judgment as to both law and facts; otherwise the order is void because in conflict with the due process clause, Fourteenth Amendment. . . . " In essence, the Supreme Court appeared to say that in rate-making cases the valuation of property presents the issue of a "constitutional" fact and this must be reviewed by the courts.

The other case was a workmen's compensation case arising under the maritime jurisdiction of the United States. The U.S. Employees' Compensation Commission could claim jurisdiction in this instance only if two basic facts were established. The Supreme Court then held that it was a responsibility of the courts *de novo* to decide the question of *jurisdictional* fact, that is, whether the accident had occurred on navigable waters and whether the master-servant relationship was involved, both questions of fact being necessary to determine the authority of the Employees' Compensation Commission to make an award against the employer.[16]

In yet a third kind of case the Supreme Court held that the proof of citizenship in a deportation case was a factual matter for the courts to determine; it could not be finally determined by the administrative officers entrusted with enforcement of the immigration laws.[17]

In the intervening years the Supreme Court has appeared to retreat somewhat from these advanced positions. Increasingly that body, and other judicial bodies, have been disposed to give more weight to findings of fact by administrative agencies if supported by substantial evidence. Thus, for example, in a more recent rate-making case, the Supreme Court has said that a "presumptive validity" attaches to a rate determination if the result is just and reasonable.[18] In still another case the Supreme Court declared that it was not the court's function to supplant the judgment of a state utility commission.[19]

It is not easy to determine always, however, whether a particular issue is a question of fact or a question of statutory interpretation or applicability. In a recent case the Supreme Court was confronted with the question whether the Congress of Industrial Organizations was a national union in the meaning of the Taft-Hartley Act. The National Labor Relations Board said that the CIO was not a national union in the sense in which that term was used by the statute. The court said that it was.[20] Is this a question of fact, or is it a question of law? In another labor case, on the basis of statutory instructions contained in the Taft-Hartley Act and the Federal Administrative Procedure Act, the Supreme Court as-

[16] *Crowell v. Benson,* 285 U.S. 22 (1932).
[17] *Ng Fung Ho v. White,* 259 U.S. 276 (1922).
[18] *Federal Power Commission v. Hope Natural Gas Company,* 320 U.S. 591 (1944).
[19] *Railroad Commission of Texas v. Rowan and Nichols Oil Company,* 310 U.S. 573 (1940).
[20] *National Labor Relations Board v. Highland Manufacturing Company,* 341 U.S. 322 (1951).

serted that the courts "must now assume more responsibility for the reasonableness and fairness of Labor Board decisions than some courts have shown in the past."[21] Did this mean that courts should give more attention to the substantial evidence accumulated by administrative agencies to ensure that it was substantial, or did it mean that the courts should substitute their judgment on the meaning or legal interpretation of facts?

In still another recent case, one involving the Selective Service System, where the decisions on classification of persons eligible for military service are supposed to be final with the administrative agency, the Supreme Court on a collateral attack substituted its own judgment about legal interpretation to be given to a particular set of facts. The individual involved claimed deferment from military service as a minister. The facts were that he worked some 25 hours a month as a radio repairman, for which he was paid, and some 150 hours a month as a minister for Jehovah's Witnesses, work for which he was not paid. Under the statute, a person may be deferred as a minister if he is "duly ordained" and if he is a "regular" minister of religion and not one who "irregularly and incidentally preaches and teaches the principles of religion." The Supreme Court ruled that the individual met the statutory criteria; it was of no importance to the court that the sect concerned was unorthodox or that the person ministered primarily to the poor, for which he was unpaid. The court said there was no affirmative evidence to support the local draft board's decision that the man was only "irregularly and incidentally" a minister.[22] This decision, on which the justices were divided six to three, represented a borderline case.

At best, attempts by the judiciary to recognize a difference between questions of fact and of law have created a good deal of uncertainty. In general, the courts have insisted that they may substitute their judgment on questions of law for that of administrative agencies but have deferred to the judgment of administrative bodies on matters of fact. Indeed, when matters of fact are reviewed by the courts, they usually confine their attention to the record of the administrative agency rather than undertaking *de novo* to consider all the evidence in some case or controversy. But the courts are definitely concerned to determine that findings of fact are supported by substantial evidence, and in the process of so inquiring the courts can and do reach conclusions different from those of an administrative agency. It may well be, as one legal scholar has insisted, that "the distinction between law and fact thus remains at the heart of the principal formula for judicial review of administrative action."[23] But the distinction is often difficult to define, and may be cast aside, especially in

[21] *Universal Camera Corporation v. National Labor Relations Board,* 340 U.S. 474 (1951).

[22] *Dickinson v. United States,* 346 U.S. 389 (1953).

[23] Kenneth Culp Davis, in *American Political Science Review,* vol. 48 (September, 1954), p. 938.

instances where troublesome issues of public policy arising from statutory interpretation confront the courts.

SCOPE OF REVIEW: QUESTIONS OF LAW

In general, it is customary to say that the courts review the legality of administrative decisions, legality being both a matter of procedure and a matter of constitutional or statutory interpretation. Many years ago, the Supreme Court asserted in one case that a state might make the judgments of an administrative tribunal final even on a legal question, declaring that "due process is not necessarily judicial process."[24] More recently, the courts would probably be somewhat more cautious in making any such statement. Rather, the judiciary conceives its purpose as one of reviewing administrative action to ensure that the procedure followed meets the standards of due process of law, and that the results are within the scope of authority of the agency and generally reasonable. Yet in some kinds of cases the courts may be reluctant to assert their review role; unless a person is clearly being deprived of life, liberty, or property, the courts are unwilling to assert a constitutional basis of judicial review.[25]

The Federal Administrative Procedure Act attempts to define the scope of judicial review in terms of compelling agency action unlawfully withheld or unreasonably delayed and of setting aside any agency action found to be (1) capricious, arbitrary, or an abuse of discretion, (2) contrary to constitutional right or immunity, (3) in excess of statutory jurisdiction or authority, and (4) without observance of proper procedure. In addition, the law mentions any finding not supported by substantial evidence or unwarranted by the facts "to the extent that the facts are subject to trial *de novo*. . . . " These provisions do little more than recognize positions which the judiciary had already taken in relation to administrative agencies.

To some extent, the attitude of the courts toward administrative action has depended upon the nature of the subject matter itself. In such fields as the granting of title to public lands, the eligibility of an individual for veterans' benefits, the determination whether an article sought to be patented is new or useful, the granting or withholding of a liquor license —here the courts tend to intervene only to a limited extent. In immigration matters, the courts have often been willing to insist upon careful standards of procedure but have acquiesced in statutory demands that rulings of the immigration authorities be final. And in tax matters the courts give a substantial degree of finality to administrative determinations. On the other hand, where questions of property rights are involved,

[24] *Reetz v. Michigan,* 188 U.S. 505 (1903).
[25] Cf. Nathaniel L. Nathanson, "Central Issues of American Administrative Law," *American Political Science Review,* vol. 45 (June, 1951), p. 348.

such as in matters of trade practice and the fixing of rates, the courts have recognized a need for more extensive review. In fields where the nature of government action is more nearly one of policing certain standards of conduct, as in labor relations and investment banking, the courts again have tended to restrict somewhat the scope of their review.[26]

Undoubtedly, the attitude of courts toward administrative decisions is determined also in part by the respect in which they hold the administrative procedure regularly followed. In federal tax matters, the Tax Court of the United States is recognized as a separate administrative court. Its members have specialized knowledge of tax questions. They do not investigate or prosecute cases; they hear controversies brought by aggrieved individuals or referred by Treasury officials. For some reason this court is still regarded as an administrative tribunal, whereas the Court of Customs and Patent Appeals and the Court of Customs are regarded as specialized courts of the nation's judiciary system.

A CASE STUDY

It may be particularly instructive, in seeking to understand the role of the courts in supervising administrative agencies, to study the record of the Federal Trade Commission. Obviously we can do no more here than to suggest some of the major elements in that story. When the Federal Trade Commission Act was passed by Congress in 1914, it represented a departure in government relation to economic enterprise in the United States. The Sherman Antitrust Act of 1890 provided a statutory basis for the federal government to bring suits to dissolve monopolies or penalize monopolistic business practices. Otherwise, the only restraints upon business operations in general were common-law remedies such as those for the misappropriation of trade secrets, for the sale of damaged or defective merchandise, and for the deceitful diversion of patronage. As one study has pointed out: "These common-law rules became increasingly inadequate as railroads replaced canals, steam and electricity replaced water and animal power, factories replaced workshops, and national markets replaced purely local markets."[27] In an economic system of large corporations, medium-sized businesses, small individual proprietors, and millions of consumers; in a trade system of widely varying and ingeniously contrived competitive practices—in such a world, new methods of business control appeared desirable. Certainly it was not enough to dissolve monopolies. The issue was whether monopolies could be prevented from developing in the first place.

In particular, the Federal Trade Commission Act declared "unfair

[26] Cf. Cooper, *op. cit.,* chap. 18.
[27] George W. Stocking and Myron W. Watkins, *Monopoly and Free Enterprise* (New York: The Twentieth Century Fund, Inc., 1951), p. 346.

methods of competition" to be unlawful. The Commission was established to police competitive business practices which might result in the eventual elimination or diminution of competition. The Commission was given authority to investigate business practices which might be regarded as unfair competition, to hold hearings on such charges, and to issue cease and desist orders requiring a business enterprise to halt those practices deemed to be unfair methods of competition. The statute declared as a matter of public policy that unfair methods of competition should be illegal, but it did not undertake to define just what practices in particular were to be regarded as unfair. The Federal Trade Commission was left to define the subject on a case-by-case basis in the process of exercising its regulatory authority.

The 1914 statute did not provide any direct penalty for a failure to abide by the terms of a cease and desist order. Rather, the law specified that if a respondent failed to comply with a Commission order, then the Commission might petition a court of appeals for enforcement of its order. If the court issued an enforcement order, then definite penalties were attached to the failure of a business concern to abide by the court's decision. But in the process of issuing an enforcement order, the courts were given the opportunity, indeed the responsibility, to review the Commission's procedure, findings, and conclusions. In this way the judicial system was given a major voice in the regulatory process.

In the intervening years, the Federal Trade Commission has dealt with a wide variety of practices considered by it to constitute unfair methods of competition. There have been cases on deceptive practices, such as the use of well-known names on products in order to suggest reliability (like Mayo Brothers vitamins which had no connection with the famous Mayo Brothers Clinic of Rochester, Minnesota); on misrepresentation of the geographical origin of a product (like the use of the word Havana on cigars made in this country); on misrepresentation of the nature of a seller's business; and on misrepresentation of professional or other approval of products, and the misbranding of a product (like labeling cotton goods woolens). There have been cases on restrictive trade agreements which tended to limit production, fix prices, or to divide trade areas on a geographical basis. There have been cases on trade discrimination, such as contracts which require a supplier in order to obtain one line of merchandise to purchase certain other commodities as well. There have been cases involving differential price arrangements, such as the lower prices given by a well-known tire manufacturer for tires sold to Sears, Roebuck and Company for distribution under the distributor's rather than the manufacturer's name. There have been cases involving the use of advertising allowances which, in effect, were secret rebates to particular distributors of a manufacturer's product. There have been cases where there appeared to be a concerted plan to drive some distributors out of business, such as when a candy manufacturer gave special price concessions to vending machine operators. These and many other types of cases have occupied the attention of the Federal Trade Commission.

In a field involving government regulation of general business on a very broad scale, employing new concepts and new administrative techniques, it seems natural indeed that the courts should have examined the work of the Federal Trade Commission with a good deal of care. Indeed, a number of studies made of the Commission within the first twenty years of its experience pointed out that the courts had been quite cautious in approving Commission orders. There was almost the suggestion of judicial hostility to the whole administrative effort of the Federal Trade Commission.[28] Since the public policy being charted by the Commission was new and since the scope of its authority was so extensive, it is easy to understand why the courts should have been so hesitant in upholding Commission orders. Moreover, it seems likely that the courts had some reason to believe that Commission procedure often expressed crusading zeal rather than objective analysis. The fact, too, that the task of the Commission was to apply statutory prohibitions to specific sets of facts encouraged the courts to express their own judgment about whether the actions complained of really met the statutory description of an unfair trade practice. Each amendment to the 1914 law made the statute more specific but gave the court even more reason for careful statutory interpretation.

In recent years, however, there has been general agreement that the courts have taken an increasingly favorable attitude toward the work of the Federal Trade Commission. Partly, this reflects a growing judicial— and popular—understanding of the nature of and need for the administrative process of regulation. Little by little the courts have adapted their point of view to accommodate this new administrative procedure. Partly, the change reflects greater *expertise* by the Federal Trade Commission in handling its work—that is, the Commission has accumulated a vast knowledge of trade practices and a certain skill in obtaining and presenting evidence for administrative action. Partly, the change reflects improved administrative procedures by the Commission which have given the essentials of a fair hearing to every respondent. As a result one student has commented:[29]

> . . . The present trend is toward a narrower scope of review. While still recognizing the early established doctrine that what is an unfair method of competition is a question for the courts, the decisions are coming to empha-

[28] Cf. Gerard C. Henderson, *The Federal Trade Commission: A Study in Administrative Law and Procedure* (New Haven, Conn.: Yale University Press, 1924); Thomas C. Blaisdell, Jr., *The Federal Trade Commission* (New York: Columbia University Press, 1932); and Carl McFarland, *Judicial Control of the Federal Trade Commission and the Interstate Commerce Commission, 1920–1930* (Cambridge, Mass.: Harvard University Press, 1933).

[29] Cooper, *op. cit.*, pp. 369–370.

size the great weight to be given to the findings and experienced judgment of the Commission in determining this question. Similarly, the rule reserving to the courts the determination as to whether public interest is involved, is coming to be tempered by the readiness of the courts to accept the finding of the Commission that the requisite public interest is present.

THE OBJECTIVES OF JUDICIAL REVIEW

The broad purposes of judicial review of administrative decisions were well summarized in the report of the Attorney General's Committee on Administrative Procedure in 1941. First, judicial review should be expected to check, but not to supplant, administrative action, especially by ensuring that action does not go beyond lawfully delegated authority. Secondly, judicial review should be expected "to speak the final word on interpretation of law, both constitutional and statutory." Thirdly, judicial review should be expected to require administrative agencies to use fair procedure in the handling of adjudicative cases. In the fourth place, judicial review should be expected to prevent extremes of arbitrariness or incompetence in administrative adjudication.[30]

In general, this has been the historical role of the judiciary in relation to administration and especially in relation to regulatory administration. Both statutory and constitutional power have been used by the courts to assert and perform this supervisory task. The courts themselves, rather than legislative enactment, have defined the area and scope of review which they will undertake. The courts themselves have had to decide certain statutory directives, such as what shall be "substantial evidence" in support of administrative findings.

A good deal of attention has been given in recent years to improving the procedures of regulatory agencies. Apart from the work done by the Committee on Administrative Law of the American Bar Association, we should mention in particular the Attorney General's Committee on Administrative Procedure (1941), the first Hoover Commission (1949),[31] and the second Hoover Commission (1955).[32] The Federal Administrative Procedure Act of 1946 helped in codifying proper standards for administrative agencies to observe. The task of the courts has been immeasurably aided by greater attention on the part of administrative agencies to the essentials of fair procedure.

In 1955 the second Hoover Commission and its task force on legal services and procedure recommended that the scope of judicial review be

[30] Sen. Doc. 8, 77th Cong., 1st Sess., pp. 77–78.

[31] Commission on Organization of the Executive Branch of the Government, *Regulatory Commissions,* and appendix N, "Task Force Report on Regulatory Commissions" (Washington: Government Printing Office, 1949).

[32] Commission on Organization of the Executive Branch of the Government, *Legal Services and Procedure,* and *Task Force Report on Legal Services and Procedure* (Washington: Government Printing Office, 1955).

enlarged somewhat. In the first place, it recommended elimination of the two clauses in the Federal Administrative Procedure Act restricting judicial review. One of these clauses made an exception in those circumstances where existing statutes precluded judicial review, and the other clause exempted "agency action . . . by law committed to agency discretion." The task force and the Commission argued that every citizen should be entitled to demonstrate to a court whether he had been injured wrongly by administrative action. The task force reported that there were at least six kinds of cases involved under the first exemption, including packers and stockyard cases, veterans' affairs, international civil aviation, international claims, and compensation claims of federal employees. The task force asserted that it was not its intention to substitute judicial judgment for administrative judgment; it was concerned rather to enable any citizen to assert before a court that an agency decision was obviously in error to the extent that it amounted to an abuse of discretion or an unwarranted exercise of discretion.

In so far as the second exemption was concerned, the argument was somewhat technical. In a later section, the 1946 law provided that the courts might set aside agency action found to be an abuse of discretion. The task force appeared to believe that the two provisions of the Federal Administrative Procedure Act were contradictory, and that repeal of the exemption would do no more than open the way for judicial review of any administrative abuse of discretion. It was not intended, the task force asserted, to restrict administrative discretion exercised within the limits of statutory authorization.

The task force also proposed a number of other changes. One of these was that, whenever agency action was not based on a formal hearing and record, the courts should be permitted to institute trial *de novo* in the reviewing court. The purpose of this was to provide a check upon any administrative disposition in informal hearings to rely upon irrelevant or incompetent evidence. Another proposal would have enlarged the general scope of judicial review by including judicial determination of whether agency action constituted "an abuse or *clearly unwarranted exercise* of discretion." The words "clearly unwarranted exercise" of discretion would have been new. Furthermore, the task force wanted the phrase "unsupported by substantial evidence" changed to read "cases . . . clearly erroneous in view of the reliable, probative, and substantial evidence." Other recommendations dealt with simplifying the form of action for bringing about judicial review, the timing of judicial review, and the elimination of any duplication of hearings before an administrative body and a trial court.[33]

The recommendations of the second Hoover Commission would have to be studied with some care before it could be determined whether the

[33] *Ibid.*, pp. 206–220.

proposals are essentially technical and perfecting in purpose or whether substantially they would enlarge judicial review at the expense of administrative effectiveness. Certainly the tone of the task force reasoning suggested only the limited objective of perfecting present practices. But the statutory language recommended to achieve this end might well be interpreted greatly to enlarge the role of the judiciary. It is probably for this reason that the Congress has been cautious about amending that part of the Federal Administrative Procedure Act defining the scope of judicial review.

The role of the judiciary in supervising administrative action is a sensitive one. The concern of the courts might be expressed in language employed on one occasion by Arthur W. Macmahon: "The task of administrative justice is to create within the administrative system the equivalents of caution, detachment, and uniformity, while advancing the virtues of quickness, cheapness, firmness, and due specialization of knowledge."[34] The courts must be concerned no less than administrative agencies to achieve the ends of administrative justice. To do otherwise would be to destroy administrative specialization on the one hand, and on the other hand, to confer all administrative authority upon the courts themselves. The concern of the courts with justice for the individual is not an excuse for blocking society in the pursuit of a public or general interest.

The courts remain the bulwark of justice for the person. As such they must and do play a vital role in supervising administrative performance. But the courts confront limitations as well. The protection of the individual is an important part of government in a free society. Yet it is not the sum total of such government. A free society is not an anarchy. It must have government able and competent to administer its work. In the process of judicial review the courts endeavor to ensure that administrative agencies shall operate within the limits of their authority and that their actions shall be reasonable and fair in their impact upon the individual. The courts can do this much—and this much is essential. The courts themselves recognize that their role is not to determine or administer public policy. The judiciary is one branch and only one branch of a great system of government.

[34] Arthur W. Macmahon, "The Ordeal of Administrative Law," *Iowa Law Review,* vol. 25 (March, 1940), p. 425.

Conclusion

Chapter 25

The Goal: Responsible Bureaucracy

We commonly speak of the public employee as a civil servant. The administrative work of government is presumably servant to a master. That master is not simply the people of the United States. That master, if a master does in truth exist, must be the representative institutions of government established by American constitutionalism. Only if those institutions function fully and effectively can we hope to achieve in our society the goal of a responsible bureaucracy.

It scarcely seems necessary here to debate whether a responsible bureaucracy is desirable or not. It is enough to remind ourselves that if we value a free society and a democratic polity, then we must have institutions of government which are limited, which promote the public welfare without stooping to tyranny, and which are adequate to keep bureaucracy within the lead-strings of political direction and control.

Moreover, the existence of a bureaucracy in and of itself is not necessarily an indication that a free society and a democratic polity are threatened. If this proposition were true, then we have already lost any hope of preserving our democracy. There can be no government without some degree of administrative apparatus; and in a highly complex, industrial society of today, and in a world where the peace and security of our national existence is threatened, a highly organized, extensive bureaucracy is seemingly a necessity.

Woodrow Wilson wrote in 1887: "There is no danger in power, if only it be not irresponsible."[1] And in referring to the administrative work of government he spoke of the need "to crown its duties with dutifulness." Large-scale administrative organization is not in and of itself irresponsible, or lacking in dutifulness. The challenge is whether the institutions of our government are adequate to make the power of large-scale public administration politically responsible. The challenge is whether those in-

[1] Woodrow Wilson, "The Study of Administration," *Political Science Quarterly*, vol. 2 (1887), reprinted in vol. 56 (December, 1941), p. 481.

stitutions are adequate to crown the duties of administrative agencies with dutifulness.

We have observed that American constitutionalism has not been especially concerned with defining the status of bureaucracy, or with specifying the organization and operation of administrative agencies. Rather, the broad outlines of governmental structure established by our federal and state constitutions are concerned primarily with the exercise of political power. These constitutions created three great branches of government to share the policy-making function. These constitutions, again using the words of Wilson, "properly concern themselves only with those instrumentalities of government which are to control general law." In thus concentrating attention upon the exercise of power, our constitutions assume that that power, properly structured in the interests of freedom, will be adequate to keep bureaucracy politically responsible.

Much of American constitutional commentary has concentrated attention upon the separation of power into legislative, executive, and judicial branches and upon the conflict which at times appears to delay timely, decisive action in meeting the urgent political issues of our day.[2] On occasion, this conflict does assume importance, although the conflict itself is often exaggerated and the constructive purpose served by such conflict is frequently overlooked. But as a result of observing too narrowly only the disagreements which have arisen in the history of our government, we fail to perceive another, even more vital, feature of our constitutional system. Legislature, executive, and judiciary in combination present the full panoply, the full majesty of government in our society. We need to give more attention to what the three achieve in concert and somewhat less attention to how the three on occasion disagree.

It is the three branches of government in concert which provide the instrumentalities for keeping bureaucracy responsible. No one branch is more important than the other. Each branch is different in its relation to the administrative work of government. Each has a different role or function. Each must do its part in maintaining an administrative apparatus which is servant, not master, of our democracy.

THE ROLE OF THE LEGISLATURE

In our system of government basic issues of public policy are embodied in statutory enactment. To some degree this is not entirely true in the case of foreign affairs and of national defense, although even in these

---

[2] "This conflict between the Executive and Congress is the most significant fact about the American government of today. Unless something is done to cure it, it may prove to be a tragic fact." Thomas K. Finletter, *Can Representative Government Do the Job?* (New York: Reynal & Hitchcock, Inc., 1945), p. 17. This statement by a distinguished lawyer and public servant is cited as illustrative of many such commentaries.

areas of policy our government increasingly depends upon legislative support to provide the resources required to achieve policy objectives. In general, however, the tasks to be undertaken by the state are determined through political activities which culminate in the passage of legislation. Much of this political endeavor occurs outside the formal legislative process as such, involving as it does the activity of political party organization, of interest groups, of media of mass communication, of public discussion, and of influential citizens. Nonetheless, all of this endeavor comes to focus finally upon the legislative process itself, where the necessary statutes are formally enacted.

In this process of consideration and enactment the bureaucracy necessarily must participate. Administrative officials have ideas and experience which are essential to public discussion and legislative consideration. To deny to the public at large and to legislators the benefit of administrative points of view on such issues as credit control, atomic fallout, public health, public education, urban redevelopment, and foreign relations is to carry on discussions and to make decisions half-informed. Administrative officials, both those who are political appointees and those who are professional public servants, must be heard. They cannot be isolated from the political process or the legislative process.

There are undoubtedly limits of law and of propriety beyond which administrative officials cannot go. By law administrative officials are forbidden to use the resources of their position to engage in direct pressure tactics to influence legislative votes, such as urging citizens to write their representatives or denouncing particular legislators. Administrative officials politically selected have greater leeway in behavior than professional administrative officials. The latter are expected to be more restrained in public discussion, considering issues on their merits and avoiding partisan or personal references. Moreover, once a policy issue has been resolved, even temporarily, administrators are expected to be loyal in carrying out the decision even though they have reservations about its wisdom and subsequently may again express their doubts. Within the limits fixed by law and custom, administrators do and must participate in the consideration of public policy.

Statutory enactment is the foundation of public policy decision because it provides the basis of administrative action. Administrators draw their authority from law. They are expected to behave in accordance with law. Their actions are subject to challenge in a court of law and can be defended only upon the basis of law. Furthermore, administrators find the objectives of their action in law; here is the source of guidance for what they are expected to achieve. And in law administrators find the standards and the procedures by which they are expected to act. The work of government begins with statutes.

The public policy which guides the multitude of governmental activities today must not be thought of as some simple, coherent set of objectives for administrative action. At times in our political history there have been dominant political figures, often the executive, who have urged broad general goals toward which all governmental activity should be directed. In our national political history we have experienced some degree of coherent policy objectives under executives, such as Jefferson, Jackson, Lincoln, Theodore Roosevelt, Wilson, Franklin Roosevelt, and Eisenhower. But individual actions have been taken which by no means could fit any unified, coherent enunciation of objectives attempted by one of these executives. Public policy is never a single doctrine; our scheme of government knows rather an extensive set of policy decisions embracing the many different activities of government.

Public policy needs to be thought of realistically in terms of the governmental objectives in such fields of endeavor as foreign affairs, housing, agriculture, natural resources, transportation, welfare, health, economic growth, and education. Beyond these broad categories, we should speak of foreign *policies* rather than policy, since our relations with other countries entail different concepts of national interest under varying circumstances and in different parts of the world. Transportation policy may mean one set of objectives in terms of highways, something else in terms of ocean shipping, something still different in terms of air transport, and yet something else again in terms of the railroads. Public policy is, therefore, a discrete aggregation of many varied objectives of governmental action which have been decided through the legislative process at various times and under various pressures.

Yet one characteristic of this term public policy remains constant amid the variety of subject-matter content. Public policy spoken primarily through the legislative process is the beginning, the fount, of administrative action. Public administration starts with policy decisions which establish the broad purposes or objectives of governmental action. And this policy decision making stems from the legislative process. Administrators make policy decisions which supplement, or implement, the broad legislative process of decision making. Administrators may also advise about desirable broad policies. But administrators do not decide these broad policies. They administer them.

The legislative process does more than determine the broad policies to guide administrative action. It also provides the appropriations which determine the magnitude and scope of administrative endeavor. The important decisions about the size of a governmental budget are policy decisions. If the legislative process decides upon agricultural price support at 100 per cent of parity, then certain budget decisions must necessarily follow. If a state legislature decides that the state shall provide financial assistance to local school districts at so much per pupil in average daily attendance or at so much per classroom unit, then certain budget decisions must necessarily follow. If a government has a debt of certain size, then debt service charges automatically follow in the magnitude required to support that debt. A legislature may reduce administrative requests for appropriations within certain limits, but any substantial reduction depends upon the repeal or modification of previous policy decisions which have determined that there shall be a certain activity and at a certain general level. Yet the fact remains that the legislative process, not administrative agencies themselves, decides what shall be spent each year or each biennium for various activities.

Furthermore, the legislature may watch over the disbursement of public funds, taking various precautions to make sure that expenditures conform with legislative intentions. Sometimes, by law or by constitutional requirement there is a system of separate check upon administrative disbursement. Sometimes a statute may permit certain modifications in expenditure plans if these are approved by the executive, or by a joint legislative-executive body. Sometimes, the legislature by statute places certain safeguards around the disbursement of funds by all administrative agencies, or by particular agencies. And when new appropriations are made the legislature may express its displeasure about the way expenditures have been handled in the past by reducing the amount made available.

Beyond this, the legislature may prescribe organizational arrangements for the conduct of administrative activities and set forth various operating procedures, such as those for the appointment and retention of personnel, for the purchasing of supplies, for the planning and building of public facilities, and for the handling of legal cases. Administrative agencies are then required to operate within the context of these procedures. A failure to do so may open an agency to legal suit or other sanctions.

And in the exercise of its legislative power the legislature may inquire into any administrative behavior which it considers appropriate. Administrative officials may be required to answer any questions directed to them and to produce papers, except as instructed not to do so by the executive. Administrators may be investigated in detail, but the legislature can alter any unsatisfactory situation only by statutory enactment.

This is a substantial array of authority vested in the legislature. The role of the legislative process is to provide the legal basis for public administration in our government. There can be no continuing, or temporary, administrative activity without this statutory base. The power to enact law is the power to determine what administration shall undertake to do, how it shall do it, and how much it shall spend. Only the legislative process, with certain exceptions in the realm of foreign affairs and national defense, can make these basic decisions.

THE ROLE OF THE EXECUTIVE

In general, the executive has a peculiar position. He is a participant, and an important participant, in the legislative process which has just been reviewed. He may guide or influence legislative action in fixing the policy objectives of governmental action, in determining appropriations, and in setting forth organizational and procedural arrangements. If dissatisfied with action by the legislature on any of these matters, the executive may disapprove. The legislature may make its will effective over executive veto only by a two-thirds vote. In many instances a majority of this size may not be obtainable.

In addition, the executive may have a substantial impact upon legislative action through his political role. As leader of a national or state political organization, no matter how loosely organized, the executive may still be an important figure in various political decisions which can affect the career of individual legislators. Furthermore, the executive may mobilize public opinion in behalf of his own legislative program, thus encouraging some particular action by the legislature.

The executive, accordingly, is a direct participant of substantial stature in the legislative process. Accordingly, he shares in the legislative power which provides the policy, expenditure, organizational, and procedural framework for the administrative activity of government in our society.

Beyond this, the executive has still further authority to supervise the conduct of administrative agencies. In the federal government, it is the President who is chief diplomat. It is he personally who decides what foreign nations this country shall recognize, and it is he personally who decides what treaties to negotiate. It has followed in practice that the executive is the source of broad policy objectives in our foreign relations, even though the legislature must provide the necessary machinery. In addition, the President is Commander in Chief of the Armed Forces, holding the power to determine the broad strategic objectives to be realized by military objectives, even though it is the Congress which must declare war and provide the means for raising and supporting the nation's Armed Forces.

In general, the executive exercises a continuing oversight of administrative activity. He appoints vital personnel who provide the necessary political leadership in an administrative agency. Sometimes, he appoints such personnel for a statutory term of office and may not remove an appointee except for cause involving malfeasance or other misconduct. In most instances, the selection of key personnel is subject to senatorial approval. Sometimes, the executive may select a substantial number of administrative personnel. Sometimes, a state constitution establishes certain administrative agencies headed by persons directly elected to office. Whatever the situation, through his power to appoint and to remove key administrative personnel, the executive provides an important element within the administration sympathetic to his point of view.

The executive may consult with department and agency heads to the extent that he desires to do so. Such consultation may be concerned with the desirability of some additional legislative enactment. Such consultation may be concerned with appropriation, organizational, or procedural matters requiring legislative consideration. Such consultation may be concerned with particular programs or supplementary policies required in order to carry out statutory directives. The executive's sanction for such consultation may be his role as participant in legislative matters or his role in appointing and removing key personnel.

In most units of government the executive has become an institution. He requires assistance in preparing budget recommendations for submission to the legislature. He requires assistance in considering personnel, organizational, and procedural improvements to suggest to the legislature. He requires assistance in selecting and appointing key personnel. He requires assistance in arranging for consultation with heads of agencies on matters of mutual interest. The burden of the executive is great, and he can no longer give personal attention to the myriad of details and the complex issues which he is expected to handle.

An institutionalized executive has perhaps in some instances lost something of the personal effectiveness which an energetic, forceful, and able individual might bring to the office. Yet the office of the executive has gained something in ability to supervise and direct the administrative agencies of government. Much of executive effectiveness now depends upon the quality of the assistance which he enjoys in the exercise of his high office.

The executive is the general manager of public administration, but general manager in a peculiar or unique sense. He is not a chief administrator who exercises continuing oversight of all administrative detail, or who bears responsibility for the conduct of all administrative agencies. He does not expect every administrative agency of the federal or of the state government to consult with him about every major decision. Some agencies enjoy a considerable degree of administrative autonomy conferred by constitution or by statute. Sometimes an executive finds it convenient to let the political defense of administrative action rest with the administrative agency involved rather than to assume the responsibility himself. Nor even if he were disposed to do so could an executive assume full responsibility for administrative activity; by the nature of his office and by the requirements of the constitution which he protects and defends, he must share responsibility with legislature and judiciary.

In regulatory administration, for example, where the authority for policy making within the broad framework of statutory direction has been vested in a commission or board, the executive does not supervise the decisions made in individual cases or approve every exercise of the rule-making power. In state government, where substantial discretion has been delegated to boards of trustees for the management of state-supported institutions of higher education, the executive does not presume to supervise the many decisions which enter into the operation of these colleges and universities.

Even where the executive's relationship to administrative agencies has not been placed in some special category, the executive must, of necessity, leave a great array of discretionary authority to the heads of individual administrative bodies. The executive is disposed by the nature of his role and the limitations of time to give his concern primarily to those aspects of administration which raise major issues of public policy. He must watch carefully over budget matters, because appropriations are a major element in the fiscal and economic policies of government. He must consult at length on policies which require legislative attention and which are likely to arouse much public discussion and opposition, because these issues affect his own and his party's political future. He must be prepared to intervene whenever there is a serious breakdown in the administrative performance of any agency, because administrative failure, or widespread allegation of administrative failure, becomes necessarily a major political issue. Varying circumstances and conditions determine just what aspects of public administration the executive shall single out for his special attention.

In recent years there has been a growth of central service and control agencies in government whose purpose is not to deal with the public at large but rather with other administrative agencies. The civil service commissions which grew up with the reform movement of the 1880s and later are examples. In more recent years there have been planning commissions, public building agencies, budget offices, records offices, and others supervising the work of the operating agencies or performing specific tasks for them. The executive has had a new task to perform as a result of this development. Whenever there is a major conflict between these centralized service and control agencies and the operating agencies, the executive is often asked to intervene and facilitate some adjustment.

The executive represents all the people of the nation or state in his single person. He has become the dominant individual in our system of government. He combines in his position political, legislative, and administrative authority of far-reaching scope. He is able to watch over the behavior of administrative agencies in terms of the fundamental political point of view which he represents, and for whose exercise he is responsible to the voters at large. His power and his influence are such that, in matters of basic public policy, administrative agencies must necessarily accept his leadership.

THE ROLE OF THE JUDICIARY

The judicial power speaks through decisions in cases and controversies coming before the courts for their consideration. The judiciary is concerned to keep the exercise of governmental power within constitutional limits while promoting the general welfare. In this concern for constitutional limitations, the judiciary stands guardian of the separation of power, and supervises administrative behavior to make sure that administrative judgment meets the standard of legality and that administrative procedures meet the standard of due process of law. On occasion, the interpretation of constitutional limitations and of legal standards may be influenced by the judges' own conceptions of desirable public policy. Yet rigorous training in the traditions of the law helps judges to keep in check their own personal predilections. Nonetheless, the canons of judicial process and of constitutional interpretation are not so exact as to prevent the courts, too, from sharing in the exercise of political power. And possessing as they do their measure of political power, courts participate in the supervision and control of administrative agencies.

In the United States, the judiciary does not function, as in England and France, in the presence of an all-powerful legislature. In theory limited to the jurisdiction conferred by the Constitution and laws of the United States, the power of the federal judiciary in practice has appeared to be so little subject to effective restraint by the legislative and executive power that some persons have been led to speak of "judicial supremacy" in our scheme of government. When the court speaks, its decisions may be overruled only by a higher court (or in the case of the Supreme Court of the United States by a later Supreme Court) or by constitutional amendment. Sometimes the attitude of the Supreme Court on constitutional questions may be affected by the kind of judge appointed by the President and approved by the Senate. This is at best a slow and somewhat uncertain process of affecting judicial change. Sometimes Presidents have refused any assistance in enforcing court decisions. Sometimes the legislature has sought by law to change court decisions or to alter the jurisdiction of the court system. On one occasion, in 1937, President Franklin D. Roosevelt made a frontal attack upon the Supreme Court by proposing to the legislature that the number of judges be increased. Although the Congress rejected the suggestion, the Supreme Court also helped the situation by somewhat altering its attitude on certain legislative enactments of the Roosevelt period. The threat of such action remains under extreme circumstances as a possible means of influencing court decisions, especially where there are political differences about desirable public policy.

From time to time, it is necessary for the legislative and executive branches of government to remind the judiciary that they share power with the courts. Otherwise, the courts may come to believe that the whole burden of political decision making and of supervising the bureaucracy falls upon the judiciary. So exclusive a role was not assigned to the judiciary by the Constitution. To be sure, the courts perform an essentially political function, but they do not perform this function without the possibility of restraint from the other two branches of government. The judiciary is not an unfettered participant in the governmental process.

THE ENFORCEMENT OF POLITICAL RESPONSIBILITY

The institutions of legislature, executive, and judiciary in our scheme of government exist and function external to the bureaucracy itself. The legislature is made up of numerous members elected from local districts. The executive is elected by the voters at large. Judges are either appointed by the executive and confirmed by the upper chamber of the legislature, or are separately elected by the voters. These basic institutions for the exercise of political power function in accordance with constitutional prescription and tradition. They are responsible to the people.

Administrative agencies do not select legislators, the executive, or judges. Administrative agencies do not enact laws, do not determine how much they shall spend, do not determine their own organization, do not select their own heads, do not render the final decision in controversies with individual citizens. In these respects, the bureaucracy is responsible to the legislature, to the executive, and to the judiciary.

Nor is this power exercised by legislature, executive, and judiciary merely formal. It is also real. There is a high degree of coincidence between the institutional framework of political power in our society and its actual exercise. The legislature is influenced by pressure groups, by local desires, and by particular individuals. But the legislature is not subservient to some single individual or to some small group enjoying a monopoly of political power. The executive is the servant of the people. The judiciary is dedicated to the tradition of Western justice and the rule of law. The power exercised by our political institutions is both formal and actual.

To be sure, the power of American political institutions reflects in turn the structure of political power within our society. The essential characteristic of the power structure is its pluralism. Political parties are organized on a local basis. Economic power is shared by large corporations and by hundreds of thousands of small enterprises. Labor is organized into many different groups, and even the federation of national unions is by no means all-inclusive. Organized religion cannot be established by the state and is in practice divided into many different denominations. There are many universities, not just one or a few, so that no monopoly in the use of intellectual power is possible. Our police force is organized on a local basis. So is our system of public elementary and secondary education. The enumeration might continue indefinitely.

The point is that American society has abhorred any monopoly of power and has thus far successfully avoided it. While this pluralistic structure of power prevails, the political institutions of our society are enabled to function in large part as envisaged by those who framed our constitutional system.

This system in its ideal model—that is, in theory—draws a sharp distinction between politics and bureaucracy. The political decisions of society are entrusted to the institutions of legislature, executive, and judiciary. The administrative work of the state is entrusted to the bureaucracy created by and responsible to these political institutions. This is the constitutional doctrine of responsible bureaucracy in our scheme of government.

In large measure, moreover, this constitutional doctrine has been realized in practice. In an imperfect society no set of political institutions functions to perfection, and no constitutional doctrine framed by and for man is necessarily beyond improvement. Yet, to a considerable degree we have kept bureaucracy responsible to these political institutions.

There can be no question but that we live in the cra of the administrative state. Large-scale governmental administration is a fact of our times, whether we like the situation or not. There are some who believe that the administrative state is in and of itself incompatible with a democratic polity and a free society. They insist we must go back to a simpler day, to a lessened governmental role. The alternative is to capitulate to the commissar, to the small group whose members combine in their persons a monopoly of political power and control of the bureaucracy. This is a gloomy prediction. It poses a choice only between government without large-scale administration and government without freedom.

It seems illusionary to believe that a society can deliberately turn its back upon the complexities wrought by the technology of our day. Moreover, in the present state of world tension, government without large-scale attention to national defense—and this means government without large-scale administration—might invite external aggression and a consequent loss of freedom. There is no national security, and no guarantee of freedom, in nostalgia for a simpler era.

We have then only the choice of government with large-scale administration which is politically responsible or government by the commissar. Americans, whom Wilson described as democrats "by inheritance and repeated choice," can have only one answer. It is to make the administrative state compatible with freedom. And this means an administrative state in which bureaucracy is kept responsible to the political institutions of constitutional government.

It is no easy task to keep bureaucracy politically responsible. The means do not lie in the direction of promoting a breakdown in the public service. Administrative leaders must be encouraged to exercise an appropriate initiative in the presentation and consideration of public policy. If external controls were to go so far as to bar the bureaucracy from the consideration of policy matters, then the political institutions of society would deny themselves the benefit of timely and expert advice. If the top talent of the public service were to be driven from the bureaucracy by inadequate salaries, slow promotion, or other unsatisfactory conditions of service, the political institutions of our society would have no answering response to their demand for administrative activity.

Sometimes administrative agencies may determine important elements of public policy because of an inability on the part of the legislature to agree upon the provisions of a statute, or because of legislative-executive-judicial conflict. The bureaucracy is not to be condemned because it acts in situations which might otherwise create the vacuum of no action at all. Nor does bureaucratic policy making under these circumstances mean irresponsible political action.

There is no danger in bureaucratic formulation of public policy so long as two conditions obtain. If the bureaucracy formulates public policy only in the absence of clear and definite instructions from the legislative, executive, or judiciary, then it has not undermined the institutions of a democratic polity. Under these circumstances, the bureaucracy may even be strengthening rather than weakening our government. The other condition is that the bureaucracy, when formulating public policy, must always recognize the power of the legislature, executive, or judiciary to step in and repeal, modify, or alter such public policy. When the legislature, executive, and judiciary do speak on matters of public policy, their voice is final and determinative in the formulation of public policy in our scheme of government.

If a bureaucracy were to be inefficient in the performance of its duties —that is, wasteful of manpower and other resources and capable of only minimum performance of its duties—then such a bureaucracy would be dangerous to the existence of a democratic polity and a free society. If a bureaucracy were in practice to seek to carry out policies other than those specifically provided by the institutions of political power in our government, then such a bureaucracy would be dangerous. If a bureaucracy were able to conceal important information from the public, or were purposefully to misinform the public, then such a bureaucracy would be dangerous. If a bureaucracy were to interfere with the functioning of the institutions of popular government, including the holding of free elections, then again such a bureaucracy would be dangerous to our democratic polity and our free society.

It must be emphasized also that one of the great protections of American society against these very dangers is something more than the existence of institutions of political power external to the bureaucracy itself. Equally vital is the absence of a highly centralized bureaucracy. The federal system for division of governmental power, and the traditions of a high degree of localism in American political life, create circumstances in which the failure of bureaucracy in any one unit of government is not necessarily fatal to the system of government as a whole. This is an important safeguard, indeed, and not one lightly to be dismissed.

In the administrative state, control of the bureaucracy by political institutions is a matter of some finesse and subtlety. Control cannot be exercised by a bludgeon. Administrative breakdown is as much to be feared in the modern state as a politically irresponsible bureaucracy. The administrative state must be well served by its administrative apparatus, and this need is as much the concern of the political institutions of government as the assurance of appropriate political direction of that apparatus.

Our constitutional system possesses the instrumentalities for adequate political control of bureaucracy. So long as the structure of political power encourages the effective operation of the political institutions of our society, and so long as the political institutions lead and encourage as well as direct and supervise the administrative work of government, that long shall we continue to have a politically responsible bureaucracy in a democratic polity and a free society.

Index

DATE DUE

GAYLORD			PRINTED IN U.S.A.